THE CHEMISTRY OF SYNTHETIC DYES

VOLUME III

CONTRIBUTORS

G. COLLIN

S. F. MASON

R. PRICE

C. V. STEAD

J. M. STRALEY

J. M. TEDDER

K. VENKATARAMAN

N. N. VOROZHTSOV, JR.

M. ZANDER

The Chemistry of
SYNTHETIC DYES

VOLUME III

Edited by

K. VENKATARAMAN

National Chemical Laboratory
Poona, India

ACADEMIC PRESS   1970   New York and London

CONTENTS

LIST OF CONTRIBUTORS

Numbers in parentheses indicate the pages on which the authors' contributions begin

G. Collin (61), Rütgerswerke AG., Duisburg-Meiderich and Castrop-Rauxel, Germany

S. F. Mason (169), Chemistry Department, King's College, London, England

R. Price (303), Research Department, Imperial Chemical Industries, Dyestuffs Division, Hexagon House, Blackley, Manchester, England

C. V. Stead (249), Research Department, Imperial Chemical Industries, Dyestuffs Division, Hexagon House, Blackley, Manchester, England

J. M. Straley (385), Research Laboratories, Tennessee Eastman Company, Division of Eastman Kodak Company, Kingsport, Tennessee

J. M. Tedder (223), The University, St. Andrews, Scotland

K. Venkataraman (1), National Chemical Laboratory, Poona, India

N. N. Vorozhtsov, Jr. (85), Institute of Organic Chemistry, USSR Academy of Sciences, Novosibirsk, USSR

M. Zander (61), Rütgerswerke AG., Duisburg-Meiderich and Castrop-Rauxel, Germany

PREFACE

For a few years I considered writing an entirely new edition of "The Chemistry of Synthetic Dyes." As a result of discussions with many friends and colleagues who are familiar with the two volumes of this work, I decided that the urgent need was not for a revision, because very little of the material had become obsolete, but for the addition of supplementary material covering the developments from 1950.

The progress made in the chemistry of synthetic dyes in the last twenty years is amazing. The discovery of reactive dyes is one major advance. There has also been extensive research on intermediates, disperse dyes, cationic dyes, cyanine dyes, and pigments, which has led to much new chemical knowledge. Consequently I realized that it was no longer possible for a single author to give accurate and authoritative accounts of the progress made in each specialized area of synthetic dyes. I have been very fortunate in the response I have had to my invitations to contribute to the additional volumes. The chapters have been written by acknowledged authorities who have worked for many years on the topics they have covered; their names have been associated with many patents and papers.

The additional volumes not only cover synthetic dyes of nearly all types, but also raw materials, intermediates, and such fundamental topics as color and electronic states of organic molecules, measurement of color, photochemistry of dyes, and physical chemistry of dyeing. A separate chapter on fluorescent brightening agents has also been included because of their close relationship to synthetic dyes.

These volumes are intended primarily for chemists and technologists who are concerned with the synthesis of dyes and their applications, but since most of the chapters constitute essays in synthetic organic chemistry, they should be of interest to organic chemists in general. An important feature is the very thorough coverage and critical assessment of patent literature as well as of publications in scientific journals. The record of achievement presented in these volumes also indicates the direction of future research.

I am deeply indebted to the authors for accepting my invitation. I must also thank the companies who made it possible for their leading scientists to spare the necessary time. The plan for this multiauthor effort took concrete shape during ten days I spent in the Research

Department of Farbenfabriken Bayer; I am greatly indebted to Professor Petersen, Dr. Delfs, and their colleagues for valuable suggestions. I am grateful to Dr. R. R. Davies of the Research Department, Imperial Chemical Industries (Dyestuffs Division), Manchester, who has helped me in many ways. My thanks are also due to Mr. J. V. Rajan who has assisted me in all the editorial work. Academic Press has handled production of the volumes with its usual efficiency, and it is a pleasure to thank the staff for their cooperation. Finally, I wish to make grateful acknowledgment of the hospitality of the National Chemical Laboratory provided by the Director, Dr. B. D. Tilak, and the Director-General of Scientific and Industrial Research, Dr. Atma Ram, without which I could not have undertaken this project.

K. VENKATARAMAN

National Chemical Laboratory
Poona, India

CONTENTS OF OTHER VOLUMES

VOLUME I

Volume II

VOLUME V *(Tentative)*

List of Abbreviations

Manufacturing companies (CI abbreviations have generally been followed):

AAP	Koppers Co. Inc., Pittsburgh, Pennsylvania (American Aniline Products Inc.)
ACC	Augusta Chemical Co., Augusta, Georgia
Acna	Aziende Colori Nazionali Affini A.C.N.A., Milan, Italy
B & BASF	Badische Anilin- und Soda-Fabrik A.G., Ludwigshafen a. Rhein, Germany
BrC	British Celanese Ltd., Spondon, England
CCC	American Cyanamid Co., Bound Brook, New Jersey
CFM	Cassella Farbwerke Mainkur A.G., Frankfurt a. Main, Germany
Chinoin	Chinoin Gyogyszer-es Vegyeszeti Termelek Gyara RT, Budapest, Hungary
CIBA	CIBA Ltd., Basle, Switzerland
CL	Celanese Corporation of America, New York
CN	Compagnie Nationale de Matières Colorantes et de Produits Chimiques du Nord réunies Etablissements Kuhlmann, Paris, France
DGS	Deutsche Gold- und Silber Scheideanstalt vormals Roessler, Frankfurt, Germany
DH	Durand & Huguenin S. A., Basle, Switzerland
Dow	Dow Chemical Co., Midland, Michigan
EKCo	Eastman Kodak Co., Rochester, New York
Ethicon	Ethicon Inc., Somerville, New Jersey
FBy	Farbenfabriken Bayer A.G., Leverkusen, Germany
FH	Farbwerke Hoechst A.G., Frankfurt/Main-Hoechst, Germany
Filature Provoust	Filature de Laine Provoust, Roubaix, France
Fran	Compagnie Française des Matières Colorantes, Paris, France
FW	Farbenfabrik Wolfen, Kr., Bitterfeld, Germany
G	General Aniline & Film Corporation, New York
Gy	J. R. Geigy S. A., Basle, Switzerland
HCC	Hodogaya Chemical Co., Ltd., Tokyo, Japan

HH	Hardman and Holden Ltd., Manchester, England
HWL	Hickson & Welch Ltd., Castleford, England
IC	Interchemical Corporation, Hawthorne, New Jersey
ICI	Imperial Chemical Industries Ltd., Manchester, England
IG	I. G. Farbenindustrie A.G., Frankfurt a. Main, Germany
K	Kalle & Co., A.G., Biebrich, a. Rhein, Germany
Kewanee	Keewanee Oil Co., Bryn Mawr, Pennsylvania
KYK	Nippon Kayaku Co., Ltd., Tokyo, Japan
LBH	L. B. Holliday & Co., Huddersfield, England
MCI	Mitsubishi Chemical Industries Ltd., Tokyo, Japan
MDW	Mitsui Chemical Industry Co., Ltd., Tokyo, Japan
MLB	Farbwerke vorm. Meister, Lucius & Brüning, Hoechst a. Main, Germany
NAC	Allied Chemical Corporation, New York, New York
Nepera	Nepera Chemical Co., Inc., Harriman, New York
NSK	Sumitomo Chemical Co. Ltd., Osaka, Japan
OBM	Otto B. May, Inc., Newark, New Jersey
PCC	Peerless Color Co., Passaic, New Jersey
PHO	Phoenix Color & Chemical Co., Paterson, New Jersey
Pitt	Pittsburgh Coke & Chemical Co., Pittsburgh, Pennsylvania
RL	Rohner Ltd., Pratteln, Switzerland
S	Sandoz Ltd., Basle, Switzerland
TE	Eastman Chemical Products (Eastman Kodak Co.), Kingsport, Tennessee
Ube-Ditto	Ube-Ditto Kasai Ltd., Osaka, Japan
UCC	Union Carbide Corporation, New York, New York
VGF	Vereinigte Glanzstoff-Fabriken A.G., Wuppertal-Elberfeld, Germany
Vond	N. V. Fabriek van Chemische Producten, Vondelingenplaat, Holland
Whitten	H. A. Whitten Co., New York, New York
YDC	Yorkshire Dyeware & Chemical Co. Ltd., Leeds, England

Journals, Reports and Books:

1961 *Chemical Abstracts List of Abbreviations* has been generally followed. The following special abbreviations have also been used.

BIOS	British Intelligence Objectives Sub-Committee Final Report
CA	Chemical Abstracts
CI	Colour Index, 2nd edition, 1956
CIOS	Combined Intelligence Objectives Sub-Committee Report

CIS	Colour Index, 2nd edition, Supplement 1963
CSD	The Chemistry of Synthetic Dyes, Academic Press, 1952
FIAT	Field Intelligence Agency Technical Report
PB	Technical Report of the Office of the Publication Board, now Office of the Technical Services of the U. S. Department of Commerce
Ullmann	Ullmanns Encyclopädie der Technischen Chemie

Patents:

AustP	Austrian Patent
BeP	Belgian Patent
BP	British Patent
CP	Canadian Patent
CzechP	Czechoslovakian Patent
DAS	Deutsche Auslegeschrift
DBP	Deutsche Bundespatente
DP	Dutch Patent
DRP	Deutsche Reichspatente
EGP	East German Patent
FP	French Patent
IP	Indian Patent
JP	Japanese Patent
PolP	Polish Patent
RP	Russian Patent
SAP	South African Patent
USP	United States Patent

THE CHEMISTRY OF SYNTHETIC DYES

VOLUME III

Chapter I

INTRODUCTION

K. Venkataraman

NATIONAL CHEMICAL LABORATORY, POONA, INDIA

I. Centenaries

Because the synthetic dye industry had its birth in 1856, the period surveyed in these supplementary volumes covers the centenaries of several important events. To commemorate Perkin's discovery of Mauve in 1856, Perkin Centenary Celebrations were held in London and New York and the Proceedings have been published in two volumes,[1,2] which include papers on a wide range of topics: the life and work of Perkin, the development of the dyestuff industry and of organic chemistry, the chemistry of synthetic dyes, and many aspects of the application of dyes. As stated by Robinson,[3]

The discovery of Mauve was an example of sharp observation, but it had very little significance in itself. The really important thing was that the young Perkin had a vision of the possible future. It almost seems now that he was inspired with a sense of mission and he never faltered when this took him into the unfamiliar realms of chemical technology and commerce. The generous impulse of his young blood, his quick enthusiasm, carried him away from the pursuit of pure chemistry, though only to a certain extent. He was always busy with some researches of the kind miscalled academic, and later in life returned to the fold from which he had strayed. Nevertheless, it cannot be too strongly emphasized that William Perkin was the real pioneer of the organic chemical industry not because he discovered Mauve, but because he set to work to manufacture and to sell it.

It is a far cry from the conditions under which Perkin discovered and manufactured the first synthetic dye to the present time when the development of a new dye and its translation to technical practice can only be accomplished as part of the activities of a large dyestuff manufacturing organization.

Several other centenaries of important events occurred during the period 1950–1969. The most important, except for Kekulé's formulation of the cyclic structure of benzene,[4] is the discovery of diazotization by Peter Griess in 1858 and the coupling of diazonium salts in 1864.[5] It is only in recent years that many aspects of diazotization and coupling have been elucidated (see Tedder, Chapter V in this volume). A whole book has

---

[1] "Perkin Centenary London—100 Years of Synthetic Dyestuffs." Pergamon Press, Oxford, 1958.

[2] H. J. White Jr., ed., "Proceedings of the Perkin Centennial." Am. Assoc. Textile Chemists and Colorists, 1956.

[3] R. Robinson, *Endeavour* 15, 94 (1956).

[4] "Kekulé Centennial." Advan. Chem. Ser. No. 61. Am. Chem. Soc., Washington, D. C., 1966.

[5] R. Wizinger, *Angew. Chem.* 70, 199 (1958).

been written on azo and diazo chemistry,[6] and a full volume of Houben-Weyl has been devoted to aromatic diazonium salts and related topics.[7] A recent book includes a comprehensive account of the use of diazonium salts in photography.[8] Other centenaries are of the discoveries of Magenta and its derivatives, Cyanine Blue, Aniline Black, and synthetic Alizarin; and the birth of von Weinberg and Herz.[9]

In the Russian translation of Vols. I and II of this series (*CSD I* and *II*) it is mentioned that little attention has been paid to the work of Russian authors. This neglect was corrected in the Russian edition in a series of footnotes, one of which states that N. N. Zinin in 1842 reduced nitrobenzene to aniline.[10] According to a review by Vorozhtsov and Stepanov,[11] Y. Natanson synthesized Fuchsine two years before Verguin and six months before Perkin's discovery of Mauve.

The three major units of IG Farbenindustrie (Bayer, BASF, and Hoechst) have developed independently since 1945; Bayer and BASF have brought out volumes to celebrate their centenaries, and Hoechst, a Jubilee Volume, which contain valuable reviews of progress in the chemistry of synthetic dyes.[12]

The brief outline of the history of synthetic dyes in *CSD I* concluded with the discovery of copper phthalocyanine by ICI in 1934, phthalocyanine derivatives for dyeing and printing (1947), the Solacet dyes for acetate silk (1936), and the addition of new anthraquinonoid vat dyes by the IG during 1934–37. The war interrupted further progress, but the numerous *BIOS* and *FIAT* reports, supplemented by copied, photographed, or microfilmed documents, made available a great mass of information on the chemistry and technology of German dyes and the vast areas of research on dyes, intermediates, and related organic and inorganic chemicals carried out in the IG laboratories.[13]

[6] H. Zollinger, "Azo and Diazo Chemistry." Wiley (Interscience), New York, 1961.

[7] Houben-Weyl, *in* "Methoden der Organischen Chemie" (R. Stroh, ed.), 4th ed., Vol. X, Part 3. Thieme, Stuttgart, 1965.

[8] J. Kosar, "Light Sensitive Systems." Wiley (Interscience), New York, 1965; see also M. S. Dinaburg, "Photosensitive Diazo Compounds and Their Uses." Focal Press, London, 1967.

[9] *Chem. Ber.* **89**, I and XIX (1956).

[10] "History of Russian Chemistry." Acad. Sci., U.S.S.R., 1954.

[11] N. N. Vorozhtsov, Jr. and B. I. Stepanov, *New Books Abroad* (1963).

[12] "Beitrage zur hundertjahrigen Firmengeschichte 1863–1963." Farbenfabriken Bayer AG, 1964/5; "100 Jahre BASF—Aus der Forschung." 1965; Forschung in Hoechst, Jubilaumsjahr." 1963; E. Baumler, "A Century of Chemistry." Econ Verlag, Düsseldorf, 1968.

[13] For an index of microfilms, see F. O. Robitschek, *FIAT* 764 (4 vols.); see also *FIAT Final Rept.* 1313 (3 vols.).

II. World Production of Dyes

The world production of dyes has increased from 127,000 tons in 1920 to 539,000 tons in 1966, an increase which is surprisingly small in comparison with the increase in production of many industrial products. The more important change has been in the quality (brightness, fastness properties, suitability for modern dyeing practice) and variety (especially in the newer types). The pattern of world dyestuff manufacture from 1936–1966 is shown in Table I.

Detailed data on the production and sales of individual dyes are available only for the United States. Approximately two-thirds of the total consumption of dyes in the United States is accounted for by the textile industry, about a sixth by the paper industry, and the remainder is used chiefly for the production of pigments and in the dyeing of leather and plastics. Over 1500 dyes are manufactured and sold as paste, powders, lumps, and solutions in concentrations varying from 6% to 100%.

Japan, which is surpassed only by the U. S., West Germany, and the USSR in the dyestuff industry, produces over 1300 dyes, of which only 73 have an annual turnover of over 90 tons. There are 5 large companies (Mitsui, Sumitomo, Mitsubishi, Nippon Kayaku, and Hodogaya), besides nearly 70 small producers, and attempts are being made to reorganize production with the object of overcoming the economic disadvantages of manufacturing a large number of dyes in too small quantities. Technical collaboration agreements with foreign manufacturers account for about 2% of the production. Recently Mitsubishi and Hoechst jointly established Kasei Hoechst for the production of reactive dyes.

III. The Chemistry of Commercial Dyes

As the topic for two lectures to mark the centenary of the birth of Sir William Perkin, Rowe advisedly chose the development of the chemistry of *commercial* synthetic dyes,[14] and he drew attention to the assistance given to the dyestuff industry by academic workers who determined the constitution of commercial dyes. It was possible to include extensive additional data on the chemistry of commercial dyes in Vols. I and II of this series as the result of the publication of reports on the German industry after 1945. The present tendency on the part of dyestuff firms, in contrast to the manufacturers of ethical drugs, is to withhold structural information, and it is of interest in this connection to recall a statement

[14] F. M. Rowe, "The Development of the Chemistry of Commercial Synthetic Dyes 1856–1938." Inst. Chem., London, 1938.

TABLE I
PATTERN OF WORLD DYESTUFFS PRODUCTION[1]

Producing country	1936	1958	1962	1966
France	11,400	12,400	14,200	19,949*
West Germany	73,828[2]	32,802	46,358	77,261
Italy	15,000	11,441	21,516*	16,235*
Japan	19,116	20,711	27,962*	45,431*
Switzerland	(8,000)[3]	13,500	24,000	26,400
United Kingdom	27,765	29,000	35,800	38,500
United States	61,168	62,183	100,913*	122,592*
Total Major Producers	216,277	182,037	270,749	346,368
Bulgaria	—	—	800	(1,300)
China	—	15,000	30,000	(38,000)
Czechoslovakia	—	5,000	5,700	(9,250)
East Germany	73,828[2]	9,627	11,900	(14,500)
Hungary	—	1,000	600	(700)
Poland	2,146	8,754	12,000	(14,500)
Rumania	—	3,082	5,000	7,298*
USSR	35,100	80,000	85,600	(82,500)
Total Soviet Bloc	37,246	122,463	151,600	168,048
Argentina	—	1,299	500	(1,800)
Australia	—	152	315*	500*
Belgium	—	1,290	1,260	1,962
Brazil	—	1,000	2,000	(2,500)
Canada	—	140	—	—
Chile	—	102	150	(370)
Denmark	—	1,200	(1,200)	(1,270)
Greece	—	440	(465)	(500)
Holland	—	3,850	4,456	3,045
India	—	2,975	5,000	5,192*
Mexico	—	250	(400)	(800)
Norway	—	15	—	—
Pakistan	—	—	(240)	(240)
Portugal	—	120	201	252
Spain	—	3,500	5,634*	5,634*
Yugoslavia	—	(300)	(300)	(900)
Total—Rest of the world		16,633	22,121	24,965
World total		321,133	444,470	539,381

[1] Figures in tons. Figures in parentheses are estimates. Figures for 1936 and 1958 are from a private communication from ICI, Manchester, U. K. The rest of the figures are those submitted to the Organization for Economic Co-operation and Development (OECD), Paris, except those asterisked, which come from the official sources of the respective countries and are used in preference to those of OECD, either because they give a product group breakdown or because the strengths are more comparable with normal commercial strengths.

[2] Represents production of undivided Germany.

[3] 1936 figures for Switzerland estimated from 1932 and 1937 figures (U. S. Tariff Commission).

of Hofmann[15]: "If a chemist decides to keep the nature of his discovery secret while he markets his product, so that everybody can buy it, he must not be surprised when the secret is only of ephemeral duration. The time of the 'Arcanists' is over."

IV. Colour Index

An event of outstanding importance was the publication in 1956 of the second edition of the *Colour Index* in four volumes, followed by a Supplement in 1963 and quarterly Additions and Amendments (New Series), of which over 20 issues have appeared so far. It is believed that a third edition is in preparation and will appear in about five years. The second edition is a joint undertaking of the Society of Dyers and Colourists and the American Association of Textile Chemists and Colorists in cooperation with dye makers throughout the world, who supplied authentic information on their products. The number (241) of the "dye and pigment manufacturers" is, however, illusory, because the major producers are relatively few and the names of agents and firms who make a few dyes on a small scale or mix or "standardize" dyes have been included.

In the first edition of *Colour Index*, dyes were listed by chemical constitution, but this is now regarded as by no means the best arrangement for users of coloring matters; further, it makes no provision for dealing with dyes whose structures are unknown or have not been disclosed. Dyes in the second category are very large in number at present, because the disclosure of the structure of a new dye has come to be quite exceptional practice.

In Part I, Vols. 1 and 2, of the Second Edition of *Colour Index* dyes and pigments are classified according to their usage (Table II). From the user's point of view the most important property of a coloring matter is its hue on a given substrate, and dyes are consequently subdivided into a regular series of the hue groups (yellow, orange, red, violet, blue, green, brown, and black; also white for pigments). Each entry carries a reference number (e.g., CI Vat Blue 20); the numbers are consecutive within each group to provide for extensions as supplementary volumes and issues of Additions and Amendments appear. For each dye information is provided on all the known commercial names under which it is sold, methods of application, the more important fastness properties, and certain other basic data. Attention is drawn to the "well established custom in the dye and pigment making and using industries that all such statements are

---

[15] Cited by D. H. Wilcox, "Kekulé and the Dye Industry." Kekulé Centennial, Advan. Chem. Ser. No. 61. Am. Chem. Soc., Washington, D. C., 1966.

TABLE II

Dyes (Generic Names) in *Colour Index*, Part I, Inclusive of Supplement, 1963, and Additions and Amendments (New Series) up to No. 20, July 1968[1]

Application class[2]	Hue									Total
	Yellow	Orange	Red	Violet	Blue	Green	Brown	Black	White	
Acid	162	121	311	104	229	84	307	149	—	1467
Mordant	57	41	82	58	68	48	84	77	—	515
Basic	42	43	58	35	75	8	9	7	—	277
Disperse	88	66	132	44	127	2	8	28	—	495
Natural	28	6	32	—	3	4	12	6	1	92
Food	13	4	13	2	5	4	3	2	—	46
Direct	122	104	214	91	247	74	197	131	—	1180
Sulfur, Solubilized sulfur, Leuco sulfur	15	4	10	4	19	33	81	17	—	183
Vat, Solubilized Vat	45	26	56	21	69	43	72	54	—	386
Ingrain	1	—	—	—	12	4	—	—	—	17
Condense[3]	1	—	—	—	2	1	—	—	—	4
Azoic	19	14	61	7	25	4	20	22	—	172
Reactive	52	43	83	18	68	13	18	20	—	315
Pigment	106	39	173	33	60	40	14	22	31,[4] 6[5]	524
Solvent	90	56	128	24	69	21	44	27	—	459
Total	841	567	1353	441	1078	383	869	562	38	6132

[1] Excludes 543 Generic Names subsequently discontinued.

[2] In addition, the following Components and Chemicals and Disperse Mixtures are mentioned:

Components and Chemicals [Colorless components (i) used for the production of dyes on the fiber and (ii) which fluoresce under ultraviolet radiation. Developers are usually coupling components for azo dyes]: Azoic Diazo Components, 126; Azoic Coupling Components, 106; Oxidation Bases, 35; Fluorescent Brightening Agents, 190; Developers, 23; and Reducing Agents, 13. Total, 493.

Disperse Mixtures: Navy, 51; Green, 32; Brown, 57; Gray, 16; and Black, 46. Total, 202.

[3] Classified earlier as Ingrain Colors. The classification of condense dyes is not firmly established and may be modified. The present definition of "condense dyes" is as follows: Dyes which during or after application react covalently with themselves or other compounds, other than with the substrate, to form molecules of much increased size.

[4] Mostly inorganic.

[5] Metal powders in flake form (usually termed "bronze").

'without guarantee,' for while a maker may guarantee the quality of his products he cannot guarantee that some one else has used them correctly."

In Part II, Vol. 3, the classification is on the basis of chemical constitution (Table III), and each dye is specified by a number in five figures (e.g., CI 31505 corresponding to CI Direct Brown 132 in Part I).

In each class of coloring matters, the description is preceded by a brief account of its characteristics and references to the literature (general as well as special aspects). The structural formula of each dye is followed by a brief outline of manufacturing methods, color reactions which can assist in identification, the names of the discoverers, and literature references including patents in particular. Volume 3 also lists a number of coloring matters, distinguished by an asterisk and the absence of a Part I number, which are not now known to be manufactured; they are included because their chemistry and their relation to current products are of interest.

Part II also contains an index of intermediates including their systematic and trivial names, structural formulas, and the Part II numbers of the dyes in the manufacture of which they are used. Part III, Vol. 4, lists the abbreviations and literature references, and it also contains fastness tests data, an index of patents, a commercial names index, and tables relating the numbers in the second edition to those in the first edition and Schultz (7th edition). The commercial names index includes the names of all homogeneous dyes made by the former IG, obsolete range names, and the range names under which dyes and pigments are sold by traders.

In the Supplement, 1963, manufacturers have reported about 1250 new dyes, representing more than a quarter of the number in the Second Edition, 1956. The data in the Supplement include and supersede all the information contained in the quarterly Additions and Amendments 1–16. A completely new commercial names index is provided because of the large number of new commercial names and the numerous changes in the original index. An important feature of the Supplement is the introduction of a new usage group of reactive dyes containing 89 entries. The section on sulfur dyes has been completely rewritten, using three generic names: (1) CI Sulfur (conventional or disperse sulfur dyes), (2) CI Leuco Sulfur (dry or liquid mixtures with Na_2S or sodium formaldehyde sulfoxylate), and (3) CI Solubilized Sulfur (thiosulfonic acid derivatives prepared by the action of sodium sulfite or bisulfite on the parent sulfur dye). The section on food dyes is a record of the changes made in the permitted list in the U. K., U. S., and West Germany; and it is rightly added that the latest information on the regulations in force should be obtained from an authoritative official source.

Reference is made in the 1963 Supplement to the unification of testing

TABLE III

Dyes of Known Chemical Constitution in *Colour Index*, Part II,
Inclusive of Supplement, 1963, and Additions and Amendments
(New Series) up to No. 20, July 1968

Chemical class	Volume 3	Supplement 1963	Additions and Amendments	New structures[1]
1. Nitroso	7	—	—	1
2. Nitro	36	1	—	7
3. Monoazo	778	34	21	247
4. Disazo	806	14	10	262
5. Trisazo	247	7	3	75
6. Tetrakisazo and azo dyes of greater complexity	88	1	—	30
7. Azo dyes produced on the fiber	2	—	—	—
8. Azoic				
(a) Diazo components	57	2	—	3
(b) Coupling components	37	1	6	14
9. Stilbene	40	2	2	4
10. Diphenylmethane	2	—	1	1
11. Triarylmethane	181	1	—	53
12. Xanthene	68	—	1	16
13. Acridine	17	1	—	4
14. Quinoline	9	—	—	—
15. Methine and polymethine	20	—	—	2
16. Thiazole	4	—	—	1
17. Indamine and indophenol	6	—	—	1
18. Azine	59	—	—	10
19. Oxazine	54	—	1	6
20. Thiazine	15	—	—	—
21. Sulfur	100	5	—	32
22. Lactone	4	—	—	—
23. Aminoketone and hydroxyketone	29	—	—	6
24. Anthraquinone and related coloring matters	—	4	—	72
(a) Dyes without heterocyclic nucleus fused to central vatting system	290	—	6	—
(b) Dyes with heterocyclic nucleus fused to central vatting system	140	—	—	—
25. Indigoid	117	1	—	5
26. Phthalocyanine	19	1	1	6
27. Natural organic coloring matters	76	—	—	—
28. Oxidation bases	65	—	—	—
29. Inorganic	222	—	—	—
Total	3591	76	54	858
Grand total		3721[2]		

[1] Structures not mentioned in *CSD I* and *II*; obsolete dyes are not included.
[2] Includes 1288 obsolete dyes.

methods for fastness properties and to the two basic systems: (1) American, published annually in the Technical Manual of the American Association of Textile Chemists and Colorists (AATCC); and (2) ISO/ECE, methods developed by the International Standardization Organization (ISO) and by the Europäisch-Continentale Echtheitsconvention or Groupement d'Etudes Continental European pour la Solidite des Teintures et Impressions (ECE). However, the fastness testing methods for the cited ratings are indicated by the symbols "A" (AATCC methods); ECE; ISO; SDC (methods of the Society of Dyers and Colourists); and SNV (new Swiss national standards).

In the Additions and Amendments (New Series), the items are arranged in three main groups: (1) CI Generic Names; (2) CI Constitutions; and (3) Commercial Names Index. Although there are very few dyes for which structures are disclosed, this quarterly publication gives authentic information, of obvious value to the user, concerning new dyes added to a commercial range (new entries with a Part I number), old dyes made by an additional manufacturer, and dyes now deleted from a commercial range.

A. STRUCTURES DISCLOSED IN *Colour Index*

Most of the dyes whose structures are given in *Colour Index* and not in Volumes I and II of this series (*CSD I* and *II*) are (a) no longer manufactured, or (b) of ancient vintage prepared from well-known intermediates, or (c) dyes in the microfilms indexed in *FIAT* 764. The great majority naturally are azo dyes. Several are azoic pigments from known diazonium and coupling components. Many were discovered in the last century, and nearly all before 1950. A few examples of dyes not listed in *FIAT* 764 and of some interest may be cited. CI Acid Red 138 (CI 18073) is (p,n-dodecylaniline→ N-acetyl H-acid). CI Direct Blue 166 [CI 23165; 3,3'-dihydroxybenzidine $\rightrightarrows$ (J-acid)$_2$] is an example of dyes mentioned in *CSD* with reference to patents, but not linked to commercial names. CI Direct Green 28 (CI 14155) is mentioned in old Ciba patents and is a minor variation of the dye (VIII) in *CSD I* (p. 588). CI Acid Red 15 (CI 17930) is the only dye from o-aminobiphenyl(→ N-acetyl-γ-acid).

CI Acid Green 2 (CI 18775) is the copper complex of an azo dye from a triphenylmethane; a dye of similar type (CI Mordant Green 21; CI 43845) described in a 1909 patent is not indexed in CI Supplement. Three disazo dyes from diaminotriphenylmethanes are solvent colors (CI Solvent Yellow 30, Red 22, Red 18; CI 21240, 21250, 21260). CI Disperse Orange 13 (CI 26080; aniline → α-naphthylamine → phenol) is typical of

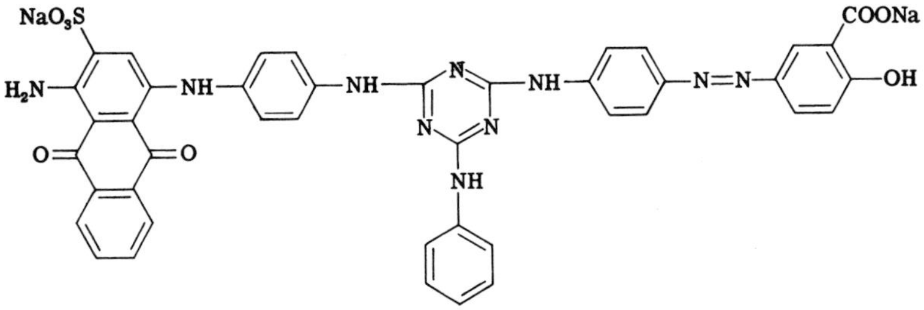

CI Direct Green 28

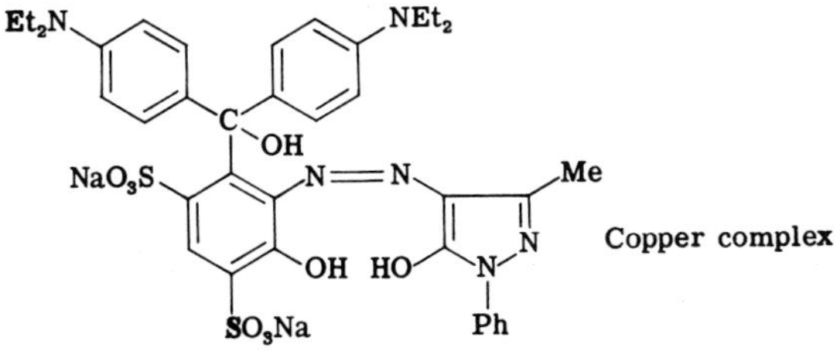

CI Acid Green 2

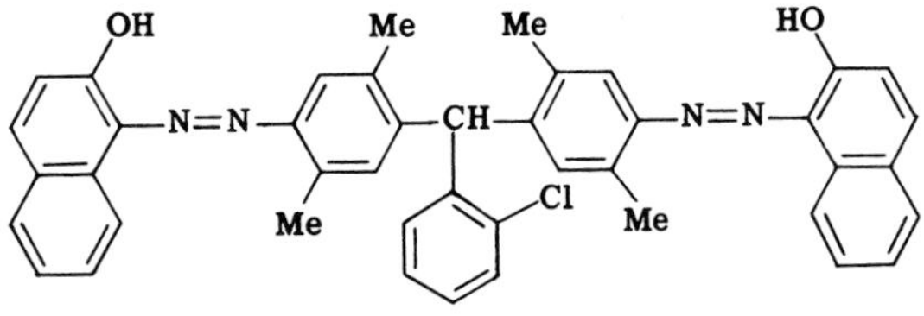

CI Solvent Red 22

dyes suitable for application to polyester fiber because of the terminal phenol group. Contrary to a statement in *CSD I*, 2-naphthylamine-4,8-disulfonic acid (A) is now an important intermediate from which 20 or more commercial dyes are made; CI Direct Yellows 50 and 34 (CI 29025 and 29060) are (A → *m*-toluidine or cresidine; phosgenated). Fast bluish gray shades on cotton are obtained from CI Direct Black 103 (CI 34179; A → α-naphthylamine → 1,7-Cleve's acid $\xrightarrow{\text{alk}}$ γ-acid).

CI Disperse Red 64 (CI 11136) is (2-amino-6-ethoxybenzothiazole → *N*-phenyldiethanolamine).

Acetylacetone is a coupling component for several acid dyes used as cobalt complexes; e.g., CI Acid Orange 100 (CI 11640) is the 2:1 cobalt complex of 2-amino-6-chloro-4-nitrophenol → acetylacetone. CI Acid

Violet 78 (CI 12205) and CI Acid Green 62 (CI 11836) are the 2:1 chromium complexes of (2-amino-4-methylsulfonylphenol → β-naphthol) and (picramic acid → p-hydroxyacetanilide), respectively.

CI Pigment Red 117 (CI 15603) is the barium salt of (3-amino-6-chlorocumene-4-sulfonic acid → β-naphthol). CI Pigment Red 77 (CI 15826) is the manganese lake of (2,3-dichloroaniline-5-sulfonic acid → 2-hydroxy-3-naphthoic acid).

The aftercoppered dye CI Direct Black 104 (CI 28685) is (2-amino-5-nitrophenol → J-acid → 8-hydroxyquinoline).

CI Azoic Coupling Components 113, 111, and 112 (CI 37567–9) are, respectively, the anilide, o-toluidide, and 4-chloro-2,5-dimethoxyanilide of 2-hydroxy-6-methoxy-3-naphthoic acid, an acid first used for this purpose; others are various anilides of 2-hydroxy-3-naphthoic acid, 3-hydroxydibenzofuran-2-carboxylic acid, or acetoacetic acid.

One of the simplest cationic dyes for acrylic fiber is CI Basic Red 18 (CI 11085).

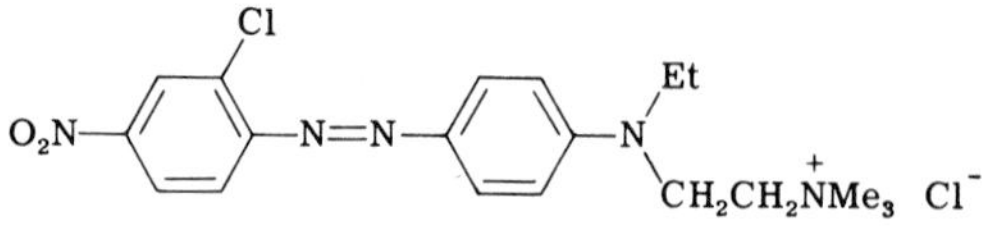

CI Basic Red 18
CI 11085

CI Pigment Yellow 101 (CI 48052) is the azine of 2-hydroxy-1-naphthaldehyde. CI Pigment Violet 19 (CI 46500) is the β-phase of linear quinacridone; but Cinquasia Red B and Y, which are in the γ-form, are included.

CI Solvent Green 7 (Pyranine; D and C Green 8; CI 59040), a very yellowish green, is prepared by the partial hydrolysis of pyrene-1,3,6,8-tetrasulfonic acid.

CI Acid Black 97 (CI 65008) is in fact the 1,1'-anthrimide. Another interesting anthraquinone derivative is CI Disperse Blue 27 (CI 60767).

The structures of 19 reactive dyes of the 1,3,5-triazine and vinyl sulfone types have become available, and have been published mainly in two papers by Allan et al. (see Panchartek et al.[16,17]). The same authors have also determined the structures of several direct dyes: CI Direct Yellow 70, Orange 94, Red 174, and Black 122.

Dyes classified as "aminoketone and hydroxyketone coloring matters"

[16] J. Panchartek, Z. J. Allan, and F. Muzik, Collection Czech. Chem. Commun. 25, 2783 (1960).
[17] J. Panchartek, Z. J. Allan, and J. Peskocil, Collection Czech. Chem. Commun. 27, 268 (1962).

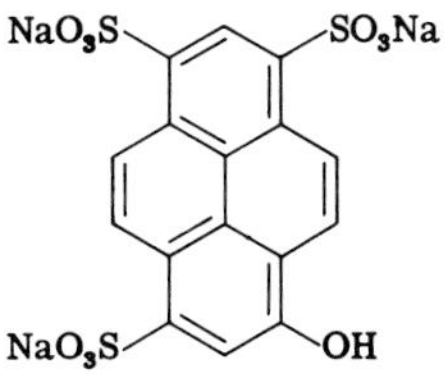

CI Solvent Green 7; CI 59040

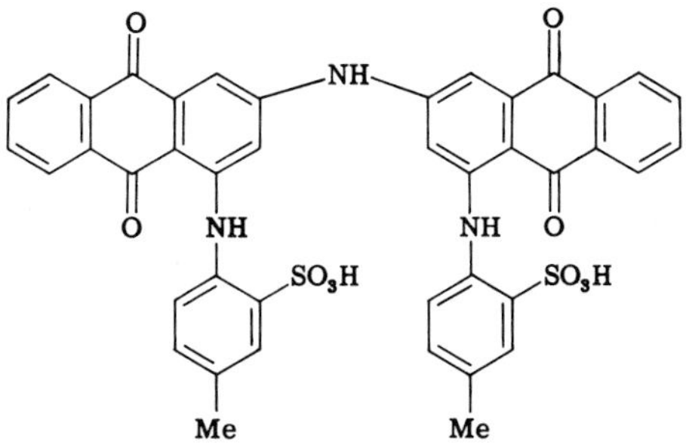

CI Acid Black 97; CI 65008

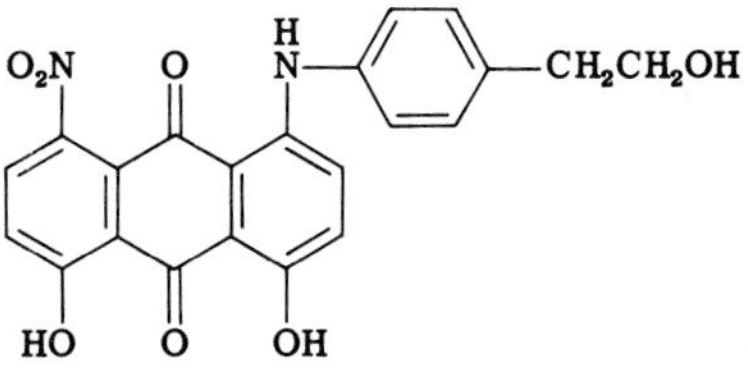

CI Disperse Blue 27; CI 60767

should perhaps be treated as derivatives of benzoquinone and naphthoquinone. In *CSD II* derivatives of naphthalic and perylene-3,4,9,10-tetracarboxylic acid were relegated to an unclassified group of "Miscellaneous Dyes." Structural formulas are assigned to dyes such as CI Vat Brown 37 (CI 56012); they are of little technical importance, but the purity of the compounds and the chemical and other evidence need to be examined before the structures are accepted.

Vat dyes in relation to *Colour Index* are discussed in Vol. VI of this series.

There are minor differences such as the position of a sulfonic group in

CI Vat Brown 37

the structures given in *CSD* and in *Colour Index* for many dyes, but mostly azo dyes, because of their vast number and variety and of the possibilities for replacing intermediates. In addition, commercial names are liable to change as well as increase in number with the advent of new manufacturers; a new dyestuff index is therefore provided at the end of these volumes, in which errors are corrected and the dyes in *CSD I* and *II* are related to CI Part I and Part II numbers.

B. NATURAL DYES AND PIGMENTS

The section on natural dyes and pigments in Part I of the *Colour Index* is of limited value because, unlike synthetic dyes, natural dyes are not standardized commercial products, except for logwood, perhaps cochineal as a food color, and two or three others to a much smaller extent. The essential basis for the *Colour Index*, which is the authentic information on their products supplied by reputable manufacturers, therefore does not exist for the natural dyes. The section in Part II dealing with the chemistry of natural organic coloring matters fulfills no real purpose. The names in Part I and the numbers in Part II cannot be correlated, since many of the former refer to more than one botanical species and many of the plants contain more than one coloring matter. As stated in the preamble, "the literature on the constitution of the components of natural dyes and pigments is extremely voluminous." As a result of the general interest in natural products and the availability of greatly improved methods of isolation and structure determination, the structures of many natural coloring matters have been proved or revised in recent years, and it is not possible for *Colour Index* to maintain the data in this field up to date, even if it is limited arbitrarily to "the colored organic materials of animal or vegetable origin which either have been or are used as dyes or pigments."

A natural coloring matter which has proved to be related to technically important dyes for polyester fiber covered by several recent patents is lac dye (CI Natural Red 25). In *Atharva-Veda*, dating back a few centuries BC, a hymn describes the medicinal properties of the deep red resinous secretion of the lac insect (*Coccus laccae; Laccifer lacca* Kerr), and for many centuries thereafter the dye was used for producing crimson and scarlet shades on wool and silk mordanted with aluminum and tin. Recent work[18] has shown that lac dye is a complex mixture, the main constituents of which are two 2-phenylanthraquinones, laccaic acids A and B (I; R = NHCOCH₃ or OH). Over 500,000 kg of crude lac dye are now washed away every year in the course of shellac manufacture, and there is a possibility of converting it into a few useful dyes.

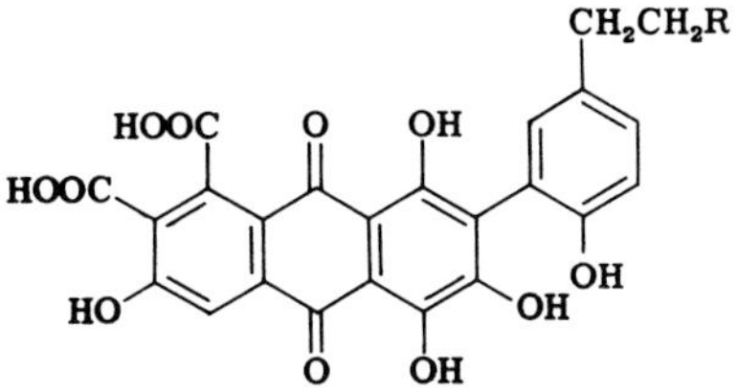

Laccaic acid A: R = NHCOCH₃
Laccaic acid B: R = OH

(I)

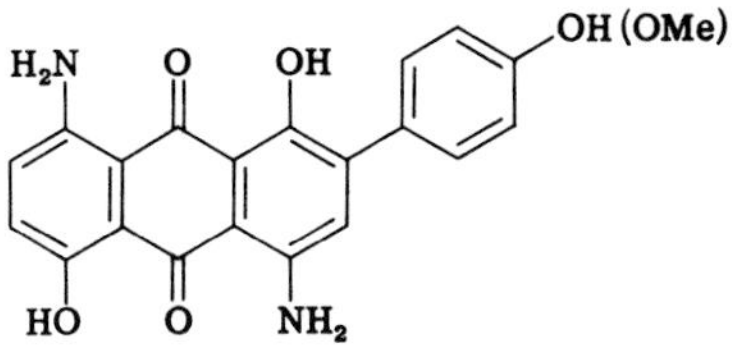

(II)

It was discovered by the IG in 1926 that when 1,5-diamino-4,8-dihydroxyanthraquinone-3,7-disulfonic acid was treated with phenol or anisole at a low temperature in the presence of sulfuric and boric acids, a remarkable nuclear phenylation with the displacement of a sulfonic group took place. The product, a monosulfonic acid of (II), was an acid dye for wool, and the reaction apparently was not exploited commercially because of the availability of cheaper acid dyes. The IG patents[19] also mentioned that the sulfonic group could be removed by treatment with aqueous sodium dithionite and ammonia and that the compounds (II), which could be used as mordant dyes, yielded valuable vat dyes by acylation of the amino groups. These claims likewise found no practical application; but 2-arylanthraquinones, such as Foron Blue (II) of Sandoz, are now marketed as fast and brilliant dyes for polyester fiber.

V. Raw Materials for Synthetic Dyes

Coal tar continues to be an important source of aromatic compounds as raw materials for the dyestuff industry, but petroleum-derived benzene, toluene, xylenes, and naphthalene have now become equally important (see Collin and Zander, Chapter II in this volume). The U. S. pro-

[18] E. D. Pandhare, A. V. Rama Rao, R. Srinivasan, and K. Venkataraman, *Tetrahedron* Suppl. 8, Part I, 229 (1966); E. D. Pandhare, A. V. Rama Rao, I. N. Shaikh, and K. Venkataraman, *Tetrahedron Letters* p. 2437 (1967); R. Burwood, G. Read, K. Schofield, and D. Wright, *J. Chem. Soc., C* p. 842 (1967).
[19] IG, *DRP* 445,269; 446,563; 456,235.

duction in 1965 of benzene, toluene, and xylenes by petroleum operators was, respectively, about 5, 18.8, and 50 times the quantities produced by coke-oven operators; naphthalene production was about 75%. However, the dyestuff industry is only a minor consumer of these hydrocarbons in comparison with their scale of production and the demands of the plastics and other industries.

Collin and Zander have referred to the impact of gas chromatography and spectroscopy on tar analysis, as a result of which the number of aromatic compounds isolated from coal tar has risen from 215 in 1951 to about 475 in 1967. Methods of isolation in large-scale practice have continually increased in efficiency. The major constituents have thus become available in larger quantities at lower prices, and in addition it has become technically feasible to separate compounds present in as low a percentage as 0.1. Some of these may find use as starting materials for the synthesis of dyes.

Cyclohexane, now produced in vast quantities from petroleum in the U. S., is comparable in price to benzene, but the purity is not adequate for oxidation to cyclohexanol–cyclohexanone (feedstock for caprolactam, adipic acid, and cyclohexylamine), and cyclohexane of high purity is still made by the hydrogenation of benzene. Processes for the preparation of intermediates such as phenol and aniline from cyclohexane are covered by patents, but technical production continues to be based on benzene. Since both hydrogenation and dehydrogenation are technically feasible, the direction in which the cycle is operated will depend on the ultimate cost of the products.

The increased use of petroleum-based raw materials and natural gas limits the availability of anthracene; but the difference in cost of anthraquinone from anthracene and from phthalic anhydride–benzene is perhaps marginal or dependent on local conditions. The importance of anthraquinone is shown by the large capital expenditure undertaken by American Cyanamid to produce anthraquinone from naphthoquinone and butadiene, finally written off in 1961.

VI. Intermediates

Colour Index, 1956, gives a list of 1110 intermediates, together with the CI numbers of the dyes for which each intermediate is used. The Supplement, 1963, lists 30 additions; and there are none in the Additions and Amendments so far. Since the intermediates relate only to dyes of known structure or known methods of preparation (such as the sulfur dyes), the limitations of the index will be realized. Intermediates vary in complexity from formaldehyde to violanthrone and 4,4′-bisbenzamido-1,1′-anthrimide ($C_{42}H_{25}N_3O_6$). Many are used for a single dye in contrast to the major intermediates (such as aniline, p-nitroaniline, β-naphthol, J-acid, and H-acid) used for a large number of dyes.

Progress in intermediates (see Vorozhtsov, Chapter III in this volume) has been in four main directions: (a) new or modified methods, with simultaneous advances in the chemical engineering aspects, for the production on a very large scale of intermediates such as phenol, phthalic anhydride, and terephthalic acid, required for the plastics, synthetic fiber, and other industries; (b) improvements in production methods for important intermediates such as H-acid and the aminoanthraquinones, which are common to many dyes; (c) new intermediates (including many heterocyclic compounds) for reactive dyes, cationic dyes, disperse dyes, pigments, etc.; and (d) a better understanding of the mechanisms of aromatic substitution and other reactions.[20]

Two new processes for phenol are from (a) benzene via cumene (isopropylbenzene) and its hydroperoxide, and (b) toluene via benzoic acid, Cu^{II} benzoate, Cu^I benzoate, and o-benzoyloxybenzoic acid. The first is much more important and is superseding all other processes in spite of the disadvantage that every ton of phenol is accompanied by 0.6 ton of acetone. Air oxidation of benzene to phenol has been extensively studied, but is technically unsuccessful so far. A patent[21] claims the direct amination of benzene to aniline by treatment with ammonia in the presence of a catalyst; its technical feasibility seems remote at present; but in view of the advances in catalysis such direct hydroxylation and amination of aromatic hydrocarbons are future possibilities. The first plant to make aniline by ammonolysis of phenol (20,000 tons per year) is to be built in Japan.[21a]

Continuous nitration and catalytic reduction of nitro compounds (in the vapor phase for nitrobenzene and the liquid phase for others) are processes in which there has been considerable progress. Under the usual reaction conditions the proportions of isomers obtained in aromatic substitutions do not always correspond to industrial needs. Attempts to in-

---

[20] In a recent review of some reactions leading to dye intermediates, K. Gerlach ("Synthese und Reaktionsmechanismen in der Farbstoffchemie," p. 48. Sauerländer AG, Aarau, 1968) has discussed naphthalene derivatives for the synthesis of amphilinked direct dyes, the preparation of diazonium compounds by processes other than diazotization, the synthesis of 2-nitronaphthalene and similar compounds from the adduct of naphthalene and hexachlorocyclopentadiene, reactions with tetracyanoethylene and related compounds, and the synthesis of isoindolenines, thienothiophthenes, isothiazoles, pyrazoles, and indazoles.

[21] L. Schmerling and Universal Oil Products Co., *USP* 2,948,755.

[21a] *Chem. Eng. News* **47**, No. 12, 37 (1969).

crease the ratio of the desired isomer (e.g., the para-compound in the nitration of toluene and chlorobenzene) by changing the reaction conditions, or by isomerization as in the Henkel reaction on the phthalic acids, have already produced useful results. The von Richter reaction, in which *p*-nitrochlorobenzene yields *m*-chlorobenzoic acid as the major product, does not appear to have been exploited for dye intermediates. A novel approach to β-substitution in naphthalene, covered by patents of the Fundamental Research Co., is by nitration or halogenation of the Diels-Alder adduct of naphthalene and hexachlorocyclopentadiene, followed by thermal dissociation of the adduct.[22] Starting from β-methylnaphthalene, 3-nitro-2-methylnaphthalene can thus be obtained and used for a new and perhaps technically feasible synthesis of 2-hydroxy-3-naphthoic acid.

Nitration, halogenation, sulfonation, and other reactions, which are involved in the synthesis of dye intermediates but are also fundamental reactions of aromatic chemistry, have been extensively investigated as part of the progress in physical organic chemistry. Among the special reactions of dye intermediates, the benzidine rearrangement is the subject of many papers, but none represents the last word on its mechanism. Rieche and Seeboth[23] have demonstrated the mechanism of the Bucherer reaction as proceeding through the tetralone sulfonic acids (see, however, Vorozhtsov, Chapter III in this volume).

A recent book on chemical carcinogenesis[24] deals in detail with the aromatic amines and azo compounds. Bladder cancer occurring in the dyestuff industry is discussed; benzidine and α- and β-naphthylamines are highly potent, and the manufacture of Magenta and Auramine is dangerous. The production and use of 2-naphthylamine have now been banned in many countries including India, but curiously enough, benzidine continues to be produced and used on a large scale. The U. S. production of benzidine in 1965 was over 1.6 million pounds. However, it is understood that the precautions taken in the manufacture of α-naphthylamine and benzidine in the U. K. (and presumably elsewhere) have been intensified. Methods have been described[25] for the determination of benzidine and β-naphthylamine in the atmosphere, the plant, and clothing. 2-Naphthylamine sulfonic acids, which are major intermediates, are now made by the Bucherer reaction on naphthol sulfonic acids; but there is no evidence for the tacit assumption that the naphthylamine sulfonic acids do not share the potency of the parent amine, and a calculated risk has been

---

[22] Fundamental Research Co. *USP* 3,309,402; *FP* 1,366,805; and others.
[23] H. Seeboth, *Angew. Chem. Intern. Ed. Engl.* **6**, 307 (1967).
[24] D. B. Clayson, "Chemical Carcinogenesis." Churchill, London, 1962.
[25] L. T. Butt and N. Strafford, *J. Appl. Chem. (London)* **6**, 525 (1956).

taken.[24] In *CSD I* (p. 95), the erroneous statement was made that the salts and sulfonic acids of the amines are innocuous.

4-Aminobiphenyl, which may be present in diphenylamine, is also a carcinogen.

VII. Dyes for New Synthetic Fibers

Nylon is the most important synthetic fiber, the combined world production of nylon 6 and 66 today being more than 3000 million pounds; but nylon textiles were well established before 1950 and dyes for nylon were therefore discussed in *CSD I*. The polyamide is the most hydrophilic of the synthetic fibers, and it can be dyed with direct, acid, and metallized dyes. Careful selection of known dyes and their reclassification from the point of view of their dyeing and fastness properties, rather than totally new synthetic effort, provided the main solution to dyeing problems; cationic or anionic auxiliary agents and pressure dyeing at high temperatures have helped in covering yarn irregularities and obtaining better wash-fastness. In addition, disperse dyes are very suitable for dyeing nylon by a simple dyeing process from aqueous dye liquors.

Apart from the discovery of the reactive dyes, progress in the development of new dyes has depended mainly on the development of two new fibers: polyester and polyacrylonitrile. There was a casual reference to Terylene in *CSD I*, together with the statement that the cold-drawn fibers were very difficult to dye. World production of polyester fiber today is over 2000 million pounds. Acrylic fibers were unknown until 1948 and acquired real importance when Orlon 42 was introduced by du Pont in 1953. The production of acrylic and modacrylic fibers (defined, respectively, as containing not less than 85% and 35–85% of polyacrylonitrile) is now over 1800 million pounds. Other synthetic fibers, modifications of polyamide and polyester fibers (e.g., both acid-dyeable and basic-dyeable polyesters), and the increasing tendency to use blends of two or more synthetic and natural fibers have created attendant problems concerning dyes and dyeing processes. A BASF process for casting a porous fabric directly from a monomer may reshape the textile industry, and will incidentally involve dyeing problems.[25a]

A. DISPERSE DYES

Disperse dyes (mainly azo dyes and anthraquinone derivatives) are used on cellulose di- and triacetate, polyester, and polyamide fibers and to

[25a] *Chem. Eng. News* **47**, No. 12, 38 (1969); C. H. Krauch, *Naturwissenschaften* **11**, 539 (1968).

some extent on acrylic fibers (see Straley, Chapter VIII in this volume). Using greatly improved methods of dispersion, many of the older acetate dyes, such as derivatives of 1,4-diamino- and 1-amino-4-hydroxyanthraquinone and the blue azo dyes from diazotized 2-bromo-4,6-dinitroaniline, have been found to be suitable for polyester fiber; but the use of carriers (biphenyl, *o*-phenylphenol, etc., as solvents and fiber-swelling agents, fulfilling the same functions as water in the dyeing of hydrophilic fibers) or high temperatures and pressures in the dyeing processes which are in technical practice at the present time, as well as the more stringent fastness requirements (for instance, toward sublimation), have led to the synthesis of many new dyes specifically designed for polyester fiber. Many are derivatives of anthraquinone containing amino and hydroxy substituents in the 1,4- or 1,4,5,8-positions with additional substituents in the 2- or 2,3-positions (including annelated ring systems); and many are azo dyes from low molecular weight heterocyclic intermediates, based for instance on the observation that the replacement of *p*-nitroaniline by 2-amino-5-nitrothiazole as the diazonium component for a monoazo dye produces a profound bathochromic shift from red to blue.

Since certain shades can only be obtained by using a mixture of disperse dyes, the compatibility of dyes in a mixture is important.[26] An interesting claim in this connection is that a mixture of the two dyes (III; R = H or Me) dyes cellulose esters and nylon in twice the depth obtained with either dye.[27]

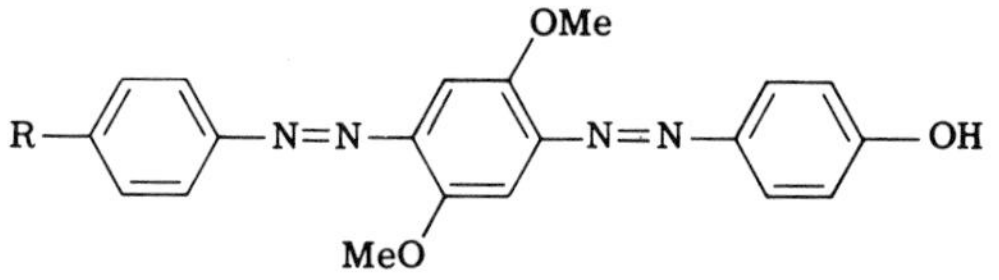

(III)

B. DYES FOR ACRYLIC FIBERS

It was nearly impossible to dye acrylic fibers when they were first marketed in 1948, but numerous dyes and several dyeing techniques are now available. Earlier methods, of limited use for dark shades, depended on the fact that under certain conditions acrylic fibers take up cuprous ion and can then be dyed with acid-mordant dyes. The dyeing properties

[26] K. Hoffmann, W. McDowell, and R. Weingarten, *J. Soc. Dyers Colourists* **84,** 306 (1968).
[27] Eastman Kodak, *USP* 3,253,876.

were then greatly improved by the introduction of cationic or anionic sites into the polymer during manufacture by copolymerization with appropriate monomers, thus imparting affinity for acid or basic dyes. The basic-dyeable acrylic fibers, such as Orlon 42, are now much more important, because they can be dyed in fast and brilliant shades.

Selected polymethine and triphenylmethane dyes, already known or modified in structure, were first used; but the need in particular for improving light fastness led to intensive research for new dyes (see Baer in Vol. IV). These "cationic dyes" belong to three main types: (a) dyes in which the cationic charge is more or less insulated from the chromophore; (b) dyes carrying a positive charge and belonging mainly to the carbocyanine and azacyanine classes; and (c) amine salts. Valuable contributions to heterocyclic chemistry have been made in this connection, and another notable development is Hünig's oxidative coupling reaction for the synthesis of diazahemicyanine dyes.[28]

C. Dyes for Polypropylene

Because of its tensile strength, excellent chemical and rot resistance, nearly total absence of moisture regain, low bulk density and low cost, polypropylene fiber is being widely used for carpets, blankets, and upholstery; it has also entered the textile apparel field. One drawback is the relatively low softening point; another is that, being an isotactic and highly crystalline alkane, it is difficult to dye. Most of the polypropylene fiber in use today is uncolored or mass-pigmented; but the production of a dyeable fiber is rapidly expanding. The main dyeing method is to incorporate a metallic compound (notably the nickel complex of an alkylated o,o'-dihydroxydiphenyl sulfide or aluminum monostearate), which also stabilizes the fiber to degradation by ultraviolet light, and dye with disperse dyes (e.g., the azo dyes: anthranilic acid → β-naphthol; p-aminoacetanilide → p-cresol) as ligand molecules. Numerous patents cover specific dye structures, such as azo dyes from heterocyclic hydrazines and 1,2-quinones, or from heterocyclic diazonium components.[29] Thus the dyes (IV) from 2-hydrazinothiazoles and 1,2-naphthoquinone dye the nickel-modified fiber a fast blue. A second method is to incorporate a basic monomer such as 4-vinylpyridine at the stage of polymerization, whereby the fiber becomes dyeable with acid dyes and metallized azo dyes, the 1:2 complexes being particularly suitable. Other dye-bond-

[28] For a recent review, see S. Hünig, *Angew. Chem. Intern. Ed. Engl.* 7, 335 (1968).

[29] FBy, *BP* 1,050,778; 1,055,489; 1,071,590; 1,086,975; 1,132,638; Nippon Kayaku Co., *JP* 3310 (1967).

ing groups can be grafted on the swollen fibers. Copolymerization of
α-acrylamidoanthraquinone and its derivatives with vinyl monomers
gives colored polymers.[30] Preformed heterocyclic polymers (e.g., a co-
polymer of N-vinylpyrrolidinone and dimethylaminoethyl methacrylate)
may be blended with polypropylene.[31] When polypropylene is modified
with a very high molecular weight polyglycol (100,000 to over 1 million),
the latter concentrates in the amorphous region of the fiber; the fiber
structure is thus opened up for the absorption of large dye molecules.[32]

Extensive work has been carried out in Japan on dyes for polypropylene. A process for improving the dyeability of unmodified polypropylene
is by chlorination or bromination; good affinity for cationic dyes is thus
obtained.[33] The affinity for dyes is increased by the addition of C_{16-18}-
amines.[34] A few disperse dyes among the large number available for
cellulose acetate and polyester fibers have been found to be suitable for
dyeing unmodified polypropylene, but actual use appears to be very
limited. The advantage of introducing hydrophobic groups into azo and
anthraquinonoid disperse dyes was demonstrated by Teramura.[35]

p-Disazobenzene derivatives (V), in which one or both the R substituents may be tert-butyl, are very suitable for directly dyeing polypropylene fibers yellow and orange shades from an aqueous dispersion.[36]
Disperse dyes containing nuclear methyl or ethyl groups or long alkyl
chains have been claimed in several patents as fast dyes for polypropylene.[37] Thus the blue dye, 1,4-bis-2′,4′,6′-triethylanilinoanthraquinone,
has affinity for polypropylene, but not the unsubstituted dianilino
compound.[38]

Two disperse dyes, Resolin Yellow 5R (CI Disperse Yellow 7; p-amino-

(IV)   (V)

[30] G. A. Voloshin and B. G. Boldyrev, Zh. Organ. Khim. 4, No. 7, 1277 (1968).

[31] J. J. Press, USP 3,316,328; 3,337,651-2.

[32] J. J. Press, USP 3,336,710.

[33] Toyo Rayon, JP 11,171 (1965).

[34] Nippon Rayon, BP 985,937.

[35] K. Teramura, S. Yokoyama, Y. Asai, and K. Tao, Sen-i Gakkaishi 21, 272 and
277 (1965).

[36] Y. Nagai and M. Matsuo, Kogyo Kagaku Zasshi 67, 88 (1964).

[37] See, e.g., Acna, BP 904,963; 905,321; 961,213; 977,229; ICI, BP 953,373-5;
Vereinigte Glanzstoff-Fabriken, BP 838,687.

[38] IC, USP 3,188,163.

azobenzene → o-cresol) and Serisol Fast Pink RGL (CI Disperse Red 22; 1-anilinoanthraquinone), and CI Solvent Yellow 2 (4-amino-4'-dimethylaminoazobenzene), have recently been examined, and it has been shown that disperse dyes capable of dyeing polypropylene fiber have high diffusion coefficients and low saturation values.[39]

VIII. Reactive Dyes

The reactive dyes represent by far the most important development in synthetic dyes after 1935 (see Siegel, Schündehütte, and Hildebrand in Vol. V).[40] The two outstanding properties of the reactive dyes which have been responsible for their phenomenal success and for the flood of patents are their ease of application and the brilliance of the shades. For the organic chemist they are of profound interest because new synthetic methods and reactions are being discovered in the course of attempts by dyestuff manufacturers to find new reactive systems and produce technically valuable reactive dyes.

For a century after Perkin's discovery of Mauve the synthetic dyes applicable to cotton were broadly of two types: (a) direct dyes which gave wash-fast shades by aggregation within the fiber or by attachment to the cellulose macromolecule by hydrogen bonding and/or van der Waals or dispersion forces; and (b) dyes precipitated in the fiber by various methods. The basic idea that the hydroxyl groups of cellulose can be used for producing colored esters or ethers was mentioned as early as 1895 by Cross and Bevan. They benzoylated soda cellulose, nitrated, reduced, diazotized, and coupled to form an azo dye, in which the original ester link with a cellulose hydroxyl was still present. Many attempts were subsequently made to combine dyes with cellulose by means of ether or ester linkages, and an example of a dye[41] capable of chemical combination with cellulose at high temperature and high alkali concentration, unsuitable for practical dyeing, is (VI).

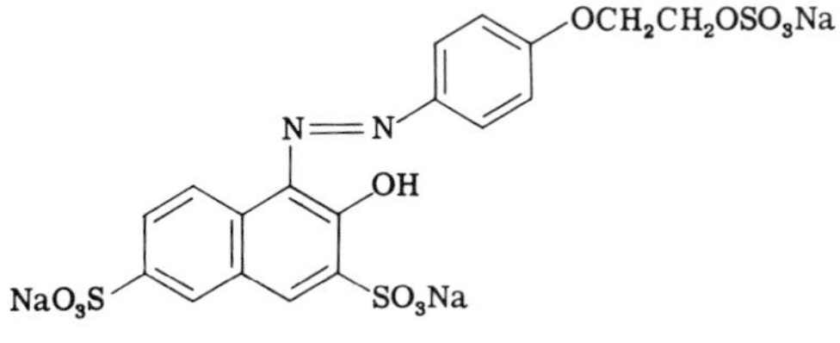

(VI)

[39] C. L. Bird and A. M. Patel, *J. Soc. Dyers Colourists* **84**, 560 (1968).
[40] See also A. Lukós and W. Ornaf, "Barwniki Reaktywne." Warsaw, 1966.
[41] J. D. Guthrie, *USP* 2,741,532; *Am. Dyestuff Reptr.* **41**, 13 and 30 (1952).

Cyanuric chloride, which has been known for over eighty years, is a remarkable substance with tremendous potentialities as an intermediate for synthesis, because the three nitrogen atoms in the aromatic ring system render the three chlorine atoms very labile and readily susceptible to nucleophilic substitution. Thus it can be condensed successively with three amines, alcohols, or phenols in the presence of a base, and innumerable products can be made in this manner. The Ciba company carried out extensive work on cyanuric chloride derivatives from about 1920; dyes containing the 1,3,5-triazine ring appeared in 1924 and they were the subject of numerous patents. Cyanuric chloride was used mainly as a convenient bridging unit for the combination of azo or other dye units or intermediates to form more complex dyes; a blue and a yellow dye could, for instance, be combined to form a green dye. Special properties were also claimed, such as high tinctorial power and purity of the shades, increase in affinity for cellulose fibers, and improvement in fastness. Ciba included such dyes in its range of Chlorantine Fast Colors, and a few anthraquinonoid dyes were among the Cibanone group of vat colors. In *Colour Index*, 1956, there are three azo dyes and two vat dyes of this type. In one of the azo dyes, Chlorantine Fast Blue 8G (CI 28500), which is now obsolete, the third chlorine atom of cyanuric chloride is unsubstituted, but the possibility of using it as a reactive dye for chemical combination with cellulose was not thought of; it is obvious now that

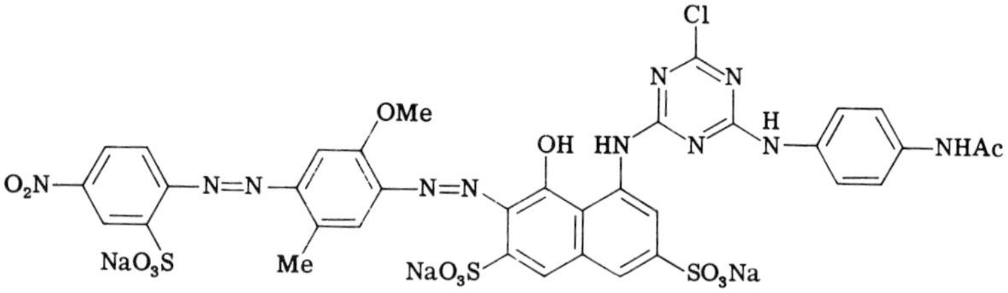

Chlorantine Fast Blue 8G (CI 28500)

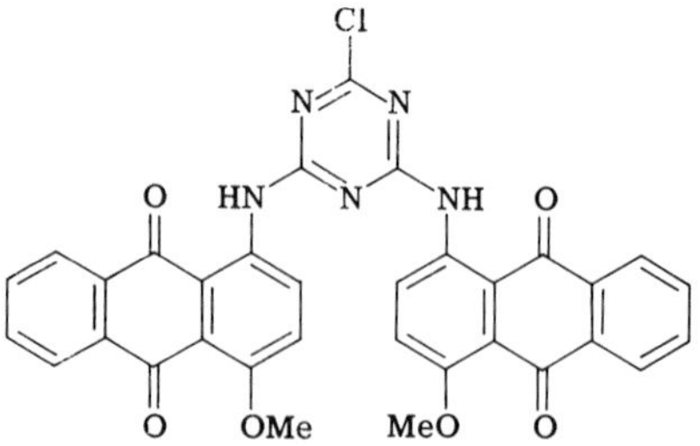

Cibanone Orange 6R (CI 65705)

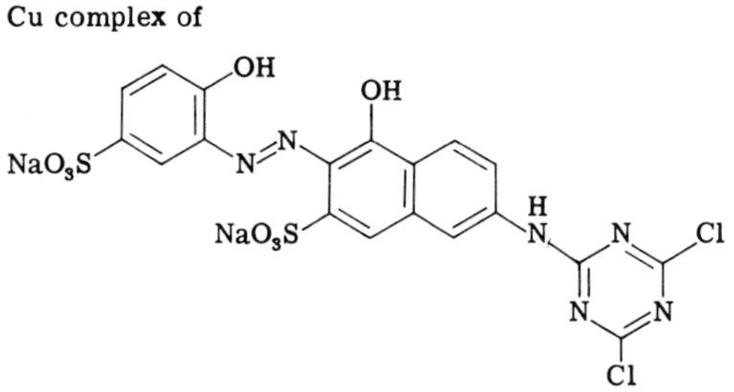

Cu complex of

(VII)

the particular structure is unsuitable for a reactive dye because of the very high substantivity of Chlorantine Fast Blue 8G. Similar vat dyes (e.g., Cibanone Orange 6R; CI 65705) must have undergone some chemical combination with cellulose when applied in printing under alkaline conditions, even allowing for some loss of halogen during vatting; but this again was apparently not noticed. Such vat dyes, applied by a special method, which are "presumed to be held by chemical linkage with the fiber," are the subject of recent patents.[42]

The copper complex of the dye (VII) was mentioned in *CSD I* (p. 587), but its potentiality as a reactive dye was not realized.

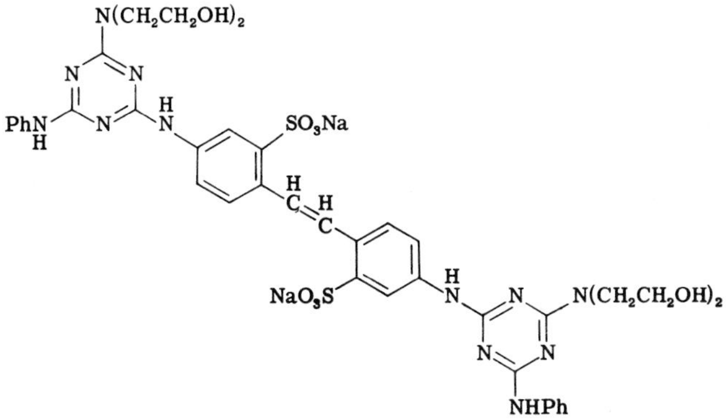

(VIII)

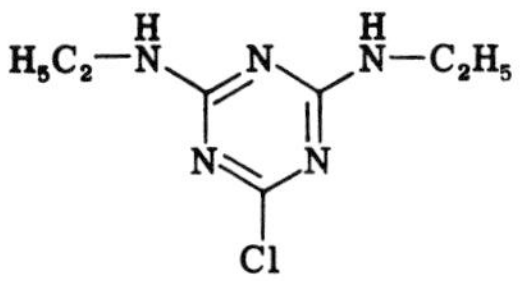

Simazine

[42] Ciba, *BP* 891,794; 892,382.

Perhaps one reason for the limited technical success of cyanurated dyes, apart from the delay in the discovery of reactive dyes, was the difficulty in preparing and using cyanuric chloride, which has now become available on a large scale at a low price, mainly as the result of process developments by Degussa in Germany and Kyowa Gas and Chemical Industries in Japan. Thousands of tons are used for the synthesis of fluorescent brightening agents [such as (VIII)], herbicides (such as Simazine), and fungicides, in addition to reactive dyes.

Stephen[43] has given a very interesting account of early work in the ICI Dyestuffs Division, based on the important discovery that highly

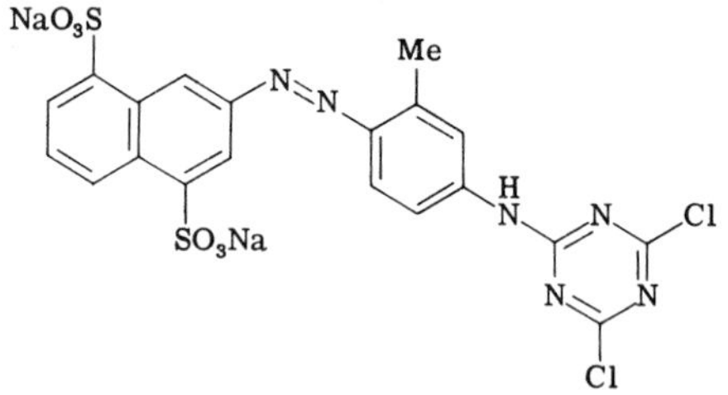

Procion Yellow R

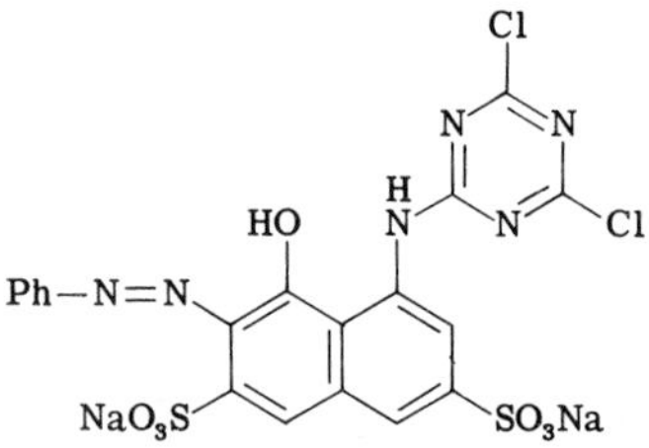

Procion Brilliant Red 5B

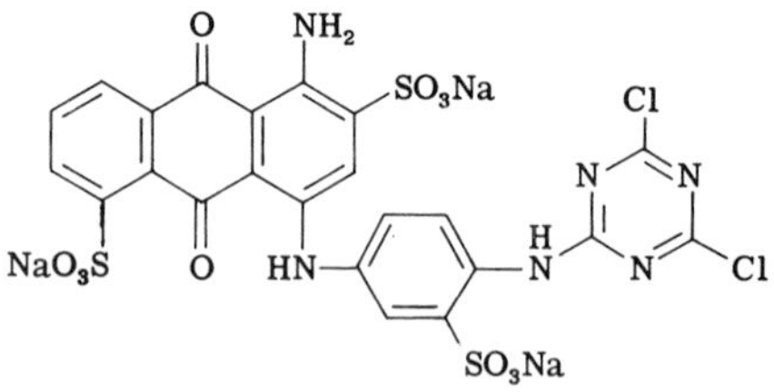

Procion Blue 3G

[43] W. E. Stephen, *Chimia* (*Aarau*) **19**, 261 (1965).

reactive dyes can be applied to cotton from an aqueous solution under conditions of dyeing practice by controlling the pH and the temperature. Three reactive dyes were first marketed: Procion Yellow R, Brilliant Red 5B, and Blue 3G. ICI also developed a second range of reactive dyes (Procion H brand), which contain only one reactive chlorine atom; they are consequently much more stable than the Procions, but they require higher pH and higher temperature for fixation.[44] Almost simultaneously Ciba marketed the Cibacron dyes, the equivalent of the Procion H brand.

In a 1947 patent Ciba described dyes of the type (IX), capable of dyeing ethers and esters of cellulose, fast nonphototropic yellow shades, as well as of dyeing polyamide and animal fibers[45]; but its usefulness as a reactive dye for cellulose was completely missed.

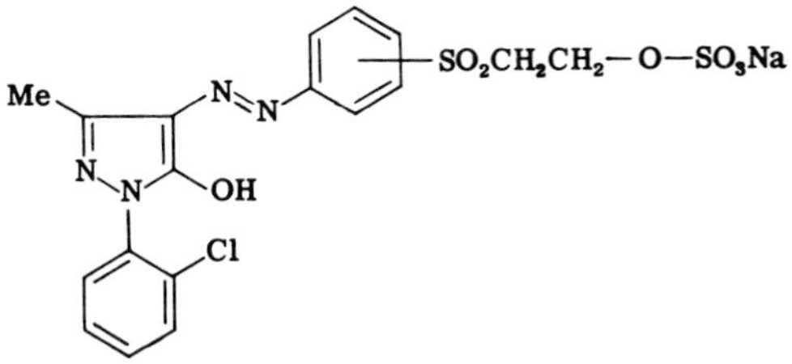

(IX)

In 1953 Hoechst marketed two dyes, Remalan Brilliant Blue B and Yellow GG, applicable to wool, silk, and polyamides. They contained the group $SO_2CH_2CH_2$—OSO_3H as the characteristic substituent, which was hydrolyzed to the vinyl sulfone ($SO_2CH=CH_2$), and then formed a strong covalent bond with the free amino or other suitable group in the fiber. It was soon realized that dyes containing the $SO_2CH_2CH_2$—OSO_3Na group linked to an aromatic nucleus are excellent reactive dyes for cellulose. The first dyes of this type, the Remazols, were marketed in 1957,

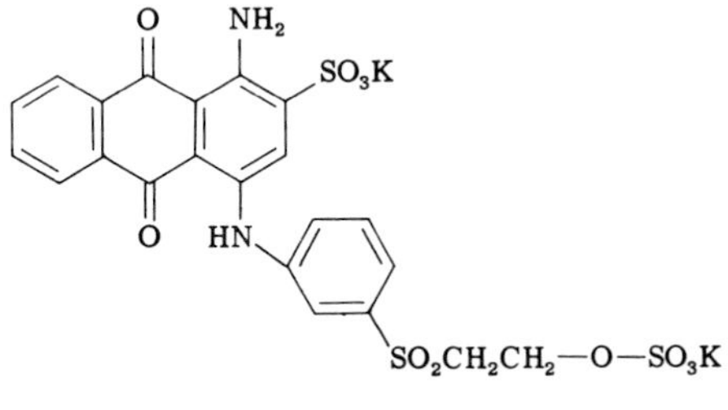

Remazol Brilliant Blue R

[44] T. Vickerstaff, J. Soc. Dyers Colourists 73, 125 (1961).
[45] W. Müller, J. Scheidegger, and Ciba, USP 2,424,493; BP 587,467.

and a wide range is now available. Perhaps the most important of the Remazols is Brilliant Blue R, which dyes a beautiful royal blue shade.[46]

Bohnert[47] has stated that "the primary reaction of the Remazol dyes leads to the formation of vinyl sulfones, and hence the vinyl-sulfonyl group can be regarded as the true reactive group of this class of dyes":

$$Dye-SO_2CH_2CH_2-O-SO_3Na + NaOH \longrightarrow Dye-SO_2CH=CH_2 + Na_2SO_4 + H_2O \quad (1)$$

$$Dye-SO_2CH=CH_2 + Cell-OH \xrightarrow{OH^-} Dye-SO_2CH_2CH_2-O-Cell \quad (2)$$

In the absence of cellulose, β-elimination to form the vinyl sulfone according to Eq. (1) is to be expected, and can be readily shown to take place very rapidly; but the validity of Eq. (2) as representing the sole mechanism of a normal dyeing process requires further investigation. Recent work[48] on the dyeing properties of Remazol Brilliant Blue R (CI Reactive Blue 19) and the corresponding vinyl sulfone has shown that the formation of the vinyl sulfone in the dyebath is unfavorable to the dyeing process. Its formation on the fiber cannot be excluded at this stage, but an alternative mechanism of dyeing needs to be considered. Adsorption of the parent sulfuric ester by cellulose and the removal of a proton from the methylene group activated by the adjacent sulfone group can result in an allylic type structure, as shown below. An S_N2 reaction then becomes feasible; and —O—SO₃Na, a very good leaving

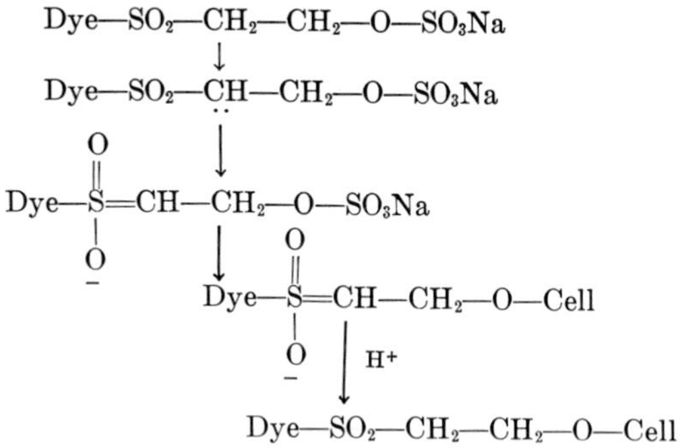

group, is replaced by the cellulose anion, a much stronger nucleophile. However, much more experimental work on a series of dyes of this type is necessary.

[46] J. Heyna, in "Recent Progress in the Chemistry of Natural and Synthetic Colouring Matters and Related Fields" (T. S. Gore et al., eds.), p. 473. Academic Press, New York, 1962; Angew. Chem. Intern. Ed. Engl. **2**, 20 (1963).

[47] E. Bohnert, J. Soc. Dyers Colourists **75**, 581 (1959).

[48] M. R. R. Bhagwanth, E. H. Daruwalla, V. N. Sharma, and K. Venkataraman, Textile Res. J. (in press).

Reactive systems containing mobile halogen other than cyanuric chloride are also in use, and over 300 reactive systems have been mentioned in the patent literature. Chromogens of nearly every type can in principle be used for reactive dyes; but those in actual use are mainly azobenzenes and phenylazopyrazolones for yellows; monoazo derivatives of J-acid and H-acid for oranges and reds; 1-amino-4-anilinoanthraquinone derivatives for blues; copper or nickel phthalocyanines for turquoise blues and greens; copper, chromium, and cobalt complexes of monoazo and disazo dyes for violets, blues, browns, grays, and blacks. One direction in which research is progressing is a search for a reactive group and optimum affinity in a dye molecule which will lead to the ideal of total fixation of a dye.

The Basazols (BASF) represent a compromise between the reactive dyes concept and the older methods of fixation of dyes on fibers by the intervention of tannin or metallic mordants. Dyes containing amino or other nucleophilic groups are applied to cellulose in the presence of a compound [such as (X)] which links the dye to the fiber; the Basazol dyes are at present very limited in number and are suitable mainly for printing.

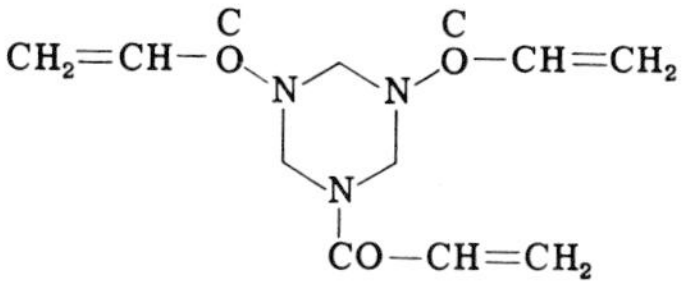

$$CH_2{=}CH{-}O\overset{C}{}\ \overset{N\diagdown\diagup N}{\diagdown}\ \overset{C}{}O{-}CH{=}CH_2$$
$$N$$
$$|$$
$$CO{-}CH{=}CH_2$$

(X)

Some of the cross-linking agents for cellulose used in textile finishing[49] have potential value in this process if dyes of appropriate structures are chosen.

The chemical reactions between reactive dyes and cellulose can be set down in general terms; but dyes with different reactive systems, and even dyes with the same reactive system which differ in solubility, affinity, and other properties influencing fixation, will vary in their dyeing properties. Application methods have therefore been investigated much more intensively than for any other class of dye, and new techniques are being developed.

Reactive dyes for wool and nylon have also been produced and examples of such dyes are the Procilan range of premetallized dyes for wool and the Procinyl disperse dyes for nylon (ICI), the Lanasols (CIBA), and the Remazolans (Hoechst).

[49] See, for example, J. G. Frick, Jr., *Am. Dyestuff Reptr.* **56**, P684 (1967).

IX. Azo Dyes

The lapse of more than a century after their discovery has not diminished the preeminence of the azo compounds among synthetic dyes. Azo dyes and their intermediates occupied more than half of Vol. I of this series; in these supplementary volumes the azo chromophore figures in nearly the whole of the chapter on metal–dye complexes and in substantial parts of the chapters on disperse dyes, reactive dyes, cationic dyes, pigments, and dye–fiber affinity. Nevertheless, Stead, in Chapter VI in this volume, has shown that an exciting story can be written about the residual chemistry of azo dyes. Physical methods have thrown new light on the structure and tautomerism of azo compounds. Azo dyes not readily obtainable by diazonium coupling can be synthesized by several other methods. One example is the azoferrocenes. There has been no slackening of research and patent activity on both water-soluble azo dyes for wool, nylon, and cotton and water-insoluble azoic colors.

X. Neutral-Dyeing Metal–Dye Complexes for Wool and Nylon

Although attention was drawn in Vol. I to Drew and Fairbairn's classical work[50] in which the complex (XI; R, R′ = H), a monobasic acid insoluble in water but soluble in aqueous alkali, was described, the great technical importance of dyes of this type was not forecast.

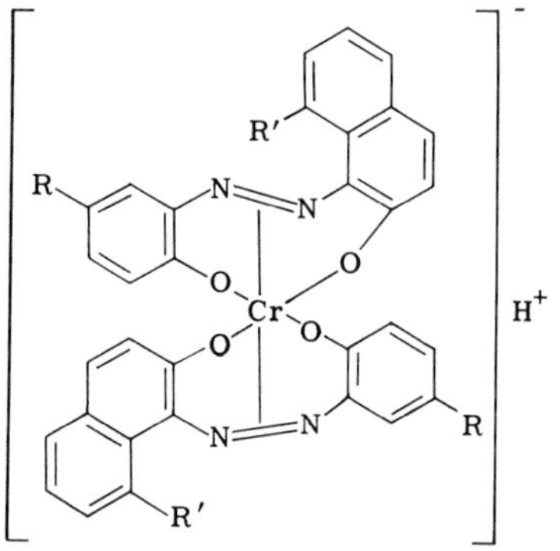

(XI)

In the first detailed account of the neutral-dyeing metal complexes of azo dyes, Schetty[51] traced the historical background which ultimately led

---

[50] CSD I, p. 561; H. D. K. Drew and R. E. Fairbairn, J. Chem. Soc. p. 823 (1939).
[51] G. Schetty, J. Soc. Dyers Colourists 71, 705 (1955).

to the discovery by Geigy that azo dyes containing SO_2CH_3 and no sulfonic groups, by treatment with ammonium chromosalicylate or oxalato-ammino-chromate, form chromium complexes which dye wool from neutral or weakly acid baths with maximum protection to the fiber.[52] The Irgalan dyes of Geigy are of the type (XI; R = SO_2CH_3, R' = $NHCOCH_3$), which is a blue dye; such 2:1 azo dye:chromium (or cobalt) complexes, in which two different azo dye molecules may be used, are now marketed by several firms and are the subject of numerous patents. In a long series of papers Schetty[53] has examined the chemistry and stereochemistry of metal–dye complexes (see Price, Chapter VII in this volume).

XI. Basic Dyes

Recent developments concerning basic dyes (see Ayyangar and Tilak in Vol. IV), apart from the "cationic dyes" for acrylic fibers, include improved processes for some of the old and well-known dyes such as Auramine and Methyl Violet; dyes with heterocyclic systems useful in photochemical processes; and leuco derivatives useful for transfer sheet materials and offset printing inks. Work has also been reported on the mechanism of reactions leading to basic dyes and on steric effects.

XII. Anthraquinonoid Dyes

Like the azo dyes, many anthraquinone derivatives are included among disperse dyes and reactive dyes, and they provide especially the blues and violets. The remaining areas of application where anthraquinonoids have a role are mordant, acid, and acid-mordant dyes (see Schoenauer, Benguerel, and Benz in Vol. VI). Quinizarin and 1,5-dihydroxyanthraquinone continue to be important intermediates for derivatives of amino- and aminohydroxyanthraquinones. *Colour Index*, 1956, records 23 dyes made from quinizarin, and the number is now undoubtedly much larger. As mordant dyes the hydroxyanthraquinones, with the minor exception of alizarin, are obsolete. The constitution of Turkey Red was revised in 1940 on the basis of careful elemental analysis, which led to the molecular formula $(Ca_3Al_2Alizarin_4)(5H_2O)$[54]; but steric and other factors

[52] Gy, *SP* 261,126; 265,102-7.
[53] G. Schetty, *Chimia (Aarau)* **18**, 244 (1964).
[54] M. Rutishauser, Dissertation, Zürich (1940).

were not considered. More recently Kiel and Heertjes[55] obtained data "from conventional analytical methods including infrared spectroscopy" for the formation of the complexes (XII); but there is need for further study, using modern physical methods, of the structures of the metal complexes of the hydroxyanthraquinones, including alizarin.[56] In contrast to the metallized azo dyes, no attempt has been made to produce preformed metal complexes of the hydroxyanthraquinones as dyes for wool and nylon; at any rate none apparently is to be found in a commercial range.

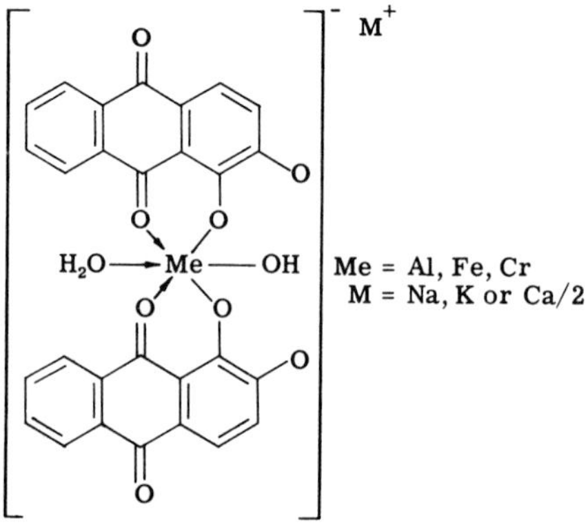

Me = Al, Fe, Cr
M = Na, K or Ca/2

(XII)

In an investigation of the Bohn-Schmidt reaction cyclic bis-sulfuric esters of 1,4,9,10-tetrahydroxyanthracenes have been isolated, indicating the mechanism of the oxidation.[57] The unique position occupied by quinizarin and leucoquinizarin as intermediates has kept alive an interest in their structures and reactions. An NMR study[58] has confirmed Zahn and Ochwat's leucoquinizarin structure. An interesting series of reactions starting from quinizarin has been described by Winkler.[59]

[55] E. G. Kiel and P. M. Heertjes, J. Soc. Dyers Colourists 79, 21, 61, 186, and 363 (1963); 81, 98 (1965).

[56] For a recent review of metal complexes of hydroxyanthraquinones and naphthoquinones, see H. Baumann and H. R. Hensel, Fortschr. Chem. Forsch. 7, 727 (1967).

[57] J. Winkler and W. Jenny, Helv. Chim. Acta 48, 125 and 193 (1965).

[58] S. M. Bloom and R. F. Hutton, Tetrahedron Letters p. 1993 (1963); see also N. R. Ayyangar, A. V. Rama Rao, and K. Venkataraman, Indian J. Chem. 7, 533 (1969).

[59] J. Winkler, Chimia (Aarau) 20, 122 (1966); see also A. Green, J. Chem. Soc. p. 1428 (1926).

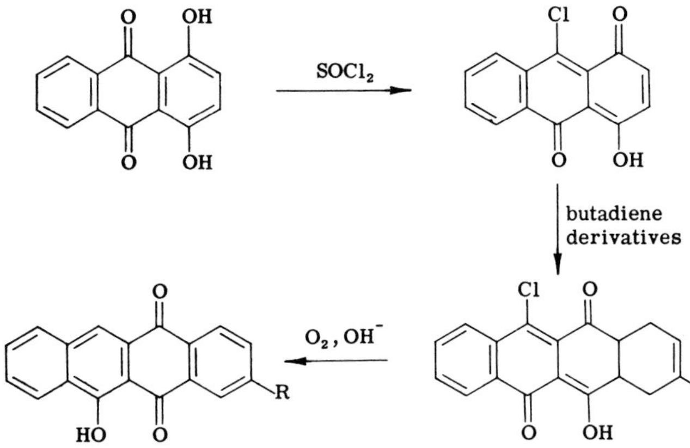

The reaction of leucoquinizarin with ethylenediamine and N-alkyl-ethylenediamines gives two series of products, (XIII) and (XIV).[60]

Among 13 acid blues for which individual U. S. production figures (1966) are available, 7 are anthraquinonoids; and among 6 acid greens, only 1 is anthraquinonoid, but quantitatively it is almost a third of the acid green total. All of them are made from 1-amino-4-bromoanthraquinone-2-sulfonic acid or 1-amino-2,4-dibromoanthraquinone or quinizarin or anthrarufin.

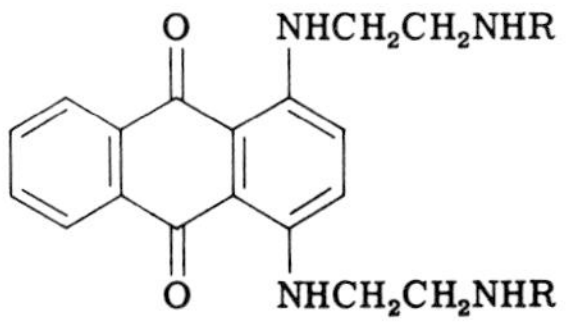

(XIII) 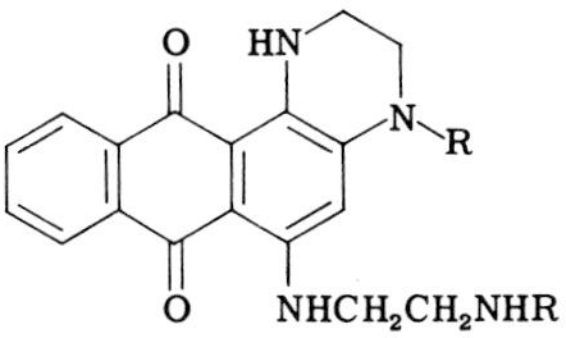   (XIV)

Blue and green acid anthraquinone dyes continue to be technically important and to be heavily covered by patents, although they only represent minor variations of well-known structures based on 1,4-diaminoanthraquinone, 1-amino-4-hydroxyanthraquinone, and 1,5-diamino-4,8-dihydroxyanthraquinone. Two arbitrarily chosen examples may be cited to show the directions in which new dyes with some advantages are being sought. The condensation products of 1-amino-4-bromoanthraquinone-2-sulfonic acid with an amino derivative of a hydrogenated cyclopentadiene dimer or trimer dye polyamide fibers in fast blue shades.[61]

[60] M. S. Simon and D. P. Waller, *Tetrahedron Letters* p. 1527 (1967); C. W. Greenhalgh and N. Hughes, *J. Chem. Soc., C* p. 1284 (1968).
[61] BASF, *FP* 1,482,615.

Dyes such as (XV) give "fast green dyeings and prints on cellulosic and polyamide materials."[62]

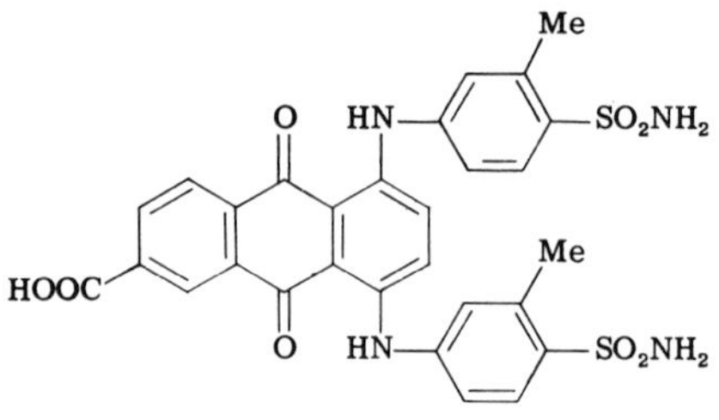

(XV)

XIII. Anthraquinonoid Vat Dyes

Notwithstanding the advent of the reactive dyes, anthraquinonoid vat dyes have maintained their position as fast dyes for cotton and viscose. Their use as pigments is limited by their cost, but recent patents suggest that this is compensated by the wide spectral range available and the fastness properties, especially for the mass pigmentation of synthetic fibers and plastics. Progress in the chemistry of anthraquinonoid vat dyes is discussed in Vol. VI of this series. Both production figures and patent literature show the sustained importance of indanthrones, violanthrones, carbazoles, and the pyridine derivatives obtained by the cyclization of the condensation product of 3-bromobenzanthrone and α-aminoanthraquinone. Numerous patents cover claims of better yields, especially in indanthrone manufacture. Suggested structural variations also relate largely to these main types. A series of CIBA patents protect the introduction of a carboxyl, sulfonic, or sulfate group in a large molecule, by which the vattability is improved.[63] Later in this chapter a brief reference is made to new approaches for investigating orientation and other problems concerning the sparingly soluble polycyclic quinones. The drastic conditions under which the indanthrones, violanthrones, and carbazoles are prepared do not lend themselves readily to experimentation leading to a precise definition of the mechanisms by which they are formed. Bradley's extensive work on indanthrone has demonstrated the difficulties and limitations of attempting to follow reaction paths by collecting qualitative data on the formation of intermediates and by-products.[64] Even the nature of the reacting species (radical, ion, radical-ion, ion pair) has not been clearly established. On the purely synthetic

[62] FBy, *BP* 1,114,956.
[63] Ciba, *BP* 952,798; 991,625; 991,811; 991,976.
[64] W. Bradley *et al., J. Chem. Soc.* p. 2129 (1951), *et sequa.*

side the isolation of pure compounds and proof of identity require such special care and new techniques that later work showed, for instance, that the earlier syntheses of linear indanthrone did not yield authentic material.[65]

The Scholl cyclization with aluminum chloride or sulfuric acid is a step in the technical production of vat dyes of the dibenzopyrenequinone and carbazole types, and it has also been used for determining the structures of polycyclic quinones. The mechanism of this important reaction, in which closure to condensed ring systems occurs by intramolecular dehydrogenation of aromatic compounds, has been reviewed recently by Balaban and Nenitzescu.[66] They have discussed their own reformulation of Baddeley's mechanism of a normal electrophilic substitution of an aromatic nucleus by its conjugate acid. They have also referred to Rooney and Pink's conclusion,[67] on the basis of ESR spectra, that "there seems little doubt that free radicals of this type (monopositive radical ions) are active intermediates in ring closure reactions of aromatic hydrocarbons catalyzed by anhydrous aluminium chloride." They rightly conclude that the number of mechanistic possibilities is thus greatly increased, and that further experimental data are needed. One factor to be considered is that two *p*-benzamido groups in the anthrimide facilitate the cyclization to the carbazole. Another aspect of the Scholl reaction is Wick's reinvestigation of Mieg's work on the dimerization of 1-aminoanthraquinone in a melt of aluminum chloride and moist pyridine, which has led to useful dyes and pigments.[68]

Several commercial dyes in which one or two anthraquinone units provide the vattable part and color variations are obtained by the attachment of heterocyclic rings were described in *CSD II*. To this group may be added Indanthrene Red F3B (CI Vat Red 31), the structure of which was determined in the course of a program of work on anthraquinone

Indanthrene Red F3B

[65] E. Leete, O. Ekechukwu, and P. Delvigs, *J. Org. Chem.* **31**, 3734 (1966).

[66] A. T. Balaban and C. D. Nenitzescu, *in* "Friedel-Crafts and Related Reactions" (G. A. Olah, ed.), Vol. II, p. 979. Wiley (Interscience), New York, 1964.

[67] J. J. Rooney and R. C. Pink, *Proc. Chem. Soc.* p. 143 (1961).

[68] A. K. Wick, *Helv. Chim. Acta* **49**, 1748 (1966), *et sequa*; FP 1,416,980; 1,509,260; 1,525,542.

derivatives[69]; it was subsequently found that the structure was disclosed in an inaccessible 1958 publication.[70]

XIV. Indigoid and Thioindigoid Dyes

Among 33 vat dyes for which individual U. S. production figures are reported (1966), only 4 are thioindigoid. There are no indigoids, and the other 29 are anthraquinonoids. The only country for which a separate figure of indigo production is reported is France (41 tons). Tetra-bromoindigo as the solubilized vat color finds considerable use in India. With the exception of halogenated indigo and a few thioindigoids (reds, violets, and browns, especially for printing), the indigoid group is steadily declining in commercial importance.

Indigo in excellent yield and purity has been obtained[71] from malono-dianilide by the following reactions:

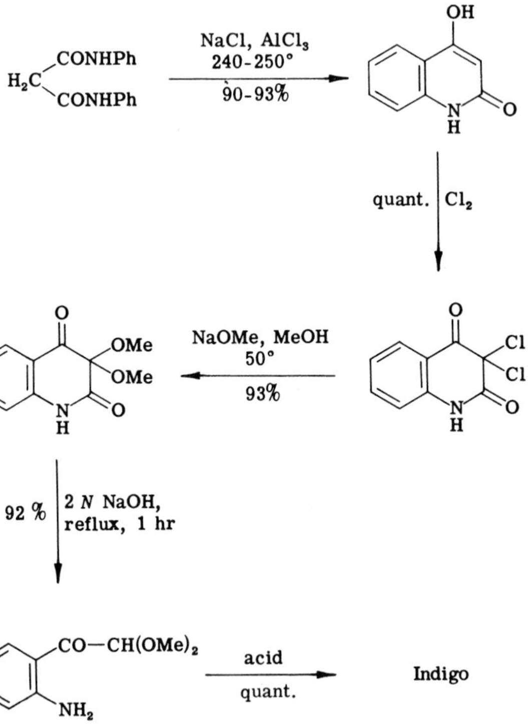

[69] T. G. Manjrekar, Ph.D. Thesis, Bombay University (1968).

[70] O. Bayer, "Die Neuere Entwicklung der Farbenchemie." Leverkusen, W. Germany, 1958; see also Ciba, *BP* 954,410, and other patents on oxadiazoles.

[71] E. Ziegler and T. Kappe, *Angew. Chem. Intern. Ed. Engl.* **3,** 754 (1964).

Cis–trans isomerization (including steric effects), electronic, fluorescence, IR and ESR spectra, photoconductance, and crystal structure of indigoid dyes have been studied. Russian and Indian workers have synthesized numerous indigoids and examined their spectral properties. Thioindigoid dyes have been prepared by thionation of 1- and 2-acetylnaphthalene.[72] The synthesis of polymeric indigo from 4,4'-di(carboxymethylamino)biphenyl-3,3'-dicarboxylic acid is perhaps the only real achievement to record in this area.[73]

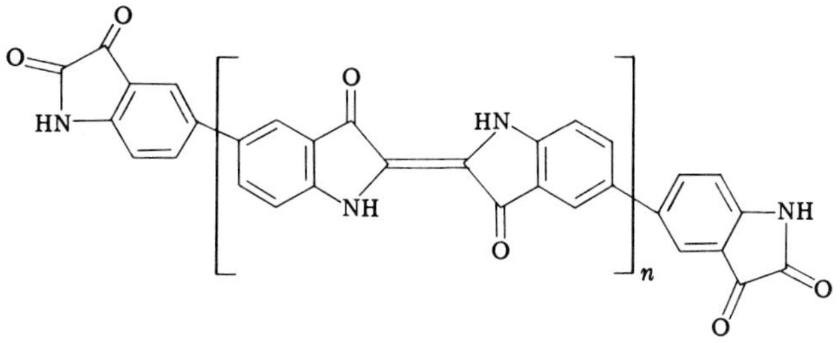

Polymeric indigo

Hardly 10 patents on the indigoids have appeared since 1950 and the following are examples. Thioindigoids containing at least one triazine residue give high wet fastness on cellulose.[74] Use of a nitroarylsulfonic acid as an oxidizing agent gives thioindigoid dyes free from impurities.[75] Indigo and thioindigo have been submitted to the known chloromethylation and pyridinium or isothiuronium salt formation to produce dyes on the Alcian Blue model.[76]

XV. Sulfur Dyes

Sulfur Black continues to be produced in large quantities, and a series of other sulfur dyes, prepared mostly by a simple process of thionation of appropriate intermediates by sodium polysulfide, are also marketed. They represented 9% of the total U. S. production of dyes in 1966; Sulfur Black production was about half of all the sulfur dyes. According to one

[72] I. A. Troyanov, G. M. Oksengendler, and E. F. Kostomarova, *Ukr. Khim. Zh.* **28,** 367 (1962).
[73] A. A. Berlin, B. I. Liogonkiĭ, and A. N. Zelenetskiĭ, *Dokl. Akad. Nauk SSSR* **178,** 1320 (1968); see also G. Manecke and G. Kossmehl, *Makromol. Chem.* **70,** 112 (1964).
[74] Ciba, *BP* 936,414.
[75] CCC, *USP* 2,804,464.
[76] G, *USP* 2,657,214; 2,728,774; see also S. Nakazawa, *Yuki Gosei Kagaku Kyokai Shi* **21,** 53 (1963).

report,[77] dyeing with sulfur dyes accounts today (in the U. S. presumably) for a major portion of the poundage of dyed cellulosic fibers both in 100% construction and in blends with polyester, polyamide, and acrylic fibers.

There have been important technical advances in the production of sulfur dyes in the form of (a) dispersions, (b) stable, clarified, reduced solutions, and (c) nonsubstantive thiosulfonic acid derivatives (CI Solubilized Sulfur dyes), as shown in the new *Colour Index* classification of sulfur dyes mentioned earlier.

Patent claims refer to "active sulfur dyes in pre-reduced liquid form," which are not merely easier to apply than the older sulfur dyes, but also yield brighter shades and higher fastness.

The preparation of a sodium polysulfide solution of "great activity" has been described.[78]

Many sulfur dyes are converted by treatment with sodium bisulfite or sulfite into water-soluble thiosulfonic acids, which have practically no affinity for cotton and are suitable for application by padding methods. The normal substantive leuco derivative is liberated by treatment of the impregnated material with sodium sulfide, and the dyeing process is then completed by oxidation as usual. Hydrosol (CFM), Thionol M (ICI), Sulphosol (JR) and Kayasol (KYK) are such solubilized sulfur dyes, which have become much more important in dyeing practice than the older sulfur dyes.[78a]

Arylthiosulfonic acids, such as (XVI), are well known as intermediates in the Bernthsen method for the synthesis of Methylene Blue and other thiazine dyes. In 1903 Green and Perkin[79] prepared the 2,5-dithiosulfonic acid (XVII) of p-phenylenediamine by treatment with aqueous sodium thiosulfate and chromate at room temperature. Oxidation of a mixture of (XVII) and a monoamine gave black and brown dyes, which behaved like sulfide colors, but had less affinity for cotton. They concluded that the products were thiols or thiosulfonic acids derived from dyes of the aniline black type.

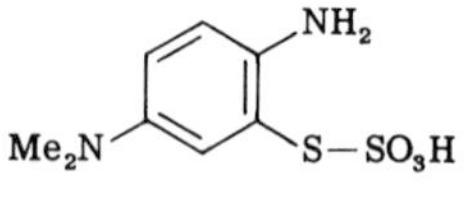

(XVI) 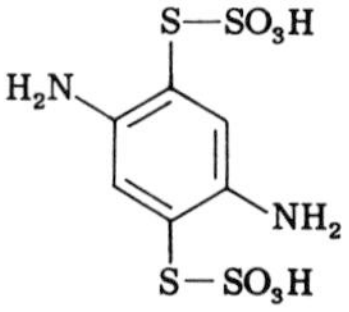   (XVII)

[77] L. Tigler, *Am. Dyestuff Reptr.* **57**, P333 (1968).
[78] L. Legradi, *Chem. & Ind. (London)* p. 1693 (1965).
[78a] See also H. Rath, *DBP* 958,585; 1,071,864; 1,264,387.
[79] A. G. Green and A. G. Perkin, *J. Chem. Soc.* **83**, 1201 (1903).

Dykolites (Southern Dyestuff Co., Division of Martin-Marietta Corporation) are sodium S-arylthiosulfates (Ar—S—SO$_3$Na). They are nonsubstantive to cellulose, but substantive to polyamides, wool, and silk from acid solution. It is claimed that fastness to wet treatments is obtained by very rapid chemical conversion of the water-soluble dyes on the fiber into water-insoluble hydrophobic dyes. One procedure for the preparation of a Dykolite is to diazotize an aromatic primary amine carrying a thiosulfate group (e.g., H$_2$NC$_6$H$_4$—S—SO$_3$Na) and couple with a component (e.g., β-naphthol, 1-phenyl-3-methyl-5-pyrazolone) free from water-solubilizing groups.

The usual process for dyeing sulfur dyes is inapplicable to the Dykolites. The fixation of the Dykolites as polysulfides requires specific conditions and the most suitable reagent apparently is sodium tetrasulfide.[79a] The extensive literature on the fission of an –S—S– bond by nucleophiles[80] shows that the difficulty in determining appropriate conditions for the fixation of arylthiosulfates in a dyeing process is the need for producing the symmetrical dye polysulfide in maximum yield.

Unlike the sulfur dyes prepared by thionation processes "azodisulfide dyes" have a definite structure, because they are prepared by coupling a diazotized disulfide, such as 4,4'-diaminodiphenyldisulfide, with two molecules of an azoic coupling component. A variation is to condense cyanuric chloride with an aminoazobenzene and then condense two molecules of the product with one of 4,4'-diaminodiphenyl disulfide. They can be applied together with sulfur dyes by special dyeing methods.[81]

In 1874 Bunte prepared sodium salts of S-alkylthiosulfates (Bunte salts) by the action of sodium thiosulfate on alkyl halides (RBr + Na$_2$S$_2$O$_3$ → RSSO$_3$Na + NaBr). Bunte salts can be converted into disulfides[82] by treatment with sodium sulfide:

$$2RSSO_3Na + Na_2S \longrightarrow R—S_3—R + 2Na_2SO_3$$
$$R—S_3—R + Na_2SO_3 \xrightarrow{(Na_2S)} RSSR + Na_2S_2O_3$$

Milligan and Swan[83] described the preparation of azo dyes such as (XVIII) and (XIX), and they made the important observation that some of them were unexpectedly good dyes for wool, especially in their washfastness. Under certain conditions of application they underwent partial

[79a] Martin-Marietta Corp., *BP* 1,146,002.

[80] W. A. Pryor, "Mechanisms of Sulfur Reactions." McGraw-Hill, New York, 1962.

[81] Martin-Marietta Corp., *BP* 1,018,459; 1,025,042; 1,025,043; 1,014,703; 1,016,850; *USP* 3,225,025; 3,299,040.

[82] H. Distler, *Angew. Chem. Intern. Ed. Engl.* **6**, 544 (1967).

[83] B. Milligan and J. M. Swan, *J. Chem. Soc.* p. 2969 (1959); *Textile Res. J.* **31**, 18 (1961); *Rev. Pure Appl. Chem.* **12**, 72 (1962); B. Milligan, B. Saville, and J. M. Swan, *J. Chem. Soc.* p. 3608 (1963).

decomposition, some dye being bound covalently to the wool and some being converted to the symmetrical dye disulfide. Wool Fast Turquoise Blue SW, the condensation product of copper phthalocyanine trisulfonyl chloride with an aminoalkylthiosulfate, dyes wool by such reactions; prints on nylon, using thiourea, thiodiethylene glycol, and ammonium sulfate, are very fast to light.[84]

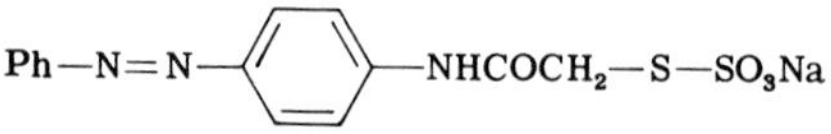

$$Ph-N=N-\underset{}{\bigcirc}-NHCOCH_2-S-SO_3Na$$

(XVIII)

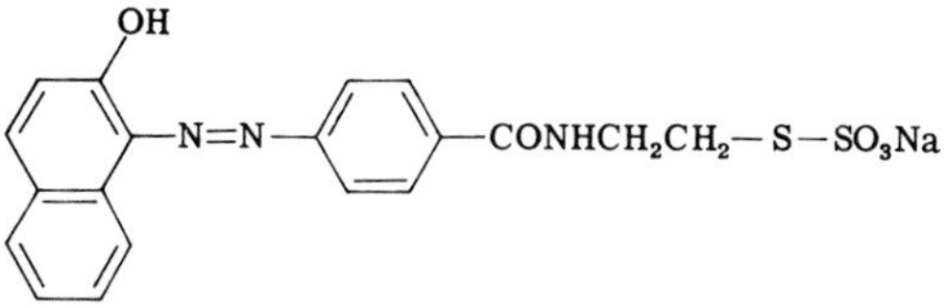

$$\underset{}{\bigcirc}\!$$

OH

—N=N—⟨⟩—CONHCH$_2$CH$_2$—S—SO$_3$Na

(XIX)

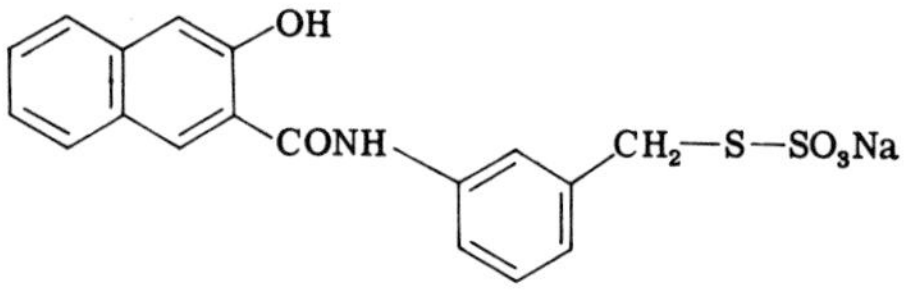

OH

CONH ... CH$_2$—S—SO$_3$Na

(XX)

When a dye which contains Bunte salt groups ($ArCH_2-S-SO_3Na$) and no other water-solubilizing groups, and which has affinity for cotton, is treated on the fiber with sodium sulfide solution at room temperature, water-insoluble disulfides are formed as polycondensation products. The shades thus produced have good wet-fastness. The aliphatic disulfide groups produced by polycondensation are unaffected by treatment with aqueous sodium sulfide, unlike the aromatic disulfide groups of conventional sulfur dyes. Dyes of this type have been prepared[84] by (a) diazotizing Bunte salts containing aromatic amino groups and coupling them with suitable components; (b) coupling diazonium salts with compounds such as (XX) containing thiosulfate groups; and (c) condensing amines

[84] K. Schimmelschmidt, H. Hoffmann, and E. Baier, *Angew. Chem. Intern. Ed. Engl.* **2**, 30 (1963); W. Schulteis *et al.*, *BP* 953,428; *USP* 3,088,790; H. Luttringhaus, *Am. Dyestuff Reptr.* **53**, P728 (1964).

containing thiosulfate groups (e.g., $H_2NCH_2CH_2$—S—SO_3Na) with dyes containing reactive halogen atoms (SO_2Cl; COCl). It is desirable to introduce two groups (–$SO_2NHCH_2CH_2$—S—SO_3Na) into a dye molecule in suitable positions, because the object is to "polycondense" the dye on cellulose to give insoluble wash-fast dyeings. Inthion Brilliant Blue I5G and other blue and green dyes are prepared by the last method. Inthion dyes can be applied by procedures simpler than those used for conventional sulfur dyes containing thiol or disulfide groups.

An ICI patent[85] describes the preparation of phthalocyanine dyes containing thiosulfate groups by the treatment of a polychloromethyl phthalocyanine with ammonium or alkali metal thiosulfate in hot dimethyl sulfoxide.

Hiyama[86] has described sulfur dyes ("Hyaman colors"), in which one molecule of a dye containing a primary amino group is condensed with one molecule of cyanuric chloride, and the remaining two chlorine atoms are converted to thiol groups. Thus green dyes of structure (XXI) were prepared from copper phthalocyanine; the dyes were greenish blue, blue-green, or green, depending on the number of pendant groups being 2, 3, or 4. Sulfur dyes were also prepared which contained the group –$SO_2NHC_6H_4SCN$. The dyes showed strong affinity for vinylon and nylon, as well as cotton and rayon, and gave clear shades unlike the common sulfur dyes. The Hyaman colors were in an early stage of technical production in 1959, but they are not mentioned in *Colour Index*.

$$\left[\begin{array}{|c|} \hline \text{Copper phthalocyanine} \\ \hline \end{array} \left\{ \begin{array}{c} \text{HN} \diagdown \diagup \text{N} \diagdown \diagup \text{SH} \\ \text{N} \diagdown \diagup \text{N} \\ \text{SH} \end{array} \right\}_{2-4} \right]$$

(XXI)

The obvious complexity of thionation reactions and the amorphous and polymeric character of sulfur dyes have deterred organic chemists generally from undertaking work on their chemical constitution. Except for the presence of groups such as thiol, sulfide, disulfide, polysulfide, sulfoxide, and thianthrene, we have no real knowledge of the structure of a single sulfur dye. The statement made by von Weinberg in 1930 and quoted by Strouse[87] is still true: "The constitution of sulfur black made

[85] ICI, *BP* 955,004.
[86] H. Hiyama, "Synthetic Sulfur Dyes." Osaka Municipal Tech. Res. Inst., Osaka, 1959. A book by this author in Japanese on sulfur dyes has recently appeared.
[87] G. C. Strouse, *Dyestuffs* **45,** 61 (1966).

from dinitrophenol is not yet known, and all that can be said with certainty is that the formulas published in papers and patents are incorrect—these formulas do not take notice of the important fact that in the color formation three mols. of dinitrophenol split off exactly one mol. of ammonia, which means that the body will probably contain three benzene rings."

The last important paper in this area appeared in 1948[88]; structures were suggested for the constituents of Immedial Yellow GG and Immedial Orange C; dyes which were similar in properties to Immedial Pure Blue and Indocarbon CL, but which had more or less authentic structures, were also synthesized. When structures are postulated which contain thianthrene rings or its oxides, it is necessary to remember their conformational flexibility[89] in relation to the high substantivity of the dyes.

It is not impossible that by the application of chromatographic techniques for isolation, combined with NMR, mass spectra, and other physical methods of structure determination, progress can be made with at least some of the relatively simple sulfur dye molecules. One example of structure determination relates to Cibanone Orange R.[90] Extensive chemical evidence[91] led to structure (XXII), which had to be ruled out as soon as the mass spectra of the dye and the NMR and mass spectra of the reductive methylation and acetylation products were determined. Structure (XXIII) agrees with the mass and NMR spectra, but not with the color and other properties.[92] The dye is now obsolete, but has

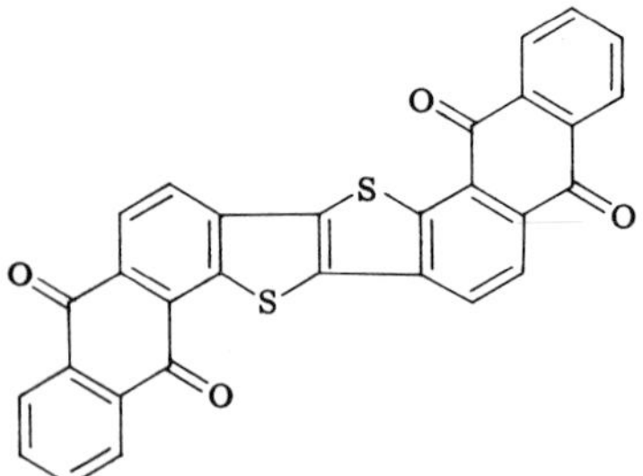

(XXII)

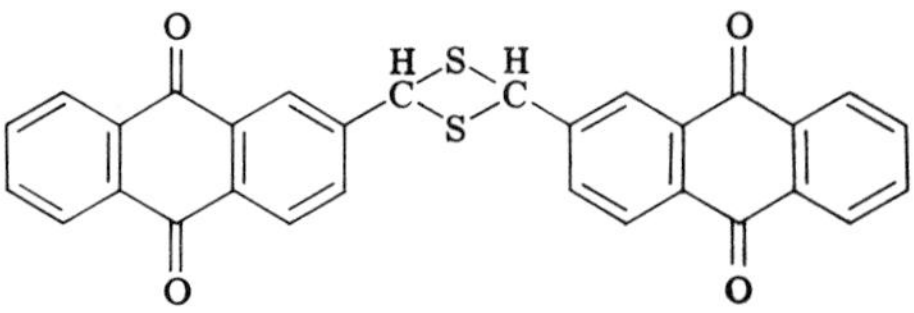

(XXIII)

[88] W. Zerweck, H. Ritter, and M. Schubert, *Angew. Chem.* **60A**, 141 (1948); see also K. H. Shah, B. D. Tilak, and K. Venkataraman, *Proc. Indian Acad. Sci.* **A28**, 111 (1948); J. Marek and D. Markova, *Collection Czech. Chem. Commun.* **27**, 1533 (1962).

[89] J. Chickos and K. Mislow, *J. Am. Chem. Soc.* **89**, 4815 (1967).

[90] *CSD II*, p. 1110.

[91] (Miss) M. D. Bhavsar, B. D. Tilak, and K. Venkataraman, unpublished work; (Miss) M. D. Bhavsar, Ph.D. Thesis, Bombay University (1958).

[92] T. G. Manjrekar, Ph.D. Thesis, Bombay University (1968); T. G. Manjrekar, A. V. Rama Rao, and K. Venkataraman, *Indian J. Chem.* (in press).

long been of great interest as the dye of choice for investigating the photochemical degradation of cellulose in the presence of quinonoid dyes.

Although very little progress has been made in determining the structures of sulfur dyes, extensive work has been carried out on ring systems such as phenoxathiin and thianthrene which are present or have been postulated in sulfur dyes[93]; it provides the basis for an extension of Zerweck's work on the stepwise synthesis of sulfur dyes with definite structures.

Current research in organosulfur chemistry from other points of view was reviewed during the second organic sulfur symposium held in 1966, which had as its central theme the reactive intermediates of organosulfur chemistry.[94] There is, of course, no mention of sulfur dyes, but prospective investigators of the challenging problems of sulfur dye structures, the progressive decomposition of some dyes on storage or on the fiber, and dye–fiber interactions, will be interested in the papers on characteristics of organosulfur compounds and intermediates (E. C. Kooyman), action of mercaptans and disulfides in free radical, photochemical, and high-energy radiation reactions (S. G. Cohen), the formation of cations and cation radicals from aromatic sulfides and sulfoxides (H. J. Shine), synthesis and properties of thiocarbonyl compounds (R. Mayer), and the oxibase scale (R. E. Davis). The mechanisms of sulfur reactions are discussed in a stimulating monograph, which also makes no reference to sulfur dyes.[80]

XVI. Technology of Dyeing and Printing

Methods of application of dyes in textile dyeing and printing have undergone modifications to meet the requirements of the new synthetic fibers and their blends with the natural fibers, new classes of dyes, and continuous production methods for lowering costs (see Glenz and Neufang in Vol. IV). In large-scale continuous dyeing processes the work of the dyer in producing a level shade to be matched against a standard has been facilitated by automation.[95] For both continuous and batch processes, the dyes and their precise proportions to be used can be determined by instrumental match prediction (IMP). Numerous papers have ap-

---

[93] D. S. Breslow and H. Skolnik, "Multi-sulfur and Sulfur and Oxygen Five- and Six-membered Heterocycles," Part II. Wiley (Interscience), New York, 1966.

[94] M. J. Janssen, ed., "Organosulfur Chemistry." Wiley (Interscience), New York, 1967.

[95] For a discussion of automation and its influence on dyeing with reactive dyes, see I. Seltzer, *J. Soc. Dyers Colourists* **81**, 251 (1965); see also *Am. Dyestuff Reptr.* **56**, P294–P304 (1967); *J. Soc. Dyers Colourists* **85**, 57 (1969).

peared on advances in instrumentation and the use of computers for shade matching.[96] Among the systems in commercial operation may be mentioned COMIC (Colorant Mixture Computer)[97] and IMP (ICI). Limited water supply, effluent disposal problems, the effectiveness of solvents in removing fats and waxes and rendering fabrics more absorptive, and the intrinsic advantages of organic solvents over water for dyeing with disperse dyes and dyes of a few other classes have led to the development of solvent dyeing processes. In the Vapocol process of ICI trichloroethylene is used as the solvent for dyeing nylon and polyester fiber. The Irga-solvent process of Geigy is for the dyeing of filament nylon.[97a] Using 1,1,1-trichloroethane as solvent and soluble derivatives of known disperse, acid and basic dyes, solvent dyeing is at present being developed for the continuous dyeing of nylon, polyester, and acrylic carpets.[97b] Dyeing processes in which neither water nor an organic solvent is used are also being developed.

XVII. Physical Chemistry of Dyeing

Advances in the technology of dyeing and printing involve an understanding of the physical chemistry of dyeing and printing processes, on which extensive work has therefore been carried out in recent years, mostly in the research departments of the large dye manufacturers. There is a growing realization that no single theory of dyeing can cover cellulose, protein, polyamide, polyester and other fibers, dyes of different structural types, and different conditions of dye application.

Recent work in the physical chemistry of dyeing has emphasized the need for more accurate experimental techniques and precise mathematical treatments (see Daruwalla in Vol. VI). Calorimetric, spectroscopic, and polarographic techniques have been widely employed to study the state of the dye in the dyebath and the influence of dyebath additives. The state of the dye in the fiber has received less attention than other aspects of the mechanism of dyeing, and only a few direct approaches have been made to quantitative evaluation. Most of the reported investigations on the kinetics of dyeing deal with long-period processes, and very little information is at present available on short-period dyeing. Theoretical

[96] See E. Rohmer, R. Lehmann, U. Gugerli, E. Atherton, and F. North, *Intern. Farbtagung Luzern* **2**, 865, 705, 839, 823 (1965).

[97] H. R. Davidson, *Am. Dyestuff Reptr.* **56**, P443 (1967).

[97a] See also B. Milićević, *SVF Fachorgan Textilveredlung* **4**, 213 (1969).

[97b] *Chem. Eng. News* **47**, No. 15, 46 (1969).

and experimental conditions in a fiber present in a dyebath have been investigated, and various approaches have been suggested to overcome the complicating factors of the dyebath becoming less concentrated during the dyeing process and the diffusion coefficient of the dye in the fiber not remaining constant. Microdensitometric methods have been employed to obtain profiles of dye penetration in films of substrate. In the thermodynamics of dyeing, new attempts have been made to determine the activity of the dye in the substrate. Attempts have also been made to apply data on the relation between orientation of functional groups in the solute molecule and the shape of adsorption isotherms for studying dyeing mechanisms. Reactive dyes have presented new and difficult problems as several simultaneous reactions are likely to take place during their application.

Dye–fiber interactions involve different types of forces, and more evidence is now available in favor of the existence of hydrophobic bonds. The mass, chemical constitution, and geometry of dye molecules have been shown to play an important role, both in the kinetics of dyeing and in imparting substantivity to textile fibers.

XVIII. Pigments

In 1950 the phthalocyanines, azoics, and anthraquinonoid vat dyes were the three main types of organic pigments. All the three continue to be used and their range has been extended, special attention having been paid to appropriate methods of preparation and conversion to suitable physical forms as factors which determine the value of a pigment. Thus some of the Chromophthals (Cromophtals, CIBA) are disazo compounds, prepared, for example, by condensation of two molecules of the acid chloride of the monoazo compound from a diazotized chlorotoluidine and 2-hydroxy-3-naphthoic acid with one molecule of benzidine.

By suitable substitution in the diazonium and coupling components the azoics can indeed offer a wide choice of pigments not substantially inferior to the phthalocyanines. In spite of the outstanding properties of the phthalocyanines as pigments, they are limited to blues and greens, and since pigments are becoming increasingly important for the mass coloration of synthetic fibers and plastics and a variety of other purposes, including, in fact, the dyeing and printing of textile fabrics, extensive research on new pigments has been in progress (see Lenoir in Vol. V).[98] There is a great demand for pigments of high light-fastness.

[98] See also N. V. Shah, *J. Soc. Dyers Colourists* **83**, 220 (1967); H. Gaertner, *J. Oil Colour Chemists' Assoc.* **46**, 13 (1963).

For special purposes, such as the coloration of polyethylene and poly-propylene, another stringent requirement is high heat stability (temperatures of about 300°). Cost, of course, is always a consideration which limits the use of vat dyes from perylene tetracarboxylic acid and similar products. Thus low-cost brilliant yellow pigments with adequate fastness properties remain to be discovered.

The dioxazine derivative, Pigment Fast Violet R Base, was mentioned in *CSD II* (p. 787) as an intermediate in the preparation of the direct cotton dye, Sirius Supra Blue FFRL, but not its importance as a pigment (CI Pigment Violet 23; CI 51319); and the dioxazines now form an important group of pigments.

A major advance is the commercial development of the quinacridones in 1958, supplementing the blue and green phthalocyanines in the orange to violet regions of the spectrum. Quinacridone was described by H. Liebermann in 1935, but its remarkable properties as a pigment were not demonstrated until more than twenty years later by the du Pont Co., which isolated three crystalline forms and converted them into yellowish red, bluish red, and violet pigments. The great insolubility and stability of the small quinacridone molecule arise from intermolecular hydrogen bonding in the solid state. Substituted quinacridones and other aspects of pigment production based on the parent quinacridone are the subject of many patents.

In view of the ready availability and reactivity of 2,3-dichloro-1,4-naphthoquinone, attempts have been made to use it for the synthesis of dyes (see CI Vat Yellow 27; CI 56080), but with little success, although they led to new and interesting heterocyclic quinonoid chromophoric systems (see Tilak in Vol. V). More recently, a few of the phthaloylpyr-rocolines obtained in the course of this work have been found to be bright pigments with excellent fastness properties and may be included in the Cromophtal range of Ciba.

Azomethines from *o*-hydroxyaldehydes, isoindolinone azomethines, and fluorubines are other important groups of pigments. Fluorubine was discovered even earlier than quinacridone (Hinsberg and Schwantes, 1903), but its value as a pigment was only realized in 1959.

XIX. Food Colors

The statement in Vol. I (p. 302) that "Indeed it is a matter for consideration whether the safest and most rational practice will not be to use as food colors the natural coloring matters present in edible plant materials" finds steadily increasing justification in the diminishing number of colors regarded as safe after further work on chronic toxicity.[99] In the U. S. which appears to have the most rational and elaborate procedures for testing and certifying food additives, 18 dyes were in the approved list in 1952. Only the 8 dyes in Table IV are in the latest certified list (Feb. 1969); a ninth dye, Ponceau SX (CI 14700; FD and C Red No. 4), is limited to use in maraschino cherries and short-term drugs. Citrus Red No. 2 (CI 12156) is limited to the coloring of mature oranges, and Orange B (the azo dye: naphthionic acid → ethyl 1-p-sulfophenyl-5-pyrazolone-3-carboxylate) to sausage casings and surfaces. Table IV also gives a list of the food colors permitted in the U. K. and the European Economic Community. The Joint FAO/WHO Expert Committee on.Food Additives has so far placed only three dyes (Amaranth, Sunset Yellow FCF, and Tartrazine) in category A, defined as colors found acceptable for use in food. The daily acceptable intake for man in milligrams per kilogram of body weight is 0–7.5.

CI Food Orange 4, 1, and 3, Yellow 12 and 8, and Brown 3 (Table IV) are made from a diazonium or coupling component not containing a sulfonic group; one of the reduction products formed in the body will therefore be an unsulfonated aromatic amine, not readily eliminated because of its solubility in fat. Azo dyes to be used as food colors should preferably contain sulfonic groups in both the diazonium and coupling components.

A total ban on synthetic dyes in food materials will be fully justified in India and other countries where large sections of the population suffer from malnutrition and where it is impossible to control the purity of the dyes, the quantity, and the conditions under which they are used. One drug, the coloring of which should be prohibited because it is consumed at a level of about 12 g/day for a year or more by tubercular patients, is p-aminosalicylic acid (sodium or calcium salt).

Mannell and his collaborators in Canada have published new data on the chronic toxicity of some food colors.[100]

Because "carotenoids . . . have always been present in the diet of man, and this seems to be a much more decisive demonstration of tolerance than toxicity tests with pigments carried out on a few generations of small laboratory animals," Isler has developed the commercial synthesis of several carotenoids useful as food colorants, and also special formulations to overcome their lipophilic character and poor solubility.[101] If

---

[99] J. Noonan, "Color Additives in Food" *in* "Handbook of Food Additives" (T. F. Furia, ed.), Chem. Rubber Publ. Co., Cleveland, Ohio, 1968.

[100] W. A. Mannell, *Food Cosmet. Toxicol.* **2**, 169 (1964); W. A. Mannell and H. C. Grice, *J. Pharm. Pharmacol.* **16**, 56 (1964); and other papers.

[101] O. Isler, R. Rüegg, and U. Schwieter, *Pure Appl. Chem.* **14**, 245 (1967).

TABLE IV
SYNTHETIC DYES PERMITTED IN FOOD[1]

Commercial name	CI Food number	CI Constitution number	U. S.	EEC	U. K.
Sunset Yellow FCF	Yellow 3	15985	√	√	√
Tartrazine	Yellow 4	19140	√	√	√
Amaranth	Red 9	16185	√	√	√
Erythrosine	Red 14	45430	√	(√)	√
Wool Violet 5BN	Violet 2	42640	√	—	—
Brilliant Blue FCF	Blue 2	42090	√	—	—
Indigocarmine	Blue 1	73015	√	√	√
Fast Green FCF	Green 3	42053	√	—	—
Ponceau 4R	Red 7	16255	—	√	√
Red FB	Red 13	14780	—	—	√
Fast Red E	Red 4	16045	—	—	√
Scarlet GN	—	14815	—	√	—
Ponceau 6R	Red 8	16290	—	√	—
Orange GGN	Orange 2	15980	—	√	—
Orange G	Orange 4	16230	—	—	√
Orange RN	Orange 1	15970	—	—	√
Oil Yellow GG	Orange 3	11920	—	—	√
Yellow 2G	Yellow 5	18965	—	—	√
Oil Yellow XP	Yellow 12	12740	—	—	√
Acid Yellow G	Yellow 2	13015	—	√	—
Chrysoine S	Yellow 8	14270	—	√	—
Quinoline Yellow	Yellow 13	47005	—	√	—
Green S	Green 4	44090	—	(√)	√
Indanthrene Blue RS	Blue 4	69800	—	√	—
Patent Blue V	Blue 5	42051	—	√	—
Violet BNP	Violet 3	42580	—	—	√
Brown FK	Brown 1	—	—	—	√
Chocolate Brown FB	Brown 2	—	—	—	√
Chocolate Brown HT	Brown 3	20285	—	—	√
Black PN	Black 1	28440	—	√	√
Black 7984	—	—	—	√	√

[1] √, Permitted; (√), provisionally permitted. Data on the U. K. and the European Economic Community (EEC) have been taken from R. G. Todd, ed., "Extra Pharmacopoeia: Martindale," 25th ed., Pharm. Press, London, 1967. The U. S. list was kindly provided by Dr. M. Dolinsky, Division of Colors and Cosmetics, U. S. Food and Drug Administration.

several reviews on carotenoid synthesis had not recently appeared, a chapter on carotenoids might well have been included in these volumes.

The introduction of nitrile groups into carotenoids produces a strong bathochromic shift. Reddish and bluish pigments of this type have been suggested as food colors[102]; but such substitution deprives them of the main attraction of the carotenoids, which is their occurrence in edible plants. A more rational approach to nontoxic food colors is the synthesis, by the Robinson method,[103] of anthocyanidins and anthocyanins whose stability has been increased by the introduction of H, alkyl, alkoxy, or phenoxy groups in the 3-position.[104]

XX. Dyes in Biology

Ehrlich's classic work on the selective staining of nerve cells by Methylene Blue and the paralyzing effect of some dyes on specific micro-organisms led to the use of a few dyes as antibacterial and chemothera-peutic agents[105] and to their much wider application in histological stain-ing. Several books are available on biological stains and staining techniques, but few attempts have been made to relate, at least in broad terms, the chemical constitution of dyes and their histological behavior (see Gurr and Unni in Vol. VI).

One aspect of dyes in biology is their use in dyeing human hair. Henna and plant extracts containing pyrogallol or the tannins have been em-ployed for this purpose from prehistoric times until the present day. It was mentioned in *CSD II* (p. 1195) that *p*-phenylenediamine is widely used as a hair dye in spite of its liability to produce dermatitis; and the reactions on the hair, when applied in conjunction with hydrogen peroxide and resorcinol or catechol, were briefly considered. More recently, prod-ucts for dyeing hair directly under suitable conditions and having no irritant or toxic effects on the scalp have become commercially important. Current trends in the synthesis of hair dyes and the chemistry of the dyeing processes are discussed by Corbett in Vol. V.

XXI. Dyes in Photography

The cyanines have attracted more patents and publications than per-haps any other group of synthetic dyes (see Ficken in Vol. IV). Some of the reasons are the rapidly increasing demand for films and plates for black-and-white as well as color photography from amateurs and pro-fessionals, the expansion of the cinema industry, the need for infrared

---

[102] N. V. Philips Gloeilampenfabrieken, *BP* 1,110,056.
[103] D. D. Pratt and R. Robinson, *J. Chem. Soc.* p. 745 (1923); and other papers.
[104] U. S. Secretary of Agriculture, *USP* 3,266,903.
[105] For an account of "Dyes in medicine and pharmacy," see R. G. Todd, ed., "Extra Pharmacopoeia: Martindale," 25th ed. Pharm. Press, London, 1967.

sensitization for scientific, exploratory, and defense purposes, and the possibility of using the cyanines in lasers, and other new devices. A monumental volume[106] on the cyanines appeared in 1964, which is invaluable for reference and deep study by the specialist, but in which it is difficult to see the wood for the trees; Ficken's much shorter review brings order into a bewilderingly complex topic for the benefit of the organic chemist. Synthetic methods and reaction mechanisms are discussed in relation to each structural type, including dyes related to the cyanines. Finally, the stereochemistry, properties, and applications of the cyanines are surveyed.

Color formers in photography were included in a chapter on miscellaneous dyes in Vol. II. Bailey and Williams provide in Vol. IV a much more adequate review of the chemistry of image formation in color prints and transparencies by oxidative coupling, and of the color developers and couplers involved.

XXII. Dyes in Physical Chemistry and Chemical Physics

On the initiative of Swiss color chemists an International Colour Symposium was first organized in 1960. Illustrative of the interest of the color chemist in the fundamental aspects of the subject and the appeal that color chemistry has to physical chemists and physicists, is the program of the second International Colour Symposium held in 1964. The topics chosen for the lectures and discussions had the general title "Optically Excited Organic Systems,"[107] and they covered various methods of treating π-electron systems in relation to the wavelength, intensity, and structure of electronic absorption bands (see Mason, Chapter IV in this volume) and to fluorescence and phosphorescence; the study of transient species by flash photolysis; variations in hue and fastness properties of dyes on different substrates; semiconductivity and photoconductivity; phototropy; modern concepts of spectral sensitization; fiber degradation by anthraquinonoid dyes; and new chromophoric systems.

The action of light on dyes and dyed fibers was reviewed in Vol. II; but a basic knowledge of the photochemistry of dyes (see Meier in Vol. IV) has become necessary for the interpretation of available data, for any attempts to correlate the chemistry of dyes and their physical state on substrates with fading, and for a planned synthesis of light-fast dyes.

It is only in a very few cases that the products of the fading of dyes by exposure to sunlight and air have been isolated and characterized.

[106] F. M. Hamer, "Cyanine Dyes and Related Compounds." Wiley, New York, 1964.
[107] "Optische Anregung Organischer Systeme." Verlag Chemie, Weinheim, 1966.

Desai and Vaidya isolated p-dimethylaminobenzophenone from Malachite Green and Michler's ketone from Crystal Violet.[108] McKeown and Waters[109] have recently used electron spin resonance spectroscopy for following the mechanism of oxidation of phthalein dyes. They have shown that when phthalein dyes are oxidized by alkaline hydrogen peroxide within the cavity of an ESR spectrometer, the spectra of substituted p-benzosemiquinone radicals can be observed, indicating that oxidation occurs by HO_2^- attack and Dakin rearrangement to break off one phenolic ring as a p-benzoquinol, leaving a substituted benzophenone.

As a technique for studying free radicals (species with one or more unpaired electrons), ESR[110] is useful in the investigation of many dye phenomena, such as the action of light and oxidizing and reducing agents on dyes and dyed fibers, the mechanism of reactions involved in the synthesis of dyes, and the stability of ring systems present or postulated in dye molecules.

In a recent review on phototropy[111] (or photochromism) azo, thio-indigo, and triphenylmethane dyes, as well as numerous other organic compounds, are discussed. Photochromic compounds (heterocyclic spiranes) are used by the National Cash Register Co. in a microimagery process for compressing bulky documents, first recorded on a 35 mm microfilm, into a minute space; this can provide a solution for the continually increasing problems of the maintenance and retrieval of information.

Electrical conductivity in organic solids has been studied extensively in recent years, partly because of its possible relation to energy transfer in biological systems and to normal and abnormal processes in the living cell. Many dyes are of interest as semiconductors and photoconductors because their molecules possess π-electrons which can be readily excited and can then migrate from molecule to molecule in the crystal. In an authoritative book on organic semiconductors[112] Gutmann and Lyons have devoted a section to organic dyes; the phthalocyanines, however, are treated separately because of the extensive work carried out on them in the form of single crystals. The statement that "dyes generally are amorphous" and the marking of cyananthrone, indanthrone, and indanthrene black as cationic dyes in the table giving data on 111 organic dyes illustrate the gap between the chemistry of synthetic dyes and their use by physicists.

[108] C. M. Desai and B. K. Vaidya, *J. Indian Chem. Soc.* **31**, 261 (1954).
[109] E. McKeown and W. A. Waters, *J. Chem. Soc., B* p. 679 (1966).
[110] For a review and references, see R. O. C. Norman and B. C. Gilbert, *Advan. Phys. Org. Chem.* **5**, p. 53 (1967).
[111] R. Exelby and R. Grinter, *Chem. Rev.* **65**, 247 (1965).
[112] F. Gutmann and L. Lyons, "Organic Semiconductors." Wiley, New York, 1967.

The ramifications of a single group of synthetic dyes into widely different areas are seen in Booth's chapter in Vol. V and the monograph of Moser and Thomas (379 pp.; 1200 references)[113] on the phthalocyanines. Some applications are the removal of traces of metals by adding metal-free phthalocyanine as a scavenger, a new crystalline form (X-form) of metal-free phthalocyanine as a photoconductive material in electro-photography,[114] nickel phthalocyanine as an oxidation catalyst, and the production of high specific activity radioisotopes of short half-life by neutron irradiation of cobalt and other phthalocyanines in the Szilard-Chalmers process. The phthalocyanines have the great advantages for investigational purposes that hundreds of compounds based on the parent phthalocyanine nucleus can be readily synthesized and that the organic framework is a ligand for metal atoms of every group in the periodic table.

According to a recent news item,[115] a liquid laser capable of producing green, yellow, orange, and red laser light has been produced by IBM scientists. The color of the beam is changed simply by refilling the liquid laser with a different dye solution. It was first noticed that a solution of chloroaluminum phthalocyanine emits a spectrally broad pulse, up to some hundreds of wavenumbers in width depending on dye concentration, cavity length, and conditions of cavity gain.[116] More recently[117] it has been reported that efficient spectral narrowing and continuous tunability in dye lasers over bandwidths large compared with the ordinary lasing action can be obtained by the use of diffraction gratings as cavity reflectors. This effect was demonstrated with xanthene and carbocyanine dyes; solid solutions of dyes in polymethylmethacrylate can also be used as practical dye laser materials. By examining other related dyes it is expected that the entire wavelength domain from 347 mμ (ruby second harmonic) to about 1 μ can be practicably spanned according to these techniques.[117]

XXIII. Fluorescent Brightening Agents

Krais[118] observed in 1929 that aesculin, the 6-glucoside of aesculetin (6,7-dihydroxycoumarin), brightened the appearance of cotton textiles

[113] F. H. Moser and A. L. Thomas, "Phthalocyanine Compounds." Reinhold, New York, 1963.

[114] Rank Xerox, *BP* 1,116,554.

[115] *Sci. J.* (*London*) 3, No. 7, 17 (1967).

[116] P. P. Sorokin and J. R. Lankard, *IBM J. Res. Develop.* 10, 162 (1966).

[117] B. H. Soffer and B. B. McFarland, *Appl. Phys. Letters* 10, 266 (1967); see this paper for earlier references. See also P. P. Sorokin *et al.*, *J. Chem. Phys.* 48, 4726 (1968); A. J. Gibson, *J. Sci. Instr. Ser. No.* 2, 2, 802 (1969).

[118] P. Krais, *Melliand Textilber,* 10, 468 (1929).

by compensating the yellowing produced by bleaching. In 1940 Wendt[119] discovered the value of derivatives of 4,4′-diaminostilbene-2,2′-disulfonic acid for this purpose; and products such as (VIII) constitute the great majority of the commercial products used at the present time. However, hundreds of patents have been taken on coumarins, benzothiazoles, benzoxazoles, benzimidazoles, pyrazolines, and other types (see Gold in Vol. VI), especially for application to synthetic fibers. During the last twenty years there has been an amazing growth in the consumption of optical whitening agents, and the U. S. production in 1966 was 23.2 million pounds compared to 219.1 million pounds of all synthetic dyes.

XXIV. Identification and Analysis of Dyes

The literature of dyes lacks a comprehensive book on the qualitative and quantitative analysis of dyes in substance and on substrates. The nearest approach is a thin volume, which adds little to the earlier edition.[120] Several useful papers have appeared, but mostly on isolated aspects.[121] An exception is a paper[122] on the identification of pigments, in which their isolation by thin-layer chromatography (TLC) is discussed and the IR spectra of 96 organic pigments are presented.

A brief account of the chromatography of dyes was given in Vol. II, and a major development is TLC, widely used in work on natural products and in organic chemistry as a whole. Several books on TLC are available, each of which has a short section or chapter on dyes.[123] Rettie and Haynes[124] have described the TLC of dyes with full experimental details, and have also discussed its qualitative and quantitative applications.

[119] B. Wendt and IG, *DRP* 752,677.

[120] E. Clayton, "Identification of Dyes on Textile Fibers." Soc. Dyers Colourists, Bradford, England 1963.

[121] See, for instance, F. Jordinson and R. Lockwood on reactive dyes: *J. Soc. Dyers Colourists* **84**, 205 (1968), and earlier papers; D. Haigh on disperse dyes: *ibid.* **79**, 242 (1963); E. G. Kiel and G. H. A. Kuypers on paper chromatography: *Tex* **23**, 66 (1964), and subsequent papers; J. Sramek on applications of chromatographic techniques: *J. Chromatog.* **15**, 57 (1964), and other papers; G. S. Egerton, J. M. Gleadle, and N. D. Uffindell on anthraquinonoid dyes: *J. Chromatog.* **26**, 62 (1967); and numerous papers on food colors.

[122] A. McClure, J. Thompson, and J. Tannahill, *J. Oil Colour Chemists' Assoc.* **51**, 580 (1968).

[123] See, for instance, J. G. Kirchner, "Thin-Layer Chromatography," pp. 393–405. Wiley (Interscience), New York, 1967.

[124] G. H. Rettie and C. G. Haynes, *J. Soc. Dyers Colourists* **80**, 629 (1964); see also J. Gasparic and A. Cec, *J. Chromatog.* **14**, 484 (1964); J. W. Copius-Peereboom and H. W. Beekes, *ibid.* **20**, 43 (1965).

XXV. Applications of NMR Spectroscopy
and Mass Spectrometry

When the need arises for determining the structure of a commercial
dye, the problem has been greatly simplified by the general progress of
organic chemistry and can often be solved in a fraction of the time required in 1950. The first step, of course, is to isolate the dye as a pure
homogeneous substance, crystalline if possible. IR, NMR, and mass spectrometry can then be used to supplement or replace the usual chemical

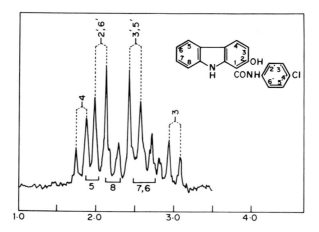

Fig. 1. NMR spectrum of Naphthol AS-LB in dimethyl sulfoxide.

methods. The possibilities of NMR spectroscopy, not merely in determining the chemical constitution of synthetic dyes, but also in investigating
steric effects, following reaction paths, and studying dye–fiber interactions, are largely unexplored, at any rate so far as published work is concerned. An example (see Stead, Chapter VI in this volume) where it gives
a straight answer to a specific problem is the constitution of Naphthol
AS-LB (CI Azoic Coupling Component 15; CI 37600), which is the
p-chloroanilide of 2-hydroxycarbazole-1-carboxylic acid, and not the
3-acid (see Fig. 1; chemical shifts on the τ-scale). Figures 2 and 3, the
NMR spectra of the pure 2,3-acid and a mixture of the two acids, show
that the latter contains 50% of each acid.[125]

The mass and NMR spectra of a series of azoic coupling components

[125] M. R. R. Bhagwanth, A. V. Rama Rao, and K. Venkataraman, *Indian J. Chem.*
7, 1065 (1969); B. S. Joshi *et al.*, *J. Chem. Soc. C*, p. 1518 (1969); R. L. M. Allen
and P. Hampson (private communication).

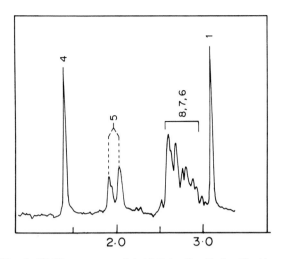

Fig. 2. NMR spectrum of Acid B in dimethyl sulfoxide.

were examined, and in the course of this work it was found that Naphthol AS-BN (CI Azoic Coupling Component 43) and RP (CI Azoic Coupling Component 39) have the indicated structures. The former was demetallized by EDTA and examined as the trimethyl ether; it is the first commercial azoic coupling component which is a copper complex. Naphthol

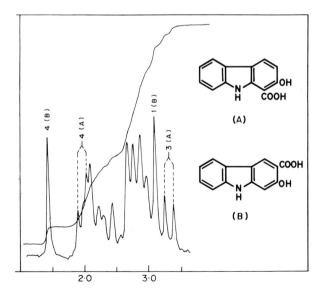

Fig. 3. NMR spectrum of a mixture of Acids A and B in dimethyl sulfoxide.

AS-RP is of interest as a tetralin derivative and nonplanar; it is recommended for use on polyamide fibers.

Cu complex of

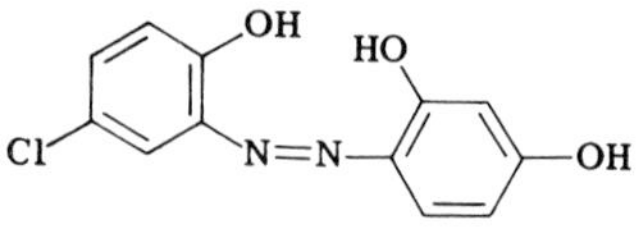

Naphthol AS-BN

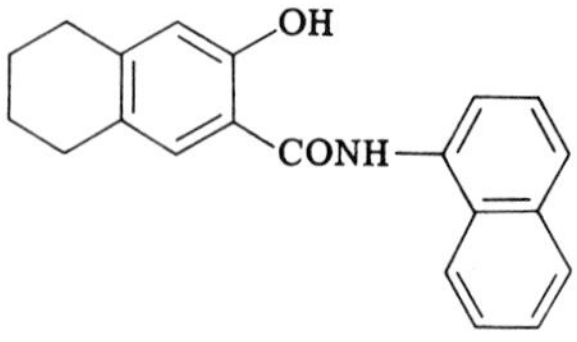

Naphthol AS-RP

The mass spectra of azoic coupling components provide data on the acid and amine moieties, the usual hydrolytic fission therefore being unnecessary for this purpose. Naphthol AS shows a base peak and a second peak of almost equal intensity corresponding to the two fragments (XXIV) and (XXV). The NMR spectrum of Naphtanilide CB (CI Azoic Coupling Component 111) in pyridine showed the presence of a methoxyl and an aromatic C-methyl group, which were located, respectively, in the hydroxynaphthoic acid and aniline halves from the mass spectrum [molecular ion at m/e 307, and the base peak corresponding to (XXIV) at m/e 200]. The NMR spectrum in dimethyl sulfoxide showed that the methoxyl group was in the 6- or 7-position in 2-hydroxy-3-naphthoic acid, and that the amine was o-toluidine; the orientation of the methoxyl group in the 6-position and not the 7-position was proved by the paramagnetic shift of an ortho-coupled doublet in the NMR spectrum of the dye obtained by coupling with diazotized aniline. Naphtanilide CB and Naphtanilide HS (CI Azoic Coupling Component 112), examined by similar methods, were thus found to have the indicated structures.[125a]

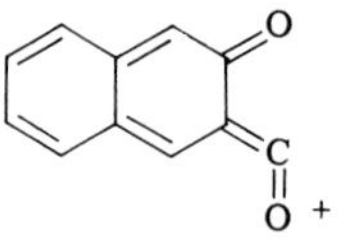

m/e 170

(XXIV)

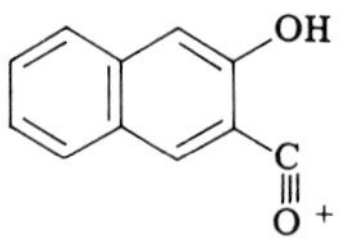

m/e 171

(XXV)

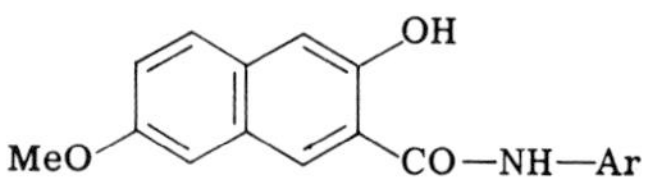

Naphtanilide

CB: Ar = o-Tolyl
HS: Ar = 4-Chloro-2,5-
        dimethoxyphenyl

[125a] M. R. R. Bhagwanth, A. V. Rama Rao, and K. Venkataraman, *Indian J. Chem.* **8** (1970) (to be published).

Another example of the use of NMR spectroscopy is azophenol–quinonehydrazone tautomerism.[126] The deshielding effect of the azo group on the ortho and/or peri protons and the lack of aromatic character in one of the rings of the hydrazone form which results in diamagnetic shifts of the protons in comparison with those of the azophenol form enable the two forms to be identified. More quantitative data can be obtained[127] by using azo compounds containing ^{15}N, or by a double irradiation technique with ^{14}N.[128]

NMR spectral evidence has shown that cellulose forms ether linkages with reactive dyes derived from vinyl sulfones and ester-type linkages with the monochloro- and dichlorotriazine dyes. NMR spectral data have also provided unequivocal evidence for the sites of attack of reactive dyes derived from vinyl sulfone on α-methylglucoside and on cellulose.[129] In dyed viscose the primary hydroxyl and the C-2 hydroxyl group of cellulose are the main sites of attack. With a particular dye and one set of experimental conditions, the primary hydroxyl and the C-2 hydroxyl groups were attacked in a relative proportion of 60–70% and 40–30%; but it is probable that the quantitative result will depend on the structure of the dye and the conditions under which the dyeing is carried out.

NMR spectra have been useful in relating color with conformation in pyrazolone azomethine dyes.[130]

Chemical shifts in the NMR spectra of polymethine dyes have been used to determine the electron densities at various points in the chain; theoretical prediction of the alternation of electron density along the chain and the all-trans configuration were confirmed.[131] Azamethincyanines were found to have the mono-cis arrangement.[132]

A disadvantage of NMR spectroscopy is that solubility of about 10% in appropriate solvents is normally required, although spectra can some-

[126] B. L. Kaul, P. Madhavan Nair, A. V. Rama Rao, and K. Venkataraman, *Tetrahedron Letters* p. 3897 (1966); see also F. A. Snavely and C. H. Yoder, *J. Org. Chem.* **33**, 513 (1968).

[127] V. Bekarek, K. Rothschein, P. Vetesnik, and M. Vecera, *Tetrahedron Letters* p. 3711 (1968).

[128] A. H. Berrie, P. Hampson, S. W. Longworth, and A. Mathias, *J. Chem. Soc.,* B p. 1308 (1968).

[129] M. R. R. Bhagwanth, A. V. Rama Rao, and K. Venkataraman, *Indian J. Chem.* **6**, 397 (1968).

[130] E. B. Knott and P. J. S. Pauwels, *J. Org. Chem.* **33**, 2120 (1968).

[131] G. Scheibe *et al., Tetrahedron Letters* p. 5053 (1966); S. Dähne and J. Rauft, *Z. Physik. Chem. (Leipzig)* **224**, 65 (1963); **232**, 259 (1966).

[132] H. J. Friedrich, *Angew. Chem. Intern. Ed. Engl.* **2**, 215 (1963).

times be obtained in such powerful solvents as sulfuric acid, perchloric acid, and arsenic trichloride. Solubility is a serious problem in many dyes, especially vat dyes of both the anthraquinone and indigoid types. It has recently been shown that many violanthrone derivatives, as their reductive methylation products, have adequate solubility in tetramethylurea.[133] By this technique it was possible, for instance, to show that bromination of 16,17-dimethoxyviolanthrone gives the 3,12-dibromo derivative. Acetyl and carbethoxy derivatives of the leuco compounds can also be used; and other derivatives, such as the trityl and trimethylsilyl ethers, are being examined. Many of the sodium salts of the sulfuric esters of the leuco compounds, available as commercial products or readily obtainable from the parent vat dyes, dissolve in dimethylacetamide, and, of course, in deuterium oxide, and can be submitted to NMR spectroscopy.

For mass spectrometry, many intermediates and dyes, such as those which contain sulfonic groups or have a high molecular weight, have to be converted to derivatives with the required volatility. Polycyclic quinones can be examined in the form of ethers of the reduction products, and sulfonic acids as their methyl esters or the dimethylamides.

XXVI. Synthetic Dyes and Organic Chemistry

The parallel development and interdependence of synthetic dyes and organic chemistry are common knowledge. In fact reactions originating with synthetic dyes are often used for synthetic purposes without awareness of their history. However, it is usual to think of aromatic carbocyclic chemistry in this connection, and the role of synthetic dyes in the advancement of heterocyclic chemistry needs to be stressed. Indigo and thioindigo, oxazines, phenazines, thiazines, pyrazolones, cyanines, and phthalocyanines belong to the era of classical dyestuff chemistry, and they opened up vast areas of heterocyclic chemistry. A recent book[134] on practical heterocyclic chemistry contains many synthetic reactions and compounds with which the dyestuff chemist is familiar. Quinolines, quinazolines, indazoles, and other heterocyclic systems can be synthesized from one old dye intermediate, isatin; partial hydrogenation converts it to oxindole, of interest in pharmacological and metabolic studies

---

[133] P. Madhavan Nair, T. G. Manjrekar, A. V. Rama Rao, and K. Venkataraman, *Chem. & Ind. (London)* p. 1524 (1967).

[134] A. O. Fitton and R. K. Smalley, "Practical Heterocyclic Chemistry." Academic Press, New York, 1968.

and as a nucleus occurring in alkaloids.[135] A novel reaction[136] with *o*-nitro-benzaldehyde for converting 17-keto steroids to steroidal indoxyls, indoles, and quinolines is a casual example from recent literature of the use of a reagent involved in Bayer's indigo synthesis in 1882. During the last twenty years the search for new dyes for old and new fibers and for photographic processes has led to a great increase in our knowledge of the synthesis and reactions of heterocyclic compounds, as shown by the massive records of progress reported in these supplementary volumes.

Interest in the universities has now shifted to physical organic chemistry, reaction mechanism, natural products, and the borderline between organic chemistry and biology. Research on synthetic dyes is therefore almost entirely confined to the research departments of the large dyestuff organizations, who also include in their program the physical chemistry of dyeing and other aspects of the properties of dyes in relation to their application. An unfortunate feature of the situation is that many valuable advances in synthetic methods are described only in patents, with their obvious limitations, or lie buried in the records of companies.

Futurology is now a subject of several books. According to a newspaper report, ICI recently concluded "a large scale forecasting exercise on the year 2000," but the results are confidential. Since ICI spends about 30 million pounds a year on research and development, the object of such speculation must be to see that profitable areas for investigation are chosen. Synthetic dyes, in comparison for instance with plastics and synthetic fibers, must occupy a relatively small proportion of the long range R & D program. In fact any major effort in synthetic dyes will be related to the commitments made in synthetic fibers and to the expansion of the textile and other color-using industries. Since dyes are numerous and of a bewildering variety, made by batch processes on a relatively small scale, basic research in organic synthesis and reaction mechanisms, as much as work planned to meet specific dyestuff requirements, will influence the new directions which the development of synthetic dyes will take.

[135] O. Bayer and W. Eckert, *in* "Methoden der organischen Chemie" (E. Müller, ed.), 4th ed., Vol. VII, Part 4, p. 5. Thieme, Stuttgart, 1968; A. H. Beckett, R. W. Daisley, and J. Walker, *Tetrahedron* **24**, 6093 (1968); G. Tacconi, *Farmaco (Pavia)*, (*Ed. Sci.*) **19**, 113 (1964).

[136] A. Hassner, M. J. Haddadin, and P. Catsoulacos, *J. Org. Chem.* **31**, 1363 (1966).

Chapter II

RAW MATERIALS

G. Collin and M. Zander

RÜTGERSWERKE AG., DUISBURG-MEIDERICH AND CASTROP-RAUXEL, GERMANY
*Translated by T. H. Goodwin, Chemistry Department, University of Glasgow,
Glasgow W.2, Scotland*

I. Coal Tar

Coal tar is still one of the most important sources of aromatic compounds and particularly of polycyclic aromatic hydrocarbons and heterocyclics. The monocyclic aromatics are also obtained, in increasing quantity, from petrochemical sources, which will be discussed in more detail in Section II.

In the last two decades research into the chemical composition of coal tar has received an enormous stimulus through the application of gas chromatography and spectroscopy (see, e.g., Sauerland and Zander[1-4]). In *CSD I*, Table I (pp. 28–32) there are listed altogether 215 aromatic compounds which, in 1951, were known to be present in coal tar. The

[1] H. D. Sauerland, *Brennstoff-Chem.* **44**, 37 (1963).
[2] H. D. Sauerland and M. Zander, *Erdoel Kohle* **19**, 502 (1966).
[3] M. Zander, *Erdoel Kohle* **19**, 278 (1966).
[4] M. Zander, *Chem. Ingr.-Tech.* **37**, 1010 (1965).

number had been more than doubled by 1967 and amounts now to some 475.[5-8]

Parallel with the development of research, progress has occurred in the techniques of isolating pure components from tar. By concentrating the working up of the tar in large, centrally located, continuously operating plants it has been possible to obtain, quite economically, even compounds which are present in proportions less than 0.1%.

In particular, the introduction of gas chromatography has greatly improved our knowledge of the quantitative composition of coal tar, which in many cases has been found to be a much richer source of raw materials than had previously been supposed. Naphthalene, the major constituent of tar, is typical. The average naphthalene content of a tar from a representative coking plant was given in 1951 as about 5–8% (*CSD I*, Table II, p. 32), since the methods of analysis then available were very similar to the processes actually used in the large-scale extraction. According to our present knowledge the average concentration of naphthalene is about 10%.

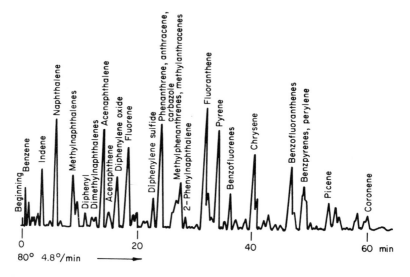

Fig. 1. Gas chromatogram of a coal tar[9]: 3 m Apiezon L; 0.3% on glass microbeads of 60–80 mesh; starting temperature, 80°; temperature-programmed, 4.8°/minute; flame ionization detector.

[5] O. Kruber, A. Raeithel, and G. Grigoleit, *Erdoel Kohle* **8**, 637 (1955).

[6] K. F. Lang, *Fortschr. Chem. Forsch.* **7**, No. 1, 172 (1966).

[7] K. F. Lang and I. Eigen, *Fortschr. Chem. Forsch.* **8**, No. 1, 91 (1967).

[8] Coal Tar Research Association, "The Coal Tar Data Book," 2nd ed. Gomersal, 1965.

[9] H. D. Sauerland, *Erdoel Kohle* **19**, 503 (1966).

Figure 1 shows a temperature-programmed gas chromatogram of the volatile components of a typical crude coal tar from a high-temperature coking plant.[9] Such chromatograms enable the principal components of the tar, with the exception of phenols and bases, to be determined directly and quantitatively from the crude tar. Fifty to 55% of the tar is obtained in the boiling range up to 550°. The rest remains unvaporized and so its constituents are not estimated; they are the high molecular weight aromatics of pitch.

Quantitative evaluation of the gas chromatogram in Fig. 1 gives the percentage compositions reported in Table I.[10] The compositions of high-

TABLE I

RESULTS OF THE GAS-CHROMATOGRAPHIC INVESTIGATION OF A
TYPICAL COKE-OVEN TAR FROM THE RUHR

Component	Weight percentage of crude tar
Compounds boiling below 215° (except phenols and bases), i.e., benzene and its homologs, indene, hydrindene, methylindenes	3.5
Naphthalene (and thionaphthene)	10.3
2-Methylnaphthalene	1.5
1-Methylnaphthalene	0.5
Diphenyl	0.4
Dimethylnaphthalenes	1.0
Acenaphthylene	2.0
Acenaphthene	0.3
Diphenylene oxide	1.4
Fluorene	2.0
Methylfluorenes	0.8
Diphenylene sulfide	0.3
Phenanthrene, anthracene, carbazole	9.0
Methylphenanthrenes, methylanthracenes	1.8
2-Phenylnaphthalene	0.3
Fluoranthene	3.3
Pyrene	2.1
Benzofluorenes and compounds boiling with them	2.3
Chrysene	2.0
Benzanthracene, triphenylene, benzofluoranthenes	1 7
Perylene, benzpyrenes, picene, coronene, and compounds boiling with them	3.5
Total	50.0

[10] H.-G. Franck and G. Collin, "Steinkohlenteer: Chemie, Technologie und Verwendung." Springer, Berlin, 1968.

temperature tars vary within certain limits and depend on the coal that has been used, on the type of coke oven, and on the temperature and duration of coking.[11]

As has already been indicated, naphthalene, which forms, on the average, 10% of the weight of coke-oven tar is its most important component. Together with 11 other compounds whose individual contributions are 1% or more, it forms about one-third of the total weight of the tar. Table II lists these principal constituents of the high-temperature tar, while

TABLE II

COMPOUNDS PRESENT IN HIGH-TEMPERATURE COAL TAR
TO THE EXTENT OF 1% OR MORE

Compound	B.p. at 760 mm. (°C)	M.p. (°C)	Average wt. % in crude tar
Naphthalene	217.955	80.290	10.0
Phenanthrene	338.4	100	5.0
Fluoranthene	383.5	111	3.3
Pyrene	393.5	150.0	2.1
Acenaphthylene	270	93	2.0
Fluorene	297.9	115.0	2.0
Chrysene	441	256	2.0
Anthracene	340	218	1.8
Carbazole	354.76	244.4	1.5
2-Methylnaphthalene	241.052	34.58	1.5
Diphenylene oxide	285.1	85	1.0
Indene	182.44	−1.5	1.0
Total of the principal components			33.2

Table III includes further important components arranged in order of decreasing proportion by weight.[10] It would exceed the space allocated to this chapter to include all the 475 compounds that have been definitely identified.

In spite of the fact that compounds that are important for synthesis of organic dyestuffs are present in relatively small amount in coal tar, the supply of raw material is great compared with the demands of the dyestuff producers. Consequently, and this applies particularly to the condensed aromatics, only a small part of the total which might be isolated is in fact obtained as pure product; the greater proportion is used

[11] W. Weskamp, W. Dressler, and E. Schierholz, *Glueckauf* **98**, 567 (1962); **103**, 215 (1967).

TABLE III

OTHER IMPORTANT COMPOUNDS FOUND IN HIGH-TEMPERATURE COAL TAR

Compound	*B.p. at 760 mm (°C)*	*M.p. (°C)*	*Average wt. % in crude tar*
Acridine	343.9	111	0.6
1-Methylnaphthalene	244.685	−30.480	0.5
Phenol	181.839	40.90	0.4
m-Cresol	202.231	12.22	0.4
Benzene	80.100	5.533	0.4
Diphenyl	255.0	69.2	0.4
Acenaphthene	277.5	95	0.3
2-Phenylnaphthalene	359.8	101	0.3
Toluene	110.625	−94.991	0.3
Quinoline	237.10	−14.2	0.3
Diphenylene sulfide	331.4	97	0.3
Thionaphthene	219.9	31.321	0.3
m-Xylene	139.103	−47.872	0.2
o-Cresol	191.003	30.99	0.2
p-Cresol	201.940	34.69	0.2
Isoquinoline	243.25	26.48	0.2
Quinaldine	247.6	−1	0.2
Phenanthridine	349.5	107	0.2
7,8-Benzoquinoline	340.2	52	0.2
2,3-Benzodiphenylene oxide (Brasan)	394.5	208	0.2
Indole	254.7	52.5	0.2
3,5-Dimethylphenol	221.692	63.27	0.1
2,4-Dimethylphenol	210.931	24.54	0.1
Pyridine	115.256	−41.8	0.02
2-Methylpyridine (α-Picoline)	129.408	−66.7	0.02
3-Methylpyridine (β-Picoline)	144.143	−18.25	0.01
4-Methylpyridine (γ-Picoline)	145.356	3.65	0.01
2,6-Dimethylpyridine (2,6-Lutidine)	144.045	−6.10	0.01
2,4-Dimethylpyridine (2,4-Lutidine)	158.403	−63.96	0.01
Total			6.6

as technical blends. The world production of coal tar in 1967 amounted to some 16 million tons, of which about one-third came from Western Europe, about one-fifth each from Eastern Europe including the USSR and from the U. S., as well as about one-seventh from the Asiatic countries. Table IV shows the production of raw coal tar by the principal producing countries in 1965.[10] About 80% of the total production is high-

TABLE IV
COAL TAR PRODUCTION BY THE MOST IMPORTANT COUNTRIES IN 1965

Country	Production in thousands of tons
Great Britain	2439
Federal Republic of Germany	1932
France	625
Belgium	282
Italy	245
Netherlands	137
Spain	120
Austria	79[1]
Sweden	40[1]
Switzerland	27[1]
Western Europe	5926
USSR[2]	2500
Poland[2]	600
Czechoslovakia[2]	400
Yugoslavia[2]	40
Eastern Europe including USSR	3540
U. S.	3350
Japan	1380
China[2]	500
India[2]	300
Canada[2]	200
Elsewhere[2]	700
World excluding Europe & USSR	6430
World Total	16,000 approx.

[1] 1964 Production.
[2] Estimated.

temperature tar and it is to this that the analytical data already given relate.

The fundamental processes for working up crude coal tars are distillation, crystallization, extraction, and polymerization. The primary fractionation is carried out almost exclusively by continuous distillation. Figure 2 gives a diagrammatic summary of the amount and method of working up of each of the resulting fractions.[10]

For the primary distillation of the coal tar there have been developed in the last 20 years numerous continuous processes depending on (a) flash vaporization and (b) recirculation of the bottom fractions and on combinations of the two.[10,12] Among the best known processes are those of

[12] G. Collin and G. Mauhs, *Ullmann* 16, 668 (1965).

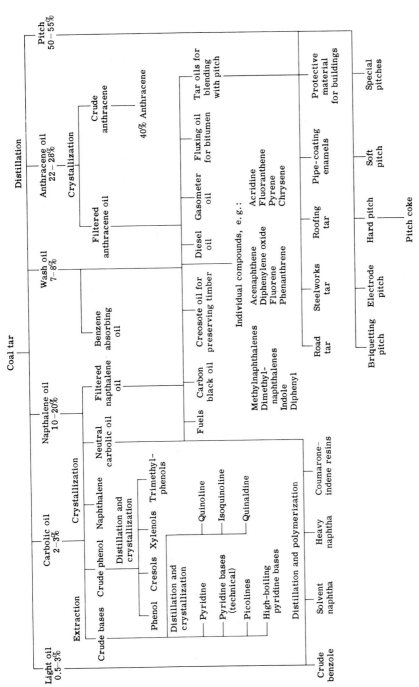

Fig. 2. Working up high-temperature tar. (From H. G. Franck and G. Collin, "Steinkohlenteer: Chemie, Technologie und Verwendung," Springer, Berlin, 1968.)

Koppers (*CSD I*, p. 34), Teerverwertung,[13,14] Rütgers,[15] Wilton,[16] Ab-der-Halden (Proabd),[17] and Foster-Wheeler as well as numerous others.[18-26] By way of example the flow diagram of the Rütgers process is reproduced in Fig. 3. This depends on recycling and, by precise division into many separate fractions, makes possible the economic recovery of particular tar ingredients in high yield. For example, up to 95% of the naphthalene

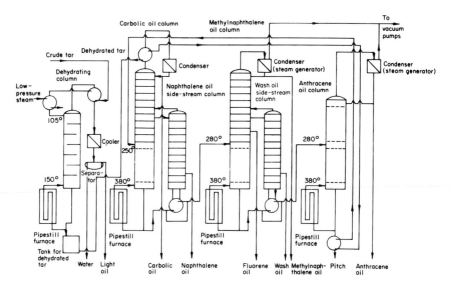

FIG. 3. Continuous tar distillation by the Rütgers process. (From H. G. Franck and G. Collin, "Steinkohlenteer: Chemie, Technologie und Verwendung," Springer, Berlin, 1968.)

[13] H. J. V. Winkler, "Der Steinkohlenteer und seine Aufarbeitung." Verlag Glückauf, Essen, 1951.
[14] Gesellschaft für Teerverwertung mbH, *DRP* 767,001; *DBP* 956,308.
[15] Rütgerswerke AG, *DBP* 940,165; 948,243.
[16] Anonymous, *Gas J.* **286**, 277 (1956).
[17] Société pour l'Exploitation des Procédés Ab-der-Halden, *BP* 961,237; *FP* 876,795.
[18] L. B. Mayoh, *Gas Times* **84**, 141 (1955).
[19] W. Fritz, *Gas-Wasserfach* **100**, 1217 (1959).
[20] Anonymous, *Gas World* **149**, 734 (1959); **151**, 323 (1960).
[21] B. E. A. Thomas and J. G. D. Molinari, *Gas J.* **304**, 19 (1960).
[22] P. von Loyen and O. M. Stührmann, *Erdoel Kohle* **13**, 758 (1960).
[23] H. S. Turnbull, *Blast Furnace Steel Plant* **50**, 411 (1962).
[24] V. E. Privalov, J. P. Isaenko, V. N. Novikov, M. G. Gaisarov, F. A. Mustafin, and G. V. Khomutinkin, *Koks i Khim.* No. 12, 34 (1964).
[25] L. N. Ermolov, *Koks i Khim.* No. 8, 36 (1966).
[26] D. McNeil, "Coal Carbonization Products." Pergamon Press, Oxford, 1966.

originally present in the crude tar is found in the naphthalene fraction, of which it forms some 85%.

A. Light Oil

Because there may be up to 5% of water in the crude tar, the light oil of the primary distillation cannot be accurately separated by fractionation. It is therefore usually first extracted with soda lye (caustic soda solution) to remove the phenols and then with sulfuric acid to remove the bases, after which it may be resolved into four fractions by redistillation:

(1) Crude benzole with a boiling range of ∼70–160°, containing benzene and its homologs as principal components.

(2) Crude solvent naphtha with a boiling range of ∼160–185°, containing besides homologs of benzene various unsaturated compounds which are copolymerizable to coumarone-indene resins.

(3) Heavy naphtha with a boiling range of ∼185–200°, which, after purification is also used as a solvent.

(4) Light oil residue, boiling over 200°, having naphthalene as its principal constituent.

The crude benzole and the nonpolymerizable portion of the solvent naphtha are conveniently worked up further in conjunction with the crude benzole fraction obtained from the coal in the coking process. After removal of the tar this crude *coke-oven benzole* is washed out of the raw gas by means of wash oil. In the last 20 years purification by the BASF-Scholven hydrorefining process has displaced the earlier wasteful acid purification technique as the method of refining the crude benzole.[10,27-36] In this impurities containing sulfur, oxygen, and nitrogen lose these catalytically as hydrogen sulfide, water, and ammonia, respectively, while the accompanying hydrocarbon fragments as well as the olefinic compounds are hydrogenated without any significant hydrogenation of the benzene nucleus itself. The material thus obtained is worked up to

[27] Scholven-Chemie AG, *DBP* 844,440.
[28] W. Urban, *Erdoel Kohle* 4, 279 (1951).
[29] W. Grothe, *Erdoel Kohle* 6, 450 (1953).
[30] H. Novak and H.-G. Liebich, *Brennstoff-Chem.* 35, 308 (1954).
[31] H. Nonnenmacher, O. Reitz, and P. Schmidt, *Erdoel Kohle* 8, 407 (1955).
[32] F. Trefny, *Tech. Mitt. Krupp* 48, 223 (1955).
[33] E. Boye, *Chemiker-Ztg.* 80, 279 (1956).
[34] M. Höring and E. E. Donath, *Ullmann* 10, 555 (1958).
[35] F. Sonntag, *Erdoel Kohle* 13, 752 (1960).
[36] J. B. Lane, *Coke Gas* 492 (1961).

pure products by redistillation in a highly efficient system of columns with, for example, 276 bubble-cap plates. In this way the aliphatic impurities are removed in the forerunnings and in the intermediate azeotropic fractions.[10,34,37] Over 95% of the *benzene* and over 90% of the *toluene* are obtained in pure form. A xylene fraction is taken off in the boiling range 138–141° and contains *m*-xylene as its chief component together with the ortho and para isomers and ethylbenzene.

The separation of these isomers is effected, for example, in the Phillips process by redistillation and crystallization.[38–40] The *o-xylene*, which boils 5.3° higher than *m*-xylene, is first separated as the bottom product in a 150-plate column while ethylbenzene, which boils 2.2° below the *p*-xylene, comes off as the top product from a 350-plate column. The individual components of the residual mixture of *m*- and *p*-xylenes differ in boiling point by only 0.7°, but by continuous low-temperature fractional crystallization between −23° and −54° pure *p-xylene* can be separated in solid form. The filtrate, containing about 80% *m*-xylene, can be worked up to 95% by redistillation in a 250-plate column. Installations for the separation of the xylenes are frequently linked with others for their isomerization in order to secure, according to the prevailing demand, optimum yields of the isomers that are required. For this purpose, after removing the isomer that is in demand, the mixture of the remaining isomers is catalytically converted into the equilibrium mixture, which is then reintroduced with the feed stock into the separation plant.[40]

There are other processes for working up the crude benzole. In the Houdry-Litol process for the refinement of coke-oven benzole by catalytic hydrogenation, besides the reactions already stated to occur in the BASF-Scholven process, the nonaromatic fractions are converted completely into gaseous hydrocarbons while the higher benzene homologs are partially hydrodealkylated and converted into benzene and lower homologs.[41] Other technically developed processes for purifying the aromatics from the paraffinic hydrocarbons make use of extractive distillation. Extraction media are aqueous diethylene glycol (Udex process), tetramethylene sulfone (Shell-Sulfolane process), aqueous monomethylformamide (Mofex process), and aqueous *N*-methylpyrrolidone (Lurgi-Arosolvan process).[42–44] To separate the mixture of xylene isomers, the

[37] F. Trefny, *Erdoel Kohle* 8, 874 (1955).
[38] J. A. Weedmann and R. A. Findlay, *Petrol. Refiner* 37, No. 11, 195 (1958).
[39] D. L. McKay, G. H. Dale, and J. A. Weedmann, *Ind. Eng. Chem.* 52, 197 (1960).
[40] E. Weingaertner, *Ullmann* 18, 733 (1967).
[41] A. K. Logwinuk, L. Friedman, and A. H. Weiss, *Ind. Eng. Chem.* 56, No. 4, 20 (1964).
[42] W. Rühl, *Ullmann* 6, 675 (1955).
[43] C. L. Dunn, *Hydrocarbon Process Petrol. Refiner* 43, 150 (1964).
[44] E. Guccione, *Chem. Eng.* 73, No. 14, 78 (1966).

formation of addition compounds, clathrates, and complexes as well as selective extraction can be made use of instead of the combination of distillation and crystallization.[40]

From the sulfuric acid extract of the light oil the *pyridine bases* are obtained by precipitation with ammonia or caustic soda. The mixture of bases gives, after azeotropic removal of the water with benzene[45] and subsequent rectification, *pyridine* and *α-picoline* as pure compounds and the following inhomogeneously boiling fractions:

β-/γ-Picoline/2,6-lutidine
2-Ethylpyridine
2,4-/2,5-Lutidine
2,3-Lutidine/3-/4-ethylpyridine/2-methyl-6-ethylpyridine
2,4,6-/2,3,6-Collidine
Aniline
o-/m-/p-Toluidine
Xylidines

The pure compounds are isolated from these fractions by the formation of addition compounds, azeotropic distillation, or selective extraction.[10,46-50]

B. CARBOLIC OIL

The carbolic oil from the primary distillation of the coal tar is usually combined with the mother liquor from the naphthalene crystallization and subjected to continuous extraction with aqueous caustic soda to remove the phenols.[10] After purification of the aqueous sodium phenolate solution by steam blowing, the crude wet phenol is obtained by precipitation with carbon dioxide.

Instead of this caustic soda process direct selective extraction of the phenol can also be applied. The Lurgi-Phenoraffin process has achieved technical importance by using an aqueous sodium phenolate solution as the selective solvent and isopropyl ether for extracting the phenolate solution when supersaturated with phenols.[10,51]

After azeotropic dehydration of the crude phenol thus obtained, its

[45] Rütgerswerke AG, *DBP* 850,006.
[46] A. Dierichs and R. Kubička, "Phenole und Basen." Akademie Verlag, Berlin, 1958.
[47] R. Oberkobusch, *Brennstoff-Chem.* **40**, 145 (1959).
[48] Gesellschaft für Teerverwertung mbH, *DBP* 1,012,603; 951,931; 1,023,040.
[49] Rütgerswerke und Teerverwertung AG, *DBP* 1,218,450.
[50] L. Kuczyński and A. Nagowski, *Przemysl Chem.* **34**, No. 11, 190 (1955).
[51] Metallgesellschaft AG, *DAS* 1,068,724; *DBP* 1,094,758; *DAS* 1,101,435; *DBP* 1,138,066; *DAS* 1,144,286; *DBP* 1,172,270; 1,175,249; 1,196,208.

rectification leads to the production of *phenol* and *o-cresol* as technically pure distillates.[10,52-54] The succeeding *m-/p*-cresol mixture is then resolved into the pure isomers by forming addition compounds with sodium acetate and oxalic acid or urea and benzidine or by alkylation of the mixture with isobutene, distilling the *tert*-butylcresols and dealkylating them.[10,46,55-57] From the higher-boiling fractions of the xylenols some compounds can be isolated relatively easily by direct crystallization, especially the *3,4-* and the *3,5-dimethylphenols*. The remaining xylenol isomers may be obtained by distillation and crystallization and also by formation of addition compounds with amines and phenols, alkylation with isobutene, selective extraction, and azeotropic distillation.[10,46]

C. Naphthalene Oil

Depending on the precision of the separation in the tar distillation process naphthalene oil has a crystallization point somewhere between 65° and 74°; this already corresponds to a naphthalene content of 73–88%. The naphthalene is conveniently separated from the compounds that boil in the same range by one of the numerous crystallization techniques developed in the last twenty years.[10,12] It can also be obtained from the oil by distillation after the phenols have been removed.[10,12,26]

New crystallization processes for naphthalene oil include the continuous GBAG screw press process,[58-62] combined indirect cooling and stirring introduced by the Teerverwertung Company,[63] direct cooling with aqueous media according to Rütgers method,[64] the continuous Proabd technique using the scraper crystallizer,[65] the Proabd zone-melting process,[66,67] and crystallization from methanol.[67-70]

[52] Rütgerswerke AG, *DBP* 925,350; *DAS* 1,150,995; 1,157,236.
[53] P. V. Clifton and W. H. A. Webb, *Ind. Chemist* **32**, 526 (1956).
[54] K. A. Adey, *Gas J.* **303**, 475 (1960).
[55] Gesellschaft für Teerverwertung mbH, *DBP* 1,118,797; 1,124,046.
[56] Rütgerswerke AG, *DAS* 1,153,027.
[57] Rütgerswerke und Teerverwertung AG, *DBP* 1,145,629.
[58] Rheinelbe Bergbau AG and Heinrich Koppers GmbH, *DBP* 945,388.
[59] Gelsenkirchener Bergwerks-AG, *DBP* 966,921.
[60] Gelsenkirchener Bergwerks-AG and Heinrich Koppers GmbH, *DBP* 1,005,050.
[61] Heinrich Koppers GmbH and Gelsenkirchener Bergwerks-AG, *DAS* 1,095,800.
[62] H. Berge, *Gas-. Wasserfach* **103**, 699 (1962).
[63] Gesellschaft für Teerverwertung mbH, *DBP* 1,022,573; 1,073,465; 1,138,378.
[64] Rütgerswerke AG, *DBP* 824,494; *USP* 2,790,017.
[65] T. G. Woolhouse, *J. Appl. Chem.* (*London*) **7**, 573 (1957).
[66] J. G. D. Molinari, *Ind. Chemist* **37**, 323 (1961).
[67] V. E. Privalov, B. S. Gurevich, and V. M. Bednov, *Koks i Khim.* No. 1, 40 (1965).

Except in the GBAG screw press process, zone melting, and the methanol recrystallization process, the naphthalene which crystallizes out is subjected to centrifugation and washed with water or aqueous media. All the procedures give technical *naphthalene* with a crystallization point that is usually above 79°, the trade quality usually required, for example, for oxidation to phthalic anhydride.

To obtain pure naphthalene with a crystallization point higher than 79.6° *thionaphthene*, which is present in proportions up to 2%, must be at least partially removed either by azeotropic distillation with glycols or by chemical methods. The latter include partial sulfonation or chlorination, partial resinification with formaldehyde and acid or with Friedel-Crafts catalysts and desulfurization with metallic sodium, or hydrorefining.[10]

D. WASH OIL

In the continuous primary distillation of tar the wash oil is removed either as a single fraction requiring redistillation or as several separate fractions. There are produced, in order of increasing boiling range, the following fractions: methylnaphthalene, diphenyl, dimethylnaphthalene, diphenylene oxide, acenaphthene, and fluorene fractions.

After removing the phenols and bases from the methylnaphthalene fraction, deep cooling and centrifuging gives *2-methylnaphthalene*. Accurate rectification of the filtrates yields *1-methylnaphthalene,* which boils 3.6° higher. If demand requires it, the methylnaphthalene fraction can be converted into naphthalene by hydrodealkylation.[10]

Diphenyl and *indole* are concentrated in the diphenyl fraction. The indole may be extracted by potassium hydroxide fusion or by azeotropic distillation with diethylene glycol or by extraction with glycols or aqueous dimethyl sulfoxide.[71-74]

The dimethylnaphthalene fraction contains 9 of the 10 isomeric forms of this compound. Of these the *2,6-, 1,6-,* and *2,3-dimethylnaphthalenes* are relatively easily obtainable by redistillation and crystallization. The whole mixture can be isomerized to the 2,6-isomer.[10]

Cooling and centrifuging the *acenaphthene* fraction enable this hy-

[68] The Midland Tar Distillers Ltd., *BP* 628,403; 630,397.
[69] Butler & Co. Ltd., *BP* 686,166.
[70] Tennants' Tar Distillers and Engineering Supplies Ltd., *BP* 755,501.
[71] Gesellschaft für Teerverwertung mbH, *DBP* 812,079; 832,155; 908,021; 1,077,665.
[72] UCC, *USP* 2,837,531; 2,916,496; 2,916,497.
[73] Houdry Process Corporation, *USP* 2,982,771.
[74] Union Rheinische Braunkohlen Kraftstoff AG, *DBP* 1,218,451.

drocarbon to be obtained in much greater quantity than is present in the original coal tar. In the course of the distillation the proportion of acenaphthene is more than doubled by the hydrogenation of acenaphthylene.[75,76]

In removing the *diphenylene oxide* fraction care must be taken to secure a complete separation from the fluorene present, since diphenylene oxide forms, on the one hand, a continuous series of mixed crystals with the fluorene (which boils 12.8° higher) and, on the other, a eutectic with the lower boiling acenaphthene. By refrigeration and centrifugation diphenylene oxide can be recovered from the fluorene-free fraction.[76,77]

Fluorene is obtained from the fluorene fraction by cooling and centrifuging after adding solvent naphtha.[10,78]

The *quinoline bases* are recovered either from the wash oil or from the methylnaphthalene and diphenyl/indole fraction after removal of the phenols, by extraction with sulfuric acid and precipitation with ammonia. The separation of the individual compounds may be achieved, for example, by rectification and the formation of addition products with water. In contrast to isoquinoline, quinoline and quinaldine form crystalline hydrates. By suitable combinations of distillation and crystallization economical recovery of pure *quinoline, isoquinoline,* and *quinaldine* is practicable.[47,79] The higher boiling *lepidine* can be isolated by means of the addition compound with *o*-cresol.[80]

E. ANTHRACENE OIL

The anthracene oil is usually taken off as two fractions during the primary distillation of the tar; the major portion is the lower boiling "anthracene oil I" and the smaller the higher boiling "anthracene oil II."

Indirect stirred cooling and centrifuging of anthracene oil I give crystalline crude anthracene. This contains 20–35% anthracene, 30–40% phenanthrene, and 12–20% carbazole. The so-called "40% anthracene," which contains more than 40% and frequently 45–55% anthracene, is obtained either by mixing the crude anthracene with hot, crude anthracene oil and crystallizing, when the greater part of the phenanthrene is removed without altering the ratio of anthracene to carbazole, or by dis-

[75] J. Jurkiewicz, J. Janczur, and H. Laskowska, *Koks, Smola, Gaz* 3, 42 (1958); 4, 97 (1959).

[76] H.-G. Franck, *Brennstoff-Chem.* 45, 1 (1964).

[77] Gesellschaft für Teerverwertung mbH, *DBP* 839,040.

[78] S. Juzwa, *Koks, Smola, Gaz* 7, 110 (1962).

[79] Gesellschaft für Teerverwertung mbH, *DBP* 910,166; 1,051,854; 1,067,817.

[80] Gesellschaft für Teerverwertung mbH, *DBP* 1,110,644.

tillation in such a way as to secure thorough removal of the carbazole.[81,82] Double recrystallization of the 40% anthracene from pyridine yields *anthracene* of about 95% purity which is used as the raw material for the production of anthraquinone.[13,81-84] Instead of pyridine the following can be used as selective solvents for the removal of the carbazole: toluene/acetone, benzene/methanol, glycols, dialkyl sulfoxides, and dialkylformamides.[85-89] To prepare the purest anthracene, the carbazole and tetracene are removed by azeotropic distillation with ethylene glycol.[90] From the phenanthrene fraction that results from the redistillation of the filtered anthracene oil or that forms the top product in the continuous distillation of crude anthracene pure *phenanthrene* may be obtained if required either by washing with sulfuric acid, recrystallizing, and redistilling or by removal of the accompanying diphenylene sulfide[91] by treating the melt with sodium and maleic anhydride.[92-96] Further possible techniques of purification are azeotropic distillation and molecular sieve adsorption.[97,98]

Carbazole is obtained, by use of selective solvents, from the carbazole fraction, which forms the bottom product in the distillation of the crude anthracene. Purification is effected by the processes indicated for anthracene.[85-90]

Extraction of filtered anthracene oil with sodium bisulfite causes the separation of the *acridine* as the sodium salt of the acridone sulfonic acid and from this the free base is liberated by caustic soda.[13]

Redistillation of the high-boiling anthracene oil II gives *phenylnaphthalene,* fluoranthene, pyrene, benzofluorene, and chrysene frac-

[81] Gesellschaft für Teerverwertung mbH, *DBP* 966,864; 963,428; 1,081,899.
[82] Stamicarbon N. V., *BP* 726,860.
[83] L. D. Gluzman, *Koks i Khim.* No. 4, 35 (1958).
[84] J. P. Isaenko and T. M. Markaczewa, *Koks i Khim.* No. 12, 35 (1958).
[85] Soc. Chimique de Gerland S. A., *FP* 976,773.
[86] E. Bellet, *Compt. Rend. Congr. Ind. Gaz* **68,** 859 (1951).
[87] Union Rheinische Braunkohlen Kraftstoff AG, *DAS* 1,046,002.
[88] J. Jurkiewicz and K. Wiszniowski, *Koks, Smola, Gaz* **5,** 117 (1960).
[89] J. Kula, W. Kuszka, and H. Šmigielski, *Koks, Smola, Gaz* **5,** 156 (1960).
[90] R. Sizmann, *Angew. Chem.* **71,** 243 (1959).
[91] Gesellschaft für Teerverwertung mbH, *DBP* 832,156.
[92] Gesellschaft für Teerverwertung mbH, *DBP* 806,437; 960,895; 1,164,385.
[93] Rütgerswerke AG, *DBP* 814,441.
[94] L. D. Gluzman, *Koks i Khim.* No. 2, 39 (1959).
[95] N. D. Rusjanova, M. V. Goftman, Z. K. Gordeeva, A. N. Zubok, and C. V. Chomutinkin, *Koks i Khim.* No. 7, 48 (1961).
[96] B. D. Blaustein and S. J. Metlin, *Anal. Chem.* **37,** 295 (1965).
[97] J. F. Feldman and M. Orchin, *USP* 2,590,096.
[98] Union Oil Co. of California, *USP* 2,967,896.

tions.[99] From the fluoranthene fraction *fluoranthene* itself is obtained by mixing with solvent naphtha and centrifuging.[13,99-101] If the pyrene fraction is recrystallized in the presence of sulfuric acid or ferric chloride to remove *2,3-benzodiphenylene oxide* (*brasan*) pure *pyrene* results,[13,102-104] while the benzofluorene fraction on recrystallization from solvent naphtha gives *1,2-* and *2,3-benzofluorene* as mixed crystals.[99] Likewise *chrysene* is recovered from its boiling fraction by crystallization, preferably with simultaneous partial sulfonation or by the introduction of chlorine.[99,105] Not only anthracene oil II but also the pitch distillate obtained in preparing hard pitch is a suitable starting material for the production of chrysene.

F. PITCH

Pitch, the residue from the coal tar distillation, is a solid mixture of similar compounds, namely, high molecular weight aromatic hydrocarbons and heterocyclics, which form a polycomponent eutectic.[106] Its principal components are aromatics with up to seven condensed rings, some of which are probably joined together by methylene groups.[106-111] On heating the pitch as a prelude to distillation these methylene bridges seem to break up more or less completely so that only the aromatics with up to seven nuclei can be detected in the fractions distilling over.

In the pitch distillate, which is obtained on further working up the pitch to "hard pitch" for pitch coking and for the manufacture of electrode pitch, there are not only the low-boiling constituents of the pitch but also secondary products formed by cracking. The distillate is, among other things, a source material for fluoranthene, pyrene, benzofluorene, and chrysene (which besides being components of the pitch are also recoverable from anthracene oil II) and for *benzofluoranthene, benzpyrene,* and *picene*. The highest boiling pure compounds which have so

[99] Gesellschaft für Teerverwertung mbH, *DBP* 817,150; 963,334.
[100] S. Bal, *Koks, Smola, Gaz* 6, 6 (1961).
[101] L. D. Gluzman and A. G. Nikitenko, *Zh. Prikl. Khim.* 34, 626 (1961).
[102] J. Szuba and U. Śmieżek, *Przemysl Chem.* 35, No. 12, 610 (1957).
[103] L. D. Gluzman, A. G. Nikitenko, and R. M. Cin, *Koks i Khim.* No. 1, 52 (1961).
[104] Rütgerswerke und Teerverwertung AG, *DBP* 1,189,961.
[105] Gesellschaft für Teerverwertung mbH, *DRP* 760,563; *DBP* 807,682.
[106] H. G. Franck, *Brennstoff-Chem.* 36, 12 (1955).
[107] O. Kruber, *Bitumen, Teere, Asphalte, Peche* 1, 177 (1950).
[108] L. J. Wood and G. Phillips, *J. Appl. Chem.* (*London*) 5, 326 (1955).
[109] A. Lissner and H. G. Schäfer, *J. Prakt. Chem.* [4] 273, 230 (1955).
[110] H. G. Schäfer, *Freiberger Forschungsh.* A51, 35 (1956).
[111] E. de Ruiter, *Erdoel Kohle* 18, 625 (1965).

far been isolated from pitch are coronene, naphtho[1,2-*b*]chrysene (3,4;8,9-dibenztetraphene) and benzo[*c*]picene (fulminene).

II. Petroleum and Synthetic Processes

Coal tar is no longer, as it was formerly, the only technically important source of raw materials for the dyestuffs industry. Nowadays many of these substances are also obtained from petroleum and by synthetic methods.

The most important starting materials for obtaining *benzene* and its homologs from petroleum are the reformates obtained catalytically or thermally from straight-run petroleum distillates boiling within the range 60–200°.[112,113] The aromatic hydrocarbons may be recovered from the reformates by extractive distillation or by adsorption on silica gel but solvent extraction is usually preferred. The benzene is isolated from the resulting mixtures by fractional distillation.

In the Udex process[114] the extraction liquids are glycols, e.g., a mixture of 75% diethylene glycol and 25% dipropylene glycol with traces of water, since, in the presence of small amounts of water glycols are highly selective solvents for aromatic hydrocarbons. Because of their considerably lower boiling points the aromatic hydrocarbons are very readily removed from the glycol phase by distillation. The resulting benzene is of very high purity. Other extraction liquids and processes which are now being used for this purpose have already been referred to in considering the working up of crude benzole (see Section I,A).

Another important method of producing benzene is the hydrodealkylation of toluene and xylenes. Both catalytic and thermal processes are known.

The catalysts that find most favor are chromium(III) oxide and platinum on aluminum oxide. The Detol process of the Houdry Process Corporation[115] is a fixed-bed catalytic method for the production of benzene from alkylbenzenes. Its working temperature is 540–650°. Related processes include that known as the Hydeal process used by the Universal Oil Products Co. and by the Ashland Oil and Refining Co.,[116]

---

[112] "Chem. Technologie" (K. Winnacker and L. Küchler, eds.), Vol. 3, pp. 250–255. Carl Hanser Verlag, Munich, 1959; F. Asinger, "Einführung in die Petrol-Chemie," pp. 131–138. Akademie Verlag, Berlin, 1960; *Brennstoff-Chem.* **46**, 316 (1965).

[113] Anonymous, *Hydrocarbon Process. Petrol. Refiner* **41**, No. 9, 164 (1962).

[114] D. Read, *Petrol. Refiner* **31**, No. 5, 97 (1952); *Oil Gas J.* **55**, No. 35, 117 (1957).

[115] Anonymous, *Hydrocarbon Process. Petrol. Refiner* **40**, No. 11, 236 (1961).

[116] Anonymous, *Hydrocarbon Process. Petrol. Refiner* **40**, No. 11, 251 (1961).

and the Bextol process of Royal Dutch Shell.[117] The yields of benzene and toluene in all these processes are very high. The five-membered ring of the indanes and indenes is opened under the conditions of the hydrodealkylation and the side chains so formed are eliminated.

A thermal hydrodealkylation process is that of the Gulf Research and Development Company.[118] In the dealkylation of toluene the yield of benzene is greater than 95%. Diphenyl and high molecular weight aromatic hydrocarbons are produced in small amounts as by-products.

A new technique of thermal hydrodealkylation which is, however, still at the experimental stage, is the MHC process of the Mitsubishi and Chiyoda Chemical Engineering and Construction Company Ltd.[119] This can use material which contains up to 30% of nonaromatic hydrocarbons, and the purity of the hydrogen used need not be very high.

Toluene is also obtained from the aromatic extracts from petroleum reformates. It is produced in the reforming process principally by the aromatization of methylcyclohexane and of dimethylcyclopentane, when simultaneous expansion of the ring takes place.

The isomeric *xylenes* are produced from the C_8 fraction of the aromatic extracts from petroleum reformates.[120] These contain, on the average, 20–24% o-xylene, with 42–48% m-xylene, and 16–20% p-xylene, and 10–11% ethylbenzene. (For the separation of the mixture of isomers see Section I,A.)

In addition to these reformates a further technically interesting source of benzene and its homologs is the pyrolysis gasoline formed during the short-time cracking of light naphtha to ethylene.[121] For every 1000 kg of ethylene formed 600–900 kg of pyrolysis gasoline is produced, composed of some 60–70% of extractable aromatics. The composition of these aromatics is closely dependent on the operating conditions of the ethylene plant. In general the benzene content is between 20% and 40%, that of the toluene between 15% and 20%, and that of the xylenes between 10% and 15%. The recovery of the aromatics is not achieved in a single step, but requires several. In the first the dienes present in the gasoline are hydrogenated to olefins. The refined material is then suitably distilled to yield a forefraction, a main fraction, and a residue. The main fraction boiling between 50° and 150° is subjected to hydrogen treatment,

[117] Anonymous, *Hydrocarbon Process. Petrol. Refiner* **42**, No. 3, 121 (1963).
[118] Anonymous, *Hydrocarbon Process. Petrol. Refiner* **40**, No. 11, 298 (1961).
[119] S. Masamune, J. Fukuda, and S. Katada, *Hydrocarbon Process. Petrol. Refiner* **47**, No. 2, 155 (1967).
[120] H. W. Haines, Jr., J. M. Powers, and R. B. Bennett, *Ind. Eng. Chem.* **47**, 1096 (1955).
[121] K. H. Eisenlohr, K. Naumburg, and H. G. Zengel, *Erdoel Kohle* **20**, 82 (1967).

whereby the olefins are saturated and the sulfur compounds are removed. The aromatic hydrocarbons are then separated by extractive distillation or liquid–liquid extraction. N-Methylpyrrolidone has become established as the solvent in both techniques.

Until 1961 *naphthalene* had been obtained almost exclusively from coal tar both in Europe and in the United States, but since then its production from petroleum has become increasingly important. By 1965 about 43% of the United States production of naphthalene was petrochemical.

Starting materials for the petrochemical manufacture of naphthalene are the higher-boiling fractions from the reforming processes, gas oil from catalytic crackers, and by-products from the pyrolysis reactions for the production of olefins.[122] These mixtures, which consist essentially of naphthalene and its homologs, are subjected to dealkylation. In the Hydeal process[123] of the Ashland Oil and Refining Company and of Universal Oil Products the starting material, obtained from the heavy reformate, is dealkylated with excess hydrogen over a chromium oxide–aluminum oxide catalyst of high purity but containing a controlled amount of sodium; the naphthalene so formed, after treatment on a clay catalyst to remove olefins, is obtained by distillation. A similar catalytic technique is the Unidak procedure of the Union Oil Company of California.[124]

Thermal dealkylation processes have been developed by the Sun Oil Company[122,124] and the Atlantic Richfield and Hydrocarbon Research.[125]

The highly condensed aromatics which are significant for the dyestuffs industry, such as pyrene or chrysene, are almost exclusively obtained from coal tar. Another possible source of these compounds would be the hydrogenation of coal, although at present this is not carried out practically. *Coronene*, in particular, can be obtained as a by-product in coal hydrogenation. It has been estimated that about 70 tons of coronene can be obtained from 100,000 tons of coal.[126]

World production of synthetic *phenol* amounts, at the present time, to about 1.6 million tons and accounts for a large proportion of the total weight of this compound which is made. Of this about two-thirds is obtained by the cumene process of Hock and Lang. Other important techniques are the Dow process (alkaline hydrolysis of chlorobenzene), the Raschig process (hydrolysis of chlorobenzene by steam), and alkali

[122] R. B. Stobaugh, *Hydrocarbon Process. Petrol. Refiner* **45**, No. 3, 149 (1966).
[123] D. S. Asselin and R. A. Erickson, *Chem. Eng. Progr.* **58**, No. 4, 47 (1962).
[124] Anonymous, *Ind. Eng. Chem.* **54**, No. 2, 32 (1962).
[125] S. Feigelman and C. B. O'Connor, *Hydrocarbon Process. Petrol. Refiner* **45**, No. 5, 140 (1966).
[126] P. W. Sherwood, *Petrol. Refiner* **29**, 106 (1950).

fusion of benzenesulfonic acid. Twenty-eight percent of the phenol synthesized is prepared by these methods.

Of less importance are the oxidative decarboxylation of benzoic acid (the Dow/California Research process) and the oxidation of cyclohexane (Scientific Design process).

Hock and Lang[127] reported, in 1944, the acid cleavage of cumene hydroperoxide to phenol and acetone. A few years later this reaction, known as either the Hock or the cumene process, had been developed on a large scale by the Distillers Company in Great Britain and by the Hercules Powder Company in the United States. Since then, plants for the synthesis of phenol by this method have been established in almost all industrial countries.

The process[128] is based on the following three reaction steps:

(1) Preparation of cumene by the alkylation of benzene with propylene.

(2) Oxidation of cumene to its hydroperoxide by means of air.

(3) Cleavage of the cumene hydroperoxide in an acid medium to phenol and acetone.

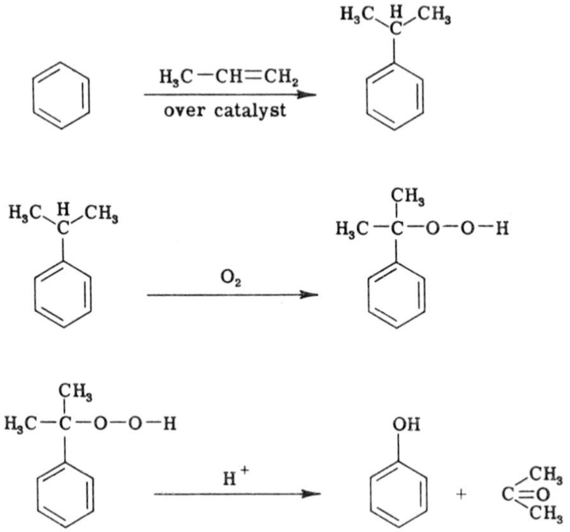

The cumene is usually prepared by vapor-phase alkylation using a phosphoric acid catalyst on a suitable carrier. The crude cumene is refined by distillation to secure the high purity (99.8%) necessary for the

[127] H. Hock and S. Lang, *Ber.* 77, 257 (1944).
[128] H. Morschel, *Ullmann* 13, 434 (1962).

subsequent reactions. It is then oxidized to its hydroperoxide in special contactors by air at a few atmospheres pressure and a temperature above 100°. In order to prevent the decomposition of the hydroperoxide by the traces of acid which are formed, a small quantity of soda is added to the reaction mixture as a stabilizer. At the same time care is taken to maintain a water vapor content of 10–20% in the vapor phase in the oxidation plant. In this way, the danger of explosion is eliminated. The oxidation mixture contains 20–25% of cumene hydroperoxide and unchanged cumene. The principal by-products are phenyldimethylcarbinol and acetophenone. It is not necessary to isolate the hydroperoxide before the cleavage stage, but in practice it is enriched by distilling off part of the cumene (again in the presence of soda as a stabilizer). For the acid-catalyzed cleavage of the cumene hydroperoxide two techniques are employed: (a) homogeneous cleavage in which use is made of acetone as solvent for both the hydroperoxide and the acid; (b) heterogeneous cleavage in which the crude hydroperoxide is dispersed in the aqueous acid phase. The catalyst is almost invariably sulfuric acid. Under favorable circumstances the yield of phenol from this decomposition is over 90%.

To work up the raw product of the cleavage reaction it is first extracted with water and dilute soda solution. The acid-free reaction product is then fractionated and in addition to phenol, the principal product, there are obtained cumene, α-methylstyrene, acetophenone, and phenyldimethylcarbinol. The residue contains larger quantities of α-cumylphenol. The phenol is then purified further.

In the Dow process,[129] which at present accounts for 7% of the world production of phenol, chlorobenzene undergoes alkaline hydrolysis. The reaction mixture is a chlorobenzene–water emulsion containing caustic soda and the process is operated at temperatures between 360° and 390° under 280 atm pressure. Diphenyl ether and o- and p-hydroxydiphenyl are the principal by-products. The chlorine needed for the manufacture of the necessary chlorobenzene is obtained by the electrolysis of sodium chloride and is the most expensive item in the Dow process.

The hydrolysis of chlorobenzene by water vapor, the Raschig method,[130] is another important source of phenol. The reaction had been known for a long time, but only received technical attention when it became possible to link the hydrolysis of the chlorobenzene with the chlorination of benzene by hydrogen chloride and air using a cyclic process in which loss of hydrogen chloride was small. For the chlorina-

[129] L. Aguello and W. Williams, *Ind. Eng. Chem.* **52,** 894 (1960).
[130] W. Mathes, *Angew. Chem.* **52,** 591 (1939).

tion stage benzene, air, and gaseous hydrogen chloride are led over a chlorination catalyst at about 230°. A large excess of benzene is used. In addition to chlorobenzene there are produced chiefly higher chloro derivatives of benzene and various decomposition products. The hydrolysis of the chlorobenzene takes place at 450–500° in the presence of a catalyst and working up of the resulting phenol involves both extraction and distillation steps.

The synthesis of phenol by sulfonation of benzene followed by alkali fusion presupposes cheap supplies of sulfuric acid and has the disadvantage of producing the relatively valueless inorganic by-products sodium sulfite and sulfate. The alkali fusion is carried out at temperatures between 320° and 340° and the reaction times are rather long.[131]

Even the *cresols* are no longer obtained exclusively from coal tar. Petrochemically they are extracted chiefly from the aqueous alkaline liquors which result from the washing of the distillates from cracked petroleum.[132] These aqueous liquors contain, for example, about 25% of phenolic compounds and about 10% of mercaptans and thiophenols. To recover the phenols and cresols their alkaline solution is first oxidized with air, the sulfur-containing compounds thus being converted into disulfides which are insoluble in alkali and can be separated by decantation. The mother liquor is then treated with carbon dioxide (flue gas) when the phenols are precipitated. The resulting mixture contains the following approximate percentages of the substances named: phenol 20; o-cresol 18; m-cresol 22; p-cresol 9; dimethylphenols 28; higher phenols 3. The mixture is resolved by fractional distillation.

In a process used by the Pittsburgh Consolidated Chemical Co.[133] the phenolic compounds are separated directly from the alkaline wash liquors by treatment with carbon dioxide. The crude product is fractionated in such a way that the components boiling below 100° and above 250° are removed. The main fraction, which contains the greater part of the phenolic substances, is then extracted with 70% aqueous methanol and a light naphtha, after which the methanol extract is freed from sulfur compounds by ion exchange. The mixture of phenols thus purified is then separated by fractional distillation to obtain the phenol and the cresols.

Several syntheses of cresols are operated on the technical scale. The hydrolysis of mixtures of o- and p-chlorotoluene under pressure at

[131] O. Lindner, *Ullmann* **13**, 427 (1962).

[132] Anonymous, *Chem. Eng.* **69**, (8), 66 (1962).

[133] Anonymous, *Chem. Eng.* **64**, (7), 228 (1957).

300–350° with aqueous caustic soda[134] provides, by partial isomeriza-
·tion, a cresol mixture containing 40–60% *m*-cresol.

The Hercules Powder Co. has studied the application of the cumene
process to the manufacture of cresols. The process has been applied
mainly to the synthesis of *p*-cresol.[135]

Alkylation of phenol with methanol in the gas phase on an aluminum
oxide catalyst leads, among other compounds, to cresols and xylenols.[136]
The reaction can be carried out so that *o*-cresol and 2,6-xylenol predominate among the products.

[134] M. Allen, *J. Am. Chem. Soc.* **54**, 2920 (1932); R. N. Shreve and C. J. Marsel,
Ind. Eng. Chem. **38**, 254 (1946).

[135] Hercules Powder Co. *USP* 2,727,796.

[136] N. M. Cullinane, W. C. Davies, and Peter Spence & Sons, Ltd., *BP* 602,257.

Chapter III

INTERMEDIATES

N. N. Vorozhtsov, Jr.

INSTITUTE OF ORGANIC CHEMISTRY, USSR ACADEMY OF SCIENCES,
NOVOSIBIRSK, USSR

I. Sulfonation

A. Mechanism of the Reaction

The characteristic property of sulfonation is the marked dependence of the rate of the reaction on the sulfuric acid concentration. The usual equation of sulfonation with sulfuric acid

$$ArH + H_2SO_4 = ArSO_3H + H_2O$$

suggests that the rate of reaction must depend linearly on the concentration of sulfuric acid. However, the experimentally measured kinetics reveal a much greater decrease of the rate on dilution with water. For example, when the concentration is reduced from 100.0% to 99.5% H_2SO_4, the rate of the reaction[1] is changed by several orders of magnitude. This is due to a change of the nature of sulfuric acid with the dilution. Anhydrous 100% sulfuric acid is ionized but to a small extent (0.2–0.3%),[2] in accord with the equations of autoprotolysis:

$$2H_2SO_4 \rightleftarrows H_3SO_4^+ + HSO_4^-$$
$$2H_2SO_4 \rightleftarrows SO_3 + H_3O^+ + HSO_4^-$$
$$3H_2SO_4 \rightleftarrows H_2S_2O_7 + H_3O^+ + HSO_4^-$$

The addition of water to 100% H_2SO_4 results in a significant increase of the H_3O^+ and HSO_4^- concentrations and in a simultaneous decrease of the $H_3SO_4^+$, SO_3, and $H_2S_2O_7$ concentrations.

The kinetics of sulfonation of p-nitrotoluene,[3] and benzene[4] and its homologs[5] by sulfuric acid of different concentrations suggests that SO_3 is most probably the sulfonating agent in aqueous sulfuric acid as well (the rate of the reaction and the concentration of SO_3 are approximately inversely proportional to the square of water concentration).

However, the data on the sulfonation of chlorobenzene[6] and the recent revision of the data available on the sulfonation kinetics have revealed that in all probability two agents take part in the sulfonation. These agents are the differently solvated molecules of SO_3. In more concentrated

---

[1] H. Cerfontain, Rec. Trav. Chim. 84, 551 (1965); for recent review see H. Cerfontain, "Mechanistic Aspects in Aromatic Sulfonation and Desulfonation" Wiley (Interscience), New York, 1968.

[2] R. J. Gillespie, J. Chem. Soc. pp. 2493 and 2516 (1950).

[3] W. A. Cowdrey and D. S. Davies, J. Chem. Soc. p. 1871 (1949).

[4] A. W. Kaandorp, H. Cerfontain, and F. L. J. Sixma, Rec. Trav. Chim. 81, 969 (1962).

[5] A. W. Kaandorp, H. Cerfontain, and F. L. J. Sixma, Rec. Trav. Chim. 82, 113 (1963).

[6] C. W. Kort and H. Cerfontain, Rec. Trav. Chim. 86, 865 (1967).

sulfuric acid, the effect of pyrosulfuric acid, $H_2S_2O_7 = SO_3(H_2SO_4)$, prevails; in the less concentrated acid (for example, 85% and less for toluene) the effect of $H_3SO_4^+ = SO_3(H_3O^+)$ cation prevails.[7]

The change of the rate of sulfonation of a number of substances with the sulfuric acid concentration best corresponds within certain limits to the activities of $H_2S_2O_7$ and $H_3SO_4^+$. With benzene in 79% H_2SO_4, both particles take equal part in the sulfonation. The presence of two active particles explains the change of the ratio of the rates of formation of certain isomers and thereby the change of the ratio of the reaction products with the concentration of H_2SO_4. The $H_3SO_4^+$ particle is more selective and the difference of the rates of the formation of the different isomers via this cation is greater than that in the sulfonation with $H_2S_2O_7$.

The mechanism of the sulfonation of benzene, for example, can be represented by the following scheme:

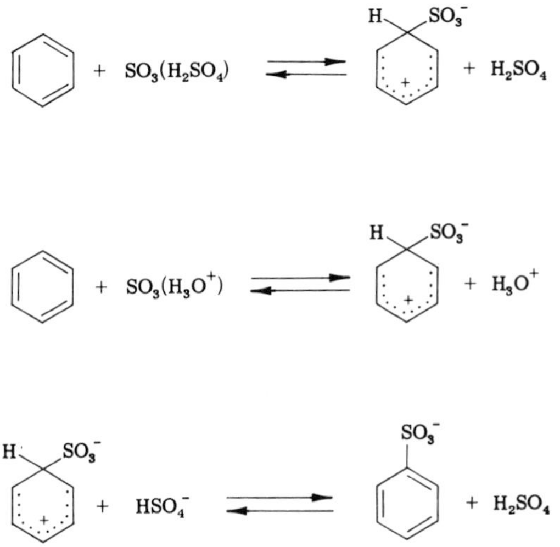

The rate-limiting step of the process is the first one, i.e., the formation of the intermediate product of the sulfuric anhydride addition to the molecule of aromatic compound. Accordingly, there is no primary isotopic effect in the reaction of sulfuric anhydride with benzene and toluene; the stage of the elimination of the proton does not affect the overall rate of the process.[8] Sulfuric anhydride is naturally the sulfonating agent of oleum.

[7] C. W. Kort and H. Cerfontain, Rec. Trav. Chim. 87, 24 (1968).
[8] H. Cerfontain and A. Telder, Rec. Trav. Chim. 84, 1613 (1965).

The characteristic property of sulfonation which distinguishes it from the other substitution reactions is the relative readiness of the inverse reaction—hydrolysis of the sulfonic acids with aqueous sulfuric acid to the starting product containing no sulfonate grouping.

The overall process of sulfonation, if water is present in the reaction mixture (that of H_2SO_4, or that formed during the reaction), must be represented by the following equation:

$$ArH + H_2SO_4 \rightleftarrows ArSO_3H + H_2O$$

Reversibility of the reaction significantly affects its result.

Obviously, the ratio of the isomeric sulfonic acids in the absence of the reverse reaction depends on the relative rates of the replacement of different hydrogen atoms. At the same time, if the reverse reaction is possible, the ratio of the isomers at equilibrium will conform to the ratio of the equilibrium constants of the corresponding isomers.[9] The ratio of the equilibrium constants is usually markedly different from that of the rate constants of the sulfonation at different positions. For this reason it is possible to obtain one or the other compound as the major product under appropriate conditions.

The kinetics of hydrolysis strongly suggest that sulfonate anion takes part in the reaction. The reaction begins with protonation of the SO_3^--bearing carbon atom, and its mechanism is reverse to that of the sulfonation with $SO_3(H_3O^+)$.[10]

An intramolecular mechanism has also been proposed to explain the isomerization of sulfonic acids, i.e., the change of the relative isomer content. However, experiments with isotopic labeling now leave no doubt that it is the reversibility of reaction that leads to sulfonic acid isomerization. For example, studies of the transformation of o-toluenesulfonic acid into the para-isomer made with compounds with a radioactive sulfur atom revealed that the process mainly involves exchange of sulfur with the medium. The extent of the isomerization proceeding without exchange with the medium is very small and may well be explained in terms of the "cage effect" rather than by the intramolecular character of the reaction.[11]

Similarly, the isomerization of 1-naphthalenesulfonic acid to the 2-

[9] N. N. Vorozhtsov, Jr., *Anilinokrasochnaya Prom.* **4**, 85 (1934); *Chem. Abstr.* **28**, 4652 (1934); *Org. Chem. Ind. (USSR)* **5**, 392 (1938); *Chem. Abstr.* **33**, 546 (1939).

[10] A. C. M. Wanders and H. Cerfontain, *Rec. Trav. Chim.* **86**, 1199 (1967).

[11] E. A. Shilov and F. M. Vainstein, *Ukr. Khim. Zh.* **21**, 58 (1955); *Chem. Abstr.* **49**, 8845 (1955); Ya. K. Syrkin, V. I. Yakerson, and S. E. Shnol, *Zh. Obshch. Khim.* **29**, 187 (1959); *Chem. Abstr.* **53**, 21764 (1959).

sulfonic acid in 75–78% sulfuric acid results in practically complete exchange of sulfur.[12]

As revealed by studies with both the ^{14}C-labeled ring and the ^{35}S label, 5–6% selective migration of the sulfo group into the neighboring β-position occurs in concentrated (91%) sulfuric acid, probably due to the intramolecular mechanism.[13] To a somewhat greater extent (13–15%) the reaction proceeds without exchange of sulfur with the medium.[14]

The most important side reaction during sulfonation is the formation of the corresponding sulfones and sulfone-sulfonic acids, which is most extensive when the process has to be performed under drastic conditions, at a high content of sulfuric anhydride or at high temperatures.

The sulfones are obviously formed by electrophilic reaction with the aromatic compound of the arylsulfonyl cation $ArSO_2^+$ that arises and enters into the reaction according to the following equations:

$$ArSO_3H + 2H_2SO_4 \rightleftarrows ArSO_2^+ + H_3O^+ + 2HSO_4^-$$
$$ArSO_2^+ + ArH \rightarrow ArSO_2Ar + H^+$$

A number of papers and patents (see Section I,B) claim that an efficient method for the suppression of sulfone formation is addition of sodium sulfate to the reaction mixture. This additive increases the content of bisulfate ion in the sulfuric acid, thus decreasing the equilibrium content of SO_3 and the rate of sulfonation. However, the concentration of sulfonyl cation (which determines the rate of sulfone formation) is inversely proportional to the square of the concentration of HSO_4^-, whereas that of SO_3 is inversely proportional to the first power of HSO_4^- concentration, so that the relative rate of sulfone formation will decrease along with the overall decrease of the rate of sulfonation.

Sulfonation with 100% SO_3 proceeds according to the equation

$$ArH + SO_3 \rightarrow ArSO_3H$$

and does not afford any water or sulfuric acid. In this case, the formation of arylsulfonylic cations and of sulfones must be due to the equilibrium

$$ArSO_3H + SO_3 \rightleftarrows ArSO_2^+ + HSO_4^-$$

To suppress sulfone formation during the sulfonation with sulfuric anhydride in SO_2, it is recommended to add carboxylic acids[15] or phos-

---

[12] S. E. Shnol, Ya. K. Syrkin, V. I. Yakerson, and L. A. Blyumenfeld, *Dokl. Akad. Nauk SSSR* **101**, 1075 (1955); *Chem. Abstr.* **50**, 3354 (1956); F. Megson, *Dissertation Abstr.* **18**, 793 (1958).

[13] V. A. Koptyug and S. A. Shkolnik, *Zh. Organ. Khim.* **1**, 1452 (1965); *Chem. Abstr.* **64**, 6445 (1966).

[14] V. A. Koptyug and S. A. Shkolnik, *Zh. Organ. Khim.* **2**, 1870 (1966); *Chem. Abstr.* **66**, 5476 (1967).

[15] Tennessee Corp., *USP* 2,798,089; 2,831,020; 2,841,612; W. H. C. Rueggeberg, T. W. Sauls, and S. L. Norwood, *J. Org. Chem.* **20**, 455 (1955).

phoric acid.[16] These compounds are bases in the medium and by forming bisulfate ions with SO_3 suppress the formation of the arylsulfonylic cations that are the source of sulfones.

Occasionally (e.g., during sulfonation with oleum of halo derivatives) sulfonic acid anhydrides, $(ArSO_2)_2O$, are formed in the reaction mixtures[17] after sulfonation along with sulfonic acids. The anhydrides readily react with water affording the free sulfonic acids.

B. Some Important Sulfonic Acids

1. Benzenesulfonic Acid

It is suggested that the sulfonation of benzene to benzenemonosulfonic acid be performed with weak oleum in an excess of benzene (up to 10%) at 190–255° and 10–30 atm. The reaction proceeds rapidly and is not complicated by any formation of disulfonic acids or of sulfones.[18] The formation of sulfones during the sulfonation with weak oleum can be suppressed by the addition of benzenesulfonic acid sodium salt; the process is performed in three stages, at increasing temperature.[19]

A number of patents describe the production of benzenemonosulfonic acid by means of 100% SO_3 as a sulfonating agent. It is suggested that the sulfonation be performed in liquid SO_2 with the addition of carboxylic acids[15] or of orthophosphoric acid.[16]

A method has been proposed for the sulfonation of benzene to benzenemonosulfonic acid with stabilized 100% sulfuric anhydride (in the absence of SO_2) in the presence of carboxylic acids having two to eight carbon atoms,[20] sodium sulfate,[21] bentonite clay treated with acid,[22] or pyridine[23] to suppress sulfone formation.

2. Benzene-m-disulfonic Acid

During sulfonation of benzene to benzene-m-disulfonic acid with oleum, the 3,3'-disulfonic acid of diphenyl sulfone is formed as a by-product. This disulfonic acid is formed both from diphenyl sulfone and from

[16] CCC, USP 3,133,117.

[17] V. O. Lukashevich, Dokl. Akad. Nauk SSSR 99, 995 (1954); Chem. Abstr. 50, 217 (1956); Dokl. Akad. Nauk SSSR 112, 872 (1957); Chem. Abstr. 51, 14591 (1957).

[18] A. A. Spryskov, Zh. Obshch. Khim. 18, 1371 (1948); Chem. Abstr. 43, 2178 (1949); Allied Chemical & Dye Corp., USP 2,697,117.

[19] UCC, USP 2,692,279.

[20] Allied Chemical & Dye Corp., USP 2,704,295.

[21] Monsanto Chemical Co., USP 2,693,487.

[22] Monsanto Chemical Co., USP 2,889,360.

[23] Monsanto Chemical Co., USP 2,889,361.

benzenemonosulfonic acid. *m*-Benzenedisulfonic acid does not form diphenyl sulfone disulfonic acid.[24]

The addition of sodium sulfate suppresses the formation of disulfonic acid of diphenyl sulfone.[25] It is pointed out that the formation of sulfones during sulfonation with 100% SO_3 can also be reduced by addition of Hg compounds.[26]

The use of 100% SO_3 is suggested in the presence of some amount of the reaction mixture obtained in the preceding sulfonation and of sodium salts to obtain benzene-*m*-disulfonic acid.[27] Continuous processes are also suggested based upon this method.[28]

On the other hand, benzene-*m*-disulfonic acid may be obtained from benzene by the action of excess 96% H_2SO_4 at a high temperature (235°) by distilling off in vacuum both the water (that of the sulfuric acid and that formed during the reaction) and the excess sulfuric acid. The residue after the distillation is pure benzene-*m*-disulfonic acid (the content is more than 98%), m.p. 137°.[29] It is also possible to add sodium sulfate or benzenesulfonate.[30]

The *m*-benzenedisulfonic acid obtained by sulfonation of benzenesulfonic acid with strong oleum does not contain any isomeric disulfonic acids—the sulfonation proceeds only in the position meta to the sulfonic group. However, when heated at 235° in sulfuric acid, *m*-disulfonic acid affords an equilibrium mixture containing about 66% *m*- and 34% *p*-benzenedisulfonic acid. In 90% sulfuric acid the equilibrium is attained after 200 hours. With the increase of the concentration of sulfuric acid, the rate of the isomerization decreases.[31]

3. *Toluenesulfonic Acids*

The reaction rate constant of the sulfonation of toluene in 91% H_2SO_4 is 30 times, and in 79% H_2SO_4, 110 times higher than that of benzene.[5] In sulfonation with 82.3% H_2SO_4 at 25°, 32% ortho, 2.9% meta, and

[24] A. P. Shestov and N. A. Osipova, *Zh. Obshch. Khim.* **29**, 595 (1959); *Chem. Abstr.* **54**, 367 (1960).

[25] A. P. Shestov, N. A. Osipova, and Z. A. Pavlova, *RP* 94,284; T. D. Shishkina, P. S. Timofeev, and A. I. Kochetova, *RP* 156,551; *Chem. Abstr.* **60**, 6791 (1964).

[26] Technion Research & Development Foundation, *USP* 3,268,578.

[27] The Vulcan Chemical Co., *USP* 2,807,641; FH, *DBP* 1,104,500.

[28] FH, *BP* 947,866; *USP* 3,097,235.

[29] Hooker Chemical Co., *BP* 1,024,496.

[30] Stepan Chemical Co., *USP* 3,227,750.

[31] S. P. Starkov and A. A. Spryskov, *Zh. Obshch. Khim.* **27**, 3067 (1957); *Chem. Abstr.* **52**, 8072 (1958).

65.1% para-isomers are formed.[32] With an increase of the concentration of sulfuric acid to 95.3% the amount of ortho isomer increases up to ~50%.

The formation of para-isomer decreases if the temperature of the reaction is less than 10°. If sulfuric acid anhydride is used instead of sulfuric acid, the amount of para-isomer increases (up to 91%).[33] The effect of different factors upon the ratio of isomers in sulfonation of toluene has been studied.[34] At high temperatures, the ratio of isomers is determined by thermodynamic factors and the more stable m-sulfonic acid is the major product.

At 141° the sulfonation with 74% H_2SO_4 results in an equilibrium sulfonic acid mixture containing 3.2% o-, 69.6% m-, and 37.2% p-toluenesulfonic acid.[35] The kinetics of sulfonation of p- and o-toluenesulfonic acid by means of concentrated H_2SO_4 and weak oleum to 2,4-disulfonic acid has been studied. At 25° the isomerization of o-toluenesulfonic acid does not, practically, occur. At 65° its isomerization is about 27% of the disulfonation.[1,36]

Pure p-toluenesulfonic acid can be obtained by sulfonation of toluene with 98% H_2SO_4 in the presence of $KHSO_4$.[37]

The formation of sulfones in the sulfonation of toluene with the solution of SO_3 in SO_2 can be decreased by the addition of acetic acid.[38] When this process goes on continuously one can obtain toluene-p-sulfonic acid containing less than 4% ortho isomer.[39]

p-Toluenesulfonic acid from the mixture of isomers obtained in the sulfonation of toluene by 96% H_2SO_4 can be isolated in the form of a crystalline monohydrate by diluting with water after neutral impurities are extracted with toluene or other solvent.[40] To isolate the p-sulfonic acid from the mixture free of H_2SO_4 and containing mainly the m- and the p-sulfonic acid, it is suggested to saturate the aqueous solution with hydrogen chloride below 0°.[41]

[32] L. Vollbracht, H. Cerfontain, and F. L. J. Sixma, Rec. Trav. Chim. 80, 11 (1961).

[33] A. A. Spryskov and B. G. Gnedin, Zh. Obshch. Khim. 33, 1082 (1963).

[34] H. Cerfontain, F. L. J. Sixma, and L. Vollbracht, Rec. Trav. Chim. 82, 659 (1963); 83, 226 (1964).

[35] A. A. Spryskov, Izv. Vysshikh Uchebn. Zavedenii, Khim. i Khim. Tekhnol. 4, 981 (1961); Chem. Abstr. 57, 16464 (1962); A. C. M. Wanders, H. Cerfontain, and C. W. Kort, Rec. Trav. Chim. 86, 301 (1967).

[36] A. A. Spryskov and T. Potapova, Izv. Vysshikh Uchebn. Zavedenii, Khim. i Khim. Tekhnol. 5, 280 (1962); Chem. Abstr. 57, 16464 (1962).

[37] P. H. R. Lion, FP 1,397,422.

[38] Tennessee Corp., USP 2,841,612.

[39] Tennessee Corp., USP 2,828,333.

[40] Chemetron Corp., DBP 1,160,433.

[41] A. A. Spryskov, RP 136,363; Chem. Abstr. 56, 3418 (1962).

4. Naphthalenesulfonic Acids

The kinetics of the reaction of naphthalene with sulfuric acid revealed that the rate of naphthalene sulfonation in 79% H_2SO_4 (at 25°) is 80 times higher than that of benzene; in 83.4% H_2SO_4 it is 43 times higher. At 25° the rate ratio of the formation of sulfonic acid isomers (1-/2-) changes from 5.9:1 to 4.1:1 with the increase of sulfuric acid concentration from 75% to 95%.

With an increase of the temperature at constant concentration of sulfuric acid this ratio decreases[42] from 5.2:1 at 0.5° to 3.3:1 at 70° (95.2% H_2SO_4).

Naphthalene-1-sulfonic acid (for the further nitration to 1,5- and 1,8-nitrosulfonic acids) can be obtained by the continuous method in three steps; the temperature is increased from 25–35° at the first step to 45–55° at the third and the concentration of H_2SO_4 decreased from 93–97% to 87–90%, respectively.[43]

Naphthalene-1-sulfonic acid which is almost free of the 2-isomer (its content is less than 2%) can be obtained by the action of an equimolar amount of chlorosulfonic acid upon naphthalene in nitrobenzene at 25° and lower. The 1-sulfonic acid is crystallized from nitrobenzene (the 2-isomer remains in nitrobenzene solution).[44] It is proposed to separate 1-sulfonic acid from the mixture obtained by sulfonation with monohydrate in the form of its o-toluidine salt.[45]

To obtain pure 2-sulfonic acid, sulfuric acid of relatively low concentration (84.5% = $H_2SO_4 \cdot H_2O$) may be applied. During the reaction the temperature is lowered from 160° to 155°. Part of the water and the unreacted naphthalene is distilled off. The yield of 2-sulfonic acid practically free of the 1-isomer, of disulfonic acids, and of sulfones is 98–100%.[46]

Sulfonation of naphthalene can be carried out by means of more dilute (60–70%) sulfuric acid with addition of substances facilitating the removal of water by distillation (hexane, for example) and at temperatures decreasing continuously from 145° to 128°. After removal of hexane, naphthalene, and water in vacuo, the residue is poured into 25–35% H_2SO_4 and the 2-sulfonic acid crystallizes out on cooling. The filtrate containing sulfuric acid, 1-sulfonic acid, and disulfonic acids is evapo-

[42] H. Cerfontain and A. Telder, Rec. Trav. Chim. 86, 527 (1967).
[43] A. N. Shebuev, N. I. Amiantov, T. S. Bekasova, A. A. Vigasin, N. P. Karrask, S. V. Marochko, A. I. Chekalina, S. P. Uarova, and I. V. Shikanova, RP 165,746; Chem. Abstr. 62, 10392 (1965).
[44] CCC, USP 3,155,716.
[45] CCC, USP 2,955,134.
[46] CIBA, DBP 1,167,333.

rated to one-third the original volume and then returned into the process. Repeated processing does not increase the amount of by-products.

The 2-naphthol obtained from 2-naphthalenesulfonic acid isolated by this method contains only 0.07–0.08% 1-naphthol.[47]

Study of naphthalene sulfonation to 2-sulfonic acid by means of concentrated (93%) sulfuric acid showed it expedient to add sodium sulfate in order to reduce the formation of 1-sulfonic acid and to eliminate the formation of disulfonic acids.[48]

Naphthalene-2-sulfonic acid free from naphthalene-1-sulfonic acid can be obtained by diluting the mixture up to 90% sulfuric acid, in which only the 2-isomer is noticeably soluble.[49] Extraction of the 1-isomer with isobutyl or amyl alcohols is also described.[50]

Both the 1- and the 2-sulfonic acids react slowly with 95% H_2SO_4 even at room temperature. The reaction rate is directly proportional to the concentration of sulfonic acid and is much less (by several orders of magnitude) compared with naphthalene. The reaction rate of naphthalene-1-sulfonic acid is 10 times smaller than that of the 2-isomer (in the 1-isomer, the 5-position of the naphthalene nucleus is deactivated, unlike that in the 2-isomer).[42] The use of oleum and SO_3 for naphthalene sulfonation results in an increase of the yield of 1,5-disulfonic acid to 75% on a naphthalene basis.[51]

5. Anthraquinonesulfonic Acids

The direct mercuration of anthraquinone to mono- and dimercuric derivatives by treatment with mercuric oxide or basic mercuric sulfate in the medium of polyphosphoric acid (and dimethyl sulfate as well) is the last link in the chain of arguments which show that the catalytic action of mercury is due to the primary formation of 1-mercuric derivatives which subsequently exchange mercury for a sulfonic group.[52]

Thallic oxide (which is able to form organic thallium compounds by interaction with aromatic compounds) also catalyzes the formation of the 1-sulfonic acid of anthraquinone.

[47] NAC, *DBP* 1,157,213.

[48] B. V. Passet and M. E. Galanov, *Zh. Prikl. Khim.* **36**, 1793 (1963); *Chem. Abstr.* **60**, 1663 (1964).

[49] A. Ito and H. Hiyama, *Kogyo Kagaku Zasshi* **67**, No. 1, 57 (1964); *Chem. Abstr.* **60**, 15793 (1964); *Kagaku To Kogyo (Osaka)* **37**, No. 1, 38 (1963).

[50] N. N. Dykhanov and G. N. Nikitenko, *RP* 162,855; *Chem. Abstr.* **61**, 13257 (1964).

[51] S. N. Chalykh, I. I. Gromova, G. B. Shchekina, and I. V. Pokrovskaya, *RP* 169,521; *Chem. Abstr.* **63**, 2941 (1965).

[52] N. S. Dokunikhin and L. A. Gaeva, *Zh. Obshch. Khim.* **33**, 2727 (1963); *Chem. Abstr.* **60**, 537 (1964).

The fact that only anthraquinone-2-sulfonic acid is formed in the absence of mercury is reasonably explained by the greater volume of the sulfonating agent molecules (compared with nitrating and chlorinating agents) which prevents them from entering the sterically hindered (by the ketone group) 1-position of anthraquinone. Steric effects in sulfonation are observed in a number of other cases. For example, peri-disulfonic acid is not formed from the 1-sulfonic acid of naphthalene (while in nitration of the 1-sulfonic acid, peri-nitrosulfonic acid is the major product).[53] Similarly, the sulfonation of tert-butylbenzene does not afford any o-sulfonic acid,[54] but the nitration of tert-butylbenzene affords 16% of the o-nitro compound.[55]

Earlier it was considered impossible to introduce more than one sulfonic group into each benzene ring of anthraquinone. It is established now that prolonged sulfonation of 2,6- and 2,7-disulfonic acids of anthraquinone with greater than usual amounts of mercury added (3–4%) at 130–200° gives rise to 1,3,5,7- and 1,3,6,8-tetrasulfonic acids of anthraquinone.[56] Similarly, from 2-chloroanthraquinone-3,7- and 3,6-disulfonic acids it is possible to obtain 2-chloroanthraquinone-3,5,7- and 2-chloroanthraquinone-3,6,8-trisulfonic acid, which also contain two sulfonic groups in one of the nuclei.[57]

Sulfonic acids and their salts isolated out of the mixture of anthraquinonesulfonic acids obtained by sulfonation in the presence of mercury contain considerable amounts (up to 1%) of mercury, whose toxicity makes their further reprocessing difficult. Many methods have been suggested for removal of mercury from sulfonic acids.

Sodium chloride or chlorosulfonic acid may be added to the sulfonated mixture at 130–140°.[58] The solution of the 1,8-disulfonic acid of anthraquinone (after the isolation of 1,5-isomer) may be treated with fine copper powder followed by hot filtration,[59] or with oxidants ($KMnO_4$, $Na_2Cr_2O_7$, HNO_3).[60] The solutions of anthraquinone-1-sulfonic acid may be treated with Fe or Cu.[61] This works well in the presence of powdered

[53] N. S. Dokunikhin, in "Recent Progress in the Chemistry of Natural and Synthetic Colouring Matters and Related Fields" (T. S. Gore et al., eds.), pp. 555–560. Academic Press, New York, 1962.

[54] J. M. Arends and H. Cerfontain, Rec. Trav. Chim. 85, 93 (1966).

[55] H. C. Brown and W. H. Bonner, J. Am. Chem. Soc. 76, 605 (1954).

[56] FBy, DBP 913,772.

[57] FBy, DBP 913,771.

[58] O. I. Kochetova and P. N. Ershov, RP 119,876; Chem. Abstr. 54, 2296 (1960); P. N. Ershov and I. E. Sharanova, RP 122,747; Chem. Abstr. 54, 7670 (1960).

[59] G, USP 2,999,869.

[60] G, USP 3,079,404.

[61] V. A. Ivanova, E. V. Popova, M. I. Gol'dfarb, N. G. Ivanova, and V. A. Khodak, RP 138,614; Chem. Abstr. 56, 9713 (1962).

anthraquinone added to the solution in an amount approximately equal to that of mercury. The mercury that falls out is adsorbed by anthraquinone and is thus better removed.[62]

The dipotassium salt of anthraquinone-1,8-disulfonic acid may be treated with KI solution and the precipitate of potassium sulfonate then separated from the mercury-containing filtrate.[63]

Until recently, only 7 were known of the 10 possible disulfonic acids of anthraquinone. Unknown anthraquinone-1,2-disulfonic acid was obtained from 1-chloro-2-nitroanthraquinone by heating it with an aqueous solution of sodium sulfite. Similarly, the 2,3-disulfonic acid was obtained from 2-chloro-3-nitroanthraquinone. The 1,3-disulfonic acid was obtained by the action of sodium sulfite upon 1-bromoanthraquinone-3-sulfonic acid.[64] Anthraquinone-1,2,3-trisulfonic acid was obtained by the action of sodium sulfite on 1-bromo-2-nitro-3-chloroanthraquinone.[64a]

C. THERMAL ISOMERIZATION OF SULFONIC ACID SALTS

For the isomerization of sulfonic acids in sulfuric acid medium it is a proven fact that the displacement of the sulfonic group is caused by reversibility of the reaction; the ratio of isomers changes from that determined by kinetic factors to that determined by thermodynamics of the reaction. The mechanism of the thermal isomerization of sulfonic acid salts is different.

This process was first discovered for the salts of amino- and hydroxysulfonic acids, mainly of the naphthalene series. Some examples are the transformation of the salt of naphthionic acid to 1-naphthylamine-2-sulfonic acid or of 1-naphthol-4-sulfonic acid to 1-naphthol-2-sulfonic acid.[65]

Study of rearrangements of this type in the presence of $Na_2{}^{35}SO_4$ showed that the labeled atom is practically not contained in the product of isomerization. Hence, free sulfuric acid or its acid salt is not the intermediate product of the reaction. A hypothesis has been put forward that the isomerization of the salt of naphthionic acid starts with the addition of a proton to the carbon atom that bears the sulfonic group, and that

[62] V. A. Ivanova, E. V. Popova, M. I. Gol'dfarb, N. G. Ivanova, and V. A. Khodak, RP 129,655; Chem. Abstr. 55, 4461 (1961).

[63] G, USP 2,900,397.

[64] N. S. Dokunikhin and L. A. Gaeva, Zh. Organ. Khim. 1, 201 (1965); Chem. Abstr. 62, 14594 (1965).

[64a] L. A. Gaeva, N. S. Dokunikhin, and I. I. Zemskova, Zh. Organ. Khim. 4, 181 (1968).

[65] V. A. Koptyug, "Isomerisation of Aromatic Compounds," p. 147. Oldbourne Press, London, 1965.

the sulfonic group is subsequently transferred to the molecule of naphthylamine. The 1-naphthylamine that is formed along with 1-naphthylamine-2-sulfonate reacts with another molecule of naphthionate.[66]

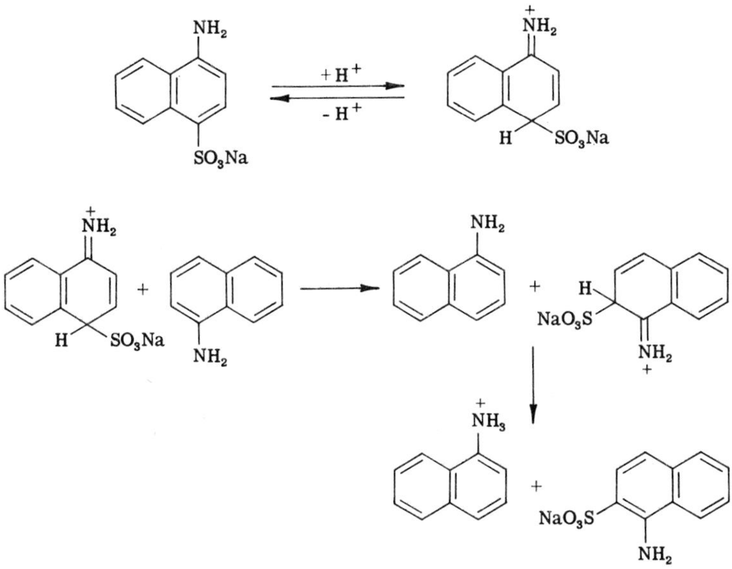

Recently, the thermal isomerizations of the salts of the unsubstituted sulfonic acids of benzene and naphthalene have been performed. Thus, the salt of the p-disulfonic acid of benzene can be obtained from the disodium salt of benzene-m-disulfonic acid by heating it to 373–600° in the presence of catalysts (mercury and chrome compounds, for example, HgO, or potassium chrome alum). It is necessary to carry out the process in an atmosphere of inert gas (N_2, CO_2). Similarly, the 2,6-isomer can be obtained from the salt of naphthalene-2,7-disulfonic acid.[67]

These and some other disulfonic acids can be also obtained by disproportionation of salts (preferably, sodium or potassium salts) of the corresponding monosulfonic acids. It was suggested to obtain in this way benzene-p-disulfonic acid,

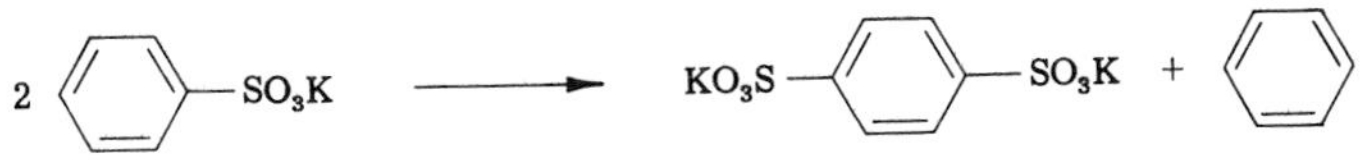

[66] E. A. Shilov, M. N. Bogdanov, and A. E. Shilov, *Dokl. Akad. Nauk SSSR* **92**, 93 (1953); *Chem. Abstr.* **48**, 10695 (1954).
[67] ICI, *USP* 2,978,499.

diphenyl-4,4'-disulfonic acid, and naphthalene-2,-6-disulfonic acid. As catalysts of the disproportionation described, antimony compounds,[68] chrome, mercury, vanadium, or silver compounds,[69] and compounds of cadmium, zinc and mercury[70] have been used.

D. DETERMINATION OF SULFONIC ACIDS

The modern methods of sulfonic acid detection and quantitative determination are completely different from those that were in common use not so long ago. Physical-chemical methods are widely applied. Their introduction markedly simplified the qualitative and quantitative analyses of the sulfonated mixtures and in a number of cases provided more precise data. Among these methods, paper chromatography is one of the most widely used.[71]

Chromatography is usually performed in solvent systems containing weak bases (bicarbonate, pyridine, ammonia) besides water, sometimes with addition of alcohols (ethyl, propyl, butyl, and amyl alcohol). Acidic systems are occasionally used, for example, butanol–water–hydrochloric acid. Both the ascending and descending techniques of chromatography are applied. Good results are obtained by the radial method.[72]

The R_f values decrease with the number of sulfonate groups and thus may be used to evaluate the latter. Location of the spots of unsubstituted sulfonic acids of aromatic hydrocarbons is sometimes difficult because of the small reactivity of these compounds.

Naphthalenesulfonic acids are detected by fluorescence excited with light of wavelength 253 mμ.[73] The spots of anthraquinonesulfonic and anthracenesulfonic acids also fluoresce in UV light.[74] Anthraquinonesulfonic acids spots are also colored by spraying with an alkaline solution of hydrosulfite.[71] A general method of sulfonic acid detection is heating of chromatograms at 200° — spots colored dark brown to black appear.[71] A general method is also detection with pinacryptol yellow; on spraying with this reagent, the spots of different sulfonic acids (those of benzene,

[68] ICI, *BP* 839,663.
[69] ICI, *USP* 2,978,500.
[70] Sun Oil Co., *USP* 3,239,559.
[71] J. Gasparič, *in* "Paper Chromatography" (I. M. Hais and K. Macek, eds.), pp. 633–639. Publishing House of the Czechoslovak Academy of Sciences, Prague, 1963.
[72] E. V. Sokolova, *Zavodsk. Lab.* **27**, 150 (1961); *Chem. Abstr.* **55**, 20789 (1961).
[73] G. Spencer and V. Nield, *Chem. Ind. (London)* p. 922 (1956).
[74] M. Večeřa, J. Gasparič, and J. Borecky, *Collection Czech. Chem. Commun.* **20**, 1380 (1955).

toluene, xylene, naphthalene) fluoresce yellow, orange, or yellow-brown on a light green background.[75]

Sulfonic acids can be eluted from the corresponding spots and estimated quantitatively by several different methods. Polarography was applied to determine the polysulfonic acids of naphthalene (the accuracy is ±3%).[76] The same method was used to determine sulfones of the benzene and naphthalene series and their sulfonic acids.[77] Obviously, the sulfones are reduced under polarography to the corresponding sulfinic acids and hydrocarbons.[77] The total amount of sulfonic acids in the mixture with sulfuric acid can be found directly by differential electrometric titration with morpholine, diphenylguanidine,[78] or (better) by tetraethylammonium hydroxide[79] in acetonitrile or acetone.

Finally, a convenient method of both identification and quantitative determination of sulfonic acids is spectrophotometry, especially in UV light. This method in combination with paper chromatography to resolve mono- from disulfonic acids has been successfully applied to the sulfonation products of naphthalene.[80] Knowing the qualitative composition of the sulfonation mixture and the absorption spectrum of each of the sulfonic acids present, it is possible to estimate the content of each component rather quickly and exactly by measuring the UV spectrum. The calculations are performed with the help of a computer.[81]

To identify and to determine sulfonic acids in mixtures, particularly the mono- and disulfonic acids of naphthalene, the IR spectra of their salts are measured in KBr tablets. The sample must be carefully dried.[82]

Recently, the method of proton magnetic resonance has been successfully applied to the identification of sulfonic acids.[83]

[75] J. Borecky, *J. Chromatog.* **2,** 612 (1959).

[76] A. P. Shestov, N. A. Osipova, and K. K. Petukhova, *Zh. Obshch. Khim.* **31,** 1780 (1961); *Chem. Abstr.* **55,** 26865 (1961).

[77] E. S. Levin and A. P. Shestov, *Dokl. Akad. Nauk SSSR* **96,** 999 (1954); *Chem. Abstr.* **48,** 13471 (1954); E. S. Levin and N. A. Osipova, *Zh. Obshch. Khim.* **32,** 2084 (1962); R. C. Bowers and H. D. Russel, *Anal. Chem.* **32,** 405 (1960).

[78] E. A. Gribova and E. S. Levin, *Zavodsk. Lab.* **24,** 1356 (1958); *Chem. Abstr.* **53,** 9904 (1959).

[79] E. A. Gribova, *Zavodsk. Lab.* **27,** 154 (1961); *Chem. Abstr.* **55,** 24375 (1961).

[80] V. A. Koptyug and S. A. Shkolnik, *Zh. Organ. Khim.* **1,** 1448 (1965); *Chem. Abstr.* **64,** 6445 (1966).

[81] J. M. Arends, H. Cerfontain, I. S. Herschberg, A. J. Prinsen, and A. C. M. Wanders, *Anal. Chem.* **36,** 1802 (1964).

[82] A. Ito, *Kogyo Kagaku Zasshi* **60,** 1004 (1957), *Chem. Abstr.* **53,** 11110 (1959); A. Ito, S. Kitahara, and H. Hiyama, *Kogyo Kagaku Zasshi* **66,** 1587 (1963); *Chem. Abstr.* **60,** 13203 (1964).

[83] H. de Vries and H. Cerfontain, *Rec. Trav. Chim.* **86,** 875 (1967).

II. Nitration

A. Mechanism of the Reaction and Its General Rules

It is now firmly established that nitration with anhydrous and aqueous nitration mixtures as well as with concentrated nitric acid involve nitronium cation, NO_2^+, as the active nitrating agent. In nitric acid the formation of nitronium cation occurs according to the equation

$$2HNO_3 \rightleftarrows NO_2^+ + NO_3^- + H_2O$$

The absence of a kinetic isotopic effect during nitration[84] is an indication of the two-stage character of the process. Commonly accepted is the following scheme of the reaction:

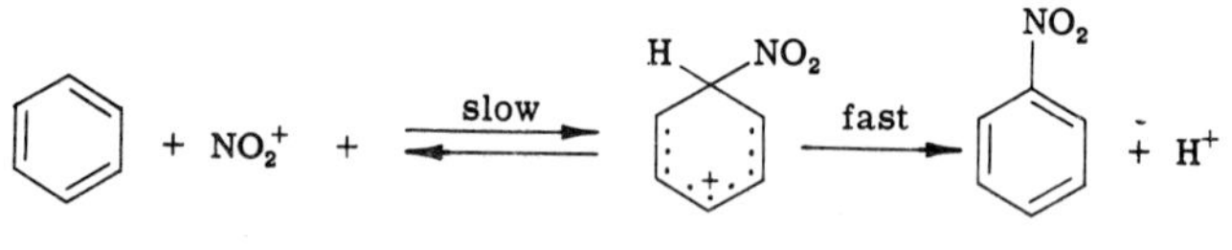

It assumes the intermediate formation of the product of nitronium cation addition to the molecule of aromatic compound. The second stage—elimination of a proton—is the most rapid one and thus not rate-limiting.

The reaction rate is usually proportional to the concentration of aromatic compound as well as to that of nitronium ion. In concentrated sulfuric acid the extent of nitric acid conversion to nitronium cation is high. Thus, a dilute $(0.2 M)$ solution of nitric acid contains practically all nitrogen in the form of nitronium cation. However, in a similar solution but in 87% sulfuric acid, only 14.7% of nitric acid is in the form NO_2^+.[85]

Still, the influence of sulfuric acid concentration upon the reaction rate is not limited to the degree of HNO_3 conversion to NO_2^+.

The rate of nitration with nitric acid in excess sulfuric acid or oleum of different concentration is minimum in 100% sulfuric acid. With the decrease of the concentration of sulfuric acid down to 90–95%, the nitration rate increases several-fold and reaches the maximum at a certain concentration; with the still further decrease of H_2SO_4 concentration, the

[84] L. Melander, *Arkiv Kemi* **2**, 213 (1950); T. G. Bonner, F. Bowyer, and G. Williams, *J. Chem. Soc.* p. 2650 (1953); W. M. Lauer and W. E. Noland, *J. Am. Chem. Soc.* **75**, 3689 (1953).

[85] G. M. Bennett, J. C. D. Brand, D. M. James, T. G. Saunders, and G. Williams, *J. Chem. Soc.* pp. 474 and 1185 (1947).

reaction rate decreases. A similar effect is produced by the addition of some salts and pyridine.[86] A probable explanation of this increase of the rate with the addition of water and salts is the fact that these additions reduce the dielectric constant of the medium. Since the formation of the above-mentioned product of the addition of nitronium ion to the aromatic nucleus depends on the distribution of charge over the nucleus, the nitration rate should increase with decreasing dielectric constant of the medium according to the general theory of solvent effect upon the rates of reactions.[87] Over a range of concentrations, this increase of the rate produces a greater effect than does the decrease of nitronium cation concentration caused by the dilution.

The increase of reaction rate necessary for nitration of the less reactive compounds is practically accomplished by the use of anhydrous mixtures, a mixture of nitric acid and oleum, for example.[88] For the extremely difficulty nitrated compounds, use of a mixture of pure SO_3 with HNO_3 is suggested.[89] Extremely active nitration agents are crystalline salts of the nitronium ion, for example, $[NO_2^+][PF_6^-]$ or $[NO_2^+][BF_4^-]$.[90] It is expedient to carry out nitration in an inert organic solvent, tetramethylenesulfone,[91] for example. Treatment with nitronium salts afforded the nitro derivatives of some nitriles.[92]

In the nitration of sufficiently reactive aromatic compounds with nitric acid in organic solvents the slowest reaction step is nitronium cation formation. In these cases the reaction rate naturally does not depend on the concentration of the aromatic compound.[93]

Some compounds of high reactivity, such as ethers of phenols, can be readily nitrated with dilute nitric acid, usually in organic solvents. The mechanism of reaction is evidently different here. For a number of examples it has been proved that the presence of nitrogen oxides in nitric acid is necessary for the reaction to proceed. It is likely that the formation of the nitro compound in this case proceeds via the nitroso compound.

[86] T. G. Bonner and F. Brown, *J. Chem. Soc., B* p. 658 (1966).
[87] R. J. Gillespie and D. G. Norton, *J. Chem. Soc.* p. 971 (1953).
[88] Atlantic Refining Co., *USP* 2,934,571.
[89] P. M. Heertjes, *Rec. Trav. Chim.* 77, 693 (1958).
[90] G. A. Olah, S. J. Kuhn, and A. Mlinkó, *J. Chem. Soc.* p. 4257 (1956); L. L. Ciaccio and R. A. Marcus, *J. Am. Chem. Soc.* 84, 1838 (1962).
[91] S. J. Kuhn and G. A. Olah, *J. Am. Chem. Soc.* 83, 4564 (1961); G. A. Olah, S. J. Kuhn, S. H. Flood, and J. C. Evans, *ibid.* 84, 3687 (1962).
[92] Dow, *USP* 3,162,675.
[93] E. D. Hughes, C. K. Ingold, and R. I. Reed, *Nature* 158, 448 (1946); *J. Chem. Soc.* p. 2400 (1950); see also T. G. Bonner, R. A. Hancock, and F. R. Rolle, *Tetrahedron Letters* 1665 (1968).

The following mechanism of the reaction involving N_2O_4 as the active species is probable:

$$ArH + N_2O_4 \rightarrow ArNO + HNO_3$$
$$ArNO + N_2O_4 \rightarrow ArNO_2 + N_2O_3$$
$$N_2O_3 + 2HNO_3 \rightarrow 2N_2O_4 + H_2O$$

N_2O_4 is not consumed and the concentration of nitric acid only decreases. By-processes of oxidation, in fact, increase the concentration of N_2O_4 and, consequently the rate of the reaction.[94] Salts of N-nitro-pyridinium (and its homologs) are good nitrating agents for labile compounds.[94a]

A few papers report the use of salts of nitric acid for nitration instead of the acid. Thus, bubbling benzene, toluene, and chlorobenzene vapor into the melted eutectic (m.p. 120°) of lithium, sodium, and potassium nitrates containing 5% potassium pyrosulfate, which gives NO_2^+ according to the equation

$$NO_3^- + S_2O_7^{2-} \rightleftarrows 2SO_4^{2-} + NO_2^+$$

affords the corresponding mononitro derivatives (temperature of the melt is 250°). It is interesting that the proportion of isomers of nitrotoluene and chloronitrobenzene is close to the usual one. Nitrobenzene at 300° affords m-dinitrobenzene; analogous treatment of pyridine results in 3-nitropyridine.[95]

X-ray irradiation of benzene and potassium nitrate smoothly affords nitrobenzene. The reaction results in potassium hydroxide, as proved by acidimetric titration.[96]

$$C_6H_6 + KNO_3 \rightarrow C_6H_5NO_2 + KOH$$

It is also suggested that nitro compounds may be obtained by substitution of nitro for carboxy groups by heating aromatic carboxylic acids with the nitrates of sodium, copper, nickel, and other metals at 260–360°.[97]

The nitration reactions are usually irreversible. It has been proposed that some known examples of acid-catalyzed nitro group migration in the derivatives of o-nitroaniline[98] and o-dinitrobenzene[99] are due to reversibility of the reaction in these cases.[100] 9-Nitroanthracene affords nitric

[94] T. G. Bonner and R. A. Hancock, *Chem. Commun.* p. 780 (1967).
[94a] C. A. Cupas and R. L. Pearson, *J. Am. Chem. Soc.* **90**, 4742 (1968).
[95] R. B. Temple, C. Fay, and J. Williamson, *Chem. Commun.* p. 966 (1967).
[96] W. W. Epstein, R. N. Kust, and D. MacGregor, *Chem. Commun.* p. 1190 (1968).
[97] California Research Corp., *USP* 2,780,657.
[98] K. C. Frisch, M. Silverman, and M. T. Bogert, *J. Am. Chem. Soc.* **65**, 2432 (1943).
[99] K. H. Pausacker and J. G. Scroggie, *Chem. Ind. (London)* p. 1290 (1964); *J. Chem. Soc.* p. 1897 (1955); I. K. Barben and H. Suschitzky, *ibid.* p. 627 (1960).
[100] P. H. Gore, *J. Chem. Soc.* p. 1437 (1957).

acid and anthraquinone along with some other products on boiling with H_2SO_4 in trichloroacetic acid. However, no anthracene was found among the reaction products.[100]

B. NITRATION TECHNOLOGY

1. General

Industrial reaction mixtures containing the usual mixed acid as nitrating agent most often (with the hydrocarbons or their chloro derivatives) are biphasic, consisting of two layers—the acidic and the organic layers. Nitric acid is distributed between the two layers and though the distribution coefficient of HNO_3 (organic phase: acid) is usually more than 1, the reaction proceeds mainly in the acidic layer.[101] The reaction rate in the acidic layer is high under optimum conditions. For toluene, for instance, at 55° and optimum concentration of nitrating acid (e.g., 40.9 mole% H_2SO_4 and 11.4 mole% HNO_3) the nitration rate in the acidic phase is 2000 g-moles/liter per hour.[102] In a recent paper the possibility is discussed that in the usual heterogeneous nitration the mass-transfer rate is of significant importance.[103]

The introduction of a nitro group markedly (by a factor of 10^5–10^7) decreases the rate of further reaction.

The high reaction rate, the considerable difference in the nitration rates (depending on the presence of nitro group), and the increasing demand for nitro compounds have stimulated the use of continuous-action plants for the large-scale production of nitrobenzene, nitrotoluene, and nitrochlorobenzene, and this principle is of major industrial importance. Many types of flow reactors for continuous nitration have been described. It is suggested that nitration be performed in a countercurrent of reagents: the hydrocarbon is fed into the lower part of the reactor, and the nitrating mixture into the upper part. The corresponding nitro compounds are taken from the upper part, and the spent acid from below.[104] Nitration can also be performed by countercurrent in a series of reactors.[105]

It seems that the systems with co-current flow of reagents are more widely applied, particularly in reactors having much in common with

[101] A. J. Barduhn and K. A. Kobe, *Ind. Eng. Chem.* **48**, 1305 (1956); Z. E. Zinkov, E. A. Budrina, and N. G. Zakharova, *Zh. Prikl. Khim.* **35**, 139 (1962); *Chem. Abstr.* **56**, 12370 (1962).

[102] H. M. Brennecke and K. A. Kobe, *Ind. Eng. Chem.* **48**, 1298 (1956).

[103] C. Hanson, J. G. Marsland, and G. Wilson, *Chem. Ind. (London)* p. 675 (1966).

[104] Dynamit Nobel A. G., *DBP* 1,062,234.

[105] Aktiebolaget Chematur, *USP* 3,087,971; 3,204,000.

those of periodic action.[106] The nitrated compound and nitrating mixture are fed into the central part of the nitrator (equipped with an efficient stirrer) and the nitro compound and the spent acid are removed continuously through an outlet in the upper part of the side wall.

Continuous-action reactors where reaction takes place in a thin film,[107] tubular reactors operated under conditions of turbulent movement,[108] and some others[109] have been proposed. It is recommended for the cases in which a solid nitro product is obtained to carry out continuous nitration in the presence of solvent so that the reaction mixture remains liquid.[110] In continuous nitration (of benzene, toluene) it is suggested that the major part of the reaction mixture be recirculated through the nitrator.[111] Continuous nitration with nitric acid (70%) alone at a high temperature (100–120°) has also been suggested.[112] In periodic nitration the substance being nitrated (benzene, toluene, chlorobenzene, anisole) may be fed into the reactor with the anhydrous nitric mixture as vapor diluted with carrier gas (N_2, CO_2).[113]

The separation of nitro compounds from the spent acid takes place in the separators, also of continuous action. The tangential supply of the reaction mass into the layer of the emulsion causes its rotation and facilitates the layer separation. Continuous layer separation is facilitated and accelerated by addition of tertiary octylamine (2-amino-2,4,4-trimethylpentane) in an amount of 0.0025–0.015% of the weight of the nitro product.[114]

The first fractions obtained by distillation of the nitro product usually contain some starting hydrocarbon and the nonnitrated admixture (the nitration is usually performed at a deficiency of HNO_3). This fraction may be returned to the process. Aliphatic admixtures are not accumulated; they are consumed due to oxidation during the nitration.[115]

The purification from acidic admixtures (nitrophenols) that are usually present in crude nitro compounds can be performed with ion-

[106] S. A. Shchekotikhin and A. G. Smirnov, *RP* 42,996 (1935); J. C. Smith, *Chem. Ind.* **62**, 929 (1948); F. Meissner, G. Wannschaff, and D. F. Othmer, *Ind. Eng. Chem.* **46**, 718 (1954).

[107] E. Dahmen, *Chem. Weekblad* **38**, 275 (1941); *Chem. Abstr.* **36**, 5465 (1942); *DP* 49,574; *Chem. Abstr.* **35**, 5126 (1941).

[108] Hercules Powder Co., *USP* 3,053,908; Atlas Chemical Industry Inc., *USP* 3,178,481.

[109] NSK, *USP* 3,160,669.

[110] U. S. Rubber Co., *BeP* 594,100.

[111] U. S. Rubber Co., *USP* 3,092,671.

[112] EKCo., *USP* 2,739,174.

[113] Dynamit Nobel A. G., *DBP* 971,523; 971,577; 972,273; 972,566.

[114] DuP, *USP* 2,791,617.

[115] FBy, *DBP* 1,129,466.

exchange resins.[116] The separation of mixtures of isomers by crystallizing the highest melting isomer can be carried out by circulation in crystallizers with ribbed tubes.[117] The purification of solid polynitro compounds (dinitrobenzene, trinitrotoluene, dinitrochlorobenzene) can be performed by crystallization from nitric acid.[118]

2. Nitration of Benzene

a. Nitrobenzene Production. To eliminate nitrobenzene and nitric acid losses treatment of the spent acid with fresh benzene and feeding of the benzene solution of nitrobenzene thus obtained into the nitrating reactor has been suggested.[119]

Nitric acid is noticeably soluble in nitrobenzene. The coefficient of its distribution between nitrobenzene and sulfuric acid increases with H_2SO_4 concentration (it is 1.9 for 74.5% H_2SO_4).[101] To eliminate the loss of nitric acid with the nitro compound it is recommended to extract nitric acid from nitrobenzene with spent acid, to treat the extract with benzene, and to return the mixture of benzene and nitrobenzene into the process.[120]

A new method of obtaining nitrobenzene, of doubtful practical importance, is nitration by heating benzene with aqueous solutions of nitrates of copper or silver under pressure at 250–360°.[121] Extremely pure nitrobenzene for use in Kerr cells as light modulator is obtained by freezing-out and zone fusion.[122]

b. Dinitrobenzene Production. Study of the isomer proportion in dinitrobenzene obtained by nitrating nitrobenzene with nitric acid in excess sulfuric acid showed that with increasing reaction temperature from 0° to 40° the content of *o-* and *p-*dinitrobenzene increases from 4.75% and 1.39% to 6.74% and 2.35%, respectively.[123] The nitration rate of nitrobenzene is 6×10^{-8} times lower than that of benzene.[124]

To obtain dinitrobenzene containing more metaisomer it is recommended to carry out the nitration in two steps; the nitrating mixture in the second step must contain 20% HNO_3 and 2% H_2O.[125]

To obtain almost colorless *m*-phenylenediamine which is stable during storage, *m*-dinitrobenzene after the usual purification with sodium sulfite

[116] FBy, *DBP* 1,222,904.
[117] DuP, *USP* 3,272,875.
[118] Aktiebolaget Bofors, *USP* 2,874,196; *DBP* 1,092,459.
[119] DuP, *USP* 2,773,911.
[120] DuP, *USP* 2,849,497.
[121] California Research Corp., *USP* 2,780,656.
[122] Askania-Werke A.-G., *DBP* 1,070,606.
[123] A. D. Mésure and J. G. Tillett, *J. Chem. Soc., B* p. 669 (1966).
[124] J. G. Tillett, *J. Chem. Soc.* p. 5142 (1962).
[125] DuP, *USP* 3,185,738.

is treated with water and detergents and then cooled to a temperature lower than its melting point.[126]

The nitration of nitrobenzene in the presence of mercury oxide affords 26% o-dinitrobenzene and 24% meta isomer. o-Dinitrobenzene is obtained in 91% yield by the action of concentrated nitric acid upon o-nitrophenylmercurichloride.[127]

3. Nitration of Toluene

a. Mononitrotoluene Production. The kinetics of mononitration of toluene by nitrating mixture has been studied in detail in a laboratory pilot plant of continuous action. The reaction proceeds mainly in the acidic phase.[102] The presence of 4% of nitrosylsulfuric acid increases the nitration rate.[128]

The amount of m-nitrotoluene in the mixture of isomers as determined by the method of isotopic dilution is 2.08% at a nitration temperature of 0° and 3.44% at 30°, 4.18% at 45°, and 4.70% at 60°. Similar results were obtained by the method of IR spectroscopy; in the mixture obtained at 30°, 3.45% m-, 44% p-, 52.5% o-, and traces of 2,4-dinitrotoluene have been found.[129]

The great demand for p-nitrotoluene (for the production of p-nitrobenzoic acid, dinitrostilbenedisulfonic acid, etc.) stimulated the elaboration of a variety of patented methods of toluene nitration that claim increase of the content of p-nitrotoluene in the isomer mixture obtained by nitration. Thus, nitration of toluene with nitric acid in the presence of dehydrated ion-exchange resin (polymeric sulfonic acid) reduces the ortho: para ratio to 0.91 (usually it is 1.2–1.7).[130] For this change of the orientation, it is necessary to take a significant amount of resin, 5–7 parts per 1 part of nitric acid (toluene is used in excess). Increase of the temperature of nitration above 50° results in formation of phenylnitromethane, among other reaction products. At 100° its amount is equal to that of o-nitrotoluene. The change of orientation is explained by the fact that the nitration involves action of the ionic pair NO_2^+ sulfonate$^-$, whose big size hinders sterically the *ortho* substitution.[131]

Other suggestions include nitration with a mixture of nitric acid with

---

[126] NAC, *USP* 3,086,063.

[127] Y. Ogata and M. Tsuchida, *J. Org. Chem.* **21**, 1065 (1956).

[128] K. A. Kobe and J. L. Lakemeyer, *Ind. Eng. Chem.* **50**, 1691 (1958).

[129] R. M. Roberts, P. Heiberger, J. D. Watkins, H. P. Browder, Jr., and K. A. Kobe, *J. Am. Chem. Soc.* **80**, 4285 (1958).

[130] Pitt, *USP* 2,948,759.

[131] O. L. Wright, J. Teipel, and D. Thoennes, *J. Org. Chem.* **30**, 1301 (1965).

aromatic mono- and polysulfonic acids[132] (it should be noted that the isomer ratio claimed in this patent is close to that obtained by nitration with nitrating mixture),[129] by alkyl nitrates and polyphosphoric acid (with neopentyl nitrate, up to 65% of the para and 32.5% of the ortho isomer are obtained),[133] with cellulose nitrate and nitric acid in the presence of mercury (up to 77% of p-nitrotoluene),[134] and with metal nitrates such as $NaNO_3$ in the presence of $AlCl_3$ or $FeCl_3$ (60% of the para isomer).[135] Nitration of toluene in the presence of fluorides of alkali metals in HF[136a] and in the presence of acetonitrile increases the ortho: para ratio.[136b]

The nitration of toluene with the usual nitrating mixture results in compounds of acidic nature in a yield 0.5–2% that of mononitrotoluene. Their major component (70–80%) is 2,6-dinitro-p-cresol. Also present are two mononitro-o-cresols, dinitro-o-cresol, mononitro- and trinitro-m-cresol, mononitro-p-cresol, p-nitrophenol, 2,4-dinitrophenol, and 3-nitro-4-hydroxybenzoic acid.[137]

b. Dinitrotoluene Production. For the special reprocessing of mononitrotoluene into dinitrotoluene with a high 2,4-/2,6-isomer ratio has been suggested that the former be obtained in a system of two reactors, with excess HNO_3 in the first one.[138] Nitration of the isolated o-nitrotoluene by the continuous method affords a mixture of 2,4- and 2,6-dinitro compounds; the ratio is 2:1.[139]

Dinitrotoluene can be obtained by continuous nitration of toluene in a system of several nitrators,[140] or by continuous nitration of nitrotoluenes.[141] When toluene is nitrated in two steps to dinitrotoluene (without the separation of mononitrotoluene isomers) the 2,4-/2,6-isomer ratio is 4:1.[142]

Another possibility is to obtain dinitrotoluene from toluene by the action of a mixture of concentrated HNO_3 (98.6%) and BF_3, in one

[132] NAC, *USP* 3,196,186.
[133] CCC, *USP* 3,126,417; S. M. Tsang, A. P. Paul, and M. P. Di Giaimo, *J. Org. Chem.* **29**, 3387 (1964).
[134] UCC, *USP* 3,149,169.
[135] Universal Oil Products Co., *USP* 3,110,738.
[136a] Universal Oil Co., *USP* 3,326,983.
[136b] O. L. Wright, *BeP* 665,610; *USP* 3,221,062.
[137] V. Dadák, J. Seitl, and K. Šmekal, *Chem. Prumysl.* **12**, 69 (1962); V. Dadák and J. Seitl, *ibid.* **12**, 352 (1962); *Chem. Abstr.* **57**, 623 (1962).
[138] DuP, *USP* 2,947,791.
[139] K. A. Kobe and J. T. Fortman, *Ind. Eng. Chem.* **53**, 269 (1961).
[140] ICI, *USP* 3,243,466; *DBP* 1,275,526.
[141] NSK, *USP* 3,157,706.
[142] ICI, *FP* 1,333,444.

stage.[143] On separation of the organic and acidic layers, the latter is treated with ethylene dichloride or propylene dichloride in continuous extractors to afford dinitrotoluene.[144] Crude dinitrotoluene can be purified by washing with water followed by dilute NaOH (1%) at 70° and then again with water.[145]

The 2,6-isomer can be obtained from the eutectic mixture by crystallization at temperatures below 0° after the addition of aniline or its N-methyl derivatives.[146]

The production of the mixture of 2,4- and 2,6-dinitrotoluene is run on a large scale for further conversion into diisocyanates which are used for polymer synthesis, particularly, of polymers of the Moltoprene type.

The nitration of mesitylene, one of the higher benzene homologs, is of a certain practical importance. To decrease tar formation it is reasonable to eliminate nitrogen oxides from the nitrating mixture by addition of NH_2SO_3H or urea during nitration.[147] Nitromesitylene is reduced to mesidine which is used in the production of acid anthraquinone dyes.

4. Nitration of Chloro Derivatives of Benzene

a. Nitration of Chlorobenzene. Similarly to nitrotoluene, p-nitrochlorobenzene is the isomer in most popular demand among nitro derivatives of chlorobenzene. In this connection a number of patents describe conditions of nitration which will increase the formation of the p-nitro isomers. It is suggested that the nitration be performed (like that of toluene) with nitric acid in the presence of ion-exchange resins,[130] sulfonic acids,[148] or the mixture of HNO_3 with acetic anhydride (it is necessary to point out that working with pure acetyl nitrate is extremely dangerous).[149] Nitration can be also carried out in the presence of a catalytic amount of sulfuric acid in aliphatic chloro solvents—CCl_4, $CHCl_2$—$CHCl_2$, etc. (up to 85% of the para isomer is formed).[150]

Moreover, nitration with nitrating mixture can be performed in the presence of carboxylic acids (with acetic acid, for example, 74.2% of the para isomer is obtained)[151] or of amines which are not nitrated. It is preferable to take primary aliphatic amines with the NH_2 group at a

[143] Secretary of the Army, U.S.A., *USP* 3,293,310.

[144] ICI, *USP* 3,232,999.

[145] ICI, *USP* 3,221,064.

[146] DuP, *USP* 2,765,348.

[147] NAC, *USP* 3,078,317.

[148] Monsanto Chemical Co., *USP* 3,077,502.

[149] W. König, *Angew. Chem.* **67**, 157 (1955).

[150] Universal Oil Products Co., *USP* 3,183,275; A. K. Sparks, *J. Org. Chem.* **31**, 2299 (1966).

[151] Universal Oil Products Co., *USP* 3,180,900; 3,253,045.

tertiary carbon atom $RC(CH_3)_2NH_2$ or tertiary cyclic amines (pyridine, 73–74% of the p-isomer).[152]

The effect of temperature and spent acid concentration upon the isomer ratio has been discussed.[153]

Isolation of p-nitrochlorobenzene from the mixture with the o-isomer by heating with aniline at 175° has been suggested. The o-isomer gives 2-nitrodiphenylamine; the p-isomer does not react.[154] Isolation of m-nitrochlorobenzene from the nitration products (after removal of the p- and o-isomers) by distillation has been recommended.[155] Pure p-nitro-chlorobenzene can be obtained from p-chlorobenzenesulfonic acid by the action of N_2O_4 at 150–180°.[156]

2,4,6-Trinitrochlorobenzene can be obtained from 2,4-dinitrochloro-benzene by heating at 140–170° with nitronium pyrosulfate (70% SO_3, 30% HNO_3).[157]

b. *Nitration of the Polychlorobenzene Derivatives.* The nitration of o-dichlorobenzene results in a mixture of 1,2-dichloro-3-nitrobenzene and 1,2-dichloro-4-nitrobenzene. 1,2-Dichloro-4-nitrobenzene can be isolated from this mixture by treatment with 7–13% oleum, which sulfonates only 1,2-dichloro-3-nitrobenzene.[158]

Dinitro-1,2,4-trichlorobenzene can be obtained from 1,2,4-trichloro-benzene by nitration with excess anhydrous, or SO_3-containing nitration mixture at 100–150°.[159]

5. Nitration of p-Chlorotoluene

To reduce the formation of dinitro compounds (which are dangerous for the distillation) the nitration of p-chlrotoluene may be carried out in the presence of aliphatic dichloro compounds, such as dichloroethane. The content of 2-nitro-4-chlorotoluene is thus increased from 65% to 72.5%.[160] The content of dinitro compounds in the mixture of mononitro derivatives of p-chlorotoluene may be reduced (e.g., from 0.4% to 0.1%) by treatment with oxidants (K_3FeCy_6, O_2, H_2O_2, $KMnO_4$) in an aqueous alkaline solution.[161]

[152] Monsanto Chemical Co., *USP* 3,076,037.
[153] H. H. Bieber and W. F. Schurig, *Abstr. Papers, 130th Meeting Am. Chem. Soc. Atlantic City*, p. 21M (1956); E. Iwata, *Chem. Abstr.* 53, 5182 (1959).
[154] CCC, *USP* 2,700,060.
[155] Phillips Petroleum Co., *USP* 3,311,666.
[156] Monsanto Chemical Co., *USP* 3,153,674.
[157] Stamicarbon, *USP* 2,733,275.
[158] G, *USP* 2,883,435.
[159] Ethyl Corp., *USP* 2,749,372.
[160] G, *USP* 2,810,000.
[161] G, *USP* 2,876,267.

6. *Nitration of Naphthalene and Its Derivatives*

The nitration of naphthalene with nitric acid in acetic anhydride affords nitronaphthalene isomers in a ratio of 1-/2- = 10 (at 0–20°).[162] Nitration in acetonitrile affords only 1-nitronaphthalene.[136] To eliminate the need for grinding naphthalene, it has been suggested that melted naphthalene be nitrated at a temperature not exceeding 90°. At higher temperatures the amount of the 2-isomer increases.[163]

1-Nitronaphthalene can be obtained in a glass column of continuous action by reaction with a countercurrent of N_2O_4 at 180° and purified by distillation at 0.25 Torr and 142–145°.[164] 1-Nitronaphthalene is also obtained by heating naphthalene with Al, Mn, and Fe nitrates.[165] The nitronaphthalene can be purified by washing with aqueous sodium carbonate and H_2O_2 followed by azeotropic distillation with ethylene glycol.[166]

A usual isomer ratio (1:2) of 1,5- and 1,8-dinitronaphthalenes is obtained by nitration of 1-nitronaphthalene with nitric acid and with nitrating mixtures containing acetic anhydride or BF_3 and acetic acid.[167] At the same time, the nitration of naphthalene with $BF_3 \cdot N_2O_4$ complex in nitroethane results in more 1,5-dinitronaphthalene (ratio 1,5/1,8 = 1.5:1).[168] A mixture of dinitronaphthalenes with the prevailing 1,5-isomer can also be obtained by continuous nitration of 1-nitronaphthalene dissolved in concentrated sulfuric acid,[169] by nitration in CCl_4 in the presence of ion-exchange resin,[130] or in acetonitrile solution.[136] The mixture of 1,5- and 1,8-dinitronaphthalenes can be resolved by recrystallization from dimethylformamide,[170] dichloroethane,[169] or cyclohexanone.[171] Countercurrent extraction with a solvent system can also be applied for this purpose.[172]

2-Nitronaphthalene can be obtained by nitrating the product of the addition of 2 moles of hexachlorocyclopentadiene to naphthalene.

[162] M. J. S. Dewar and T. Mole, *J. Chem. Soc.* p. 1441 (1956); see also A. A. Spryskov, and I. K. Barvinskaja, *Zh. Organ. Khim.* **4**, 191 (1968).
[163] Ministry of Petroleum and Chemical Industry (Rumania), *FP* 1,352,613.
[164] Rütgerswerke und Teerverwertung A.-G., *DBP* 1,240,060.
[165] W. Alama and K. Okon, *Biul. Wojskowej Akad. Tech.* **13**, No. 7, 103 (1964); *Chem. Abstr.* **62**, 3961 (1965).
[166] G. I. Mikhailov, *RP* 167,841; *Chem. Abstr.* **62**, 16162 (1965).
[167] E. R. Ward, C. D. Johnson, and L. A. Day, *J. Chem. Soc.* p. 487 (1959).
[168] G. B. Bachmann and C. M. Vogt, *J. Am. Chem. Soc.* **80**, 2381 (1958).
[169] BASF, *DBP* 1,150,965.
[170] FW, *BP* 933,680.
[171] Asahi Chemical Ind., *JP* 2551/66; *Chem. Abstr.* **64**, 14148 (1966).
[172] Asahi Kasei Kogyo Co., *JP* 6269/66; *Derwent Japan. Patent Rept.* **5**, No. 14, Sect. 5 (general organic), 3 (1966).

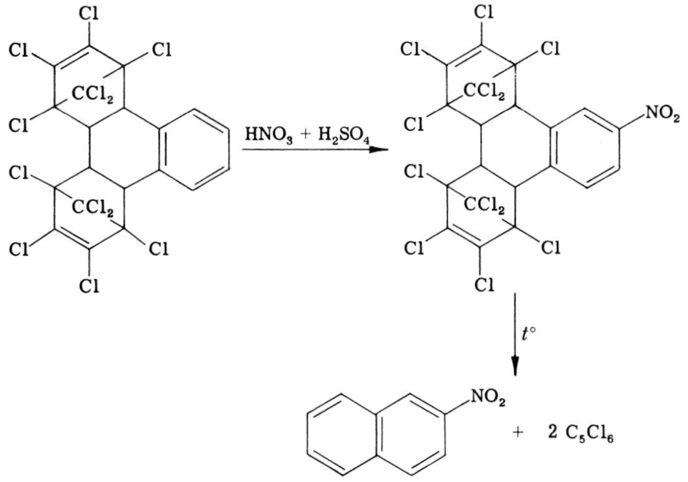

The nitration product is subsequently subjected to thermal decomposition.[173] 2,3-Dinitro- and 1,3-dinitronaphthalenes are obtained by dinitration of the addition product followed by decomposition.[174] From 2-nitronaphthalene, 1,6- and 1,7-dinitronaphthalenes can be obtained by further nitration.[175]

Studies of the nitration of naphthalene-1-sulfonic acid revealed that monosubstituted products with nitro groups at all the positions except the 2-position are formed in minor amounts along with the major products 1,8- and 1,5-nitronaphthalenesulfonic acids. The nitration of naphthalene-1,5-disulfonic acid results in its 3- and 4-nitro derivatives. The 1,7-disulfonic acid gives 3-, 4-, 5-, 6-, and 8-mononitro derivatives, and the 2,7-disulfonic acid affords all three possible nitronaphthalene-2,7-disulfonic acids.[176]

The nitration of naphthalene-1,5-disulfonyl chloride by anhydrous nitrating mixture affords its 3-nitro derivative.[177]

The mixture of 1-nitronaphthalene-6- and 1-nitronaphthalene-7-sulfonic acids obtained by nitration of naphthalene-2-sulfonic acid can be separated (after the removal of sulfuric acid by treating with chalk) by precipitation of the 1,6-isomer in the form of the barium salt (by addition to a solution of barium chloride in a small excess to the 1,6-isomer present). The filtered barium salt of 1-nitronaphthalene-6-sulfonic acid

[173] A. A. Danish, M. Silverman, and Y. A. Tajima, *J. Am. Chem. Soc.* **76**, 6144 (1954); *USP* 2,658,913.

[174] Fundamental Research Co., *USP* 3,065,278; 3,085,115.

[175] Fundamental Research Co., *USP* 3,065,277; 3,132,184.

[176] J. Latinák, *Collection Czech. Chem. Commun.* **28**, 1143 (1963).

[177] FH, *DBP* 1,176,648.

is converted into the ammonium or potassium salt (by addition of the corresponding sulfate) and the salt crystallizes on evaporation. The yield is 24% of theory. The filtrate after the separation of the barium salt of the 1,6-isomer is reduced to give 1-naphthylamine-7-sulfonic acid—a valuable intermediate for azo dyes. 1-Nitronaphthalene-6-sulfonic acid is sulfonated with 66% oleum in the presence of ammonium sulfate and the 1-nitronaphthalene-3,6-disulfonic acid is nitrated without isolation from the reaction mixture into the 1,8-dinitro-3,6-disulfonic acid. Reduction of the dinitro acid results in 1,8-diaminonaphthalene-3,6-disulfonic acid (yield 88% of the weight of the ammonium salt of 1-nitronaphthalene-6-sulfonic acid). The diamino disulfonic acid is converted to H-acid by the known route.[178]

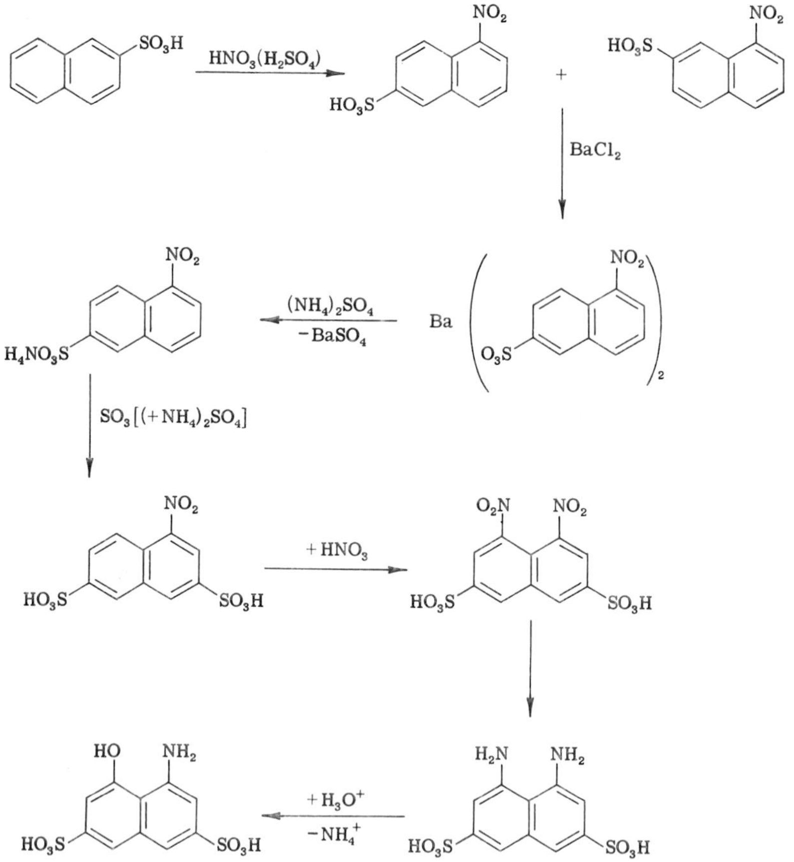

[178] FBy, *USP* 2,875,242; 2,875,243.

The nitration of 2-naphthylamine-1-sulfonic acid (Tobias acid) affords 80–85% 8-nitro- and 20–15% 5-nitro-2-naphthylamine-1-sulfonic acid. Hydrolysis of the compounds results in 8-nitro- and 5-nitro-2-naphthylamines.[179]

7. Nitration of Anthraquinone and of Its Derivatives

A method is proposed affording pure 1-nitroanthraquinone by prolonged (100 hours) treatment of anthraquinone with concentrated (90–100%) nitric acid at 20–25° (yield 95–99%).[180] Alternatively, the compound may be obtained by treatment of anthraquinone with potassium nitrate in anhydrous hydrogen fluoride at 60° under pressure.[181] The nitration of 1,4-dihydroanthraquinone affords the nitrate of 1,2,3,4-tetrahydro-2-hydroxy-3-nitroanthraquinone.

The action of mineral acid in acetic acid followed by oxidation results in 2-nitroanthraquinone.[182] Nitration of 2,3-dihalo-1,2,3,4-tetrahydro-anthraquinones and subsequent alkaline treatment results in a mixture of 1- and 2-nitroanthraquinones.[183] Nitration of 1-methylanthraquinone proceeds smoothly to give 1-methyl-4-nitroanthraquinone, m.p. 261.1–261.5°.[184]

The sulfonic group in mono- and disulfonic acids of anthraquinone can readily be replaced by a nitro group by heating with 5–10% nitric acid at 240–250° under pressure. This method afforded pure 1- and 2-nitro-anthraquinones and 1,5- and 1,8-dinitroanthraquinones. The reaction evidently proceeds by a chain radical mechanism according to the equations[53,185]

$$RSO_3^- + NO_2 \rightarrow RNO_2 + \dot{S}O_3^-$$

$$\dot{S}O_3^- + HNO_3 \rightarrow HSO_4^- + NO_2$$

C. ANALYSIS OF NITRO COMPOUNDS

Chromatography is an important modern method for analyzing the mixtures of nitro derivatives obtained by nitration. Thus, for example,

[179] D. C. Morrison and H. P. C. Lee, J. Org. Chem. **27**, 3336 (1962); Fundamental Research Co., USP 3,251,877.

[180] G, USP 2,874,168.

[181] Instytut Przemyslu Organicznego, PolP 46,428; Chem. Abstr. **59**, 13907 (1963).

[182] V. I. Gudzenko, Zh. Obshch. Khim. **32**, 618 (1962); Chem. Abstr. **58**, 488 (1963); RP 136,354; Chem. Abstr. **56**, 3434 (1962).

[183] CCC, BP 896,911.

[184] V. Ya. Fain and V. L. Plakidin, Zh. Obshch. Khim. **31**, 1588 (1961); Chem. Abstr. **55**, 24699 (1961).

[185] N. S. Dokunikhin and G. S. Lisenkova, Khim. Nauka i Promy. **3**, 280 (1958), Chem. Abstr. **52**, 20089 (1958).

column chromatography on alumina has been successfully applied to the separation and quantitative determination of nitro derivatives of naphthalene,[167] of the nitro compounds of acidic nature that are formed in the side reactions during toluene nitration,[137] etc.

Thin-layer chromatography is used, particularly, on the mixture of silica gel and gypsum.[186]

Paper chromatography is also widely applied. It is used, for example, for the analysis of the mixture of nitrotoluenes (after reduction to toluidines).[187] No reduction is needed to separate on the paper the dinitro derivatives of benzene, naphthalene, and anthraquinone. The spots are detected under a UV lamp more easily after impregnating the chromatogram with fluorescein.[167,188] Paper chromatography has been applied to detect 2-nitronaphthalene, 1,5- and 1,8-dinitronaphthalenes, and 2,4-dinitronaphthol in commercial 1-nitronaphthalene.[189]

Gas–liquid chromatography is widely used to determine the composition of the mixture of products obtained by nitration of toluene; 2,4,7-trinitrofluorenone or, better, Apiezon L is used as a stationary phase.[190] Gas–liquid chromatography can be used to determine exactly the composition of the mixture of isomers of dinitrobenzene,[123] and of mononitrobiphenyl.[191]

Occasionally, IR spectroscopy has been used to analyze the mixtures of nitro compounds. For example, the method was applied to determine the composition of the mixture of nitro derivatives of chlorobenzene[192] and of mononitrotoluenes.[133,193] In the latter case, the application of IR spectroscopy has actually given the same data as the method of isotopic dilution, which is more time consuming.[129]

Polarography is also used in the analysis of nitro compounds; it can, unlike IR spectroscopy, detect minor admixtures, for example, the admixture of dinitrobenzene in commercial nitrobenzene.[194] Polarography

[186] T. Furukawa, Nippon Kagaku Zasshi **78**, 1185 (1957); Chem. Abstr. **52**, 13364 (1958); S. Hashimoto, J. Sunamoto, and I. Shinkai, Kogyo Kagaku Zasshi **68**, No. 12, 2510 (1965); Chem. Abstr. **65**, 6278 (1966).

[187] J. Latinák, Collection Czech. Chem. Commun. **23**, 442 (1958).

[188] J. Franc, Collection Czech. Chem. Commun. **20**, 384 (1955).

[189] S. Kitahara, A. Ito, and H. Hiyama, Kagaku to Kogyo (Osaka) **37**, No. 1, 31 (1963); Chem. Abstr. **60**, 4279 (1964).

[190] J. R. Knowles, R. O. C. Norman, and G. K. Radda, J. Chem. Soc. p. 4885 (1960); J. S. Parsons, S. M. Tsang, M. P. Di Giaimo, R. Feinland, and R. A. L. Paylor, Anal. Chem. **33**, 1858 (1961).

[191] R. Taylor, J. Chem. Soc. B p. 727 (1966).

[192] N. Oi and K. Miyazaki, Yakugaku Zasshi **77**, 1027 and 1030 (1957); Chem. Abstr. **52**, 985 (1958).

[193] F. Pristera and M. Halik, Anal. Chem. **27**, 217 (1955).

[194] T. Takeuchi and M. Kasagi, J. Chem. Soc. Japan, Ind. Chem. Sect. **52**, 64 (1949); Chem. Abstr. **45**, 1916 (1951).

has been applied to analyze the mixture of mono- and dinitroxylenes.[195] The ease of the polarographic reduction of nitro compounds correlates with the readiness of their reduction by usual reducing agents.[196]

III. Halogenation

A. MECHANISM OF THE REACTION

At the ambient or slightly elevated temperatures pure benzene does not react in the dark with molecular chlorine—the most readily available and most common chlorinating agent. Yet, a vigorous reaction of the substitution of hydrogen atoms of the nucleus by chlorine occurs after the addition of catalysts to the reaction mixture. Usually, metal chlorides soluble in the compound being chlorinated are used for this purpose.[197] It is possible to perform chlorination using insoluble catalysts like Al_2O_3[198] or aluminum silicates.[199] In the presence of $FeCl_3$ the chlorination is a homogeneous catalytic reaction.[200] Obviously, the reaction is a homogeneous catalytic one in the presence of other metal chlorides as well. The mechanism of the catalysis is not yet firmly established. Most probably, the catalyst interacts with the chlorine molecule, polarizing it, and the polarized chlorine molecule subsequently reacts with the molecule of aromatic compound to form a positively charged product of the addition of chlorine cation. For example, when ferric chloride is used as a catalyst, the reaction can be presented in the following way:

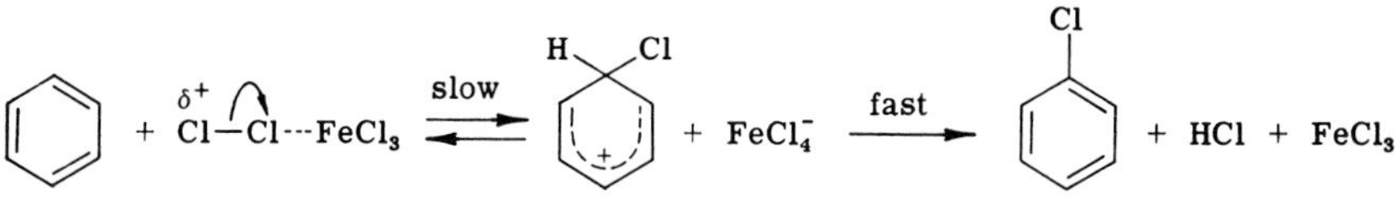

At the next stage, which is usually much faster, a proton is eliminated and the substitution product is formed along with hydrogen chloride (due to the interaction of the proton with the ion $FeCl_4^-$), and the catalyst is regenerated.

The polarization of the chlorine molecule by other catalysts can be presented similarly.

[195] C. H. Hale, *Anal. Chem.* **23**, 572 (1951).

[196] S. Hashimoto, J. Sunamoto, and I. Shinkai, *Kogyo Kagaku Zasshi* **68**, 1017 (1965); *Chem. Abstr.* **65**, 3718 (1966).

[197] *CSD* I, p. 64.

[198] N. N. Vorozhtsov and I. S. Travkin, *RP* 51,042.

[199] California Research Corp., *USP* 2,473,990.

[200] N. N. Woroshzow, "Grundlagen der Synthese von Zwischenprodukten und Farbstoffen," p. 194. Akademie Verlag, Berlin, 1966.

Chlorination differs from sulfonation and nitration in that the introduction of chlorine into the nucleus only slightly decreases the rate of the further reaction (in the case of benzene, this decrease is approximately 8-fold). Therefore, unlike other substitution reactions, chlorination affords reaction products containing significant amounts of the products of further substitution. In the cases when such products are not desirable, the reaction must often be stopped while large amounts of the starting compounds are still present in the reaction mixture.

Besides substitution into the nucleus, the synthesis of chloro derivatives substituted in the side chains, such as those of toluene and other benzene homologs, is of great practical importance. The mechanism of the reaction here is absolutely different. This reaction is initiated by irradiation and by substances that form radicals in the reaction mixture. Hence the reaction is of a typical radical nature, and the active agent is apparently atomic chlorine.

Atomic chlorine is formed from molecular chlorine by absorption of light quanta according to the scheme

$$Cl_2 + h\nu = 2Cl\cdot$$

or, alternatively, by reaction with a radical

$$Cl_2 + R\cdot = RCl + Cl\cdot$$

Chlorine atoms initiate the chain reaction according to the scheme

$$C_6H_5CH_3 + Cl\cdot \rightarrow C_6H_5CH_2\cdot + HCl$$
$$C_6H_5CH_2\cdot + Cl_2 \rightarrow C_6H_5CH_2Cl + Cl\cdot$$

It has been established that with increasing temperature the quantum yield in photochemical chlorination becomes higher. Thus, in toluene chlorination at $-80°$, 25 chlorine molecules enter the reaction with each quantum absorbed, and at $20°$ the quantum yield reaches 8×10^4.[201]

The necessity for careful purification from iron and other metal chlorides which catalyze the substitution of hydrogen atoms of the nucleus follows from the fact that the rate of catalytic chlorination into the nucleus is much higher than that of radical substitution for the hydrogens of the side chain.

The positive effect of the addition of phosphorus chlorides in side-chain chlorination is evidently due to binding of trace amounts of water (present in aromatic compounds and brought with chlorine).

It is interesting that the displacement of sulfonic groups in anthraquinonesulfonic acids by chlorine atoms in acidic aqueous solution is a radical reaction. The formation of chloroanthraquinones from anthra-

[201] M. Ritchie and W. I. H. Winning, *J. Chem. Soc.* p. 3579 (1950).

quinonesulfonic acids proceeds smoothly when these are treated with chlorine under UV illumination, or in the presence of initiators that form atomic chlorine (persulfates, isobutyroazodinitrile, ammonium chloride, some amides).[202]

The addition of chlorine to the aromatic nucleus (the formation of hexachlorocyclohexane from benzene, for example) is also a radical reaction. In the case of radical chlorination of toluene, the primary substitution into the side chain is due to the lower rate of addition to the nucleus.

B. METHODS OF SYNTHESIS OF CHLORO COMPOUNDS

1. General

The synthesis of aromatic halo compounds from the halides of carboxylic and sulfonic acids has been described. Passing the vapors of carboxylic acid halides in a stream of N_2 over palladium, platinum, copper, or nickel on charcoal as catalyst results in elimination of CO to give the corresponding halo derivatives. Benzoyl fluoride affords fluorobenzene and isophthaloyl chloride gives *m*-dichlorobenzene.[203]

Decarboxylation of acid chlorides can be carried out in a high yield by heating with chlorotris(triphenylphosphine)rhodium.[204] The halides of sulfonic acids give halo derivatives on heating at 200–300° in high-boiling, preferably halogen-containing solvents ($C_6H_2Cl_4$, $C_{12}F_{10}$, chloro derivatives of biphenyl). The reaction is catalyzed by CuCl and by palladium on charcoal.[205] Examples are the synthesis of chlorobenzene, fluorobenzene, and *p*-difluorobenzene. Halonaphthalenes are smoothly obtained from the corresponding sulfonic acid halides by heating with SO_2Cl_2 in the presence of a small amount of benzoyl peroxide (or another source of free radicals) in a solvent like CCl_4.[206]

It is possible to obtain chloro derivatives by partial dechlorination of polychloro derivatives with hydrogen in the presence of Pd on charcoal and other catalysts.[207]

The isolation of chloro derivatives from the mixture of isomers can

---

[202] N. S. Dokunikhin and L. M. Egorova, *Khim. Nauka i Promy.* **2**, 132 (1957); *Chem. Abstr.* **52**, 6297 (1958); *RP* 110,204; *Chem. Abstr.* **52**, 14694 (1958); "Organic Intermediates and Dyes," Collection of arts., Vol. 1, pp. 72–82. State Chem. Publ. House, Moscow, 1959.

[203] Monsanto Chemical Co., *USP* 3,221,069; *BP* 957,957; 976,438; Stauffer Chemical Co., *BeP* 651,529.

[204] J. Blum, *Tetrahedron Letters* No. 15, 1605 (1966).

[205] Monsanto Chemical Co., *USP* 3,256,350.

[206] Monsanto Chemical Co., *USP* 3,297,770.

[207] Ethyl Corp., *USP* 2,943,114; Hooker Chemical Corp., *USP* 2,949,491.

be achieved by repeated partial sorption and desorption[208] or by forming (at 0°) complexes with pyromellitic dianhydride.[209]

2. Chlorination of Benzene

Continuous methods of chlorobenzene production are widely used. Probably, the most interesting method is continuous chlorination without external cooling, where the heat of reaction (32 kcal/mole[210]) is spent to evaporate part of the benzene.[211] A detailed description of this and some other processes has been given.[212] It is expedient to carry out the process at 76–83°, leaving about 65% of the benzene in the reaction mixture. The yield of the polychlorides of benzene is about 3.5–4.5% of chlorobenzene.

To increase the content of para isomer in the mixture of dichlorobenzenes it is suggested that the chlorination of benzene be performed in the presence of sulfur-containing compounds (S_2Cl_2,[213] sulfonic acids,[214] organic compounds of divalent sulfur[215]) added to the usual catalyst ($FeCl_3$). These additions also increase the amount of 1,2,4,5-tetrachlorobenzene in the chlorination to the mixture of tetrachlorobenzenes, and of p-chlorotoluene in the chlorination of toluene.

Benzene chlorination can be carried out by the action of not only elemental chlorine, but also by chlorides of metals of higher valency. When a fluidized layer of $FeCl_3$ is used as the agent of chlorobenzene chlorination at 160–180°, an extremely high ratio of p- and o-dichlorobenzenes (14–20:1) is obtained.[216] The amount of para isomer is also increased when chlorination of chlorobenzene is performed by VCl_4 and $MoCl_5$. These chlorination agents possess a high selectivity, probably because the attacking particle has a large volume.[217]

A mixture of dichlorobenzenes containing 50% m-dichlorobenzene can be obtained by elimination of two molecules of HCl from benzenetetrachloride (3,4,5,6-tetrachloro-1-cyclohexene) with potassium hydroxide in ethyl alcohol. Benzenetetrachloride is obtained by the action of

[208] Union Oil Co. of California, *USP* 2,958,708.

[209] California Research Corp., *USP* 2,962,535.

[210] F. W. Kirkbride, *J. Appl. Chem.* (*London*) **6**, 11 (1956).

[211] B. E. Berkman, *RP* 63,784; J. Lee, *Chem. Eng.* **54**, 122 (1947).

[212] B. E. Berkman, "Industrial Synthesis of Chlorobenzene." State Chem. Publ. House, Moscow, 1957.

[213] Hooker Chemical Co., *BP* 988,306.

[214] Société Anonyme dite Société d'Electrochimie, d'Electro-Metallurgie et des Acieries Electriques d'Ugine, *USP* 2,976,330.

[215] Union Carbide Australia, *USP* 3,226,447.

[216] Monsanto Chemical Co., *USP* 3,029,296.

[217] P. Kovacic and R. M. Lange, *J. Org. Chem.* **30**, 4251 (1965).

chlorine upon benzene in the presence of iodine under infrared illumination.[218]

A several-fold amount of nontoxic stereoisomers of $C_6H_6Cl_6$ is obtained in the production of the insecticide lindane—the γ-isomer of hexachlorocyclohexane. Their utilization is economically important. It is obviously most reasonable to use them as starting compounds for obtaining polychloro derivatives of benzene.[219]

Hexachlorocyclohexane can be converted to a mixture of 1,2,4- and 1,2,3-trichlorobenzenes by heating it in the presence of catalysts (iron, aluminum, and their chlorides[220]). The mixture obtained after the elimination of three molecules of HCl contains up to 85% of 1,2,4-trichlorobenzene. Activated charcoal[221] and sulfur[222] are also recommended as catalysts for the dehydrochlorination. Purely thermal methods of dehydrochlorination are also suggested.[223]

The transformation of hexachlorocyclohexane to trichlorobenzene can also be realized by the action of different alkaline agents, such as CaO, NH_3, or sodium hydroxide.[219]

Hexachlorocyclohexane can be directly reprocessed to hexachlorobenzene (which is of interest as an insecticide and as an intermediate for pentachlorophenol—an important antiseptic) by passing its vapor mixed with chlorine over catalysts[224] or by the action of sulfuric anhydride.[225] Hexachlorobenzene can be obtained by chlorination of di-, tri-, and tetrachlorobenzene, more easily in the gas phase in the presence of activated charcoal.[226]

The mixture of 1,2,3- and 1,2,4-trichlorobenzenes can be separated by

[218] G. Calingaert, M. E. Griffing, E. R. Kerr, A. J. Kolka, and H. D. Orloff, *J. Am. Chem. Soc.* **73**, 5224 (1951); **75**, 4243 (1953); Ethyl Corp., *USP* 2,920,110.

[219] J. N. Bezobrazov, A. W. Molchanov, and K. A. Gar, "Hexachlorane," pp. 114–122. State Chem. Publ. House, Moscow, 1958.

[220] N. N. Vorozhtsov, *Org. Chem. Ind. (USSR)* **1**, 667 (1936); *Chem. Abstr.* **31**, 667 (1937); Dow, *USP* 2,569,441.

[221] Ethyl Corp., *BP* 741,203; Pennsalt Chemicals Corp., *USP* 2,955,142.

[222] F. Becke, *USP* 3,043,887.

[223] Commercial Solvents Corp., *USP* 2,768,216.

[224] Schering A. G., *USP* 2,886,606.

[225] BASF, *BP* 754,640.

[226] Soc. d'Electrochimie, d'Electro-Métallurgie et des Aciéries Electriques d'Ugine, *FP* 1,106,763.

its partial chlorination. The 1,2,3-isomer is chlorinated more readily. From the chlorinated mixture, pure 1,2,4-trichlorobenzene is obtained by distillation, and 1,2,3,4-tetrachlorobenzene is isolated from the residue by crystallization.[227]

1,2,4,5-Tetrachlorobenzene (important as a raw material for the herbicide 2,4,5-trichlorophenoxyacetic acid) can be obtained from the mixture with 1,2,3,4-tetrachlorobenzene and pentachlorobenzene by crystallization from tetrachloroethylene.[228]

3. Chlorination of Toluene

Chlorination of toluene in the absence of catalysts at 25° results in o- and p-chlorotoluenes whose ratio depends on the nature of the solvent. Thus in acetic acid, in trifluoroacetic acid, and in $5 M$ sulfuric acid, mixtures containing 60%, 67%, and 90% of o-chlorotoluene respectively, are formed. The para isomer predominates (up to 66% in nitromethane) when the chlorination is performed in the medium of aliphatic nitro compounds or in acetonitrile. There is no correlation between the reaction rate and the ratio of isomers. The probable explanation of the effect of solvent is that chlorination agents are in fact complexes of chlorine with solvents.[229]

The ratio of ortho to para isomers in toluene chlorination in the absence of solvents changes depending on the nature of catalyst. Chlorination of toluene in the ring in the presence of ferric chloride gives 58–63% o- and 37–42% p-chlorotoluene. The content of the para isomer can be increased to 53% by carrying out the reaction with PtO_2 as a catalyst.[230] The chlorination in the presence of $FeCl_3$ and S_2Cl_2 also increases the ratio of p- to o-chlorotoluenes.[231] The chlorides of Ti, Th, Sn, Zr, and W as catalysts direct chlorine preferably to the position ortho to the methyl group (for instance, the chlorotoluenes obtained with $TiCl_4$ contain 76.5% of ortho isomer). The major component thus obtained in dichlorotoluene is 2,5-dichlorotoluene, and in tetrachlorotoluene, the 2,3,5,6-isomer.[232]

The chlorination of toluene in the side chain with molecular chlorine is best performed in the dark, at an elevated temperature in the presence of small amounts (0.01–0.1% of the hydrocarbon weight) of substances that form radicals, such as benzoyl peroxide or azoisobutyronitrile. In this way it is possible to introduce into the side chain one, two, and three chlorine atoms. The high reaction rate enables ready preparation of

[227] Olin Mathieson Chemical Corp., USP 3,275,697.
[228] Olin Mathieson Chemical Corp., USP 2,938,929.
[229] L. M. Stock and A. Himoe, Tetrahedron Letters No. 13, 9 (1960).
[230] Tenneco Chemicals Inc., USP 3,317,617.
[231] Hooker Chemical Co., DP 6,511,484.
[232] Heyden Newport Chemical Corp., USP 3,000,975.

benzyl chloride in the reactor of continuous action.[233] The maximum yield of benzyl chloride (and of benzal chloride) when the reaction is performed under irradiation, without initiators added, and with a small excess of chlorine (7%) is 70%. The yield is lower in the continuous process.[234]

Trinitrobenzyl chloride is obtained from trinitrotoluene by the action of an aqueous solution of NaOCl upon a mixture of trinitrotoluene with tetrahydrofuran and methanol under cooling.[235]

2,6-Dichlorobenzal chloride can be obtained from the mixture of isomers containing 2,6-dichlorotoluene by chlorination in the side chain. All isomers, except the 2,6-isomer, are transformed to dichlorobenzotrichlorides. After the hydrolysis of dichlorobenzotrichlorides by steam or by heating them with diluted mineral acids, dichlorobenzoic acids are separated from 2,6-dichlorobenzal chloride by the action of alkali carbonate solution.[236]

An original method is suggested for obtaining p-cyanobenzotrichloride. Under the usual conditions (high temperature, irradiation) p-tolylnitrile is chlorinated only to p-cyanobenzal chloride. To obtain p-cyanobenzotrichloride, the chlorination of p-cyanobenzal chloride or p-tolylnitrile is performed in an aqueous suspension under irradiation at temperatures below 100°.[237]

4. Chlorination of Xylenes

4,6-Dichloro-1,3-dimethylbenzene is obtained from m-xylene by the action of a mixture of nitric and hydrochloric acids under heating.[238]

The chlorination of p-xylene with 2 moles of Cl_2 (in the presence of 1% $FeCl_3$) affords 2,5-dichloro-p-xylene as the major product (50–67%) along with the 2,3-dichloro derivatives. The 2,5-dichloro isomer is separated from the fraction of dichloro-p-xylenes by crystallization from an alcohol, e.g., isopropyl alcohol.[239]

The dichloro derivatives of both m- and p-xylene (2,5-dichloro-p-xylene) are smoothly obtained by chlorination in the medium of glacial acetic acid (in the presence of 0.5–1% $FeCl_3$). In this medium, only two

[233] N. N. Vorozhtsov, Jr. and P. N. Kulakov, RP 77,525; N. N. Vorozhtsov, Jr. and B. Ya. Libman, RP 85,577; 85,813; N. N. Vorozhtsov, Jr., R. D. Gaukhberg, and B. Ya. Libman, RP 102,806; Chem. Abstr. 52, 4686 (1958).

[234] H. G. Haring and H. W. Knol, Chem. & Process Eng. 45, 560 (1964).

[235] Secretary of the Navy, U.S.A., USP 3,267,159.

[236] Philips Gloeilampenfabriken N. V., BP 947,308.

[237] Chemische Werke Witten, DBP 1,188,073.

[238] Esso Research and Engineering Co., USP 3,326,987.

[239] Diamond Alkali Co., USP 3,035,103.

chlorine atoms enter the xylene nucleus.[240] It has been suggested that 2,3,5,6-tetrachloro derivative can be obtained by chlorination of p-xylene adsorbed on zeolite or, alternatively, in the presence of Fe and $FeCl_3$ in the solution of CCl_4. The latter process can be realized as a continuous one.[241]

5. Chlorination of Nitro Compounds

In the chlorination of nitrobenzene to m-nitrochlorobenzene, the presence of water (in amounts higher than 0.02%) is harmful. Removal of water from the reaction mixture is best performed by addition of phosphorus chlorides (usually phosphorus trichloride, 3–5 parts per part of water). Iron and iodine are recommended as catalysts. Similarly, o- and p-nitrotoluene can be chlorinated in the nucleus.[242] m-Chloronitrobenzene can be separated from the mixture obtained by chlorination by treatment with 10% SO_3, which sulfonates admixtures followed by rectification or crystallization.[243] m-Chloronitrobenzene can also be separated by sulfonation from the residue after the distillation of the major part of the compound from the reaction mixture.[244]

Pentachloronitrobenzene (pesticide) can be obtained by chlorination of mono- or polychloronitrobenzenes (preferably of o-chloronitrobenzene which is a surplus product of chlorobenzene nitration) in the medium of $ClSO_3H$ with the addition of iodine as a catalyst.[245]

The replacement of nitro groups by chlorine atoms by the action of chlorine is evidently a radical process that takes place in the vapor phase.

$$ArNO_2 + Cl\cdot \rightarrow ArCl + NO_2$$
$$NO_2 + Cl_2 \rightarrow NO_2Cl + Cl\cdot$$

It is expedient to carry out the process continuously and to remove continuously the lower-boiling reaction products. 2,4-Dichlorofluorobenzene and a mixture of 3-chloro-4-fluoro- and 2-fluoro-5-chloronitrobenzenes (where the former compound prevails) were obtained in this way from 2,4-dinitrofluorobenzene.[246]

[240] Diamond Alkali Co., USP 3,002,027.

[241] Esso Research and Engineering Co., USP 2,998,459; Standard Oil Co., USP 2,954,409.

[242] DuP, USP 3,005,031; V. I. Zetkin, R. V. Dzhagatspanyan, and E. V. Zakharov, Zh. Prikl. Khim. 38, 2379 (1965); Chem. Abstr. 64, 621 (1966).

[243] G, USP 2,795,620.

[244] G, USP 2,795,621; BP 768,077.

[245] Olin Mathieson Chemical Corp., USP 3,026,358; DBP 1,248,025.

[246] N. N. Vorozhtsov, Jr., G. G. Yacobson, N. I. Krizhechkovskaya, A. I. D'yachenko, and I. V. Shikanova, Zh. Obshch. Khim. 31, 1223 (1961); Chem. Abstr. 55, 24605 (1961).

The chlorination of 2,6-dinitrotoluene or of 2-nitro-6-chlorotoluene at 170° in the presence of 2% of pyridine results in a mixture containing 2,6-dichlorobenzonitrile (~18%) and 2,6-dichlorobenzyl chloride besides 2,6-dichlorobenzal chloride (50%).[247]

1,5-Dichloroanthraquinone in ~90% yield is obtained from 1,5-dinitro-anthraquinone (sometimes diluted with mineral salt, NaCl, for example) by treating it with chlorine at 270–290°.[248] The replacement of the nitro group by a chlorine atom in o-nitrotoluene, o-nitrobenzonitrile, and o-nitrobenzoic acid by the action of hydrogen chloride is performed by heating in dichlorobenzene.[249]

6. Isomerization of Chloro Compounds[250]

The chlorination of chlorobenzene affords a mixture of isomers. It mainly consists of p- and o-dichlorobenzenes. The content of the meta isomer is small. There is no 1,3,5-trichlorobenzene in the mixture of tri-chlorobenzenes obtained by chlorination.

The chlorination of naphthalene results in monochloronaphthalene containing 90% of 1-chloronaphthalene. Since some of the isomers that cannot be obtained by chlorination are now of practical importance or can become important in future, numerous studies have been carried out on obtaining these isomers by isomerization of the corresponding available compounds.

The isomerization of o- and p-dichlorobenzenes to m-dichlorobenzene is well studied. It is established that aluminum chloride in the presence of hydrogen chloride is a good catalyst of the isomerization. In this catalytic system, the isomerization proceeds with measurable velocity at 120°, and at 160° an equilibrium mixture containing 54% m-, 16% o-, and 30% p-dichlorobenzene is formed.[251] This composition is close to the theoretical one, evaluated from the thermodynamic data.[252]

The activity of aluminum chloride can be increased by addition of the oxides of Cr, Zn, Ti, and Mg and by the addition of mercuric chloride

[247] Shell Oil Co., *USP* 3,341,565.
[248] N. S. Dokunikhin, N. D. Genkin, and L. M. Egorova, *RP* 178,390; *Chem. Abstr.* **65**, 2191 (1966).
[249] Shell Internationale Research Mij. N. V., *BP* 987,000.
[250] V. A. Koptyug, "Isomerization of Aromatic Compounds," pp. 56–77 and 99–104. Oldbourne Press, London, 1965.
[251] A. A. Spryskov and Yu. G. Erykalov, *Zh. Obshch. Khim.* **28**, 1637 (1958); *Chem. Abstr.* **53**, 1195 (1959); *Zh. Obshch. Khim.* **29**, 2798 (1959); *Chem. Abstr.* **54**, 10906 (1960).
[252] I. N. Godnev and A. S. Sverdlin, *Zh. Fiz. Khim.* **35**, 474 (1961); *Chem. Abstr.* **55**, 17184 (1961).

or magnesium sulfate.[253] The activity of aluminum chloride increases tenfold after addition of a small amount (2.5–8%) of water. A mixture of aluminum chloride, aluminum oxide, and magnesium sulfate in the ratio 4:1:1 proved to be one of the most active catalysts.[253]

With aluminum chloride and no other addition isomerization of p-dichlorobenzene is performed at 225–250°.[254] A continuous method of isomerization of dichlorobenzene is suggested; the process is carried out in an apparatus connected with 'an efficient rectifying column. The mixture of o- and p-dichlorobenzenes and hydrogen chloride is fed at 180–185° into a reactor containing aluminum chloride. m-Dichlorobenzene containing about 10% of para isomer and boiling at a lower temperature (b.p. 172°) is distilled off through the column. Such an arrangement of the process avoids restrictions imposed by the reversibility of the reaction.[255]

The mixture of isomers, particularly the meta and para isomers (the ortho isomer can be isolated by rectification) is separated by bromination. m-Dichlorobenzene reacts with bromine while the para isomer does not. After 2,4-dichlorobromobenzene is separated from p-dichlorobenzene by rectification, m-dichlorobenzene is regenerated by treating with hydrogen in the presence of a catalyst and of an acceptor of hydrogen bromide.[256]

A method of production of 1,3,5-trichlorobenzene by isomerization has also been elaborated. Other trichlorobenzenes or their mixtures can be used as starting materials, for example those obtained from nontoxic isomers of hexachlorocyclohexane. Aluminum chloride with added water or alcohol (cyclohexanol, for example) is recommended as isomerization catalyst.[257] The equilibrium mixture contains about 25% 1,3,5-trichlorobenzene.[258] 1,3,5-Trichlorobenzene is frozen out or isolated by rectification.[258]

1-Chloronaphthalene is isomerized to 2-chloronaphthalene in the presence of aluminum chloride at 20–50°. Because of the considerable tar formation, only 60% chloronaphthalene (on weight basis) is obtained, containing ~60% of the 2-isomer.[259] The isomerization proceeds more smoothly (yield 98%) when vapor of 1-chloronaphthalene is passed over

[253] A. A. Spryskov and Yu. G. Erykalov, *Zh. Obshch. Khim.* **31**, 292 (1961); *Chem. Abstr.* **55**, 22191 (1961).

[254] UCC, *USP* 2,920,109.

[255] BASF, *DBP* 1,020,323.

[256] Dow, *USP* 3,170,961.

[257] BASF, *DBP* 947,304.

[258] Yu. G. Erykalov, A. A. Spryskov, and E. M. Efimova, *Zh. Obshch. Khim.* **32**, 4025 (1962); *Chem. Abstr.* **59**, 418 (1963).

[259] E. Koike and M. Okawa, *Rept. Govt. Chem. Ind. Res. Inst., Tokyo* **50**, 6 (1955); *Chem. Abstr.* **50**, 11297 (1956).

silica-alumina catalyst or, in a current of hydrogen chloride, over aluminum oxide. The isomerized mixture contains 55–60% 2-chloronaphthalene. From this mixture, 2-chloronaphthalene can be obtained by crystallization with cooling. The mother liquor (eutectic mixture of chloronaphthalenes) can be repeatedly isomerized and in this way 1-chloronaphthalene can be entirely transformed to 2-chloronaphthalene.[260]

The isomerization of *peri*-chloro-substituted naphthalenes proceeds readily. Thus 1,8-dichloronaphthalene heated with anhydrous 2-naphthalenesulfonic acid isomerizes to 1,7-dichloronaphthalene.[261] The change of the position of the chlorine atom is also possible in some *peri*-substituted chloronaphthalenes. 1-Chloronaphthalene-8-sulfonic acid under heating in an $AlCl_3$–NaCl melt at 150° is completely converted to 2-chloronaphthalene-8-sulfonic acid.[262] Under the same conditions, 2-chloro-8-naphthoic acid is obtained from 1-chloro-8-naphthoic acid.[262] It is interesting that the isomerization of 8-substituted 1-chloronaphthalene is practically irreversible. This is due to the steric hindrance arising in *peri*-substituted naphthalenes.[250]

The mechanism of the isomerization of halo derivatives is at present established exactly. Isomerization of *o*-dichlorobenzene in the presence of chlorobenzene-1-^{14}C or using $Al^{36}Cl_3$ as catalyst gives practically no radioactive products of isomerization. Thus, the isomerization is an intramolecular reaction; the migration of the chlorine atom occurs without rupture of its bond with the aromatic nucleus, rather by consecutive 1,2-shifts.[263] The reaction begins by addition of a proton to the carbon atom bearing the chlorine substituent:

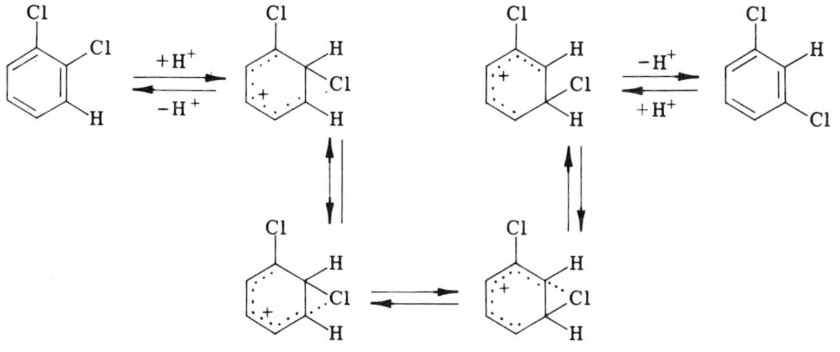

[260] N. N. Vorozhtsov, Jr. and A. M. Beskin, *RP* 72,496; *Zh. Obshch. Khim.* **24,** 657 (1954); *Chem. Abstr.* **49,** 5403 (1955).

[261] V. A. Koptyug, V. G. Shubin and V. A. Plakhov, *Zh. Obshch. Khim.* **31,** 4023 (1961); *Chem. Abstr.* **57,** 9754 (1962).

[262] A. M. Komagorov and V. A. Koptyug, *Zh. Obshch. Khim.* **33,** 3040 (1963); *Chem. Abstr.* **60,** 1665 (1964).

It has been established using 1-chloronaphthalene-1-^{14}C, that more than 90% of the chlorine is transferred, but to the β-position (neighboring to the formerly occupied α-position) in the isomerization of 1-chloronaphthalene to 2-chloronaphthalene. This may be only if the reaction is intramolecular according to the above-outlined mechanism. In the case of an intermolecular mechanism, uniform distribution of chlorine atoms among all four β-positions of the naphthalene nucleus would be the case.[264] The chloronium ion is possible as intermediate in the isomerization of the proton addition product.

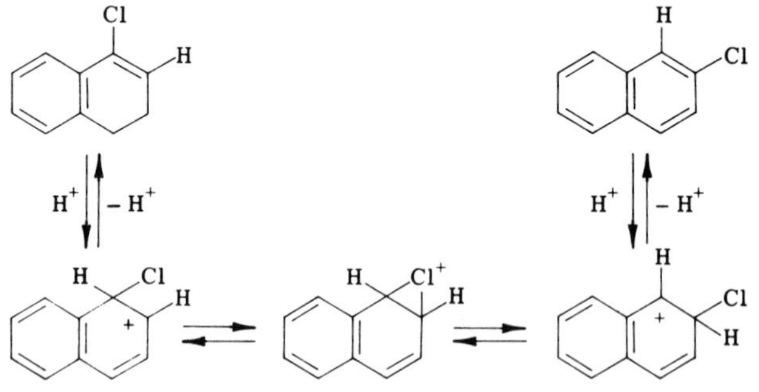

The further replacement of halogen atom (to position 3) is hindered because the formation of the corresponding intermediate compound should lead to loss of aromaticity of the second benzene ring.

C. Analysis of Chloro Compounds

Gas–liquid chromatography has found wide application to the analysis of chloro derivatives. With the help of this method it is possible to separate and to determine quantitatively chloro compounds having close boiling points. Good results are obtained in the analysis by gas–liquid chromatography of the chloro derivatives of benzene,[265] naphthalene,[266] and anthraquinone.

[263] V. A. Koptyug, I. S. Isaev, N. A. Gershtein, and G. A. Berezovskii, *Zh. Obshch. Khim.* **34**, 3779 (1964); *Chem. Abstr.* **62**, 8955 (1965); V. A. Koptyug. I. S. Isaev, Yu. G. Erykalov, and A. A. Spryskov, *Zh. Organ. Khim.* **1**, 2081 (1965); *Chem. Abstr.* **64**, 11107 (1966); see, for comparison Yu G. Erykalov, A. A. Spryskov, G. Bekker, and A. P. Belokurova, *Zh. Organ. Khim.* **4**, 1247 (1968).

[264] N. N. Vorozhtsov, Jr. and V. A. Koptyug, *Zh. Obshch. Khim.* **28**, 1646 (1958); *Chem. Abstr.* **52**, 335 (1958).

[265] R. A. Troupe and J. J. Golner, *Anal. Chem.* **30**, 129 (1958).

[266] P. B. D. de la Mare, R. Koenigsberger, and J. S. Lomas, *J. Chem. Soc. B* p. 834 (1966).

Paper chromatography can be used for the analysis of less volatile chloro compounds (e.g., chloroanthraquinone).[267] For the identification of halogeno derivatives and for the quantitative analysis of their mixtures, IR spectroscopy is successfully applied. In this way mixtures of dichlorobenzene and polychlorobenzenes have been analyzed and the content determined of admixtures in benzyl chloride,[268] and the isomeric composition of mixtures of dihalo-naphthalenes have been determined.[261]

It is also possible to determine aromatic chloro derivatives polarographically. In this way chloro derivatives of benzene and naphthalene[269] and of anthraquinone[267,270] have been determined. Polarography enables separate determination of isomers when these are present in the same mixture.

IV. Amination

A. REDUCTION OF NITRO COMPOUNDS

1. Reduction with Iron

Among the methods of reduction of nitro compounds to amines, the reduction with cast iron borings in electrolyte solutions still remains important. The method under optimum conditions affords high yields of amines not contaminated with any by-products (unlike, e.g., the reduction with tin, which sometimes results in the formation of considerable amounts of amines, chlorinated in the nucleus[271]). The rate of reduction depends on the nature and concentration of the electrolyte. It is highest in the presence of NH_4Cl, followed by $FeCl_2$ and $(NH_4)_2SO_4$.[272] Increas-

[267] M. Nepras, M. Večeřa, J. Borecky, and M. Jureček, *Collection Czech. Chem. Commun.* **28**, 2706 (1963); N. S. Dokunikhin, B. N. Kolokolov, and O. A. Egorova, *Zh. Analit. Khim.* **21**, 888 (1966); N. S. Dokunikhin and B. N. Kolokolov, *Zh. Vses. Khim. Obshchestva im. D. I. Mendeleeva* **7**, 597 (1962); *Chem. Abstr.* **58**, 6759 (1963); *Zh. Analit Khim.* **20**, 398 (1965); *Chem. Abstr.* **63**, 1205 (1965).

[268] R. L. Hudson, *Anal. Chem.* **29**, 1717 (1957); S. K. Freeman, *ibid.* p. 63.

[269] E. S. Levin and Z. I. Fodiman, *Zh. Fiz. Khim.* **28**, 601 (1954). *Chem. Abstr.* **48**, 11218 (1954); P. Zuman, *Chem. Listy* **56**, 219 (1962); *Chem. Abstr.* **56**, 12664 (1962).

[270] L. J. Kheifets, V. D. Bezuglyi, N. S. Dokunikhin, and B. N. Kolokolov, *Zh. Obshch. Khim.* **37**, 299 (1967); V. D. Bezuglyi, L. J. Kheifets, N. A. Sobina, N. S. Dokunikhin, and B. N. Kolokolov, *Zh. Obshch. Khim.* **37**, 783 (1967); *Chem. Abstr.* **67**, 96270 (1967).

[271] G. R. Robertson and R. A. Evans, *J. Org. Chem.* **5**, 142 (1940).

[272] V. O. Lukashevich and M. A. Voroshilova, *Dokl. Akad. Nauk SSSR* **2**, 394 (1935); *Chem. Abstr.* **29**, 6820 (1935); V. A. Zasosov and A. M. Tsyganova, *Med. Prom. SSSR* **15**, No. 8, 38 (1961); *Chem. Abstr.* **57**, 7158 (1962); T. Lesiak, D. Huszcza, and K. Sujkowska, *Przemysl Chem.* **40**, 506 (1961).

ing the concentration of electrolyte increases the rate of the reaction to a certain limit; in the case of $FeCl_3$, this is arrived at 0.8 N. The concentration of electrolyte decreases during the reduction due to absorption on iron oxides. The reaction goes mainly on the surface of iron. A lag period occurs, followed by a zero-order reaction (at the end, first order if large amounts of amine are present). Naturally, the solubility of the nitro compound in water is important, as it determines the concentration.[273]

The mechanism of the reaction is not yet firmly established. The reduction proceeds in weakly alkaline media. Obviously the first stage is the oxidation of iron by nitro compounds to ferrous oxide. This stage has been observed experimentally. The agitation of fine iron powder with nitrobenzene and water in the cold yields a precipitate of ferrous hydroxide that slowly enters into the following reactions.[272] At elevated temperatures, usual during the reduction with Fe, the ferrous oxide subsequently reduces the nitro compound (in weakly alkaline media) at a very high rate. It is considered desirable to add pyridine during the reduction with iron[274] or to use the coordinated compounds of bivalent iron with pyridine as electrolytes. The coordinated compounds themselves are reductants of the nitro compounds.[275]

The composition of the iron oxides formed during the reduction depends to a certain extent on the nature of the electrolyte. In the presence of NH_4Cl, the amount of ferric oxide formed is 49.7%, whereas in the presence of $FeCl_2$ it is 74.7%. The ferrous hydroxide formed initially in the presence of the above (and of some other) electrolytes is transformed further into $Fe(OH)_2 \cdot n\ Fe_2O_3$ and Fe_3O_4. However, in the presence of aluminum chloride, ferrous hydroxide affords the light yellow α-form of ferrous hydroxide, $FeO(OH)$, as the only product. It is for this reason that aluminum chloride is used to obtain yellow pigments from iron sludge during the reduction of nitrobenzene.[276]

2. Reduction with Sulfides

The oldest method of reduction, with sulfides, also retains its importance. The reduction with sulfides is widely applied to obtain from nitro compounds amines insoluble in water (amino anthraquinones, etc.), and also for the partial reduction of polynitro compounds.

[273] S. Yagi, T. Miyauchi, and C. Y. Yeh, *Bull. Chem. Soc. Japan* **29**, 194 (1956).
[274] CIBA, *FP* 1,261,497; Boruta, *PolP* 42,933.
[275] CIBA, *DBP* 1,171,431; *USP* 3,123,645.
[276] I. Riskin, *J. Appl. Chem. USSR* **19**, 148 and 569 (1946); *Chem. Abstr.* **41**, 871 and 2256 (1947); I. Riskin and I. Velikoslavinskaya, *J. Appl. Chem. USSR* **19**, 262 and 271 (1946); *Chem. Abstr.* **41**, 871 and 872 (1947).

The mechanism and the kinetics of the reduction with Na_2S, $NaSH$, and Na_2S_2 have been studied in detail. It has been established that the reduction of nitro compounds with aqueous sodium sulfide proceeds stepwise, in two stages. Sodium sulfide, reducing the nitro compound, is first oxidized into sodium tetrasulfide.

$$ArNO_2 + 4Na_2S + 4H_2O = ArNH_2 + Na_2S_4 + 6NaOH$$

The tetrasulfide formed in the alkaline medium reduces the nitro compound and affords sodium thiosulfate.

$$5ArNO_2 + 3Na_2S_4 + 6NaOH + 2H_2O = 5ArNH_2 + 6Na_2S_2O_3$$

Summation of the two equations results in the known equation:[277]

$$4ArNO_2 + 6Na_2S + 7H_2O = 4ArNH_2 + 3Na_2S_2O_3 + 6NaOH$$

Studies of the reduction of nitrobenzene in a diluted ($0.015 M$ or less) aqueous solution with excess $NaSH$ revealed that the reduction is a bimolecular reaction (first order for each of the reagents). The primary product of the nitrobenzene reduction is phenylhydroxylamine, which is reduced with SH^- much more slowly than nitrobenzene. However, the reduction of the nitro compound affords HS_2^-, which reduces nitrobenzene 7 times faster than does SH^-, and reduces phenylhydroxylamine 2–3 times faster than nitrobenzene. For this reason, at the end of reaction the mixture contains only the starting compound and the final product, i.e., the nitrocompound and the amine.[278]

The rate of the reduction of nitrobenzene with Na_2S_2 in diluted aqueous-methanolic solution is also directly proportional to the concentrations of Na_2S_2 and nitrobenzene. In the more concentrated solution, a third-order reaction is the case—the rate is proportional to the square of the concentration of Na_2S_2. The rate constant grows linearly with increasing concentration of alkali. This increase of the rate is due to shift of the hydrolysis.

$$S_2^{2-} + H_2O \rightleftarrows OH^- + HS_2^-$$

The active reducing particle is the doubly charged anion S_2^{2-}. Probably, the third order of the reaction is in fact only apparent and is explained by shift of the equilibrium increasing the disulfide concentration.

The effect of substituents in the aromatic nucleus is in good accord with the Hammett equation. The ρ-constant of the reaction is $+3.55$. This high sensitivity of the reaction to the nature of the substituents may be due to the double charge of the active reducing particle S_2^{2-}. The positive sign and the large value of ρ well explain the successful use of

[277] S. T. Rachevskaya, *J. Gen. Chem. USSR* **10**, 1089 (1940); *Chem. Abstr.* **35**, 3985 (1941).

[278] O. J. Cope and R. K. Brown, *Can. J. Chem.* **40**, 2317 (1962).

sulfides for the selective partial reduction of polynitro compounds. For example, m-nitroaniline must be further reduced more than 10^3 times more slowly than m-dinitrobenzene.[279]

Patents continue to appear suggesting hydrogen sulfide as a reducing agent. For example, the nitro compounds may be reduced to the amines by passing hydrogen sulfides through their solutions in the presence of amines such as $C_6H_{11}NH_2$ added as catalysts.[280]

The reduction of nitro compounds with hydrogen sulfide can also be performed in the vapor phase at normal pressure at 100–500° over aluminosilicate zeolite catalysts having monodisperse pores of diameter greater than 5 Å and containing exchangeable metal cations with a great affinity for sulfur.[281]

Performance of the partial reduction of polynitro compounds to nitroamines under the pressure of the calculated amount of H_2S in the presence of amphoteric oxides of Th, Zn, and Al has been suggested.[282] 2-Amino-5-chloro-4-nitrophenol has been obtained by partial reduction of 5-chloro-2,4-dinitrophenol with $Na_2S_2O_4$; disulfides are not satisfactory in this case.[283]

The reduction of nitro compounds with aqueous Na_2S_2 solutions has been performed in a flow reactor. The reductions with this continuous method of 1-nitronaphthalene to 1-naphthylamine[284] and of m-chloronitrobenzene to m-chloroaniline have been described.[285]

3. Reduction to Hydrazo Compounds

The reduction with sodium and potassium of various nitro compounds in 1,2-dimethoxyethane involves migration of an electron of a metal atom to a molecule of the nitro compound as the primary act, affording an anion-radical; in the case of nitrobenzene, for example, it has the following structure:[286]

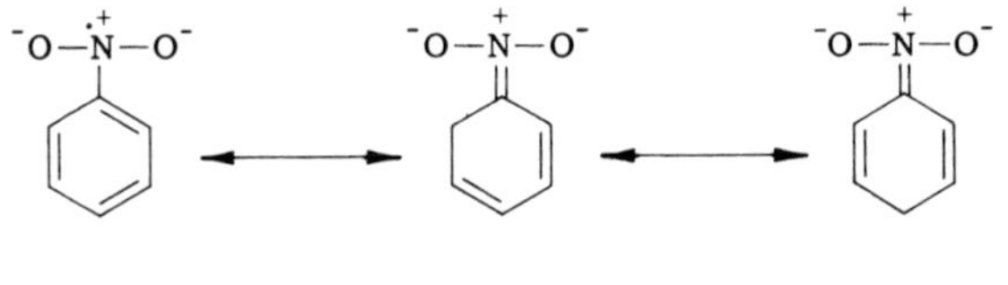

[279] M. Hojo, Y. Takagi, and Y. Ogata, *J. Am. Chem. Soc.* **82**, 2459 (1960).
[280] ICI, *BP* 907,042.
[281] Socony Mobil Oil Co., *USP* 3,253,038.
[282] Lummus Co., *FP* 1,389,061.
[283] FW, *BeP* 616,561; *BP* 911,809; *FP* 1,301,473.
[284] G. A. Timokhin and B. I. Kissin, *Khim. Prom.* p. 255 (1960); *Chem. Abstr.* **55**, 13386 (1961).

The same anion-radical is formed on the cathode during electrochemical reduction of nitro compounds.[287]

The anion-radical forms an intimate ionic pair with the metal cation so that the alkali metal ion interacts with the spin density of a nitro group.

The action of the second metal atom results in products of the addition of two metal atoms, which have been isolated individually. When the reduction is performed in ether, they are precipitated as double compounds of the formula $ArNO_2Na_2 \cdot ArNO_2$. During reduction in the presence of water, the disodium compounds are rapidly decomposed. The primary products of the hydrolysis are hypothetical "dihydroxyamines" that eliminate water and afford the nitroso compounds:[288]

$$ArNO_2Na_2 \xrightarrow[-2\,NaOH]{+2\,H_2O} \left[Ar-\overset{\overset{\displaystyle H}{|}}{\underset{\underset{\displaystyle O^-}{|}}{N^+}}-OH \right] \xrightarrow{-H_2O} ArNO$$

The action of sodium amalgam subsequently leads to addition of at first one sodium atom, resulting in the corresponding anion-radical,[289] which thereafter adds the second atom of sodium and is transformed into a disodium derivative of arylhydroxylamine, $ArNONa_2$. The latter is hydrolyzed to give arylhydroxylamine.[288] The reduction proceeds in the same manner with other metals, e.g., with zinc.

Arylhydroxylamines in the alkaline medium react with the nitroso compounds, affording azoxy compounds. The accumulation of arylhydroxylamines during the reduction must be avoided, because they can be transformed into amines—an undesired reaction. Hence, the reduction must be performed under conditions most favorable for increasing the rate of the arylhydroxylamine reaction with the yet unreduced nitroso compound. It has been established that the rate of the azoxy coupling increases with increasing concentration of alkali and with temperature. For this reason, the reduction with metals in alkaline media to the stage of azoxy com-

[285] G. A. Timokhin and B. I. Kissin, *Khim. Prom.* p. 258 (1966); *Chem. Abstr.* **64**, 19454 (1966).

[286] T. E. Chu, G. E. Pake, D. E. Paul, J. Townsend, and S. I. Weissman, *J. Phys. Chem.* **57**, 504 (1953); R. L. Ward, *J. Am. Chem. Soc.* **83**, 1296 (1961).

[287] R. D. Allendoerfer and P. H. Rieger, *J. Am. Chem. Soc.* **88**, 3711 (1966); D. H. Geske and A. H. Maki, *ibid.* **82**, 2671 (1960).

[288] V. O. Lukashevich, *Usp. Khim.* **17**, 692 (1948); *Chem. Abstr.* **43**, 7918 (1949); V. O. Lukashevich, *J. Gen. Chem. USSR* **11**, 1007 (1941); *Chem. Abstr.* **40**, 1150 (1946).

[289] T. Kauffman and S. M. Hage, *Angew. Chem.* **75**, 295 (1963).

pounds must be performed at high concentrations of alkali (up to 50% NaOH is applied).[290] In selected cases, when the rate of the nitroso compound transformation to hydroxylamines is high, e.g., when the reduction is performed with sodium in ethanol, another path is possible, leading to azoxy compounds via reaction of arylhydroxylamine with nitro compounds:

$$3ArNHOH + ArNO_2 \rightarrow 2Ar\text{---}N\text{==}N(O)\text{---}Ar + 3H_2O$$

The route sometimes may appear the major one affording the azoxy compound.[291]

The last stages of the reduction—the conversion of azoxy compounds to the azo and hydrazo compounds by reaction with zinc powder—are best performed at low temperatures and at small alkali concentrations.

Studies of the effect of the quality of the zinc powder upon nitro compound reduction revealed that the admixture of cadmium and the form and size of particles do not affect the yield of hydrazo compounds. The presence of iron in the powder decreases the yield, but the presence of lead (up to 2.5%) abolishes the action of iron and increases the yield of hydrazo compounds.[292]

At the same time, a number of nitro compounds have been successfully reduced to hydrazo compounds with iron[293] or with iron alloys, e.g., with ferrosilicon alloy containing 15% of silicon, or with an alloy of iron with aluminum (1:2).[294]

Studies of the electrochemical reduction of nitrobenzene to hydrazobenzene demonstrated that the best result (90% yield) is obtained with the lead cathode covered with metal soluble in alkali, like spongy zinc or tin. It is possible that the metal itself is the reducing agent, and that the electric current is needed merely to regenerate it.[295]

An electrochemical method affording o-hydrazoanisole has been elaborated. A set of rotating (1800 rpm) steel disks serves as the cathode. The catholite was 10% NaOH containing 1% of PbO, the anolite was 25% NaOH. The cathode current density was 30 amp/dm². After pass-

[290] V. O. Lukashevich, *Anilinokrasochnaya Prom.* **4**, 605 (1934); *Chem. Abstr.* **29**, 2527 (1935).

[291] V. O. Lukashevich, *Dokl. Akad. Nauk SSSR* **20**, 137 (1938); *Chem. Abstr.* **33**, 1683 (1939).

[292] Y. Tajima and H. Sasuga, *J. Chem. Soc. Japan, Ind. Chem. Sect.* **57**, 116 (1954); *Chem. Abstr.* **49**, 11577 (1955).

[293] FH, *BP* 773,187.

[294] H. Iida and K. Konisi, *J. Chem. Soc. Japan, Ind. Chem. Sect.* **57**, 47 and 830 (1954); *Chem. Abstr.* **49**, 10873 (1955); H. Iida and S. Fuse, *J. Chem. Soc. Japan, Ind. Chem. Sect.* **56**, 964 (1953); *Chem. Abstr.* **49**, 6858 (1955).

[295] K. Sugino and T. Sekine, *Chem. Zentr.* **129**, 7073 (1958).

ing 90% of the current needed, xylene was added to prevent the precipitation of the hydrazo derivative.[296]

A three-stage continuous method of reduction with sodium and potassium amalgams has been described.[297]

The known methods of reduction of nitro to azoxy and hydrazo compounds by the action of hydroxy compounds and aldehydes in an alkaline medium have been improved by introduction of quinones as reduction promoters.[298]

A method has been elaborated and is accomplished on the industrial scale for the continuous reduction of nitrobenzene to hydrazobenzene with zinc powder in alkaline solution in a cascade of three reactors involving the separation of the large crystals of hydrazobenzene from the zinc oxide suspension by filtration through a metal screen.[299]

4. The Benzidine Rearrangement

The mechanism of the rearrangement of hydrazo compounds to diamines of the biphenyl series has attracted the attention of many workers. Now many features of the mechanism of this reaction are firmly established. Proven first of all was the intramolecular character of this reaction. The use of very different methods has always finally led to the conclusion that the two benzene rings that are bound by carbon–carbon bonding in diaminodiphenyl are those that were formerly bound by a nitrogen–nitrogen bond in the starting hydrazo compound.

Studies of the kinetics have revealed that the rate of hydrazobenzene rearrangement in acidic medium is directly proportional to the square of the acid concentration.[300] The behavior of the unstable monohydrochlorides of hydrazobenzene and m-hydrazotoluene also suggests that the bis salts of hydrazo compounds are involved in their rearrangement.[301] Storage of the mono salt of hydrazobenzene in ethereal solution results in slow (during a day) accumulation of a complex mixture of products, of which the majority are formed by redox disproportionation (aniline

[296] K. S. Udupa, G. S. Subramanian, and H. V. K. Udupa, Bull. Chem. Soc. Japan 35, 1168 (1962); Chem. Abstr. 58, 2392 (1963).

[297] FH, DBP 1,004,190; 1,005,525; 1,012,305.

[298] Allied Chemical & Dye Corp., BP 780,631; 780,632; USP 2,804,452; 2,804,453.

[299] B. E. Berkman, "Industrial Syntheses of Aromatic Nitrocompounds and Amines," p. 218. Publ. House "Chemistry," Moscow, 1964.

[300] G. S. Hammond and H. J. Shine, J. Am. Chem. Soc. 72, 220 (1950); E. D. Hughes and C. K. Ingold, J. Chem. Soc. p. 1638 (1950); R B. Carlin and R. C. Odioso, J. Am. Chem. Soc. 76, 100 and 2345 (1954); for a review see M. F. Shine, "Aromatic Rearrangements," pp. 124–179. Elsevier Publ. Co., Amsterdam, 1967.

[301] L. G. Krolik and V. O. Lukashevich, Dokl. Akad. Nauk SSSR 93, 663 (1953); Chem. Abstr. 49, 1615 (1955).

and azobenzene). At the same time, in excess acid the monohydrochloride is rapidly involved in the benzidine rearrangement. These data suggest the following equations as the major stages of the reaction:

$$C_6H_5NH-NHC_6H_5 + H^+ \rightleftarrows C_6H_5\overset{+}{N}H_2-NHC_6H_5$$

$$C_6H_5\overset{+}{N}H_2-NHC_6H_5 + H^+ \rightleftarrows C_6H_5\overset{+}{N}H_2-\overset{+}{N}H_2C_6H_5$$

$$C_6H_5\overset{+}{N}H_2-\overset{+}{N}H_2C_6H_5 \xrightarrow{\text{Slowly}} NH_2C_6H_4-C_6H_4NH_2 + 2H^+$$

The driving force of the bis-protonated hydrazo compound rearrangement is the electrostatic repulsion of the two neighboring positive charges.

There are a number of concepts concerning the transition state in the last stage of the rearrangement.

Experimentally well grounded is the theory of a polar transition state. This theory assumes that after double protonation the N—N bond is to a large extent heterolyzed. After heterolysis, one of the aromatic nuclei bears almost two positive charges, and is bound to the second nucleus containing a very small charge mainly by electrostatic forces. In the former nucleus, one positive charge is localized on the nitrogen atom, and the second charge is mainly on the para carbon atom (partially on the ortho carbon atoms). The structure of this nucleus is of the quinoid type. The second quasi-neutral nucleus due to the mesomeric shift of the aniline type is bipolar with the δ^+ on nitrogen, and the δ^- on the ortho and para carbons. The following formula shows this transition state:

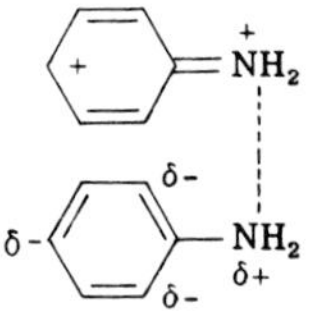

The formation of C—C bonding is facilitated by the direction of valencies of the nitrogen atoms (in the hydrazo compound the distance between the p-p' carbon atoms is about 1.5 Å, i.e., but a little greater than that between 1–1' atoms in benzidine[302]) as well as by flexibility of the C—N—N—C chain that makes possible a still closer contact.[303]

The isomerization of hydrazobenzene proceeds exclusively via the bis-protonated particle. However, examples are known (hydrazonaphtha-

[302] D. L. Hammick and S. F. Mason, J. Chem. Soc. p. 638 (1946); p. 1939 (1949).
[303] D. V. Banthorpe, E. D. Hughes, and Sir Christopher Ingold, J. Chem. Soc. p. 2864 (1964); see also D. V. Banthorpe, C. K. Ingold, and M. O'Sullivan, J. Chem. Soc. B., p. 624 (1968) and references cited therein.

lenes) of the isomerization of mono salts. In this case, in the transition state one-half of the molecule bears one positive charge distributed between the ortho and para carbons, and the other half is neutral.[303]

Cases are also known of fractional order of reaction. This may be due to coexistence of the single- and the double-proton mechanisms.[303]

Other formulations have been proposed to describe the transition state, e.g., a π-complex,[304,305] or a combination of two symmetrical cation-radicals.[306] It will be noted that the attempted observation of radicals by EPR or by initiation of polymerization reactions has been a failure.[303]

Studies of the products of the rearrangement of hydrazobenzene have revealed that, along with the amines formerly found, some 2,2'-diamino-biphenyl is also formed.[307]

Increase of the acidity of the medium in H_2SO_4 over a range of concentrations from 40% to 95% leads to decrease of the yield of benzidine.[305]

In 75% H_2SO_4 the maximum yield of benzidine has been obtained at $+15°$ ($\sim45\%$). At the same time, 96–97% of benzidine is formed on treatment of a 2.5% toluene solution of hydrazobenzene with 50% H_2SO_4.[308]

In aqueous ethanol the rearrangement induced by HCl results in different diaminobiphenyl yields at different ethanol concentrations (minimum at 90%). However, the ratio benzidine–diphenyline (60:40) does not depend on nature of solvent, nor on the concentration of acid and temperature (0–30°).[309]

The peculiar hydrazo compound, N-phenyl-N'-8-carboxynaphthyl-1-hydrazine, obtained by dissolution in alkali of 1-phenylaminobenz[cd]-indoline-2-one, affords the corresponding diphenyline as the major product along with the corresponding benzidine (isomeric aminophenyl-naphthostyrils) and benzocarbazole carboxylic acid.[310]

[304] M. J. S. Dewar, in "Theoretical Organic Chemistry," p. 195. Butterworths Scientific Publications, London, 1959; J. S. Clovis and G. S. Hammond, J. Org. Chem. 28, 3290 (1963).

[305] Z. J. Allan and V. Chmátal, Collection Czech. Chem. Commun. 29, 531 (1964).

[306] V. Štěrba and M. Večeřa, Collection Czech. Chem. Commun. 31, 3486 (1966).

[307] V. O. Lukashevich and L. G. Krolik, Dokl. Akad. Nauk. SSSR, 63, 543 (1948); Chem. Abstr. 43, 3809 (1949); M. Večeřa, J. Petranek, and J. Gasparič, Chem. & Ind. (London) p. 99 (1956); Collection Czech. Chem. Commun. 22, 1603 (1957).

[308] Z. J. Allan and J. Rakušan, Collection Czech. Chem. Commun. 31, 3555 (1966).

[309] S. Hashimoto, I. Shinkai, and J. Sunamoto, Kogyo Kagaku Zasshi 69, No. 2, 290 (1966), Chem. Abstr. 65, 7019 (1966).

[310] N. S. Dokunikhin and G. I. Bystritskii, Zh. Obshch. Khim. 33, 680 (1963); Chem. Abstr. 59, 8685 (1963).

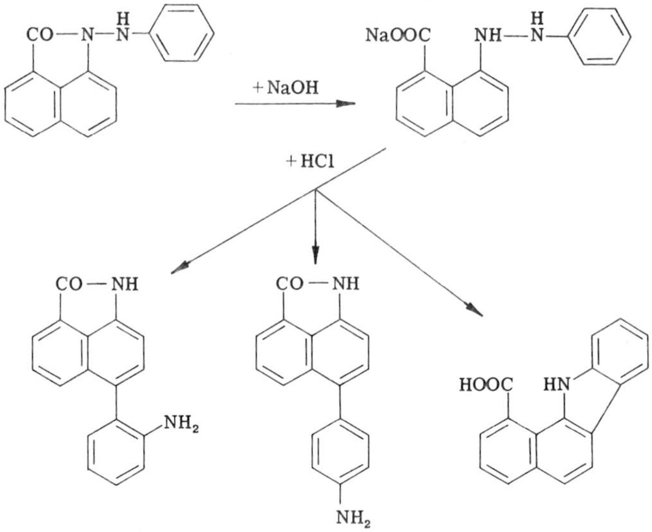

5. Catalytic Reduction

Reduction with hydrogen in the presence of catalysts gains increasing importance as a method of preparation of amines from aromatic nitro compounds, and has replaced in some instances the usual method of reduction with cast iron borings. The reason for this is the increasing demand for aromatic amines and the better susceptibility of the hydrogenation method to automation compared with the cast iron borings method. Finally, cast iron borings have become a deficient product due to the introduction of modern technology in the machine building industries.

Many metals and their compounds and combinations have been proposed as catalysts for nitrobenzene reduction to aniline in the vapor phase (Cu, Ni, Pb, Cd, Mo, etc.). Good results are obtained with nickel catalyst combined with vanadium and aluminum oxides. This catalyst affords a very high yield of aniline (97–99% of the theory). It works over a wide temperature range (240–300°), is stable (works without regeneration for 20 days), and is readily regenerated by oxidation with air.[311] Similar properties are exhibited by the catalyst obtained from nickel–aluminum alloy containing about 0.3–1.5% of vanadium.[312]

The production of aniline using a mobile layer of catalyst (copper on silica gel) has been described. Using fluidized catalyst one can more

---

[311] B. E. Berkman, "Industrial Syntheses of Aromatic Nitrocompounds and Amines," pp. 198 and 200. Publ. House "Chemistry," Moscow, 1964.

[312] J. Hruby and J. Radek, *CzechP* 86,540.

readily remove the great heat of the reaction (112 kcal/mole for the reduction of nitrobenzene to aniline with hydrogen in the vapor phase). Heat may also be efficiently removed by using converters with the intertube space filled with a high-boiling organic heat carrier.[311]

The scope of vapor-phase reduction is limited to nitro compounds that can be evaporated and remain stable at the relatively high temperatures.

Liquid-phase reduction can be performed at lower temperatures (from about 20°) in a variety of solvents and thus may be applied to a large number of nitro compounds. Nickel and noble metals (Pt, Pd, Rh, Os), can be used as catalysts for the purpose.

Some difference has been noted between the modes of action of the nickel and platinum catalysts. On nickel catalyst, the rate of the process depends on the hydrogen activation rate, whereas on platinum the rate-limiting factor is the activation of nitro compounds. Hence, hydrogenaton of strongly adsorbed nitro compounds proceeds more readily on platinum catalyst, whereas nickel is better for the more weakly absorbed compounds.[313]

The effect of substituents on the aromatic nucleus of nitro compounds upon the rate of their reduction with rhodium catalyst is insignificant.[314]

Promotion of supported platinum catalyst by addition of silver distributed in the liquid rather than in the form of an alloy with platinum has been suggested.[315]

It has been established that the Pd/C catalyst is poisoned by copper salts.[316] Higher resistance to poisoning with sulfur-containing compounds is exhibited by Ni catalyst containing the carbonates of Zn and Ca.[317]

One of the most important processes of catalytic reduction is the reduction of a mixture of dinitrotoluenes to toluylenediamines, which are used as intermediates in the synthesis of diisocyanates for porous plastics production. The catalytic reduction is the major route to these diamines.

Mixed dinitrotoluenes (obtained by nitration of o-nitrotoluene) are reduced in methanolic solution (with the reaction mixture of the preceding operation added to reduce the heating of the reaction mixture) at 100–170° with Raney nickel as catalyst. The pressure of the reaction is

[313] D. V. Sokol'skii and V. P. Shmonina, Dokl. Akad. Nauk SSSR **78**, 721 (1951); Chem. Abstr. **45**, 8337 (1951); Sbo. Statei po Obshch. Khim., Akad. Nauk SSSR **2**, 1186 (1953); Chem. Abstr. **49**, 3632 (1955).

[314] L. Hernandes and F. F. Nord, J. Colloid Sci. **3**, 363 (1948); Chem. Abstr. **43**, 27 (1949).

[315] Engelhard Industries Inc., BP 971,287; USP 3,253,039.

[316] H. Greenfield, J. Org. Chem. **28**, 2434 (1963).

[317] Office Officiel Industriel de l'Azote, BeP 646,607.

50–100 atm.[318] It has also been suggested to reduce dinitrotoluene in aqueous emulsion at atmospheric or slightly elevated pressure with Pd/C or Ni on silica gel as catalysts,[319] or alternatively in aqueous ethanol with Pd/C or Pt catalyst.[320]

Hydrogenation of dinitrotoluene and of other dinitro compounds (e.g., of m-dinitrobenzene) can be performed in the presence of solvents that dissolve both the starting compound and the diamine formed, such as morpholine, its N-alkyl derivatives, dimethylformamide, or pyridine.[321]

Another interesting example of the application of liquid-phase catalytic reduction is the production of mono- and polychloroanilines, which are interesting both as intermediates for dyes and as starting compounds for pesticide synthesis. The catalytic reduction of chloronitro compounds is sometimes complicated by the side reaction of dehalogenation. For this reason the catalysts and the reaction conditions must provide selective reduction of the nitro group without touching the halogen substituent. For the purpose, Pt/C is applied in minor amounts as the catalyst (the nitro compound:platinum ratio is more than 10,000), and minor amounts of magnesium oxide or hydroxide are added to the reaction mixture.[322] Patented as catalysts for the reduction of chloronitro compounds are Rh in benzene solution,[323] copper-chrome catalyst,[324] and some other catalysts.[325]

Catalytic reduction also affords phosphorus-containing amines that are used as intermediates, such as the tris-p-aminophenyl esters of phosphoric or thiophosphoric acid.[326]

The reduction of nitro sulfonic acids in an aqueous solution to the corresponding amino sulfonic acids has been performed successfully with Ni catalyst obtained by heating to 250° nickel formate in a mixture of paraffin wax and paraffin oil.[327] Reduction by hydrogen with Ni catalyst at 10–15 atm was used in the production of 2-amino-4-trifluoromethyl-

[318] FBy, *DBP* 948,784; 1,044,099; *FP* 1,112,653.

[319] NAC, *BP* 832,153.

[320] ICI, *BP* 852,144; 907,154; Societe Industrielle des Dérivés de l'Acétylène, *FP* 1,290,268.

[321] G, *USP* 2,894,036.

[322] DuP, *BP* 859,251.

[323] Columbia-Southern Chemical Corp., *USP* 2,772,313.

[324] Columbia-Southern Chemical Corp., *USP* 2,791,613.

[325] W. H. Davenport, V. Kollonitsch, and C. H. Kline, *Ind. Eng. Chem.* **60**, No. 11, 11 (1968); VEB Leuna Werke W. Ulbricht, *DBP* 1,118,796; Dow, *BP* 960,046; G, *USP* 3,148,217.

[326] FBy, *DBP* 1,122,075.

[327] F. Allisson, J. L. Compte, and H. E. Fierz-David, *Helv. Chim. Acta* **34**, 818 (1951).

amide of metanilic acid. The
n at 60–90°.[328]
statu nascendi is also applied
for example, the compounds
presence of Raney nickel[329]

hydrogen in the presence of
nd sodium hydroxide solution

Y AN AMINO GROUP

in the Absence of Catalysts

y an amino group is usually
ives with aqueous ammonia,
an autoclave). Although the
lic substituents (halobenzenes,
queous ammonia, the reaction
nantly) in the aqueous layer.
nd the temperature (and, con-
bility. For example, the solu-
)° is about 5%; at 200°, 13%;

udies of the kinetics of the substitution of a chlorine atom by an
amino group that occurs when heating o- and p-nitrochlorobenzenes with
aqueous solutions of ammonia have revealed that (when the chloro
compound is dissolved completely) this is a usual bimolecular reaction
(as revealed by kinetic studies, the solubility per 100 ml of 25% NH_3
is more than 6.6 g of p-nitrochlorobenzene at 160°[334] and more than 4.95 g
for o-nitrochlorobenzene at 150°).[335] The rate of this reaction (the con-

[328] BIOS 1153, 160; FIAT, 1313, II, 227.

[329] D. Balcom and A. Furst, J. Am. Chem. Soc. 75, 4334 (1953).

[330] M. J. S. Dewar and T. Mole, J. Chem. Soc. p. 2556 (1956); P. M. G. Bavin,
Can. J. Chem. 36, 238 (1958).

[331] DuP, USP 2,194,938.

[332] DuP, BP 528,317; USP 2,344,244.

[333] N. N. Vorozhtsov, Jr. and V. A. Kobelev, Dokl. Akad. Nauk SSSR 3, 109
(1934); Chem. Abstr. 28, 6706 (1934); J. Gen. Chem. USSR 8, 1106 (1938); Chem.
Abstr. 33, 3769 (1939).

[334] N. N. Vorozhtsov, Jr. and V. A. Kobelev, J. Gen. Chem. USSR 8, 1330 (1938);
Chem. Abstr. 33, 4114 (1939).

[335] N. N. Vorozhtsov, Jr. and V. A. Kobelev, J. Gen. Chem. USSR 9, 1043 (1939);
Chem. Abstr. 33, 8580 (1939).

venient temperature interval is 140–180°) is directly proportional to the concentrations of both ammonia and the chloro derivative. The activation energy for p-nitrochlorobenzene is 21.4 kcal/mole[334] and it is 20.5 kcal/mole for o-nitrochlorobenzene.[335,336]

Introduction of a trifluoromethyl group into the position para to chlorine in o-nitrochlorobenzene results in a considerable increase of the rate of reaction with aqueous ammonia.[336]

m-Nitrochlorobenzene does not react with aqueous ammonia below 200°.[337] The earlier data[338] on the high mobility of chlorine in m-nitrochlorobenzene are erroneous.[339]

The same kinetic rules as those of the reaction of o- and p-nitrochlorobenzenes with ammonia are valid for the reaction of 2-chloroanthraquinone with aqueous ammonia at 200–210° which affords 2-aminoanthraquinone.[340]

Obviously, the reaction with aqueous ammonia of aromatic chloro compounds containing a mobile chlorine atom is, like the reaction of these chloro derivatives with amines,[341] a two-stage reaction. The rate-limiting step is the addition of ammonia to the chloro derivative.

The intermediate addition product is dipolar, and its probable formation from p-nitrochlorobenzene, e.g., is described by the following scheme:

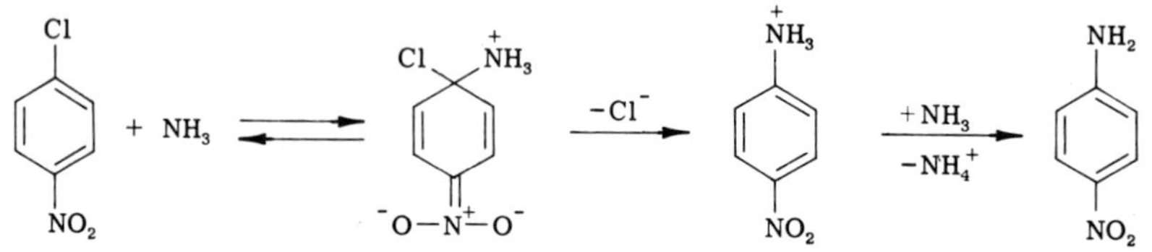

The addition product is rapidly transformed into the ammonium salt (with recovery of the nucleus aromaticity), and then affords the free amine on reaction with ammonia.

Opposing the synchronous S_N2 mechanism is the much higher mobility

[336] S. M. Shein, L. A. Kozorez, and N. N. Vorozhtsov, Jr., *Kinetika i Kataliz* **5**, 732 (1964); *Chem. Abstr.* **61**, 13163 (1964).

[337] N. N. Vorozhtsov, Jr. and V. A. Kobelev, *J. Gen. Chem. USSR* **9**, 1465 (1939); *Chem. Abstr.* **34**, 2688 (1940).

[338] M. Sprung, *J. Am. Chem. Soc.* **52**, 1656 (1930).

[339] N. N. Vorozhtsov, Jr. and V. A. Kobelev, *J. Gen. Chem. USSR* **9**, 1047 (1939); *Chem. Abstr.* **33**, 8581 (1939).

[340] N. N. Vorozhtsov, Jr. and V. A. Kobelev, *J. Gen. Chem. USSR* **9**, 1515 (1939); *Chem. Abstr.* **34**, 2688 (1940).

[341] J. F. Bunnett and R. E. Zahler, *Chem. Rev.* **49**, 273 (1951); C. F. Bernasconi and H. Zollinger, *Helv. Chim. Acta* **49**, 103 (1966); **50**, 3 (1967).

of a fluorine atom on an aromatic nucleus compared with that of chlorine. For example, the action of ammonia on m-chlorofluorobenzene afforded m-chloroaniline, and analogous treatment of pentachlorofluorobenzene gave rise to pentachloroaniline.[342]

In the aliphatic series, where the reaction proceeds by a synchronous mechanism and thus depends on the strength of the bond between the halogen and carbon atoms, the fluoro compounds react with nucleophilic agents much more slowly compared with the chloro derivatives.

2. Kinetics and Mechanism of the Reaction in the Presence of Catalysts

Chlorobenzene, as well as 1-chloronaphthalene, 1-chloronaphthalene-4-sulfonic acid, and p-chloroaniline, in the absence of the compounds of copper do not enter into the reaction with aqueous ammonia when autoclaved at 235°. In the presence of the compounds of copper (cuprous compounds are preferred) all the above substances, and also m-nitrochlorobenzene, smoothly afford the corresponding amines when heated at 200° in aqueous ammonia solution. Studies of the kinetics of these reactions[333,337,343] have revealed that the rate of reaction is directly proportional to the concentrations of both copper and the chloro derivative, and, unlike the rate of the noncatalytic reaction of nitrochlorobenzene with ammonia, does not depend on the concentration of ammonia. Hence it may be assumed that the reaction is a two-stage one, and that the first stage is the formation of the addition product of the catalyst and the chloro compound.

$$ArCl + Cu(NH_3)_2^+ \rightarrow ArCl \cdot Cu(NH_3)_2^+$$

This stage is the slowest and the rate-limiting one. In this complex cation chlorine is mobile enough, and the intermediate rapidly reacts with ammonia, hydroxyl ion, and with the aromatic amine according to the following scheme:

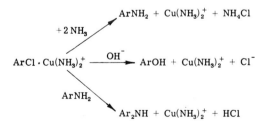

[342] N. N. Vorozhtsov, Jr., G. G. Yacobson, and T. D. Rubina, *Dokl. Akad. Nauk SSSR* **134**, 821 (1960); *Chem. Abstr.* **55**, 6415 (1961).

[343] N. N. Vorozhtsov, Jr. and V. A. Kobelev, *J. Gen. Chem. USSR* **9**, 1569 (1939); *Chem. Abstr.* **34**, 2688 (1940).

to afford the amine, the phenol, and the diarylamine (and regenerate the catalyst).

The rate of the overall process does not depend on the concentration of ammonia, but the proportion of each reaction product ($ArNH_2$, $ArOH$, and Ar_2NH) is determined by the ratio of the concentrations of ammonia, hydroxyl ions, and the aromatic amine. Specifically, the following equation has been experimentally proved valid for the reaction of chlorobenzene with ammonia:

$$\frac{[C_6H_5NH_2]}{[C_6H_5OH]} = K\frac{[NH_3]}{[OH^-]}$$

In agreement with the equation, the formation of phenol decreases with increasing concentration of ammonia (due to increase of the $[NH_3]/[OH^-]$ ratio). The activation energy of the reaction of chlorobenzene with ammonia in the presence of $Cu(NH_3)_2^+$ is about 17 kcal/mole.

The three isomeric chlorofluorobenzenes smoothly react with ammonia in the presence of the compounds of cuprous oxide to afford the corresponding fluoroanilines.[344] This selective activation of the chlorine atom suggests that the diamminecuprous cation $Cu(NH_3)_2^+$ reacts directly with the halogen atom.

It is possible that the diamminecuprous cation adds coordinatively to the unshared electron pair of the chlorine atom. In the complex

$$C_6H_5—\overset{\delta^+}{\underset{..}{Cl}}: \rightarrow Cu(NH_3)_2^+$$

the halogen atom gains a positive charge, and its conjugation with the nucleus weakens, along with an increasing inductive effect. This facilitates the addition of ammonia (and of other nucleophilic agents) to the carbon atom that bears the halogen substituent, and the subsequent fission of halogen. Obviously, the ease of the addition of cuprous ion to a halogen atom must be inversely related to the electronegativity of the halogen. For this reason fluorobenzene[344] fails to react with ammonia in the presence of diamminecuprous cation, and the chlorine atoms are replaced selectively in fluorochlorobenzenes. In p-chlorobromobenzene, the bromine atom can be substituted selectively, without touching the chlorine atom.[345]

Hence, the mobility of the halogen atom in the catalytic substitution of an amino group for halogen falls into the following sequence: $F \ll Cl < Br$,[344] contrary to the $F > Cl$ sequence observed in the noncatalytic reaction.[342]

[344] N. N. Vorozhtsov, Jr., G. G. Yacobson, and T. D. Rubina, *Dokl. Akad. Nauk SSSR* **127**, 1225 (1959); *Chem. Abstr.* **54**, 349 (1960).

[345] Dow, *USP* 1,729,775; 1,935,515.

C. MECHANISM OF THE BUCHERER REACTION: STRUCTURE OF BISULFITE COMPOUNDS

New and interesting results have been obtained during the studies of the naphthol bisulfite derivatives, and they have completely changed previous concepts concerning their structure. All the reactions and the IR spectrum (well-resolved bands of the 1-tetralone carbonyl group) strongly suggest that the product of the reaction of bisulfite with 1-naphthol is 1-tetralone-3-sulfonic acid.[346] The formation of this product obviously occurs because of the addition of bisulfite to the double bond of the 1-naphthol keto form, e.g.,

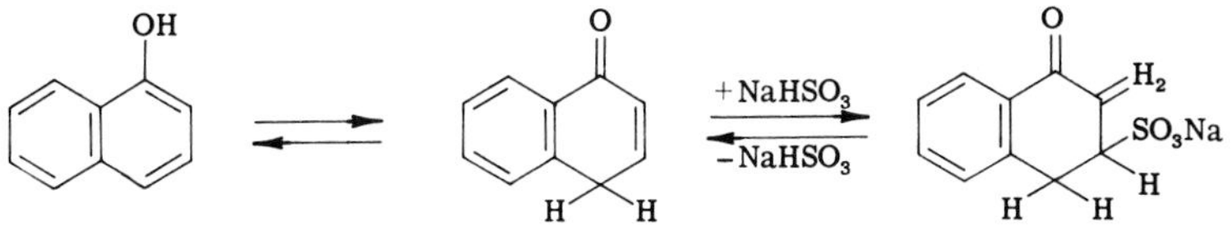

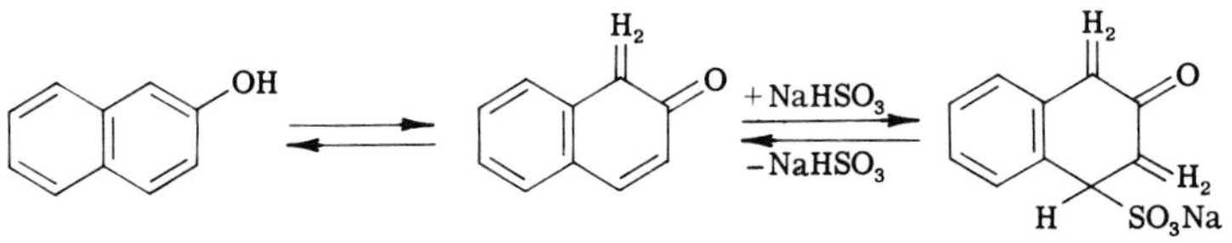

The addition at the 3-position, rather than at the 4-position, is due to the shift of electrons inducing (due to the presence of the C—O group) a positive charge (decrease of electron density) at carbon atom 3, which facilitates the addition of HSO_3^- anion at this point. Similarly, bisulfite adds to 2-naphthol to give 2-tetralone-4-sulfonic acid.

A tetralone structure had been proposed earlier for the bisulfite derivative of 1-nitroso-2-naphthol.[347] The product of bisulfite addition to 1-anthrol is also a ketosulfonic acid.[348]

The isolation of tetralonesulfonic acids and of their derivatives after the interaction of naphthols and related compounds with bisulfite led the authors of these interesting studies to the conclusion that the same tetralone derivatives are intermediates of the Bucherer reaction—replacement

[346] S. V. Bogdanov and N. N. Karandasheva, *Zh. Obshch. Khim.* **26**, 3365 (1956); *Chem. Abstr.* **51**, 9544 (1957); A. Rieche and H. Seeboth, *Ann.* **638**, 43 (1960); **671**, 70 and 77 (1964); H. Seeboth, *Angew. Chem.* **79**, 329 (1967).

[347] S. V. Bogdanov, *J. Gen. Chem. USSR* **2**, 9 (1932); *Chem. Abstr.* **26**, 5297 (1932).

[348] S. V. Bogdanov and M. V. Gorelik, *Zh. Obshch. Khim.* **29**, 136 (1959); *Chem. Abstr.* **53**, 21899 (1959).

of a hydroxy group with an amino group which occurs on heating of naphthols with aqueous ammonia in the presence of bisulfites (and also the reverse reaction). These authors believe that the replacement of a hydroxy group with an amino group proceeds by transformation of keto-sulfonic acids into ketimidesulfonic acids which subsequently eliminate bisulfite molecules to afford the amines. In the reverse reaction, the replacement of an amino by a hydroxy group proceeds via hydrolysis of the previously formed ketimidesulfonic acids to tetralonesulfonic acids, which subsequently eliminate bisulfite to give naphthols.

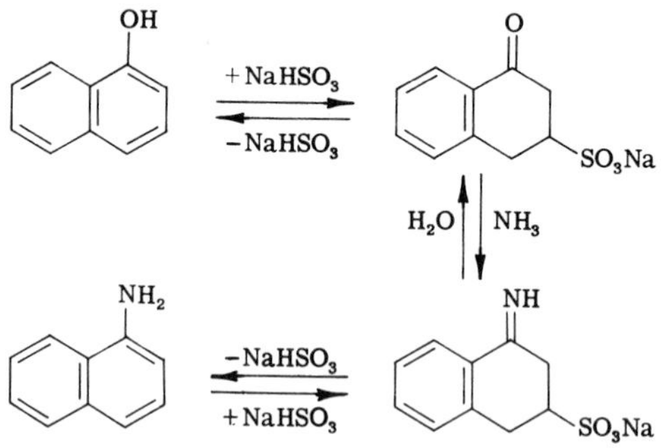

In our opinion, the mechanism is not yet finally established. It is known that the isolation of a compound from the reaction mixture is not a de-cisive argument that the compound is the intermediate product. The weak point of the mechanism seems to be the transformation of ketone-sulfonic acid into ketimidesulfonic acid. Reactions of this type usually take place under anhydrous conditions, and sometimes in the presence of dehydrating agents. Contrary to this, the Bucherer reaction takes place in an aqueous medium. The extreme ease of replacement of the hydroxy group with an amino group in *gem*-hydroxysulfonic acids—the bisulfite derivatives of aldehydes and ketones—is also well known.

Hence, it seems quite reasonable that along with the above more stable bisulfite addition products to the carbon–carbon double bond, the Bucherer reaction also involves, in accord with the earlier concept,[349] the formation of the less stable and more reactive addition products to the carbonyl (or ketimido) group that contain a reactive hydroxy or amino group. It may also be that another bisulfite molecule adds to tetralone-sulfonic acid, affording a reactive and unstable bis disulfite compound. Hence, the reaction of 2-naphthol with bisulfite and ammonia leading to

[349] *CSD* I, p. 80; N. N. Woroshzow, "Grundlagen der Synthese von Zwischen-produkten und Farbstoffen," p. 489. Akademie Verlag, Berlin, 1966.

2-naphthylamine can proceed by one of the two following alternative pathways:

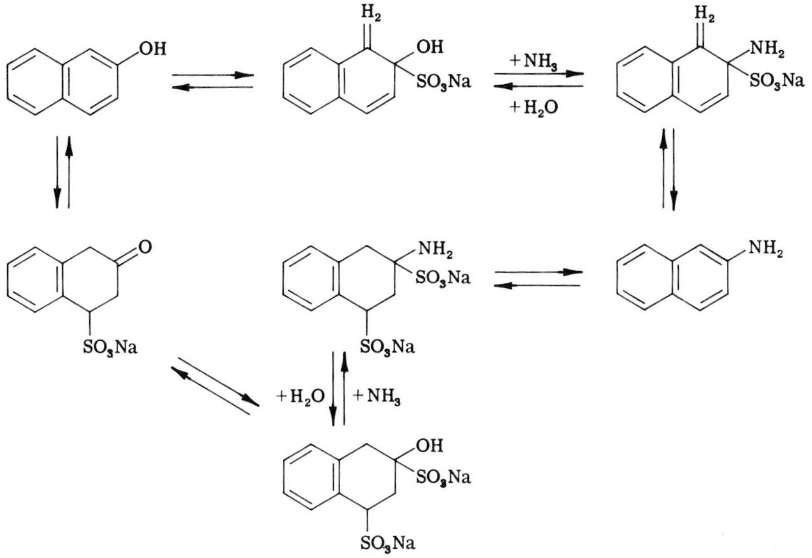

The stable compounds isolated from the reaction mixture are 2-naphthol, tetralonesulfonic acid, and the final product, 2-naphthylamine. However, the reactive compounds that react, in fact, with ammonia affording the amines may be the hydroxysulfonic acid of dihydronaphthalene or tetralol disulfonic acid, which contain hydroxy and sulfo groups in the *gem* position.

It is well known that studies of the reaction mechanism often reveal the participation of very unstable intermediates (such as the above-mentioned bis salts of hydrazo compounds in the benzidine rearrangement; see Section IV,A,4).

The data on the kinetics of the Bucherer reaction are few. The kinetic data obtained by investigation of the reaction of 1-naphthol-5-sulfonic acid with ammonia and ammonium sulfite show that the reaction rate is proportional to the concentrations of hydroxy compound and of sulfite and ammonium ions. The rate of reaction is independent of the ammonia concentration, but by doubling the sulfite ion concentration the rate of reaction increases fourfold.[350] Lack of dependence on ammonia concentration and proportionality to the second power of sulfite concentration suggest that in this case the reaction involves addition of two sulfite

---

[350] *CSD I*, p. 81.

ions to the molecule of hydroxy compound. The rate of formation of this adduct is the slowest stage of the reaction and is followed by a faster reaction with ammonia. This kinetic evidence strongly supports the assumption that tetralol disulfonic acids are intermediates in the Bucherer reaction.

Contrary to the data for 1-naphthol-5-sulfonic acid, the rate of formation of 2-naphthylamine from 2-naphthol is proportional to the first power of the concentrations of the hydroxy compound and of the bisulfite ion (and as in the previous case does not depend on the concentration of ammonia[351]). This result confirms that the first stage of the reaction is the addition of bisulfite ion to 2-naphthol.

It may well be found, however, that the difference between the kinetics of the two reactions is in fact due to different rates of some stages of the reaction rather than to their different mechanisms. Thus, for the mechanism of the Bucherer reaction to be firmly established, further studies of the kinetics and equilibria involved need to be carried out.

V. Hydroxylation

A. Synthesis of Hydroxy Compounds from Sulfonic Acids

Alkaline fusion of a benzenesulfonic acid salt with the sulfo group at a ^{14}C-labeled carbon atom revealed that the hydroxyl in the phenol formed is attached to the same carbon atom (more than 97%). Hence, the aryne mechanism of nucleophilic substitution does not play any role in this reaction. This is also confirmed by the fact that only p-cresol is obtained from p-toluenesulfonic acid.[352]

The action of $Na^{18}OH$ or $K^{18}OH$ upon a salt of benzenesulfonic acid results in incorporation of ^{18}O into the phenol hydroxyl. Thus, the phenol oxygen is supplied by alkali rather than by the sulfo group.[352,353]

Recently results have been published for the alkaline fusion of 1,2- and 1,4-benzenedisulfonic acids and of o- and p-phenolsulfonic acids, thoroughly purified from the isomers. It appears that the previously reported formation of resorcinol[354] from these compounds is erroneous and was probably due to the admixture of m-isomers in the starting compounds.[355]

---

[351] V. V. Kozlov and I. K. Veselovskaya, Zh. Obshch. Khim. **28**, 3333 (1958); Chem. Abstr. **53**, 14063 (1959).

[352] S. Oae, N. Furukawa, M. Kise and M. Kowanishi, Bull. Chem. Soc. Japan **39**, 1212 (1966); Chem. Abstr. **65**, 8693 (1966).

[353] I. A. Makolkin, Acta Physicochim. URSS **16**, 88 (1942).

[354] H. E. Fierz-David and G. Stamm, Helv. Chim. Acta **25**, 364 (1942).

[355] L. R. Buzbee, J. Org. Chem. **31**, 3289 (1966).

The o-disulfonic acid of benzene affords o-phenolsulfonic acid, pyrocatechol, and some phenol on alkaline fusion. The p-disulfonic acid of benzene affords only p-phenolsulfonic acid (and phenol as by-product). No hydroquinone could be obtained from the p-disulfonic acid of benzene or from p-phenolsulfonic acid. p-Phenolsulfonic acid is relatively stable under the alkaline fusion conditions and is rather slowly converted into products other than hydroquinone. This may not be due to subsequent reactions of the hydroquinone formed—the latter is almost completely stable under the alkaline fusion conditions.[355]

Good yields of a number of hydroxy derivatives of benzene and naphthalene have been obtained when the reaction is performed in aqueous alkali under pressure. The reaction with benzene and naphthalene monosulfonic acids proceeds at a rate satisfactory for industrial application at about 350° at ~200 atm.[356]

Studies of the kinetics of the reactions of benzenesulfonic acid and of a number of naphthalenesulfonic acids with aqueous sodium hydroxide (autoclaved under pressure) revealed that the order of reaction is 2 for the majority of sulfonic acids, and is close to 3 in the cases of benzenesulfonic acid and of 2-naphthol-6- and 7-sulfonic acids (first order for the sulfonic acid and second order for the alkali).

The reaction kinetics suggest that the alkaline fusion is a two-stage reaction. The first stage is the addition of hydroxyl ion to sulfonic salt anion; this reversible reaction results in a doubly charged anion.

$$ArSO_3^- + OH^- \rightleftarrows (ArSO_3 \cdot OH)^{2-}$$

The addition product reacts with another OH^- ion to give phenolate ion, sulfite ion, and water.

$$(ArSO_3 \cdot OH)^{2-} + OH^- \rightarrow ArO^- + SO_3^{2-} + H_2O$$

The reaction is apparently of the second order when the slower, rate-limiting stage is addition of the first hydroxyl to sulfonic acid anion. When the slower stage is the transformation of the addition product to phenolate ion, the reaction apparently becomes third order. The equilibrium concentration of the addition product is in fact equal to

$$[(ArSO_3 \cdot OH)^{2-}] = K[ArSO_3^-][OH^-]$$

and the rate of phenol formation

$$d[ArO^-]/dt = k[(ArSO_3 \cdot OH)^{2-}][OH^-]$$
$$= kK[ArSO_3^-][OH^-]^2$$

[356] N. N. Vorozhtsov, Jr., *Org. Chem. Ind. USSR* **6**, 422 (1939); *Chem. Abstr.* **34**, 2606 (1940); *Khim. Prom.* No. 1, 15 (1957); *Chem. Abstr.* **51**, 11019 (1957); R. N. Shreve and F. R. Lloyd, *Ind. Eng. Chem.* **42**, 811 (1950).

The possible structure of the intermediate for benzenesulfonic acid, for example, is as follows:

$$\text{HO} \quad \text{SO}_3^-$$

The participation of two negatively charged ions in the formation of an intermediate explains why the reaction proceeds only at high temperatures. The structure of the intermediate explains the high stability of p-phenolsulfonic acid to alkaline fusion and the impossibility of hydroquinone formation.[355] In this case the formation of the intermediate would result in a negative charge on the carbon atom that bears the negatively charged oxygen. Obviously, the intermediate must be formed with great difficulty.

The rate of the reaction of the 1-isomer of naphthalenesulfonic acid is somewhat greater (at 300°, about 3 times greater) than that of the other isomer. Introduction of another sulfonic group into the sulfonic acid molecule remarkably (by a factor of 10–30) increases the rate of reaction. Naphtholsulfonic acids react much more slowly compared with not only the disulfonic acids, but also with the corresponding monosulfonic acids. For this reason, it is possible to obtain naphtholsulfonic acids as the major reaction products by alkaline fusion of disulfonic acids (e.g., of 1,5- and 2,7-naphtholsulfonic acids). Introduction of the methyl group (in the case of 2-methyl-6-naphthalenesulfonic acid) to a certain extent also decreases the rate of reaction (about 3 times at 300°).

The activation energies of all the alkaline fusion reactions are relatively high and vary between 34.2 kcal/mole (for 2-methylnaphthalene-6-sulfonic acid) and 47 kcal/mole (for benzenesulfonic acid).[356,357]

The fusion of 2-naphthalenesulfonic acid, as noted earlier, led to formation of minor amounts of naphthalene, which was explained by the hydrolytic side reaction affording naphthalene and sodium sulfate that takes place along with the major substitution of hydroxyl for the sulfo group. However, the determination of the amounts of sulfite and sulfate ions showed that no sulfate ion was formed, whereas a quantitative yield of sulfite ion ($\geqslant 99.5\%$) was obtained. The amount of naphthalene increases while the amount of naphthol decreases on more prolonged treatment of sulfonic acid with aqueous sodium hydroxide. Large amounts of naphthalene (up to 20% of the theoretical) are obtained when 2-naph-

[357] N. N. Vorozhtsov, Jr. and S. M. Shein, *Ukr. Khim. Zh.* **24**, 208 and 213 (1958); *Chem. Abstr.* **52**, 20075 (1958); *Ukr. Khim. Zh.* **26**, 341 (1960); *Chem. Abstr.* **55**, 3530 (1961); S. M. Shein and N. N. Vorozhtsov, Jr., *Ukr. Khim. Zh.* **24**, 643 and 757 (1958); *Chem. Abstr.* **53**, 12252 and 18921 (1959).

thol is heated with sodium hydroxide solution at 395–400°. *o*-Toluic and *o*-tolylpropionic acids are formed, among other naphthol degradation products, particularly, liquid hydrocarbons. Obviously, naphthalene and the other by-products of alkaline fusion of 2-naphthalenesulfonic acid are formed by redox transformation of 2-naphthol under the reaction conditions.[358]

2-Naphthol of higher purity is obtained, as claimed in a patent, when the sodium salt of 2-naphthalenesulfonic acid is mixed with a less than 10% excess of sodium hydroxide at 255–275° and the mixture is then carefully heated to 310–350°.[359]

To obtain hydroxyanthraquinones from the corresponding sulfonic acids, a dilute (3–6%) solution of sodium hydroxide at ~150° can be applied instead of the usual milk of lime. The substitution of hydroxyls for the sulfonic groupings proceeds without the introduction of additional hydroxy groups under the conditions. The method may be applied to obtain 2,6-dihydroxyanthraquinone or its mixture with the 2,7-isomer.[360]

Interest in increasing the scale of production of the most important aromatic hydroxy compounds (phenol, resorcinol, 2-naphthol)—not induced, however, by the demands of the dye industry—stimulated research aimed at increasing the productivity of the alkaline fusion reactors, particularly on the elaboration of continuous-action reactors. Preparation of phenol and 2-naphthol in tube reactors at high pressure (200 atm) with aqueous sodium hydroxide solutions has been suggested.[356]

Also suggested were continuous processes of alkaline fusion of benzenesulfonic acid in continuous-action reactors that work at atmospheric pressure with anhydrous sodium hydroxide.[361] A continuous-action reactor with a 6000 rpm stirrer has been proposed for the production of resorcinol by reaction of melted sodium hydroxide with anhydrous 1,3-benzenedisulfonic acid salt in a stream of nitrogen heated to 500°.[362]

B. Synthesis of Hydroxy Compounds from Chloro Compounds

Studies of the kinetics of the reaction of chlorobenzene with diluted (10% and less) aqueous solutions of sodium and potassium hydroxides at

[358] F. Hofmann, L. Boente, W. Steck, and J. Amende, *Naturwissenschaften* **20**, 403 (1932); N. N. Vorozhtsov, Jr. and S. M. Shein, *Ukr. Khim. Zh.* **26**, 490 (1960); *Chem. Abstr.* **55**, 8361 (1961).

[359] CIBA, *FP* 1,326,175.

[360] S. M. Shein, V. A. Ignatov, and N. N. Vorozhtsov, Jr., *Zh. Prikl. Khim.* **39**, 1867 (1966); *Chem. Abstr.* **66**, 19807 (1967); *RP* 159,861; *Chem. Abstr.* **60**, 11964 (1964).

[361] B. E. Berkman, "Sulfonation and Alkali Fusion in Industrial Organic Syntheses," p. 88. State Chem. Publ. House, Moscow, 1960.

[362] AAP, *FP* 1,319,454.

$\sim 300°$ have revealed, contrary to earlier statements,[363] that the substitution of hydroxyl for the chlorine atom is a usual bimolecular reaction of the S_N2 type.[364] Under these reaction conditions, the conversion of chlorobenzene to phenol proceeds extremely smoothly. At present it is not yet clear whether the reaction proceeds via intermediate addition of hydroxyl ion to chlorobenzene (as is the case with many nucleophilic substitution reactions of chloronitro compounds) or whether it goes by the synchronous mechanism accepted in the aliphatic series.

A by-product when there is a deficiency of alkali or at short reaction periods is diphenyl ether $(C_6H_5)_2O$. Contrary to some statements,[363] its alkaline hydrolysis to phenol is irreversible (it also proceeds by a bimolecular mechanism):

$$(C_6H_5)_2O + 2NaOH \rightarrow 2C_6H_5ONa + H_2O$$

In the aqueous alkaline solution, sodium phenolate affords no diphenyl ether. The apparent cessation of new diphenyl ether formation when it is previously added to the reaction mixture is because the presence of the compound in an amount equal to 15–20% of that of chlorobenzene from the very beginning of the reaction results in consumption of diphenyl ether due to hydrolysis approximately equal to its accumulation.[364]

At increased concentrations of alkali (15–20%) and at higher temperatures (340°) the reaction proceeds by another mechanism, the so-called aryne mechanism, as shown by experiments with 1-^{14}C-chlorobenzene. The carbanion formed by the action of hydroxyl ion upon chlorobenzene eliminates chlorine ion and affords dehydrobenzene, which adds a molecule of water and gives phenol:

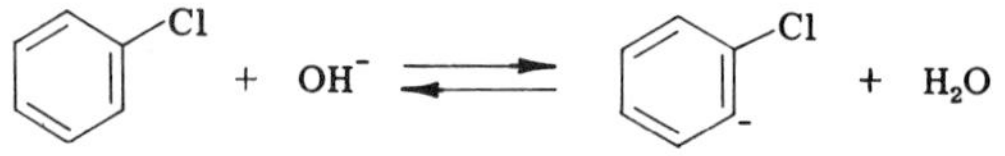

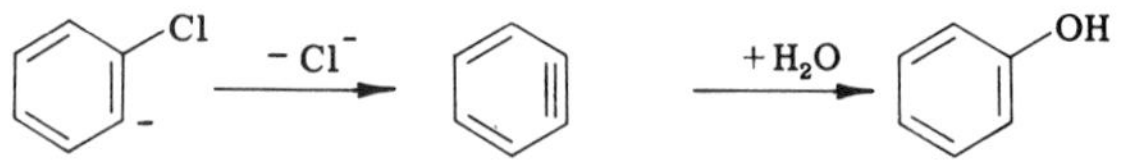

Simultaneously, the usual substitution takes place (in $4N$ NaOH at

[363] W. J. Hale and E. C. Britton, *Ind. Eng. Chem.* **20**, 114 (1928).

[364] N. N. Woroshzow, "Grundlagen der Synthese von Zwischenprodukten und Farbstoffen," pp. 421 and 422. Akademie Verlag, Berlin, 1966.

$340°$, 16%).[365] The intermediate formation of dehydrobenzene also explains the fact that a mixture of cresols with m-cresol predominating is formed when individual chlorotoluene isomers are treated with sodium hydroxide $(4\,N)$.[366]

The formation of the by-products of chlorobenzene hydrolysis, which are, besides diphenyl ether, o- and p-hydroxybiphenyls (and their phenyl ethers) and 2,6-diphenylphenol, is due to the addition of dehydrobenzene to the atoms of phenolate ion taking part in the negative charge distribution (the atom of oxygen and the o- and p-carbon atoms) :[367]

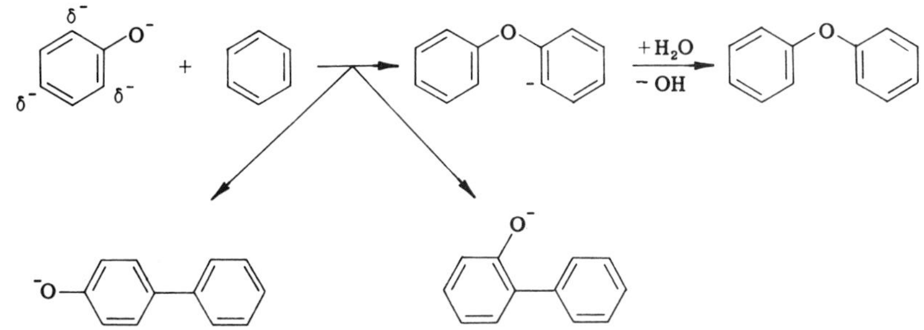

The subsequent interaction of dehydrobenzene with o- and p-hydroxybiphenyl anions results in the other above-mentioned products.

Heating 1- or 2-chloronaphthalene with an aqueous $(0.95\,N)$ solution of sodium hydroxide results in a mixture of both the naphthol isomers (containing 40% of the 2-isomer when starting with 1-chloronaphthalene, and 20% of 1-naphthol when starting with 2-chloronaphthalene). Hence, here again the bimolecular reaction is complicated by the elimination leading to intermediate dehydronaphthalene. The different extent of isomerization must be due to the different ratio of the rates of the elimination and of the direct substitution of hydroxyl group for chlorine atom.

Using copper or its compounds as catalysts, it is possible to convert chloronaphthalene to the corresponding naphthol without the side formation of the other isomer.[368]

The polychlorobenzene derivatives by treatment with alkali (usually in ethanolic solution) may be converted to chloro derivatives of phenol— from monochloro- to pentachlorophenol. The reaction of the halo com-

[365] A. T. Bottini and J. D. Roberts, *J. Am. Chem. Soc.* **79**, 1458 (1957); A. Lüttringhaus and D. Ambros, *Ber.* **89**, 463 (1956).

[366] R. N. Shreve and C. J. Marsel, *Ind. Eng. Chem.* **38**, 254 (1946).

[367] R. Huisgen and J. Sauer, *Angew. Chem.* **72**, 91 (1960).

[368] S. M. Shein, V. A. Ignatov, V. V. Pupin, I. K. Korobeinicheva, and E. D. Krivousova, *Izv. Sibirsk. Otd. Akad. Nauk SSSR.* No. 12, 67 (1967).

pounds with alkali in a solution of alcohols involves two stages: the ether of phenol (and of the corresponding alcohol) is formed initially and subsequently split with metal alcoholate to afford phenolate and the ether,[369] e.g.,

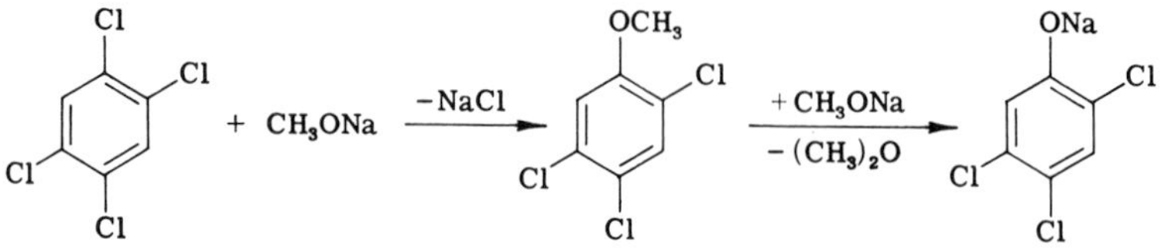

It should be mentioned that the alkali in alcohol solutions is mainly in the form of the alcoholate.[370] It was proved that the splitting of phenol ethers and of the derivatives thereof proceeds by an S_N2 mechanism with cleavage of the bond between alkyl and oxygen.[371] Increasing the number of chlorine atoms in the benzene molecule increases the rate of the reaction with sodium methylate, mainly due to a decrease of the activation energy (from 34–36 kcal/mole in hexachlorobenzene).[372]

Both 1- and 2-chloronaphthalenes react with sodium methylate in the same manner as do the derivatives of benzene. The formation of methoxynaphthalenes is followed by their conversion to naphthols.[373]

Preparation of resorcinol from m-dichlorobenzene (and from m-chlorobromobenzene) by heating at 250–300° in the presence of copper compounds with metal fluoride solutions, e.g., with potassium fluoride, has been suggested.[374]

C. SYNTHESIS OF HYDROXY COMPOUNDS
   VIA ISOPROPYL DERIVATIVES

Rather recently, a new method of preparation of phenol via cumene (isopropylbenzene) has been proposed and it is now applied in industry

[369] P. W. de Lange Rec. Trav. Chim. 38, 101 (1919); S. M. Shein and V. A. Ignatov, Zh. Obshch. Khim. 32, 3220 (1962); Chem. Abstr. 58, 11183 (1963).

[370] E. F. Caldin and G. Long, J. Chem. Soc. p. 3737 (1954); W. C. Woodland, R. B. Carlin, and J. C. Warner, J. Am. Chem. Soc. 77, 340 (1955).

[371] S. M. Shein and V. A. Ignatov, Zh. Obshch. Khim. 32, 3220 and 3223 (1962); Chem. Abstr. 58, 11183 (1963); Zh. Obshch. Khim. 33, 2667 (1963); Chem. Abstr. 60, 1557 (1964).

[372] S. M. Shein and V. A. Ignatov, Zh. Organ. Khim. 2, 1070 (1966); Chem. Abstr. 65, 15177 (1966).

[373] S. M. Shein and V. A. Ignatov, Zh. Organ. Khim. 2, 704 (1966); Chem. Abstr. 65, 8702 (1966).

[374] N. N. Vorozhtsov, Jr., T. D. Rubina, and G. G. Yacobson, RP 144,489; Chem. Abstr. 57, 12384 (1962).

along with those starting with benzenesulfonic acid and with chlorobenzene. The method simultaneously affords acetone.

The first plant producing phenol and acetone from cumene was in-
stalled in the USSR in 1949.[375] In the U. S., this method of phenol production was first applied in 1954. The apparent overwhelming advantages
of the new process led to almost all the development of phenol production
in the U. S. being based on the cumene method. In 1965, more phenol was
produced via cumene than by any other method (43% of the output of
synthetic phenol in the U. S.), and it is believed that the contribution of
this method to total phenol output must become still greater in spite of
the elaboration of other novel methods.[376]

Cumene needed for phenol production is obtained by reaction of benzene with propylene (propane-containing) in the presence of aluminum
chloride in the liquid phase or, more often, in the vapor phase in the
presence of a catalyst containing phosphoric acid:

$$C_6H_6 + CH_3CH{=}CH_2 \xrightarrow[(H_3PO_4)]{} C_6H_5CH(CH_3)_2$$

The cumene obtained is separated from excess benzene and purified by
rectification (99.8% purity). Pure cumene is oxidized by air, usually in
the presence of alkali at 130° and at slightly elevated pressure. The oxidation results in the relatively stable hydroperoxide.

$$C_6H_5CH(CH_3)_2 + O_2 \rightarrow C_6H_5C(CH_3)_2(OOH)$$

The hydroperoxide is formed by a chain oxidation reaction. The chain
initiation stage is probably the formation of $C_6H_5\overset{\cdot}{C}(CH_3)_2$ from cumene
after the elimination of a hydrogen atom by some hydrogen acceptor.
The radical reacts with an oxygen molecule to give hydroperoxide radical,
which subsequently gives rise to hydroperoxide and to the starting radical
after reaction with another cumene molecule:

$$C_6H_5CH(CH_3)_2 \rightarrow C_6H_5\overset{\cdot}{C}(CH_3)_2 \overset{O_2}{\rightarrow} C_6H_5{-}\underset{|}{\overset{\overset{\displaystyle OO\cdot}{|}}{C}}{-}(CH_3)_2 \xrightarrow{+C_6H_5CH(CH_3)_2}$$

$$C_6H_5{-}\underset{|}{\overset{\overset{\displaystyle OOH}{|}}{C}}(CH_3)_2 + C_6H_5\overset{\cdot}{C}(CH_3)_2$$

Cumene hydroperoxide is a relatively stable compound which may be
stored unchanged for several years at room temperature. It may be distilled without decomposition *in vacuo* at 5 mm Hg (or less) at about 90°.

[375] B. D. Kruzhalov and B. I. Golovanenko, "Combined Synthesis of Phenol and
Acetone." State Chem. Publ. House, Moscow, 1963.
[376] H. Hock and H. Kropf, *Angew. Chem.* **69**, 313 (1957); R. B. Stobaugh, *Hydrocarbon Process. Petrol. Refiner* **45**, No. 1, 143 (1966).

At the same time, the hydroperoxide rapidly and almost quantitatively decomposes in the presence of strong acids to give phenol and acetone:

$$C_6H_5-\overset{\overset{\displaystyle OOH}{|}}{C}(CH_3)_2 \xrightarrow{[H^+]} C_6H_5OH + (CH_3)_2CO$$

A mechanism of this reaction is proposed assuming that the rearrangement occurs in the initially formed cation with the positive charge on the oxygen atom:[377]

$$C_6H_5\overset{\overset{\displaystyle OOH}{|}}{\underset{\underset{\displaystyle CH_3}{|}}{C}}-CH_3 \xrightarrow[-H_2O]{+H^+} C_6H_5-\overset{\overset{\displaystyle O^+}{|}}{\underset{\underset{\displaystyle CH_3}{|}}{C}}-CH_3 + C_6H_5-O-\overset{+}{\underset{\underset{\displaystyle CH_3}{|}}{C}}-CH_3 \xrightarrow{+C_6H_5\overset{|}{C}(CH_3)_2}$$

$$C_6H_5OH + (CH_3)_2CO + C_6H_5-\overset{\overset{\displaystyle O^+}{|}}{C}(CH_3)_2$$

The carbonium ion formed by the rearrangement affords phenol and acetone on interaction with another hydroperoxide molecule and regenerates a radical with positively charged oxygen atom.

In industry, the oxidation of cumene is performed to a small extent of the conversion. The hydroperoxide-containing reaction mixture is decomposed with 10–25% sulfuric acid at 55–65°. After washing with water, the decomposition product contains 76% cumene and only 14% phenol and 8% acetone. Sometimes, highly concentrated hydroperoxide is obtained before the decomposition. The by-products of thermal hydroperoxide decomposition formed during its preparation are minor amounts of α-methylstyrene and acetophenone. The advantage of the method is the minimum consumption of reagents. To transform benzene into phenol, one needs propylene (which affords acetone) and air.

Similarly, substituted phenols such as nitrophenols[378] may be obtained, or p-cresol may be prepared from p-isopropyltoluene.[379] Polyhydroxybenzenes such as resorcinol, hydroquinone, or phloroglucinol can be obtained from polyisopropylbenzenes.[380]

2-Naphthol can be obtained from 2-isopropylnaphthalene.[381]

[377] M. Kharasch, A. Fono, and W. Nudenberg, J. Org. Chem. 15, 748 (1950).

[378] Hercules Powder Co., USP 2,774,796.

[379] L. F. Marek, Ind. Eng. Chem. 43, 1992 (1951); 44, 2046 (1952).

[380] Hooker Electrochemical Co., BP 751,598; Distillers Co., 775,813; 775,896; ICI, FP 1,111,244; BP 754,864; F. Seidel, M. Schulze, and H. Baltz, J. Prakt. Chem. [4] 3, 278 (1956).

[381] Distillers Co. Ltd., DBP 866,941; 871,011; BP 654,035; CCC, USP 2,727,927.

D. SYNTHESIS OF HYDROXY COMPOUNDS FROM AROMATIC CARBOXYLIC ACIDS

A new and interesting method of phenol preparation starting with benzoic acid has been elaborated. A number of other hydroxy compounds can also be prepared from different aromatic carboxylic acids. It was known earlier[382] that heating cupric benzoate leads to a mixture of products containing phenol, salicylic acid, and the phenyl ester of benzoic acid.

Detailed investigation of the thermal conversion of the copper salt of benzoic acid resulted in elucidation of the mechanisms involved, and optimum conditions were found for the preparation of the products desired. For example, cupric benzoate when heated in inert organic solvents at 250–260° is involved in a rapid oxidation of the aromatic nucleus by cupric ions. The reaction leading to salicylic acid proceeds according to the following equation:

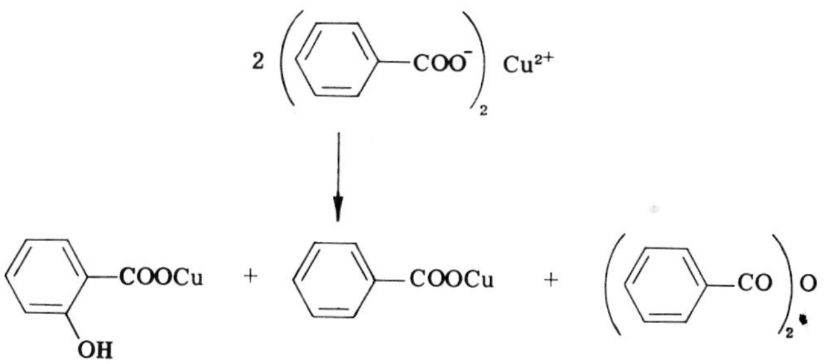

Aliphatic hydrocarbons, mixtures of hydrocarbons (for example, mineral oil), fluoro hydrocarbons, cyclohexane, etc., may be used as solvents. Cyclohexane is volatile, and the reaction in it must be performed under pressure, but it is easier to remove it from the products compared with the high-boiling solvents.

The reaction proceeds in several stages. It is probable that cyclohexadienyl radical is initially formed by transfer of an electron from an oxygen atom to a copper atom. The radical can subsequently react with benzoic acid to give cuprous salts of O-benzoylsalicylic and of benzoic acids, and also free benzoic acid. The intermediate formation of the salt of O-benzoylsalicylic acid is proved by its isolation from the reaction mixture. Subsequently, benzoic acid reacts with the cuprous salt of benzoylsalicylic acid, affording the salt of salicylic acid and benzoic anhydride (the latter was also found among the reaction products):

[382] E. M. Bamdas and M. M. Shemyakin, *Zh. Obshch. Khim.* **18**, 324 (1948); *Chem. Abstr.* **43**, 124 (1949).

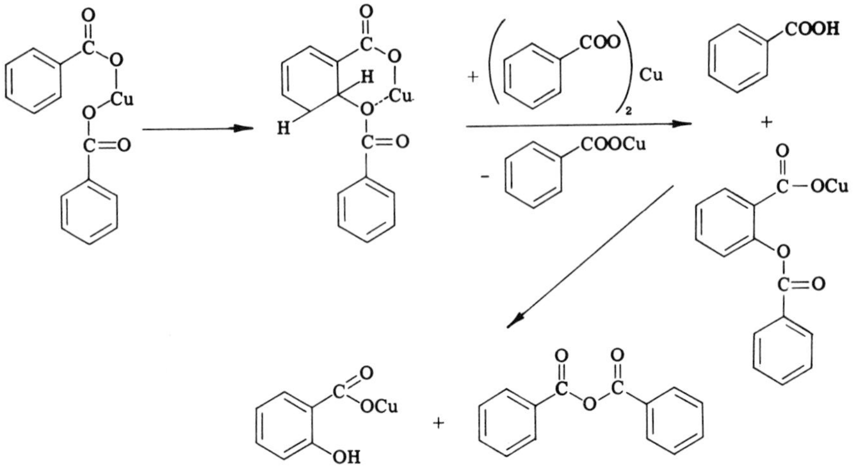

The extent of conversion to salicylic acid can be increased by adding excess basic cupric carbonate, which transforms benzoic acid formed in the course of the reaction to the starting cupric salt. Water eliminated after salt formation hydrolyzes the benzoic anhydride. The extent of the conversion can also be increased by bubbling air into the reaction mixture to oxidize the cuprous to cupric salts.

The mixture of acids isolated from the reaction contains up to 63% salicylic acid. To separate it from benzoic acid extraction with organic solvents after binding of salicylic acid into a complex compound with iron(III) has been suggested.

Similarly, other hydroxy carboxylic acids have been obtained from the homologs of benzoic acids and from some of its derivatives. The hydroxyl group enters only into the position ortho to the carboxyl (the content of isomeric hydroxy acids in salicylic acid if present is lower than 1%). A by-product is phenol, formed by decarboxylation.[383]

When aromatic compounds, such as toluene and other benzene homologs, or some substituted benzene derivatives (fluoro- and chlorobenzene, nitrobenzene, diphenyl ether) are used as solvents, the reaction sometimes proceeds mainly in another direction. The action of cupric benzoate upon a molecule of solvent results in substitution of a benzoyloxy group for a hydrogen atom of the solvent. A mixture is formed of isomeric benzoyloxy compounds where the meta isomer always prevails (in the presence of

[383] W. W. Kaeding and G. R. Collins, *J. Org. Chem.* **30**, 3750 (1965); Dow, *USP* 3,159,671; 3,337,616.

o-, *p*-, as well as of *m*-orientating substituents). The overall reaction follows the equation:

$$2(C_6H_5COO)_2Cu + C_6H_5R \rightarrow C_6H_5COOC_6H_4R + 2C_6H_5COOCu + C_6H_5COOH$$

The independence of the distribution of isomeric products of the nature of the substituents suggests a radical mechanism of the reaction.

The following mechanism, similar to that of salicylic acid formation discussed above, is proposed:

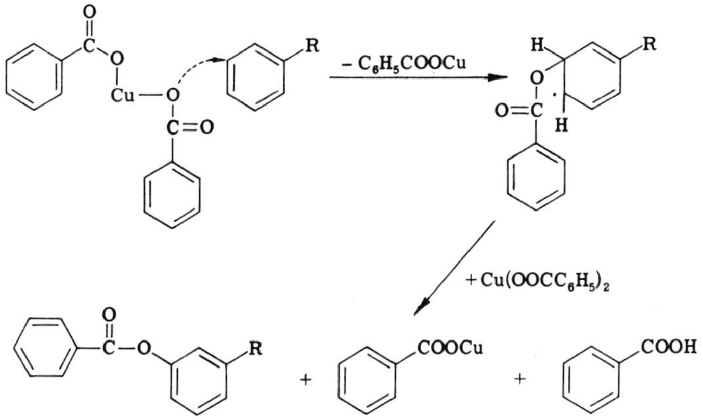

The yield of benzoyloxy compound is about 50% of theory. Salicylic acid and phenol are always formed as by-products.

In this reaction, the extent of the conversion of benzoic acid to the benzoyl derivative of the oxy compound can also be increased by adding cupric oxide and by bubbling air, which regenerates cupric benzoate from benzoic acid and cuprous benzoate. Bubbling of air makes it possible to use catalytic amounts of copper, and the overall reaction goes according to the equation:

$$C_6H_5COOH + C_6H_5R + \tfrac{1}{2}O_2 \xrightarrow{[Cu^{2+}]} C_6H_5COOC_6H_4R + H_2O$$

Hydrolysis of the benzoic acid derivative affords the substituted phenol.

In benzene homologs, the benzoyloxy group to some extent enters the side chain to give the derivatives of benzyl alcohol.[384]

The most interesting practical results are obtained when cupric salts of carboxylic acids are decomposed in proton-containing solvents. Under appropriate conditions, phenol appears as the major (and almost the

[384] W. W. Kaeding, H. V. Kerlinger, and G. R. Collins, *J. Org. Chem.* **30**, 3754 (1965).

only) product of the reaction. The hydroxyl group enters the position ortho to the carbon atom that formerly bore the carboxyl, as shown by experiments with benzoic acid labeled by ^{14}C at the benzene ring.[385] The same conclusion follows from the isomer ratio obtained with substituted benzoic acids. Water may be used as proton-containing solvent (under pressure above 200°).[386] However, the solvent most interesting practically is benzoic acid. The process is performed at 220–250° with bubbling air and steam. The reaction goes according to the following equation:

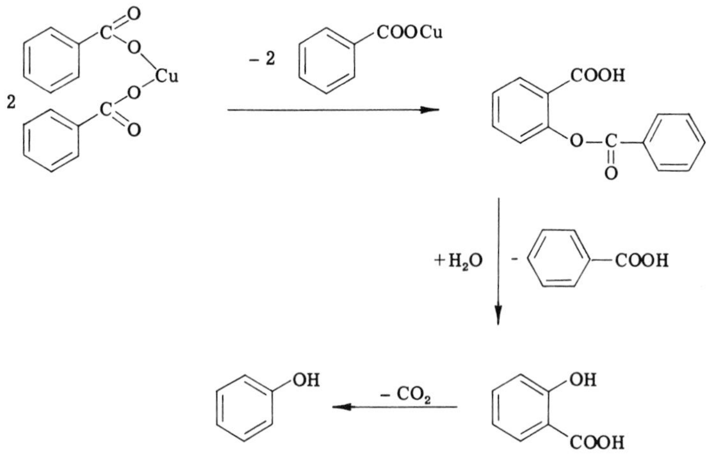

Cupric benzoate is regenerated from the cuprous salt and free benzoic acid by the action of air.

$$2C_6H_5COOCu + 2C_6H_5COOH + \tfrac{1}{2}O_2 \rightarrow 2(C_6H_5COO)_2Cu + H_2O$$

The overall equation of the process is

$$C_6H_5COOH + \tfrac{1}{2}O_2 \xrightarrow{\;[Cu^{2+}]\;} C_6H_5OH + CO_2$$

The primary product here may be the cyclohexadienyl radical of the structure shown above, where the reaction leading to salicylic acid was discussed. The further course of the reaction differs in that free O-benzoylsalicylic acid rather than the salt is formed in the excess of benzoic acid. Benzoylsalicylic acid in the presence of water is hydrolyzed and the resulting salicylic acids rapidly decarboxylated (the half-life time is a few seconds) to phenol.

As seen in the overall equation, no copper salts are consumed in the

---

[385] W. Schoo, J. V. Veenland, J. A. Bigot, and F. L. J. Sixma, *Rec. Trav. Chim.* **80**, 134 (1961).

[386] W. W. Kaeding, *J. Org. Chem.* **26**, 3144 (1961); Dow, *USP* 2,764,587.

reaction, i.e., these are homogeneous catalysts of the reaction. In practice, magnesium salts are added to copper salts as promoters of copper action. The temperature of reaction is higher than the boiling point of phenol, and the latter is continuously distilled off with steam. The mixed vapors are fed into a column. Toluene is added to remove water by azeotropic distillation, and phenol is subsequently purified by distillation.

To remove the tar accumulated in the oxidation reactor, a part of its content is by-passed to extract it with water. The insoluble tar is removed, and the aqueous extract containing benzoic acid and its copper and magnesium salts is recycled. A 95% yield of phenol is claimed.[387] The process is in operation at three plants: one in the U. S. (output 18,000 tons annually), one in Canada, and one in the Netherlands.[388] This method of phenol production is interesting in that it starts with the more readily available toluene rather than with benzene.

To reduce the formation of tar in the process, the use of antioxidants has been suggested. Performing the reaction in biphenyl, bis(4-hydroxy-3,5-tert-butylphenyl) sulfide, and analogous compounds have been tested as antioxidants.[389]

The method can be applied to prepare phenol homologs from benzoic acid derivatives. The hydroxyl group always enters the position ortho to the site occupied formerly by carboxyl. For this reason, m-cresol is obtained from both o- and p-toluic acids, whereas m-toluic acid affords a mixture of o- and p-cresols (ratio 40:60).[390]

E. DIRECT REPLACEMENT OF HYDROGEN ATOMS BY HYDROXYL GROUPS

Studies of the mechanism of vapor-phase benzene oxidation to phenol have revealed that the reaction is of a radical nature and that its kinetics may be described in terms of a degenerated explosion. Increasing the surface of the reactor inhibits both the overall rate of reaction and the formation of phenol, which is induced by oxidation of some other organic compounds. Along with phenol comparatively large amounts of the benzene and phenol pyrolysis products are formed.[391]

[387] W. W. Kaeding, R. O. Lindblom, R. G. Temples, and H. I. Mahon, *Ind. Eng. Chem., Process Design Develop.* **4**, No. 1, 97 (1965).

[388] W. W. Kaeding, *Hydrocarbon Process. Petrol. Refiner* **43**, No. 11, 173 (1964).

[389] D. M. Albright, C. Perlaky, and P. X. Masciantonio, *Ind. Eng. Chem., Process Design Develop.* **5**, No. 1, 71 (1966).

[390] W. W. Kaeding, R. O. Lindblom, and R. G. Temple, *Ind. Eng. Chem.* **53**, 805 (1961).

[391] I. I. Ioffe, *Zh. Fiz. Khim.* **28**, 772 (1954); *Chem. Abstr.* **49**, 6697 (1955); I. I. Ioffe, Ya. S. Levin, E. V. Sokolova, I. G. Kronich, and N. I. Shirokova, *Zh. Fiz. Khim.* **28**, 1386 (1954); *Chem. Abstr.* **49**, 8674 (1955).

It has been suggested that phenols may be obtained from aromatic hydrocarbons by the action of oxygen at 100–120° under pressure in the presence of catalysts and of hydrofluoric or of fluoroboric acid at small extents of conversion. The yields, as patents claim, are high. *o*-Cresol is thus obtained from toluene, 2-naphthol from naphthalene.[392] The preparation of phenol by oxidation of benzene with oxygen at 650–750° and 1.5–2 atm in the presence of minor amounts of water and hydrogen bromide (or of the substances that produce the latter compound) has recently been described.[393]

Phenol can be obtained from benzene by oxidation with atomic oxygen *in vacuo*.[394] Ozonation of benzene vapor in dry air gives only 25–30% phenol on the basis of consumed benzene (a small part of the benzene reacts).[395]

Oxidation of benzene in aqueous solutions of metal salts under γ-irradiation results in a 9% yield of phenol on the basis of the benzene present.[396] Radiation-induced oxidation of crude benzene results in a better yield of phenol compared with the pure hydrocarbon. It is believed that the impurities present are autooxidized and act as initiators of the chain oxidation process.[397]

An industrial method for oxidation with air or oxygen of an aqueous emulsion of benzene under γ-irradiation (^{60}Co) has been elaborated. The temperature of reaction is about 200°. A disadvantage of this method is the formation of tar (due to the side reactions and further transformation of phenol and dihydroxybenzene).[398]

Preparation of phenol by oxidation of benzene at 673° in the presence of water vapor with oxygen on an inert fluidized catalyst at elevated pressure has been suggested.[399] Minor amounts of phenol are obtained when air is bubbled through benzene containing $TiCl_3$.[400] Toluene and naphthalene can be oxidized in the same way.[401] (For the oxidation of toluene to cresol see also ref. 402.)

[392] Standard Oil Co. of Indiana, *USP* 2,499,515; Phillips Petroleum Co., *USP* 2,530,369; 2,632,027; L. F. Marek, *Ind. Eng. Chem.* 43, 1991 (1951).

[393] Gulf Research and Development Co., *USP* 3,360,572.

[394] C. J. Chin and D. F. Othmer, *Ind. Eng. Chem.* 45, 1266 (1953).

[395] K. Sugino and E. Inoue, *J. Chem. Soc. Japan, Pure Chem. Sect.* 71, 518 (1950); *Chem. Abstr.* 45, 9499 (1951).

[396] A. Danno, *Hydrocarbon Process. Petrol. Refiner* 43, No. 4, 131 (1964).

[397] N. Suzuki and H. Hotta, *Bull. Chem. Soc. Japan* 37, 244 (1964).

[398] *Chem. Age (London)* 88, 233 (1962).

[399] Detjen & Co., *BP* 903,868.

[400] K. Ziegler, *DBP* 1,184,772.

[401] UCC, *USP* 3,033,903.

[402] Anonymous, *Chem. Eng. News* 42, No. 36, 39 (1964); H. Pichler and F. Obenaus, *Brennstoff-Chem.* 45, 97 (1965).

There is indication in the literature that the Schenectady Chemical Co. has succeeded in industrial oxidation of benzene to phenol in a plant with an annual output of 10,000 tons.[376]

It has been suggested that naphthols may be obtained by oxidation of naphthalene in the liquid phase at elevated pressure and temperature in the presence of iron, silver, and copper oxides with continuous azeotropic distillation of the water formed.[403]

Hydroxyanthraquinones can be obtained by heating anthracene or anthraquinone in the liquid phase at 220–300° under pressure with water and a source of bromide ion.[404]

Methods of direct introduction of the hydroxyl group into an aromatic nucleus by the action upon aromatic compounds of oxidants other than oxygen, such as organic peroxides, have been described. The oxidation of aromatic hydrocarbons to phenols with organic peroxides in the presence of boric acid as catalyst gives a higher yield of hydroxy compounds when catalytic amounts of pyridine are added.[405] Cresols and the hydroxy derivatives of polyalkylbenzenes, anisole, and polyalkoxybenzenes are obtained by action of diisopropyl peroxydicarbonate in the presence of catalysts of the Friedel-Crafts type. The method is useful in the preparation of 2,4-dimethoxyphenol and 2,4,6-trimethoxyphenol. The orientation of the hydroxyl group points to the electrophilic character of the substitution.[406]

Minor amounts (15%) of phenol and pyridine were obtained by UV irradiation of the benzene solution of pyridine N-oxide. The mechanism of the reaction is unknown. Probably, oxepin is the primary product; it is known that this compound isomerizes to phenol by the action of pyridine.[407]

Direct hydroxylation of the aromatic nucleus can also sometimes be accomplished as a result of the reduction of another substituent present. For example, 1,8-dinitronaphthalene is smoothly converted by the action of dilute alkali into 4-nitroso-5-nitronaphthol due to reduction of one of the nitro groups.[408]

[403] I. I. Ioffe, V. V. Suchkov, V. I. Sushenaya, and E. A. Migge, *RP* 176,915; *Chem. Abstr.* **64**, 12601 (1966).

[404] BASF, *DBP* 1,160,124; 1,165,180.

[405] Rhone-Poulenc, Suppl. *FP* 85,435.

[406] P. Kovacic and S. T. Morneweck, *J. Am. Chem. Soc.* **87**, 1566 (1965); P. Kovacic and M. E. Kurz, *J. Org. Chem.* **31**, 2011 (1966); *J. Am. Chem. Soc.* **87**, 4811 (1965).

[407] J. Streith, B. Danner, and C. Sigwalt, *Chem. Commun.* p. 979 (1967).

[408] N. N. Vorozhtsov, Jr. and A. I. Ryulina, *RP* 108,897; *Chem. Abstr.* **52**, 11941 (1958).

VI. Synthesis of Aromatic Carboxylic Acids

A. Synthesis by Oxidation

Recently, the scale of production of benzoic acid and benzene di- and polycarboxylic acids has considerably increased. The methods of production by oxidation, usually with the cheapest oxidant—oxygen of the air—have become widely applied.

Benzoic acid, the demand for which has considerably increased with the elaboration of the method of its transformation to phenol (see Section V,C), is usually produced by the oxidation of toluene with air in the liquid phase in the presence of cobalt salt. The oxidation is performed at 130–140° and at the corresponding pressure. The equation is

$$C_6H_5CH_3 + 1\tfrac{1}{2}O_2 \xrightarrow{[Co]} C_6H_5COOH + H_2O$$

The oxidation is stopped when the content of toluene in the reaction mixture is still high. Besides benzoic acid and the intermediate products of toluene oxidation—benzyl alcohol, benzaldehyde, and the benzyl ether of benzoic acid—minor amounts of biphenyl and all three isomers of methylbiphenyl are present in the reaction mixture. The formation of the products is due to the radical character of the reaction.

Large-scale industrial production of benzoic acid as an intermediate for phenol synthesis is performed on the basis of this method.[388] Recycling the products of incomplete oxidation has been suggested.[409] Tertiary alkyl-substituted benzoic acids are obtained in this way from tertiary alkyl-substituted toluenes.[410]

It has been suggested that p-nitrobenzoic acid can be obtained from p-nitrotoluene by oxidation with air (or ozone) under pressure in propionic acid and in the presence of $CoBr_2$ and $MnBr_2$ as catalysts.[411] The oxidation of xylenes under the same conditions as applied to toluene gives rise to the corresponding toluic acids. To oxidize m- and p-xylenes directly to isophthalic and terephthalic acids, respectively, a method has been elaborated based on reaction with air at 125–275° in the liquid phase at 40 atm with acetic acid as solvent and heavy metal (Co, Mn, Mo) bromides as catalysts. The method is used in industry.[412,413]

Benzenedicarboxylic acids can be obtained from the corresponding

[409] Alpine Chemische A.-G., *AustrianP* 191,410.

[410] G. W. Hearne, T. W. Evans, V. W. Buls, and C. G. Schwarzer, *Ind. Eng. Chem.* **47**, 2311 (1955).

[411] ICI, *BP* 814,487.

[412] D. E. Burney, G. H. Weisemann, and N. Fragen, *Petrol. Refiner* **38**, No. 6, 186 (1959).

[413] R. Landau, *Ind. Eng. Chem.* **53**, No. 10, 36A (1961).

diethylbenzenes by oxidation with oxygen in carboxylic acid medium in the presence of compounds of manganese.[414]

It has been suggested that terephthalic acid can be obtained from *p*-diisopropylbenzene by oxidation with air.[415]

The most common raw material for terephthalic acid synthesis is, however, *p*-xylene. Two-stage oxidation is also used in industry. Xylene is first oxidized to *p*-toluic acid, the latter esterified with methyl alcohol, and the other methyl group then oxidized. Terephthalic acid is an important intermediate for polyester fiber synthesis and is sometimes applied in dye synthesis.[413]

A review has been published on the oxidation of aromatic hydrocarbons and their derivatives in the liquid phase with oxygen and oxygen-containing gases.[416] Oxidants other than air are sometimes used to obtain carboxylic acids from benzene homologs. For example, preparation of benzoic, isophthalic, and terephthalic acids by oxidation of toluene and xylenes with aqueous nitric acid at temperatures above 150° under pressure has been suggested. Substituted benzoic acids are thus obtained from substituted toluenes.[417]

The duPont Co. produces *p*-terephthalic acid by oxidation of *p*-xylene with nitric acid.[413]

It has been suggested that terephthalic acid can be obtained from *p*-diisopropylbenzene by oxidation with nitric acids[418]; similarly benzophenone-3,4,3′,4′-tetracarboxylic acid can be obtained from 1,1-bis(3,4-dimethylphenyl)ethane[419]; and sulfonated benzoic acids from cumene sulfonic acids.[420]

To obtain the carboxylic acids of polycyclic hydrocarbons such as naphthalene from the corresponding homologs, it is convenient to use aqueous sodium dichromate solution as oxidant at 250° in an autoclave. The yields are usually higher than 90%.[421] It is known that oxidation under other conditions with other oxidants usually results in oxidation of an aromatic nucleus in polycyclic hydrocarbons rather than in the oxidation of the alkyl group. Quinone homologs are formed.

The most important carboxylic acid of the aromatic series remains

[414] Chempatents Inc., *BP* 777,761.

[415] N. V. de Bataafsche Petroleum Mij., *BP* 772,635; *FP* 1,112,152; Chempatents Inc., *BP* 762,849; 774,835.

[416] H. L. Riley, *Chem. Ind.* (*London*) p. 980 (1966).

[417] E. B. Bengtsson, *Acta Chem. Scand* 7, 774 (1953); BASF, *FP* 1,024,048; DuP, *SP* 282,253; *BP* 655,074; Aktiebolaget Bofors, *SP* 274,843; Monsanto Chemical Co., *USP* 2,766,280; 2,766,281.

[418] ICI, *FP* 1,099,276; BASF, *FP* 1,106,130.

[419] Gulf Research and Development Co., *BeP* 654,012.

[420] BASF, *DBP* 953,701.

[421] L. Friedman, D. L. Fishel, and H. Schechter, *J. Org. Chem.* 30, 1453 (1965).

phthalic acid. The world annual industrial capacity of the production of its anhydride by oxidation of naphthalene and o-xylene in the vapor phase over vanadium-containing catalyst is more than 1 million tons. The large scale of the production has stimulated the design of plants of high productivity.

Systems with a fluidized layer of catalyst have found wide application in the production of phthalic anhydride. The advantages of this method are the improvement of heat removal, the possibility of designing converters with an annual output of more than 30,000 tons, improved safety of the work, and reduction of the air:naphthalene ratio, which facilitates the condensation of phthalic anhydride.[422] It was reported that in 1966 in the U. S. more than 50% of the phthalic anhydride obtained was produced in plants with fluidized catalyst.

The stationary layer of catalyst is usually applied in the production of phthalic anhydride from o-xylene. It is, however, reported that a fluidized catalyst was elaborated and applied industrially for both o-xylene and naphthalene, as well as their mixtures.[423]

The various methods of phthalic anhydride production are considered in a special monograph.[424]

Oxidation with air over vanadium catalyst can be applied to obtain the dianhydride of pyromellitic (1,2,4,5-benzenetetracarboxylic) acid from durene (1,2,4,5-tetramethylbenzene) and from some higher benzene homologs; the compound is now an important raw material for polymer synthesis.[425]

Catalytic methods have been elaborated for obtaining nitriles from benzene homologs by the action of ammonia. The temperature of the process is 525–550° at atmospheric pressure; molybdenum- and nickel-containing catalysts are recommended.[426] Nitriles can also be produced by the action of air and ammonia upon benzene homologs.[427] Nitriles can be used as intermediates to obtain the corresponding acids (e.g., terephthalic acids from p-xylene)[428] or other compounds, such as 2,4,6-triphenyl-1,3,5-triazine from toluene via benzonitrile.[429]

[422] H. L. Riley, *Chem. Ind.* (*London*) p. 1464 (1956); p. 979 (1966); *Brit. Chem. Eng.* **2**, No. 1, 8 (1957).

[423] *Chem. Ind.* (*London*) p. 893 (1960); *Chem. Eng. News* **44**, No. 14, 24 (1966).

[424] D. A. Gurevich, "Phtalic Anhydride." Publ. House "Chemistry," Moscow, 1968.

[425] Standard Oil Development Co., *USP* 2,509,855; California Research Corp., *USP* 2,576,625; 2,625,555; Gelsenberg Benzin A.-G., *BeP* 655,686.

[426] W. I. Denton, R. B. Bishop, H. P. Caldwell, Jr., and H. D. Chapman, *Ind. Eng. Chem.* **42**, 796 (1950); Socony-Vacuum Oil Co., *USP* 2,478,464.

[427] H. L. Riley, *Chem. Ind.* (*London*) p. 985 (1966); Socony-Vacuum Oil Co., *USP* 2,540,788; 2,540,789; BASF, *BP* 972,122; Knapsack-Griesheim A.-G., *BeP* 651,562.

[428] Anonymous, *Chem. Age* (*London*) **93**, 538 (1965).

[429] Pure Oil Co., *USP* 3,071,586.

B. Synthesis by Isomerization of Salts of Carboxylic Acids[430]

It has long been known that hydroxycarboxylic acids of the aromatic series can be transformed by migration of carboxyl to isomeric compounds. At present it has been established that analogous isomerization may occur also with unsubstituted carboxylic acids of the aromatic series but at higher temperatures. One of the most interesting examples of isomerization of this kind is the preparation of terephthalic acid from phthalic and isophthalic acids:

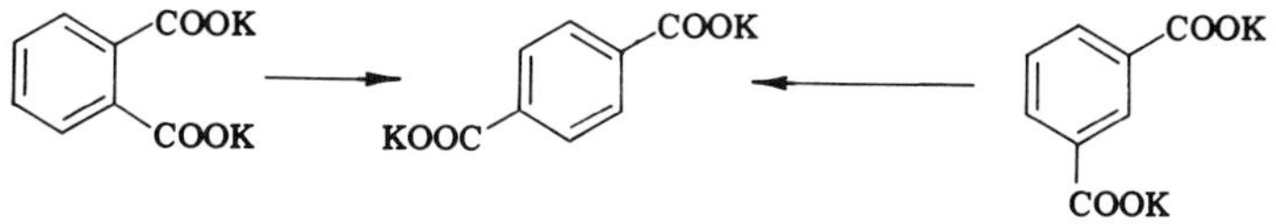

The isomerization is usually performed with the potassium salt of benzene dicarboxylic acid. The temperature of the process is 400–450°. The absence of water and of free acid is essential. The process is usually performed under carbon dioxide pressure (up to 50 atm). The reaction is catalyzed by some metal salts, and one of the best catalysts is cadmium iodide. It is reported that the yield of terephthalic acid is more than 95%. Isophthalic acid is isomerized less readily than the ortho isomer.

A number of other acids can also be obtained by isomerization. For example, 4,4'-biphenyl dicarboxylic acid can be obtained from diphenic acid. Napthalic acid affords naphthalene-2,6-dicarboxylic acid.

Intermolecular transfer of the carboxyl is also possible. For example, the potassium salt of benzoic acid under conditions similar to those considered above is converted to the dipotassium salt of terephthalic acid and benzene.

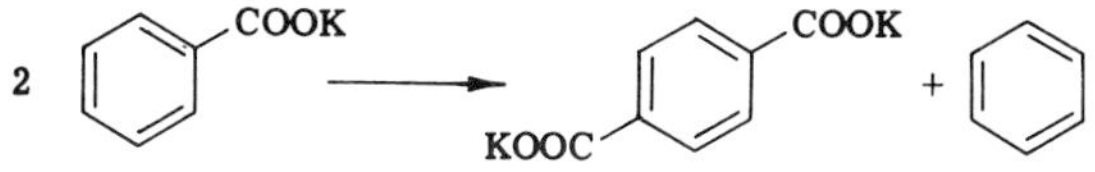

It is interesting that when strontium and barium benzoates are used as starting compounds, the disproportionation affords the salt of phthalic acid.

2,6-Naphthalenedicarboxylic acid was prepared by disproportionation of the potassium salt of either 1- or 2-naphthoic acid.[431] The nature of the products of the disproportionation depends on the reaction temperature. Thus, at 400°, 2,3-naphthalenedicarboxylic acid is formed from the

[430] V. A. Koptyug, "Isomerization of Aromatic Compounds," pp. 157–174. Oldbourne Press, London, 1965.
[431] E. McNelis, J. Org. Chem. 30, 1209 (1965).

potassium salt of 2-naphthoic acid, whereas the 2,6-isomer is formed at 450°. Only the 2,3-isomer is obtained from the sodium salt of 2-naphthoic acid (at temperatures up to 500°).[432] The barium salts of both the naphthoic acids afford on disproportionation a mixture of naphthalene dicarboxylic acids with the relative ortho and peri positions of the carboxyl groups—1,2-, 1,8-, and 2,3-naphthalene dicarboxylic acids.[431]

Dicarboxylic acids of the heterocyclic series can be also obtained by this method.

The mechanisms of the isomerization and disproportionation reactions are probably similar. Studies of the isomerization and disproportionation in an atmosphere of ^{14}C-labeled carbon dioxide revealed that ^{14}C is incorporated into terephthalic acid carboxyls. The probable mechanism of the isomerization of, e.g., phthalic to terephthalic acid, may involve primary formation of carbanion by elimination of carbon dioxide. The negative charge of the carbanion subsequently migrates to the position para to carboxyl.

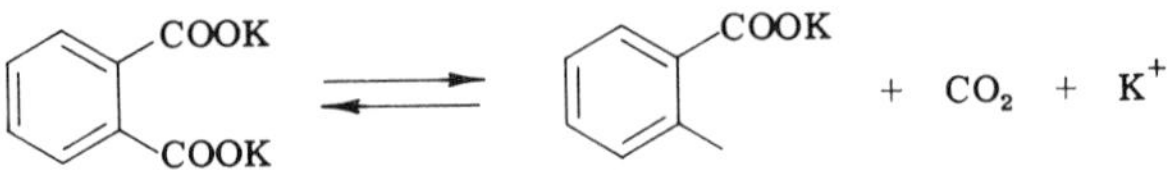

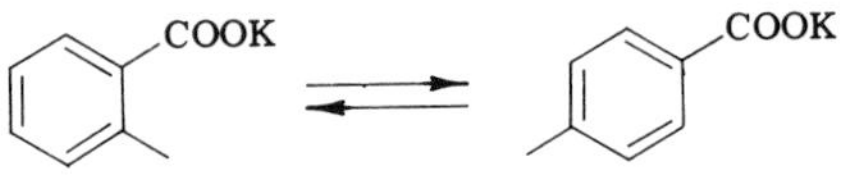

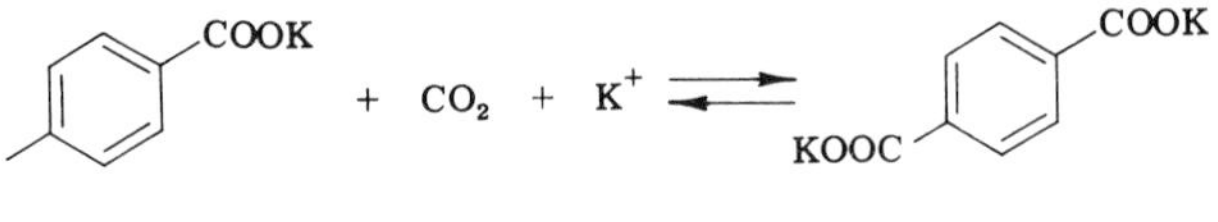

In the disproportionation (e.g., of benzoic acid salt) the anion $C_6H_5^-$ formed initially after carbon dioxide elimination reacts with another molecule of benzoate, deprives it of a proton, and thus gives rise to benzene. The anion, formed from potassium benzoate by proton elimination with the negative charge at the position para to the COO^- group, adds CO_2 and K^+ according to the following scheme and gives rise to the dipotassium salt of terephthalic acid.

---

[432] J. W. Patton and M. O. Son, *J. Org. Chem.* **30**, 2869 (1965).

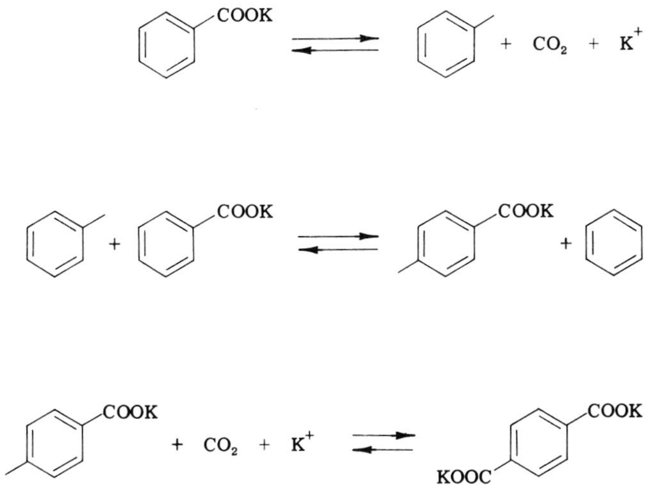

A plant for manufacturing terephthalic acid using phthalic or benzoic acid as starting material with an annual output of about 5000 tons was put in action in Japan in 1958. Potassium phthalate is isomerized to terephthalate, usually at 420° with zinc or cadmium salt catalyst. It is claimed that the yield of terephthalic acid is over 95%. Potassium hydroxide is recovered and recycled.[433]

[433] *Chem. Eng.* **65,** September 22, p. 69 (1958); P. W. Sherwood, *Chem. Ind.* (*London*) p. 1096 (1960).

CHAPTER IV

COLOR AND THE ELECTRONIC STATES OF
ORGANIC MOLECULES

S. F. Mason

CHEMISTRY DEPARTMENT, KING'S COLLEGE, LONDON, U.K.

I. Introduction

Studies of the relations between the color and the constitution of organic molecules fall broadly into two main periods which are characterized principally by the current levels of theory and instrumentation. Although the Beer-Lambert law governing absorption intensities[1] was well established and widely used in quantitative colorimetry the measurement of absorption wavelengths, using photographic spectrographs, was of primary interest in the early period, the results being interpreted in terms of the classical bond or electron oscillation theory of the light-absorption process. During the later period, covering the past two or three decades, photographic techniques have been augmented by photoelectric instrumentation, which has substantially facilitated the measurement of absorption intensities. At the same time absorption intensities have assumed

[1] A. Beer, *Ann. Phys. Chem.* **163**, 78 (1852).

a greater diagnostic and theoretical importance with the development of a new interpretative procedure, the wave-mechanical treatment of large polyatomic molecules. The achievements of the classical period were fully reviewed in the first volume of this series,[2] and in the present chapter we shall be concerned mainly with subsequent developments in the field of the electronic spectroscopy of organic dyes.

II. Factors Governing the Absorption of Light

A. CLASSICAL LAWS

In the practice of absorption spectroscopy a collimated beam of mono-chromatic light with wavelength λ and frequency ν enters at normal incidence a cell of pathlength l (cm) containing the absorbing species at a concentration c (mole liter^{-1}) in an appropriate transparent solvent. The integrated fraction of light absorbed by the assembly of molecules in the cell is measured by the optical density or absorbance d which, according to the Beer-Lambert law,[1] is proportional to the number of absorbing systems in the light path, namely,

$$d = \log(I_0/I) = \epsilon cl \qquad (1)$$

where I_0 and I are, respectively, the intensities of the light incident upon and emergent from the cell. The constant ϵ is the decadic molar extinction coefficient or molar absorbancy index in mole^{-1} cm^2 at the wavelength λ. In the electronic spectrum of an absorbing species the extinction coefficient has maximum values ϵ_{max} at specific wavelengths λ_{max} which characterize the species in its particular solvent environment.

The extinction coefficient has the dimensions of an area, and for a system with unit optical density at a wavelength λ_{max} we have, by substituting Eq. (1),

$$\epsilon_{max} \simeq 10^4 pa \qquad (2)$$

where a is the area of the absorbing molecules in (angstroms)^2 and p is the probability of absorption. Thus the extinction coefficient of a dye molecule absorbing a photon with unit probability[3] is expected to be $\sim 10^5$.

The maximum extinction coefficient of an absorption band may be affected markedly by a change of phase or of solvent, but a decrease in the coefficient due to an environmental change is frequently compensated by an increase in the width of the band. The area of a band, represented

[2] CSD Vol. I, Chapter VIII, pp. 323–400.
[3] E. A. Braude, *J. Chem. Soc.* p. 379 (1950).

by the integral of the extinction coefficient over the frequency range of the absorption, $\int \epsilon \, dv$, is accordingly less sensitive to the particular solvent environment and it affords a better measure of the intrinsic absorption intensity. The band area is related to the oscillator strength, f, which, in the classical electron vibration theory, is the number of oscillators each of mass m and charge e giving rise to the absorption band,

$$f = (10^3 mc^2 \ln 10/\pi e^2 N) \int \epsilon \, dv \qquad (3)$$
$$\simeq 4.31 \times 10^{-9} \, \epsilon_{max} \, \Delta \bar{\nu}$$

where $\Delta \bar{\nu}$ is the bandwidth at half-maximum extinction in wavenumbers (cm^{-1}).

B. QUANTUM THEORY

According to the quantum theory, when a molecule absorbs visible or ultraviolet radiation with a frequency v a valency electron is promoted from a lower to a higher energy level in the molecule, the energy-level difference ΔE being given by the well-known relationship $\Delta E = hv$. The lower level may be a lone-pair nonbonding electronic orbital n or a bonding σ- or π-orbital, and the higher level an unoccupied orbital of the σ- or π-type. For small polyatomic molecules the nonbonding lone-pair electrons have the least binding energy, and in the bonding levels π-electrons have higher energies than σ-electrons, whereas in the antibonding levels that order is reversed (Fig. 1). Thus the absorption bands of simple molecules due to $n \rightarrow \pi^*$ transitions generally lie at

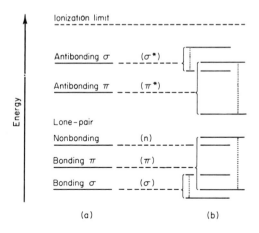

FIG. 1. The relative energies of the σ, π, and lone-pair orbitals in (a) a simple and (b) a complex unsaturated molecule.

longer wavelengths than those arising from $\pi \rightarrow \pi^*$ excitations, and $\sigma \rightarrow \sigma^*$ absorption bands usually lie in the far-ultraviolet region.

In dye molecules and other large unsaturated systems there are as many π-levels as there are conjugated atoms, and the π-orbitals of both the bonding and the antibonding set are spread over a range of binding energies. The higher-bonding π-orbitals now have energies above those of the nonbonding lone-pair levels (Fig. 1), so that the $n \rightarrow \pi^*$ bands, which are intrinsically weak, are submerged under the stronger $\pi \rightarrow \pi^*$ bands and are not observed.

In the quantum-mechanical treatment the intensity of an absorption band depends upon the form and the magnitude of the charge displacement produced by the promotion of a valency electron from the lower, occupied, orbital to the higher, unoccupied, level. The charge distribution of the promoted electron is different in the two orbitals, and the absorption of light gives rise to a transient moment in the molecule due to the rearrangement of the electronic charge density over the atomic centers. The most intense absorption bands are associated with an electric-dipole transition moment produced by a linear charge displacement in the absorption process. Rotatory charge displacements, giving magnetic-dipole transition moments, or charge displacements producing multipole moments, are generally less important as they give rise to an intrinsic absorption which is weaker by a factor of 10^{-5} or less than that due to an electric-dipole transition.[4] However, magnetic-dipole transition moments are important in optical activity which arises from the displacement of a valency electron through a helical path in the light-absorption process. A helical charge displacement, which is possible only in molecules devoid of a secondary element of symmetry, generates a concurrent and collinear electric and magnetic dipole transition moment and produces circular dichroism, i.e., the differential absorption of left and right circularly polarized light.[5]

The area of an absorption band depends in the quantum theory upon the line strength which represents the sum of the squares of the various transition moments. For the absorption of isotropic or plane-polarized light by polyatomic molecules only the first term of the sum is significant, namely, the electric dipole strength, D, which is given by,

$$D = \mu^2 = (3hc10^3 \ln 10/8\pi^3N) \int (\epsilon/\nu) \, d\nu \qquad (4)$$
$$\simeq 92 \times 10^{-40} \, \epsilon_{max} \, \Delta\bar{\nu}/\bar{\nu}_{max}$$

where μ is the electric-dipole transition moment expressed, like D, in cgs units.

[4] S. F. Mason, *Quart. Rev. (London)* 15, 287 (1961).
[5] S. F. Mason, *Quart. Rev. (London)* 17, 20 (1963).

The electric-dipole transition moment may be calculated theoretically by molecular orbital methods from the wavefunctions of the ground state ψ_0 of the molecule and the excited electronic state ψ_n produced by the optical-absorption process,

$$\mu_{0n} = e \int \psi_0 \left(\sum_i \mathbf{r}_i \right) \psi_n \, d\tau \tag{5}$$

where $\mathbf{r}_i$ is a vector defining the position of the electron i relative to a fixed origin. In general we need consider only the two levels of the molecule connected by the electronic transition, namely, the bonding space-orbital ψ_b and the antibonding space-orbital ψ_a, which are doubly occupied and unoccupied, respectively, in the electronic ground state. If we allow for the promotion of either of the two electrons in ψ_b and for a possible change of electron spin the transition is represented by

$$[\psi_b(1)\psi_b(2)] \xrightarrow{h\nu} [\psi_b(1)\psi_a(2) \pm \psi_a(1)\psi_b(2)]/\sqrt{2} \tag{6}$$

The positive and negative signs in Eq. (6) refer to the transition without change of spin (singlet) and with change of spin (triplet), respectively, in accord with the Pauli principle which requires that the total wavefunction, covering both space and spin orbitals, be antisymmetric with respect to the interchange of electrons (1) and (2). The electric-dipole moment of the transition is then given by

$$\mu_{0n} \simeq \mu_{ba} = e \left[\int \psi_b(2)\mathbf{r}_2\psi_a(2) \, d\tau_2 \pm \int \psi_b(1)\mathbf{r}_1\psi_a(1) \, d\tau_1 \right]/\sqrt{2} \tag{7}$$

and since the two electrons are indistinguishable the moment for the singlet transition is

$$\mu_{ba} = e \sqrt{2} \int \psi_b(\mathbf{r})\psi_a \, d\tau \tag{8}$$

whereas for the triplet transition the moment vanishes.

The singlet $\pi \to \pi^*$ transition of ethylene (Fig. 2) is the prototype of the majority of significant electronic transitions in dye molecules, and in this the bonding ψ_b and antibonding ψ_a molecular π-orbitals connected by the transition have the respective forms

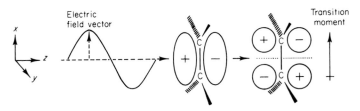

Fig. 2. The π-orbital changes and the orientation of the electric-dipole excitation moment in the $\pi \to \pi^*$ transition of ethylene.

$$\psi_b = (\phi_1 + \phi_2)/\sqrt{2} \tag{9}$$

and

$$\psi_a = (\phi_1 - \phi_2)/\sqrt{2} \tag{10}$$

where ϕ_1 and ϕ_2 are the $2p\pi$ atomic orbitals of the two carbon atoms. From Eqs. (8)–(10) the moment of the singlet $\pi \rightarrow \pi^*$ transition of ethylene is

$$\mu_{\pi\pi^*} = e(\mathbf{R}_1 - \mathbf{R}_2)/\sqrt{2} \tag{11}$$

where $\mathbf{R}_1$ and $\mathbf{R}_2$ are the position vectors of the two carbon atoms, the difference between $\mathbf{R}_1$ and $\mathbf{R}_2$ being equal to the carbon–carbon bond length in ethylene. The theoretical $\pi \rightarrow \pi^*$ transition moment of ethylene accordingly is 4.5×10^{-18} cgs (4.5 Debye), which corresponds to a classical oscillator strength of 0.60, compared with the experimental value[6,7] of 0.30–0.34. In general, theoretical absorption intensities calculated by the simple molecular orbital method are too large by a factor of about 2, but the relative values show satisfactory agreement with experiment.[4–9]

C. Selection Rules

A number of general selection rules determine in principle whether the moment of an electronic transition is finite or zero, the transitions being termed "allowed" or "forbidden," respectively. We have seen from Eq. (7) that the transition moment vanishes if there is a change of electron spin when a molecule absorbs radiation. In practice spin-forbidden absorption bands due to a transition from a singlet ground state to a triplet excited state are very weak with oscillator strengths of the order of 10^{-6} or less in molecules composed of the lighter atoms. Spin-forbidden transitions occur only to the degree that the nominal singlet and multiplet states are mixtures of singlet and multiplet configurations so that both states have components with the same spin multiplicity. Spin–orbit coupling, which mixes electronic configurations with different spin multiplicities, is more important in the heavier atoms and in molecules containing heavy atoms. Even solvents containing heavy atoms, such as ethyl iodide, enhance the intensities of the spin-forbidden absorption

[6] N. S. Bayliss, *Quart. Rev. (London)* **6**, 319 (1952).

[7] A. Maccoll, *Quart. Rev. (London)* **1**, 16, (1947).

[8] H. H. Jaffé and M. Orchin, "Theory and Applications of Ultraviolet Spectroscopy." Wiley, New York, 1962.

[9] J. N. Murrell, "The Theory of the Electronic Spectra of Organic Molecules." Methuen, London, 1963.

bands of solutes composed solely of light atoms, such as the aromatic hydrocarbons.[10]

In addition to its spin, an electron has a spatial orbital motion and a general selection rule governs the types of space orbital which may be connected by an allowed electronic transition. As a transition moment is a measurable physical property of a molecule it must be independent of any rotation, reflection, or inversion of the coordinate frame of the molecular system.[11] This condition requires that the combination of the symmetry species of the space orbitals ψ_a and ψ_b connected by an electronic transition and that of the vector $\mathbf{r}$ [Eq. (8)] must be invariant with respect to all symmetry elements of the molecule. If not, the transition moment [Eq. (8)] vanishes, and the transition is forbidden. Similarly the combination of the symmetry species of the ground and the excited-state wavefunctions, ψ_0 and ψ_n, and of the electronic position vectors, $\mathbf{r}_i$ [Eq. (5)], must be totally symmetric for an allowed electric-dipole transition.

The symmetry elements of ethylene, for example, consist of an inversion center, three twofold rotation axes, x, y, and z, and three reflection planes xy, xz, and yz (Fig. 2). In the case of the $\pi \to \pi^*$ transition of ethylene we find that the combination of the symmetries of the π- and π^*-orbitals with that of the x component of the vector $\mathbf{r}$ [Eq. (8)], which gives the direction of the transition moment (Fig. 2), is symmetric with respect to each of these symmetry elements. The combination is therefore invariant under all symmetry operations of ethylene and is totally symmetric, indicating that the $\pi \to \pi^*$ transition is allowed and has a nonzero moment in the x direction (Fig. 2). The π- and π^*-orbitals are antisymmetric and symmetric, respectively, under inversion, but the vector $\mathbf{r}$ [Eq. (8)] is also antisymmetric with respect to inversion, and the combination of the two antisymmetries gives a resultant symmetric behavior for the binary product ($\pi \mathbf{r}$) and thus for the triple product ($\pi \mathbf{r} \pi^*$) entering into the expression for the transition moment [Eq. (8)]. On the other hand the $\sigma_{CC} \to \pi^*$ transition of ethylene is forbidden since the carbon–carbon bonding σ-orbital and the antibonding π-orbital are symmetric under inversion, whereas the vector $\mathbf{r}$ is antisymmetric, and since antisymmetry appears an odd number of times in the triple product of the symmetry species of ($\sigma_{CC} \mathbf{r} \pi^*$) the combination as a whole is antisymmetric with respect to inversion.

The general symmetry rule implies that high-intensity absorption arises from an electronic transition to a higher-energy orbital with one more nodal plane or surface than the lower occupied orbital from which

---

[10] M. Kasha and S. P. McGlynn, *Ann. Rev. Phys. Chem.* **7**, 403 (1956).
[11] M. Sponer and E. Teller, *Rev. Mod. Phys.* **13**, 75 (1941).

the electron is promoted.[12] In the $\pi \rightarrow \pi^*$ transition of ethylene, for example, a new nodal plane is generated at the center of the carbon–carbon bond perpendicular to the bond direction (Fig. 2). The node is created by the linear displacement of electronic charge from the center of the carbon–carbon bond, and the transition moment is directed along the bond perpendicular to the new nodal surface.

Weak absorption results if an electron is promoted from a lower occupied orbital to a higher-energy orbital with more than one additional node, since the component transition moments, perpendicular to the new nodal surfaces, tend to have opposed directions and so partly cancel one another. The cancellation is particularly complete in molecules with a

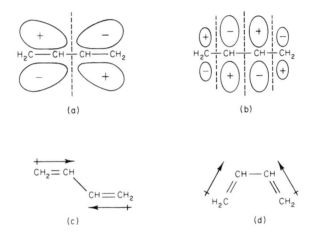

FIG. 3. The nodal changes involved in the transition of an electron from (a) the higher bonding to (b) the higher antibonding π-orbital of butadiene, and the instantaneous orientation of the component transition moments in (c) *trans*-butadiene and (d) *cis*-butadiene.

center of symmetry if the nodes change by an even number on excitation. This parity selection rule is illustrated by the transition of an electron from the higher occupied to the higher unoccupied π-orbital of butadiene, $\pi_2 \rightarrow \pi_4^*$ (Fig. 3), where the orbitals are numbered in the order of decreasing bonding. The component transition moments of the $\pi_2 \rightarrow \pi_4^*$ transition of butadiene give a vanishing vector sum for the *s-trans* isomer, which has a center of symmetry, but give a net resultant in the *s-cis* isomer, which is not centrosymmetric (Fig. 3). In conformity with the parity rule the *cis*-polyenes are found generally to give a characteristic weak absorption, the "*cis* peak" on the short-wavelength side of the main absorption band, but the *trans* isomers do not (Fig. 4).

[12] E. J. Bowen, *Quart. Rev. (London)* **4**, 236 (1950).

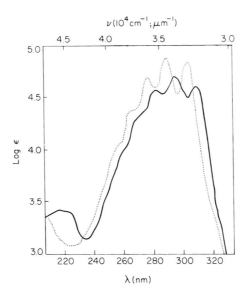

FIG. 4. The absorption spectra in hexane of all-*cis*-deca-2,4,6,8-tetraene (———)
and of all-*trans*-deca-2,4,6,8-tetraene (·····). From D. Holme, E. R. H. Jones,
and M. C. Whiting, *Chem. & Ind. (London)* p. 928 (1956).

Each π-orbital of a conjugated molecule has, in general, one more
node than the π-level immediately beneath it in the energy scale, the
most-bonding π-orbital having no nodes perpendicular to the molecular
plane. Thus the lowest unoccupied π-orbital normally has one more node
than the highest occupied π-orbital, and the lowest-energy $\pi \to \pi^*$ transition of dye molecules is generally expected to have a large intensity. For
linear molecules such as the polyenes (I) and the simple cyanines (II)

$$R-[-CH=CH-]_n-R \qquad R_2\overset{+}{N}=CH-[-CH=CH-]_n-NR_2$$

$$\text{(I)} \qquad\qquad\qquad\qquad \text{(II)}$$

the long-wavelength absorption band should contain the majority of the
absorption intensity in the whole of the accessible electronic spectrum.
In cyclic molecules, such as the aromatic hydrocarbons and macrocyclic
dyes, degeneracies in the π-orbital energies modify these expectations,
which now apply to the lower-energy system of absorption bands in
which the shorter-wavelength component may have the higher intensity.
Dyes consisting of a conjugated chain terminated by aromatic groups
also exhibit high-intensity absorption at shorter wavelengths, due to
transitions largely localized in the aromatic residues, in addition to the

main absorption band in the visible deriving from the π-system as a whole.

D. POLARIZATION DIRECTIONS

A molecule having an allowed transition with an excitation energy satisfying the quantum condition, $\Delta E = h\nu$, does not absorb light of frequency ν unless the oscillating electric field of the radiation is parallel to the direction of the transition moment. In the $\pi \rightarrow \pi^*$ transition of ethylene, electronic charge is linearly displaced from the center of the double bond towards the carbon atoms and the electric-dipole transition moment is directed or polarized along the carbon–carbon bond. Thus radiation with the energy required for the $\pi \rightarrow \pi^*$ transition of ethylene (162 nm; 61,700 cm^{-1}), propagated in the z direction, may be either x- or y-polarized or contain both polarizations, but only x-polarized light is absorbed for the orientation of the ethylene molecule depicted (Fig. 2) in which the carbon–carbon bond, and hence the $\pi \rightarrow \pi^*$ transition moment, lie along the x axis of the coordinate frame.

The polarization directions of the transition moments of a given dye molecule may be determined by a number of methods,[13] all of which involve spectroscopic measurements on dye molecules with a particular orientation relative to the direction of propagation of the light and to the plane of polarization if the radiation is not isotropic. In general the relative polarization directions of the several transition moments of a particular dye molecule are more readily determined than the absolute directions in the molecular coordinate frame, since absolute measurements require a knowledge of the orientation of the molecular axes of the dye in a laboratory coordinate frame.

In a single crystal with a known structure the individual molecules have determinate orientations, but the measurements of the absorption spectrum of a dye crystal with plane-polarized light is complicated by the high intensity of absorption, necessitating the use of thin crystals (<1 μm), and by interactions between adjacent dye molecules.[14] The crystal absorption spectra of aromatic hydrocarbons have been extensively investigated in connection with both the polarization of the transition moments and the intermolecular interactions,[14-18] but relatively few

[13] F. Dörr, Angew. Chem. Intern. Ed. Engl. **5**, 478 (1966).

[14] A. S. Davydov, "Theory of Molecular Excitons" (transl. by M. Kasha and M. Oppenheimer, Jr.), McGraw-Hill, New York, 1962.

[15] D. S. McClure, "Electronic Spectra of Molecules and Ions in Crystals." Academic Press, New York, 1959.

[16] H. C. Wolf, Solid State Phys. **9**, 1 (1959).

[17] T. N. Misra, Rev. Pure Appl. Chem. **15**, 39 (1965).

studies of dye systems have been reported.[17] Notable examples are the polarized absorption crystal studies of the linear quinolinocyanines[19] and the cyclic phthalocyanines.[20]

The problem of high absorption intensity may be overcome by measuring the specular reflection spectrum of a single crystal of a dye with plane-polarized light.[21] When isotropic radiation is incident normally upon the face of a molecular crystal the ordered aggregate of molecules preferentially reflect light with the polarization and frequency that the corresponding molecules in dilute solution would absorb, were they to retain their crystal orientations. The specular or metallic reflection spectrum of a single crystal is of a different nature from the so-termed diffuse reflectance spectrum of the corresponding powdered crystal.[22] In the latter case the light is reflected internally from the rear surface of the particles, passing through each particle two or more times, and the diffuse reflectance spectrum is essentially an absorption curve if the particle size is small. If not there is specular reflection from the front surface of each particle as well as diffuse internal reflection from the rear and the resultant spectrum is complex.[22]

The diffuse reflectance spectrum, like the isotropic absorption spectrum, affords no polarization data, but the specular reflection spectrum of a single crystal provides the absolute polarization directions of the transition moments of the molecule if the crystal structure is known, as in the case of the all-*trans* tetraene carboxylic acid, β-ionylidene crotonic acid.[23] Otherwise the technique yields the relative polarization directions of the electronic transitions of the molecule, as in the case of auramine (III; $R = NH_2$), where the weak shorter-wavelength bands at 316 and 372 nm have been shown by specular reflectance[21] to be polarized perpendicular to the strong lowest-energy band at 440 nm. Theoretical studies suggest[24] that the 440 nm band of auramine is long-axis-polarized while the 316 and 372 nm bands are polarized along the short axis of the molecule [the x and y direction, respectively, in (III; $R = NH_2$)].

Both the problem of high absorption and that of interaction with other molecules of the same kind in the crystal may be overcome by studying the polarized spectrum of a single mixed crystal. The dye is introduced

[18] D. P. Craig and S. H. Walmsley, "Excitons in Molecular Crystals." Benjamin, New York, 1968.

[19] W. Hoppe, *Kolloid-Z.* **109**, 27 (1944).

[20] L. E. Lyons, J. R. Walsh, and J. W. White, *J. Chem. Soc.* p. 167 (1960).

[21] B. G. Anex, *Mol. Cryst.* **1**, 1 (1966).

[22] W. W. Wendlandt and H. G. Hecht, "Reflectance Spectroscopy." Wiley (Interscience), New York, 1966.

[23] L. J. Parkhurst and B. G. Anex, *J. Chem. Phys.* **45**, 862 (1966).

[24] F. C. Adam, *J. Mol. Spectry.* **4**, 359 (1960).

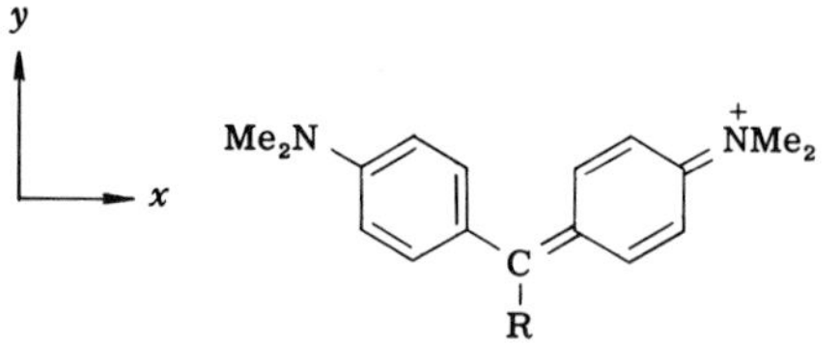

(III) 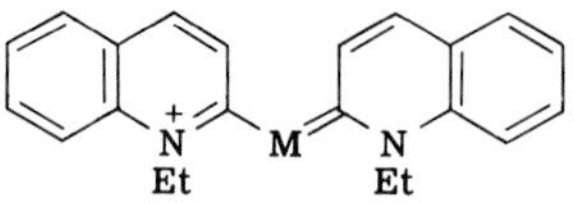   (IV)

in low concentration as a guest molecule in a host lattice of molecules which absorb at a higher frequency. Thus the iodide of pseudoisocyanine (IV; M = CH) forms mixed crystals with its "half-molecule," quinaldine ethiodide, and the spectrum of a dilute mixed crystal shows that the long-wavelength band of monomeric pseudoisocyanine at 530 nm is long-axis-polarized.[25]

Liquid crystals, which become uniformly ordered in one or two dimensions in a magnetic field, may be used as a host lattice or solvent for polarized spectroscopic measurements.[26] The majority of known liquid crystals are composed of large unsaturated molecules which absorb in the visible region,[27] but mixtures of cholesteryl esters have good optical transmission properties and serve as nematic solvents which, with their dye solutes, assume a preferred molecular orientation in a magnetic field.[26] The polarization of the long-wavelength bands of β-carotene, 4-dimethylamino-4'-nitroazobenzene, and octa-$tert$-butyldibenzoquinone, have been determined by this technique.[26]

In a nonpolar solvent a dye molecule with a permanent electric-dipole moment becomes statistically orientated in a static electric field, and the directions of the transition moments of the molecule relative to that of the permanent moment are readily determined with polarized light propagated perpendicular to the field. This method was first used[28] to show that the long-wavelength band of p-nitrosodimethylaniline is polarized parallel to the direction of the permanent dipole moment of the molecule, and similar studies of a wide range of analogous polar molecules have been carried out subsequently.[29]

Long-chain molecules, notably soluble polymers, are statistically orientated in solution under streaming conditions, and the transition-moment directions of the solute molecules may be determined with polar-

[25] G. Scheibe, *Angew. Chem.* **52**, 631 (1939).

[26] E. Sackmann, *J. Am. Chem. Soc.* **90**, 3569 (1968).

[27] G. W. Gray, "Molecular Structure and the Properties of Liquid Crystals." Academic Press, New York, 1962.

[28] W. Kuhn, H. Dührkopp, and H. Martin, *Z. Physik. Chem.* **B45**, 121 (1939).

[29] H. Labhart, *Tetrahedron* **19**, Suppl. 2, 223 (1963).

ized light propagated perpendicular[30] or parallel[31] to the flow direction. The polymer of pseudoisocyanine (IV; M = CH) has been studied[30] by this method, which is particularly useful for the investigation of dye molecules bound to soluble polymers.[31,32]

The absorption of polymer films which have been dyed is generally dichroic, and the dichroism is enhanced if the film is stretched, either before or after the dyeing process. The dichroism is particularly marked

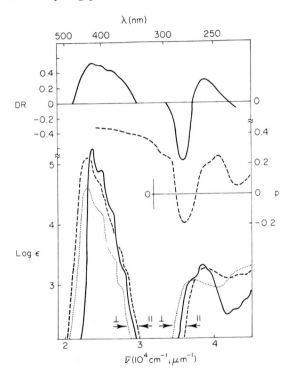

FIG. 5. The spectra of α,ω-di(N-pyrrolidinyl)pentamethinecyanine [II; $R_2 =$ $(CH_2)_4$] in methanol solution (———) and in a stretched poly(vinyl alcohol) film with the electric vector of the radiation parallel $\parallel$ (— — —) and perpendicular $\perp$ (·····) to the direction of stretching (bottom curves). The resultant dichroism ratio is DR $= (\epsilon_{\parallel} - \epsilon_{\perp})/(\epsilon_{\parallel} + \epsilon_{\perp})$ for the film measurements (top curve), and the degree of fluorescence polarization is $p = (I_{\parallel} - I_{\perp})/(I_{\parallel} + I_{\perp})$ for polarized excitation through the frequency region of absorption (middle curve). Adapted from G. Scheibe, J. Kern, and F. Dörr, Z. Elektrochem. 63, 117 (1959); F. Dörr, J. Kotschy, and H. Kausen, ibid. 69, 11 (1965).

[30] G. Scheibe, Z. Elektrochem. 47, 73 (1941).
[31] S. F. Mason and A. J. McCaffery, Nature 204, 468 (1964).
[32] C. Nagata, M. Kodama, Y. Tagashira, and A. Imamura, Biopolymers 4, 409 (1966).

in the case of elongated dye molecules, such as the linear cyanines (II) (Fig. 5), and it is presumed to arise from a preferred orientation of the long axis of the dye along the stretching direction of the film. Measurements of the absorption spectrum of the film with plane-polarized light give $\epsilon_\parallel$ and $\epsilon_\perp$, the extinction coefficient for light polarized, respectively, parallel and perpendicular to the stretching direction, and the linear dichroism at a particular wavelength is expressed as the ratio, $(\epsilon_\parallel - \epsilon_\perp)/(\epsilon_\parallel + \epsilon_\perp)$. Positive values of the linear dichroism ratio, which may be close to unity in commercial polarizing films, e.g., Polaroid, correspond to electronic transitions polarized parallel or at a small angle to the stretching direction, while negative values of the ratio are associated with a transverse polarization.[33] In the case of α,ω-di(N-pyrrolidinyl)pentamethinecyanine [II; $n = 2$, $R_2 = (CH_2)_4$] adsorbed on a stretched poly(vinyl alcohol) film the dichroism spectrum suggests (Fig. 5) that the intense long-wavelength band at 420 nm is long-axis-polarized, whereas the weak shoulder at 275 nm is polarized in a transverse direction.[34]

The most general method for the determination of the relative polarization directions of the transition moments of an organic molecule is the measurement of the polarized excitation and luminescence of the molecule in a viscous or solid isotropic solution. This method does not depend upon a particular molecular property, such as a permanent dipole moment or an elongated shape, as almost all molecules in a glassy solution at low temperature luminesce when irradiated. Exceptions are labile species subject to photolysis with unit quantum yield.

If plane-polarized light is incident upon a glassy solution only those

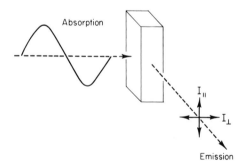

Fig. 6. The relative orientation of the directions of propagation and of polarization of the absorbed and emitted light in polarized excitation and emission measurements.

[33] A. Jablonsky, *Acta Phys. Polon.* **3**, 421 (1934).
[34] G. Scheibe, J. Kern, and F. Dörr, *Z. Elektrochem.* **63**, 117 (1959).

solute molecules whose transition moments have a component parallel to the plane of polarization absorb radiation and subsequently luminesce[35] (Fig. 6). The polarized exciting light selects the suitably orientated solute molecules, and if they do not reorientate during the lifetime of the excited electronic state the luminescence is polarized. As the emission probability is related to the corresponding absorption probability, the lifetime of an excited state is inversely proportional to the intensity of the absorption producing that state, namely,

$$1/\tau_0 = 29 \times 10^{-10} \, \bar{\nu}_{max}{}^2 \epsilon_{max} \, \Delta\bar{\nu} \tag{12}$$

where τ_0 is the intrinsic or radiative lifetime in seconds. For allowed transitions with $\epsilon_{max} \simeq 10^5$ the excited state has a lifetime of $\sim 10^{-8}$ second and the corresponding emission, fluorescence, is likewise short-lived. However, for spin-forbidden transitions with $\epsilon_{max} < 1$ the excited triplet state has a substantially longer lifetime, up to ~ 10 seconds in the case of aromatic hydrocarbons, and the corresponding emission, phosphorescence, is temporally more persistent. Thus the polarization of fluorescence may be observed in solvents of low viscosity, even in water at room temperature in the case of some large dye molecules,[35] whereas the measurements of polarized phosphorescence requires generally the use of solid solutions.[13]

Fluorescence occurs in general only from the lowest-energy excited singlet state of an organic molecule, and phosphorescence only from the lowest triplet state. If an assembly of solute molecules are excited to a higher singlet state with light of the appropriate frequency they lose the excess electronic energy and reach the lowest-energy excited singlet state within $\sim 10^{-12}$ second. The excited molecules then fluoresce, or cross over to a triplet state, or lose energy nonradiatively, during their lifetime of $\sim 10^{-8}$ second.

If the solute molecules are excited into their lowest-energy singlet excited state the absorption and fluorescence transition moments are one and the same, and the fluorescence observed along an axis perpendicular to the direction of propagation of the exciting light and of its oscillating electric field is polarized predominantly parallel to the polarization direction of the exciting light (Fig. 6). On the other hand, if the molecules are excited into a higher singlet state with a transition moment perpendicular in the molecular frame to that of the lowest-energy excited singlet state the fluorescence has a polarization predominantly perpendicular to that of the absorbed light.

[35] P. P. Feofilov, "The Physical Basis of Polarised Emission." Consultants Bureau, New York, 1961.

The degree of polarization of the luminescence, p, is defined by the relation

$$p = (I_{\parallel} - I_{\perp})/(I_{\parallel} + I_{\perp}) \tag{13}$$

where $I_{\parallel}$ and $I_{\perp}$ are the emission intensities polarized parallel and perpendicular, respectively, to the polarization direction of the exciting light. If the angle between the absorption and the emission transition moment is α the degree of polarization is given by[36]

$$p = (3 \cos^2 \alpha - 1)/(\cos^2 \alpha + 3) \tag{14}$$

the limiting values of p being $+\frac{1}{2}$ and $-\frac{1}{3}$ for parallel and perpendicular transition moments, respectively. However, in molecules with a threefold or higher rotational axis of symmetry the absorption and emission moments may be doubly degenerate, in which event the upper limiting value of the degree of polarization is $+\frac{1}{7}$.

The polarization excitation and emission spectra of a wide variety of dye molecules have been reported,[35] and the relative polarization directions of the transition moments of a given dye obtained by this and other methods are in substantial agreement, e.g., α,ω-di-(N-pyrrolidinyl)-pentamethinecyanine [II; $n = 2$, $R_2 = (CH_2)_4$] (Fig. 5). In the case of crystal violet (III; $R = p\text{-Me}_2\text{NPh}-$) the degree of polarization is found[35] to change from $+0.4$ to -0.1 in the region of the long-wavelength absorption band between 620 and 500 nm, the positive value being larger than the limit of $+\frac{1}{7}$ required for a doubly degenerate absorption and emission transition. Thus crystal violet does not possess a threefold rotational axis of symmetry in the lowest excited state nor, possibly, in the ground state, and the x- and y-polarized components of the lowest-energy transition in (III; $R = p\text{-Me}_2\text{NPh}-$) have slightly different energies although their absorption lies under a common band envelope.

E. VIBRATIONAL STRUCTURE

The main long-wavelength absorption band of a number of dyes exhibits a structure due to vibrational modes active in the electronically excited state. The vibrational structure appears because the equilibrium nuclear configuration of the molecule in the excited electronic state differs from that of the ground state. The promotion of an electron from a bonding to an antibonding orbital gives rise to an increase in the average bond length, producing generally an increase in the size of the molecule. In addition the molecule may change its shape, as in the case

[36] A. Jablonsky, *Z. Physik* **96**, 236 (1935).

of acetylene which is trans-bent in its first excited state,[37] or formaldehyde which has a pyramidal shape in both its lowest singlet[38,39] and lowest triplet state.[40]

According to the uncertainty principle, $\Delta E \ \Delta t \simeq h$, the absorption of a photon with a visible or ultraviolet frequency occupies a time of $\sim 10^{-15}$ second. During this period the movement of the atomic nuclei is negligible, and in the immediately formed excited electronic state they still retain the ground-state equilibrium configuration (Fig. 7). The atomic nuclei then find themselves displaced from the new excited-state equilibrium configuration, in positions corresponding to the turning points of a vibrational mode or modes (Fig. 7), and they become centered upon the new configuration in the space of a vibrational period ($\sim 10^{-13}$ second). These modes appear in the electronic absorption band system as a progression of bands which are each separated from their nearest neighbors by the vibration frequency of the mode in the excited electronic state (Figs. 4, 7, and 8).

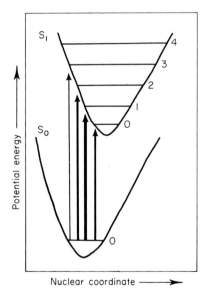

FIG. 7. The potential energy curves of the ground state, S_0, and the first excited electronic state, S_1, and the relative intensities, denoted by the relative breadths of the vertical arrows, of the vibrational bands in the $S_0 \rightarrow S_1$ electronic band system.

[37] C. K. Ingold and G. W. King, *J. Chem. Soc.* pp. 2702, 2704, 2708, 2725, and 2745 (1953).

[38] J. C. D. Brand, *J. Chem. Soc.* p. 858 (1956).

[39] G. W. Robinson, *Can. J. Phys.* **34**, 699 (1956).

[40] G. W. Robinson and V. E. DiGiorgio, *J. Chem. Phys.* **31**, 1678 (1959).

Progressions of vibrational bands in an electronic band system occur mainly from the zero vibrational level of the electronic ground state to a series of successive vibrational levels, $n = 0,1,2,3 \ldots$, of the electronically excited state, and they appear only for totally symmetric vibrations, namely, the modes which change the size but not the shape of the molecule. Nontotally symmetric modes, which change the shape of the molecule, appear only in double or even-numbered vibrational quantum changes, $0 \rightarrow 2,4,6$ etc., in allowed electronic transitions, but odd-numbered quantum changes in one or more of these modes may appear in a forbidden electronic transition and render that transition partly allowed by deforming the equilibrium shape of the molecule, e.g., by removing a center, axis, or plane of symmetry.

Progressions of vibrational bands are observed in an electronic band system only if one or a small number of vibrational modes are active in the absorption process, as with the polyenes (I), where an interval of about 1200 cm^{-1} is found between successive members of the vibrational progression of the long-wavelength absorption band, corresponding to the carbon–carbon stretching vibration frequency in the electronically excited state (Fig. 4). If many vibrational modes are active in the electronic excitation the various progressions overlap and only the envelope is observed as a smooth absorption curve, e.g., the first member of the cyanine series [II; $n = 0$, $R_2 = (CH_2)_5$] (Fig. 8).

The width of the visible absorption band of a dye, and thus the "brightness" or "dullness" of the color, is determined by the length or the number of members of the progressions in the vibrational modes of the excited state. The length of the vibrational progressions in an electronic band depends upon the extent of the change in the configuration of the atomic nuclei induced by the electronic excitation. If there is little or no change in the molecular size and shape on electronic excitation the absorption intensity is concentrated in the $0 \rightarrow 0$ member of the vibrational progression, but with an increasing change of nuclear configuration accompanying the excitation this member becomes weaker and the electronic absorption intensity is spread over the higher members of the progression. In the former case the total electronic bandwidth is small and in the latter it is larger.

In a series of related dyes, such as the cyanines (II), the larger molecules have generally smaller bandwidths and so exhibit a brighter color than the smaller members of the series (Fig. 8). In the larger dye molecules the loss of binding energy due to the lowest-frequency excitation is smaller, as is shown by the larger wavelength of absorption, and the loss is shared out by a larger number of π-bonds, so that each bond is lengthened to a lesser degree. The disparity between the equilibrium nuclear

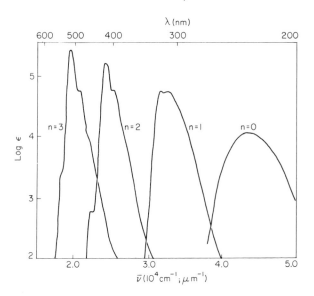

Fɪɢ. 8. The absorption spectra of the α,ω-di(N-piperidinyl)polymethine cyanines [(II); $R_2 = (CH_2)_5$, $n = 0$–3], in ethanol at 100°K. From G. Scheibe, *in* "Optische Anregung Organischer Systeme. 2 Internationales Farbensymposium" (W. Foerst, ed.), p. 109. Verlag Chemie, Weinheim, 1966.

configuration in the ground state and that in the excited state is accordingly smaller and the vibrational progressions in the absorption band system are correspondingly shorter the larger is the π-electron system of the molecule. In addition fewer vibrational modes are active in the absorption process, and the larger members of the dye series show vibrational structure in their absorption bands, whereas the smaller members give only smooth broad bands (Fig. 8).

For dyes of comparable size, the molecules containing an odd number of conjugated atoms give brighter colors than those containing an even number. In the even-numbered polyene series (I) there is a unique classical valency structure for the ground state, consisting of alternating formal single and double carbon–carbon bonds. On electronic excitation the alternation of single- and double-bond character is reversed, so that large changes in the equilibrium nuclear configuration occur and relatively long progressions in the excited-state carbon–carbon stretching vibration are observed (Fig. 4). In contrast, there are two equivalent classical valency structures for the ground state of the odd-numbered cyanine series (II), so that the carbon–carbon bond lengths are nearly equal in the ground state and they remain so, with a small average increase, on excitation. The absorptions of the longer members of the cyanine series

(II) have bandwidths at half-maximum extinction of about 1000 cm^{-1}, compared with some 4000 cm^{-1} for corresponding members of the polyene series (I) (Figs. 4 and 8). Thus the colors of the cyanine dyes are characteristically sharp and bright, whereas those of the carotenoid pigments are typically broad and dull.

III. Quantum Theories of Color

A. THE VALENCE BOND METHOD

In the early days of quantum chemistry two principal treatments were evolved for the calculation of the electronic properties of polyatomic molecules, the valence bond and the molecular orbital method. The first to be developed and applied to dye molecules, notably the cyanines,[41-45] was the valence bond method but in recent years it has been largely superseded by the various orbital treatments. The valence bond method derived historically from the classical resonance theory of conjugation in unsaturated organic molecules, in which it is supposed that there is an oscillation of bonding between formal Kekulé structures.

Two classical structures of identical energy can be written for the symmetrical cyanines (II), and it is assumed in the simple valence bond treatment that the actual molecule is a hybrid or superposition of these

$$\overset{+}{L}=CH-[-CH=CH-]_n-R \qquad\qquad L-[-CH=CH-]_n-CH=\overset{+}{R}$$

(Va)   (Vb)

$$L-\overset{+}{C}H-[-CH=CH-]_n-R$$

(Vc)

two structures, (Va) and (Vb), where the left-hand, L, and right-hand, R, terminal groups are equivalent. The wavefunction ψ_0 of the ground state of the cyanine is given by the symmetric combination of the wavefunctions ϕ_1 and ϕ_2 of the individual structures (Va) and (Vb),

$$\psi_0 = (\phi_1 + \phi_2) \tag{15}$$

[41] T. Förster, Z. Elektrochem. 45, 548 (1939); Z. Physik. Chem. B47, 245 (1940); B48, 12 (1941).

[42] L. Pauling, Proc. Natl. Acad. Sci. U. S. 25, 577 (1939).

[43] K. F. Herzfeld, J. Chem. Phys. 10, 508 (1942).

[44] A. L. Sklar, J. Chem. Phys. 10, 521 (1942).

[45] K. F. Herzfeld and A. L. Sklar, Rev. Mod. Phys. 14, 294 (1942).

and a higher-energy excited state ψ_n by the corresponding antisymmetric combination

$$\psi_n = (\phi_1 - \phi_2) \tag{16}$$

The interaction between the two classical structures (Va) and (Vb) has an energy α given by

$$\alpha = \int \phi_1 H \phi_2 \, d\tau \tag{17}$$

where H is the Hamiltonian of the system, and the hybrid electronic states ψ_0 and ψ_n are stabilized and destabilized, respectively, by the energy increment α relative to the classical structures (Fig. 9a). An elec-

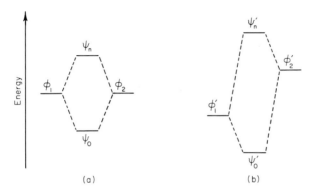

FIG. 9. The energy relations between the classical structures, ϕ_1 and ϕ_2, and the resulting hybrid states, ψ_0 and ψ_n, for the case (a) structures of similar energy and (b) structures with different energies.

tronic transition from the ground state ψ_0 occurs if the cyanine absorbs a photon with the appropriate frequency, $h\nu = 2\alpha$.

Similar considerations apply to other symmetrical odd-atom systems, such as the oxonols (VI), but for symmetrical even-atom systems, like

$$O = CH[CH=CH]_n O^-$$

(VI)

$$Me_2\ddot{N}[CH=CH]_n CHO$$

(VII)

the polyenes (I), or unsymmetrical odd-atom systems, such as the mero-cyanines (VII), the two classical valency structures which can be written for each molecule are not identical and they have different energies (Fig. 9b). The transition from the ground state ψ'_0 to the excited state ψ'_n now requires the energy difference between the two classical structures ($E_1 - E_2$) in addition to the interaction energy $2\alpha'$, and the absorption of a photon with a higher frequency is necessary (Fig. 9b). Thus molecules designed to absorb at low frequencies should be hybrids of classical structures with comparable energies and, other factors being equal, higher-frequency absorption should result the larger the energy difference between those stuctures (Fig. 9).

The extensive research of Brooker and his collaborators[46] has shown that the unsymmetrical cyanines (V; $L \neq R$) generally absorb at a shorter wavelength than the mean of the absorption wavelengths of the corresponding two symmetrical cyanines with equivalent end groups, L and R, respectively (V; $L = R$). The deviation of the absorption wavelength of an unsymmetrical cyanine from the mean is very small if the end groups L and R are so similar electronically that the classical structures (Va) and (Vb) have the same energy, or nearly so (Fig. 9a). The mean or isoenergetic wavelength λ_I may be represented[47] by a sum of contributions λ_L and λ_R from the two end groups and λ_C from each carbon atom of the polymethine chain joining them (V), namely,

$$\lambda_I = N\lambda_C + \lambda_L + \lambda_R \tag{18}$$

where N is the number of carbon atoms in the polymethine chain and λ_C has a value of $\sim$50 nm, both theoretically[47] and experimentally,[46] e.g., the series (II; R = Me) and (V) in Table I.

If the electronic properties of the two end groups L and R are not similar the classical structures (Va) and (Vb) have different energies (Fig. 9b), and the deviation of the absorption frequency of the unsymmetrical cyanine from the isoenergetic value given by the mean of the absorption frequencies of the two symmetrical analogs is large. Theoretically the deviations should be the greater the larger is the energy difference between the classical structures (Va) and (Vb). Brooker and his co-workers placed the end groups studied in an order of electronic "basicity" which represents the tendency of a given group to form a double bond to the polymethine chain.[46] Thus if (Va) contributes more to the ground-state resonance hybrid than (Vb) the bonds joining the end groups L and R to the polymethine chain have a larger and a smaller double-bond character, respectively, and L is more "basic" than R.

The absorption frequency $\bar{\nu}$ of an unsymmetrical cyanine has been shown by Platt[47] to be related to the isoenergetic frequency $\bar{\nu}_I$ by

$$\bar{\nu} = [\bar{\nu}_I{}^2 + (b_L - b_R)^2]^{\frac{1}{2}} \tag{19}$$

[46] L. G. S. Brooker, A. C. Craig, D. W. Heseltine, P. W. Jenkins, and L. L. Lincoln, *J. Am. Chem. Soc.* **87**, 2443 (1965); Color and Constitution. Part XIII; earlier parts, *ibid.* **73**, 1087, 5332, 5350, and 5356 (1951); **67**, 1869, 1875, and 1889 (1945); **64**, 199 (1942); **63**, 3192, 3203, and 3214 (1941); **62**, 1116 (1940).

[47] J. R. Platt, *J. Chem. Phys.* **25**, 80 (1956).

TABLE I

WAVELENGTH (λ) AND EXTINCTION COEFFICIENT (ϵ) OF LONGEST-WAVELENGTH
BAND MAXIMUM IN ELECTRONIC SPECTRA OF POLYENES (I; R = H)
SYMMETRICAL CYANINES (II; R = Me), OXONOLS (VI),
AND MEROCYANINES (VII)

	(I; R = H)[a]		(II; R = Me)[b]		(VI)[b]		(VII)[c]	
n	λ(nm)	$10^3\epsilon$	λ(nm)	$10^3\epsilon$	λ(nm)	$10^3\epsilon$	λ(nm)	$10^3\epsilon$
1	162	~10	312.5	64	267.5	27	283	37
2	203.5	~20	416	119	362.5	56	361.5	51
3	268	35	519	207	455	75	421.5	56
4	304	~70	625	295	547.5	(63)	462.5	65
5	334	121	734.5	352	(644)	—	491.5	68
6	364	138	848	(220)	—	—	512.5	72

[a] Values for the 0–0 vibrational band. Vapor-phase values for $n = 1$ and 2. Values for paraffin solutions, $n = 3$–6; F. Sondheimer, D. A. Ben-Efraim, and R. Wolovsky, *J. Am. Chem. Soc.* **83**, 1675 (1961).

[b] Values for methylene dichloride solution; S. S. Malhotra and M. C. Whiting, *J. Chem. Soc.* p. 3812 (1960).

[c] Values for dimethylformamide solution given in footnote b to this table.

where b_L and b_R are the basicities, in frequency units (cm^{-1}) of the left and right end groups, L and R (V), respectively. The electronic basicities of some 60 end groups have been listed for three- and five-carbon chains, correlating the spectra of more than 100 cyanine dyes.[47]

Most merocyanines are electronically unsymmetrical and show large Brooker deviations. Each member of the merocyanine series (VII), for example, absorbs consistently at a shorter wavelength than the isoenergetic value obtained from the absorption wavelengths of corresponding members of the symmetric cyanine (II; R = Me) and oxonol (VI) series (Table I). Of the two principal structures contributing to the hybrid ground and excited state of a merocyanine one, in general, is nonpolar and the other is zwitterionic, e.g., (VIIIa) and (VIIIb), respectively, for the case of phenol blue. The zwitterionic structure is stabilized in polar media whereas the energy of the nonpolar structure is relatively insensitive to the solvent environment, and large wavelength shifts result from a change of solvent.[41,46] The absorption of phenol blue undergoes a red shift from 552 nm in cyclohexane solution to 668 nm in water,[46] indicating that the nonpolar structure (VIIIa) has the lower energy and makes the

(VIIIa)   (VIIIb)

major contribution to the ground state in nonpolar solvents. The energy of the zwitterionic structure (VIIIb) is lowered in a polar solvent and the contributions of the two structures to the hybrid states of phenol blue become more nearly equal, producing a red shift (Fig. 9).

In contrast the absorption of the merocyanine (IX) undergoes a blue shift from 732 nm in toluene to 458 nm in water,[46] as the zwitterionic structure (IXa) is the more stable and makes the major contribution to the ground state of the dye even in nonpolar solvents. On changing to a polar solvent the zwitterionic structure (IXa) is further stabilized and its energy separation from the nonpolar structure (IXb) is increased, resulting in a blue shift of the absorption (Fig. 9b).

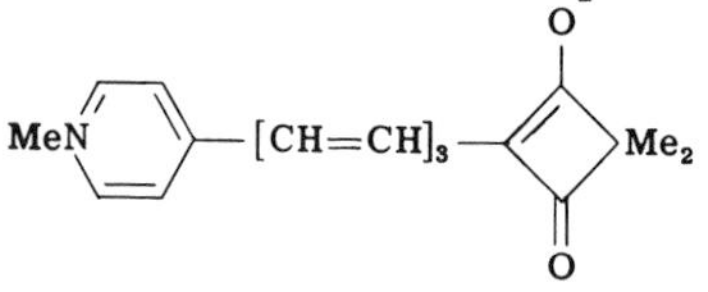

(IXa) 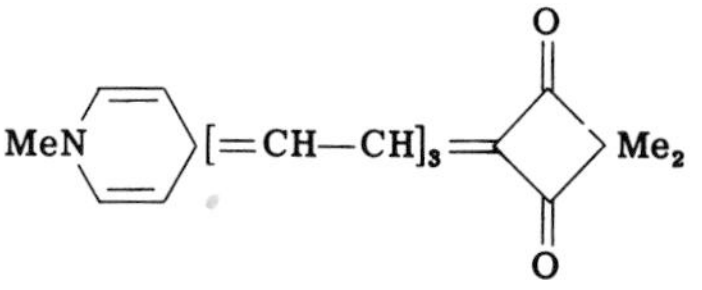   (IXb)

The absorption of merocyanine dyes in which the nonpolar and the zwitterion structures have comparable energies exhibit striking solvent effects,[46] e.g., (X). The zwitterionic structure (Xa) appears to be more stable than the neutral structure (Xb) in polar solvents but less stable in

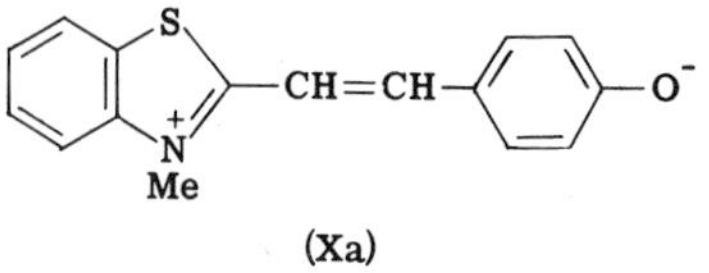

(Xa) 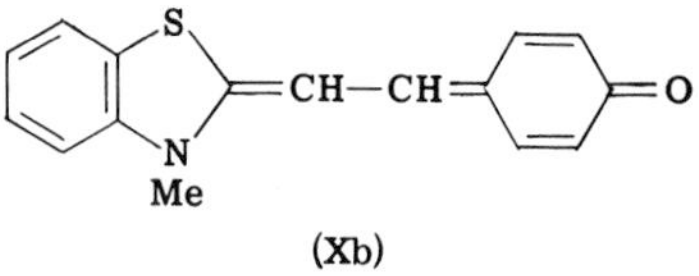   (Xb)

nonpolar solvents, so that first a red shift and then a blue shift is observed as the solvent polarity is progressively increased[46,48] (Fig. 10). At the same time the extinction coefficient of the absorption rises and then falls (Fig. 10) but compensating changes in the bandwidth maintain an approximate constancy in the band area.[48]

In the particular solvent with a polarity giving rise to the maximum value of the wavelength and the extinction coefficient of the absorption (Fig. 10) the two structures (Xa) and (Xb) are isoenergetic (Fig. 9a) and there are no major changes in bond order on excitation, since the two structures contribute equally to the ground and the excited state. In consequence there are no important changes in the relative positions of the

[48] E. G. McRae, *Spectrochim. Acta* **12**, 192 (1958).

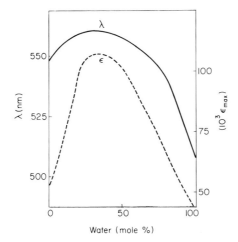

Water (mole %)

FIG. 10. The variation of the wavelength (————) and of the extinction coefficient (— — — —) of the absorption maximum of the merocyanine (X) with solvent composition in dioxane–water mixtures. From data reported by E. G. McRae, *Spectrochim. Acta* **12**, 192 (1958).

atomic nuclei on excitation and the 0–0 vibrational band appears strongly in the absorption, to the virtual exclusion of higher members of the excited-state vibrational progressions (Fig. 7). A high maximum extinction coefficient and a small bandwidth are thereby produced. In nonpolar or in highly polar solvents, on the other hand, a change in the bond alternation along the conjugated chain occurs on excitation, owing to the unequal contributions of the structures (Xa) and (Xb) to the ground and excited state of the dye. Not only the 0–0 but also the higher members of the upper-state progressions in the stretching vibrations are then involved in the absorption, giving a broadened band and a reduced maximum extinction coefficient, together with a blue shift.[48]

Although the valence bond approach provides a satisfactory qualitative account of the color of cyanine dyes the method becomes increasingly complex when refined and made more quantitative. Pauling[42] demonstrated that pairs of classical structures, such as (Va) and (Vb), cannot interact appreciably one with the other directly. The interaction takes place indirectly through a series of structures with a higher energy, where the positive charge is located upon a carbon atom, such as (Vc). The more refined the calculations become, the greater is the range of classical structures that must be considered. Calculations of this kind have been carried out by Förster[41] and by Herzfeld[43,45] and Sklar,[44,45] who showed that the absorption wavelength should increase linearly with increasing chain length for the symmetrical cyanines [Eq. (18)] but should increase only asymptotically to a limit for the unsymmetrical dyes, e.g., the limiting wavelength $[1/(b_L - b_R)]$ [Eq. (19)].

B. Molecular Orbital Treatments

1. Levels of Approximation

The electronic states of a dye molecule are built up from occupied one-electron energy levels in the molecular orbital method, in contrast to the valence bond treatment where they are regarded as combinations of classical structures. The molecular orbital approach to the question of color is accordingly a more direct one, for we are able to ascribe an absorption band to the transition of an electron from one molecular orbital to another in a dye molecule, but not from one classical valence bond structure to another.

There are a number of molecular orbital treatments of color, but basic to each of them is the assumption that, for a multielectron system, it is possible to formulate one-electron energy levels or orbitals. Strictly speaking this is not possible, for the electrons of a molecule so correlate their motions that the interelectron repulsion is minimized, and we can study directly only the multielectron states of a molecule, the one-electron energy levels being essentially heuristic approximations. However, the electron-correlation energy is not greatly different for the ground and the excited states of a polyatomic molecule, and the difference is negligible compared with other energy quantities which are usually ignored in the simpler treatments.

In all wave-mechanical treatments of color we are concerned with the energy difference between the ground and an excited electronic state of a molecule, with the wavefunctions ψ_0 and ψ_n, respectively. The wavefunctions ψ are solutions of the operator equation

$$\mathcal{3C}\psi = E\psi \tag{20}$$

where $\mathcal{3C}$ is the quantum-mechanical Hamiltonian of the molecule. If we separate the electronic and nuclear motions, on the reasonable assumption that the velocity of the electrons is so large that they adjust themselves instantaneously to the positions of the nuclei, we have the multielectron Hamiltonian

$$\mathcal{3C}(1,2, \ldots i,j, \ldots n) = -\frac{1}{2} \sum_i \nabla_i^2 - \sum_{i\mu} \frac{Z_\mu}{R_{i\mu}} + \sum_{ij} \frac{1}{r_{ij}} \tag{21}$$

in which e, m, and $(h/2\pi)$ have been taken to be units of electronic charge and mass and of action, respectively. The first term on the right-hand side of Eq. (21) is the Laplacian operator for the kinetic energy of electron i, and the other terms refer to the Coulombic potential energy; the second to the attraction of nucleus μ with an effective positive charge Z_μ for electron i, and the third to the repulsion between electrons i and j, the sums being taken over all electrons and all nuclei.

In the simplest of the molecular orbital treatments, that of the free-electron model,[6] it is assumed that the potential energy terms of Eq. (21) are constant over the length of the conjugated chain for a π-electron moving in a molecular orbital of an unsaturated system. Only the Laplacian operator for the kinetic energy of a π-electron [Eq. (21)] is considered, and the solutions obtained have the form of standing waves in a one-dimensional box. The assumptions of the free-electron model are drastic and, in particular, the distinction between the atoms and the bonds in a molecule is generally ignored, so that the method is not well suited to the treatment of detailed relations between color and molecular structure.

At an equivalent level of approximation the Hückel method[8,9] distinguishes between the atoms and bonds of a molecule, and indeed between different types of atoms and different kinds of bonds. In this method each one-electron π-orbital of a conjugated system ψ_i is represented by a linear combination of atomic $2p_\pi$ orbitals, ϕ_μ,

$$\psi_i = \sum_\mu c_{\mu i}\phi_\mu \tag{22}$$

where the numerical coefficients, $c_{\mu i}$, have the significance that $c_{\mu i}^2$ represents the fraction of the charge density of an electron in the molecular orbital ψ_i located upon the atom μ. The individual atoms are considered explicitly, for Eq. (22) is based on the assumption that an electron in the molecular orbital ψ_i behaves as though it were in the atomic orbital ϕ_μ when it is in the vicinity of the atomic nucleus μ.

Formally the many-electron Hamiltonian is broken down into a sum of equivalent one-electron Hamiltonians in the Hückel theory by assuming that the two-electron term in Eq. (21), referring to the interelectron repulsion, has some average constant value. However, the energy parameters required in the Hückel approximation are evaluated empirically in practice, namely, the Coulomb, α, and resonance integral, β, defined by,

$$\alpha_\mu = \int \phi_\mu H \phi_\mu \, d\tau \tag{23}$$

and

$$\beta_{\mu\nu} = \int \phi_\mu H \phi_\nu \, d\tau \tag{24}$$

where H is the effective one-electron Hamiltonian, and the atoms μ and

ν are bonded. The Coulomb integral α_μ is a measure of the effective electronegativity of atom μ, and the resonance integral $\beta_{\mu\nu}$ a measure of the π-bonding energy between atoms μ and ν.

Interactions between nonbonded atoms are not considered in the Hückel theory, nor in the free-electron model, and from both treatments it transpires that the topology of a π-electron system, i.e., the form of the network of conjugated bonds, is the major determinant of the relative energies of the molecular orbitals. According to both of these methods s-*cis*- and s-*trans*-butadiene have the same set of π-orbitals, but cyclobutadiene has a quite distinct and very different set.

A distinction between the π-electron energies of geometrical isomers emerges at the next level of approximation, that of the self-consistent field π-electron method.[9] In this approach the two-electron repulsion term in the many-electron Hamiltonian [Eq. (21)] is retained for the π-electrons although, for tractability, the set of repulsions between the charge densities on no more than two atomic centers is considered explicitly. The self-consistent π-orbitals [Eq. (22)] are obtained iteratively by successive approximation from Hückel orbitals, since the energy and atomic orbital coefficients of one π-orbital now depend upon the form of all of the other occupied π-orbitals.

In addition to energy parameters corresponding to the Coulomb and resonance integral of the Hückel theory [Eqs. (23) and (24)] the self-consistent field method requires values for the one- and two-center electron repulsion integrals, $\gamma_{\mu\nu}$. Where the atoms μ and ν are separated by several angstroms $\gamma_{\mu\nu}$ may be calculated from Coulomb's law, but the one-center, γ_{11}, and near-neighbor two-center integrals, γ_{12} and γ_{13}, are generally determined empirically, e.g., from the electronic spectrum of benzene.

The number of parameters required for a self-consistent field π-electron calculation is a minimum for homonuclear π-electron systems with π-bond lengths which are equal, or nearly so, and the method has been applied with the greatest success to the interpretation of the electronic spectra of the aromatic hydrocarbons.[9] The corresponding calculations for heteroatomic π-electron systems are less precise and discriminating as each type of heteroatom λ requires an individual set of parameters, α_λ, $\beta_{\lambda\mu}$, and $\gamma_{\lambda\mu}$. Relatively few dyes have been studied by means of the self-consistent π-electron method, notable examples being the symmetrical cyanines[49,50] and the merocyanines,[50] $n = 1$–3 in the series (II) and (VII), respectively. The calculated frequencies and intensities of the

[49] S. P. McGlynn and W. T. Simpson, *J. Chem. Phys.* **28**, 297 (1958).
[50] M. Klessinger, *Theoret. Chim. Acta* **5**, 251 (1966).

several bands in the spectrum of each member of these series show satisfactory agreement with the experimental values[51] (Table II).

Recently both the Hückel method[52] and the approximate self-consistent field treatment[53] have been extended to cover the σ- as well as the π-electrons in the valency shells of the atoms in relatively small molecules. In addition "complete" quantum-mechanical calculations have been

TABLE II

EXPERIMENTAL ABSORPTION WAVELENGTHS (λnm) AND OSCILLATOR STRENGTHS
(f) OF ACCESSIBLE BANDS IN SPECTRA OF SYMMETRICAL CYANINES
(II; R = Me)[a]

$$\overset{+}{Me_2N}=CH[CH=CH]_nNMe_2$$

n	λ_{expt}[b]	f_{expt}[b]	λ_{SCF}[c]	f_{SCF}[c]	λ_{HMO}[d]
1	312.5	0.86	287	0.86	316
	227.5	—	169	0.01	—
2	416	1.11	381	1.34	439
	254	0.04	219	0.03	231
	228.5	—	205	0.06	—
3	519	1.30	469	1.80	512
	309	0.05	262	0.03	290
	266.5	0.06	245	0.05	195
	235	—	205	0.01	—

[a] Corresponding theoretical values calculated by the Hückel molecular orbital (HMO) and self-consistent field (SCF) methods.

[b] S. S. Malhotra and M. C. Whiting, *J. Chem. Soc.* p. 3812 (1960).

[c] M. Klessinger, *Theoret. Chim. Acta* **5**, 251 (1966).

[d] M. J. S. Dewar, *J. Chem. Soc.* p. 2329 (1950).

reported[54] for molecules as large as pyridine, considering all inner shell as well as all valency electrons. Analogous calculations will be feasible in the near future for larger molecules, and the theoretical spectroscopic properties of potential dyes will be accessible by means of a computer. Each *ab initio* computation refers, however, to an individual molecule, and the general relations between color and molecular and electronic structure are the more evident from the less rigorous molecular orbital treatments.

[51] S. S. Malhotra and M. C. Whiting, *J. Chem. Soc.* p. 3812 (1960).

[52] R. Hoffmann, *J. Chem. Phys.* **39**, 1397 (1963).

[53] J. A. Pople, D. P. Santry, and G. A. Segal, *J. Chem. Phys.* **43**, Suppl. p. 129 (1965).

[54] E. Clementi, *J. Chem. Phys.* **46**, 4731 (1967).

2. The Relations between Color and Structure

There are two main sets of factors governing the color of a dye in relation to its molecular and electronic structure. The first and principal set relates to the size and topology of the π-electron system, covering the number of conjugated atoms and the form of the bonding network between them, linear, branched, or cyclic. The second set concerns substitution and atom-replacement effects, which are dependent upon the electronegativities and π-bonding propensities of the conjugated atoms. Both groups are amenable to treatment by the free-electron model and by the Hückel approximation, but the former theory provides a more direct interpretation of the first set and the latter of the second.

In the free-electron model, which was developed independently by Bayliss,[55] Kuhn,[56] Platt,[57] and Simpson,[58] it is assumed that the σ-bond framework of a conjugated molecule provides a constant-potential box in which the π-electrons move freely. The cross-sectional area of the box, like the potential within it, is a constant, and the important variables are the length of the box and its linear, branched, or cyclic shape. The π-electrons set up standing waves in the box with a wavelength λ_e dependent upon the electronic momentum p through the de Broglie relationship, $\lambda_e = h/p$. For a linear conjugated system the electron wavelengths λ_e must be congruent with the length L of the box, so that a given π-electron has a kinetic energy E_j given by,

$$E_j = h^2 j^2 / 8mL^2 \tag{25}$$

where m is the electronic mass and j, a positive integer, is the quantum number of the π-orbital ψ_j with the energy E_j. As the π-electron charge density ψ_j^2 vanishes at the boundaries of the box the electronic wavefunctions have the sine form

$$\psi_j = (1/\sqrt{L}) \sin \pi j(x/L) \tag{26}$$

where x is the variable coordinate along the length of the box.

The π-orbitals ψ_j from the one with lowest kinetic energy ($j = 1$) upwards (Fig. 11) are occupied by two π-electrons having opposed spins so that, for a polyene chain of N atoms containing N π-electrons, the highest occupied level is $\psi_{N/2}$. For the promotion of a π-electron from the highest occupied ($j = [N/2]$) to the lowest unoccupied ($j = [(N/2) + 1]$) molecular orbital the absorbed photon has a frequency

[55] N. S. Bayliss, J. Chem. Phys. **16**, 287 (1948).

[56] H. Kuhn, Z. Elektrochem. **53**, 165 (1949); Helv. Chim. Acta **31**, 1441 (1948); **32**, 2247 (1949); J. Chem. Phys. **16**, 840 (1948); **17**, 1198 (1949).

[57] J. R. Platt, J. Chem. Phys. **17**, 484 (1949).

[58] W. T. Simpson, J. Chem. Phys. **16**, 1124 (1948); **17**, 1218 (1949).

$$\nu = h(N + 1)/8m\ d^2N^2 \qquad (27)$$

where d is the effective average bond length, which is determined by the overall distance between the ends of the all-*trans* polymethine chain with the usual carbon–carbon spacing ($d = 1.40 \cos 30°$ Å), as projected on the x axis. Inserting values for the universal constants and the effective bond length d the corresponding absorption wavelength is found to be

$$\lambda = 49N\,(\mathrm{nm}) \qquad (28)$$

in the limit of large N for both odd- and even-atom chains.

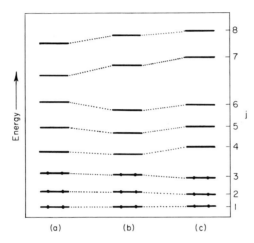

FIG. 11. The energy levels of a linear delocalized system with six conjugated atoms and six π-electrons according to (a) the simple free-election model, (b) the model with atom–bond potential alternation, and (c) the same with alternant bond–bond potential alternation.

In general the insertion of an additional vinyl group into the conjugated chain of a cyanine dye or of other odd-atom linear systems increases the wavelength of maximum absorption by $\sim$100 nm, as Eq. (28) requires (Tables I–III). The absorption wavelengths of the polyenes (I) converge, however, to a finite limit ($\sim$740 nm) for the infinite chain, and the same holds for series of other conjugated systems in which the π-electron bond orders are not uniform.

In a polyene a π-electron surmounts a potential barrier on passing over a formally single carbon-carbon bond and enters a potential trough when moving over a formal double bond, whereas in a cyanine the bond potentials are approximately equal. For a polyene of N conjugated carbon atoms there are ($N/2$) potential barriers due to bond order alter-

TABLE III
Experimental Wavelength (nm) of Lowest-Energy Band Maximum in Spectra
of N-Ethyl-2-Quinolinium (IV) and the N-Alkyl-2-Benzthiazolium (XI)
Methine- and Azacyanines, and Corresponding Theoretical Values[a]

Carbanion	Chain (M)	2-Quinolinium (IV)		2-Benzthiazolium (XI)	
		λ_{expt}[b]	λ_{theor}[c]	λ_{expt}[b]	λ_{theor}[b]
(XVI)	C	522	521	426	410
	N	421.5	450	375	360
	P[d]	—	—	478.5	—
	As[d]	642	—	491	—
(XVII)	CCC	605	613	550	480
	CNC	631	633	596	540
	NCN	430	488	412	400
	NCC	519	543	466	430
	NNC	—	557	495	480
	NNN	471	499	484	450
(XVIII)	CCCCC	708	719	667	580
	CCNCC	596	549	554	—
	NNCNN	630	704	670	—
	NNNNN	513	540	553	550

[a] Calculated by the Hückel perturbation method for the series (IV) and by the free-electron method for the series (XI).

[b] Except where otherwise specified the experimental data are taken from S. Hunig and the theoretical free-electron data from H. Kuhn, in "Optische Anregung Organischer Systeme: 2 Internationales Farbensymposium" (W. Foerst, ed.), p. 55 (p. 208) Verlag Chemie, Weinheim, 1966.

[c] Calculated by Eq. (36) from the Hückel π-orbitals of the corresponding carbanions with $\beta = 28{,}000$ cm^{-1} (2.8 μm^{-1}) and $\Delta\alpha_{NR} = 0.5\beta$ for the alkylated ring nitrogen atoms and $\Delta\alpha_N = 0.3\beta$ for the nitrogen atoms in the exocyclic chain.

[d] G. Märkl and F. Lieb, Tetrahedron Letters No. 36, 3489 (1967).

nation, and this periodic potential has the effect[56] of breaking up the free-electron energy levels into bands, each containing $(N/2)$ π-orbitals (Fig. 11). For all values of N there is an energy gap between successive bands of levels, and in consequence the energy required for the transition of an electron from the top level of the first band, consisting of the $(N/2)$ occupied π-orbitals, to the bottom level of the second band, made up of $(N/2)$ empty orbitals, remains finite even for the infinite polyene (Fig. 11). If the bond order alternation in the polyene series is explicitly considered,[56] Eq. (27) is modified to

$$\nu = \nu_l(1 - 1/N) + h(N + 1)/8m\ d^2N^2 \qquad (29)$$

where ν_l is the convergence frequency for the infinite polyene ($\sim$13,500 cm^{-1}) and is equal to the amplitude of the bond potential alternation.[56]

For all conjugated systems, whether of the polyene (I) or the cyanine (II) type, there is an additional atom–bond alternation, the potential energy of a π-electron having minima at the positions of the atomic nuclei and maxima at the bond centers. However, this potential alternation only has the effect of separating the free-electron energy levels into bands of N π-orbitals, the $(N/2)$ occupied and lowest $(N/2)$ empty orbitals being in the first band (Fig. 11). The energy intervals between the levels in the lowest band are reduced but retain their relative values, so that Eq. (27) remains valid in good approximation for odd-atom linearly conjugated series.

Bond order alternation does not greatly affect the calculation of absorption intensities by means of the free-electron model. The electric-dipole moment of the transition $\psi_j \rightarrow \psi_k$ in a linear conjugated system, obtained from Eqs. (8) and (26), is given by

$$\mu_{jk} = \sqrt{2} \, eL8jk/[\pi(k^2 - j^2)]^2 \tag{30}$$

if $(k - j)$ is odd. For even changes in the quantum number j the moment vanishes, and the moment has its largest value for a unit change, i.e., for the transition from the highest occupied to the lowest unoccupied π-orbital, $\psi_{N/2} \rightarrow \psi_{N/2+1}$. The oscillator strength of this particular transition, which is responsible for the lowest-energy band, is given by the simple expression

$$f = 8(N + 1)/3\pi^2 \tag{31}$$

from the general relation between the classical measure of absorption intensity and the quantum-mechanical dipole strength

$$f_{0n} = 8\pi^2 m v_{0n}\mu_{0n}^2/3he^2 \tag{32}$$

In general it is found that the intensity of the long-wavelength band greatly exceeds that of other bands in the spectrum of a simple linear conjugated system (Table II). The relative values of the oscillator strength of the lowest-energy band in a series of such molecules, notably the polyenes (I) and the cyanines (II), are reproduced by Eq. (31) which affords, however, absolute values that are too large by a factor of $\sim$2 (Table II).

More substantial agreement with experiment, in regard to both the wavelength and intensity of absorption, is afforded by a free-electron treatment in which the standing-wave forms of the π-electrons are quantized in the two dimensions of the molecular plane, and both the atom–bond and the bond order potential alternation are explicitly considered.[59] Kuhn, who has developed an analog computer for free-electron

[59] H. Kuhn, W. Huber, G. Handschig, H. Martin, F. Schäfer, and F. Bär, *J. Chem. Phys.* **32**, 467 and 470 (1960).

systems, has calculated the spectroscopic properties of a wide variety of molecules by the free-electron method,[60] including diphenylmethane, acridine, phenazine, and oxazine dyes, as well as the methine- and aza-cyanines (XI) for which theoretical and experimental absorption wavelengths are listed in Table III.

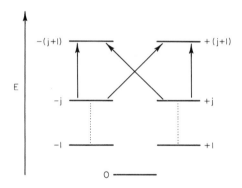

(XI)

When the terminal atoms of a linear conjugated chain are linked to form a cyclic π-electron system the manifold of free-electron energy levels is profoundly changed[57] (Figs. 11 and 12). In a cyclic conjugated sys-

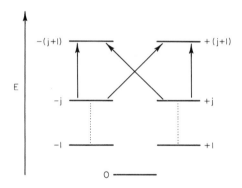

Fig. 12. The free-electron energy levels of a cyclic conjugated system and the electronic transitions responsible for the L_b, L_a, B_a, and B_b bands of cyclic polyenes and aromatic hydrocarbons.

tem the standing-wave functions of a π-electron may take the form of either sine or cosine waves, corresponding to a clockwise or anticlockwise motion of the electron round the ring. The boundary condition requires that a whole number, j, of electronic wavelengths are congruent with the circumference of the ring. This criterion is satisfied for a given value of j by a sine and a cosine wave, so that the free electron energy levels are doubly degenerate, apart from the unique case of $j = 0$, corresponding to a stationary π-electron with an infinite standing wavelength (Fig. 12). Explicitly the allowed kinetic energies of a π-electron with a mass m moving in a ring with a circumference length L are given by

[60] H. Kuhn, in "Optische Anregung Organischer Systeme. 2 Internationales Farben-symposium" (W. Foerst, ed.), p. 55. Verlag Chemie, Weinheim, 1966.

$$E_j = h^2 j^2 / 2mL^2 \qquad (33)$$

where the quantum number j has the values, 0, ± 1, ± 2, etc. Accordingly $(4n + 2)$ π-electrons are required to form a closed shell in a cyclic polyene, as was first pointed out by Hückel.[61]

For a cyclic system with $(4j + 2)$ π-electrons, the lowest-energy electronic transitions take place between the π-orbitals with quantum numbers $\pm j$ and $\pm (j + 1)$ (Fig. 12). The transitions, $+j \rightarrow + (j + 1)$ and $-j \rightarrow - (j + 1)$, involve a change of one unit of electronic angular momentum round the ring and are allowed, whereas the transitions, $-j \rightarrow + (j + 1)$ and $+j \rightarrow - (j + 1)$, involve changes of $(2j + 1)$ units of angular momentum and are forbidden. The orbital energy changes are the same for the four transitions and, from Eq. (33), they give rise to absorption bands centered on the average wavelength, λ in nm,

$$\lambda = 8.26L^2 / (2j + 1) \qquad (34)$$

where the perimeter length L is expressed in angstroms. In the case of benzene, $j = 1$ and $L = 8.4$ Å, so that $\lambda = 194$ nm, which agrees tolerably well with the wavelength value (~ 200 nm) for the center of gravity of the lowest-energy group of three absorption bands given by benzene.

The three principal long-wavelength absorption bands exhibited by benzene, and by aromatic hydrocarbons generally (Fig. 13), are termed, in order of increasing frequency, the L_b, L_a, and $B_{a,b}$ bands in the free electron nomenclature of Platt,[57] or the α, p, and β bands in the earlier nomenclature of Clar,[62] based on a consideration of resonance structures. The L_b and L_a bands have only a weak to moderate intensity and they are due to the two forbidden transitions. The high-intensity $B_{a,b}$ band of benzene arises from the two allowed transitions, which are generally split in the case of the polycyclic aromatic hydrocarbons giving separate B_a and B_b bands, each with a large intensity. The subscripts a and b refer to the atom or bond location of the nodes in the π-electron distribution of the excited state produced by the transition. In the upper state of the L_b and L_a transitions $(2j + 1)$ nodes pass through opposite pairs of atoms (XII) or pairs of bonds (XIII), respectively, and the B_a and B_b states

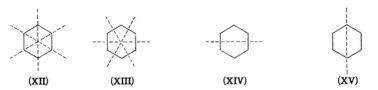

| (XII) | (XIII) | (XIV) | (XV) |

[61] E. Hückel, Z. Physik **70**, 204 (1931); **76**, 628 (1932); Z. Elektrochem. **43**, 752 (1937).

[62] E. Clar, Ber. **69**, 607 (1936); "Polycyclic Hydrocarbons." Springer, Berlin, 1964.

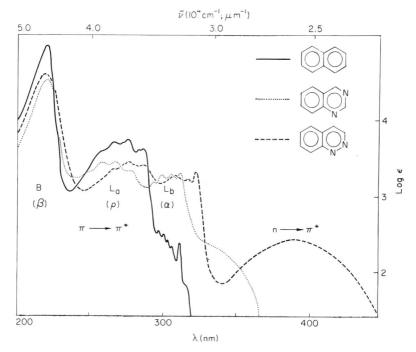

FIG. 13. The absorption spectra in cyclohexane of naphthalene (———), and of its 1,3-diaza derivatives, quinazoline, (·····) and 1,2-diaza derivative, cinnoline, (— — — —).

are bisected by a single nodal plane passing through bonds (XIV) and through atoms (XV), respectively.

The L_b and L_a transitions have a lower energy than the B_a and B_b transitions on account of the larger change in the π-electron angular momentum produced by the excitation. The larger electronic angular momentum of the L_b and L_a excited states implies that the π-electrons tend to circulate round the ring in the same direction to a greater degree than in the B_a and B_b states, and so they keep out of each others' way and reduce the interelectronic repulsion.

The L_b and L_a transitions are degenerate in odd-membered cyclic systems, such as the tropylium cation or the cyclopentadienyl anion, but in the cyclic polyenes or aromatic hydrocarbons with $(4n + 2)$ conjugated carbon atoms as well as $(4n + 2)$ π-electrons the nodal patterns of the L_b and L_a excited states match the molecular structure, so that the nodal planes pass only through atoms (XII) or only through bonds (XIII), respectively. The potential energy of a π-electron circulating round the ring is lower when it is at the position of an atomic nucleus than when it is passing over the center of a bond, and this potential alternation reduced the energy of the L_b state (XII) relative to that of the L_a state (XIII).

The introduction of a weakly conjugating substituent into an aromatic nucleus, or the replacement of a ring carbon atom by a heteroatom, breaks the degeneracy of the π-orbitals of the parent hydrocarbon (Fig. 12) although the general features of the low-energy group of aromatic band systems are retained[63] (Fig. 13). The general effect of substitution or atom replacement is an enhancement of the absorption intensity of the long-wavelength L_b band, which is usually, but not invariably, accompanied by a red shift of this band (Fig. 13). In addition, a new absorption band, due to an $n \rightarrow \pi^*$ transition, may appear at the long-wavelength edge of the aromatic $\pi \rightarrow \pi^*$ absorption system[63] (Fig. 13), although the weak $n \rightarrow \pi^*$ band or bands are usually overlaid by the stronger $\pi \rightarrow \pi^*$ absorption in dye molecules.

If a strongly conjugating group is substituted into an aromatic hydrocarbon or a heterocyclic nucleus the absorption spectrum is more profoundly changed and it has a form intermediate between those characteristic of linear and cyclic homonuclear conjugated systems. In general the long-wavelength band has a greatly enhanced intensity and it is strongly shifted to the red. Thus the lowest-frequency band of a linear conjugated system usually has a higher intensity and lies at a longer wavelength than that of a cyclic analog with a similar size and composition.

The aromatic hydrocarbons and the linear polyenes belong to the general class of alternant π-electron systems which are characterized in the Hückel theory by the property that if alternant conjugated atoms are labeled, or starred, no two starred atoms are directly bonded nor are any two unstarred atoms.[64,65] If the Hückel Coulomb integral, α [Eq. (23)], i.e., the energy of an electron in a $2p_\pi$ atomic orbital, is taken as a zero of energy, it is found[64] that for each bonding molecular orbital ψ_j with an energy E_j in an alternant system there is a paired antibonding molecular orbital $\psi_{j'}$ with an energy, $E_{j'} = -E_j$. Moreover the atomic orbital coefficients [Eq. (22)] in the bonding molecular orbital have the same absolute value as those in the paired antibonding π-orbital, but the coefficients of an unstarred atom have opposed signs in the two π-orbitals whereas those of a starred atom have the same sign.[65]

The aromatic hydrocarbons are even-alternant systems with an even

[63] S. F. Mason, *Phys. Methods Heterocyclic Chem.* **2**, 1 (1963).

[64] C. A. Coulson and G. S. Rushbrooke, *Proc. Cambridge Phil. Soc.* **36**, 193 (1940).

[65] C. A. Coulson and H. C. Longuet-Higgins, *Proc. Roy. Soc.* **A192**, 16 (1947).

number of π-orbitals so that each bonding orbital has a paired anti-bonding counterpart. The conjugative substitution of an aromatic hydro-carbon with a methylene group, e.g., the formation of the benzyl system from benzene (Fig. 14) generates an odd-alternant system with an odd number of π-orbitals. After the bonding and antibonding π-orbitals of an odd-alternant system have been paired, one π-orbital is left over and it is paired with itself, remaining a nonbonding molecular orbital at the center of gravity of the π-electron manifold (Fig. 14). As the non-bonding π-orbital is self-paired the atomic orbital coefficients of the unstarred atoms are zero, being equal to their own negative, and the electronic charge is distributed only over the starred atoms in this π-orbital.[66] In an odd-alternant system the starred and unstarred group of atoms are the major and the minor set, respectively (Fig. 14).

The conjugative substitution of an aromatic nucleus transforms the set of π-electron energy levels (Fig. 14) from the characteristically cyclic (Fig. 12) to the typically linear form (Fig. 11). In particular the electronic transition from the ground to the lowest-energy excited state

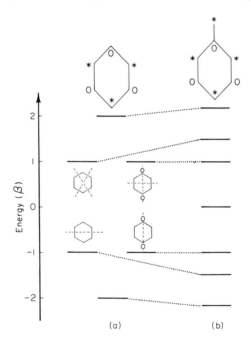

FIG. 14. The Hückel energies of the π-orbitals of (a) benzene and (b) the benzyl system.

[66] H. C. Longuet-Higgins, *J. Chem. Phys.* **18**, 265 (1950).

has a smaller frequency and it becomes allowed (Fig. 14). Many dye
molecules contain strongly conjugative substituents in an aromatic
nucleus and are odd-atom systems analogous to aryl methylene anions.
The spectroscopic effects of further substitution, or of atom replacements,
in dye molecules may be interpreted qualitatively from the properties
of the nonbonding molecular orbital of the corresponding carbanion,
or even semiquantitatively if the energies and atomic orbital coefficients
of the π-orbitals of the carbanion are known.[67-69]

The long-wavelength absorption band of an aryl methylene anion is
due to the transition of an electron from the nonbonding molecular
orbital to the lowest antibonding π-orbital. If a carbon atom of the
carbanion is replaced by a heteroatom there is, in general, a change in
the energy of both of these orbitals and the wavelength of the absorption is shifted. The change in the energy ΔE_i of the π-orbital ψ_i [Eq.
(22)] due to the replacement of the carbon atom μ is given by

$$\Delta E_i = C_{\mu i}{}^2 \Delta \alpha_\mu \tag{35}$$

where $\Delta \alpha_\mu$ is the difference between the values of the Coulomb integral
[Eq. (23)] for carbon and for the heteroatom. If the heteroatom is more
electronegative than carbon the energy of the orbital is lowered, and if
it is less electronegative the orbital is destabilized.

In the nonbonding molecular orbital ψ_0 of a carbanion, such as the
di(2-naphthyl)methine anion (XVI) which is the odd-alternant system
analogous to pseudoisocyanine (IV; M = CH), the one-electron charge
density $c_{\mu 0}{}^2$ [Eq. (35)] is zero on the unstarred atoms and correspondingly large on the starred atoms. However the one-electron charge
density is more uniformly spread over both the starred and unstarred
atoms in the lowest antibonding π-orbital. Accordingly the replacement
of an unstarred carbon atom by a more electronegative heteroatom does
not affect the energy of the nonbonding molecular orbital but it lowers
that of the first antibonding π-orbital, producing a red shift of the
absorption. Conversely the replacement of a starred carbon atom by a
more electronegative heteroatom lowers the energy of the nonbonding
orbital to a greater degree than that of the lowest antibonding π-orbital,
giving rise to a blue shift of the absorption. The exocyclic conjugated
carbon atom of pseudoisocyanine (IV; M = CH) lies at a starred position (XVI), and its replacement by the more electronegative nitrogen
atom produces a blue shift or, by the less electronegative arsenic atom,
a red shift (Table III).

[67] M. J. S. Dewar, J. Chem. Soc. p. 2329 (1950); pp. 3532 and 3544 (1952).
[68] D. A. Brown and M. J. S. Dewar, J. Chem. Soc. p. 2134 (1954).
[69] M. J. S. Dewar, Chem. Soc. (London), Spec. Publ. 4, 64 (1956).

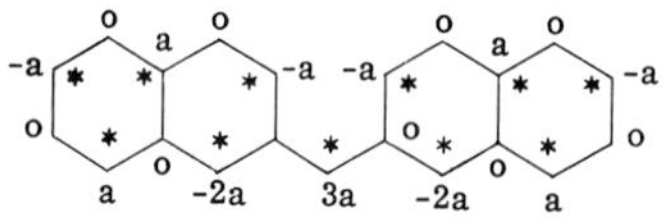

(XVI)

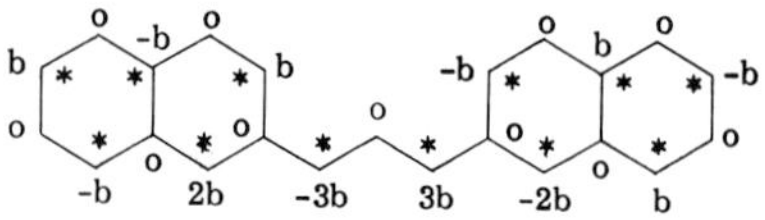

(XVII)

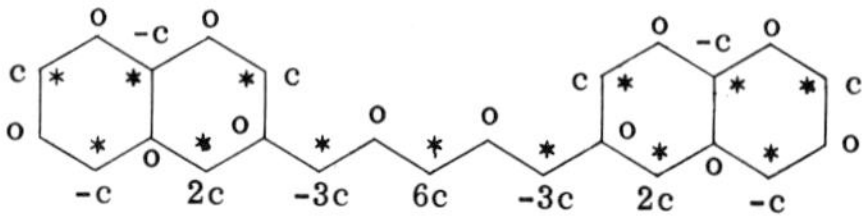

(XVIII)

Structures XVI–XVIII. The relative atomic orbital coefficients of the nonbonding molecular π-orbital in the odd-alternant hydrocarbon systems analogous to the mono-, tri-, and penta-carbocyanine dyes with end groups made up of bicyclic six-membered ring systems.

The central carbon atom in the conjugated exocyclic chain of the carbanion (XVII) corresponding to pyocyanine [(IV); $M = (CH)_3$] is unstarred and replacement of that atom by nitrogen gives rise to a red shift, whereas a similar replacement of the adjacent starred atoms produces a blue shift (Table III). In the same way the replacement of carbon atoms in the pentamethine cyanine [IV; $M = (CH)_5$] by nitrogen atoms gives rise to wavelength shifts with a direction anticipated from the positions of the starred and unstarred atoms in the corresponding carbanion (XVIII) (Table III). In the latter structure (XVIII) the replacement of the central carbon atom in the pentamethine chain produces a much larger wavelength shift than the replacement of other chain atoms (Table III) as more than one-half of the electronic charge in the nonbonding orbital is located at that atom.

The atomic orbital coefficients of a nonbonding molecular orbital, $c_{\mu o}$, are given without recourse to detailed Hückel calculations by the condition[66] that the coefficients of the starred atoms directly bonded to a given unstarred sum to zero. Hence the relative values of the coefficients in a nonbonding π-orbital, which are given in (XVI), (XVII), and (XVIII) for the carbanion analogs of the cyanines (IV) considered, are obtained by inspection. The absolute values are then readily evaluated from the requirement that the fractional electronic charge densities on the atoms, $c_{\mu o}^2$, sum to unity for the nonbonding as for each other π-orbital. Thus for the nonbonding molecular orbitals (XVI), (XVII), and

(XVIII) the constants are, $a^2 = 1/25$, $b^2 = 1/34$, and $c^2 = 1/70$, respectively.

Further, the nonbonding π-orbitals (XVI) and (XVIII) are symmetrical with respect to reflection in the perpendicular mirror plane which bisects these structures. Accordingly the adjacent levels are antisymmetric, and for each carbanion the coefficient of the central carbon atom of the exocyclic chain in the lowest antibonding π-orbital is zero. Thus the replacement of the central carbon atom in (XVI) or (XVIII) by a nitrogen atom leaves the energy of the lowest antibonding π-orbital unchanged, but the energy of the nonbonding π-orbital is drastically lowered since the central carbon atom carries the largest fraction of the electronic charge density in that orbital. The other starred atoms in the exocyclic chain of the carbanion (XVIII) corresponding to the pentamethine cyanine [IV; M = $(CH)_5$] carry only one-quarter of the charge located on the central atom in the nonbonding π-orbital, and the charge on those atoms in the lowest antibonding π-orbital is nonzero, so that the replacement of these carbon atoms by nitrogen produces a smaller blue shift (Table III).

With a knowledge of the energies and coefficients of the Hückel π-orbitals, notably for the lowest antibonding level, in each of the corresponding carbanions this approach may be made semiquantitative (Table III). Hückel orbitals for a wide variety of conjugated systems are available from dictionaries,[70-72] or they may be computed by standard procedures.[73] The difference between the energies of the nonbonding ψ_0 and lowest antibonding π-orbital ψ_l of the corresponding carbanion is given by the energy of the latter, E_l, since the former lies at the zero of energy. The addition of the corrections for the orbital energy changes due to the replacement of carbon by heteroatoms [Eq. (35)] then gives the frequency of the lowest-energy absorption band of the dye as

$$\nu = E_l + \sum_\mu (c_{\mu 0}{}^2 - c_{\mu l}{}^2) \, \Delta\alpha_\mu \tag{36}$$

where the sum is taken over all carbon atoms of the carbanion replaced by heteroatoms in the dye. The orbital energy, E_l, is expressed in units

[70] C. A. Coulson and A. Streitwieser, Jr., "Dictionary of π-electron Calculations." Pergamon Press, Oxford, 1965.

[71] A. Streitwieser, Jr. and J. I. Brauman, "Supplemental Tables of Molecular Orbital Calculations." Pergamon Press, Oxford, 1965.

[72] E. Heilbronner and P. A. Straub, "Hückel Molecular Orbitals." Springer, Berlin, 1966.

[73] A. Streitwieser, Jr., "Molecular Orbital Theory for Organic Chemists." Wiley, New York, 1961.

of the Hückel resonance integral, β [Eq. (24)], which is a disposable empirical parameter, together with the increments, $\Delta\alpha_\mu$, in the Coulomb integrals of the heteroatoms. The calculated absorption wavelengths [Eq. (36)] of the methine- and aza-cyanines (IV) recorded in Table III depend upon three parameters, β, $\Delta\alpha_{NR}$, and $\Delta\alpha_N$, since the partly positively charged alkylated ring nitrogen atoms have a larger effective electronegativity than the formally neutral nitrogen atoms in the exocyclic chain.

The properties of odd-alternant π-electron systems provide an interpretation for the spectroscopic effects of substitution as well as of atom replacement in dye molecules.[67-69] From an analysis of the absorption data of the diphenyl- and triphenylmethane dyes, G. N. Lewis[74] drew up a list of the wavelength shifts due to changes in the structure (XIX) (Table IV), which he interpreted in terms of the classical electron oscillation theory of light absorption and the relative basicities of the various substituents. The dyes considered by G. N. Lewis are substituted analogs of the odd-alternant carbanion (XX), in the highest occupied level of which, the nonbonding molecular orbital, the one-electron charge density is confined to the starred atoms. The charge density is more uniformly spread over the conjugated atoms in the lowest unoccupied π-orbital and, from Eq. (35), a large red or blue shift is expected to result from the replacement of an unstarred or starred atom,

TABLE IV

WAVELENGTH SHIFTS RELATIVE TO MICHLER'S HYDROL BLUE
(III; R = H) (λ_{max} = 610 nm)[a]

Structural change	Shift in λ(nm)
Replace R by H	-10
Replace both NR_2 by O^-	-60
X = O, or S	-70
X = NR	-130
Y = NH_2-	-180
Y = p-R_2N—Ph–	-20
Y = p-Ph–	$+10$
Y = $p\overset{+}{R_3N}$—Ph	$+20$
Replace C—Y by N	$+120$

[a] Due to substitutions and atom replacements in (XIX). Adapted from G. N. Lewis, *J. Am. Chem. Soc.* **67**, 770 (1945). Malachite green (III; R = Ph) (λ_{max} = 620 nm) is the reference dye in the original paper.

[74] G. N. Lewis, *J. Am. Chem. Soc.* **67**, 770 (1945).

(XIX)   (XX)   (XXI)

respectively, by a more electronegative heteroatom. Thus Binschedler's green (III; CR = N) absorbs at 740 nm, and phenol red (XXI) at 553 nm, compared with 610 and 620 nm for the respective reference dyes, Michler's hydrol blue (III; R = H) and malachite green (III; R = Ph).

The general effect of conjugative substitution is illustrated by the formation of the benzyl system from benzene (Fig. 14). The substitution of methylene into benzene introduces a new π-orbital with the same energy as the $2p_\pi$ atomic orbital of methylene, i.e., the nonbonding molecular orbital, and it repels the bonding orbitals of benzene to lower energies and the antibonding orbitals to higher energies if those orbitals carry a nonzero atomic orbital coefficient at the position of substitution. If that coefficient is zero the orbital remains unchanged and has the same energy (Fig. 14). Thus the substitution of an amino group into the exocyclic carbon atom of Michler's hydrol blue (III; R = H), which is unstarred in the corresponding carbanion (XX), leaves the energy of the highest occupied level unchanged but repels the lowest unoccupied level to a higher energy, and gives rise to the large blue shift observed from 610 to 440 nm, on passing from (III; R = H) to auramine (III; R = NH₂).

The new level of (III; R = NH₂) corresponding to the $2p_\pi$ atomic orbital of the amino group introduced into (III; R = H) lies below the highest occupied π-orbital on account of the substantial electronegativity of nitrogen. However, if we substitute the p-dimethylaniline group into the exocyclic carbon atom of (III; R = H), generating crystal violet (III; R = p-Me₂NPh), we introduce seven new π-orbitals, one being the analog of the nonbonding π-orbital of the benzyl system (Fig. 14), degenerate with the nonbonding π-orbital of the carbanion (XX). We cannot distinguish the newly introduced p-dimethylaniline group from the corresponding groups present in the original Michler's hydrol blue molecule, and general symmetry considerations indicate[75] that the highest occupied and lowest unoccupied levels in a symmetrical triarylmethyl system have the same energies as those of the corresponding symmetrical diarylmethyl system and those of the analogous diarylphenylmethyl system. Thus crystal violet (III; R = p-Me₂NPh) and

[75] S. F. Mason, in "Steric Effects in Conjugated Systems" (G. W. Gray, ed.), p. 52. Butterworth, London and Washington, D. C., 1958.

malachite green (III; R = Ph) have absorption maxima in the visible displaced by no more than 20 nm from that of Michler's hydrol blue (III; R = H).

The substitution of an oxygen or a nitrogen atom into the unstarred nuclear positions (XX) of Michler's hydrol blue (III; R = H) to give pyronine G (XXII) (λ 547 nm) and acridine orange (XXIII) (λ 491 nm) similarly give rise to a blue shift, which is larger for the latter dye on account of the greater basicity or electron-donating capacity of the nitrogen atom; or in Hückel terms, $\beta_{CN} > \beta_{CO}$. A striking converse red shift is observed, however, if those unstarred nuclear carbon atoms are directly bonded together to give the fluorene dye (XXIV), which

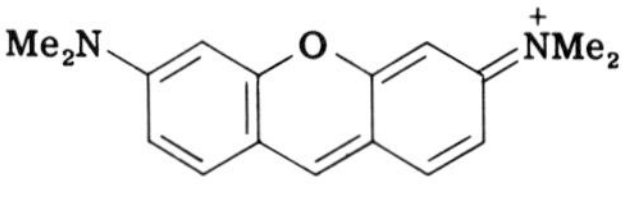

(XXII) 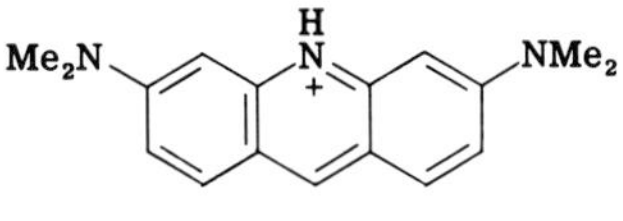　　　　　　　　　　　　(XXIII)

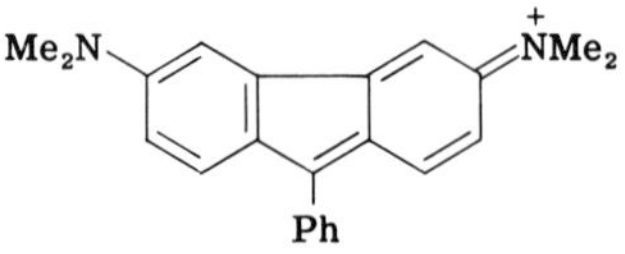

(XXIV)

absorbs at 954 nm.[68] The nonbonding molecular orbital of the carbanion (XX) corresponding to Michler's hydrol blue (III; R = H) is anti-symmetric with respect to the mirror plane bisecting the system, imply-ing that the lowest empty orbital is symmetric to reflection. In that event the coefficients in the lowest unoccupied π-orbital of the unstarred nuclear atoms which are joined to form the fluorene nucleus (XXIV) have the same sign, so that the introduction of a bond between them generates a stabilizing π-interaction, substantially lowering the energy of the lowest antibonding π-orbital. As these atoms are unstarred the introduction of a bond between them does not affect the energy of the highest occupied π-orbital, and accordingly the lowest-energy absorption band of the fluorene dye (XXIV) lies in the near-infrared.

The simple perturbation treatment of the color of dye molecules, based on the properties of odd-alternant π-systems and their nonbonding molecular orbitals, was introduced by M. J. S. Dewar[67] who, in addition, has reported extensive Hückel calculations of the absorption wavelengths of dyes with the general structure (XIX), notably (III; R = H) (III;

$R = Ph$), (III; $R = p\text{-}Me_2NPh$), (III; $CR = N$) and (XXIII), as well as the cyanine series (II), $n = 1$–3 (Table II).

IV. Electronic Interactions between Dye Molecules

It has long been known[76] that organic dyes in aqueous solution generally do not obey Beer's law[1] closely, and that the absorption spectra of dyes bound to polymers are often substantially changed.[77] The deviations from Beer's law are due to the formation by the dye molecules of dimers and higher aggregates, which have different absorption properties. The formation of dimers and oligomers by dye molecules in solution has been attributed[78] to the London[79] dispersion forces. These forces are approximately proportional to the square of the oscillator strength and to the cube of the wavelength of absorption,[78] and so they are relatively strong for dye molecules.

When two dye molecules aggregate in solution or are bound to adjacent sites on a macromolecule the dimer forms a new light-absorbing system with absorption properties different from those of the monomeric dye. Relative to the absorption of the monomeric dye, determined in dilute aqueous or in nonaqueous solution, the absorption of the dimer usually shows a loss of intensity and a shift in the wavelength of absorption or a splitting of the absorption (Figs. 15 and 16). The wavelength shift may be to the blue, as with acridine orange (XXIII) (Fig. 15) or, less commonly, to the red, as with pseudoisocyanine (IV; $M = CH$) (Fig. 16), which forms a gelatinous polymer at 10^{-2} M in aqueous solution, each polymer aggregate containing some 10^5 dye molecules.[80–82]

There are corresponding changes in the polarized absorption and in the emission spectra. The strong green fluorescence of monomeric acridine orange (XXIII) is substantially quenched and shifted to the red in the dimer species (Fig. 15), whereas pseudoisocyanine (IV; $M = CH$) does not fluoresce in the monomeric form at room temperature, and becomes

[76] S. E. Sheppard, *Proc. Roy. Soc.* **A82**, 256 (1909); *Rev. Mod. Phys.* **14**, 303 (1942).

[77] L. Michaelis and S. Granick, *J. Am. Chem. Soc.* **67**, 1212 (1945).

[78] E. Rabinowitch and L. F. Epstein, *J. Am. Chem. Soc.* **63**, 69 (1941).

[79] F. London, *Z. Physik. Chem.* **B11**, 222 (1930).

[80] E. E. Jelley, *Nature* **138**, 1009 (1936); **139**, 631 (1937).

[81] G. Scheibe, *Angew. Chem.* **50**, 212 (1937).

[82] G. Scheibe, *in* "Optische Anregung Organischer Systeme. 2 Internationales Farbensymposium" (W. Foerst, ed.), p. 109. Verlag Chemie, Weinheim, 1966.

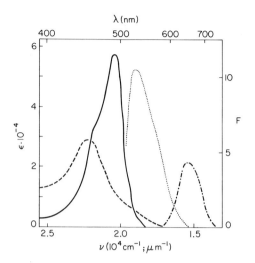

FIG. 15. The absorption spectra of acridine orange (XXIII) in water at $10^{-6}\,M$ (————) and at $10^{-2}\,M$ (— — — —), and the fluorescence spectra of the dye in water at $10^{-6}\,M$ (· · · · ·) and at $10^{-2}\,M$ (—·—·—·—).

strongly fluorescent only on aggregation.[80–82] Pseudoisocyanine is a planar molecule, but in the presence of an optically active anion, such as tartrate, the dye aggregate becomes optically active, showing Cotton effects in the wavelength region of the polymer absorption bands of the

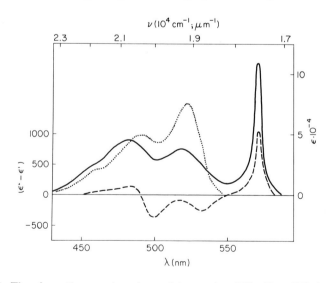

FIG. 16. The absorption spectra of pseudoisocyanine (IV; M = CH) in water at $10^{-6}\,M$ (· · · · ·) and at $10^{-2}\,M$ (————), and the circular dichroism of the dye in water at $10^{-2}\,M$ with (−)-tartrate as the counterion (— — — —).

dye[83] (Fig. 16). Other planar dyes, including acridine orange, give similar Cotton effects when bound to soluble optically active polymers, notably polypeptides,[84] polysaccharides,[85] and polynucleotides,[86] in dilute aqueous solution.

These various effects arise from the cooperative absorption of light by both of the dye molecules in a dimer or all of the N molecules in a polymer.[87-89] If two equivalent dye molecules, A and B, have ground-state wavefunctions ϕ_a and ϕ_b and excited-state functions ϕ'_a and ϕ'_b, respectively, the ground state of the dimer AB is represented unequivocally by

$$\psi_0 = \phi_a \phi_b \qquad (37)$$

However there are two possible excited configurations, $\phi'_a \phi_b$ and $\phi_a \phi'_b$ and a true stationary excited state must contain both of these, since the two molecules of the dimer each have the same probability of absorbing light and of carrying the excitation energy at any instant. Two stationary excited states are possible, ψ_+ and ψ_-, representing an in-phase and an out-of-phase combination, respectively, of the two excited configurations

$$\psi_\pm = (\phi'_a \phi_b \pm \phi_a \phi'_b)/\sqrt{2} \qquad (38)$$

In each excited state, both molecules carry an averaged excitation, and the excitation energy is rapidly interchanged between the two molecules during the lifetime of the excited dimer state.

The energies of the two dimer excited states, ψ_+ and ψ_-, differ from one another and from that of the excited state of the monomer, ϕ', owing to the classical electrostatic interaction between the transition dipole moments of the two molecules in the dimer. The interaction is attractive for one dimer excited state, decreasing the transition energy, and repulsive for the other, increasing the frequency of the photon required for the transition.

If the absorption frequency of the monomer dye molecule is ν_0 the dimer absorption frequencies to the two excited states are given by

$$\nu_\pm = \nu_0 \pm V \qquad (39)$$

[83] S. F. Mason, *Proc. Chem. Soc.* p. 119 (1964).

[84] L. Stryer and E. R. Blout, *J. Am. Chem. Soc.* **83**, 1411 (1961).

[85] A. L. Stone, *Biopolymers* **2**, 315 (1964).

[86] D. M. Neville and D. F. Bradley, *Biochim. Biophys. Acta* **50**, 397 (1961).

[87] J. Franck and E. Teller, *J. Chem. Phys.* **6**, 861 (1938).

[88] E. G. McRae and M. Kasha, *in* "Physical Processes in Radiation Biology" (L. G. Augenstein, R. Mason, and B. Rosenberg, eds.), p. 23. Academic Press, New York, 1964.

[89] T. Förster, *in* "Modern Quantum Chemistry. Istanbul Lectures" (O. Sinanoğlu, ed.), Part III, p. 93. Academic Press, New York, 1965.

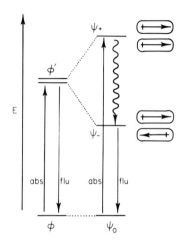

Fig. 17. The energy level diagram for a sandwich dimer.

where V is the exciton-splitting energy in frequency units. The exciton-splitting energy is given in good approximation by the classical expression for the Coulombic interaction between two transition dipoles μ separated by a distance d

$$V = \mu_a\mu_b G/d^3 \tag{40}$$

where G is a geometric factor depending upon the orientation of the transition dipoles of the individual dye molecules, μ_a and μ_b, relative to the line joining their centers. The geometric factor has the value of

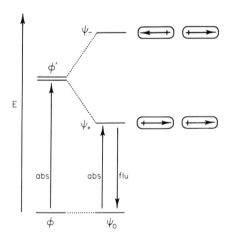

Fig. 18. The energy level diagram for a head-to-tail dimer.

$+1$ for a sandwich dimer with parallel transition-dipole moments (Fig. 17) and -2 for the head-to-tail dimer with collinear transition-dipole moments (Fig. 18).

In the sandwich dimer (Fig. 17) the transition dipoles are antiparallel in the lower-energy dimer excitation, $\psi_0 \to \psi_-$, so that the moments mutually cancel and the absorption intensity is very small. On the other hand the transition dipoles are parallel and give a large vector sum in the higher-energy dimer transition, $\psi_0 \to \psi_+$, which accordingly has a high intensity. The overall effect of sandwich dimer formation is a shift of the absorption towards the blue, as is observed with acridine orange (XXIII) (Fig. 15). More detailed consideration of the interaction in a sandwich dimer between the visible transition moment of molecule A and the ultraviolet transition moments of molecule B, and *vice versa,* leads to the conclusion that absorption intensity is transferred from the visible to the ultraviolet region in the spectrum of the dimer, accounting for the observed hypochromism of the acridine orange dimer absorption in the visible (Fig. 15).

As the lower-energy dimer excitation, $\psi_0 \to \psi_-$, is forbidden, or very weak, the excited state ψ_- has a correspondingly long lifetime [Eq. (12)]. Accordingly the dimer in the fluorescent state, the lowest-energy excited state ψ_-, is subject to collisions with quenching molecules, and other interactions which remove the excitation energy nonradiatively, for a longer period than the corresponding excited state of the monomeric dye. Thus the fluorescence of a sandwich dimer is shifted towards the red and is weak (Fig. 17), as is observed in the case of acridine orange (Fig. 15).

Contrasting effects result from the interactions between the dye molecules of a head-to-tail dimer (Fig. 18). The dimer transition from the ground state, ψ_0, to the higher-energy excited state, ψ_-, is now forbidden, since the transition moments in the two dye molecules are opposed, head-to-head, and mutually cancel. The transition moments of the dimer reinforce one another in the dimer transition to the lower-energy excited state, $\psi_0 \to \psi_+$ (Fig. 18). Thus the absorption of a dye forming a head-to-tail dimer is shifted towards the red when the dye aggregates. The lifetime of the lowest excited state, ψ_+, in a head-to-tail dimer is shorter than that of the corresponding monomer by about one-half, so that the dimer is less subject to quenching effects and fluoresces with greater efficiency.

In the pseudoisocyanine polymer the dye molecules do not form an exact head-to-tail array, since the polymer is optically active.[83] However, the marked red shift of the polymer absorption band relative to that of the monomeric dye (Fig. 16), and the distinct fluorescence of the polymer, suggest that the arrangement of the dye molecules in the pseudoisocyanine aggregate approximates more closely to a head-to-tail (Fig. 18) than to a sandwich configuration (Fig. 17).

The long-wavelength absorption band of the pseudoisocyanine polymer has a very small width (Fig. 16), which is due to the distribution of the loss of binding energy, arising from the absorption of light, over all of the $\sim 10^5$ dye molecules in the aggregate. The change in the equilibrium nuclear configuration of any one individual dye molecule when the polymer absorbs light is vanishingly small, so that no vibrational modes are involved in the electronic absorption process. At the temperature of liquid nitrogen (80°K) most of the dye molecules in the pseudoisocyanine aggregate are confined to the zero vibrational level of the electronic ground state, and the polymer band then has a width at half-maximum extinction of only 2 nm (100 cm^{-1}) as almost all of the absorption intensity lies in the 0–0 vibrational band[90] (Fig. 7).

The sandwich and the head-to-tail stacking of dye molecules are limiting forms of molecular aggregation, and in general the transition dipoles of the two molecules in the dimer are noncoplanar. Dye molecules forming dimers and aggregates when bound to macromolecules tend in particular to adopt a noncoplanar mutual disposition as the configuration of the dimer or aggregate is determined primarily by the location of the binding sites on the macromolecule.

For the general noncoplanar dimer case (Fig. 19), electronic transitions in the dimer from the ground state, ψ_0, to both of the excited states, ψ_+ and ψ_-, are allowed, and the dimer is, at least potentially, optically active. Optically active molecules have different refractive indexes, and different extinction coefficients, for left and right circularly polarized light, the circular birefringence giving rise to the rotation of the plane of linearly polarized light by optical isomers.[5] In left and right circularly polarized light the electric field vector of the radiation rotates about the direction of propagation, tracing out in space a left- or a right-handed helical envelope, respectively.

If a valency electron of a molecule is stereochemically constrained to move through a helical path on the absorption of light, the two circular components of the radiation are absorbed to different degrees. The circular dichroism $(\epsilon_l - \epsilon_r)$ is positive if the electron is displaced through a right-handed helical path by the absorbed photon, or negative if that path is left-handed. In an optically active molecule the helical charge-displacement path in a given electronic transition is right-handed for one optical isomer and left-handed for its enantiomer, so that the circular dichroism associated with the corresponding absorption band reflects the absolute stereochemistry of the isomer.[5]

[90] R. W. Matton, *J. Chem. Phys.* **23**, 268 (1944).

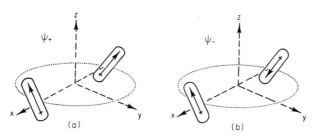

FIG. 19. The coupling modes of the monomer excitation dipole moments (a) in-phase, and (b) out-of-phase, in a dimer with noncoplanar chromophores.

Most dye molecules have a secondary element of symmetry, notably the molecular plane, and so are optically inactive. Exceptions are the azo dyes synthesized by Adams and Brode[91,92] with the object of investigating the possible differential binding of the two enantiomers to optically active fibers, such as wool, silk, or cotton. No evidence for the preferential binding of one dye enantiomer relative to its antipode was discovered in the early work[91] but subsequently it was found that simpler dissymmetric molecules, notably D- and L-mandelic acid, are differentially adsorbed by wool.[92]

When planar dye molecules form a dimer or a higher aggregate in which the individual molecules are regularly ordered but are not related by a center, a plane, or a rotation-reflection axis, the aggregate as a whole is dissymmetric and exists in two stereochemically enantiomeric configurations. The simplest case is a dimer consisting of two dye molecules with noncoplanar transition dipole moments (Fig. 19). The resultant dimer transition, $\psi_0 \rightarrow \psi_+$ (Fig. 19a) entails an overall left-handed helical charge displacement along and about the z axis, resulting in a negative circular dichroism absorption for the particular absolute stereochemical configuration of the dimer depicted. The other dimer transition, $\psi_0 \rightarrow \psi_-$ (Fig. 19b), entails a resultant right-handed helical charge displacement along and around the y axis, giving a positive circular dichroism absorption for the same dimer configuration. If the dimer has the enantiomeric configuration, the mirror image of that depicted (Fig. 19), the signs of the circular dichroism bands are reversed although they lie at the same wavelengths and have the same absolute magnitudes. The two circular dichroism bands are identified by their relative absorption frequencies [Eq. (39)], so that the particular stereochemical configuration of the dimer may be assigned from the observed optical activity.

Dye molecules bound to optically active polymers commonly give two

[91] R. Adams and W. R. Brode, *J. Am. Chem. Soc.* **46**, 2032 (1924); **48**, 2193 and 2202 (1926).

[92] W. R. Brode, *Chem. Soc. (London), Spec. Publ.* **4**, 1 (1956).

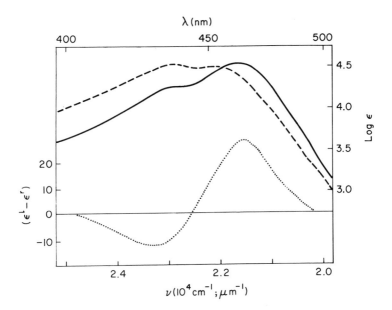

FIG. 20. The absorption spectrum of proflavin (3,6-diaminoacridine) in water at
$10^{-5} M$ (— — — —) and bound to DNA (desoxyribonucleic acid) in water (————),
and the circular dichroism of the dye–polymer complex (·····).

circular dichroism bands of opposite sign associated with the long-
wavelength absorption of the dye (Fig. 20). An optically active polymer
is essential, for although a dye may bind to a racemic polymer in an
ordered dissymmetric array, the resulting dye aggregates bound to the
polymer constitute a racemic mixture and no optical activity is detectable.

Similarly the gelatinous polymer formed by pseudoisocyanine (IV;
M = CH) and similar dyes[82] consists of an equal number of left-handed
and right-handed helical aggregates unless it is formed in the presence of
an optically active anion, or some other dissymmetric system favoring
the formation of one of the two helical configurations.[83] The circular
dichroism of the pseudoisocyanine polymer (Fig. 16) is more complex
than expected for the simple dissymmetric dimer (Fig. 19), as the aggregate contains a large number of dye molecules. However the circular
dichroism has been analyzed to show that the pseudoisocyanine polymer
formed in the presence of (−)-tartrate has a right-handed helical form
with an average helix radius of 4 Å and eight dye molecules per turn of
the helix.[83] The structures of soluble dye polymer complexes, such as
acridine orange (XXIII) bound to poly-L-glutamic acid[93] and to poly-

[93] R. E. Ballard, A. J. McCaffery, and S. F. Mason, *Biopolymers* 4, 97 (1966).

nucleotides,[94] have been similarly studied by circular dichroism and flow dichroism methods.

In general, the use of polarized light, whether linear or circular, for the spectroscopic investigation of dyes has been especially informative in recent years, adding the property of polarization direction to the more traditional measures of absorption wavelength and band intensity in characterizing an absorption process. All three properties emerge from quantum-mechanical calculations, which now provide a good understanding of the relation between color and molecular and electronic structure in the cyanine dyes and the wide range of basic and acidic dyes related to them. However, the azo dyes have not been extensively investigated theoretically, although the light-absorption properties of the azobenzene chromophore and its simple derivatives are well understood,[8] and the relations between the color and constitution of the vat dyes await detailed study.

[94] S. F. Mason and A. J. McCaffery, *Nature* **204**, 468 (1964); B. J. Gardner and S. F. Mason, *Biopolymers* **5**, 79 (1967).

CHAPTER V

DIAZOTIZATION AND COUPLING

J. M. Tedder

THE UNIVERSITY, ST. ANDREWS, SCOTLAND, U.K.

Since the publication of Volume I of this series in 1952, there have been three major developments in the chemistry of diazonium salts. First is the elucidation of the sometimes complex kinetics of the diazotization reaction and a discussion of these results will form the first section of the present chapter. Second is the development of a method for "the direct introduction of the diazonium group" which, now that the reaction is largely understood, could better be called "the nitroso route to diazonium salts," and a discussion of these reactions forms the second section. The third development has come in a greater understanding of the coupling reaction of diazonium salts and the fine details of the mechanism of the reaction have been studied. This work, which throws an important light on aromatic substitution reactions as a whole, is described in the final section.

I. The Mechanism of Diazotization

Bamberger[1] was probably the first to suggest that diazotization involves the N-nitrosation of the amine.

$$\text{ArNH}_2 \xrightarrow[\text{Slow}]{\text{NO—X}} \text{Ar—NH—NO} \xrightarrow[\text{Fast}]{} \text{Ar—N}{=}\text{N—OH} \xrightarrow[\text{Fast}]{\text{Acid}} \text{Ar}\overset{+}{\text{N}}{\equiv}\text{N}$$

Clusius has shown that under normal reaction conditions diazotization with H^{15}NO_2 leads to a diazonium salt in which the labeled nitrogen atom appears in the β-position,[2] as required by the Bamberger mechanism. The significance of this result is to some extent lessened by the observation of E. S. Lewis and co-workers that scrambling of the nitrogen atoms in a diazonium salt can occur.[3] However all the evidence

$$\text{Ar—}^{15}\text{NH} \xrightarrow[]{\text{HNO}_2} \text{Ar—}^{15}\overset{+}{\text{N}}{\equiv}\text{N} \rightleftarrows \text{Ar}\overset{+}{\underset{N}{\overset{15N}{\diagdown}}} \rightleftarrows \text{Ar—}\overset{+}{\text{N}}{\equiv}^{15}\text{N}$$

suggests that the Bamberger mechanism provides a correct overall picture. Particularly relevant is the observation that the rate of N-nitrosation of N-methylaniline from 0.002–6.5 M perchloric acid parallels exactly the rate of diazotization. There are three changes of mechanism and two different nitrosating agents for both reactions over this range of acidity. The similarity of the two reactions provides the strongest evidence that the rate-determining step of diazotization is also on N-nitrosation.[4] This makes the suggestion that the arylammonium ion reacts with undissociated nitrous acid (see references cited on p. 214 of CSD I) most unlikely. All the known reactions of amines with acid derivatives

[1] E. Bamberger, Ber. 27, 1948 (1894).

[2] K. Clusius and M. Hoch, Helv. Chim. Acta 33, 2122 (1950); K. Clusius and U. Lüthi, ibid. 40, 445 (1957).

[3] I. M. Insole and E. S. Lewis, J. Am. Chem. Soc. 85, 122 (1963); 86, 32 and 34 (1964); E. S. Lewis and R. E. Holliday, ibid. 88, 5043 (1966); but see also A. K. Bose and I. Kugajevsky, ibid. p. 2325.

[4] E. Kalatzis and J. H. Ridd, J. Chem. Soc., B p. 529 (1966).

are rationalized by the assumption that the amine behaves as a nucleo-phile, donating the "lone pair" of electrons of the nitrogen atom to the electrophilic acid derivatives, i.e.,

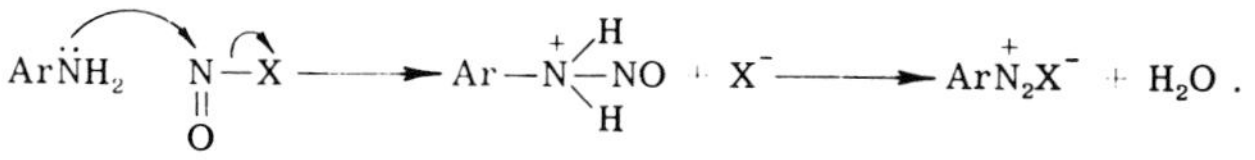

If this kind of picture is correct then the problem of the mechanism of diazotization centers not around the amine but with nitrous acid and its derivatives. This is exactly what the work of Ingold and his col-laborators showed.

We can visualize the following possible derivatives of nitrous acid:

X—NO			
X = HO	i.e.,	HO—N=O	Nitrous acid
X = NO$_3$	i.e.,	N$_2$O$_3$	Nitrous anhydride
X = Cl(Br)	i.e.,	NOCl	Nitrosyl chloride

together with the following possible ionic derivatives

NO$^+$	nitrosonium ion
H$_2$NO$_2{}^+$	nitrous acidium ion

All these five species are probably involved though it is the latter four for which most direct evidence can be obtained.

A. Nitrous Anhydride as Reagent

Evidence that nitrous anhydride (N$_2$O$_3$) is the effective diazotizing agent in dilute nitrous acid prepared from aqueous sodium nitrite and either sulfuric or perchloric acid was first obtained by Schmid.[5] He showed that the reaction in dilute sulfuric acid was third order

$$\text{Rate} = \frac{k_1[\text{ArNH}_3{}^+][\text{HNO}_2]^2}{K_b[\text{H}_3\text{O}^+]} = k_1[\text{ArNH}_2][\text{HNO}_2]^2$$

This kinetic result was also obtained by Ingold and co-workers using dilute perchloric acid.[6] The explanation of the rate law was provided by Hammett.[7] The second power observed for the nitrous acid is actually due to the equilibrium between nitrous acid and its anhydride.

[5] H. Schmid, Z. *Elektrochem.* **42**, 579 (1936); H. Schmid and G. Muhr, *Ber.* **70B**, 421 (1937).

[6] E. D. Hughes, C. K. Ingold, and J. H. Ridd, *J. Chem. Soc.* pp. 58 and 65 (1958).

[7] L. P. Hammett, "Physical Organic Chemistry," p. 294. McGraw-Hill, New York, 1940.

$$2HNO_2 \underset{Fast}{\overset{}{\rightleftarrows}} N_2O_3 + H_2O$$

$$ArNH_2 + N_2O_3 \underset{Slow}{\longrightarrow} Ar\overset{+}{N}H_2NO + NO_3^-$$

$$ArNH_2NO \underset{Fast}{\longrightarrow} ArN_2^+$$

By carrying out the reaction in very dilute acid Ingold and co-workers were able to change the rate law for third order to second order.

$$Rate = k_1[HNO_2]^2$$

This corresponds to a condition where the free amine is present in sufficient excess to react with the nitrous anhydride as fast as it is formed. In other words the inorganic reaction, though fast compared with the N-nitrosation stage, can in the presence of excess amine become rate-determining.[6,8] Under these conditions the rate of diazotization is independent of the concentration and nature of the amine provided that the pK_a of the amine is greater than 4. Second-order kinetics for diazotization had originally been observed by Hantzsch and Schümann,[9] who mistakenly assumed the reaction was first order in each reactant. The correct explanation was not forthcoming until the work of Hughes and Ridd.

Further evidence for the formation of nitrous anhydride has been obtained from a study of the ^{18}O exchange between nitrous acid and water.[10] At very low acidities and at high concentrations of the nitrite ion, exchange is second order in nitrous acid. It was subsequently reported that the rates of diazotization and oxygen exchange under identical conditions are almost the same.[11] These combined observations necessarily require nitrous anhydride to be the nitrosating species.

The logarithm of the third-order rate constants for the diazotization of aniline, p-anisidine, p-chloroaniline, and p-trimethylammoniumaniline plotted against Hammett σ-values[12] gave a straight line and from the slope a value of -1.6 can be calculated for ρ.[13] The negative value of ρ means that the reaction is favored by a high electron density at the reaction center, i.e., the amino nitrogen atom. This confirms that the reaction involves nucleophilic attack of the amine on the nitrosating agent.

[8] E. D. Hughes and J. H. Ridd, *J. Chem. Soc.* p. 70 (1958).

[9] A. Hantzsch and M. Schümann, *Ber.* **32**, 1691 (1899).

[10] C. A. Bunton, D. R. Llewellyn, and G. Stedmann, *J. Chem. Soc.* p. 568 (1959).

[11] J. H. Ridd, *Quart. Rev. (London)* **15**, 418 (1961).

[12] L. P. Hammett, "Physical Organic Chemistry," p. 184. McGraw-Hill, New York, 1940.

[13] L. F. Lankworthy, *J. Chem. Soc.* p. 8116 (1959).

B. "Mixed" Nitrous Anhydrides as Reagents

If nitrous acid can react with itself to form nitrous anhydride and water, it seems probable that it will react with other acids to form

$$2HNO_2 \rightarrow N_2O_3 + H_2O$$

a "mixed" or unsymmetrical anhydride. If the second acid is very strong

$$HNO_2 + HX \rightarrow NOX + H_2O$$

then there will be little tendency to form a molecular unsymmetrical anhydride (if it exists at all it would tend to ionize, $NOX \rightleftarrows NO^+ + X^-$). Thus with perchloric and sulfuric acids, molecular unsymmetrical anhydrides are unlikely to be important nitrosating agents. With weaker acids, however, unsymmetric anhydride formation can occur and the possibility that the unsymmetrical anhydride is the effective nitrosating agent has to be considered.

The strongest evidence for the participation of unsymmetrical anhydrides in diazotization reactions again comes from kinetics, and again it was Schmid who performed the first crucial experiment. He found that chloride ions exerted a catalytic effect when diazotization was performed in the presence of hydrochloric acid. Again it was Hammett who

$$\text{Rate} = \frac{k[\text{Ar}\overset{+}{\text{N}}\text{H}_3][\text{HNO}_2]^2}{[\text{H}_3\text{O}^+]} + k_c[\text{Ar}\overset{+}{\text{N}}\text{H}_3][\text{HNO}_2][\text{Cl}^-]$$

rewrote this rate expression, and so provided the correct explanation of the catalytic effect of chloride. He proposed that

$$\text{Rate} = k[\text{ArNH}_2][\text{N}_2\text{O}_3] + k_c[\text{ArNH}_2][\text{NOCl}]$$

the chloride ions were reacting with nitrous acid to yield nitrosyl chloride and that this was an additional nitrosating agent. Hughes and Ridd sought to isolate the inorganic reaction by having excess amine present as they had in the case of nitroso anhydride.[14] They were unable to do this with chloride ions, but with bromide ions they were able to make the inorganic reaction rate-determining, i.e.,

$$\text{Rate Br}^- \text{ catalyzed} = k_c[\text{H}^+][\text{HNO}_2][\text{Br}^-]$$

this being due to the comparatively slow formation of nitrosyl bromide:

$$HNO_2 + H^+ + Br^- \rightleftarrows NOBr + H_2O$$

The equilibrium constants for these reactions are known and Schmid and co-workers used this data to obtain the rate constants of the actual nitrosation reaction.[15]

---

[14] E. D. Hughes and J. H. Ridd, *J. Chem. Soc.* p. 82 (1958).

[15] H. Schmid and E. Hallaba, *Monatsh. Chem.* **87**, 560 (1956); H. Schmid and M. G. Forrad, *ibid.* **88**, 631 (1957); H. Schmid and C. Essler, *ibid.* 1110.

$$V = k[\text{ArNH}_4][\text{NOX}]$$

Hughes and Ridd found that acetate and phthalate buffers also provided a weak catalytic effect.[7] This is probably also due to the formation of unsymmetric anhydride molecules (e.g., CH_3COONO). However, the catalyzed rate is dependent on the second power of the nitrous acid concentration, i.e.,

$$\text{Rate } CH_3CO_2^- \text{ catalyzed} = k'_c[HNO_2]^2[CH_3CO_2^-]$$

Ingold and co-workers therefore conclude that the "nitrosyl acetate" catalyzes the formation of nitrous anhydride rather than nitrosating the amine directly.[16]

$$NO_2^- + CH_3COONO \rightleftharpoons N_2O_3 + CH_3CO_2^-$$

At the beginning of this section we briefly considered the possibility that the unsymmetrical anhydrides between nitrous acid and the strong acids such as sulfonic and perchloric acids were unlikely. Such species have, however, been proposed,[17] but the evidence that they contribute to diazotization is extremely doubtful[18] and in the opinion of the present writer must be discounted.

C. DIAZOTIZATION BY THE NITROUS ACIDIUM ION

Diazotization by nitrous anhydride should reach its maximum rate when the concentration of free amine is maximum. An increase in acidity should lower the rate by reducing the concentration of free base. Such a decrease is observed for small increases in acidity but further addition of strong acid results in an increase in diazotization rate. This result implies the onset of an additional mechanism of nitrosation, which Ingold and co-workers found to obey the following rate law:[19]

$$\text{Rate acid-catalyzed reaction} = k[ArNH_2][NHO_2][H^+]$$

This rate equation could be explained either simply due to nitrosation by the nitrous acidium ion ($H_2NO_2^+$) or by the nitrosonium ion formed as a result of a slow equilibrium:

$$H^+ + HNO_2 \xrightarrow{\text{Fast}} H_2NO_2^+$$

$$H_2NO_2^+ \underset{\text{Slow}}{\rightleftharpoons} NO^+ + H_2O$$

[16] E. D. Hughes, C. K. Ingold, and J. H. Ridd, *J. Chem. Soc.* p. 88 (1958).
[17] H. Schmid and C. Essler, *Monatsh. Chem.* **90**, 222 (1959); **91**, 484 (1960).
[18] B. C. Challis and J. H. Ridd, *J. Chem. Soc.* p. 5208 (1962).
[19] E. D. Hughes, C. K. Ingold, and J. H. Ridd, *J. Chem. Soc.* p. 77 (1958).

Ingold and co-workers argue that there is strong circumstantial evidence that this acid-catalyzed reaction involved nitrous acidium ions and not nitrosonium ions.[16] The most important of their arguments being that the ^{18}O exchange rate coincided with the formation of nitrous anhydride under these conditions, and there was no evidence of an additional exchange mechanism that the formation of the nitrosonium ion would provide. As we would expect, the nitrous acidium ion proves considerably less discriminating than nitrous anhydride, i.e., the rates of diazotization of weakly basic amines differ very little.[20]

D. DIAZOTIZATION IN MODERATELY STRONG ACID MEDIA

Weakly basic amines such as p-nitroaniline and 2,4-dinitroaniline are normally diazotized by fairly strong acid. Challis, Lankworthy, and Ridd sought to distinguish between diazotization by the nitrous acidium ion or by the nitrosonium ion in these moderately strong acid media, by examining the effect of acidity on the rate. At its simplest level the rate of nitrosation involving the nitrous acidium ion should be proportional to Hammett's acidity H_0 whereas the rate of nitrosation involving the nitrosonium ion should be proportional to H_r ($H_0 = - \log h_0$ and $H_r = - \log h_r$).

$$H^+ + HNO_2 \rightleftarrows H_2NO_2^+$$
$$\text{Rate} = k[ArNH_2][HNO_2]h_0$$

$$H^+ + HNO_2 \rightleftarrows NO_2^+ + H_2O$$
$$\text{Rate} = k'[ArNH_2][HNO_2]h_r$$

In practice the system proved much more complicated than these simple equations suggest. The reactions are no longer being studied in dilute solution and salt effects were found to be important. However, the authors reached the conclusion that even at these acidities the nitrous acidium ion was still the main nitrosating agent.[21] In these fairly strong acid solutions additional complications arise and as the acidity is increased further the possibility of nitrosation of the arylammonium ion ($Ar\overset{+}{N}H_3$) has to be considered. There is controversy over the interpretation of the kinetic results obtained in this region. Schmid and co-workers[17,22] provide a complex rate equation which appears to imply that molecular nitrosyl perchlorate is involved. This is most improbable, but

[20] L. F. Lankworthy, *J. Chem. Soc.* p. 3304 (1959).
[21] B. C. Challis, L. F. Lankworthy, and J. H. Ridd, *J. Chem. Soc.* p. 5203 (1962).
[22] H. Schmid and A. F. Sami, *Monatsh. Chem.* **86**, 904 (1955).

the alternative explanation of Ridd and his co-workers,[23] namely, nitrosation of arylammonium ion, is hardly less attractive. However, Challis and Ridd provide evidence for a strongly acid catalyzed reaction involving H_0 to the second power. The correct interpretation

$$\text{Rate} = k[\text{ArNH}_2][\text{HNO}_2]h_0{}^2 \equiv k'[\text{Ar}\overset{+}{\text{N}}\text{H}_3][\text{HNO}_2]h_0$$

of reactions occurring in concentrated solutions of this type is inevitably difficult. The evidence of Ridd and his co-workers for the nitrosation of the anilinium ions is good and pending further results we must regard this as yet a further mechanism. Whether the nitrosating agent is the nitrous acidium ion or the nitrosonium ion in solutions of this acidity is to some extent an academic queston. Thus nitrosonium ion will certainly be solvated though not necessarily by a water molecule.

E. DIAZOTIZATION IN VERY STRONG ACID MEDIA

In Volume I[24] mention is made of the diazotization of 2,4,6-trinitroaniline and other very weak bases by a solution of nitrosyl sulfuric acid in glacial acetic solution. In these mixtures of sulfuric acid and acetic acid there can be little doubt that the effective nitrosating agent is the nitrosonium ion, but no kinetic studies have been made and the interpretation of any such work would be extremely difficult.

F. SUMMARY

Diazotization involves the initial N-nitrosation of the amine. There are a number of nitrous acid derivatives which can effect nitrosation and these include N_2O_3, NOX (X = Cl, Br, I), $H_2NO_2{}^+$, and NO^+. In dilute neutral media nitrous anhydride is the main agent. Halide ions can be effective catalysts due to the formation of nitrosyl halides. In more acidic media the nitrous acidium ion is the predominant nitrosation agent. When the medium becomes very acidic there is no free amine present and nitrosation of the arylammonium ion may be important. In nonaqueous media of high acidity the nitrosonium ion is probably the effective nitrosating agent but no direct evidence for its participation is yet available.

There are two excellent reviews on the subject of the mechanism of diazotization[11,25] which discuss the literature up to 1961.

[23] B. C. Challis and J. H. Ridd, *J. Chem. Soc.* p. 5208 (1962); E. C. R. de Fabrizio, E. Kalatzis, and J. H. Ridd, *J. Chem. Soc.,* B p. 533 (1966).

[24] *CSD I,* p. 212.

[25] H. Zollinger, "Azo and Diazochemistry," Chapter 2, p. 24. Wiley (Interscience), New York, 1961.

II. The Nitroso Route to Diazonium Salts

An aromatic compound is normally converted into a diazonium salt in a three-step process nitration, reduction to the amine, followed by diazotization. However, as far back as 1871 it was known that phenols treated with nitrous acid would give diazonium salts, in one experimental step.[26] For the next eighty-six years occasional reports of the direct formation of diazonium salts appeared but it was usually regarded as an unwanted side reaction. In 1957 a serious investigation of the "direct introduction of the diazonium group into aromatic nuclei" was begun.[27] It was quickly established that the reaction was not restricted to phenols but was one of the widest applicability. The experimental conditions vary for each class of compound and so it will be convenient to deal with them separately.

A. Phenols and Their Derivatives

Reports that diazonium salts occur as by-products in the preparation of nitrosophenols (quinone-monoximes) date back to work of Weselsky already referred to.[26] Other reports include limited but thorough investigations by Rodionov and Matweew[28] and by Morel and Sisley,[29] together with a number of brief reports in which diazonium salts were unwanted side reactions.[30-32] One, at least, of these reports was substantially wrong in detail,[31] but they all pointed to the conclusion that diazonium salts could be prepared from phenols simply by treating them with excess nitrous acid.

When this work came to be reinvestigated it was quickly established that by using the right conditions the yields of phenolic diazonium salt could be almost quantitatively.[33,34] For simple phenols very high yields of diazonium salt were obtained using buffered solutions of nitrous acid in aqueous acetone solution with a vast excess of sodium nitrite (15-fold excess over phenol, 10-fold excess over hydrochloric acid). It is probable that the main function of this excess nitrite is simply to act as a buffer and so maintain a relatively high pH (pH 3–4). Since the reaction in-

[26] P. Weselsky, *Ber.* **4**, 613 (1871) ; **8**, 98 (1875).
[27] J. M. Tedder, *Tetrahedron* **1**, 270 (1957).
[28] W. Rodionov and W. Matweew, *Ber.* **57**, 1711 (1924).
[29] A. Morel and P. Sisley, *Bull. Soc. Chim. France* **41**, 1217 (1927).
[30] H. H. Hodgson, *J. Chem. Soc.* p. 1494 (1931) ; p. 866 (1932).
[31] J. St. L. Philpot and P. A. Small, *Biochem. J.* **32**, 534 (1938).
[32] A. Kraaijeveld and E. Havinga, *Rec. Trav. Chim.* **73**, 537 and 549 (1954).
[33] J. M. Tedder, *J. Chem. Soc.* p. 4003 (1957).
[34] J. M. Tedder and G. Theaker, *J. Chem. Soc.* p. 2573 (1958).

volves initial nitrosation, the position of the diazonium group in the salt is where normal electrophilic attack

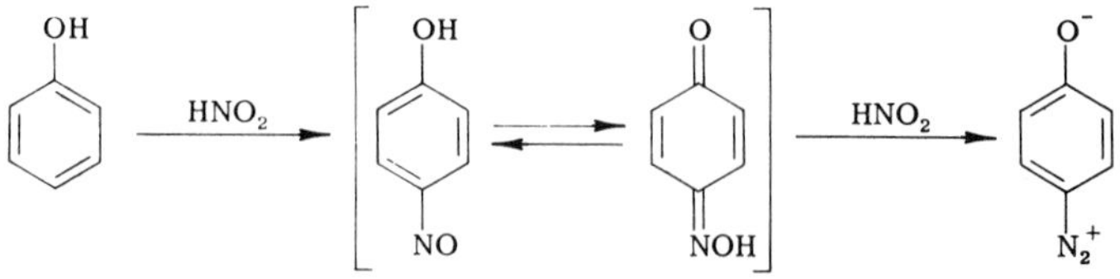

would be expected, i.e., para to the hydroxy group if this position is vacant, otherwise ortho to the hydroxy group. With α-naphthol the reaction halts at the nitrosonaphthol stage, undoubtedly because the nitroso compound is stabilized as the quinone-monoxime tautomer.

If the nitrosation is carried out in alcoholic solution using ethyl nitrite as the source of nitrous acid the product diazonium salt is that derived from the corresponding phenol ether.[34,35] Treatment of m-hydroxybenzoic acid under the same conditions as other phenols gave the expected diazonium

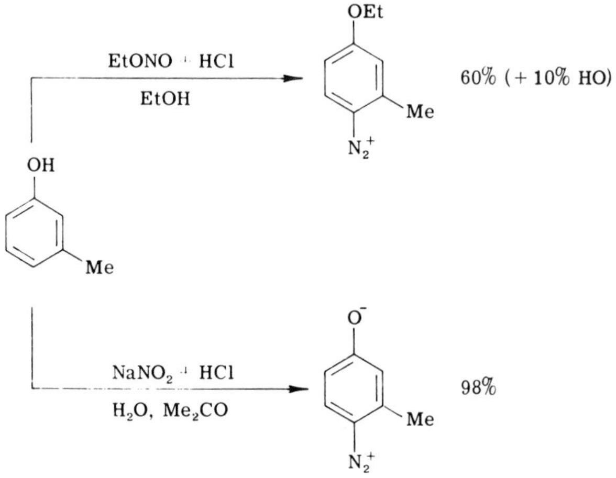

salt in moderate yield similar to other phenols containing deactivating groups. p-Hydroxybenzoic acid or salicylic acid behaved differently. The former gave exclusively p-hydroxybenzenediazonium salt while the latter gave a mixture.[36]

[35] J. M. Tedder and G. Theaker, Chem. Ind. (London) p. 1485 (1957).
[36] J. M. Tedder and G. Theaker, J. Chem. Soc. p. 257 (1959).

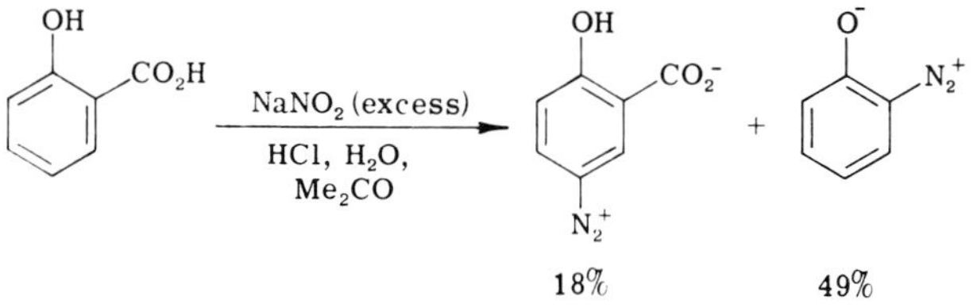

18%   49%

The nitrosation of salicyclic acid has been the subject of a number of contradictory publications. An early patent claimed the preparation of 5-nitrososalicyclic acid by direct nitrosation,[37] which Friedländer recorded with scepticism.[38] Lésniański reported the only product from nitrosation to be the nitrosophenol,[39] but five years later Gulinov claimed to have prepared 5-nitrososalicylic acid by nitrosation.[40] In 1958 Henry, apparently having failed to read the relevant literature, reported decarboxylation.[41] The first report that nitrosation of salicylic acid could yield a diazonium salt came from Nemodurk.[42,43] The decarboxylation of hydroxyaromatic acids when treated with electrophilic reagents in dilute aqueous solution is well known. For example, p-hydroxybenzoic acid undergoes decarboxylation when coupled with diazonium salts.[44] Thus the nitrosation is in no sense exceptional. The complications in the case of salicylic acid are mainly due to the fact that o-hydroxy nitroso compounds can be trapped by transition metals, and hence good yields of nitroso compound obtained.[43]

B. TERTIARY AROMATIC AMINES AND RELATED COMPOUNDS

N,N-Dimethylaniline can be converted into the corresponding 4-nitroso compound almost quantitatively, provided the solution is kept strongly acid. In buffered solution, however, the principal product is the diazonium salt[27,33,45] (see p. 234). The first report that tertiary amines could be converted directly into diazonium salts appears to have been a patent.[46] However, employing the methods described in the patent only trace amounts of diazonium salts are found, and the importance of acidity

[37] German Patent 48,491
[38] *Friedländer* **2**, 221 (1891).
[39] W. Lésniański, *Przemysl Chem.* **6**, 349 (1922); *Chem. Zentr.* **VI**, 496 (1923).
[40] J. G. Gulinov, *Zh. Khim. Prom.* **4**, 909 (1927); *Chem. Abstr.* **22**, 3648 (1928).
[41] R. A. Henry, *J. Org. Chem.* **23**, 648 (1958).
[42] A. A. Nemodurk, *Zh. Obshch. Khim.* **26**, 3283 (1956).
[43] A. A. Nemodurk, *Zh. Obshch. Khim.* **28**, 1082 (1958).
[44] E. Grandmongin and H. Freimann, *Ber.* **40**, 3453 (1907).
[45] H. P. Patel and J. M. Tedder, *J. Chem. Soc.* p. 4889 (1963).
[46] W. M. Hinman and W. G. Hollmann, *USP* 2,178,585.

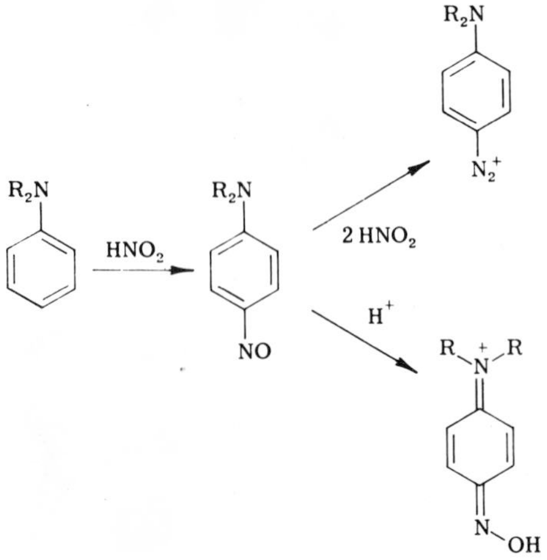

was not appreciated until much later.[33] There are more by-products produced in these reactions than in the corresponding nitrosations of phenols, and the yields reported so far are somewhat lower (e.g., ~55% for N,N-dialkylanilines). However, no detailed study of reaction conditions has yet been made. An attempt to use this one-step process in place of the conventional three-step process for the preparation of *tert*-aminoaryldiazonium tetrafluoroborates[47] showed that better yields were obtained by the conventional route. Undoubtedly if the reaction is to have practical value much greater attention will have to be given to reaction conditions and media.

When Fischer first reported the rearrangement of N-nitroso-N-alkylamines to p-nitroso-N-alkylamines (the Fischer-Hepp reaction) he was aware that small amounts of diazonium salt were formed as a result of the C-nitroso compounds reacting with the nitrous acid present.[48] By adding further nitrous acid it is possible to utilize the rearrangement as a method for preparing p-(N-alkyl-N-nitrosoamino)benzenediazonium salts.[49]

C. POLYALKYLBENZENES AND PHENOL ETHERS

It will be evident that in the nitrous acid solutions effective in converting phenols and tertiary aromatic amines into diazonium salts, the nitrosating agents are almost certainly nitrous anhydride (N_2O_3) or

[47] C. Sellers and H. Suschitzky, *J. Chem. Soc.* p. 6186 (1965).
[48] O. Fischer and E. Hepp, *Ber.* **19**, 2991 (1886); **20**, 2476 (1887).
[49] H. P. Patel and J. M. Tedder, *J. Chem. Soc.* p. 4894 (1963).

nitrosyl chloride (NOCl). (See Section I of this chapter.) In general these reagents are insufficiently reactive to C-nitrosate aromatic hydrocarbons or even phenol ethers. Polyalkoxybenzenes are more reactive and both resorcinol dimethyl ether and phloroglucinol trimethyl ether can be converted into diazonium salts in moderate yield ($\sim$50%) by treatment with buffered nitrous acid in aqueous acetone solution.[50] These aqueous solutions have no effect on anisole but anisole can be nitrosated and hence converted into p-methoxybenzenediazonium salt by using more acidic media. The first reagent shown to be capable of this reaction was a solution of ethyl nitrite in trifluoroacetic anhydride.[51] Nitrosonium ions were believed to be present in such solutions and it is possible that these provide the actual nitrosating agent. If nitrosonium ions are effective then the most obvious system would be nitrosyl sulfuric acid ($NO^+HSO_4^-$). Solutions of nitrosyl sulfuric acid in sulfuric acid prepared simply by dissolving sodium nitrite in sulfuric acid proved effective in giving low yields of diazonium salt from phenol ethers and alkylbenzenes, but the products were contaminated with nitro compounds. Purer diazonium salts and very much better yields were obtained for the more reactive aromatic compounds by using nitrosyl sulfuric acid suspended in nitrobenzene. By this means sym-trimethylbenzenediazonium salt was prepared in 78% yield, but the yield from less reactive compounds such as toluene was only a trace.[33]

Other nitrosonium salts would be expected to be effective and $NO^+BF_3NO_3^-$ (prepared from N_2O_4 and BF_3) has been found to be so.[52] Nitrosyl chloride and aluminum chloride, contrary to expectation, are not effective, but this is almost certainly due to the further reaction of the nitroso compound rather than the failure of the system to act as a nitrosating agent.[50]

D. Aromatic Sulfonic Acids, Carboxylic Acids, and Nitro Compounds

Since the nitrosonium ion is insufficiently reactive to attack benzene at normal temperatures the chances of employing the nitroso route for the preparation of diazonium salts from deactivated aromatic compounds at first sight appear remote. However, such compounds can be mercurated and aryl mercury compounds treated with nitrous anhydride[53] or nitrosyl

[50] J. M. Tedder and K. H. Todd, unpublished work (1968).
[51] E. J. Bourne, M. Stacey, J. C. Tatlow, and J. M. Tedder, J. Chem. Soc. p. 1695 (1951).
[52] J. M. Tedder, J. Am. Chem. Soc. 79, 6090 (1959).
[53] E. Bamberger, Ber. 30, 506 (1897).

chloride[54-56] yield nitroso compounds and diazonium salts. Mercuration followed successively by nitrosation and diazonium salt formation was found to occur during "oxynitration."[57,58] Very much earlier a patent specifically claiming the preparation of diazonium salts probably involved this process, although in the experiments reported oxidation occurred as well.[59]

In practice a catalytic amount of mercuric sulfate added to a solution of sodium nitrite in excess nitrosyl sulfuric acid provides a system effective in introducing the diazonium group into aryl sulfonic acids, nitro compounds, etc.[60] In some examples good yields of diazonium salt were obtained (e.g., 75% from p-nitroanisole). The catalytic function of the mercury is clear, but at first sight it is surprising that any nitroso com-

$$ArH + Hg^{2+} \rightarrow ArHg^+ \xrightarrow{NO^+} ArNO + Hg^{2+}$$

pound survives heating in concentrated sulfuric acid solution. The success of these reactions carried out at 70° is probably due to the formation of complexes between the aryl nitroso compounds and nitrosonium ions.[61] Similar complexes have been proposed for nitrosoamines.[62]

$$Ar-N=O + NO^+ \rightleftharpoons Ar-\overset{+}{N}=O$$
$$\underset{\text{N}=O}{|}$$

(Green)   (Red-brown)

Diazonium salts are not formed in these sulfuric acid solutions, the conversion of the nitroso compound into the diazonium salt occurring when the reaction mixture is poured into water. If the reaction mixture is poured instead into an aqueous solution of sulfamic acid, the free aryl nitroso compound can be isolated in a slightly higher yield than the yield of diazonium salt formed when the reaction mixture is poured into water.[61]

[54] E. Kunz, Ber. 31, 1528 (1898).

[55] L. I. Smith and F. L. Taylor, J. Am. Chem. Soc. 57, 2460 (1935).

[56] L. G. Makarova and A. N. Nesmeyanov, J. Gen. Chem. USSR 9, 771 (1939); Chem. Abstr. 34, 391 (1940).

[57] F. H. Westheimer, E. Segel, and R. Schramm, J. Am. Chem. Soc. 69, 773 (1947).

[58] M. Carmack, M. M. Baizer, G. R. Handrick, L. W. Kessinger, and E. H. Specht, J. Am. Chem. Soc. 69, 785 (1947).

[59] Bayer, BP 27,373.

[60] J. M. Tedder and G. Theaker, J. Chem. Soc. p. 4008 (1957).

[61] J. M. Tedder and G. Theaker, Tetrahedron 5, 288 (1959).

[62] C. C. Addison, N. Hodge, and J. C. Sheddon, Chem. Ind. (London) p. 1338 (1953).

E. HETEROCYCLIC COMPOUNDS

1. *Diazopyrroles*

It is customary to emphasize the similarity in chemical reactions of pyrroles and phenols. The formation of phenolic diazonium salts by treatment with buffered nitrous acid in aqueous acetone solution is described above. If the analogy can be applied, then treating pyrroles with the same medium should yield pyrrolediazonium salts. Basically, this is exactly what does happen.[63,64] At first we must take the analogy still further. Phenolic diazonium salts are converted into "diazo oxides" in alkaline media.

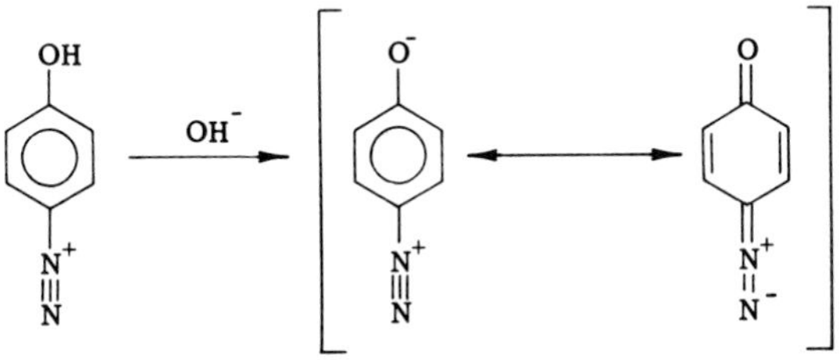

In an exactly similar way pyrrole diazonium salts are converted into "diazopyrroles." [63] Diazopyrroles are extremely stable substances which may have application in the photocopying industry, either in "lithography" [65]

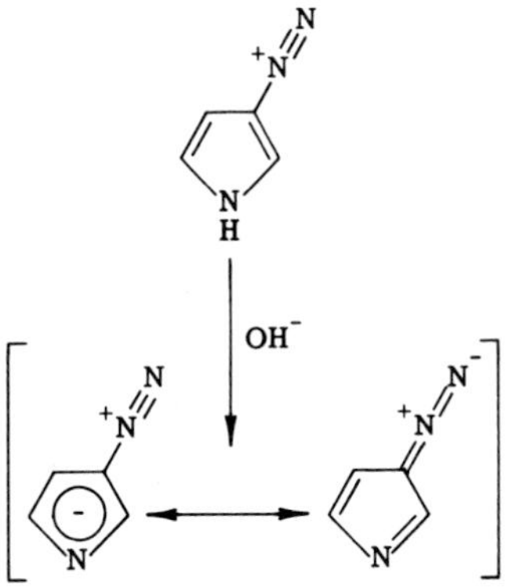

or "dye-line" processes.[66] 3-Diazopyrroles can be prepared by diazotiza-

[63] J. M. Tedder and B. Webster, *J. Chem. Soc.* p. 3270 (1960).
[64] J. M. Tedder, *Advan. Heterocyclic Chem.* **8**, 1 (1967).
[65] BP 816,382.
[66] BP 977,326; 988,221.

tion of the appropriate amine but aminopyrroles are unstable substances and there is little doubt that in most cases the nitroso route is preferable. 2-Aminopyrroles are very unstable and do not yield diazonium salts but 2-diazopyrroles can be prepared by the nitroso route.[67] On the other hand 3-diazoindoles which can be prepared from 3-aminoindoles cannot be prepared by the nitroso route, presumably because the nitrosoindole exists entirely in the oximino form.[68]

Pyrazole has a chemistry very similar to that of pyrrole and 3(5)-diazopyrazoles have been prepared directly from the parent heterocyclic compound via the nitroso route in one experimental step.[69,70] Diazopyrazoles are very similar to diazopyrroles, though as expected they are considerably more basic.

2. *Indolizine Diazonium Salts and Related Compounds*

Indolizine diazonium salts would, on current theories, be expected to be particularly stable, but aminoindolizines are reported to be unstable in air and no reports of their successful diazotization are available. Nitrosoindolizines are known, however, and these have successfully been converted into the corresponding diazonium salts.[71]

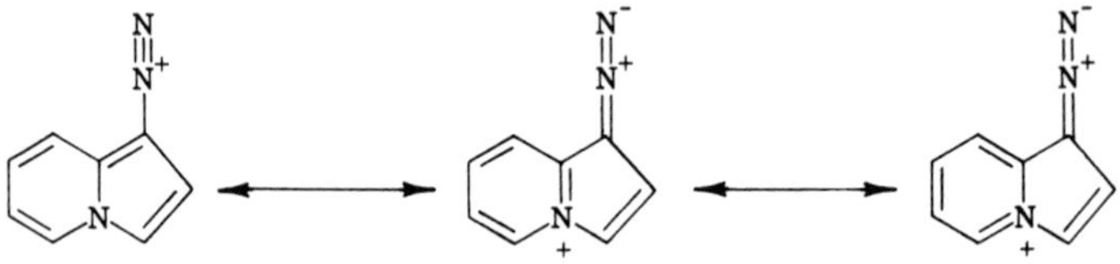

1-Nitroso compounds are converted into diazonium salts readily, but 3-nitrosoindolizines fail to react with nitric oxide. Pyrrolothiazole diazonium salts have been synthesized in a similar way.

F. SPECIAL APPLICATIONS OF THE NITROSO ROUTE: THE PREPARATION OF AN ACETYLENE DIAZONIUM SALT

In the previous section mention was made of the use of the nitroso route to diazonium salts when the corresponding amino compound was unstable or hard to come by. The nitroso route can provide access to diazonium salts which could never be prepared by diazotization because the required primary amine cannot exist. An example of such a diazo-

[67] J. M. Tedder and B. Webster, *J. Chem. Soc.* p. 1638 (1962).
[68] H. P. Patel and J. M. Tedder, *J. Chem. Soc.* p. 4593 (1963).
[69] H. P. Patel, J. M. Tedder, and B. Webster, *Chem. Ind.* (*London*), p. 1163 (1961).
[70] H. P. Patel and J. M. Tedder, *J. Chem. Soc.* p. 4589 (1963).
[71] J. M. Tedder and K. H. Todd, *Chem. Commun.* p. 424 (1967).

nium salt is an acetylenic diazonium salt, where the corresponding amino compound does not exist because it would instantly tautomerize to the cyanide. 1-Hexynediazonium nitrate has been prepared by treating the nitrosoacetylene[72,73] with nitric oxide.[74]

$$2C_4H_9C{\equiv}CH \xrightarrow{\text{HgO}} (C_4H_9C{\equiv}C)_2Hg \xrightarrow{\text{NOCl}} C_4H_9C{\equiv}C{-}NO \xrightarrow{\text{NO}} C_4H_9C{\equiv}C{-}\overset{+}{N}{\equiv}N\ NO_3^-$$

G. Mechanism of the Nitroso Route

In spite of the wide variety of conditions employed there is little doubt that in all the reactions where an aromatic compound is converted into a diazonium salt by a nitrous acid solution the aromatic nitroso compound is a necessary intermediate.[61]

The mechanism of the nitrosation process will vary depending on the nature of the nitrosating medium. From the work on diazotization (see Section I of this chapter) it is possible to suggest that in dilute aqueous nitrous acid the main nitrosating agent is nitrous anhydride (N_2O_3) or nitrosyl chloride (NOCl) if chloride ions are present. Thus the reactions involving phenols, tertiary amines, and pyrroles probably all involve initial nitrosation by one of these two reagents. The less reactive compounds such as polyalkylbenzenes and phenol ethers are probably nitrosated by either the nitrous acidium ion ($H_2NO_2^+$) or more likely in some cases the nitrosonium ion (NO^+). The nitroso compound initially formed in these cases combines with nitrosonium ions forming deep red-brown complexes which prevent the nitroso compound being decomposed by the strong acid medium.

We can summarize the various reactions as follows:

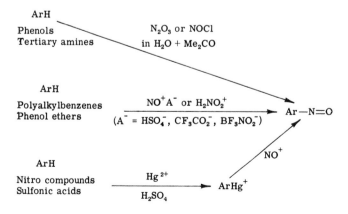

[72] E. Robson and J. M. Tedder, *Proc. Chem. Soc.* p. 13 (1963).
[73] E. Robson, J. M. Tedder, and D. J. Woodcock, *J. Chem. Soc.* p. 1324 (1968).
[74] E. Robson and J. M. Tedder, *Proc. Chem. Soc.* p. 344 (1963).

The conversion of the nitroso compound into the diazonium nitrate, has been shown to require either 2 moles of nitric oxide[61] or 3 moles of nitrite in acetic acid.[32] The first result can be rationalized as follows:

$$\text{Ar—N=O} + \text{NO} \longrightarrow \text{Ar—N—N=O} \ \underset{\overset{|}{O}}{} \ \xrightarrow{\text{NO}} \ \text{Ar—N—N=O} \ \underset{\overset{|}{O_{\diagdown N}}}{} \ \overset{\|}{O}$$

$$\text{Ar—N—N=O} \ \underset{\overset{|}{O_{\diagdown N}}}{} \ \overset{\|}{O} \longrightarrow \ \underset{\text{NO}_2}{\text{Ar—N=N—O}\cdot} \longrightarrow \left[\begin{array}{ll} \text{Ar—N=N—O—NO}_2 \\ \text{Ar—}\overset{+}{\text{N}}\text{≡N} \qquad \text{NO}_3^{-} \end{array} \right]$$

Alternatively the rearrangement can be entirely intramolecular:

$$\text{Ar—N} \underset{\overset{|}{O_{\diagdown N:}}}{\overset{\frown}{\underset{\diagdown}{}}} \overset{\frown}{\text{N}} \diagdown O \ \underset{\overset{\|}{O}}{} \longrightarrow \left[\begin{array}{ll} \text{Ar—N=N—O—}\overset{+}{\text{N}}\diagup\overset{O^{-}}{\diagdown O} \\ \text{Ar—}\overset{+}{\text{N}}\text{≡N} \qquad \text{NO}_3^{-} \end{array} \right]$$

In solution nitric oxide is probably formed via nitrous anhydride and this will explain the apparent difference in stoichiometry.

H. Importance of the Nitroso Route in Dyestuff Preparation

Although the existence of the nitroso route to diazonium salts was discovered only twenty years after the first preparation of a diazonium salt by Peter Griess, little attempt to utilize this route was made until one hundred years after Griess' discovery. During the intervening eighty years the technology of nitration, reduction, and diazotization had advanced so far that the fact that the nitroso route often involved a single experimental step instead of three, no longer gave it an overwhelming advantage. As far as the present author is aware no attempt has been made to develop the nitroso route for the industrial manufacture of a dyestuff. The circumstances which could change this situation is the development of a new dyestuff, difficult to prepare conventionally but readily available by the nitroso route. That such compounds do exist is shown by the preparation of diazopyrroles and indolizine diazonium salts. To a dyestuff chemist the nitroso route is thus a possible method to be considered when conventional methods fail or are difficult. To the researcher the nitroso route opens up the possibility of synthesizing compounds inaccessible by any other method.

III. Diazo-Transfer Reactions

The two methods of preparing diazonium salts we have discussed so far involve a two-stage introduction of nitrogen either via the amine which nitrosated or via the nitroso compound which is treated with nitric oxide. This section is concerned with reactions in which both nitrogen atoms are introduced simultaneously. Such reactions may reasonably be called diazo-transfer reactions.

$$R—M + \begin{bmatrix} \overset{+}{N} \equiv \overset{}{N}—X^{-} \\ {}^{-}N=\overset{+}{N}=X \end{bmatrix} \longrightarrow R—\overset{+}{N} \equiv N \ + \ MX$$

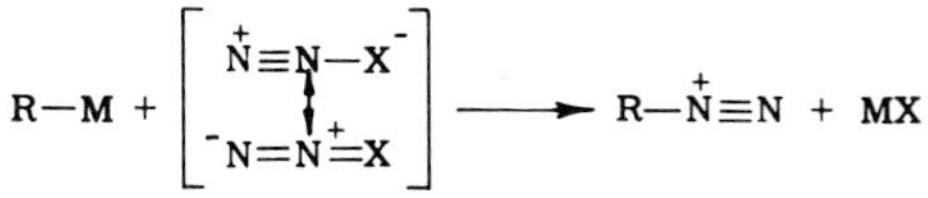

The most important diazo-transfer reagents are aryl sulfonyl azides and these are discussed in the first section. Nitrous oxide can also act as a diazo-transfer reagent and the few reports of this reagent are briefly discussed in the second section.

A. Aryl Sulfonyl Azides as Transfer Reagents

In 1926, during his extensive study of derivatives of hydrazoic acid, Curtius showed that benzenesulfonyl azide will couple with dimethyl malonate in the presence of a base,[75] the resulting triazolone breaking down on acidification to yield methyl diazomalonate amide.

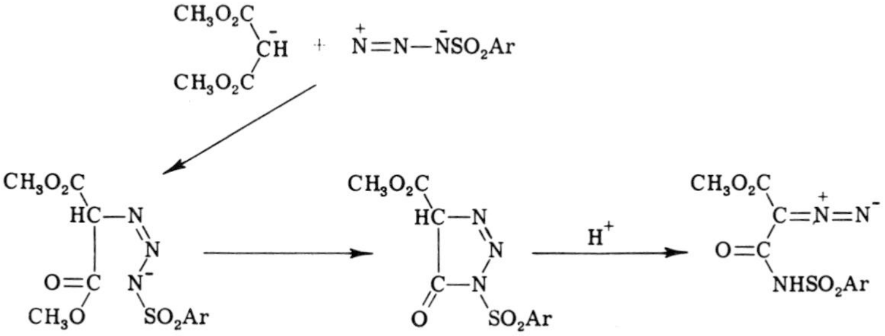

[75] T. Curtius and W. Klavehn, *J. Prakt. Chem.* [2] **112,** 65 (1926).

The reaction of p-toluenesulfonyl azide with enolate anions has recently been used quite extensively to prepare aliphatic diazo compounds.[76]

If p-toluenesulfonyl azide will couple with enolate anions it is reasonable to expect it to couple with phenoxide anions. In practice it will couple readily with naphthoxide ions to yield diazo oxides, but under the basic conditions the diazo oxide reacts with uncharged naphthoxide ions to yield the corresponding azo dyestuff.[77]

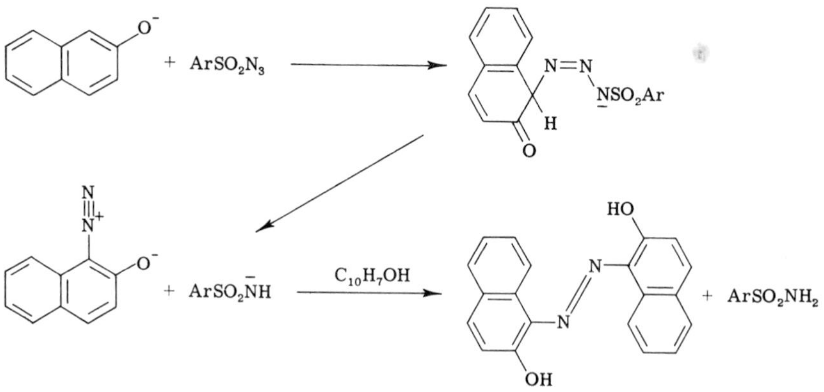

By adding the naphthoxide to an excess of the sulfonyl azide the diazo oxide can be isolated, but even then some of the symmetrical azo dye is formed.[78] When the same procedure was attempted with α-naphthol the diazo oxide isolated was the 2,1-diazo oxide not the expected 1,4-isomer. Presumably the sulfonyl azide coupled at both positions but the 1,4-diazo oxide coupled very rapidly with unchanged α-naphthol so that the less reactive 2,1-isomer was all that was isolated. The principal azo dye does, however, appear to be the 4,4'-azo-naphthol and not the 2,2'-isomer as suggested by Pelz. The reaction works with resorcinol and resorcinol monomethyl ether, but phenoxide ions react with p-toluenesulfonyl azide to yield phenyl p-toluenesulfonate and sodium azide. o-Cresol behaves similarly.[78]

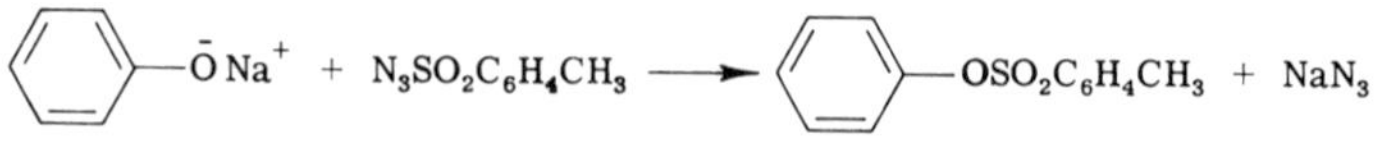

[76] M. Regitz, *Angew. Chem. Intern. Ed. Engl.* **6**, 733 (1967); see also J. B. Hendrickson and W. A. Wolf, *J. Org. Chem.* **33**, 3610 (1968).

[77] W. Pelz, BeP 562,524.

[78] J. M. Tedder and B. Webster, *J. Chem. Soc.* p. 4417 (1960).

On the other hand, Pelz has shown that the reaction is applicable not only to other naphthol derivatives but also to heterocyclic molecules such as pyrazolones.[77] In this work only the symmetrical azo compounds were isolated. On the other hand true diazo oxides were obtained from 3-aminoindenones[79,80] and thionaphthen-3-one.[81]

Diazo transfer from azides has also been much used in the synthesis of pseudoaromatic salts of a betaine type, the most important example being diazocyclopentadiene. The original authors prepared the cyclopentadienyl anion[82] using phenyllithium, but later work showed that diethylamine as solvent was sufficiently basic to promote coupling.[83,84]

$$\text{\begin{array}{c}\text{cyclopentadiene}\end{array}} + \text{ArSO}_2\text{N}_3 \xrightarrow{\text{Et}_2\text{NH}} \left[\begin{array}{c} \overset{H}{\underset{N=NNHSO_2Ar}{}} \end{array} \right] \longrightarrow \overset{(-)}{\bigcirc}-\text{N}_2^+ + \text{ArSO}_2\text{NH}_2$$

Aryl sulfonyl azides add to triple bonds and with ethoxyacetylene, an ethyl α-diazo-N-arenesulfonylacetimidate is formed.[85]

$$\begin{array}{c} \text{HC}\equiv\text{C}-\text{OEt} \\ \overset{+}{\text{N}} \underset{\diagdown \text{N}}{\quad} \overset{-}{\text{NSO}_2\text{Ar}} \end{array} \longrightarrow \begin{array}{c} \text{OEt} \\ \text{N} \diagdown \text{N} \\ \diagdown \text{N} \diagdown \text{SO}_2\text{Ar} \end{array} \longrightarrow \overset{-}{\text{N}}=\overset{+}{\text{N}}=\text{CH}-\overset{\text{OEt}}{\underset{\text{NSO}_2\text{Ar}}{\text{C}}}$$

With an acetylide anion, however, the aryl sulfonyl azide adds twice to yield a 1,2,3-triazolediazonium salt. In practice the free diazonium

$$\text{R}-\text{C}\equiv\text{C}-\text{N}=\text{N}-\overset{-}{\text{NSO}_2\text{Ar}} \longleftarrow \text{RC}\equiv\overset{-}{\text{C}}\text{Li}^+ + \text{N}_3\text{SO}_2\text{Ar}$$

$$\Big\downarrow \text{ArSO}_2\text{N}_3$$

$$\begin{array}{c} \text{R} \quad \text{N}=\text{N}-\overset{-}{\text{NSO}_2\text{Ar}} \\ \text{C}=\text{C} \\ \text{N} \diagdown \text{N} \\ \diagdown \text{N} \diagdown \text{SO}_2\text{Ar} \end{array} \xrightarrow{2\,\beta\text{-C}_{10}\text{H}_7\text{OH}} \begin{array}{c} \text{R} \quad \text{N}=\text{N}-\text{C}_{10}\text{H}_7\text{O}^- \\ \text{C}=\text{C} \\ \text{N} \diagdown \text{NH} \\ \diagdown \text{N} \end{array} + \text{ArSO}_3\text{C}_{10}\text{H}_7 + \text{ArSO}_2\text{NH}_2$$

[79] M. Regitz, Tetrahedron Letters p. 3287 (1965).
[80] M. Regitz, Angew. Chem. Intern. Ed. Engl. 4, 710 (1956).
[81] M. Regitz, Ber. 98, 36 (1965).
[82] W. von E. Doering and C. H. De Puy, J. Am. Chem. Soc. 75, 5955 (1953).
[83] F. Klages and K. Bott, Ber. 97, 735 (1964).
[84] T. Weil and M. Cars, J. Org. Chem. 28, 2472 (1963).
[85] P. Grümanger, P. V. Finzi, and C. Scotti, Ber. 98, 623 (1965).

salt is not released, but addition of β-naphthol to the reaction mixture yields the expected azo dyestuff.[86]

Diazo-transfer reactions of this type are unlikely to find wide application in the dyestuffs industry because they involve not only azide, but its conversion to a derivative which will be more electrophilic. Even the aryl sulfonyl azides are only sufficiently electrophilic to attack by very nucleophilic centers so that the whole scope of the reaction is limited. It is, however, a reaction of importance for the synthesis of special diazo compounds and will probably be further developed in the future.

B. Nitrous Oxide as Transfer Reagent

At first sight nitrous oxide looks an ideal diazo-transfer reagent, particularly if it would accept a proton. Unfortunately,

$$[\bar{N}{=}\overset{+}{N}{=}O \leftrightarrow N{\equiv}\overset{+}{N}{-}\bar{O}] \xrightarrow{\text{H}^+} [N{\equiv}\overset{+}{N}{-}OH \leftrightarrow \overset{+}{N}{=}N{-}OH]$$

attempts by the present author and others to effect electrophilic attack by protonated nitrous oxide have so far failed, and all the reported reactions involve the reactions of reactive carbanions (i.e., very strong nucleophiles) with neutral nitrous oxide. The difficulty of such reactions is that they lead to diazonium salts (or rather to diazoates) being formed in the presence of nucleophilic species with which they will couple, so that the products of the reaction are azo compounds rather than diazonium salts. The first investigation of the nitrous oxide reaction with organometallic compounds was made by Schlenk and Bergmann in 1928[87] but the phenyllithium and nitrous oxide reaction was first reported by Meier and by Beringer in 1953. Meier reported the phenol, benzidine, diphenyl, azobenzene, triphenylhydrazine, and hydrazobenzene as products.[88] However, Beringer detected lithium benzene diazotate in addition to the above products by coupling the aqueous washings with resorcinol.[89] The yield was very low, presumably due to further reaction of the diazoate with phenyllithium. Meier and Frank attempted to account for all the variety of products assuming that the initial reaction is the formation of the diazoate.[90]

$$C_6H_5Li + N_2O \rightarrow C_6H_5{-}N{=}N{-}OLi$$

This reaction clearly merits further study, although the chances of its proving a viable synthesis of diazonium salts at present looks meager.

[86] E. Robson, J. M. Tedder, and B. Webster, *J. Chem. Soc.* p. 1863 (1963).
[87] W. Schlenk and E. Bergmann, *Ann.* **464**, 1 (1928).
[88] R. Meier, *Ber.* **86**, 1483 (1953).
[89] F. M. Beringer, J. A. Fau, and S. Sands, *J. Am. Chem. Soc.* **75**, 3984 (1953).
[90] R. Meier and W. Frank, *Ber.* **89**, 2747 (1956).

IV. The Coupling Reaction: Recent Developments

Many theories were developed for the mechanism of the coupling reaction of diazonium salts with aromatic nuclei to yield diazonium salts. These have been discussed both by Saunders[91] and by Zollinger[92] in their monographs. The idea that the reaction involves attack by the diazonium cation originated with work of Sir Robert Robinson in 1917[93] although it was left to Bartlett[94] and to Hauser[95] to independently define the mechanism of the reaction in 1941. Since this work has been discussed by both Saunders and Zollinger we will not repeat such a discussion here. It is sufficient to remark that by 1952 when Volume I of this series was published the coupling reaction was recognized as an electrophilic substitution, analogous to aromatic nitration, sulfonation, etc.[96]

$$E^+ \; + \; \bigcirc \; \underset{k_{-1}}{\overset{k_1}{\rightleftarrows}} \; \left[\begin{matrix} E \quad H \\ \bigcirc^+ \end{matrix} \right] \; \underset{k_{-2}}{\overset{k_1}{\rightleftarrows}} \; \bigcirc^E \; + \; H^+$$

E = Electrophile, i.e., NO_2^+, etc.

The relative reactivity of the various coupling components can be readily understood in terms of this mechanism.

A. THE EFFECT OF SUBSTITUENTS

The establishment of diazo coupling as a typical electrophilic substitution clarifies the effect of substituents in both coupling components. Electron-accepting or electron-attracting groups in the diazonium salt will increase its reactivity compared with unsubstituted benzenediazonium salt. Similarly electron-donating or -repelling groups in the phenol or teritary amine will accelerate the reaction. A qualitative measure of the effect of substituents in the diazonium salt is given by the Hammett $\sigma\rho$ relation.[97] Zollinger has determined the relative rate of coupling of a number of meta- and para-substituted benzene diazonium salts with

[91] K. H. Saunders, "The Aromatic Diazo Compounds," 2nd ed., pp. 230–235. Arnold, London, 1949.
[92] H. Zollinger, "Azo and Diazo-Chemistry," pp. 221–283. Wiley (Interscience), New York, 1961.
[93] G. M. Robinson and R. Robinson, J. Chem. Soc. p. 963 (1917).
[94] R. Wiston and P. D. Bartlett, J. Am. Chem. Soc. 63, 413 (1941).
[95] C. R. Hauser and D. S. Breslow, J. Am. Chem. Soc. 63, 418 (1941).
[96] CSD I, p. 411 et seq.
[97] L. P. Hammett, "Physical Organic Chemistry," p. 186. McGraw-Hill, New York, 1940.

2-naphthylamine-6-sulfonic acid.[98] He obtained a good linear relation with a value of the reaction constant $\rho = +4.26$, characteristic of processes involving a large electron demand similar to other electrophilic substitutions. The effect of substituents in the other coupling component is discussed in Volume I, and there is little new which has not also been discussed by Zollinger or Saunders in their monographs. Diazo coupling is of considerable interest in studies of the effect of substituents because the reaction can often be carried out in alkaline media. The reaction of cationic species with organic molecules carrying a negative charge (i.e., phenoxide ion) cannot be studied in any other system.

The effect of pH on coupling is complex and varies from system to system. Normal moderately reactive diazonium salts couple rapidly with phenoxide ions, but only very slowly with the undissociated phenol. The overall rate of coupling therefore increases with increasing pH, although the specific rate of coupling of diazonium salt and phenoxide ion remains the same. The overall reaction rate increases because increasing basicity increases the concentration of phenoxide ion. When all the phenol is converted to phenoxide a further increase in pH might be expected to have little effect and in some cases this is observed. In other cases a further increase in pH causes a rapid drop in the overall coupling rate. This is attributed to the formation of the diazoate (via the transient diazohydroxide).

$$\underset{\text{Diazonium salt}}{Ar—\overset{+}{N}{\equiv}N} \; + \; OH^- \rightleftarrows \underset{\text{Diazo hydroxide}}{[Ar—N{=}N—OH]} \rightleftarrows \underset{\text{Diazoate}}{Ar—N{=}N—O^-} + H^+$$

A good example of this phenomenon is provided by the coupling of diazotized metanilic acid with 2-naphthol-6-sulfonic acid.[99]

B. Recent Studies on the Mechanism of the Reaction

Electrophilic aromatic substitution is not a substitution in the true sense, i.e., it is not similar to an S_N2 reaction and although frequently referred to as an S_E2, it is really nothing of the kind. The reaction is in fact

$$E^+ + \underset{}{\overset{|}{C}—X} \longrightarrow \overset{\delta+}{E}{\text-}{\text-}{\text-}\overset{|}{\underset{}{C}}{\text-}{\text-}\overset{\delta+}{X} \longrightarrow E—\overset{|}{\underset{}{C}} + X^+ \quad S_E2$$

An Aliphatic S_E2 Reaction

an addition similar to an addition of an olefin followed by an elimination. The important difference between the two reactions is that in olefin

[98] H. Zollinger, *Helv. Chim. Acta* **36**, 1732 (1953).

[99] C. Wittwer and H. Zollinger, *Helv. Chim. Acta* **37**, 1954 (1954).

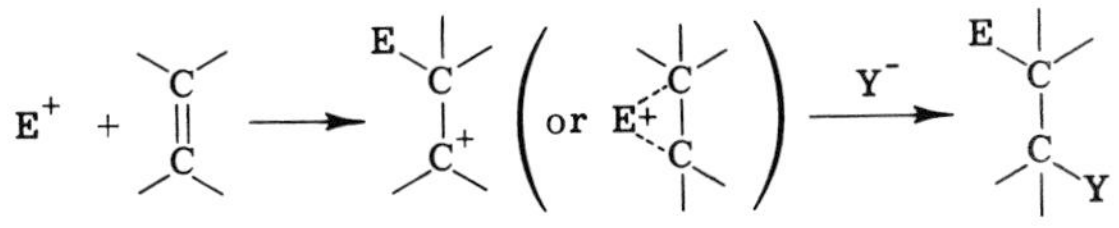

Electrophilic Addition to Olefin

addition the intermediate carbonium ion is stabilized by the addition of an anion, whereas in so-called electrophilic aromatic substitution the intermediate carbonium ion ejects a proton thus regenerating a stabilized aromatic nucleus.

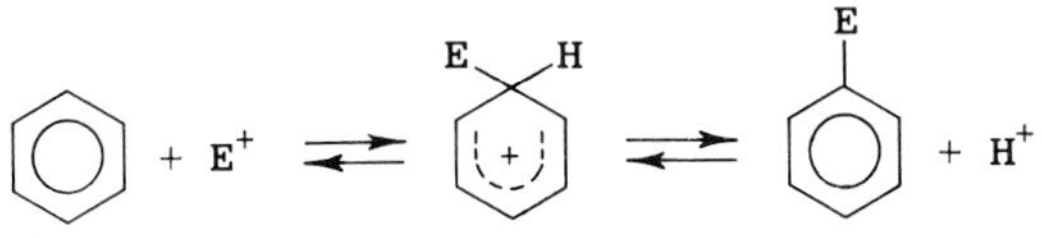

So-Called "Electrophilic Aromatic Substitution"—Really
"Electrophilic Addition-with-Elimination"

The evidence for this mechanism of aromatic addition-with-elimination reactions rests partly on studies involving diazo coupling. The technique used involves the detection of a kinetic isotope effect. The present chapter is not the place in which to discuss the causes of the kinetic isotope effect. Suffice it to say that if the rate-determining stage of a reaction involves the fission of a bond between the group R and atom A $(R—A \rightarrow R + A)$ then the reaction will be retarded if A is replaced by a heavier isotope. The kinetic isotope effect depends to a large extent on the difference in mass between the two isotopes and is largest for hydrogen and tritium, the ratio of k^H/k^T being approximately 15–30 at normal temperatures while the ratio k^H/k^D is 7 at normal temperatures.

Melander found that tritiated aromatic hydrocarbons were brominated and nitrated at the same rate as the ordinary protium compounds.[100] Since then many similar studies have been made, particularly involving nitration.[101,102] These observations confirm that so-called electrophilic aromatic substitution is not a true S_E2 replacement, because fission of the carbon–hydrogen bond is not rate-determining.

Zollinger discovered that while the coupling between the 2-methoxy-benzenediazonium cation and 1-naphthol-4-sulfonic acid showed no isotope effect, coupling between the 4-chlorobenzenediazonium cation and 2-naphthol-6,8-disulfonic acid showed almost the theoretically maximum

---

[100] L. Melander, *Arkiv Kemi* **2**, 211 (1951).
[101] T. G. Bonner, F. Bowyer, and G. Williams, *J. Chem. Soc.* p. 2650 (1953).
[102] W. M. Laver and W. E. Noland, *J. Am. Chem. Soc.* **75**, 3689 (1953).

isotope effect. The same reaction is strongly base-catalyzed.[103] This can be rationalized as follows:

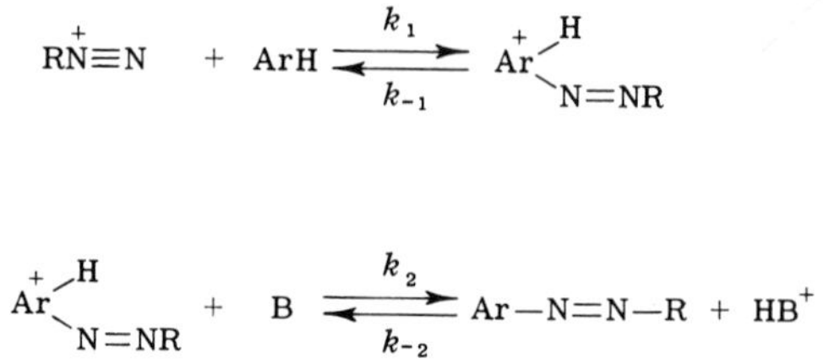

$$\overset{+}{R}N\equiv N \ + \ ArH \ \underset{k_{-1}}{\overset{k_1}{\rightleftarrows}} \ \overset{+}{Ar}\overset{H}{\underset{N=NR}{\diagdown}}$$

$$\overset{+}{Ar}\overset{H}{\underset{N=NR}{\diagdown}} \ + \ B \ \underset{k_{-2}}{\overset{k_2}{\rightleftarrows}} \ Ar-N=N-R \ + \ HB^+$$

If we neglect k_{-2} and invoke a "steady state" argument (i.e., $d[ArHN_2\overset{+}{R}]/dt = 0$) then the rate of formation of azo dye is given by

$$\frac{d[ArN_2R]}{dt} = \frac{k_1(k_2/k_{-1})[B]}{1 + (k_2/k_{-1})[B]} [ArH][R-\overset{+}{N}\equiv N]$$

If k_{-1} is very small then the expression reduces to

$$\frac{d[ArN_2R]}{dt} \approx k_1[ArH][R-\overset{+}{N}\equiv N] \qquad k_{-1} \ll k_2[B]$$

i.e., coupling between 2-methoxybenzenediazonium cation and 1-naphthol-4-sulfonic acid. If, however, $k_2[B] < k_{-1}$, then in the extreme case the observed rate will become proportional to the concentration of base and to k_2. It thus shows both base catalysis and a large isotope effect, i.e., coupling between 4-chlorobenzenediazonium cation and 2-naphthol-6,8-disulfonic acid. The three factors, k_2, k_{-1}, and [B] vary so that the extent of isotope effect and base catalysis can vary from the extreme case to zero.[104]

Small isotope effects have also been observed for sulfonation[105,106] and for some aromatic halogenations.[107,108] The explanation in each case is probably the same. This combination of isotope effect and base catalysis can be regarded as providing the complete verification of the addition-with-elimination mechanism for aromatic substitution.

[103] H. Zollinger, *Helv. Chim. Acta* **38**, 1597 and 1617 (1955).

[104] R. Ernst, O. A. Stamm, and H. Zollinger, *Helv. Chim. Acta* **41**, 2274 (1958).

[105] U. Berglund-Laisson, *Arkiv Kemi* **10**, 549 (1957).

[106] J. C. D. Brand, A. W. P. Jarvie, and W. C. Homing, *J. Chem. Soc.* p. 3488 (1959).

[107] E. Grovenstein and D. C. Kilby, *J. Am. Chem. Soc.* **79**, 2972 (1957).

[108] E. A. Shilov and F. M. Wernstein, *Nature* **182**, 1300 (1958).

CHAPTER VI

AZO DYES

C. V. Stead

RESEARCH DEPARTMENT, IMPERIAL CHEMICAL INDUSTRIES, DYESTUFFS DIVISION,
HEXAGON HOUSE, BLACKLEY, MANCHESTER, ENGLAND

This chapter consists of two main parts. In the first aspects of the chemistry of azo compounds relevant to their use in dyestuffs are discussed. The second part deals with research aimed at producing azo dyestuffs which fall outside the ambit of the various other chapters dealing with special dyestuff classes. The scope of the first part encompasses advances made at isolated points across a well-established field and to help weld these isolated but interdependent advances together headings are kept to a minimum and liberally interpreted.

I. Chemistry of Azo Compounds

A. STRUCTURE

Azobenzene is well known to exist in both a stable trans form and an unstable cis form.[1] These two forms differ greatly in their planarity, the trans form being very nearly planar in the solid state whereas in

[1] N. Campbell, A. W. Henderson, and D. Taylor, *J. Chem. Soc.* p. 1281 (1953).

the cis isomer the phenyl rings are twisted through an angle of roughly 56° about the C—N bond.[2] The cis form is prepared by photoisomerization of the trans form, the quantum yield of this process depending upon the wavelength of the light employed[3] and the relative proportion of isomers present in the equilibrium mixture produced by irradiation with light of a particular frequency being temperature-dependent.[4] The cis form reverts to the trans form by what is normally a thermal process and this reversion can be catalyzed by a variety of substances which function either as electron donors or electron acceptors.[5] Interconversion of cis and trans forms is responsible for certain azo compounds exhibiting phototropism, a phenomenon which is more frequently associated with other classes of dyestuffs but which is also encountered in azo dyestuffs, particularly in the case of simple disperse dyes.

In addition to azobenzene itself, the cis form of which was isolated in 1938, a number of other simple substituted azobenzenes have been isolated in the cis configuration, but generally as the molecule becomes more complex steric factors tend to control the configuration exclusively in the trans form. In the case of the azonaphthalenes, for instance, while the cis-2,2' and cis-1,2' compounds can be prepared by ultraviolet irradiation of solutions of the trans form, isolated by alumina chromatography at low temperatures, and characterized by their absorption spectra, the cis-1,1' isomer, although characterized in irradiated solutions containing up to 60% of the cis form, has defied isolation.[6]

Introduction of a hydroxy group located ortho or para to the azo link raises the possibilities of azophenol–quinone hydrazone tautomerism and for many years this phenomenon has yielded an interesting field of investigation. In recent years extensive use has been made of spectroscopic methods to build up a coherent picture of this tautomerism. The bulk of the information has evolved from ultraviolet and visible spectroscopy, techniques which are well suited to investigations of this nature. Indeed this has been the most interesting area of application of these techniques in azo chemistry, the many other publications dealing with the positions of peaks relative to various substituents in the molecule seeming of much less value. The ideal situation for these techniques is where a tautometric mixture is encountered since in these cases a peak due to each form is observed, the relative heights varying from solvent to solvent. The for-

[2] D. J. W. Bullock, C. W. N. Cumper, and A. I. Vogel, *J. Chem. Soc.* p. 5316 (1965); D. L. Beveridge and H. H. Jaffé, *J. Am. Chem. Soc.* **88**, 1948 (1966).

[3] G. Zimmerman, L.-Y. Chow, and U.-J. Paik, *J. Am. Chem. Soc.* **80**, 3528 (1958).

[4] E. Fischer, *J. Am. Chem. Soc.* **82**, 3249 (1960).

[5] D. Schulte-Frohlinde, *Ann.* **612**, 131 and 138 (1957).

[6] M. Frankel, R. Wolovsky, and E. Fischer, *J. Chem. Soc.* p. 3441 (1955).

mation of an isobestic point by the absorption curves measured in a variety of solvents is perhaps the clearest available demonstration that tautomerism is occurring. If one form only is present, comparison of the spectrum with that of the O- and N-methyl derivatives will often indicate the nature of that form. Infrared spectroscopy has also played a part in investigation of azo compounds, although these compounds, because of the symmetry of the azo link, are not well suited to investigation by this technique. The weak intensity of absorption prevents the assignment of a definite wavelength for N=N stretching; the azo absorptions are also quite variable and often obscured by phenyl ring vibrations. In all, little can be said about the azo peak assignments other than that the weak peaks occurring at 1410 ± 30 cm^{-1} may be due to the azo group.[7] Because of this the most useful information available from infrared spectroscopy is concerned with features of the molecule other than the azo link, such as the presence or absence of a carbonyl group in a suspected quinone-hydrazone form. Application of the alternative technique of Raman spectroscopy, which is often of more value than infrared spectroscopy in dealing with a symmetrical structural feature such as an azo link, has been investigated using a series of azobenzenes and azonaphthalenes. Some assignments of azo group vibrations have been made but so far no further use has been made of this interesting line of approach.[8]

Nuclear magnetic resonance spectroscopy offers a most valuable technique in structural investigations. The deshielding effect of the azo group on the ortho and peri protons and the diamagnetic shifts due to the lack of aromatic character in the rings of the hydrazone form have been used in an investigation of the structures of a variety of simple azo compounds which has served to confirm many of the structures previously assigned by spectroscopic methods.[9] This method, in addition, presents for the first time the possibility of determining quantitatively the relative amounts of each tautomer present in a tautomeric mixture. The difficulties encountered so far with this approach have been that insufficient solubility can sometimes preclude measurements in a sufficient variety of solvents and that the tautomerism is sometimes too rapid for the distinct forms to be observed. Neither of these difficulties should prove insurmountable and a wider application of nuclear magnetic resonance spectroscopy to the study of azo compounds will no doubt be a future trend.

[7] E. R. Champlin and R. L. Fyans, *Am. Dyestuff Reptr.* **54**, 1000 (1965); P. Bassignana and C. Cogrossi, *Tetrahedron* **20**, 2361 (1964).

[8] H. Hacker, *Spectrochim. Acta* **21**, 1989 (1965).

[9] B. L. Kaul, P. M. Nair, A. V. Rama Rao, and K. Venkataraman, *Tetrahedron Letters* **32**, 3897 (1966).

These techniques, together with studies of dipole moments[10] and magnetic susceptibilities,[11] have helped build up a much more coherent picture of which form predominates in a wide range of azo compounds. This depends, of course, on the relative stabilities of the alternative forms. In the case of the phenylazonaphthols, which present the most interesting group, the formation of an isobestic point by the visible absorption curves measured in a variety of solvents clearly demonstrates the tautomeric nature of 4-phenylazo-1-naphthol.[12] Infrared spectra further confirm such tautomerism in both the solid state and in solution with 1-phenylazo-2-naphthol, 2-phenylazo-1-naphthol, and 4-phenylazo-

(I)

1-naphthol and indicate that canonical forms such as (I) contribute to the structure of the hydrazone form.[13] Polar solvents and electron-withdrawing substituents in the phenyl ring displace the position of the equilibrium towards the hydrazone form. Suggestions that in the case of 1-phenylazo-2-naphthols no distinction can be drawn between the azo and hydrazone forms and that the labile proton is equally shared between the oxygen and nitrogen atoms have been clearly disproved and are probably quite unjustifiable on theoretical grounds. The interaction between the mobile atom and its adjacent oxygen and nitrogen atoms has been described as best represented by a hydrogen bond whose potential energy curve displays a double rather than a single minimum. The tautomeric equilibria existing in these phenylazonaphthols are made possible because the total bond energies of the two forms are comparable. Despite the loss of a fully aromatic ring in the hydrazone form this structure is, at most, only 2 kcal/mole higher in energy than the azo form.[14] This contrasts with the situation opposite 2-phenylazo-3-naphthol,[15] where in a quinone form (II) both of the rings of the naphthalene portion would have to lose their fully aromatic character; this compound,

[10] A. E. Lutskiĭ, L. A. Kochergina, and B. A. Zadorozhnyĭ, Zh. Obshch. Khim. 30, 4080 (1960); Chem. Abstr. 55, 21062d (1961).

[11] Y. Matsunaga, Bull. Chem. Soc. Japan 29, 308 (1956); Chem. Abstr. 50, 12572h (1956).

[12] A. Burawoy, A. G. Salem, and A. R. Thompson, J. Chem. Soc. p. 4793 (1952).

[13] K. J. Morgan, J. Chem. Soc. p. 2151 (1961); D. Hadži, ibid. p. 2143 (1956).

[14] E. Fischer and Y. F. Frei, J. Chem. Soc. p. 3159 (1959).

[15] H. E. Fierz-David, L. Blangey, and E. Merian, Helv. Chim. Acta 34, 846 (1951).

therefore, exists solely in the azo form. Similarly, in the case of 2- and 4-hydroxyazobenzene and 1-phenylazo-2- and -4-anthrol one structure is clearly more stable than the other and again tautomerism is not observed. The former compounds exist purely in the azo form and the latter in the hydrazone form [e.g., (III)].[16] With 5-arylazo-8-hydroxyquinolines hydrogen bonding onto the heterocyclic nitrogen atom stabilizes the azo form so that, while tautomerism still occurs, the compound is mainly in the azo form (IV). In the corresponding quinoline N-oxide the hydrogen bond is much stronger and here little or no tautomerism occurs.[17]

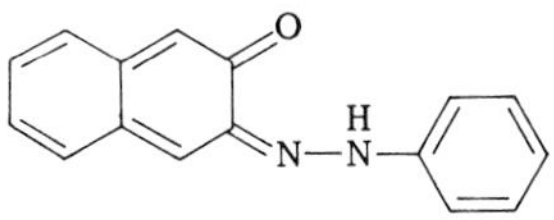

(II)

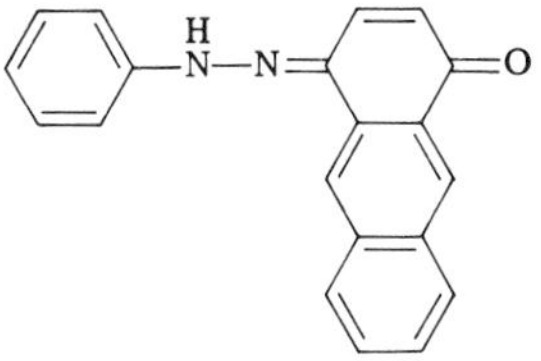

(III)

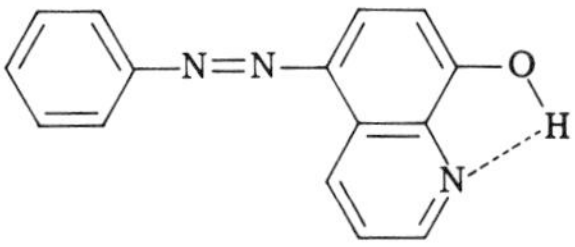

(IV)

The position with regard to 4-arylazopyrazol-5-ones has until recently been more obscure and the exact structures of these compounds has been the subject of some controversy. Although tautomerism has been proposed for these compounds[18] spectroscopic studies indicate one form only to exist. The occurrence of peaks associated with a carbonyl grouping in the infrared spectra of these compounds rules out the azophenol form which had been suggested[19] and indicates that one of the possible quinonoid forms is the correct structure. This might be expected in view of the smaller degree of resonance stabilization of the enol form in the case of a pyrazolone ring compared with, say, a naphthol ring. On the basis of infrared evidence structure (V) was proposed,[20] but the most likely

[16] J. N. Ospenson, *Acta Chem. Scand.* **5**, 491 (1951).

[17] G. M. Badger and R. G. Buttery, *J. Chem. Soc.* p. 614 (1956); E. Sawicki, *J. Org. Chem.* **22**, 743 (1957).

[18] P. E. Gagnon, J. L. Boivin, and R. N. Jones, *Can. J. Chem.* **31**, 1025 (1953); D. Biquard and M. P. Grammaticakis, *Bull. Soc. Chim. France* **8**, 246 (1941).

[19] W. Pelz, W. Z. Uschel, H. Schellenberger, and K. Loffler, *Angew. Chem.* **72**, 967 (1960).

[20] F. A. Snavely, W. S. Trahanovsky, and F. H. Suydam, *J. Org. Chem.* **27**, 994 (1962).

structure, the hydrogen-bonded lactam hydrazone (VI) is to be preferred since it agrees well with the infrared spectra and is the only one compatible with the NMR evidence, in particular accounting for the presence of a highly deshielded proton.[21] This structure is similar to that proposed for phenylazoacetoacetanilides, which have been deduced from spectroscopic evidence to be in the form (VII),[22] and also to the 3-methyl-4-arylhydrazonoisoxazol-5-one structure (VIII) which has been established for the product of coupling diazotized aniline onto 3-methylisoxazol-5-one.[23]

Turning to more complex structures, very interesting information relevant to the structure of dyes obtained by acid coupling onto Gamma-acid

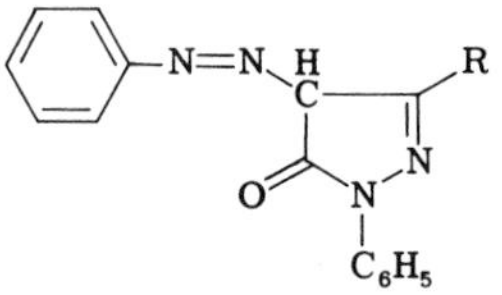

(V)

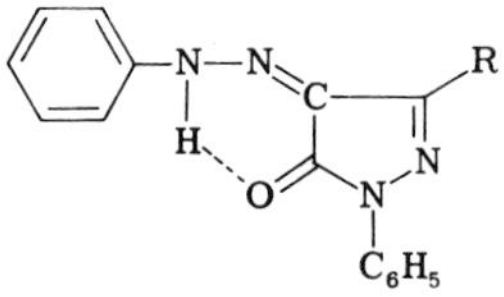

(VI)

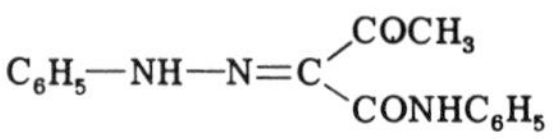

(VII)

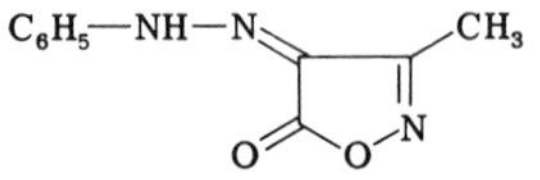

(VIII)

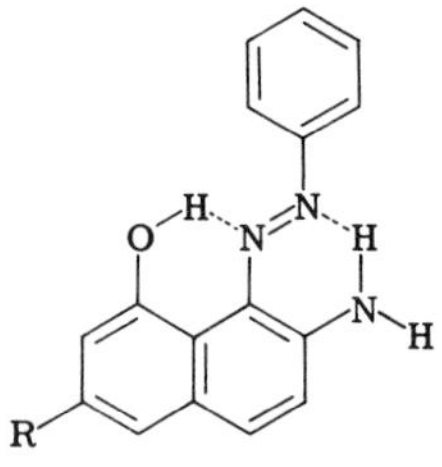

(IX)

[21] R. Jones, A. J. Ryan, S. Sternhill, and S. E. Wright, *Tetrahedron* **19**, 1497 (1963); S. Toda, *Nippon Kagaku Zasshi* **80**, 402 (1959); *Chem. Abstr.* **55**, 4150 (1961).

[22] Y. Yagi, *Bull. Chem. Soc. Japan* **36**, No. 5, 487, 492, 500, 506, and 512 (1963); *Chem. Abstr.* **60**, 4964d (1964).

[23] L. A. Summers, P. F. H. Freeman, and D. J. Shields, *J. Chem. Soc.* p. 3312 (1965).

has been supplied by an investigation into the structure of 1-phenylazo-2-amino-8-naphthol. The visible spectrum of this compound is the same whether measured in acidic or basic solution, showing that both the amino and hydroxy groups are hydrogen-bonded onto the azo linkage (IX; R = H). From the spectroscopic evidence it is concluded that the strength of the hydrogen bond formed by the peri hydroxy group is about 7 kcal/mole. The peri hydroxy group has a highly bathochromic effect when the compound is compared with 1-phenylazo-2-naphthylamine, thus contrasting with an 8-acetoxy substituent which produces a hypsochromic shift. The hydrogen bond formed between the 8-hydroxy group and the azo link serves to lock the molecule in a planar azo configuration and this exaggerates the effects of substituents in the phenyl ring.[24] These findings supply confirmation of bonding of both the hydroxy and the amino group to the azo linkage in dyes prepared by acid coupling onto Gamma-acid (IX; R = SO_3H); this type of bonding is the feature of these dyes responsible for the particularly high lightfastness (up to 6–7) which they are capable of achieving. A further consequence of the bonding of the peri hydroxy group is to make alkaline coupling onto an already acid-coupled Gamma-acid extremely difficult. Such coupling is, however, not completely precluded as had previously been thought for it can be accomplished in 2.5 N sodium hydroxide, leading to the twice-coupled product.[25] Alternatively such second coupling can be achieved by O,N-diacylation of an acid-coupled Gamma-acid dye using acetic anhydride in the presence of sulfuric acid. Cautious hydrolysis removes the O-acetyl group and in the resultant 1-arylazo-2-acetylamino-8-naphthol hydrogen bonding of the 8-hydroxy group is markedly lessened, enabling this compound to couple easily with diazotized arylamines to give brown disazo compounds whose color can be deepened by further hydrolysis to remove the N-acetyl group.[26]

B. PROTONATION

The problems encountered with the structures of simple azo compounds finds a parallel in considerations of the effects of protonation on azo compounds. Dissolution of *cis*- and *trans*-azobenzenes in strong acid results in protonation yielding two conformationally distinct conjugate acids (X) and (XI) and not a common conjugate acid such as (XII).[27,28]

[24] D. L. Ross and E. Reissner, *J. Org. Chem.* **31**, 2571 (1966).
[25] Z. J. Allan and J. Podstata, *Collection Czech. Chem. Commun.* **25**, 1337 (1960).
[26] S, *BP* 643,054.
[27] J. H. Collins and H. H. Jaffé, *J. Am. Chem. Soc.* **84**, 4708 (1962).
[28] G. E. Lewis, *J. Org. Chem.* **25**, 2193 (1960).

Indeed, noncommittal structures such as (XII) have, where postulated, invariably been shown subsequently to be incorrect and are to be treated with the greatest suspicion. In the course of a few days in the dark the cis conjugate acid (X) changes into the trans isomer (XI). On irradiation the cis conjugate acid is transformed into benzo[c]cinnoline but since this cyclization reaction is much slower than the equilibration process no difference is observed in the relative cyclization rates of the cis and trans forms.[27] When aminoazobenzenes are protonated it is clear from examination of ultraviolet and visible spectra that a tautomeric mixture of ammonium (XIII) and azonium (XIV) forms exists in nearly every case, the azonium form being stabilized by resonance as shown.[29]

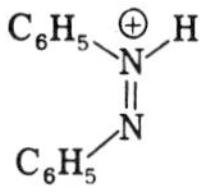

(X) 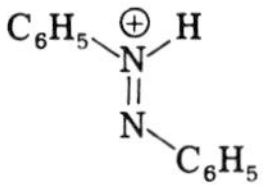   (XI) 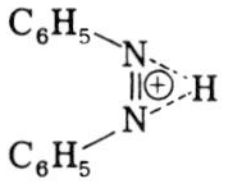   (XII)

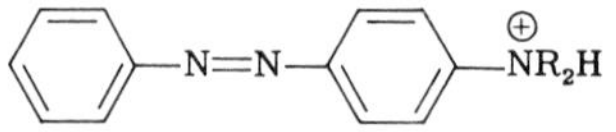

(XIII)

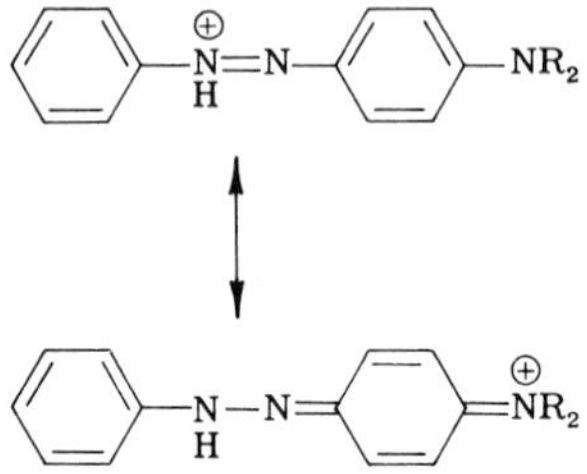

(XIV)

This resonance stabilization necessitates the proton being positioned on the β- and not the α-nitrogen atom of the azo linkage and the spectroscopic evidence does indicate that this is in fact the case.

C. Alternative Preparations

The preparation of azo compounds by diazotization and coupling, which is, of course, the all important method of making these compounds, is dealt with elsewhere. However, in addition to this method of preparation there are several alternative procedures which are of some interest.

[29] G. E. Lewis, *Tetrahedron* **10**, 129 (1960); M. Isaks and H. H. Jaffé, *J. Am. Chem. Soc.* **86**, 2209 (1964).

The well-known reaction of *p*-phenylenediamines with aromatic amines and phenols to yield, in the presence of an oxidizing agent, indamine and indophenol [e.g., (XV)] dyestuffs has been extended by

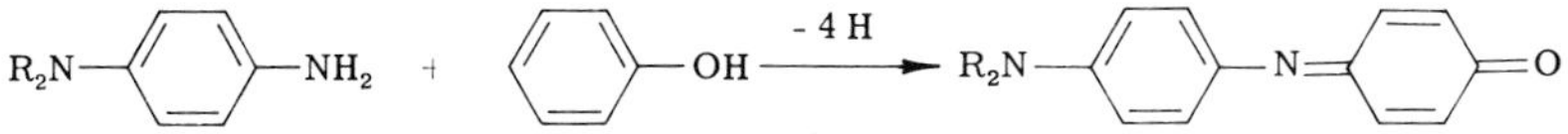

$$R_2N-\!\!\!\bigcirc\!\!\!-NH_2 \ + \ \bigcirc\!\!\!-OH \xrightarrow{-4\,H} R_2N-\!\!\!\bigcirc\!\!\!-N=\!\!\!\bigcirc\!\!\!=O$$

(XV)

$$\!\!>\!\!N-\!\!\underset{|}{C}=NNH_2 \qquad\qquad >\!\!N-\!\!\underset{|}{C}=\!\!\underset{|}{C}-\!\!\underset{|}{C}=NNH_2$$

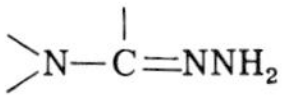

(XVI) 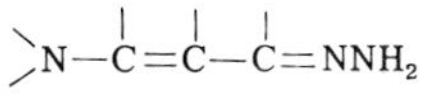   (XVII)

the use of amidrazones (XVI) and their vinylogues (XVII) which oxidatively couple with a wide variety of coupling components leading to azo compounds.[30] The following are typical examples of the reaction.

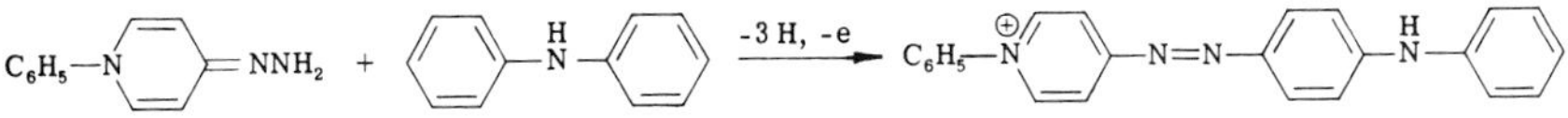

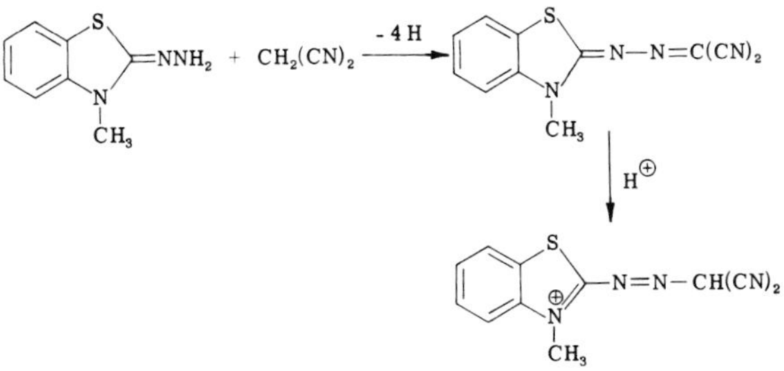

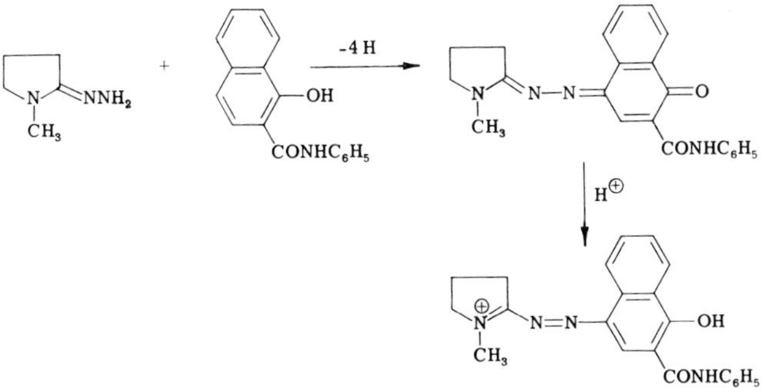

$$C_6H_5-N\!\!\bigcirc\!\!=NNH_2 \ + \ \bigcirc\!\!-\!\!\underset{H}{N}-\!\!\bigcirc \xrightarrow{-3\,H,\,-e} C_6H_5-\overset{\oplus}{N}\!\!\bigcirc\!\!-N=N-\!\!\bigcirc\!\!-\!\!\underset{H}{N}-\!\!\bigcirc$$

$$\bigcirc\!\!\!\underset{\underset{CH_3}{N}}{\overset{S}{\bigcirc}}\!\!=NNH_2 \ + \ CH_2(CN)_2 \xrightarrow{-4\,H} \bigcirc\!\!\!\underset{\underset{CH_3}{N}}{\overset{S}{\bigcirc}}\!\!-N-N=C(CN)_2$$

$$\downarrow H^{\oplus}$$

$$\bigcirc\!\!\!\underset{\underset{CH_3}{\overset{\oplus}{N}}}{\overset{S}{\bigcirc}}\!\!-N=N-CH(CN)_2$$

$$\bigcirc\!\!\!\underset{CH_3}{N}\!\!=NNH_2 \ + \ \underset{CONHC_6H_5}{\overset{OH}{\bigcirc\bigcirc}} \xrightarrow{-4\,H} \underset{CH_3}{N}\!\!-N-N=\!\!\underset{CONHC_6H_5}{\overset{O}{\bigcirc\bigcirc}}$$

$$\downarrow H^{\oplus}$$

$$\underset{\underset{CH_3}{\overset{\oplus}{N}}}{N}\!\!-N=N-\!\!\underset{CONHC_6H_5}{\overset{OH}{\bigcirc\bigcirc}}$$

[30] S. Hünig, H. Balli, K. H. Fritsch, H. Hermann, G. Köbrich, H. Werner, E. Grigat, F. Müller, H. Nöther, and K. H. Oette, *Angew. Chem.* **70**, 215 (1958); S. Hünig, H. Balli, F. Brühne, H. Geiger, E. Grigat, F. Müller, and H. Quast, *ibid.* **74**, 818 (1962).

The reaction is especially useful in the preparation of heterocyclic azo compounds which cannot be conveniently obtained by the normal techniques of diazotization and coupling. The mechanism entails oxidation of the amidrazone to a resonance-stabilized form (XVIII) which after reaction with the nucleophilic coupling component undergoes further oxi-

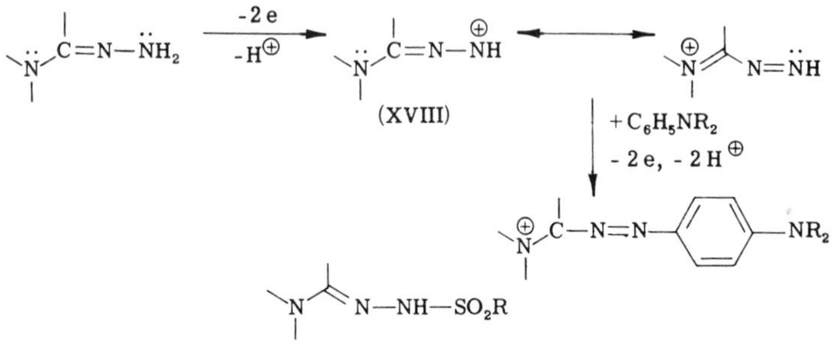

(XIX)

dation leading to the azo compound. Sulfonylamidrazones (XIX) which undergo less side decomposition at high pH values than the unsubstituted amidrazones have been found to be of particular value in this synthesis.[31]

A most useful synthesis has been described wherein a *syn*-diazosulfonate is reacted with a diazonium salt to produce an unsymmetrical azo compound with concomitant evolution of nitrogen.[32] If a *syn*-diazotate is used instead of the *syn*-diazosulfonate the product of the reaction is an *ortho*-hydroxyazo compound: In the first of these reactions it is pre-

$$R_1-N{=}N-O-SO_2^{\ominus} + R_2-\overset{\oplus}{N}{\equiv}N \longrightarrow R_1-N{=}N-R_2$$

$$R_1-N{=}N-O^{\ominus} + R_2-\overset{\oplus}{N}{\equiv}N \longrightarrow R_1-N{=}N-R_2-OH$$

ferred that R_2 is a naphthyl group, although the reaction will proceed when a benzene diazonium salt free from electronegative substituents is used; in the second reaction it is essential for one of the reactants to be of the naphthalene series. Initial attempts to explain the mechanism of these reactions invoked the formation of intermediates $R_1N{=}NOSO_2N{=}NR_2$ and $R_1N{=}NON{=}NR_2$ which were then trans-

[31] S. Hünig, W. Brenninger, H. Geiger, G. Kaupp, W. Kniese, W. Lampe, H. Quast, R. D. Raschenbach, and A. Schütz, *Angew. Chem.* **80**, 343 (1968).

[32] F. Suckfull and H. Dittmer, *Chimia (Aarau)* **15**, 137 (1961); FBy, *BP* 887,262.

formed into the products.[33] In the o-hydroxyazo synthesis it was necessary to postulate the azoxy compound (XX) as a further intermediate.

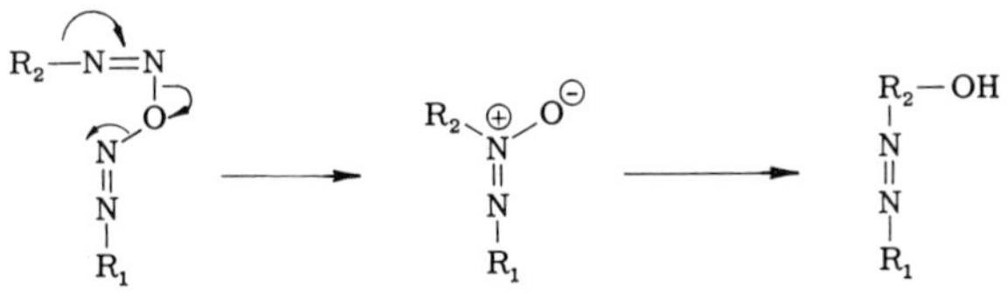

(XX)

This cannot, however, be correct since the preformed azoxy compound does not undergo the necessary Wallach rearrangement under the reaction conditions. Investigation of the reaction between o-chlorophenyl syn-diazotate and diazotized 1-naphthylamine-4-sulfonic acid leading to 1-(o-chlorophenylazo)naphthalene-4-sulfonic acid and that between β-benzoylaminophenyl syn-diazotate and diazotized α-naphthylamine leading to 1-(p-benzoylaminophenylazo)-2-naphthol using isotopically labeled nitrogen has shown the azo nitrogen to come exclusively from the phenyl diazo component. These results are interpreted[34] in terms of rapid initial diazonium salt $\rightleftharpoons$ syn-diazosulfonate and diazonium salt $\rightleftharpoons$ syn-diazotate equilibrations whereby the phenyl component is in each case converted predominantly into the diazonium ion. The reactions then take place thus:

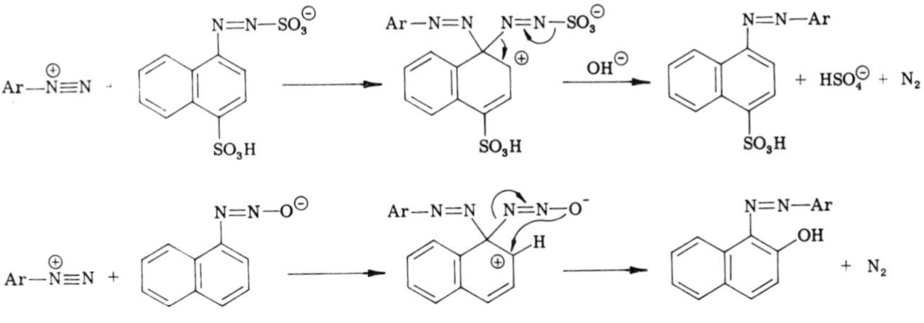

Kinetic studies on the well-known acid-catalyzed condensation of nitrosobenzenes with arylamines suggest a mechanism which involves, as a rate-determining step, attack by a protonated or acid-activated nitrosobenzene on the nitrogen atom of the free amine.[35]

[33] O. A. Stamm and H. Zollinger, *Chimia (Aarau)* **15**, 535 (1961).
[34] M. Christen, L. Funderbuck, E. A. Halevi, G. E. Lewis, and H. Zollinger, *Helv. Chim. Acta* **49**, 1376 (1966).
[35] Y. Ogata and Y. Takagi, *J. Am. Chem. Soc.* **80**, 3591 (1958).

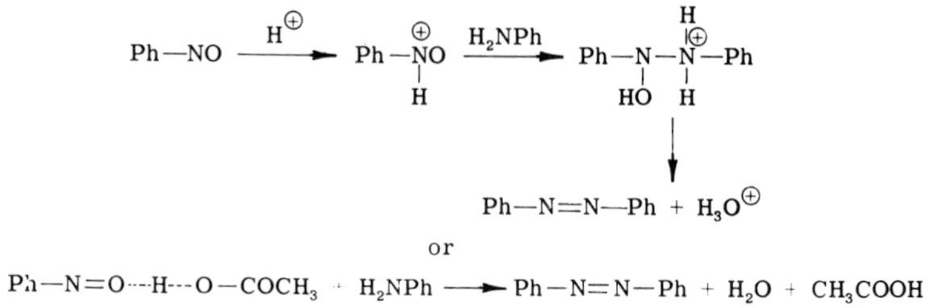

$$Ph—NO \xrightarrow{H^{\oplus}} Ph—\overset{\oplus}{\underset{H}{N}O} \xrightarrow{H_2NPh} Ph—\overset{H}{\underset{HO}{N}}—\overset{\overset{H}{|\oplus}}{\underset{H}{N}}—Ph$$

$$\downarrow$$

$$Ph—N{=}N—Ph + H_3O^{\oplus}$$

or

$$Ph—N{=}O\cdots H\cdots O—COCH_3 + H_2NPh \longrightarrow Ph—N{=}N—Ph + H_2O + CH_3COOH$$

The possibility of activation of the nitrosobenzene by loose attachment of an un-ionized acid molecule may account for the particular efficacy of acetic acid as a catalyst in this reaction. A novel condensation reaction has been employed in the preparation of the difficulty accessible 3-phenylazo-2-naphthol. After failure of the usual preparative methods this compound was successfully obtained by condensation of the N-sulfinylamine (XXI), prepared from 2-hydroxy-3-naphthylamine and thionyl chloride, with N-phenylhydroxylamine.[15]

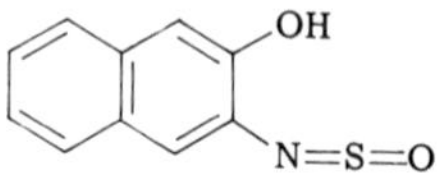

(XXI)

Investigations into the oxidation of aromatic amines to azo compounds have continued to attract interest and a variety of novel reagents, including lead tetraacetate[36] and sodium perborate,[37] have been used for this purpose. The most useful appears to be active manganese dioxide, which smoothly oxidizes simple arylamines to the corresponding azo compounds in benzene medium.[38] Sodium hypochlorite, which is an efficient reagent for this purpose, has been found most effective for the preparation of the interesting totally substituted decafluoroazobenzene from pentafluoroaniline.[39] Simple primary arylamines can also be aerially oxidized to azo compounds in the presence of cuprous chloride and pyri-

[36] K. H. Pausacker and J. G. Scroggie, J. Chem. Soc. p. 4003 (1954); E. Baer, and A. L. Tosoni, J. Am. Chem. Soc. 78, 2857 (1956).

[37] S. M. Mehta and M. V. Vakilwala, J. Am. Chem. Soc. 74, 563 (1952).

[38] M. Z. Barakat, M. F. Abdel-Wahab, and M. M. El-Sadr, J. Chem. Soc. p. 4685 (1956); O. H. Wheeler and D. Gonzalez, Tetrahedron 20, 189 (1964); O. H. Wheeler, Chem. Ind. (London) 1769 (1965).

[39] J. Burdon, C. J. Morton, and D. F. Thomas, J. Chem. Soc. p. 2621 (1965).

dine.[40] These techniques, and a variety of other oxidizing agents all failed, however, to yield 2,2'-dianilinoazobenzene from o-aminodiphenylamine, whereas reduction of the corresponding nitro compound with zinc and caustic soda yielded the desired product.[41] Azo compounds have also been prepared by oxidation of isocyanates with hydrogen peroxide,[42] the reaction proceeding thus:

$$2 \ R-NCO \xrightarrow{H_2O_2} R-NH-\underset{\underset{O}{\|}}{C}-O-O-\underset{\underset{O}{\|}}{C}-NH-R$$

$$R-N{=}N-R \xleftarrow{H_2O_2} R-NH-NH-R \longleftarrow 2 \ R-NH-\underset{\underset{O}{\|}}{C}-O$$

D. ANALYSIS

Analysis of a dyestuff invariably involves as a first step preparation of a pure sample of the dyestuff. Water-insoluble azo dyes can be purified in the same manner as simple azo compounds by crystallization from a suitable solvent. Similarly, cationic dyes can often be purified by crystallization from a suitable polar solvent, usually water. Such a procedure is, however, often not possible with a sulfonated azo dye. In these cases a suitable purification which consists essentially of removal of diluents and elimination of minor amounts of more soluble colored impurities can often be most satisfactorily achieved by repeated precipitation from an aqueous solution with potassium acetate. This salt has the advantage that it can be employed as precipitant in the form of a filtered, highly concentrated aqueous solution and can subsequently be removed from the purified dyestuff by extraction with ethanol. Ion exchange has also been mentioned as a possible aid to purification[43] and a procedure has been described whereby a dye is adsorbed onto cotton from a concentrated aqueous solution and then extracted from the fiber by water or aqueous pyridine.[44]

Chromatography is, of course, invaluable in investigating the purity

[40] A. P. Terent'ev and Y. D. Mogilyanskii, *Dokl. Akad. Nauk SSSR* **103**, 91 (1955); *Chem. Abstr.* **50**, 4807e (1956); K. Kinoshita, *Bull. Chem. Soc. Japan* **32**, 777 and 780 (1959); *Chem. Abstr.* **55**, 19741e (1961).
[41] L. T. Allan and G. A. Swan, *J. Chem. Soc.* p. 3892 (1965).
[42] H. Esser, K. Rastädter, and G. Reuter, *Ber.* **89**, 685 (1956).
[43] C. H. Giles and J. J. Greczek, *Textile Res. J.* **32**, 506 (1962).
[44] C. F. Goldthwaite and R. D. Kirby, *Am. Dyestuff Reptr.* **55**, 625 (1966).

of azo compounds and following the progress of any purification. Simple paper chromatographic techniques for use with sulfonated dyes have been reviewed.[45] Most mono and disazo dyes of this type can conveniently be examined between plates, using water, 0.05% brine and 0.5% brine as eluant, the increasing brine strength serving to exaggerate the band separation of the components in a mixture. Alternatively suitable solvent mixtures can be used to prepare ascending paper chromatograms from dyes of various types. Recommended solvent mixtures[46] and the type of chromatography are as follows:

Acid dyes
   (a) 160 cc Ethanol; 40 cc water (adsorption)
   (b) 125 cc Butanol; 24 cc ethanol; 53.5 cc water; 1.5 cc 0.88 ammonia (adsorption)
   (c) 200 cc Benzyl alcohol; 100 cc dimethylformamide; 100 cc water (adsorption)
Direct dyes
   90 cc Benzyl alcohol; 60 cc dimethylformamide; 60 cc water (adsorption)
Disperse dyes
   (a) 200 cc Cyclohexane; 192 cc acetic acid; 8 cc water (partition)
   (b) 200 cc Cyclohexane; 150 cc formic acid; 50 cc water (partition)
   (c) 200 cc Chloroform; 200 cc acetic acid; 200 cc water (inverse phase partition)
   (d) 150 cc Cyclohexane; 50 cc dimethylaniline (adsorption)
2:1 Metal complex dyes
   150 cc Butanol; 30 cc formic acid; 60 cc water

Some correlations of the structure of dyes and their R_f values have been attempted, particularly in the case of disperse dyes[47] and recently thin-layer chromatography,[48] which offers the advantages of speed and sharper resolution with less tailing of the bands, has found wider application in the dyestuffs field.

In a chemical analysis of an azo dye, determination of the azo group is of the utmost importance. Although this is standard practice in industrial research it is quite often ignored in much published work on azo compounds, presumably since the classical method involves the use of a titanous salt solution which is prone to aerial oxidation and therefore requires handling in special apparatus. Alternative methods of determining the azo link based on oxidation with stable solutions have been investigated, but offer no advantage over the classical method. In one, the nitrogen evolution from oxidation of an azo dye with potassium dichro-

---

[45] C. McNeil, *J. Soc. Dyers Colourists* **76**, 272 (1960).

[46] J. C. Brown, *J. Soc. Dyers Colourists* **76**, 536 (1960).

[47] J. Štámek, *J. Soc. Dyers Colourists* **78**, 326 (1962); C. D. Johnson and L. A. Telesz, *ibid.* p. 496.

[48] G. H. Rettie and C. G. Haynes, *J. Soc. Dyers Colourists* **80**, 629 (1964).

mate is measured[49,50]; this again involves the use of complicated apparatus. In the other, decolorization of the azo compound with ceric sulfate is employed,[50] but this suffers from the fact that a considerable proportion of the azo dyes investigated do not undergo quantitative oxidation. In addition to these procedures, addition of standard benzidine hydrochloride solution, removal of the insoluble dye-benzidine salt, and titration of the excess benzidine in the filtrate has been proposed as a simple, rapid, and accurate method of determining the sulfonic acid group content of an anionic dyestuff.[51]

The well-established methods of elemental analysis, scission with sodium hydrosulfite, and identification of the resulting fragments remain of most value in elucidating the constitution of a sulfonated azo dye. In the case of water-insoluble and cationic dyes they have, however, been powerfully reinforced by modern techniques, particularly mass spectrometry, which can yield an unequivocal molecular weight value and elemental composition, and nuclear mass resonance spectroscopy, which yields invaluable information about the protons present in the molecule.

E. Color

Little new has been added to the general principles of the relation between the color of azo compounds and their constitution but in one particular area there has been a technically important development. This has occurred in the case of simple monoazo dyes prepared by coupling a diazotized arylamine with a p-coupling amine. Dyes of this type are of paramount importance as disperse dyes. The need to produce blue dyes of very low molecular weight, so that their dyeing efficiency will be maintained, has involved the investigation of highly polar dye molecules of this pattern capable of achieving the marked bathochromic shift necessary to produce these deep shades. Increasing substitution of the diazo component by electron-attracting groups produces this required polarity, thus enabling blue shades to be obtained from structures such as (XXII) and (XXIII). Utilization of such powerful diazo components poses practical difficulties in avoiding excessive diazo decomposition during the coupling stage. In these dyes great assistance in producing the deep shade is obtained from the coupling components which contain elec-

[49] L. Nicholas and J. Mansel, *Chim. Anal. (Paris)* **42**, 171 (1960); *Chem. Abstr.* **54**, 16287i (1960).

[50] F. M. Arshid, N. F. Desai, C. H. Giles, and G. K. McLintock, *J. Soc. Dyers Colourists* **69**, 11 (1953).

[51] B. M. Bogoslovskii, *Zh. Prikl. Khim.* **28**, 659 (1955); *Chem. Abstr.* **49**, 13651h (1955).

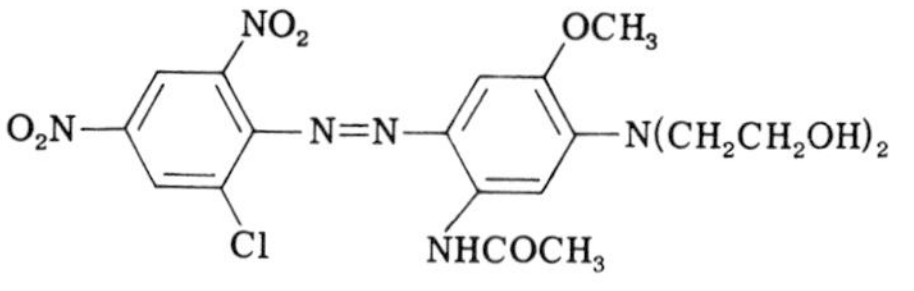

(XXII)

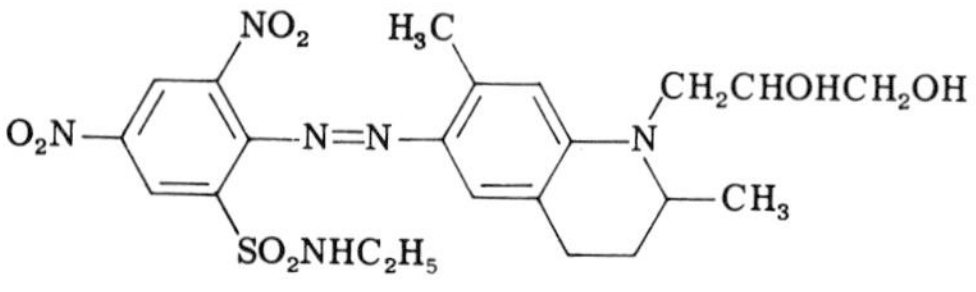

(XXIII)

tron-repelling groups located ortho- to the azo linkage. These groups enhance the polarity and therefore the bathochromic shift; this effect can be further exaggerated by incorporation of the amino group into a heterocyclic ring, as in the coupling component of (XXIII).[52] A greater effect than can be achieved with these highly substituted aniline diazo components can be obtained by using certain heterocyclic diazo components which are capable of producing remarkable bathochromic shifts compared with the corresponding benzenoid compounds. Thus the dyes prepared by coupling diazotized 5-substituted-2-amino-3-nitrothiophenes[53] (XXIV) or 2-amino-5-nitrothiazoles[54] (XXV) with the simple arylamine coupling component (XXVI) are blue to greenish blue in color. In these dyes the utilization of heteroatoms in place of negative substituents enables deep shades to be successfully obtained from dyes of very low molecular weight.

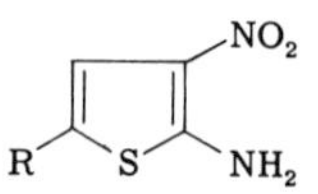

(XXIV) 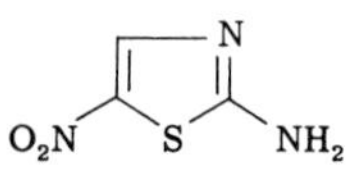　　　　　(XXV) 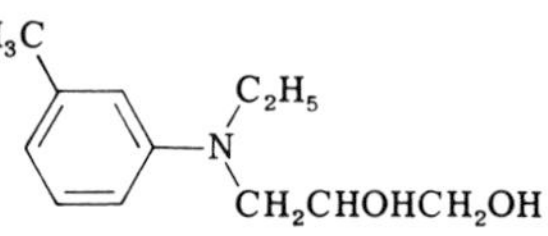　　　　　(XXVI)

[52] J. B. Dickey, E. B. Towne, D. G. Hedberg, D. J. Wallace, M. A. Weaver, and J. M. Straley, *Am. Dyestuff Reptr.* **54,** 596 (1965).

[53] J. B. Dickey, E. B. Towne, M. S. Bloom, B. H. Smith, and D. G. Hedberg, *J. Soc. Dyers Colourists* **74,** 123 (1958).

[54] J. B. Dickey, E. B. Towne, M. S. Bloom, W. H. Moore, H. M. Hill, H. Heynemann, D. G. Hedberg, D. C. Sievers, and M. V. Otis, *J. Org. Chem.* **24,** 187 (1959).

F. Novel Azo Compounds

From the large number of azo compounds described in the literature the following classes are selected as of interest on account of structural novelty.

1. Azoferrocenes

Reaction of ferrocene with a diazonium salt leads only to arylation[55] and attempted diazotization of aminoferrocene completely destroys the ferrocene nucleus.[56] Because of this the synthesis of azoferrocenes by conventional methods is not possible and these compounds remained inaccessible for some time. Eventually 1,1'-di(phenylazo)ferrocene (XXVII) was prepared by reaction of diazocyclopentadiene with phenyl-

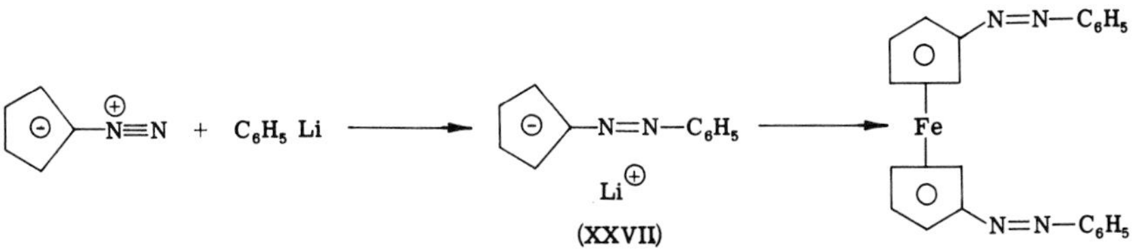

lithium and treatment of the product with anhydrous ferric chloride.[57] Monophenylazoferrocene (XXVIII) has been prepared by treating a mixture of cyclopentadienyllithium and phenylazocyclopentadienyllithium with anhydrous ferric chloride and separating from the symmetrical reaction products and also by reaction of nitrosobenzene with ferrocenylamine.[58] This latter method has also been used for the preparation of m- and p-ferrocenylazobenzene (XXIX) and the preparation of the

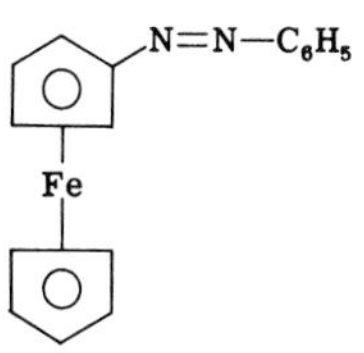

(XXVIII) 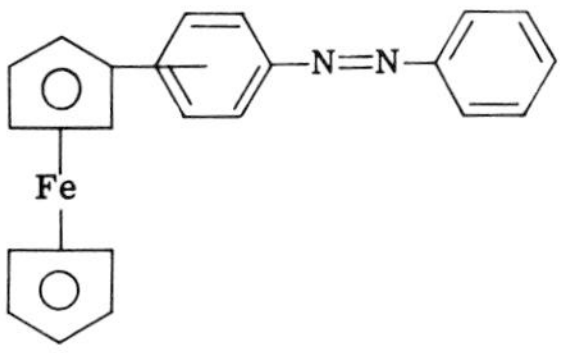   (XXIX) 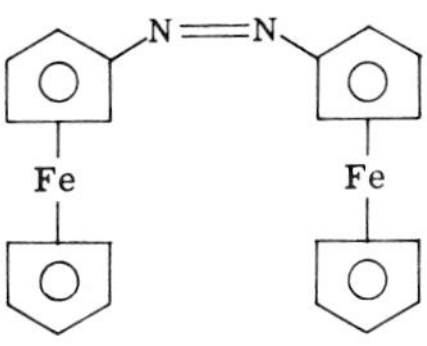   (XXX)

[55] G. D. Broadhead and P. L. Pauson, *J. Chem. Soc.* p. 367 (1955).

[56] A. N. Nesmeyanov and E. G. Perevalova, *Usp. Khim.* **27**, 3 (1958); *Chem. Abstr.* **52**, 14579c (1958).

[57] G. R. Knox, *Proc. Chem. Soc.* p. 565 (1961).

[58] A. N. Nesmeyanov, E. G. Perevalova, T. V. Nikitina, and N. I. Kuznetsova, *Izv. Akad. Nauk SSSR, Ser. Khim.* No. 12, 2120 (1965); *Chem. Abstr.* **64**, 9762h (1966).

interesting azoferrocene (XXX) by reaction of ferrocenyllithium with nitrous oxide has been described.[59]

2. Macrocyclic Azo Compounds

The macrocyclic azo compound (XXXI) is said to be formed by diazotization and self-coupling of the aminoazo compound N-m-aminobenzoyl-H-acid → N-m-aminobenzoyl-H-acid.[60] Evidence in favor of structure (XXXI) is given which would be more convincing had it included a titanometric estimation of azo group content coupled with elemental analysis. A similar cyclic structure (XXXII) was advanced for the analytical reagent calcichrome, which is prepared by the self-coupling of com-

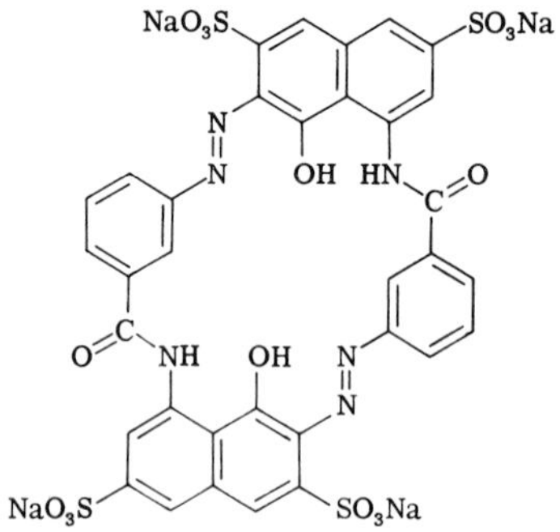

(XXXI) 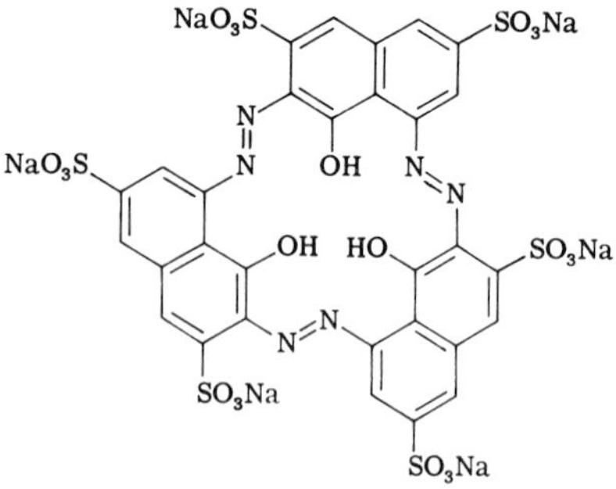   (XXXII)

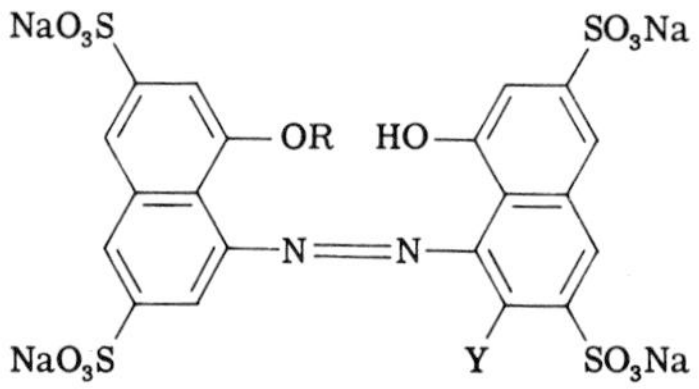

(XXXIII) 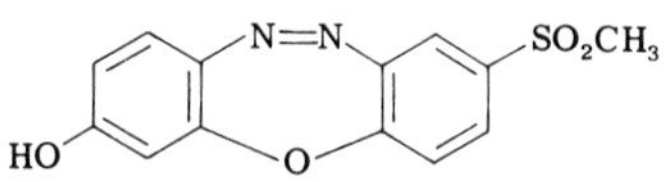   (XXXIV)

pletely diazotized H-acid.[61] This structure was subsequently disputed and an H-acid → H-acid → chromotropic acid structure advanced after a study of the color reactions of various azo compounds prepared by cou-

[59] A. N. Nesmeyanov, E. G. Perevalova, and T. V. Nikitina, Dokl. Akad. Nauk SSSR 138, 1118 (1961); Chem. Abstr. 55, 24707c (1961).

[60] J. Jarkovsky and Z. J. Allan, Angew. Chem. 75, 979 (1963).

[61] R. A. Close and T. S. West, Talanta 5, 221 (1960).

pling diazotized H-acid with H-acid and chromotropic acid.[62] Neither structure is, in fact, correct for calcichrome. Elemental analysis coupled with titanometric estimation clearly shows 20 carbon atoms, two nitrogen atoms, and four sulfur atoms for each azo group resolving the structure into a naphthalene-azo-naphthalene type. Nuclear magnetic resonance spectroscopy shows seven aromatic protons and 3 labile protons. These data accord with structure (XXXIII; R = H, Y = OH) which has been shown to be the correct structure for calcichrome by an independent synthesis from O-tosyl H-acid → 2R acid (XXXIII; R = $-SO_2C_6H_4CH_3$, Y = NH_2) which on alkaline hydrolysis undergoes both de-tosylation and replacement of the amino group by hydroxyl leading directly to calcichrome.[62a] It is apparent from its structure that calcichrome is formed from diazotized H-acid by a novel variation of the reaction between a diazonium salt and a *syn*-diazotate to form an *o*-hydroxyazo compound (see Section I,C). Both reactants are presumably supplied under the alkaline conditions from the diazotized H-acid. Smaller cyclic azo compounds, such as the oxadiazepine (XXXIV), are claimed as the products of the self-coupling of diazotized amines of the type 2-amino-4-methylsulfonyl-3'-hydroxydiphenyl ether.[63]

3. *Silicon-Containing Azo Dyes*

Dyes containing alkyl or alkoxysilane groups have been prepared by either coupling a diazotized amine with an aryl aminoalkyl silane (XXXV)[64] or, alternatively, coupling a diazotized aminoaryl alkoxy silane (XXXVI) with conventional coupling components[65] under substantially anhydrous conditions. If the reactions are carried out in aque-

$$Aryl-N{\overset{R}{\underset{C_nH_{2n}SiY_3}{}}}$$

Y = Alkyl or alkoxy

(XXXV)

$$NH_2-Aryl-C_nH_{2n}Si(O\ alkyl)_3$$

(XXXVI)

ous medium or if the final products are treated with water[66] hydrolysis of the silane grouping occurs resulting in a polysiloxane azo dye. These products, besides being substantive towards the conventional fibers, are

[62] A. M. Lukin, K. A. Smirnova, and B. Zavarikhina, *Zh. Analit. Khim.* **18**, 444 (1963); *Chem. Abstr.* **59**, 3301e (1963).

[62a] C. V. Stead, *J. Chem. Soc.* (to be published).

[63] Gy, *BP* 980,232.

[64] P. C. Canovai and UCC, *BP* 882,602.

[65] D. L. Bailey, R. M. Pike, and UCC, *BP* 894,415.

[66] D. L. Bailey, R. M. Pike, and UCC, *BP* 882,066.

claimed to possess the remarkable property of dyeing glass cloth and silica from an aqueous dyebath.

II. Azo Dyestuffs

A. WATER-SOLUBLE AZO DYESTUFFS

The period under review has seen the introduction of fiber-reactive dyes which present an entirely new class of water-soluble dyestuffs. These dyes combine easy application with a very high level of wet-fastness and have had a considerable effect on conventional water-soluble dyes. While reactive dyes are outside the scope of this chapter it will be advantageous to indicate the repercussions of this major advance when dealing with the various types of conventional dyes. The enormous technical literature describing water-soluble, sulfonated azo dyestuffs which has evolved over the years can be divided into discrete classes depending on the use to which the dyestuff is to be put. The various fibers demand certain structural characteristics from the dyes and thus a treatment of the subject according to fiber discloses well-defined groups into which the patent literature falls. There are in practice three main groups within the scope of this discussion. The first consists of fairly simple mono- and disazo dyes carrying a limited number (usually one or two) of sulfonic acid groups which are designed to dye wool. There is a second similar but slightly different group designed to dye nylon and a third group consisting of much larger and more complex dyestuffs which find application as direct dyes for cotton.

1. Wool Dyes

Progress in nonreactive metal-free wool dyes has mainly centered on extensions of the Carbolan type of dye which was evolved in the 1930s to meet the dyeing requirements of the wool fiber. These dyes [e.g., Carbolan Crimson B (XXXVII)] are simple water-soluble azo dyes into which has been built a large, hydrophobic group, known as the weighting group, with the object of discouraging subsequent desorption from the fiber and hence yielding adequate fastness to washing. These dyes can be applied to wool at near neutral pH values and possess very good wet-fastness properties. Recent research has been focused on the problem of achieving a better level of lightfastness from these dyes. To this end the azo combinations encountered in the patent literature lay particular emphasis on the use of those coupling components which are capable of yielding the highest level of lightfastness values in the various regions of the shade range. These coupling components are Gamma-acid (acid-coupled) in the case of red dyes, 2-naphthylaminesulfonic acids for orange dyes, and 5-pyrazolones or 5-aminopyrazoles for yellow dyes, making lightfastness values of 6–7, 5–6, and 6–7 attainable in these respective shade regions.

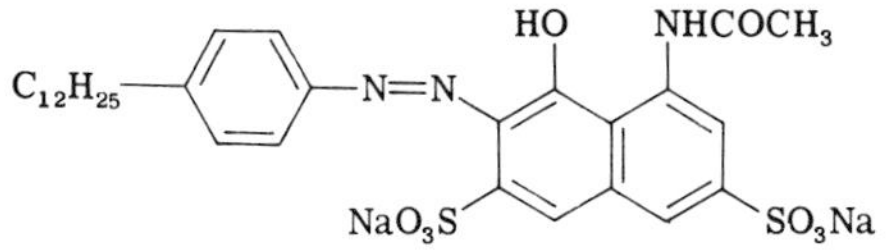

(XXXVII) 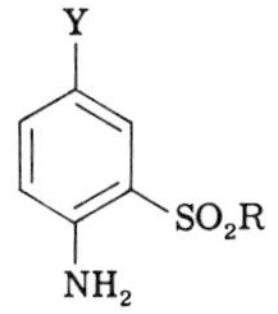   (XXXVIII)

To enable Gamma-acid and the 2-naphthylaminesulfonic acids (notably the 5, 6, and 7-monosulfonic acids) to be used as acid-coupling components in monosulfonated azo dyes one approach has been to carefully design the diazo component so as to attach the necessary weighting group, usually via an electron-attracting substituent, to the arylamine. A favored mode of attachment is via a sulfone, sulfonamide, or sulfate ester linkage. In this way, 2-amino-4-acylaminobenzenesulfonarylamides (XXXVIII; R = N(Alkyl)Aryl, Y = NHAcyl) and 2-amino-4-acyl-aminodiphenylsulfones (XXXVIII; R = Aryl, Y = NHAcyl);[67] 2-aminodiphenylsulfone-3'-sulfonic acid esters (XXXVIII; R = $C_6H_4SO_2O$-Acyl; Y = H);[68] 2-aminobenzenesulfondialkylamides (XXXVIII; R = NAlkyl$_2$, Y = H)[69] and their 4-phenoxy derivatives [XXXVIII; R = N(Alkyl)$_2$, Y = H][70] and 2-aminobenzenesulfonic acid aryl esters (XXXVIII; R = OAryl, Y = H)[71] have been used as diazo components in the preparation of fast to light, orange to bluish red dyes. In diazo components of this type carrying a sulfonamide linkage ortho to the azo group a bluish red shade is obtained by acid coupling onto Gamma-acid; a much smaller bathochromic shift is obtained by locating the linkage meta to the azo group and thus m-aminobenzenesulfonarylamides have been used to give more neutral red shades with Gamma-acid.[72] In addition to these electron-attracting groups, diazo components in which a sulfide link is used to attach the weighting group have been used in the

[67] CIBA, *BP* 705,959.
[68] FBy, *BP* 917,725.
[69] Gy, *BP* 831,843.
[70] O. Schmid, M. Hürbin, and Gy, *BP* 878,129.
[71] Gy, *BP* 739,934; S, *BP* 922,162.
[72] F. Frisch and S, *BP* 953,544.

preparation of bluish red dyes.[73] This linkage also figures in a series of disazo orange and bluish red dyes prepared by acid coupling tetrazotized diamines of the general formula (XXXIX)[74] with 2 equivalents of Gamma-acid or a naphthylaminesulfonic acid; similarly, disazo dyes have been prepared from tetrazo components of formula (XL).[75] In these disazo dyes the lack of conjugation across the central link results in shades being obtained which are similar to those of the analogous monoazo dyes. Contrastingly, disazo dyes based on aminoazo compounds of formula (XLI) diazotized and acid-coupled onto Gamma-acid yield blue shades on wool.[76]

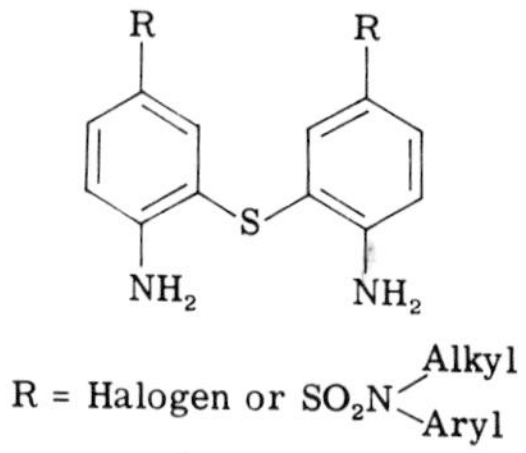
R
R
S
NH2
NH2
R = Halogen or SO2N Alkyl Aryl

(XXXIX)

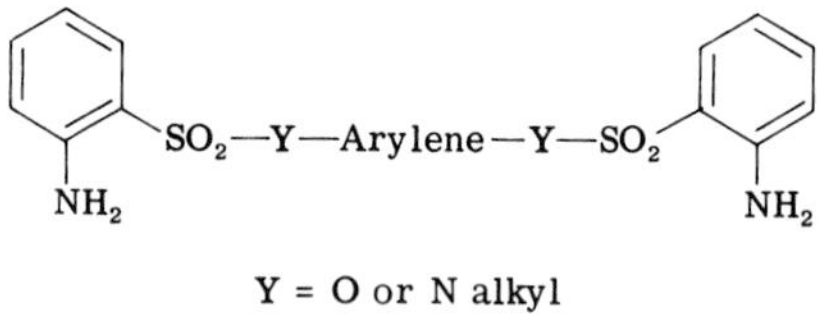
SO2—Y—Arylene—Y—SO2
NH2
NH2
Y = O or N alkyl

(XL)

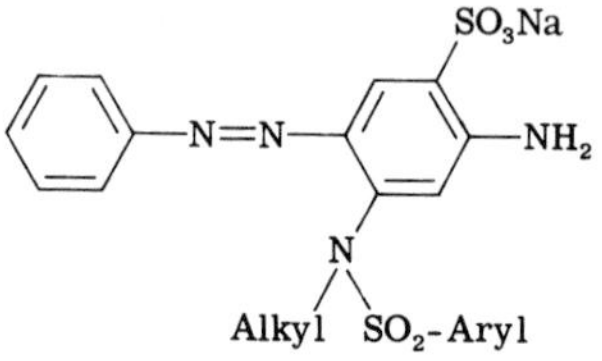
SO3Na
—N=N—
—NH2
N
Alkyl SO2-Aryl

(XLI)

While Gamma-acid and the 2-naphthylaminesulfonic acids are favored for the preparation of orange to bluish red azo dyes for wool, the attraction of having the sulfonic acid group of a monosulfonated azo dye ortho to the azo linkage in order to further advance lightfastness has led to the exploitation of the much less readily accessible substituted amides of these coupling components. Preparation entails protection of the amino (and hydroxy) group while the sulfonic acid group is converted via the sulfonyl chloride into the substituted sulfonamide followed by removal of

[73] Gy, *BP* 715,549.
[74] Gy, *BP* 695,768; FBy, *BP* 769,618.
[75] Gy, *BP* 828,698.
[76] S, *BP* 660,056.

the protective groups and thus these intermediates are considerably more costly than the sulfonic acids themselves. They are, nevertheless, attractive components for the preparation of this type of dye and consequently have been exploited. In conjunction with these compounds, aniline-2-sulfonic acids carrying alkoxycarbonylamino (XLII; R = NHCOOAlkyl)[77] and 5-arylsulfonyloxy (XLII; R = OSO$_2$Aryl)[78] groups have been used as diazo components. In the case of the amides of Gamma-acid, 5-arylsulfonyl — (XLII; R = SO$_2$Aryl) and 5-aryloxy-sulfonylaniline-2-sulfonic acids (XLII; R = SO$_2$Aryl)[79] as well as 4-amino-4'-acylaminodiphenyl-3-sulfonic acids (XLIII; R = NHCOCH$_3$) and the corresponding 4'-alkoxycarbonylamino compounds (XLIII; R = NHCOOAlkyl)[80] have found use as diazo components. A variation on this type of dye is represented by dyes of the type aniline-o-sulfonaryl-amide → (acid) Gamma-acid arylamide carrying a single sulfonic acid group in the pendant aryl residue of the coupling component[81] and the corresponding naphthylamine sulfonarylamide analogs.[82] Dyes devoid of sulfonic acid groups but possessing sufficient solubility in hot water to make them useful in the dyeing of wool have been prepared by incorporating the strongly acidic disulfimide group into the diazo component [e.g., (XLIV)] and acid coupling onto an amide of Gamma-acid or a naphthylaminesulfonic acid.[83]

A further method of incorporating a weighting group into the molecule of a lightfast bluish red dye lies in the use of a suitable N-aryl Gamma-acid. Using this type of intermediate, excellent disulfonated monoazo dyes for wool can be prepared if sufficient weight is incorporated into the molecule to overcome the presence of two sulfonic acid groups, as with, for example, the dye (XLV).[84]

Dyes of this type are capable of giving excellent light- and wet-fastness properties on wool. An even higher level of fastness to severe wet treatments can be obtained by employing dye–fiber reaction. Since, however, wool would be dyed by any unreactive species arising from hydrolysis rather than fixation it is necessary to achieve as near as possible total fixation by employing low reactivity groups relatively resistant to hydrolysis. Further, it is advantageous to incorporate into the

[77] Gy, BP 905,383.
[78] S, BP 924,995.
[79] Gy, BP 864,742.
[80] S, BP 850,844.
[81] Gy, BP 886,629.
[82] G, BP 877,180.
[83] Gy, BP 840,182.
[84] S, BP 756,624.

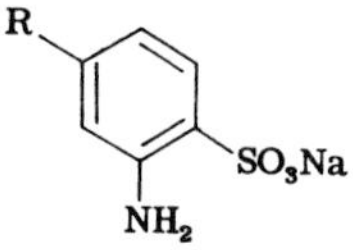

(XLII)

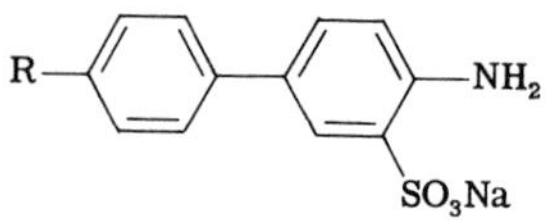

(XLIII)

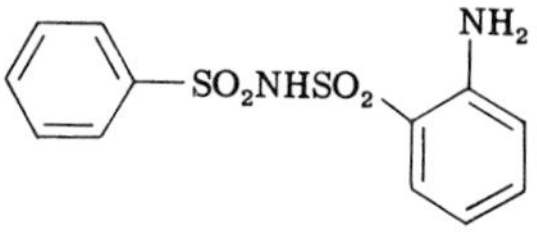

(XLIV)

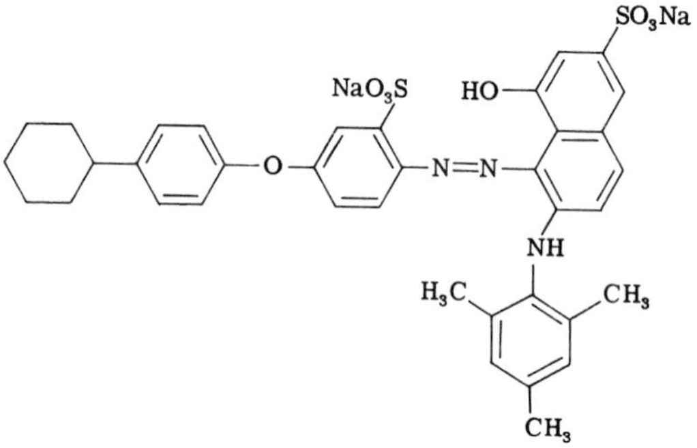

(XLV)

reactive dye molecule a suitable weighting group to ensure both satisfactory dye uptake and to minimize any deleterious effect of traces of hydrolyzed dye on fastness properties. The incorporation of a weighting group and correct choice of structure for attainment of adequate light-fastness can clearly be seen to have influenced the structure of reactive acrylamide dyes of formula (XLVI)[85] and the possibly reactive mono-chloro-s-triazinyl dyes (XLVII).[86]

Mention of alkaline-coupled acyl J-acid and acyl Gamma-acid[87] as coupling components in patents relating to orange and red dyes based on the disulfimide diazo component (XLIV) serves to show that there is still interest in dyes in these shade regions where in lower lightfastness

[85] C. V. Stead and ICI, *BP* 1,037,648.
[86] CIBA, *BP* 818,957.
[87] FBy, *BP* 806,938; 918,366.

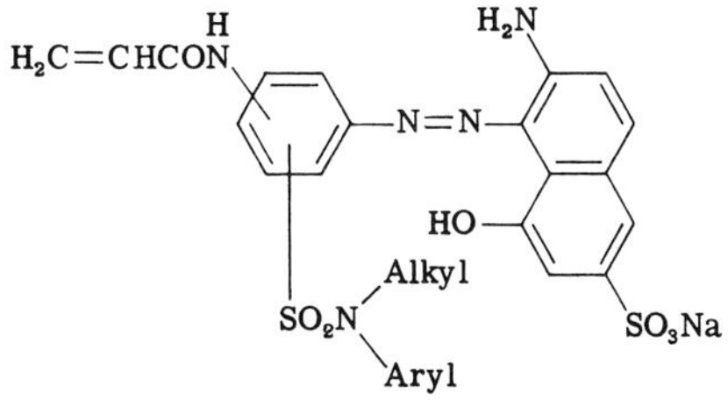

(XLVI)

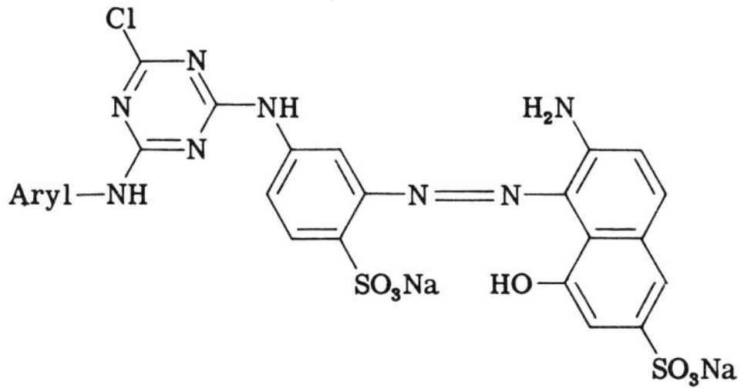

(XLVII)

can be tolerated in the interests of obtaining a more desirable shade. In the case of orange dyes based on *N*-acyl J-acid as coupling component these are only marginally inferior to those with a 2-naphthylamine-sulfonic acid as coupling component; dyes of this type which have been described for the dyeing of wool include dyes wherein a diazotized aniline-*o*-sulfonic acid is coupled onto, for example, *N*-decanoyl-J-acid,[88] or wherein 4-trifluoromethylaniline-2-sulfonic acid is used as diazo component.[89] A more pronounced deficiency in lightfastness is shown in the red shade region wherein dyes based on *N*-acyl H- or *N*-acyl K-acid can attain a maximum lightfastness of about 5 compared with the value of 6–7 attainable from acid-coupled Gamma-acid dyes. Here again the brightness of shade obtainable from *N*-acylated components is sufficiently attractive to make the dyes desirable for certain applications. Dyes of this type which have been claimed include (XLVIII)[90] and (XLIX),[91] both based on 2-aminodiphenyl ether diazo components. Use has also been made of H-acid as a diazo component in the preparation of red dyes with a *p*-coupling amine as coupling component, the necessary

[88] S, *BP* 716,007.
[89] A. H. Knight and ICI, *BP* 732,121.
[90] CIBA, *BP* 705,961.
[91] FBy, *BP* 732,949.

weighting substituent being carried on the nitrogen atom of the coupling component.[92] Similarly excellent blue wool dyes of the pattern (L) have been described.[93]

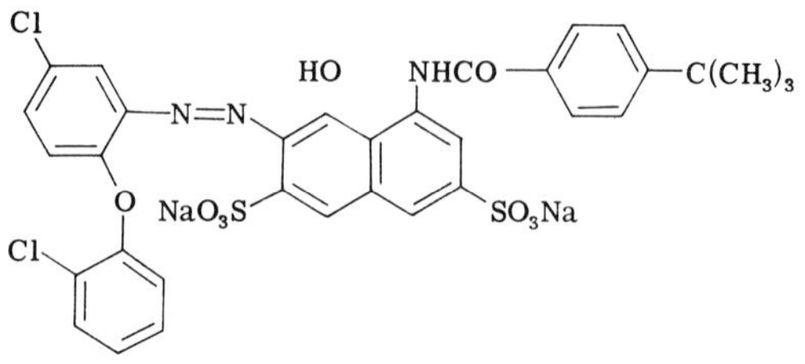

(XLVIII)

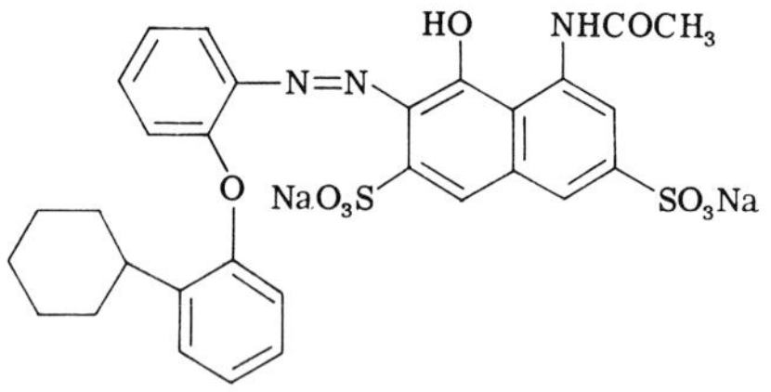

(XLIX)

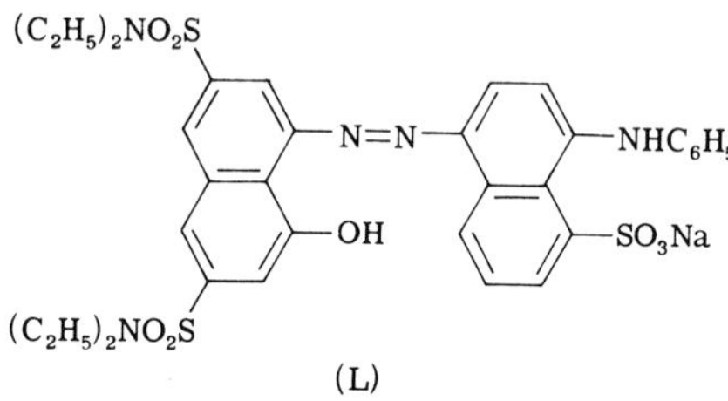

(L)

In the yellow shade region the choice of coupling components is more limited. Here, 5-pyrazolones and 5-aminopyrazoles are the coupling components of major commercial interest for they are capable of yielding dyes which combine brightness of shade with high lightfastness. The 5-pyrazolones are the more readily accessible of the two classes and these are therefore the most convenient to use, although on occasion the less easily prepared 5-aminopyrazoles are capable of yielding wool dyes of superlative properties and for this reason figure extensively in the patent literature. To achieve the required performance from both classes an electron-attracting substituent in the diazo component is most helpful.

[92] Gy, *BP* 725,814.
[93] P. W. Barker, T. L. Dawson, and ICI, *BP* 913,670.

Thus long-chain alkyl esters[94] and alkylphenoxy esters[95] of anthranilic acid have been used as diazo components in conjunction with 1-sulfoaryl-3-methyl-5-pyrazolones. Substituted arylamides and aryl esters of anilinesulfonic acids have been similarly employed with 1-aryl-3-methyl-5-aminopyrazoles.[96] Occasionally bis coupling components [e.g., (LI)] have been used in the preparation of disazo yellow dyes,[97] although disazo dyes are more usually obtained from a tetrazotized diamine.[98] Diamines such as (LII), for use with a wide variety of coupling components[99] including 1-sulfoaryl-3-methyl-5-aminopyrazoles,[100] serve to illustrate how correct weighting of the dyestuff can be achieved by skillful use of readily available intermediates.

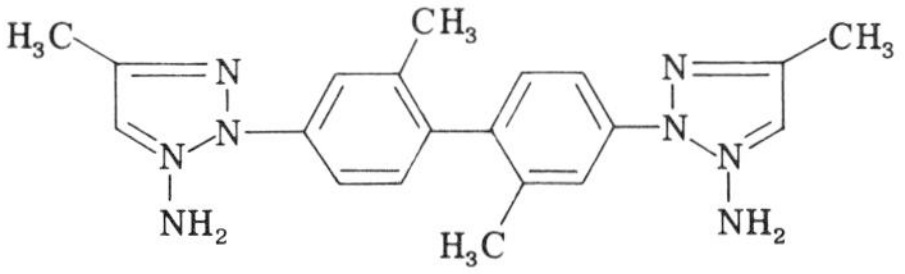

(LI)

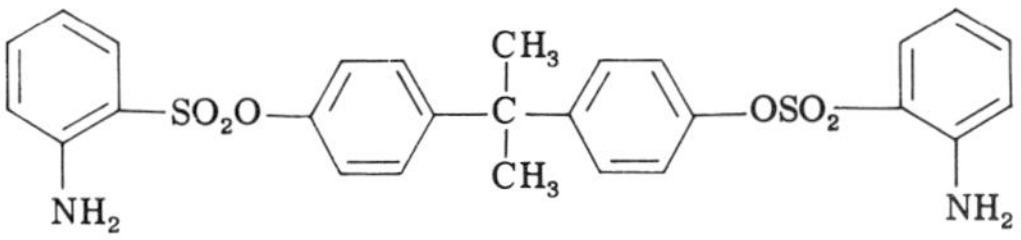

(LII) 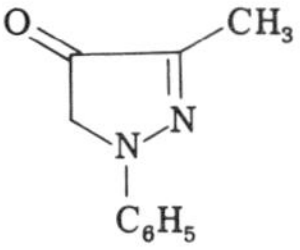   (LIII)

Use of novel 1-phenyl-3-methyl-4-pyrazolones (LIII) as coupling components for wool dyes has been described. Compared with products based on the isomeric 5-pyrazolones the products differ by a considerable displacement of the absorption to longer wavelengths, thus giving a marked bathochromic shift which is claimed to enable brown, blue, and black shades to be obtained from relatively small dye molecules. Thus the combination sulfanilic acid → 1-phenyl-3-methyl-4-pyrazolone is said to give a brown dyeing on wool.[101]

[94] Gy, BP 727,199.
[95] S, BP 756,296.
[96] Gy, BP 844,427; 868,474; FBy, BP 888,499.
[97] A. H. Knight and ICI, BP 791,443; Gy, BP 995,368.
[98] A. H. Knight and ICI, BP 706,427; 706, 857; Gy, BP 993,756.
[99] FBy, BP 810,246.
[100] FBy, BP 805,777.
[101] BASF, BP 858,562.

2. Nylon Acid Dyes

Synthetic polyamide fibers, notably nylon, can be dyed with a large variety of dye types. In the metal-free azo field the two most useful classes are the disperse dyes and the acid dyes, these two types being complementary in properties. The disperse dyes, which are dealt with elsewhere, have the better dyeing properties but are somewhat deficient in fastness properties; the acid dyes have much better fastness properties but are generally inferior in dyeing behavior. The good fastness properties of the acid dyes result from the amino groups in the fiber anchoring the dye molecule by means of salt linkages. The inferior dyeing properties are the result of irregularities in the nylon fiber. These irregularities are caused either by chemical variations in the spun filament or variations in tension in the knitting or weaving of nylon which cause an increase in the number of crystalline regions in the fiber. Many simple acid azo dyes, of the acid wool type, do not penetrate these crystalline regions sufficiently during the dyeing operation to produce level dyeings. The resulting objectionable barré effects may also be emphasized by temperature variations in the heat setting of nylon goods.

With the call for acid dyes for nylon, the dyestuff manufacturers have responded mainly by making a judicious selection from their ranges of acid wool dyes and recommending the selected dyestuffs for application to nylon. As time has progressed, acid dyes specifically designed for application to nylon have appeared and now trends are discernible in the type of structure which stands a chance of success as a nylon dye. Roughly, monosulfonated azo dyes with molecular weights in the 400–500 region and disulfonated dyes wherein the molecular weight is about 800 are most likely to have the desired properties. Too high a molecular weight exaggerates uneven dyeing, too low a molecular weight diminishes wash-fastness properties. Structural features encouraging hydrogen bond formation, such as hydroxy or acylamino groups, boost wash-fastness but tend to cause unlevelness. The patent literature relating to acid dyes for nylon can be viewed as a search for the optimum properties within these crude guide lines.

Typical acid dyes for nylon are those disclosed in patents emanating from Crompton and Knowles, who produce the Nylanthrene range which is specifically designed for application to nylon. These patents disclose greenish yellow dyes obtained by coupling diazotized 5-benzoylamino-aniline-2-sulfonic acid with a 1-aryl-3-methyl-5-pyrazolone (LIV)[102] and scarlet dyes obtained from diazotized 5-acetylaminoaniline-2-sul-

[102] Crompton & Knowles Corp., BP 985,160.

fonic acid and a 2-hydroxy-3-naphthoic aryl amide (LV).[103] Disazo orange dyes result from O-tosylation of dyes of the pattern metanilic acid → α-naphthylamine → phenol (LVI)[104] and lightfast red dyes are available from acid coupling of diazotized 3-benzoylaminoanilines with Gamma-acid (LVII).[105] This last-named dye exploits Gamma-acid as an acid-coupling component in order to achieve satisfactory lightfastness, a trend which has been remarked upon in the field of wool dyes. Dyestuffs of this type possessing superlative lightfastness have been obtained using, for example, 4-chloro-2-trifluoromethylaniline (LVIII)[106] as diazo component.

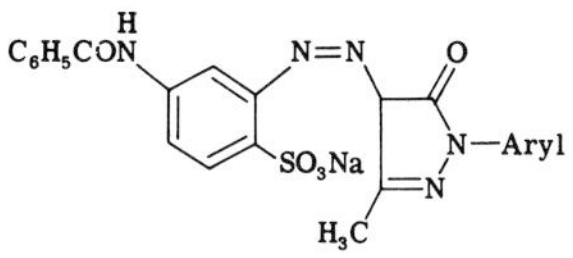

(LIV)

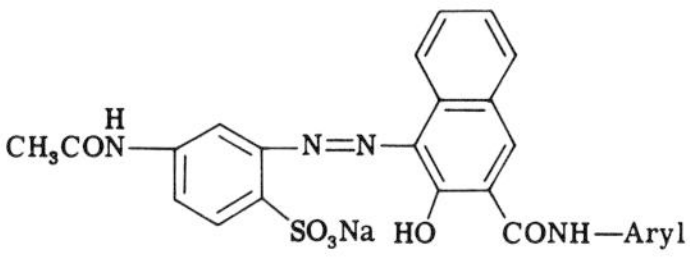

(LV)

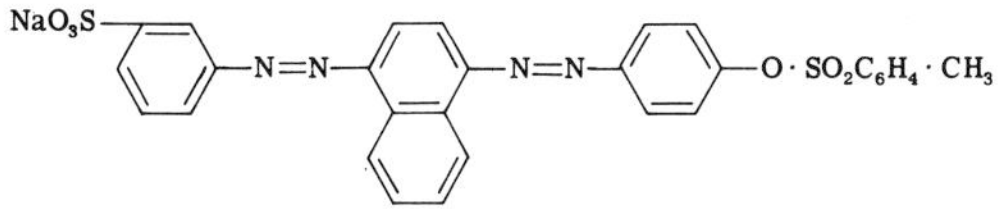

(LVI)

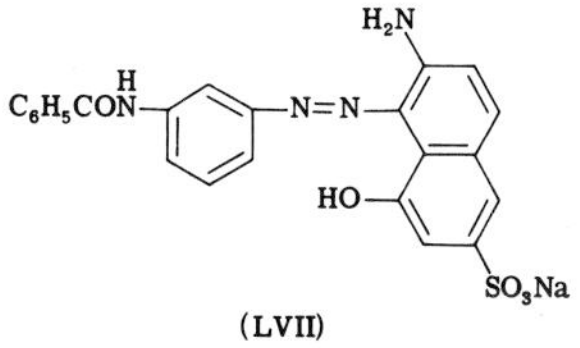

(LVII)

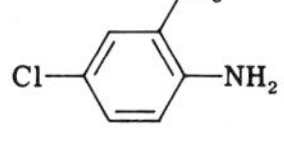

(LVIII)

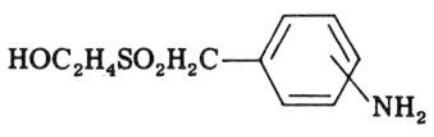

(LIX)

Claims have been advanced for the utility of hydroxyethylsulfonylmethylanilines (LIX) and their O-sulfate esters as diazo components in the preparation of yellow sulfonated pyrazolone,[107] orange naphthol-

[103] Crompton & Knowles Corp., BP 1,053,313.
[104] Crompton & Knowles Corp., BP 1,090,945.
[105] J. F. Feeman and Crompton & Knowles Corp., BP 1,035,916.
[106] J. I. Ambler, W. M. Sokol, I. M. S. Walls, and ICI, BP 761,468.
[107] H. B. Freyermuth, D. I. Randall, D. M. Buc, and G, BP 1,031,482.

monosulfonic acid,[108] and red N-acetyl H-acid dyes,[109] these dyestuffs being said to exhibit little or no barré behavior in dyeing of nylon. Aniline sulfonguanidide has been used with sulfonated coupling components to prepare nylon dyes[110] and aminoazobenzene → indole dyes carrying one or two sulfonic acid groups have been claimed.[111] Dyes in which aminoazobenzene is used as diazo component are said to be especially useful, on account of their high tinctorial strength, in the dyeing of polyamides based on undecanoic acid which, due to the increased alkyl content and consequently diminished amino group content, take up much less dyestuff than does ordinary nylon.[112]

3. Direct Dyes

Fiber-reactive dyes have made their main impact on the dyeing of cellulosic goods. This development has, of course, had repercussions on the direct dye field although these are not as great as might be thought. Reactive dyes are a superior but more costly product aimed at providing a much higher standard of wet-fastness than is possible with direct dyes. They have thus made a greater impact on azoic dyes against which they offer brightness of shade and a superlative standard of wet-fastness obtainable by a simpler application method.

The effect of reactive dyes on direct dyes has been mainly to emphasize that the role of direct dyes is to cheaply supply a method of dyeing an article to minimum standards of wet-fastness. In this role the low cost of direct dyes and their short batchwise dyeing process time are considerations of prime importance. There is a considerable demand for this type of dyeing, for instance, in the dyeing of viscose rayon linings where fastness is not of paramount importance. Direct dyes also find a major outlet in the coloration of paper where fastness is immaterial. The complexity of direct dyes makes them particularly suited to the production of deep, drab shades where metallization can be used to attain sufficiently high lightfastness to satisfy applications which demand lightfastness but not wet-fastness. New outlets, such as that opened up by the extensive use of viscose rayon in carpeting, have benefited this type of direct dye.

Improved treatments of the fiber with thermosetting resins for the purpose of conferring properties such as crease resistance or water repel-

---

[108] H. B. Freyermuth, D. I. Randall, D. M. Buc, and G, *BP* 1,031,535.
[109] H. B. Freyermuth, D. I. Randall, D. M. Buc, and G, *BP* 1,031,536.
[110] M. Jirou, and CN, *FP* 1,392,484.
[111] D. Leuchs, H. Baumann, R. Krallmann, and BASF, *BP* 975,356.
[112] M. Jirou and Fran, *BP* 937,864.

lancy[113] to the material have assisted in concealing wet-fastness deficiencies of direct dyes. At their best, coppered direct dyes have adequately high lightfastness and much work has been concentrated on maintaining this level of lightfastness after crease-resist processing. In common with all other classes of azo dyes, direct dyes sometimes show a marked drop in lightfastness[114] when the fiber is subjected to a resin treatment. The effect on any particular dye often varies depending on which resin system is used. Thus, selecting two of the many resin systems available,[115] the system (LX)/formaldehyde has a drastic effect on certain dyes while the system (LXI)/formaldehyde usually has little or no effect. The action of light on these resin systems has been shown to

(LX)   (LXI)

induce formation of an oxygen-rich intermediate in the resin and there is correlation between the ease of formation of this intermediate and the accelerated fading effect. It has, therefore, been postulated that accelerated fading is caused by photochemical oxidation of the resin in its ground state to give peroxides which are long-lived in comparison with the excited-state lifetime of the dye. In accordance with these findings (LX) in methanol forms a peroxide much more readily than does (LXI).

A major weakness which will probably increasingly tell against direct dyes in the future is that although well suited to batchwise application they do not lend themselves to easy continuous application. In addition they maintain their usefulness in spite of the presence of a superior product (reactive dyes) chiefly on economic grounds. Without doubt the availability of cheap reactive dyes would lead to a marked decline in the demand for direct dyes. The various factors outlined have led to a great diminution in direct dye research as the dyestuff manufacturers have moved the bulk of their research effort into the more rewarding area of reactive dyes. Research on direct dyes is now prosecuted on a greatly reduced scale, centering on coppered or after copperable dyes, particularly in the blue shade region. In this review much of the work reported at the beginning of the period covered will therefore be only briefly mentioned and the emphasis placed on research in those areas

[113] A. R. Smith, *J. Soc. Dyers Colourists* 77, 416 (1961).
[114] *Am. Dyestuff Reptr.* 43, 6 (1954).
[115] W. Ingamells, *J. Soc. Dyers Colourists* 79, 651 (1963).

where direct dyes are still useful or where interesting aspects of azo dye chemistry are encountered.

  a. Metal-Free Direct Dyes. Work in this field has been chiefly aimed at producing new substantive yellow monoazo dyes since in this region óf the spectrum adequate lightfastness without resort to metallization can be achieved. A noticeable feature has been the frequent use of 2-naphtho[1,2-*d*]triazolyl groups (LXII) which are introduced by coupling a diazotized amine onto a suitable 2-naphthylamine and oxidizing the resulting *o*-aminoazo compound. Thus, this group,[116] as well as acylamino,[117] has been employed as a 4'-substituent in greenish yellow dyes derived from 4-aminostilbene- or aminobenzoylaminostilbene-2,2'-disulfonic acid → acetoacetanilide chromophores. Care has been taken with the position and degree of sulfonation of the yellow dyes 4-(sulfonaphthotriazolyl)-4'-aminostilbene-2,2'-disulfonic acid → *m*-toluidine → 2-naphthylaminesulfonic acid, triazolized a second time, to achieve minimum staining on nylon.[118] The interesting intermediate 6-nitro-2-naphthylamine-4,8-disulfonic acid, which has been prominent in the metallized direct dye field, has been the starting material for yellow bis(sulfonaphthotriazolyl) monoazo dyes, e.g., (LXIII).[119]

  The use of phosgene[120] and similar diacid chlorides, such as tereph-

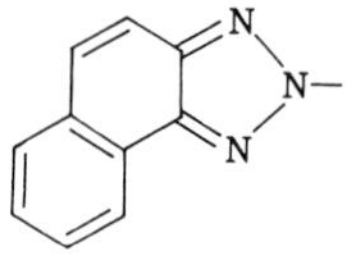

(LXII)

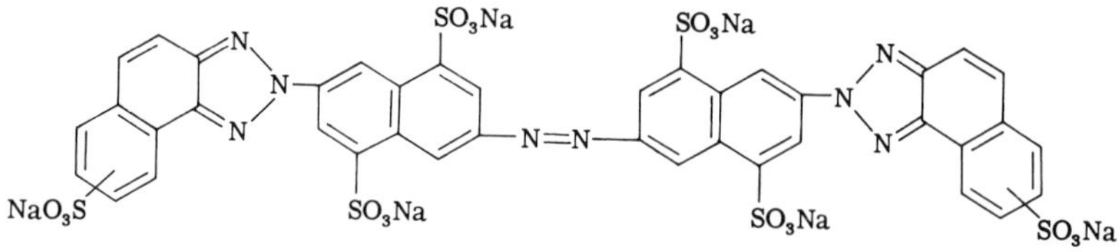

(LXIII)

[116] CIBA, *BP* 814,391; NAC, *BP* 944,072.

[117] CIBA, *BP* 810,927.

[118] NAC, *BP* 1,023,799; G. Manz and FBy, *BP* 1,073,220.

[119] FBy, *BP* 853,013; H. Nickel, F. Suckfull, K.-H. Schundehutte, and Bayer, *BP* 1,081,797.

[120] FBy, *BP* 713,217; 727,421; 784,622; H. Riat and CIBA, *BP* 846,487; J. F. Freeman and Althouse Chem. Co., *USP* 2,795,577-8.

thaloyl chloride,[121] for the linking together of two molecules of a simple aminoazo compound into a substantive entity is a well-known technique of direct dye chemistry. Further novel linking components which have been described for use in this manner are the diacid chlorides of stilbene-4,4'-dicarboxylic acid[122] and butadiene-1,4-dicarboxylic acid.[123] Fumaroyl chloride has been used for linking a blue aminoanthraquinone to a yellow aminoazo compound for the preparation of green dyes;[124] a homogeneous product is not, of course, obtained from this reaction but as with similar mixed phosgenations the asymmetric product is heavily contaminated with the two symmetrical alternatives. A stepwise method of preparing asymmetric ureas (LXIV) has, however, been described wherein one amino-containing dyestuff is reacted with an aryl chloroformate and the resulting urethane condensed with a second, different amino-containing dye.[125]

$$\text{Dye}_1\text{—NH}_2 + \text{ClCOOAr} \longrightarrow \text{Dye}_1\text{—NHCOOAr} \xrightarrow{\text{dye}_2\text{NH}_2} \text{Dye}_1\text{—NHCONH—Dye}_2$$

(LXIV)

Moving to the more complex dis- and trisazo dyes, a number of early patents disclose further permutations of intermediates leading to chiefly orange and red direct dyes.[126] In this classic type of direct dye, built up by a succession of diazotization and coupling stages, it is common practice to make use of pyridine as a coupling assistant. Various explanations have been advanced as to the manner in which pyridine facilitates coupling but the role of this base is probably very complex and probably still not fully understood. Possible modes of action are by stabilizing the diazonium salt against decomposition during a slow coupling stage and by exerting a solubilizing effect on the reactants by diminishing their tendency to form aggregates. From a study of the reaction of p-chlorobenzenediazonium chloride with 2-naphthol-6,8-disulfonic acid kinetic data have been obtained suggesting that pyridine plays the part of an efficient proton acceptor in the conversion of the thermodynamically metastable intermediate (LXV) into the azo compound.[127] In addition to pyridine, a wide variety of other basic substances have been investi-

[121] Gy, BP 817,871.
[122] R. S. Long, S. M. Tsang, and CCC, USP 2,877,218.
[123] S, BP 757,927.
[124] S, BP 713,580.
[125] FBy, BP 879,635.
[126] CIBA, BP 672,400; S, BP 717,000; 762,844; 766,015; Gy, BP 824,327.
[127] H. Zollinger, Helv. Chim. Acta 38, 1597, 1617, and 1623 (1955).

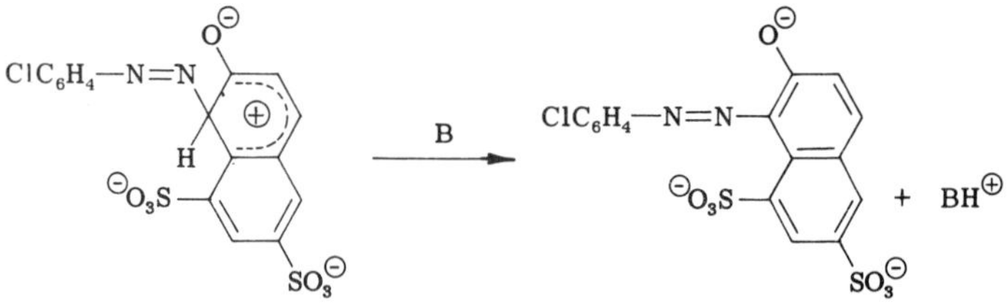

(LXV)

gated as coupling accelerators in the preparation of trisazo dyes.[128] A very obvious drawback to the use of pyridine as a coupling accelerator in manufacturing processes is the unpleasant smell and possible health hazard which it presents. To avoid these disadvantages, the use of urea[129] and related compounds[130] as coupling accelerators has been mentioned in some patents. These compounds are said to exert both a stabilizing effect on the diazonium salt and a solubilizing effect.

In the trisazo dye field combinations of the pattern A → H-acid ← D → E have been further investigated for the preparation of green[131] and black[132] leather dyes. Particular interest has been shown in variations in the M and E components used in the black tetrakisazo dye 4,4'-diaminodiphenylamine-3-sulfonic acid ⇒ (Gamma-acid → m-phenylenediamine)$_2$, the object being to improve the solubility, nylon reserve, and shade of this technically important dye.[133]

Novel coupling components for the preparation of blue to yellow-green direct dyes have been prepared by condensing copper phthalocyanine tetrasulfonchloride with an acetoacetarylamide or pyrazolone coupling component carrying an amino group; during this condensation the coupling position is protected by O-tosylation, the protecting group being subsequently removed by hydrolysis.[134]

b. Copper Complex Direct Dyes. The formation of a copper complex of an azo dye diminishes the solubility of the dyestuff in water and therefore offers the possibility of a somewhat higher standard of wet-fastness. This can be achieved by aftercoppering a low-solubility direct dye on

[128] V. Chmatal and Z. J. Allan, *Collection Czech. Chem. Commun.* **30**, 1205 (1965).

[129] S, *BP* 1,107,597.

[130] H. Ischer and S, *BP* 1,117,774.

[131] BASF, *BP* 785,101; G. Lange, W. Brunkhorst, and BASF, *BP* 870,698; FH, *BP* 858,556.

[132] CFM, *BP* 796,790; D. C. Wilson and YDC, *BP* 854,957.

[133] CFM, *BP* 703,446; 743,957; 1,019,467; 1,105,350; G. F. Garcelon and Crompton & Knowles Corp., *USP* 2,935,507.

[134] FBy, *BP* 830,920; 844,419.

the fiber, thus depressing the water solubility of the dyestuff still further and leading to an improvement in wet-fastness properties. In the early part of the period under review a novel development of this dyeing method in which the coppering process stripped the molecule of its solubilizing groups was of considerable interest. The process entailed the preparation of sulfate or phosphate[135] esters of unsulfonated azo dyestuffs, the esterifying group being located on a hydroxy group which would eventually participate in metal complex formation. Thus dyes of the patterns (LXVI)[136] and (LXVII),[137] wherein D represents the residue of a conventional substantive diamine free solubilizing groups and HOHR—RHOH is a water-insoluble, substantive coupling component capable of coupling in two positions, were prepared either by sulfating an 8-hydroxyquinoline dye [leading to (LXVII)] or use of an o-aminophenol sulfate ester [leading to (LXVI)]. The readily water soluble products were applied to the fiber in the normal manner and then aftercoppered, forming, on the fiber, the water-insoluble bis copper complexes (LXVIII) and (LXIX). In the case of the 8-hydroxyquinoline derivatives, polymerization during metallization as shown in (LXVIII) was a further factor in enhancing wet-fastness and it is noteworthy that this terminal metallization also improves the lightfastness of the dye. This development would no doubt have made a considerable impact had not the discovery of fiber-reactive dyes provided a more complete solution to the problem of achieving high wet-fastness from a water-soluble dyestuff. The introduction of reactive dyes forced research on after-metallizable direct dyes, on a much diminished scale, back to the cheaper conventional dyes carrying nuclear sulfonic acid groups. Such dyes, containing terminally metallizable salicyclic acid[138] or 8-hydroxyquinoline[139] components, figure in the recent patent literature. These components contain the two systems commonly used in terminally metallized dyes. An interesting alternative, the o-hydroxynitroso system, has been described in dyes obtained by nitrosating arylamine → resorcinol dyes.[140] Dyes which can be both terminally and radially coppered also attract attention.[141] Typical of this type is the

[135] A. R. Todd, R. R. Davies, and ICI, BP 785,038; A. R. Todd, G. Booth, R. R. Davies, and ICI, BP 785,457.

[136] R. R. Davies and ICI, BP 761,776; H. F. Andrew, H. C. Boyd, R. R. Davies, and ICI, BP 786,567; H. F. Andrew, R. R. Davies, and ICI, BP 787,646.

[137] R. R. Davies and ICI, BP 747,872; N. Legg and ICI, BP 786,745.

[138] S, BP 695,758; CIBA, BP 708,663; 784,879; 807,575; O. Senn and Westminster Bank, BP 977,710.

[139] CIBA, BP 697,136; 733,361.

[140] J. R. Atkinson, D. A. Plant, and ICI, BP 668,474.

[141] CIBA, BP 760,347; 784,613.

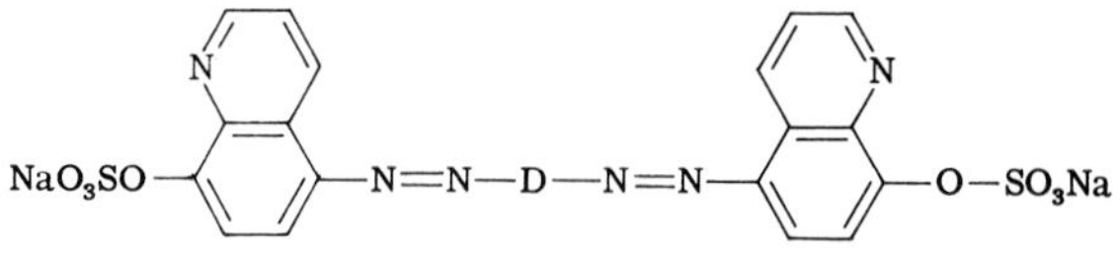

(LXVI)

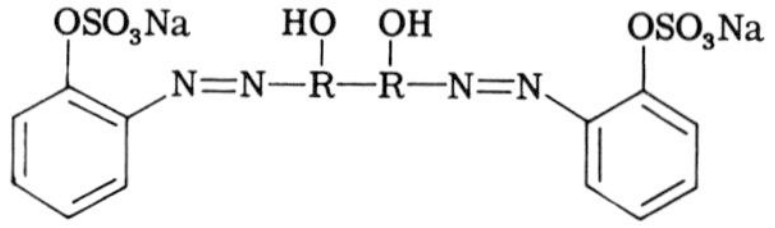

(LXVII)

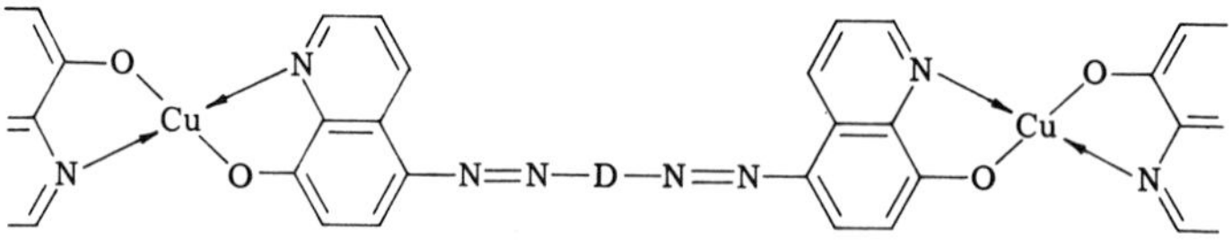

(LXVIII)

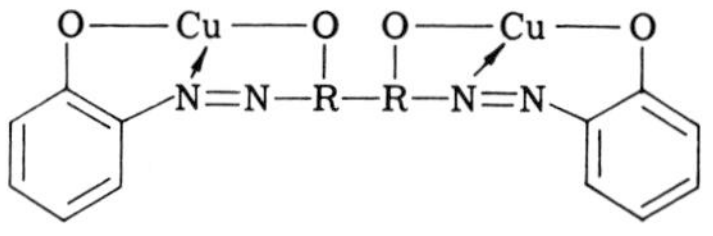

(LXIX)

dye (LXX).[142] They are converted into the radial copper complex either
by selective metallization across the azo linkage or by complete metallization followed by partial removal of the metal. This latter operation is

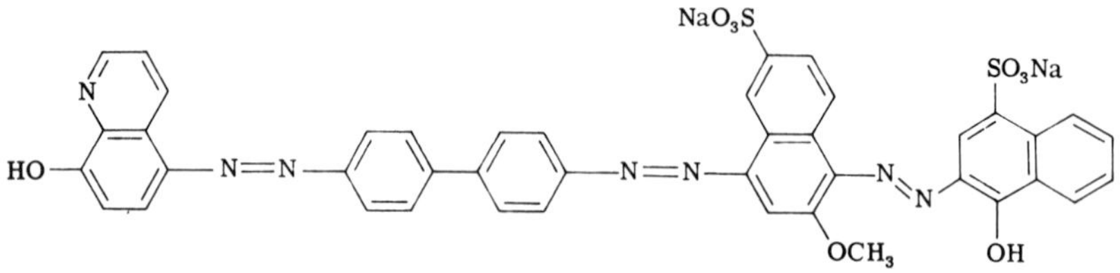

(LXX)

[142] CIBA, *BP* 1,021,944.

accomplished either by treatment with an acid or with a sequestering agent.[143] The complexes are applied to the fiber in this form and subsequently aftercoppered to involve the terminal metallizable system in metal complex formation.

Turning to the constitutions of the dyestuffs which have been described as metal complex direct dyes, the patent literature discloses seemingly endless permutations of largely the same intermediates. These dyes are particularly useful in producing dark shades and a major interest has been in the blue and navy blue shade region. The most important group of direct dyes of this type are the twice-coppered dyes of the pattern

$$E_1 \leftarrow D \rightarrow E_2$$

wherein the central diamine is dianisidine and the end components are naphthol or aminonaphthol sulfonic acids. Their importance is reflected by the disclosure of about 50 constitutions of dyes of this class, which are or have been commercially available in the Colour Index (CI 24140–24420). Patent claims made relate mainly to variations in the end components to achieve better lightfastness after crease-resist processing[144] and better level dyeing properties.[145] Purer shades are claimed to be obtained when the end components are both N-alkyl H-acid[146] and reduction of the degree of sulfonation from the usual four sulfonic acid groups to two sulfonic acid groups in conjunction with two sulfonamide groups has been used to provide aftercopperable dyes of improved fastness properties.[147] Use of various J-acid derivatives as E_1 is also claimed to improve wet-fastness.[148] Wide variations are possible in the choice of end components without changing the color and thus blue dyes are still obtained when one end component is a pyrazolone[149] and one or both end components are acid-coupled J-acid dyes.[150] Navy blue aftercopperable tetrakisazo dyes result when end Gamma-acid components are subsequently diazotized and coupled onto 8-hydroxyquinoline[151] and aftercopperable blue trisazo dyes result from pairing a pyrazolone with a 4'-amino-3'-sulfophenyl-J-acid → 8-hydroxyquinoline end compo-

[143] V. Urne and Fran, *BP* 866,443.

[144] CIBA, *BP* 674,707; 756,190; 824,284; Gy, *BP* 710,797; 786,918; 886,576; G. A. Rowe and ICI, *BP* 740,570; 744,930; E. L. Johnson, G. A. Rowe, and ICI, *BP* 742,731; 745,082; E. L. Johnson, F. L. Rose, G. A. Rowe, and ICI, *BP* 748,611; FBy, *BP* 845,491; 893,882.

[145] Gy, *BP* 840,898; CFM, *BP* 944,416.

[146] CIBA, *BP* 766,014.

[147] CIBA, *BP* 746,877.

[148] S, *BP* 792,734; Gy, *BP* 1,076,727.

[149] G, *BP* 700,701.

[150] S, *BP* 727,745; 760,705; 775,320; 791,532; 794,366.

[151] CIBA, *BP* 778,233.

nent.[152] Shades other than blue and navy blue can, however, be obtained from dyes of this pattern, especially when E_1 is either an acetoacetarylamide or pyrazolone. Thus, gray shades, claimed to have good lightfastness, are obtained when E_2 is a triazolized acid-coupled J-acid component.[153] Alternatively E_2 can be an acid-coupled H-acid unit[154] or an acetoacetylaminonaphthol which has first been coupled on the reactive methylene group with a diazotized o-aminophenol,[155] resulting in gray trisazo dyes. Gray thrice-coppered trisazo dyes are also obtained using an oxidatively coppered J-acid → naphthol sulfonic acid as end component[156] and black aftercoppered dyes arise from the use of the related tetrazotized 4,4'-diaminodiphenyl-3,3'-dicarboxylic acid coupled first with a suitable acid-coupled J-acid and second with a ketomethylene component.[157]

The substantivity of azo dyes obtained by alkaline coupling onto J-acid is well known in direct dye chemistry. The important feature of this molecule which is responsible for the substantivity is the 2,6-orientation of the azo linkage and the amino group (LXXI). In these dyes the amine → J-acid unit gives a fairly high substantivity which is raised to the level required for a direct dye by steps such as phosgenation, or diazotization and further coupling. These dyes still figure occasionally in the patent literature[158] as, for instance, in the case of the brown and green coppered disazo triazoles prepared from arylamine → J → p-coupling amine → 2-naphthylaminesulfonic acid combinations.[159]

Recently the scope of intermediates used to establish the desired 2,6-orientation has been considerably widened and the ingenuity of some of this work merits attention. Thus, in the disazo triazole dyes just mentioned 2-amino-5-naphthol-4,8-disulfonic acid (LXXII; R = H) has been used in place of J-acid either by coupling onto it and then diazotizing and further processing the aminoazo dye obtained or by diazotizing and coupling 5-benzenesulfonyloxy-2-naphthylamine-4,8-disulfonic acid (LXXII; R = $SO_2C_6H_5$), hydrolyzing, and finally introducing the first azo linkage by coupling. (LXXII; R = $SO_2C_6H_5$) and the related naphthasultone (LXXIII) have also been used to produce, by diazotization and coupling with a naphthol sulfonic acid followed by oxidative coppering and saponification, monoazo compounds[160] useful as coupling

[152] CIBA, *BP* 777,200.
[153] S, *BP* 736,180.
[154] CFM, *BP* 820,990.
[155] Gy, *BP* 755,571.
[156] S, *BP* 799,925; 809,279.
[157] S, *BP* 793,086.
[158] S, *BP* 687,328; 771,331; CIBA, *BP* 710,734; FBy, *BP* 897,437.
[159] FBy, *BP* 954,100.
[160] FBy, *BP* 879,235.

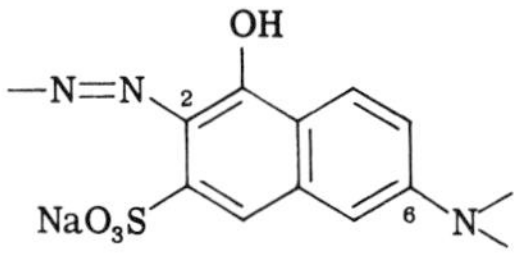

(LXXI)

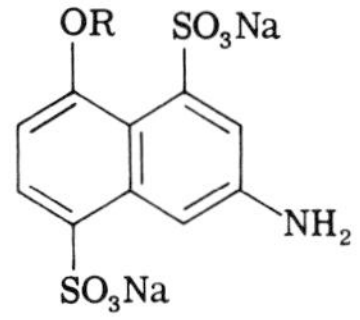

(LXXII)

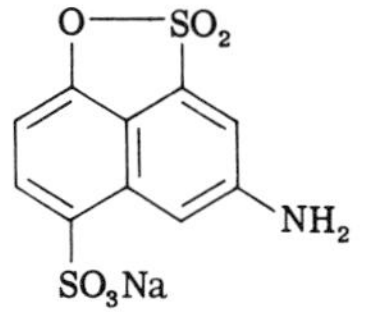

(LXXIII)

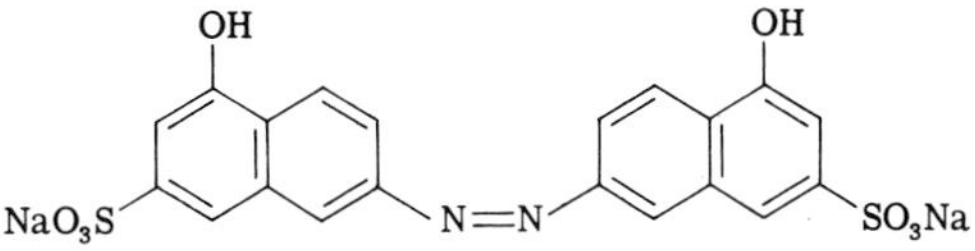

(LXXIV)

components for the preparation of gray or green polyazo dyes.[161] Reaction of diazotized O-benzenesulfonyloxy-J-acid with sulfites to form the symmetrical 5,5'-dihydroxy-2,2'-azonaphthalene-7,7'-disulfonic acid (LXXIV) and the use of this intermediate in the preparation of metallized direct dyes is described.[162] Similarly, the copper complex of (LXXV), obtained by reduction of diazotized 5-benzenesulfonyloxy-2-amino-1-naphthol-7-sulfonic acid with an ammoniacal cuprous salt[163] is a blue compound which gives green dyes with two equivalents of a diazotized arylamine.[164] Condensation of 6-nitro-1,2-naphthoquinone-4-sulfonic acid (LXXVI) with arylhydrazines carrying a metal complex-forming substituent in the ortho position has been employed to form dihydroxyazo compounds (LXXVII; R = H), the copper complexes of which can be converted into blue, violet, and gray direct dyes.[165] Alternatively, the dihydroxyazo intermediates (LXXVII; R = H or SO$_3$Na) can be more conventionally prepared from diazotized 6-nitro-2-amino-1-naphthol-4,8-disulfonic acid[166] or by coupling onto 6-nitro-1-naphthol-4-sulfonic or -4,8-disulfonic acid[167] as well as by hydrolytically coppering the coupling products of diazotized 1-chloro-6-nitro-2-naphthylamine-4,8-disulfonic acid.[168]

[161] FBy, *BP* 901,927.
[162] FBy, *BP* 872,685.
[163] FBy, *BP* 802,098.
[164] FBy, *BP* 818,008.
[165] FBy, *BP* 907,382.
[166] FBy, *BP* 907,383.
[167] FBy, *BP* 907,384.
[168] FBy, *BP* 885,042.

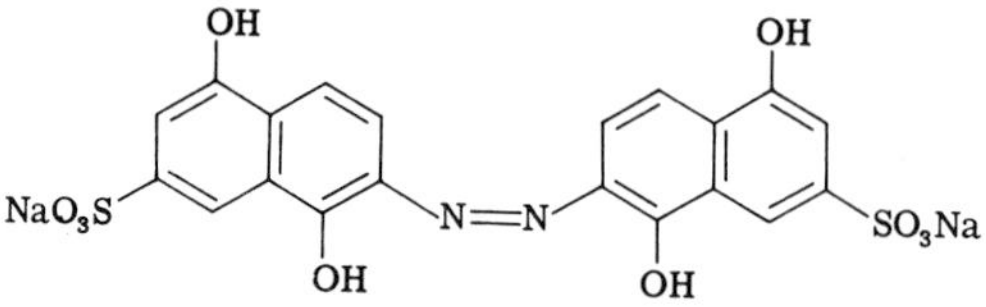

(LXXV) 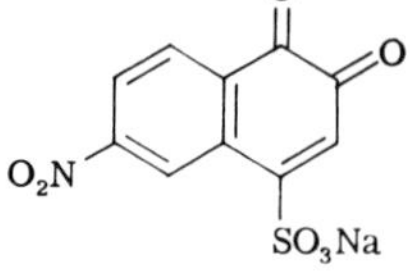   (LXXVI)

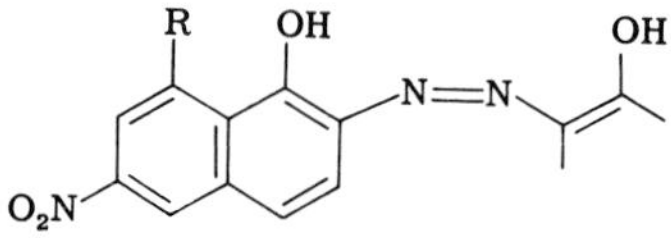

(LXXVII) 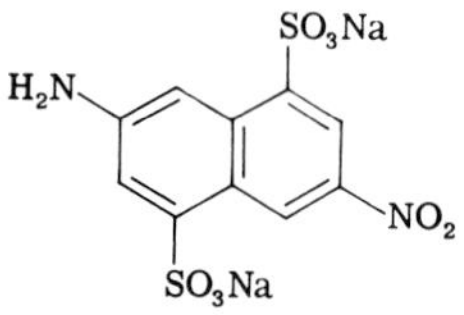   (LXXVIII)

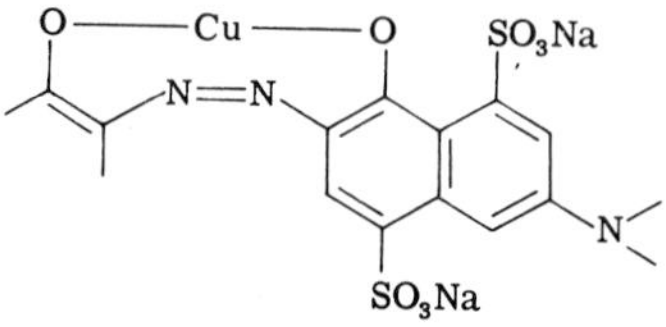

(LXXIX)

A most interesting aspect of work in this area has been concerned with the exploitation of the intermediate 6-nitro-2-naphthylamine-4,8-disulfonic acid (LXXVIII), of which mention has already been made. This intermediate has the nitro and amino groups in the correct 2,6-orientation to confer substantivity on its azo derivatives and furthermore is symmetrical, thus making it possible to arrive at the same compound by conversion of either the amino or nitro group into the azo linkage. The molecule also invites oxidative coppering and presents a most easy way in which to obtain coppered azo derivatives of the general formula (LXXIX). Thus diazotization and coupling of (LXXVIII) onto a naphthol or keto-enolic coupling component followed by oxidative coppering yields the nitro monoazo product

$$(\text{LXXIX};\!-\!\text{N}\diagdown^{\diagup} = -\text{NO}_2).$$

Useful blue and gray dyes result from joining together two molecules of this type by reducing the nitro group to an azo or azoxy link.[169] Alternatively, the nitro group can be reduced, diazotized, and coupled onto an anisidine which on further diazotization and coupling leads to blue twice-coppered trisazo dyes.[170] Co-reduction of coppered nitroazo compounds of formula

$$(\text{LXXIX;}-\text{N}\diagup_{\diagdown} = -\text{NO}_2).$$

with the nitronaphthotriazole (LXXX; R = NO$_2$), converting the nitro groups to azo or azoxy links, yields a green dyeing mixture of isomers.[171] Green coppered disazo triazoles have also been prepared starting from (LXXX; R = NH$_2$).[172] The copper complexes of suitable arylamines → (LXXXI) can be condensed to yield direct dyes of various shades[173]

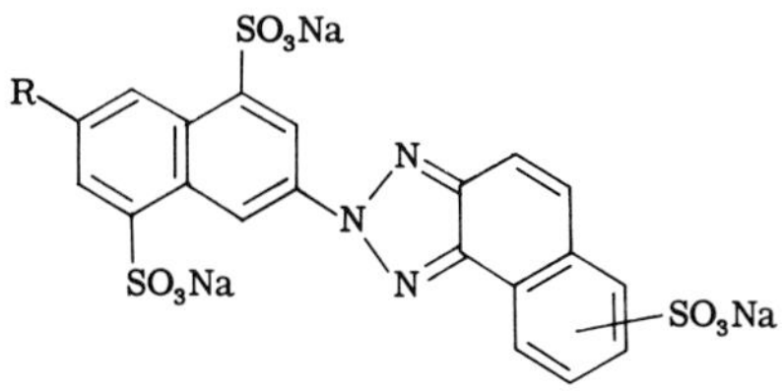

(LXXX) 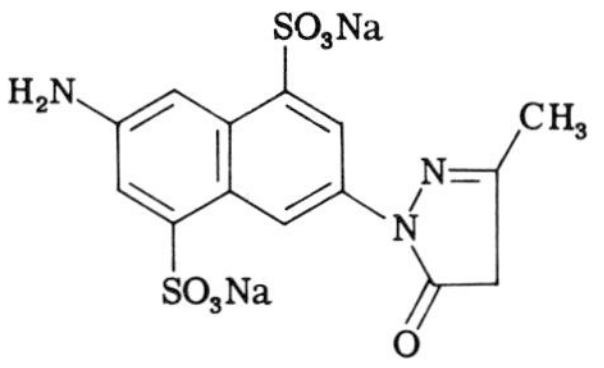   (LXXXI)

and used as A component in the scheme A → anisidine → naphthol sulfonic acid to give twice-coppered trisazo greens.[174]

In addition to these two main areas of research the patent literature has included many further examples of aminoazo compounds converted into substantive entities by reaction with phosgene,[175] fumaroyl chloride,[176] and cyanuric chloride,[177] as well as the use of substantive bis coupling components[178] such as the bis(acetoacetarylamide) derived from 4,4'-diaminostilbene-2,2'-disulfonic acid.[179] Numerous trisazo green and

[169] FBy, *BP* 820,472.
[170] FBy, *BP* 837,996.
[171] FBy, *BP* 864,276.
[172] FBy, *BP* 841,413.
[173] FBy, *BP* 875,672.
[174] FBy, *BP* 901,900.
[175] CIBA, *BP* 684,527; 744,829; 781,484; S, *BP* 695,748; 733,747; 775,048; 835,490; 839,673; FBy, *BP* 819,841.
[176] S, *BP* 698,008; 701,709; 731,199; 733,452; 738,598.
[177] CIBA, *BP* 697,416; S, *BP* 786,663.
[178] S, *BP* 692,465; 726,726; CIBA, *BP* 701,241; 820,950; 823,064; Gy, *BP* 721,486; 813,646.
[179] CIBA, *BP* 679,604.

olive dyes have been described[180] and substantive aminoarylpyrazolones[181] and aminoacetoacetarylamides[182] have been used as a basis for further olive dyes.

A variety of heterocyclic diazo components including 5-amino-1,2,4-triazole and 4-aminobenztriazole[183] as well as aminoindazoles, aminoimidazoles, and aminothiazoles[184] have been used in twice-coupled J-acid schemes to obtain chiefly gray dyes. 4-Benzthiazolylanilines → anisidine → naphthol sulfonic acids have yielded green and olive dyes[185] and 4-benzthiazolyl-2-aminophenol sulfonic acids have been used in brown trisazo dyes.[186] Among the unusual coupling components which have been employed in direct dye synthesis have been 4-benzthiazolylphenyl J- and Gamma-acid,[187] 1-indazyl-3-methyl-5-pyrazolones,[188] hydroxyindazoles, hydroxyacridines, hydroxybenzthiazoles,[189] and 2-hydroxy-4-methyl-(hydroxysulfobenz)quinolines.[190]

B. Azoic Colors

Azoic dyeing and printing have developed over the years as major methods for the coloration of vegetable fibers, in particular cotton, and it is on cotton that these methods remain of prime interest. In recent years, however, the techniques have been varied to meet needs in the synthetic fiber field. Because of differing aims and utility it will be convenient to treat these two fiber groups separately.

1. Cotton

In the azoic process a diazonium salt and a coupling component are caused to react together on the fiber with the production of a water-insoluble azo compound. Two main techniques are available, namely dyeing and printing. In the dyeing method the fiber is impregnated with a substantive coupling component and then passed through a solution

[180] Gy, BP 685,104; 825,431; 828,826; S, BP 722,949; 766,381; CIBA, BP 744,406; 902,228; M. Jirou, V. Urne, and Fran, BP 875,654; 942,151.

[181] CIBA, BP 744,666.

[182] S, BP 723,637; Gy, BP 774,682.

[183] C. Taube, E. Messmer, K.-H. Freytag, and FBy, BP 936,895.

[184] CIBA, BP 695,330; 719,363; 774,916; 806,050.

[185] CIBA, BP 756,599; 781,086.

[186] CIBA, BP 823,053.

[187] CIBA, BP 677,204.

[188] R. R. Davies, N. Legg, and ICI, BP 753,573; R. R. Davies and ICI, BP 760,710.

[189] R. R. Davies, N. Legg, and ICI, BP 748,507; R. R. Davies and ICI, BP 757,727; 760,595.

[190] Gy, BP 822,096.

of diazonium salt. In the printing method the coupling component and a stabilized diazonium salt may most conveniently be applied together and color formation subsequently caused to occur by steaming. Research has had as its chief aims extension of the color range which can be produced by these azoic methods and, particularly in printing, simplification of the method. Recent years have seen considerable progress made in both these respects.

The introduction of the Rapidogen range of azoic colors for printing applications in 1930 marked a considerable step forward in the case of application. This range consisted of standardized mixtures of coupling components of the Naphtol AS type and stabilized diazonium salts. Stabilization of the diazonium salt was achieved by conversion to a water-soluble diazoamino compound (triazene) by reaction with a secondary amine such as sarcosine (LXXXII) containing a carboxylic acid or sulfonic acid group. Other stabilizers included *N*-methyltaurine (LXXXIII) and 2-*N*-ethylamino-5-sulfobenzoic acid (LXXXIV), sec-

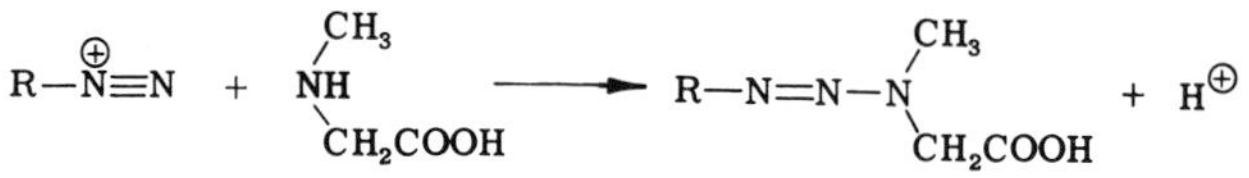

(LXXXII)

$CH_3NHCH_2CH_2SO_3Na$

(LXXXIII)

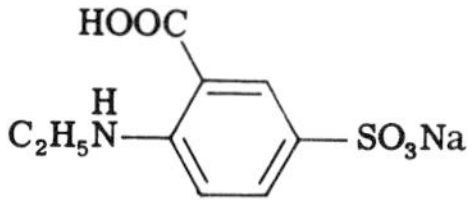

(LXXXIV)

ondary amines being chosen so that prototropy could not lead to the alternative diazoamino compound derived from the diazonium salt of the stabilizer.

The method of application was to print the Rapidogen mixtures onto the cloth and then develop the color by means of an acid steam treatment, acetic or formic acid vapor in the steam regenerating the diazonium salt from the diazoamino compound with resultant coupling to produce the coloration. Since they represented a major advance in ease of application the Rapidogens achieved considerable success. However, they suffered from the disadvantage that the method of development entailed an acid steam treatment which resulted in heavy corrosion of the plant employed. They had the further drawback that they could not be applied simultaneously with vat dyestuffs since these colors require alkaline conditions. A partial solution was afforded by the appearance of the Rapidogen N range in 1952 wherein the use of a modified stabilizer of the type (LXXXV) yielded more labile diazoamino compounds, making the preparations capable of being developed in neutral steam. A satisfactory result could, however, only be obtained when the alkali

HN-Alkyl
COOH
SO$_2$N⟨Alkyl / Alkylene-SO$_3$Na

(LXXXV)

NHCH$_2$COOH
COOH

(LXXXVI)

NHCH$_2$COOH
Cl — COOH
Cl

(LXXXVII)

incorporated in the print paste was kept to the minimum required to dissolve the Naphtol. In the same year a more complete solution was provided by the advent of the Neutrogene range[191] which utilized as stabilizer 2-carboxyphenylglycine (LXXXVI) and its halogenated derivatives such as (LXXXVII).[192] These products were superior both as regards alkali tolerance and also color yield when developed in neutral steam. The ease of scission of the diazoamino compound associated with neutral steam development is, of course, only achieved at the expense of some lowering of the storage stability but this remains quite adequate and does not pose a major disadvantage. The facile splitting of these diazoamino compounds is due, no doubt, partly to the low basicity of the nitrogen atom of the stabilizer and partly to the steric strains, especially in the 2,6-disubstituted alkylaniline structure (LXXXVII). In this context, it is worth noting that not only the stabilizer but also the diazonium salt employed are important in determining the ease with which the diazoamino compound undergoes scission. Thus the diazonium salt derived from 5-chloro-2-methylaniline stabilized with sarcosine (LXXXVIII) splits only slowly, whereas that derived from 5-methyl-2-methoxyaniline (LXXXIX) is much more labile.[193] In general, increasing the basicity of the parent amine of the diazonium salt and decreasing the basicity of the stabilizer lead to easier scission of the derived diazoamino compound. In the development of a uniform series of products both of these factors need to be taken into consideration and a satisfactory balance achieved.

[191] B. Jomain, J. Soc. Dyers Colourists 69, 661 (1953); P. Petitcolas and G. Thirot, Teintex 26, 693 (1961); W. Siegrist, ibid. p. 887; W. Siegrist, Textil-Rundschau 16, 184 (1961).

[192] P. Petitcolas, A. P. Richard, R. F. M. Sureau, R. P. V. Roe, J. E. Develotte, and Fran, BP 729,157; P. Petitcolas, A. P. Richard, R. F. M. Sureau, R. P. V. Roe, and Fran, BP 766,730; 866,510.

[193] C. Streck, Am. Dyestuff Reptr. 53, 865 (1964).

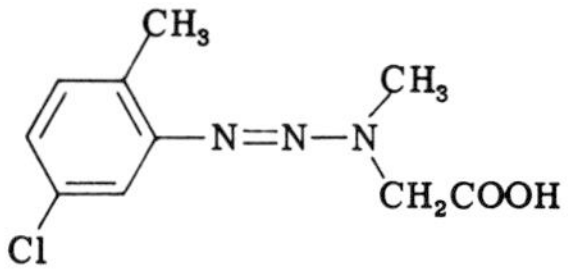

(LXXXVIII)

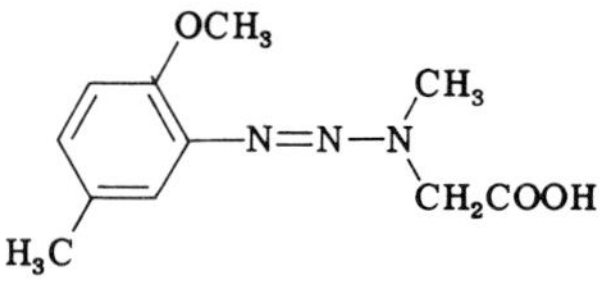

(LXXXIX)

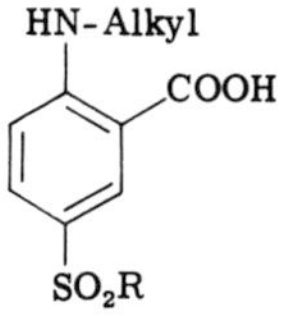

(XC)

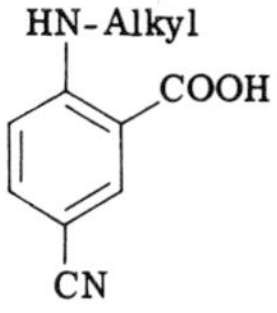

(XCI)

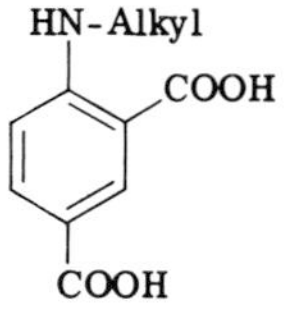

(XCII)

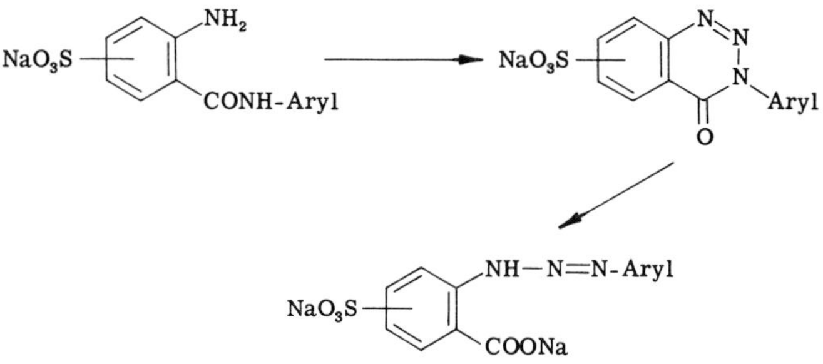

(XCIII)

The attainment of satisfactory neutral steam development by the use of diazoamino compounds based on substituted alkylanthranilic acids as stabilizers has been reflected in the patent literature, which contains numerous examples of compounds of this type. Among those which have been described[194] are the sulfones (XC; R = Alkyl)[195] and sulfonamides [XC; R = NHAlkyl[196] or N(Alkyl)$_2$[197]], 5-cyano-2-alkylaminobenzoic acids[198] (XCI), and 4-alkylaminoisophthalic acids[199] (XCII). In addi-

[194] P. Petitcolas, R. F. M. Sureau, A. P. Richard, R. P. V. Roe, and Fran, *BP* 740,759; P. Petitcolas, R. F. M. Sureau, and Fran, *BP* 771,070; CIBA, *BP* 795,339; FBy, *BP* 808,262; FH, *BP* 897,738.

[195] FBy, *BP* 864,829.

[196] FBy, *BP* 907,817.

[197] RL, *BP* 947,603.

[198] FBy, *BP* 913,100.

[199] P. Petitcolas, R. F. M. Sureau, T. Kantor, and Fran, *BP* 766,609.

tion, reexamination of the sulfonated alkylanthranilic acids [e.g., (LXXXIV)] has shown that they also can function in this way.[200] A novel variation has been the use of the cyclic compounds (XCIII) obtained by treating arylamides of sulfonated anthranilic acids with nitrous acid.[201] These react with caustic alkali in the print paste, forming a diazoamino compound which leads to color development in the normal manner on steaming, the liberated diazonium salt being derived from what was initially the arlyamide fragment. Improved stability is claimed for these cyclic compounds but it is not clear whether this is gained at the expense of neutral steam development properties. This system was used for members of the Pologen range of azoic colors. To further facilitate the work of the printer, solutions of diazoamino compounds and coupling components have been provided[202] containing all the ingredients required in the preparation of a print paste. These solutions, in a suitable organic solvent, e.g., ethylene glycol, reduce print paste preparation to a single weighing and thus avoid possible errors on the part of the printer as well as relieving him of the task of working with solid diazoamino compounds, which can be unpleasant to handle.

Research on azoic combinations aimed chiefly at widening the shade range which can be obtained has covered a wide area. An important feature of azoic dyeing is the high substantivity displayed by many of the arylamides of 2-hydroxy-3-naphthoic acid (Naphtols). This substantivity varies according to the arylamine which is condensed with 2-hydroxy-3-naphthoic acid; a measurement of the substantivity can conveniently be obtained from the R_f values of these compounds on paper chromatography.[203] The literature reveals a variety of further arylamines such as 5-aminoacenaphthene,[204] 6-aminoindazoles,[205] 4- and 5-aminobenzimidazolones,[206] and 2-aminothiophenes[207] which have been used for this purpose. 4-Aminodiphenyl yields a very substantive Naphtol capable of giving blacks and deep browns of good fastness properties[208] and

[200] FBy, BP 762,269; 771,812; 778,928; 788,689; 788,689; 843,241.

[201] S. Pizon and Instytut Barwnikow I Polyproduktow, BP 996,243.

[202] P. Petitcolas, A. P. Richard, and Fran, BP 900,402.

[203] S. Plesnik and I. Cepciansky, Sb. Ved. Praci, Vysoka Skola Chem.-Technol., Pardubice Part 1, 89 (1961); Chem. Abstr. 58, 5821h (1963).

[204] K. Murata and H. Mitoguchi, Hiroshima Daigaku Kogakubu Kenkyu Hokoku 10, 69 (1961); Chem. Abstr. 56, 1556e (1962).

[205] D. A. W. Adams, E. G. Bainbridge, H. B. Bradley, R. R. Davies, and ICI, BP 707,897; FH, BP 864,228.

[206] FH, BP 978,094; 996,075.

[207] R. S. Long and CCC, USP 2,625,542.

[208] T. Maki and K. Obayashi, J. Chem. Soc. Japan, Ind. Chem. Sect. 55, 401 (1952); Chem. Abstr. 48, 1005g (1954).

condensation of 2-hydroxy-3-naphthoic acid with 1-aminophenyl-3-methyl-4-arylazo-5-pyrazolones yields Naphtols (XCIV) capable of giving green shades with diazotized 2-alkoxy-4-arylazo-1-naphthylamines.[209] The structure of Naphtols has been varied by using new o-hydroxycarboxylic acids as well as new arylamides, the aim being the production of brown shades. Thus the benztriazole[210] (XCV) and benzonaphthofuran[211] (XCVI) derivatives have been used as a basis for browns and an improvement in properties of the carbazole browns results from the use of the pendant arylamine shown in what is said to be (XCVII);[212] recent NMR studies show, however, that the parent hydroxycarbazole carboxylic acid is the 2:1 isomer and not the 2:3 isomer as previously assumed.[212a,b,c]

These are classic azoic coupling component structures; similarly the yellow-producing components benz(4-acetoacetylamino)anilide[213] and 2-acetoacetylaminothiophen[214] are of conventional design. A number of more novel coupling components have been described, for example, 4,4'-

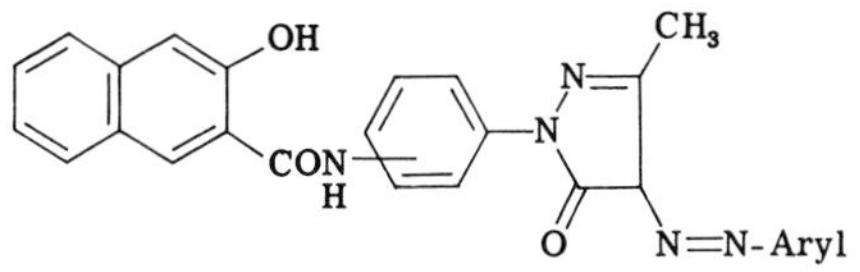

(XCIV)

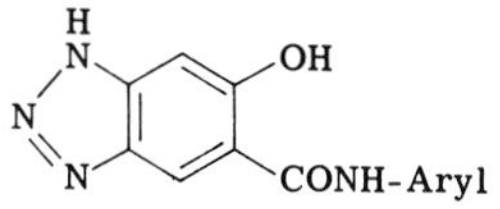

(XCV)

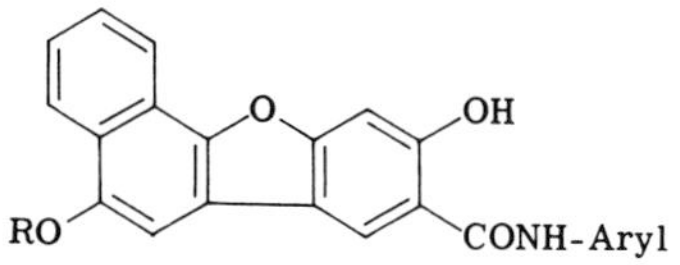

(XCVI)

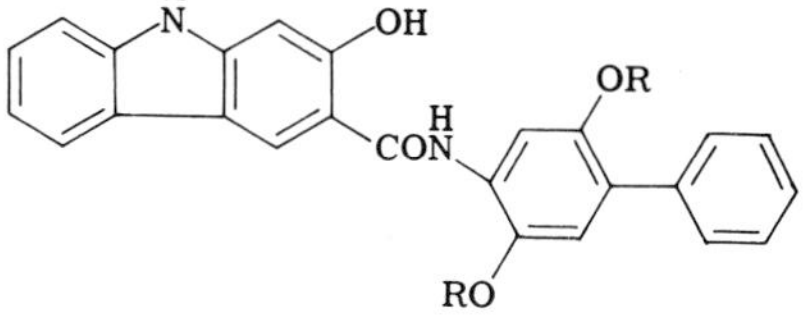

(XCVII)

[209] FH, *BP* 759,353.

[210] M. Scalera, F. H. Adams, and CCC, *USP* 2,675,376.

[211] R. S. Long, B. G. Buell, and CCC, *USP* 2,893,986.

[212] FBy, *BP* 851,538.

[212a] R. L. M. Allen and P. Hampson, private communication (1968).

[212b] B. S. Joshi, V. N. Kamat, and D. F. Rane, *J. Chem. Soc.* C, 1518 (1969).

[212c] M. R. R. Bhagwanth, A. V. Rama Rao, and K. Venkataraman, *Indian J. Chem.* **7**, 1065 (1969).

[213] CIBA, *BP* 821,029.

[214] R. S. Long and CCC, *USP* 2,625,541.

diphenylolpropane[215] (XCVIII), which is said to have a substantivity of the same order as the simple Naphtols,[216] and the polymeric arylamide (XCIX) derived from 4-amino-2-hydroxybenzoic acid.[217] 5-Arylamino-2-naphthols[218] including dimeric products formed from polyfunctional acylating agents such as terephthaloyl chloride[219] and cyanuric chloride[220] have been employed, as well as 8-arylazo-5-amino-2-naphthols, which give olives, browns, and blacks.[221] 3-Hydroxydiphenylamine[222] or 3-hydroxydibenzofuran[223] applied together with a Naphtol give full black shades on development with tetrazotized dianisidine.

Parallel research into diazo components has similarly covered a wide field. In simple arylamines, fluorine and trifluromethyl substituents are said to encourage brightness of shade.[224] The interest in deep shades is evidenced by the use of 2-amino-1,4-dimethoxyacridone[225] (C), 4-benzoxazol-2'-ylamino-2,5-dimethoxyaniline[226] (CI), and the related 4-2'-quinonyl compound[227] as diazo components and the diaminobenzanthrone[228] (CII) as tetrazo component for the preparation of blue azoic dyeings with Naphtols. The aminoazo compound (CIII) obtained by reduction of 4-nitro-2,5-dimethoxyaniline → acetoacetanilide also yields blue shades with Naphtols[229] and red dyeings with acetoacetarylamides[230] and a series of o-aminoazo compounds of structure (CIV)[231] have been described for the production of green and brown azoic dyeings.[232]

In other classes of dyestuffs, metallization of suitably substituted azo

[215] V. N. Klyuev and L. A. Dogadkina, Izv. Vysshikh Ucheb. Zavedenii, Tekhnol. Tekstil'n. Prom. No. 5, 113 (1961); Chem. Abstr. 56, 10325g (1962).
[216] V. N. Klyuev and T. S. Meshkova, Izv. Vysshikh, Ucheb. Zavedenii, Tekhnol. Tekstil'n Prom. No. 3, 113 (1960); Chem. Abstr. 54, 25839g (1960).
[217] H. Z. Lecher, B. G. Buell, and CCC, USP 2,841,575.
[218] CIBA, BP 700,024.
[219] FH, BP 706,586.
[220] FH, BP 718,560.
[221] Hooker Chemical Corp., BP 893,216.
[222] FH, BP 900,854.
[223] FH, BP 897,738.
[224] K. Inukai and K. Hosokawa, Kogyo Kagaku Zasshi 59, 441 (1956); Chem. Abstr. 52, 2412c (1958); J. Nishino, N. Kuroki, and K. Konishi, ibid. 62, 709 (1959); Chem. Abstr. 57, 13921g (1962); FH, BP 866,781.
[225] F. Brody and CCC, USP 2,725,375.
[226] F. Brody, R. S. Long, and CCC, USP 2,725,377.
[227] F. Brody and CCC, USP 2,725,376.
[228] S. M. Tsang and CCC, USP 2,821,533.
[229] FH, BP 780,484.
[230] FH, BP 760,574; 770,046.
[231] FH, BP 850,317; 896,111.
[232] FH, BP 860,995; 893,166; 896,112; 905,040.

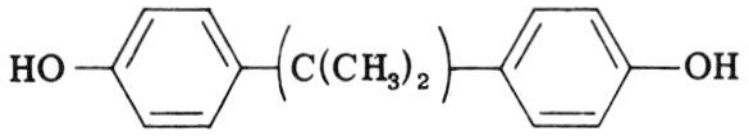

HO—⟨ ⟩—(C(CH₃)₂)—⟨ ⟩—OH

(XCVIII)

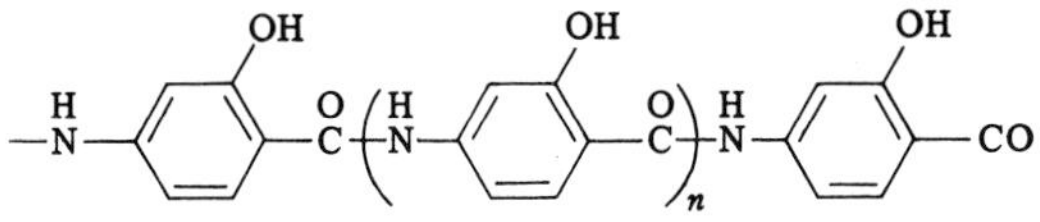

(XCIX)

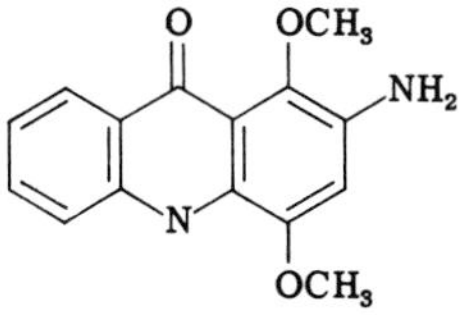

(C)

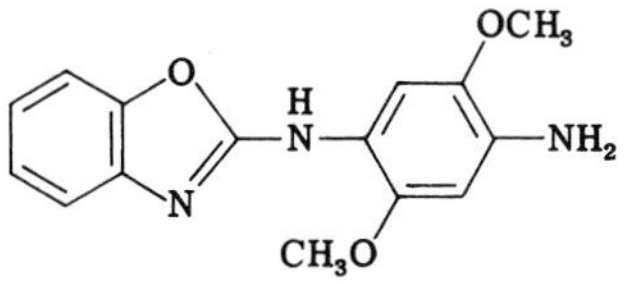

(CI)

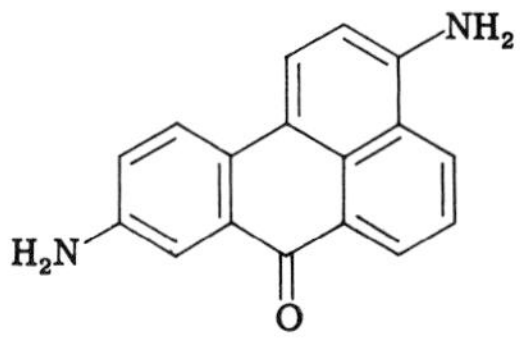

(CII)

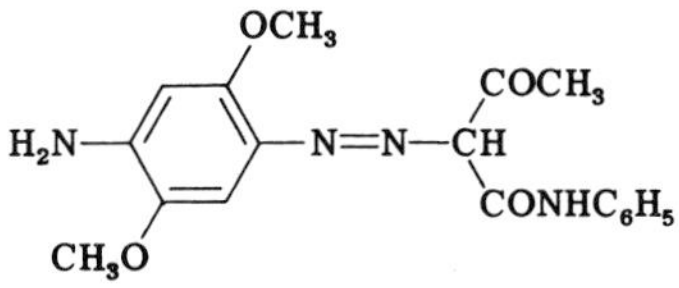

(CIII)

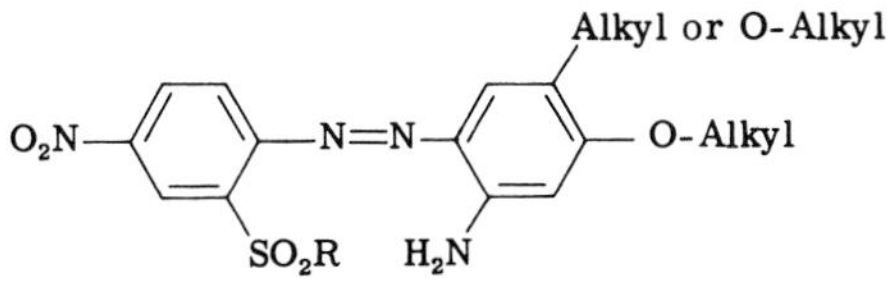

(CIV)

compounds has been invaluable as a method for attaining deep shades of high lightfastness. Recently, chiefly with the aim of achieving this type of shade, considerable interest has been displayed in building into azoic dyes metal complex-forming systems. Work has proceeded in two ways. In the first approach attempts to use coupling components which already contain a metallized azo linkage in azoic dyeing have been made. Initially metal complexes of simple o-aminophenols → resorcinol were suggested.[233] Thus the copper complex of 4-chloro-2-aminophenol → resorcinol applied to the fiber and developed with diazonium salts yields yellow-brown shades. Variations which have been explored involve the use of heterocyclic amines → resorcinol[234] as, for instance, in the case of the copper complex of 7-amino-5-chlorobenzimidazole → resorcinol, which yields browns and blacks with diazonium salts, and the copper complex of o-aminophenols → 2,4-dihydroxybenzophenone, which again develops to brown with a diazonium salt.[235] So far this method appears to have met with little success, probably because the coupling components employed have too low an order of substantivity for satisfactory performance in the azoic dyeing process. The alternative approach has been to design suitable azoic diazo components containing a metal complex-forming substituent located ortho to the amino group. These can then be used in conjunction with a conventional Naphtol coupling component and the dyeing after metallized. This has been the more successful approach and three such diazo components, Variogen Bases I, II, and III, have been introduced commercially by Hoechst.[236] The first of these yields deep green shades and the other two produce browns when the azoic dyeings are aftertreated with a variety of metals including copper, chromium, and cobalt. The patent literature discloses a variety of amino heterocyclic compounds[237] which are described for this purpose. These include the aminocarbazole (CV),[238] 7-aminobenzimidazoles (CVI; X = CH) and 7-aminobenztriazoles (CVI; X = N),[239] and the triazole

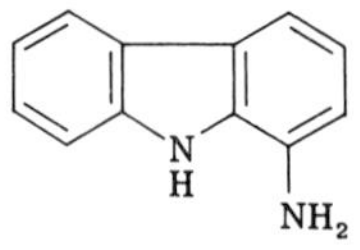

(CV) 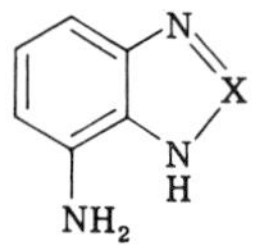   (CVI) 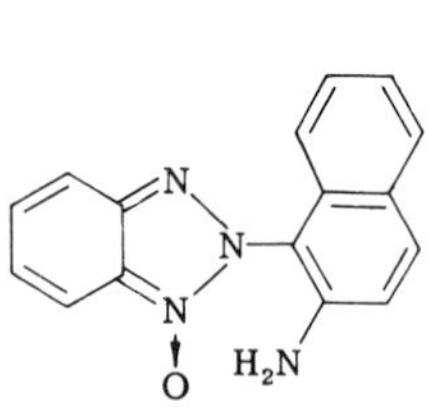   (CVII)

[233] C. Streck and G, USP 2,515,743; P. Petitcolas, R. F. M. Sureau, J. N. Cyna, and Fran, BP 830,970.

[234] R. F. M. Sureau, J. N. Blum, and Fran, BP 806,166; Fran, BP 1,062,776.

[235] FH, BP 893,574.

[236] D. Gross, Textil-Praxis 15, 1046 (1960); W. Staab, Melliand Textilber. 44, 978 (1963).

[237] FH, BP 974,108; 976,082; 976,399; 996,242.

[238] F. Muth, K. H. Gehringer, and FBy, BP 939,454.

[239] FH, BP 973,356.

oxides (CVII),[240] which yield dark, predominantly brown shades on after-metallization.

The phthalocyanine system, with its excellent shade and lightfastness properties, has also attracted attention and new ways to utilize this chromophore in azoic dyeing have been sought. The approach has been to build the copper phthalocyanine nucleus into an azoic coupling component by either treating aminomethyl phthalocyanines[241] with diketene and thus introducing a number of acetoacetylaminomethyl groups[242] or to condense a phthalocyanine sulfonyl chloride with an aminoacetoacetanilide, aminopyrazolone, or aminonaphthol.[243] When the coupling system built on is of the acetoacetanilide or pyrazolone type green shades can be produced.[244] Some success would seem to have attended these efforts, both the green-producing coupling component Naphtol AS-FGGR and the azoic printing combination Rapidogen Brilliant Green N-16G being probably based on components of this type.

2. Synthetic Fibers

The advent of synthetic fibers saw the development of special classes of dyestuffs designed for their coloration; while the dye classes which can be applied vary from fiber to fiber according to its nature, the disperse dyes emerge as a fairly common denominator for application to the majority of synthetic fibers and indeed with some of the fibers are practically the only useful class of dyestuff. The disperse dyes initially were of fairly small molecular size in order to achieve satisfactory dye uptake by the fiber and it was difficult to prepare dyes of this type capable of yielding the deep shades, particularly navy blue and black. For this reason and also because of the general utility of azoic colors in providing these shades on cotton azoic dyeing, processes were developed, rather as a necessary evil, for the production of deep shades on synthetic fibers.

On cotton, azoic dyeing owes its efficiency to the high substantivity of many of the Naphtol AS derivatives and their excellent exhaustion from alkaline solution onto the hydrophilic cotton fiber. This phenomenon, of such advantage on cotton, is directly contrary to what is required with a hydrophobic synthetic fiber. Such fibers, e.g., polyester, normally satisfactorily adsorb only dispersed, water-insoluble organic substances. Of the components used in the azoic process, the one which would ob-

[240] FH, *BP* 951,452; 973,884.
[241] FBy, *BP* 717,137; 724,212.
[242] FBy, *BP* 858,070.
[243] FBy, *BP* 811,221.
[244] FBy, *BP* 811,222.

viously be most satisfactorily adsorbed is the amine. At first this was made use of by employing an inverse azoic method wherein the amine was adsorbed onto the fiber, diazotized on the fiber, and color subsequently developed by treatment with an azoic coupling component. This process, on cellulose acetate, was the first widely used azoic process. The difficulty of adsorption of the coupling component was, however, only postponed in this process and still had to be faced later on. To achieve satisfactory uptake it was necesssary to move away from the classic type of coupling component and instead use a fine dispersion of 2-hydroxy-3-naphthoic acid, which could be satisfactorily adsorbed at about pH 3.5, to develop the color. This method was also applied to nylon, where azoic dyes give satisfactory coverage of barré nylon allied to high wet-fastness. On nylon the diazotization step was difficult and presented a further drawback to the process. Obsolescence of the method saved polyester fibers and cellulose triacetate from being dyed by this process.

The logical extension from this state of affairs was to progress to a simultaneous technique in which dispersions of the amine and 2-hydroxy-3-naphthoic acid were applied together and, when satisfactory adsorption of the two components had taken place, the adsorbed amine was diazotized and the color developed. While apparently satisfactory this method suffered from the drawback of formation of tars in the initial bath by interaction of the basic amine with the acidic coupling component. This necessitated a retrograde switch to a two-bath adsorption technique, the components being adsorbed onto the fiber each in a separate vessel. This type of process ousted the inverse method for azoic dyeing of synthetic fibers and was applied to cellulose acetate, nylon, cellulose triacetate, and polyester fibers. The simultaneous process outlined was still far from ideal but could conveniently be improved in the modified simultaneous process. In this process the coupling component and a diazoamino compound free from water-solubilizing groups are adsorbed and the color developed by steaming.[245] Suitable diazoamino compounds can be prepared by reacting the diazotized arylamine with secondary amines such as diethylamine[246] or diethanolamine[247] or with cyanamide or guanidine.[248] This modified simultaneous method remains the most convenient manner in which to carry out azoic dyeing on a wide range of synthetic fibers. Further improvements in both simultane-

[245] T. C. Nichol, G. S. J. White, and ICI, BP 539,195; H. R. Hadfield and ICI, BP 712,414.
[246] FBy, BP 874,118.
[247] FH, BP 833,669.
[248] H. R. Hadfield, N. Legg, and ICI, BP 730,653.

ous techniques have been gained by the use of carriers such as diethyl-phthalate, tetrahydronaphthalene,[249] and aryl benzoates[250] to aid adsorption of the coupling component. This has permitted more choice of coupling components and in particular has allowed 2-hydroxy-3-naphthoic arylamides to be used in the processes. High-temperature applications to polyester fiber have also allowed this greater selection of coupling components to be used in the simultaneous method.

In the patent literature conventional combinations are exemplified for the production of deep shades by these methods. Several patents relate to aminoazo compounds which have good affinity for polyester fiber at high temperatures as diazo components.[251] In addition, a number of novel coupling components such as 2-hydroxy-3-naphthoic alkyl-

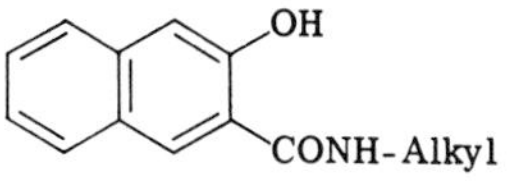

(CVIII) 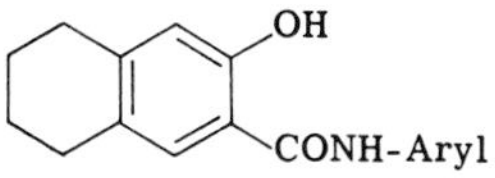   (CIX)

amides (CVIII)[252] and 2-hydroxy-3-tetrahydronaphthoic acid aryl-amides (CIX)[247] have been designed to facilitate adsorption by the fiber. Coupling components containing an amino group have been specified for application to the fiber, diazotization, and self-coupling,[253] and reaction of a nitroso compound and amine on polyester fiber to produce a black has been described.[254]

---

[249] FH, *BP* 872,948.
[250] FH, *BP* 824,269.
[251] FH, *BP* 874,025; 876,000; 896,605; 910,026.
[252] FH, *BP* 809,221.
[253] FH, *BP* 863,329.
[254] C. M. Harmuth and DuP, *USP* 3,081,141.

CHAPTER VII

THE CHEMISTRY OF METAL COMPLEX DYESTUFFS

R. Price

RESEARCH DEPARTMENT, IMPERIAL CHEMICAL INDUSTRIES, DYESTUFFS DIVISION,
HEXAGON HOUSE, BLACKLEY, MANCHESTER, ENGLAND

I. Introduction

One of the most fascinating features of modern chemistry is the ever-increasing academic and commercial interest enjoyed by metal complexes of organic compounds. Their importance is well known in many fields including catalysis, biology, and the technology of dyes and pigments, where considerable progress has been made during the past few decades. Some indication of the importance of metal complexes in the latter field is afforded by the wide variety of metal complex dyes and pigments which have been employed commercially. These include copper, chromium, and cobalt complexes of *o,o'*-dihydroxyazo (I), *o*-carboxy-*o'*-hydroxyazo (II), and *o*-amino-*o'*-hydroxyazo (III) dyestuffs, various metal lakes of *o*-hydroxyazo compounds (IV), copper complexes of arylazo-8-hydroxyquinolines (V) and arylazosalicylaldoximes (VI), chromium complexes of arylazosalicylic acid (VII), iron complexes of nitrosonaphthols (VIII) and nitrosohydroxyindazoles (IX), copper, nickel, and iron complexes of nitrosated arylazoresorcinols [(X) and

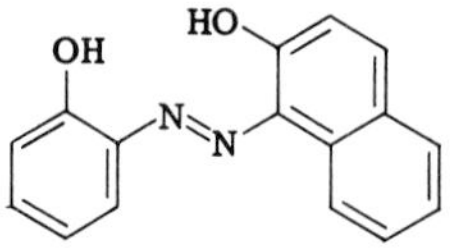

(I) 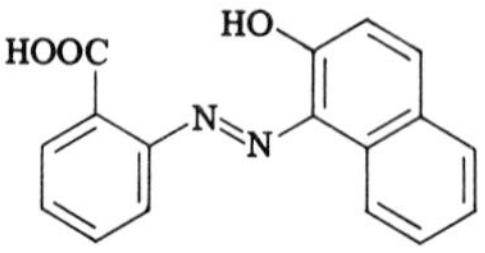   (II) 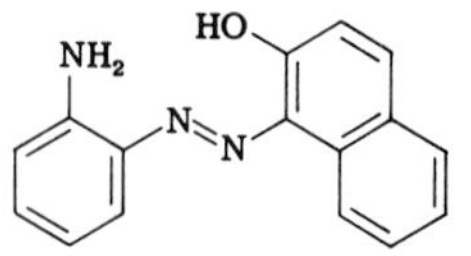   (III)

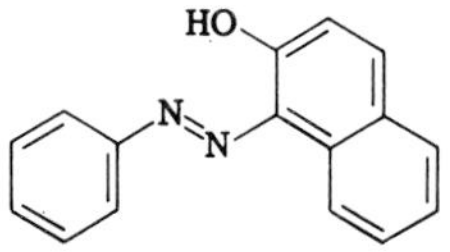

(IV) 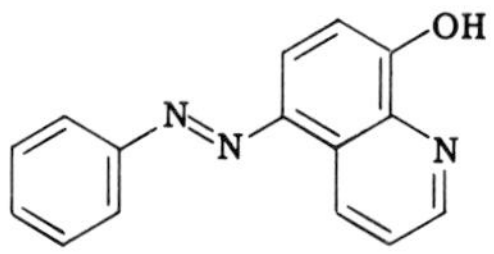   (V) 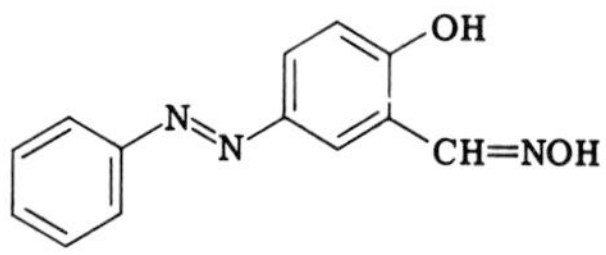   (VI)

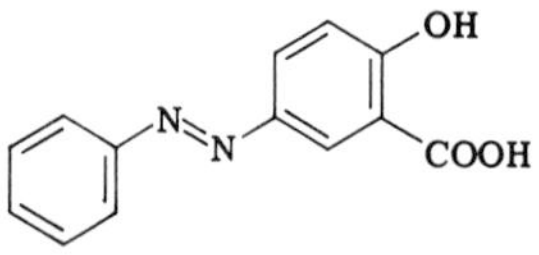

(VII) 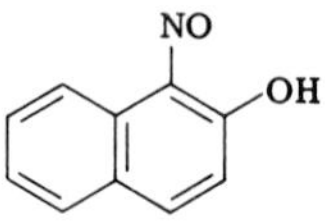   (VIII) 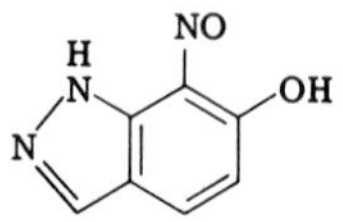   (IX)

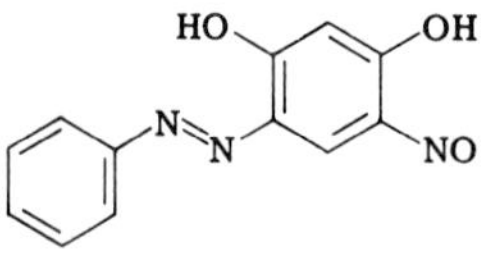

(X) 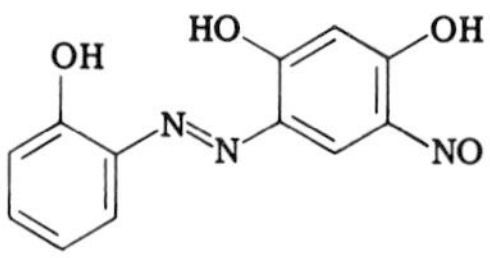   (XI) 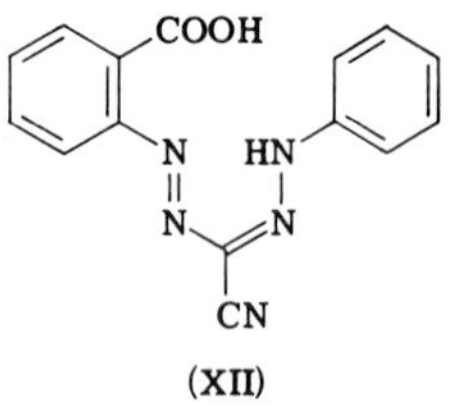   (XII)

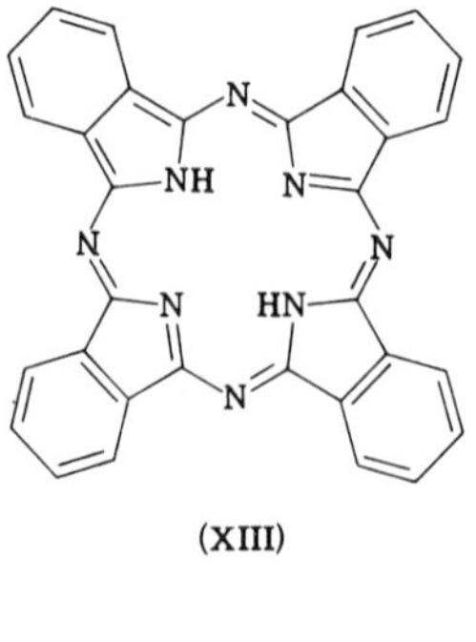

(XIII)

(XI)], copper, chromium, and cobalt complexes of formazans [e.g., (XII)], and the copper complex of phthalocyanine (XIII).

Throughout the history of synthetic dyestuffs one of the aims of the dyestuffs chemist has been to simplify the work of the dyer by improving dyeing methods and making possible the achievement of consistent results in an economic manner. A good example of the success that has been achieved is provided by the premetallized chromium complex dyestuffs. These were developed to replace metallizable dyes which were applied to mordanted wool or were metallized on the fiber in a single bath process (metachrome process), or by an aftertreatment process (afterchrome process). Although dyeings with excellent fastness properties were obtained by these methods the achievement of consistent results, particularly in the afterchrome process, was complicated by the shade change which occurred on metallization.

The first step towards achieving this success was taken as long ago as 1919 when the Swiss firm CIBA, and the IG in Germany introduced their Neolan and Palatine Fast ranges of 1:1 chromium complex azo dyestuffs, e.g., (XIV). Although dyestuffs of this type are still widely used their main disadvantage is that their application to wool requires a strongly acid dyebath which results in damage to the wool and impairment of its soft handle.

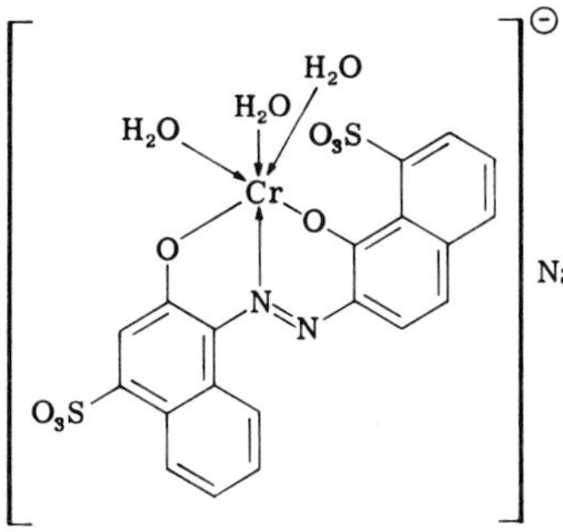

(XIV) 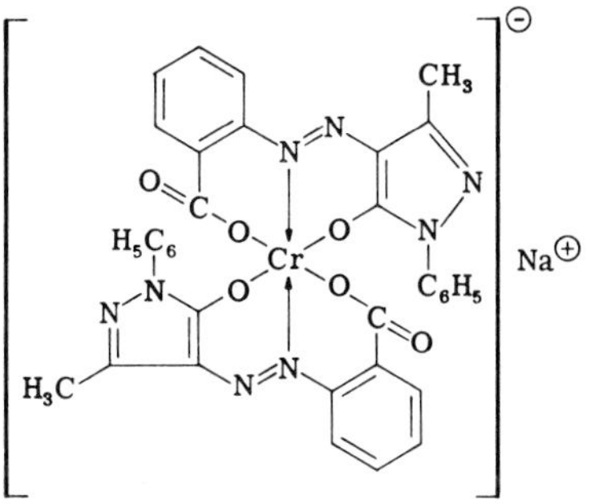   (XV)

In the late 1930s the German dyestuffs manufacturers began to place on the market a limited range of 2:1 chromium, e.g., (XV), and cobalt complexes for the dyeing of nylon, an application for which they were particularly suitable since they could be applied from an almost neutral dyebath. For the dyeing of wool they were applied from a moderately acid dyebath which did not impair the softness of the wool. However, the solubility of complexes of this type was rather inadequate for wool dyestuffs and in 1949 Geigy introduced the first example of a 2:1 chromium complex dyestuff having enhanced solubility derived from nonionic solubilizing groups. This was to become the first member of their Irgalan range of dyestuffs which are 2:1 chromium and cobalt complex dyestuffs containing methylsulfonyl groups and which are recommended for the fast dyeing of wool from neutral or weakly acid baths. The history of this development is well documented[1] and forms the subject of an excellent review by Schetty.[2] This lead was quickly followed by other dyestuffs manufactures with ranges of neutral dyeing 2:1 chromium and cobalt complex azo dyestuffs containing nonionic solubilizing groups such as the sulfonamide group.

A further advance followed from the observation[3] that 1:1 chromium complex dyestuffs react with a second molecule of the metal-free azo dyestuff to give 2:1 chromium complexes. In an extension of this[4] 1:1 chromium complex dyestuffs are treated with an equimolecular quantity of a different metallizable azo dyestuff to obtain unsymmetrical 2:1 chromium complexes (Section II,C,4,a,vi) containing a single sulfonic acid group. Dyestuffs of this type dye wool in level shades of good fastness properties from neutral or weakly acid dyebaths. In addition to extending the range of shades available, this advance permitted the preparation of dyestuffs having adequate water solubility and good dyeing properties without recourse to the use of relatively expensive intermediates containing sulfonamide or alkyl sulfonyl groups.

More recently the use of premetallized 2:1 chromium complex dyestuffs containing fiber-reactive groups has been established by ICI with their Procilan range.[5] Dyes of this type combine chemically with the wool fiber to give dyeings having wet-fastness properties which are superior to those of dyeings derived from nonreactive premetallized dyestuffs, particularly to repeated washing and severe wet treatments such as potting.

2:1 Chromium and cobalt complex azo dyestuffs have little or no affinity for cellulosic fibers and until recently their use has been restricted

---

[1] J. G. Grundy, *Dyer* **108**, 685 (1952); W. Widmer and E. Krähenbühl, *Textil-Praxis* **8**, 491 (1953); R. Casty, *SVF Fachorgan Textilveredlung* **8**, 132 and 189 (1953); C. Weidmann, *Am. Dyestuff Reptr.* **43**, 167 (1954); T. Eggar and R. Casty, *Teintex* **19**, 227 (1954); H. F. Clapham, *Am. Dyestuff Reptr.* **43**, 200 (1954); H. Pfitzner, *Melliand Textilber.* **35**, 649 (1954); J. F. Gaunt, *J. Soc. Dyers Colourists* **74**, 569 (1958); H. Zollinger, *Textil-Rundschau* **13**, 217, (1958); A. J. Hall, *Textile Recorder* **80**, 52 (1962); W. Beal, *Dyer* **131**, 198 (1964).

[2] G. Schetty, *J. Soc. Dyers Colourists* **71**, 705 (1955).

[3] H. D. K. Drew and R. E. Fairbairn, *J. Chem. Soc.* p. 823 (1939).

[4] CIBA, *BP* 765,355.

[5] *Dyer* **130**, 891 (1963); A. N. Derbyshire and J. G. Graham, *ibid.* **131**, 31 (1964); M. D. R. Lemin, *Teintex* **31**, 19 (1966); A. N. Derbyshire and G. R. Tristram, *J. Soc. Dyers Colourists* **81**, 584 (1965).

to wool and nylon. With the introduction by ICI of the Procion ranges of reactive dyes, however, their use was extended to cellulosic fibers on which they give prints of excellent fastness to light and to wet treatments.

Notable advances have also been made in the field of copper complex azo dyestuffs, early work on which has been reviewed by several authors.[6] It has been known for many years that the lightfastness of certain dyes such as (XVI) can be improved by aftertreatment with copper salts but on repeated washing the lightfastness falls. This is due to the lack of stability of the copper complexes formed on the fiber by the aftertreatment process. Dyestuffs containing the *o*-alkoxy-*o'*-hydroxy azo system can be demethylatively coppered to give the copper complex of the corresponding *o*-*o'*-dihydroxyazo compound which is quite stable (Section II,C,4,*c,i*). Under the relatively mild conditions employed in the aftercoppering process, however, demethylation does not occur and the products which are obtained are complexes in which the azo compound functions as a bidentate [*o*-hydroxyazo (Section II,B,1)], or a feeble tridentate [*o*-methoxy-*o'*-hydroxyazo (Section II,C,5,*b*)] ligand and which are unstable to repeated washing.

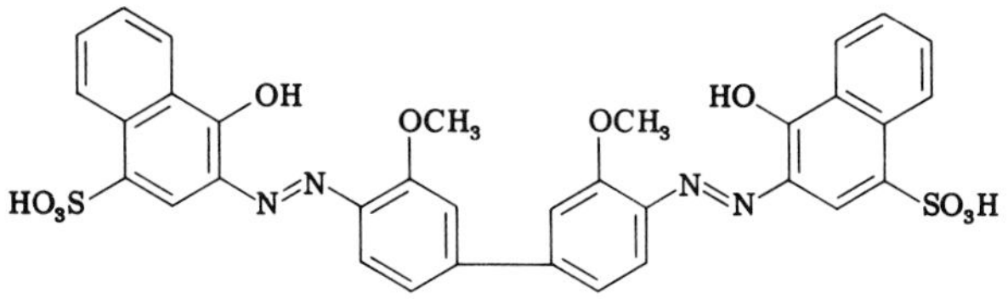

(XVI)

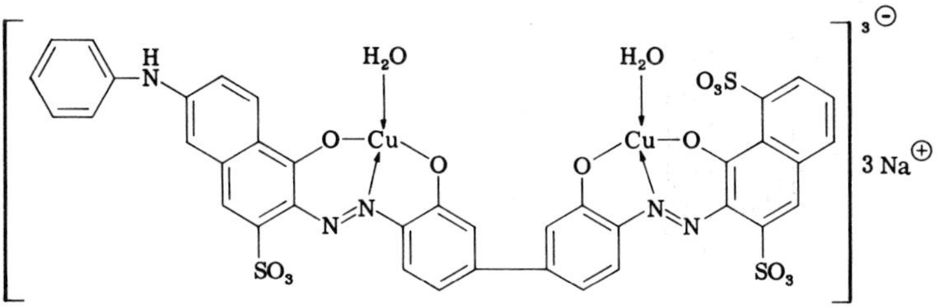

(XVII)

[6] E. D. G. Frahm, *Chem. Weekblad* **48**, 127 (1952); H. C. Puper, *Tex* **21**, 322 (1962).

The term "stability" is widely used throughout this review and in order to avoid confusion the sense in which it is used will be clarified at this stage. The statement that a particular metal complex has inadequate stability to be of value as a dyestuff in no way implies that the complex is thermodynamically unstable, but simply that it undergoes demetallization under dyebath conditions or during aftertreatment processes. For example, copper complexes of o-hydroxyazo dyestuffs are thermodynamically stable compounds and can be crystallized unchanged from a variety of solvents. They are, however, readily demetallized under relatively mild conditions and this makes them of no value as dyestuffs.

Following this observation a large number of water-soluble copper complexes of tridentate azo dyestuffs such as Sirius Supra Blue FBGL (Bayer) (XVII) were marketed. Such dyes are generally very fast to light but only moderately fast to washing because of the solubility of the complexes. This problem was met by the Benzo Fast Copper (IG), the Coprantine (CIBA) and the Cuprophenyl (Geigy) dyes, which are applied by the usual method for direct cotton dyes and converted to insoluble copper complexes on the fiber by an aftertreatment with a copper salt. However, a disadvantage of dyes of this type is that in many cases copper complex formation is accompanied by a considerable change in color, making shade matching difficult. Further work in this field (Section II,B,2) culminated in copper complex dyestuffs containing fiber-reactive groups, such as certain members of ICI's Procion ranges, which give dyeings on cellulosic fibers having excellent fastness to light and to wet treatments.

One interesting application of metallizable dyestuffs is in the dyeing of polypropylene. Polypropylene is a very hydrophobic fiber and contains no dye-receptor sites and cannot, therefore, be dyed with conventional dyestuffs. Since it has been forecast[7] that annual consumption of polypropylene in the United States alone may well reach 175–200 million pounds by 1970, dyestuffs manufacturers have been inspired to devote a considerable amount of research effort to attempts to solve this problem. One solution has been to use water-insoluble metallizable dyestuffs which become fixed within the fiber by coordination with small amounts of metal salts which may be present as residual catalysts or as additives.[8] The patent literature on this subject covers a wide variety of metallizable azo dyestuffs in addition to other metallizable dyes, such as anthra-

[7] Daily News Record [8] p. 27 (1962).

[8] F. L. Sievenpiper, R. Dawson, N. L. Andrews, and P. Stright, Dyer 128, 667 (1962); H. Leube, Melliand Textilber. 46, 743 (1965); H. P. Baumann, Am. Dyestuff Reptr. 52, 527 (1963).

quinones, in conjunction with a variety of metals, the most favored being nickel.

It is not the purpose of this review to present a detailed account of the history and technology of metal complex dyestuffs, since many comprehensive reviews on this subject are available,[2,9,9a,b] but advances such as these illustrate the value of the large amount of research which has been carried out on this subject over the years. It is as a result of this research that metal complex dyestuffs today occupy a very important place in dyestuffs technology and find application in many other fields, such as analysis. It is the aim of the author to survey and review the more recent advances in the field of metal complex dyestuffs with special reference to mechanistic and structural aspects of the subject matter.

II. Metal Complexes of Azo Dyestuffs

There can be little doubt that, with the possible exception of copper phthalocyanine, metal complex azo compounds are by far the most important and widely used metal complex dyes and pigments. Metal complex azo compounds may be divided conveniently into two classes: those in which the azo group forms a part of the metallizable system, and those in which it does not. The former class is the more important and is derived from azo dyestuffs having metallizable substituents in at least one ortho position relative to the azo group (XVIII). Substituents other than those in (XVIII) are encountered (Sections II,C,4,c,iv,b–f) but have little commercial application. Other dyestuffs of this type have a heterocyclic nitrogen atom in an appropriate position relative to the azo group for chelation to occur (Section II,C,5,c,iv,a).

Metal complex azo dyestuffs in which the azo group does not form a part of the chelating system are far less important commercially, and are obtained from azo dyes derived from metallizable coupling components such as salicylic acid (XIX), 8-hydroxyquinoline, salicylaldehyde, and salicylaldoxime.

The metals most commonly used are chromium and cobalt in the field

[9] R. Specklin, *Teintex* **15**, 451 (1950); K. Venkataraman, "The Chemistry of Synthetic Dyes," Vols. I and II. Academic Press, New York, 1952; H. Pfitzner, *Melliand Textilber.* **35**, 649 (1954); R. D. Johnson and N. C. Nielsen, *in* "The Chemistry of the Coordination Compounds" (J. C. Bailar, ed.), p. 743, Reinhold, New York, 1956; O. Stallmann, *J. Chem. Educ.* **37**, 220 (1960); H. Zollinger, "Chemie der Azofarbstoffe." Birkhäuser, Basel, 1958; H. Wahl, *Teintex* **28**, 257 (1963); P. Stright, *Dyestuffs* **44**, 252 (1963).

[9a] H. Pfitzner, *Angew. Chem.* **62**, 242 (1950).

[9b] W. Wittenberger, *Melliand Textilber.* **32**, 454 (1951).

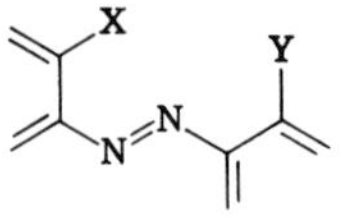

$$
\begin{array}{cc}
X & Y \\
-OH & -H \\
-NH_2 & -H \\
-OH & -OH \\
-OH & -COOH \\
-OH & -NH_2 \\
-OH & -OCH_2COOH
\end{array}
$$

(XVIII)

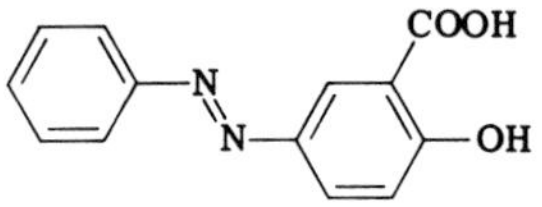

(XIX)

of wool dyestuffs, and copper in the field of cotton dyestuffs. Copper complexes find little application as wool dyestuffs because of their rather low stability to acid treatments but, with the advent of fiber-reactive dyestuffs chromium and cobalt complexes are gaining importance as dyestuffs for cellulosic fibers (Section I).

A. Coordination of the Azo Group

It is not proposed to discuss the principles of coordination here since the historical background and fundamental concepts of this subject, and the nature of the bonding in metal complexes have been extensively described elsewhere.[10,10a,b] However the evidence for, and mode of coordination of, the azo group will be discussed since this has been a subject of controversy in the past.

The donor properties of the azo group are weak and its ability to co-

[10] D. P. Craig and R. S. Nyholm, in "Chelating Agents and Metal Chelates" (F. P. Dwyer and D. P. Mellor, eds.), p. 51. Academic Press, New York, 1964; L. E. Orgel, "An Introduction to Transition Metal Chemistry: Ligand Field Theory." Methuen, London, 1960; C. J. Ballhausen, "Introduction to Ligand Field Theory." McGraw-Hill, New York, 1962; T. M. Dunn, in "Modern Coordination Chemistry" (J. Lewis and R. G. Wilkins eds.), p. 229. Wiley (Interscience), New York, 1960; J. S. Griffiths, "The Theory of Transition Metal Ions." Cambridge Univ. Press, London and New York, 1961.

[10a] D. P. Mellor, in "Chelating Agents and Metal Chelates" (F. P. Dwyer and D. P. Mellor, eds.), p. 1. Academic Press, New York, 1964.

[10b] C. K. Jørgensen, "Absorption Spectra and Chemical Bonding in Complexes." Pergamon Press, Oxford, 1961.

ordinate with metals was originally inferred from the fact that while azo compounds having a hydroxyl or an amino group in a position ortho to the azo group form metal complexes, those having hydroxyl or amino groups in meta or para positions do not.[11] However, the nature of the bond between the azo group and the metal was not clear and as recently as 1952 this uncertainty was indicated[12] by a bracket enclosing the entire azo group (XX).

In 1936 Kharasch and Ashford[13] isolated a compound which they formulated as $(C_6H_5N:NC_6H_5)_2PtCl_4$ by the interaction of azobenzene and platinic chloride. Werner[14] proposed a π-bonded structure for this compound (XXI). However this work has recently been repeated[15] and examination of the product by modern techniques has shown it to be a salt derived from hydrazobenzene, having the formula $(C_6H_5NHNH_2C_6H_5)_2[PtCl_6] \cdot H_2O$.

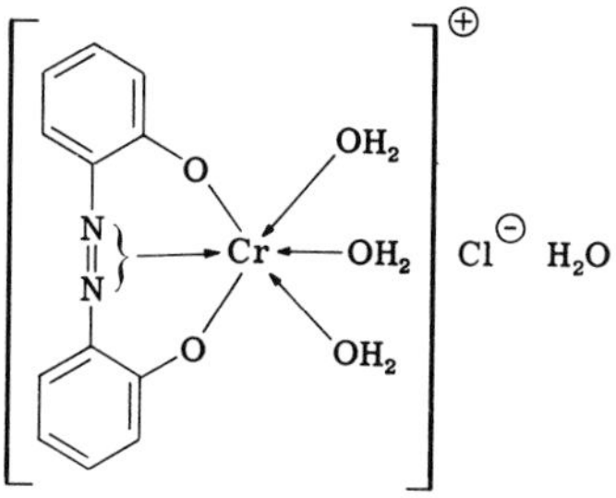

(XX) 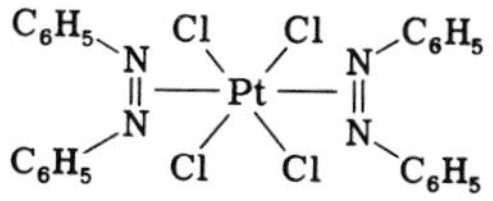   (XXI)

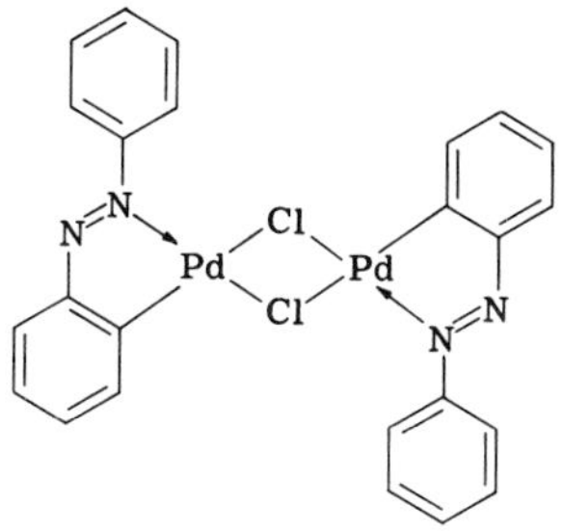

(XXII)

[11] G. T. Morgan and J. D. Main Smith, *J. Chem. Soc.* **125**, 1731 (1924).

[12] C. F. Callis, N. C. Nielsen, and J. C. Bailar, *J. Am. Chem. Soc.* **74**, 3461 (1952); J. C. Bailar and C. F. Callis, *ibid.* p. 6018.

[13] M. S. Kharasch and T. A. Ashford, *J. Am. Chem. Soc.* **58**, 1733 (1936).

[14] A. E. A. Werner, *Nature* **160**, 644 (1947).

[15] R. Murray, ICI, private communication (1967).

More recently silver and palladium complexes of azobenzene[16] and 5,6-benzocinnoline,[17] which may be compared with *cis*-azobenzene, have been isolated. No information on the structures of these complexes is available but their formation effectively demonstrated coordination of the azo group in the absence of other donor groups in the ligand molecules. A number of authors[18-21] have prepared complexes of azobenzene having a metal–carbon bond in a position ortho to the azo group. It is not clear based on available evidence which nitrogen atom of the azo group is bonded to the metal in their complexes, e.g. (XXII), but, since *o*-metallation occurs with *N,N*-dimethylbenzylamine[22] but not with *N,N*-dimethylaniline, Heck[20] concludes, by analogy, that the β-nitrogen atom of the azo group is involved in coordination. Recent X-ray crystal structure determinations on the copper complex of 1-phenylazo-2-naphthol (see next section), the copper complex of 1-pyrid-2-ylazo-2-naphthol (Section II,C,5,*c,iv,a*), and the chromium complexes of two *o,o'*-dihydroxyazo dyestuffs (Section II,C,3) and an *o*-carboxy-*o'*-hydroxyazo dyestuff (Section II,C,3) have confirmed that only one nitrogen atom of the azo group is involved in coordination. In the case of the copper complex of the bidentate azo compound, 1-phenylazo-2-naphthol, the β-nitrogen atom of the azo group is bonded to the metal which forms a part of a six-membered chelate ring.

B. BIDENTATE AZO DYESTUFFS

1. *Medially Metallized Types*

Metal complexes derived from bidentate azo dyestuffs in which the azo group forms a part of the metallizable system find their main application in the pigment field and are little used as dyestuffs. This is due to their relatively low stability in comparison with metal complexes of tridentate azo dyestuffs. They will, however, be considered in some detail since their relative simplicity compared with the latter facilitates the study of their structures, stabilities, and mechanism of formation, providing information which can be applied in the technologically very important tridentate series.

[16] R. H. Nuttall, E. R. Roberts, and D. W. A. Sharp, *J. Chem. Soc.* p. 2854 (1962).

[17] J. J. Porter and J. L. Murray, *J. Am. Chem. Soc.* **87**, 1628 (1965).

[18] A. C. Cope and R. W. Sieckman, *J. Am. Chem. Soc.* **87**, 3272 (1965).

[19] J. P. Kleiman and M. Dubeck, *J. Am. Chem. Soc.* **85**, 1544 (1963).

[20] R. F. Heck, *J. Am. Chem. Soc.* **90**, 313 (1968).

[21] M. M. Bagga, P. L. Pauson, F. J. Preston, and R. I. Reed, *Chem. Commun.* p. 543 (1965).

[22] A. C. Cope, J. M. Kliegman, and E. C. Friedrich, *J. Am. Chem. Soc.* **89**, 287 (1967).

The first example of a substantially pure metal lake of an azo dye appears to have been prepared as long ago as 1893 when Caberti and Peco[23] obtained a brown pigment by the interaction of p-nitrobenzene-azo-β-naphthol and copper salts. Following this observation a number of workers[24,24a-c] examined the reaction of o-hydroxy and o-amino azo dyestuffs with metal salts and succeeded in isolating copper, nickel, and cobalt complexes of both types of dyestuff. However, it was not until the classical work of Drew and his co-workers[25] that the structures of these complexes was established with any degree of certainty. Drew and Land-quist[25] confirmed that o-hydroxy and o-amino azo compounds formed complexes having 2:1 stoichiometry with divalent copper, nickel, and cobalt and in which a proton was lost from each molecule of the azo

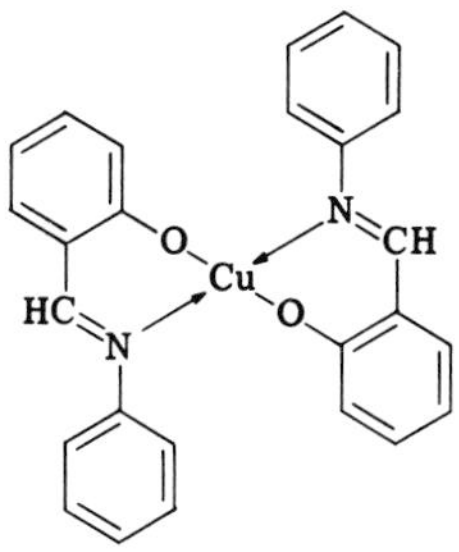

(XXIII)

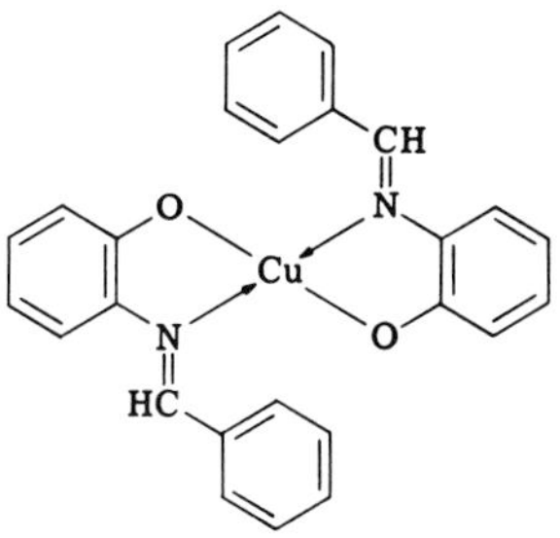

(XXIV)

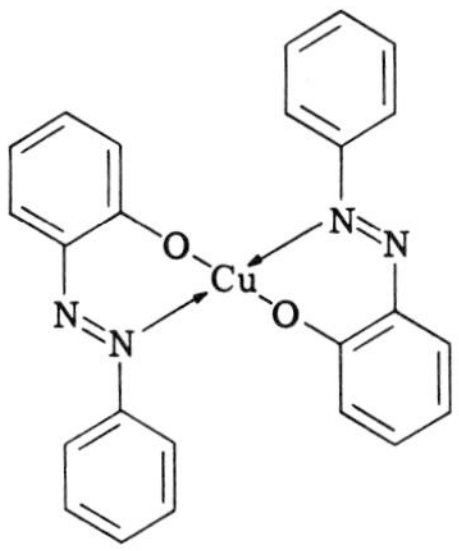

(XXV)

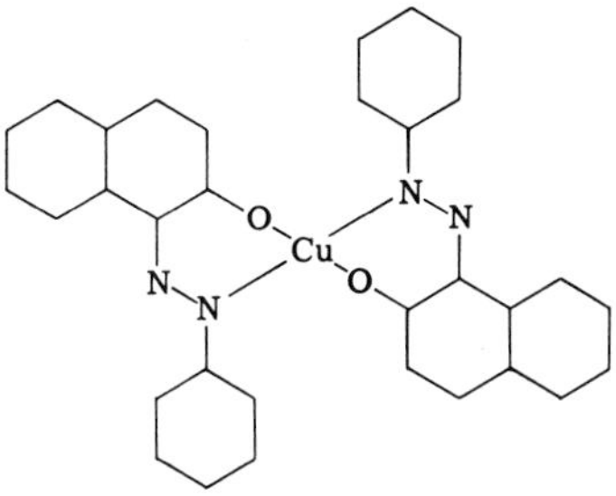

(XXVI)

[23] L. Caberti and C. Peco, *Faerbertzg.* p. 333 (1893–1894).

[24] E. Bamberger, *Ber.* **33**, 1957 (1900) ; V. G. Schaposchnikoff and V. Svientoslavski, *Z. Farb.- u. Textilchem.* **3**, 422 (1904). O. Baudisch, *Z. Angew. Chem.* **30**, 133 (1917).

[24a] G. Charrier and A. Berretta, *Gazz. Chim. Ital.* **56**, 865 (1926).

[24b] G. B. Crippa, *Gazz. Chim. Ital.* **57**, 20, 497, and 593 (1927) ; **58**, 716 (1928).

[24c] A. Cremonini, *Gazz. Chim. Ital.* **58**, 372 (1928).

[25] H. D. K. Drew and J. K. Landquist, *J. Chem. Soc.* p. 292 (1938).

compound. As a result of a comparison of the properties of the copper complexes of *N*-phenylsalicylideneimine (XXIII) and benzylidene-*o*-aminophenol (XXIV) with those of the copper complex of *o*-hydroxyazo-benzene, these authors proposed structure (XXV) for the latter. This was subsequently confirmed by the work of Davies[26] and Jarvis[26a] on the X-ray crystal structure of the copper complex of benzeneazo-β-naphthol. This complex[26a] consists of two molecules of benzeneazo-β-naphthol centrosymmetrically disposed about the central copper ion, the two oxygen atoms and the β-nitrogen atoms of the azo groups forming a square (XXVI). It is of interest to note that the molecule as a whole is not planar, the azo group lying out of the plane of the β-naphthol residue and of that of the benzene ring.

Despite the clarification of the structures of the copper complexes of *o*-hydroxyazo compounds the situation regarding cobalt complexes remained somewhat confused. Thus, certain authors[24a,24c,25,27] reported the isolation of complexes having 2:1 stoichiometry while others[12,28] reported complexes having 3:1 stoichiometry. The oxidation state of the cobalt in these complexes was also in dispute. This situation has recently[29] been clarified by the use of modern techniques to study the products obtained by the interaction of benzeneazo-β-naphthol and various cobalt salts and complexes. The results of this work are summarized in Chart 1. Thus, benzeneazo-β-naphthol and related compounds react with cobalt(II) acetate to form cobalt(II) complexes having 2:1 stoichiometry and in which one proton is lost from each molecule of the azo compound. Mag-

CHART 1

Reactions of Benzeneazo-β-Naphthol with Cobalt Compounds

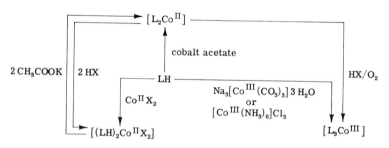

LH = Benzeneazo-β-naphthol; X = Cl, Br

[26] R. R. Davies, ICI, private communication.
[26a] J. A. J. Jarvis, *Acta Cryst.* **14**, 961 (1961).
[27] M. L. Ernsberger and W. R. Brode, *J. Org. Chem.* **6**, 331 (1941).
[28] M. Elkins and L. Hunter, *J. Chem. Soc.* p. 1598 (1935).
[29] R. Price, *J. Chem. Soc.*, A p. 415 (1967).

netic susceptibility measurements[30] show these complexes to have tetrahedral geometry and, by analogy with the copper complex of benzeneazo-β-naphthol,[26a] they have been assigned structures in which the β-nitrogen atom of the azo group is involved in coordination.

With sodium tris(carbonato)cobaltate(III)[31] neutral, diamagnetic, cobalt(III) complexes having 3:1 stoichiometry are obtained. The 2:1 cobalt(II) complexes can be converted into these complexes by treatment with mineral acid in the presence of atmospheric oxygen, and this no doubt explains the variable results obtained by earlier workers.

A novel type of complex of formula $(LH)_2Co^{II}X_2$ (Chart 1), in which no proton loss occurs from the azo compound, is produced when the latter reacts with anhydrous cobalt halides in dry ethanol. The magnetic susceptibilities and electronic conductances of these compounds support their formulation as octahedrally coordinated cobalt(II) complexes. By analogy with the neutral 2:1 cobalt(II) complexes $(L_2Co^{II}$, Chart 1), into which they are readily converted by treatment with potassium acetate, it is assumed that the metal forms a part of a 6-membered chelate ring and structure (XXVII) is proposed for these complexes. The formation of complexes of this type and their ready conversion into neutral tetrahedral 2:1 cobalt(II) complexes offers a possible mechanism for the formation of the latter.

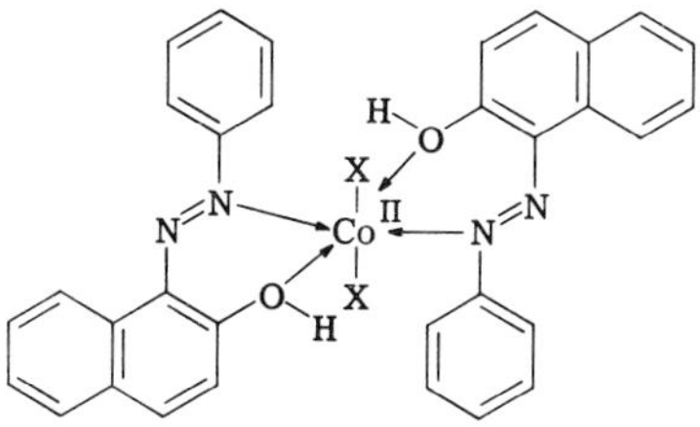

(XXVII) 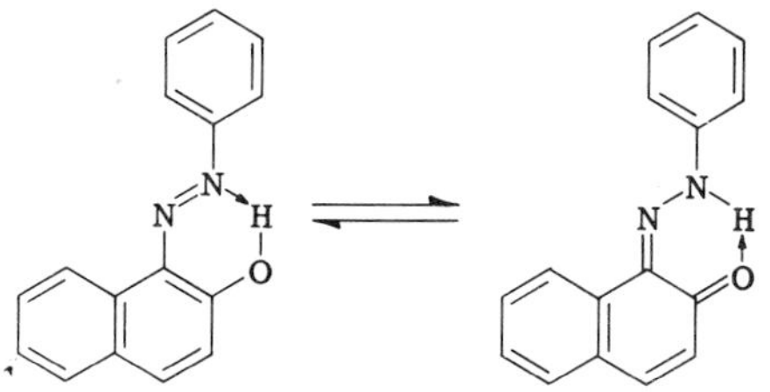   (XXVIII)

The azo–hydrazone tautomerism of o-hydroxyazo compounds and the factors that influence this have been studied by a number of workers[32] and it is concluded that benzeneazo-β-naphthols exist as strongly chelated structures (XXVIII). In view of this the mechanism outlined in

[30] B. N. Figgis and J. Lewis, *Progr. Inorg. Chem.* **6**, 37 (1964).

[31] H. F. Bauer and W. C. Drinkard, *J. Am. Chem. Soc.* **82**, 5031 (1960); *Inorg. Syn.* **8**, 202 (1966).

[32] A. Burawoy, A. G. Salem, and A. R. Thompson, *J. Chem. Soc.* p. 4793 (1952); B. L. Kaul, P. Madhaven Nair, A. V. Rama Rao, and K. Venkataraman, *Tetrahedron Letters* p. 3897 (1966); G. Schetty, *Helv. Chim. Acta* **50**, 1039 (1967).

CHART 2

Mechanism for Formation of $(LH)_2Co^{II}X_2$ and L_2Co^{II}

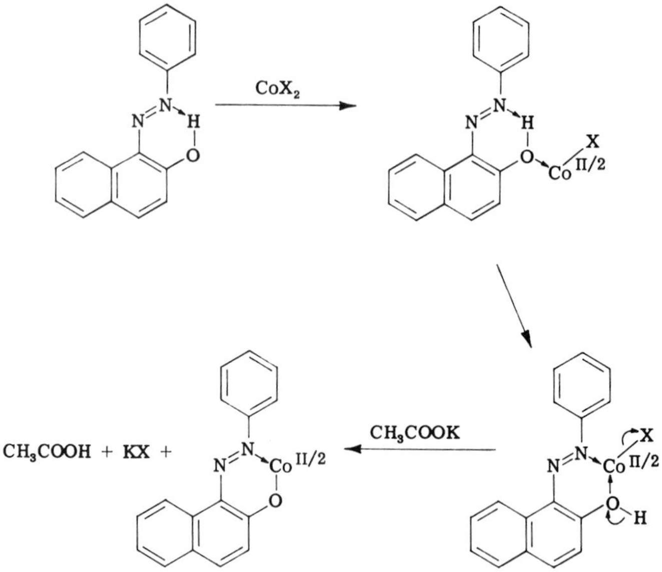

CoX$_2$

CH$_3$COOH + KX +

CH$_3$COOK

Chart 2 is proposed for the formation of complexes of the type $(LH)_2Co^{II}X_2$ and, from them, the complexes L_2Co^{II}.

No evidence was obtained for the intermediate formation of a protonated complex in the reaction of benzeneazo-β-naphthol with cobalt acetate to give a complex of the type L_2Co^{II}. In this case, it is possible that at the higher pH ionization of the o-hydroxyazo compound precedes complex formation, as has been suggested by Peters[33] and his co-workers. However, the formation of complexes of o-hydroxyazo compounds in which deprotonation of the azo compound does not occur is of considerable importance in connection with problems encountered in the manufacture of chromium complexes of tridentate metallizable azo dyestuffs. The significance of this is discussed in Section II,C,5,a,i.

Drew[25] proposed structures (XXIX) for the copper, nickel, and cobalt complexes of benzeneazo-β-naphthylamine which were analogous to those (XXV) of the corresponding complexes of benzeneazo-β-naphthol. Recent work,[34] however, casts doubt on this formulation since, in contrast to the 2:1 cobalt(II) complex of benzeneazo-β-naphthol, which has tetrahedral geometry, the 2:1 cobalt(II) complex of benzeneazo-β-naph-

[33] A. Johnson, M. S. Mort, R. H. Peters, and M. J. Wada, Tex 21, 453 (1962).
[34] R. Price, J. Chem. Soc., A p. 2048 (1967).

thylamine has square-planar geometry. In view of this and other evidence, the formulation (XXX) is preferred.[34]

In general, metal complexes derived from bidentate azo compounds in which the azo group forms a part of the chelating system have inadequate stability to be of value as dyestuffs. However, certain exceptions

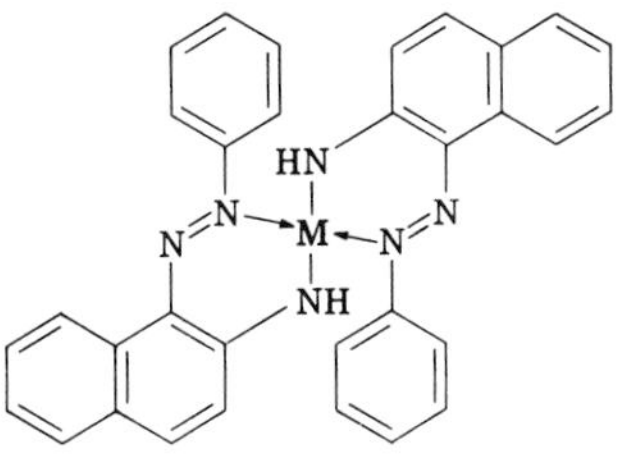

(XXIX) 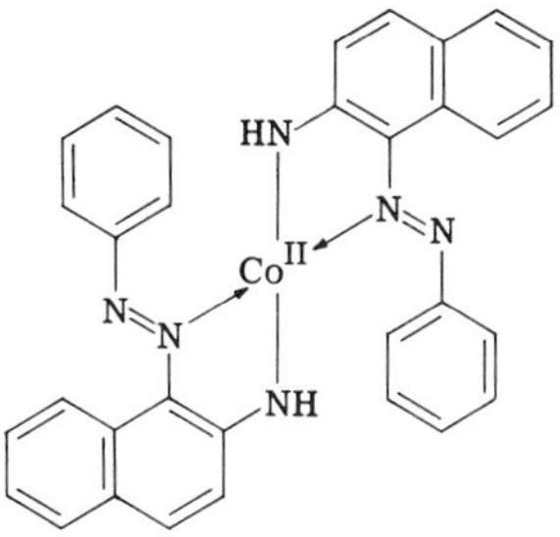   (XXX)

appear in the patent literature. These include the nickel complex of 1-(4'-nitrophenylazo)-2-hydroxy-3-naphthoic acid (XXXI), which is reported[35] to give bordeaux lacquer prints which are extremely fast to light on cotton. It is significant that in this, and other examples, the o-hydroxyazo system is not the sole chelating function in the molecule, and it is conceivable that dyes of this type function as terminally metallizable dyestuffs with complex formation occurring at the o-hydroxycarboxy system. In this context it is noteworthy that Uhlemann and Dietze[36] have recently demonstrated that 3-benzeneazo-2-hydroxyacetophenone forms two series of metal complexes (XXXII) depending upon the nature of the metal used.

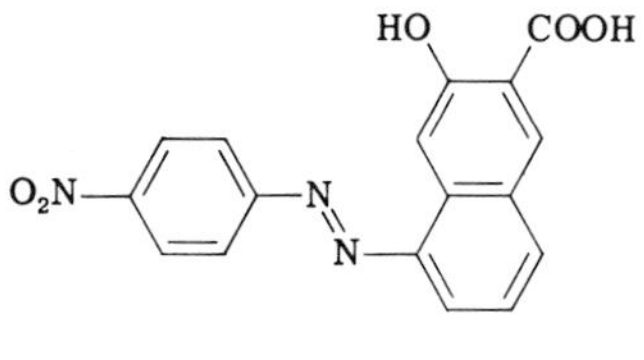

(XXXI) 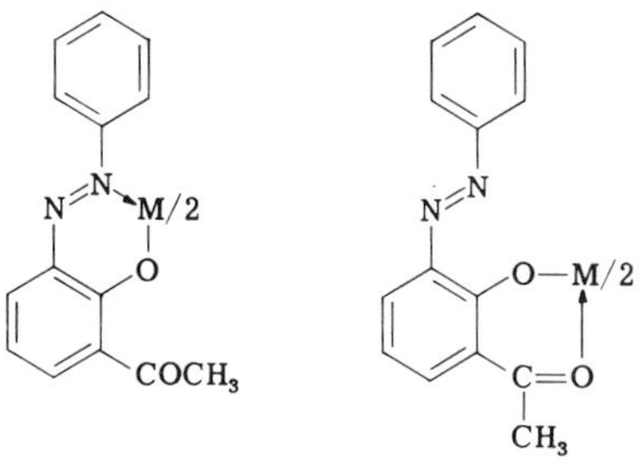   (XXXII)

[35] DuP, *USP* 2,396,328.

[36] E. Uhlemann and F. Dietze, *Z. Anorg. u. Allgem. Chem.* **353**, 26 (1967).

2. Terminally Metallized Types

Azo dyes derived from compounds such as salicylic acid and 8-hydroxyquinoline have been known to form metal complexes for many years. The early work in this field was reviewed in the previous volume; therefore, it is not proposed to discuss this in detail here but merely to comment that, in general, metal complexes derived from dyestuffs of this type are brighter in hue than those derived from azo compounds in which the azo group forms a part of the metallizable system. In contrast to dyestuffs in which the azo group forms a part of the metallizable system, terminally metallizable dyes derived from salicylic acid undergo little shade change on metal complex formation and little enhancement of lightfastness occurs.[9a] The lightfastness of terminally metallizable dyes derived from 8-hydroxyquinoline and related compounds, however, is markedly increased on copper complex formation.[26,37,38] This is attributed[26] to conjugation of the azo group to the metallizable system since the effect is nullified in dyestuffs in which this conjugation is broken.

The principal advance in this field came with the discovery[37] that azo dyestuffs containing the system (XXXIII) give dyeings of bright hue and excellent fastness properties when applied on cellulosic fibers in conjunction with an aftercoppering treatment. The dyes used are disazo types containing two systems such as (XXXIII) and derive their solubility from the sulfate ester groups, e.g., (XXXIV). The excellent washfastness properties of aftercoppered dyeings derived from dyestuffs of this type is attributable to loss of the solubilizing groups and the formation of polymeric copper complexes (XXXV). The hydrolysis of the sulfate ester groups is catalyzed by cupric ions and, as a result of a kinetic study of the cupric ion-catalyzed hydrolysis of 8-hydroxyquinoline sulfate, Hay and Edmonds[39] have proposed the intermediate formation of a complex such as (XXXVI). The formation of a complex of this type assists the transfer of electrons from the sulfur–oxygen bonds undergoing cleavage, thus facilitating hydrolysis.

Dyestuffs of this type have been prepared[37] from compounds other than 8-hydroxyquinoline. These include 4-hydroxyacridine, 4-hydroxybenzothiazole, 8-hydroxycinnoline, and 4-hydroxy-2-methylbenzoxazole. The sulfuric ester group has also been replaced by a phosphonic ester group[38] (XXXVII).

Dyestuffs containing both terminal and medial metallizable systems

[37] R. R. Davies and ICI, BP 761,776.
[38] A. R. Todd, R. R. Davies, and ICI, BP 785,038.
[39] R. W. Hay and J. A. G. Edmonds, Chem. Commun. p. 969 (1967).

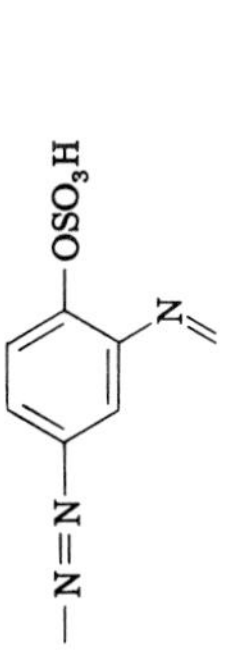

(XXXIII)

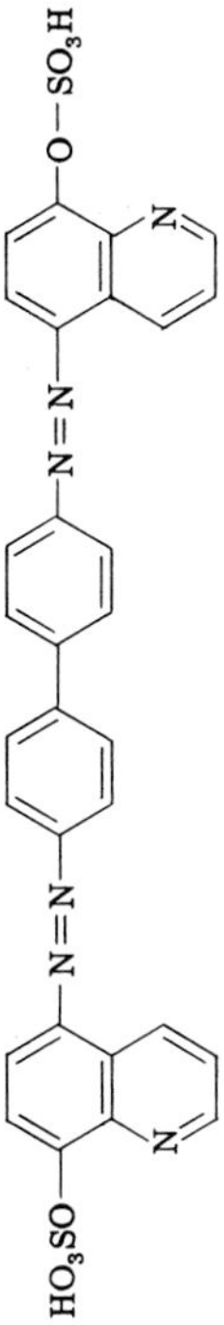

(XXXIV)

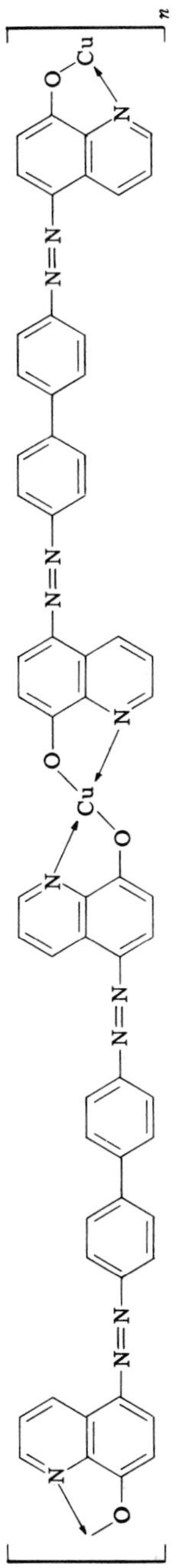

(XXXV)

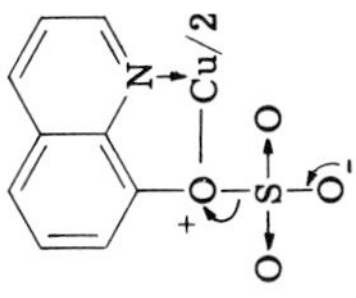

(XXXVI)

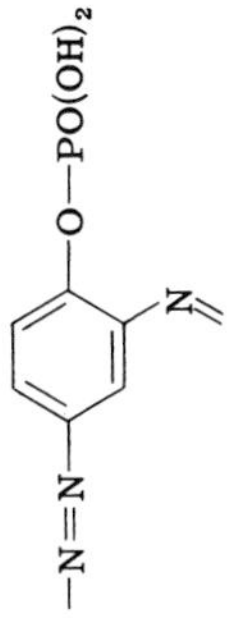

(XXXVII)

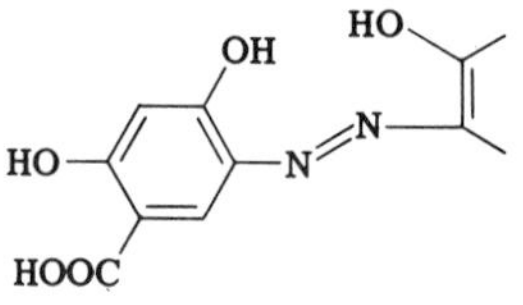

(XXXVIII) 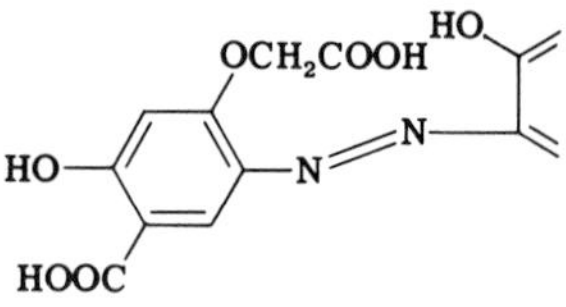   (XXXIX)

have been described.[40,41] It is claimed that dyes of this type, e.g., (XXXVIII) and (XXXIX) can be converted to metal complexes in which only the medially metallizable system is involved in complex formation and the terminal metallizable system remains free. Aftercoppered dyeings derived from such complexes are reported to have excellent fastness properties.

C. Tridentate Azo Dyestuffs

The most important types of azo compounds in this series are those containing the o,o'-dihydroxyazo, the o-carboxy-o'-hydroxyazo, and the o-hydroxy-o'-aminoazo systems. The structures of the copper (XL), 1:1

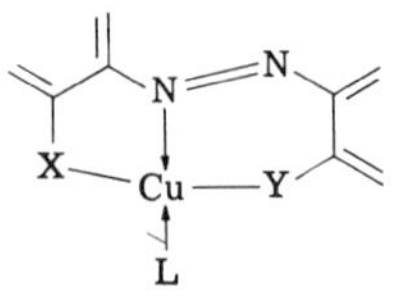

X = $-$O$-$, $-$COO$-$
Y = $-$O$-$, $-$NH$-$
L = H_2O, etc.

(XL)

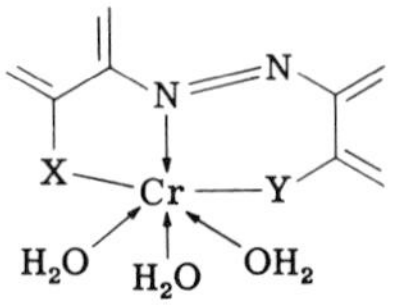

X = $-$O$-$, $-$COO$-$
Y = $-$O$-$, $-$NH$-$

(XLI)

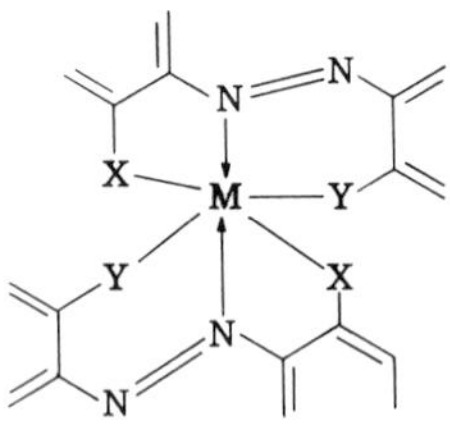

X = $-$O$-$, $-$COO$-$
Y = $-$O$-$, $-$NH$-$
M = Cr^{III}, Co^{III}

(XLII)

[40] DH, *BP* 893,353.
[41] DH, *BP* 901,748.

chromium (XLI), and 2:1 chromium and cobalt (XLII) complexes of these compounds have been discussed by many authors[3,9,9a,b,42] and recently those of the 2:1 chromium complexes of o,o'-dihydroxyazo[43] and o-carboxy-o'-hydroxyazo dyes[44] have been confirmed by X-ray crystal structure determinations. Therefore, it is not proposed to discuss early work in the field in detail, but to concentrate on more recent developments and aspects of the subject which are of theoretical importance.

1. o-Amino-o'-hydroxyazo Dyestuffs

The ability of o-amino-o'-hydroxyazo dyes to react with transition metal salts to form complexes in which two protons are lost from the azo compound was first observed[42] with the formation of the copper complex of 1-(2'-hydroxyphenylazo)-2-naphthylamine. The analytical results quoted by Beech and Drew are in good agreement with their formulation of the product (XLIII) so presumably the coordination sphere of the copper atom is completed by bridging through the oxygen atoms. Bridging of this type in which the oxygen atom is coordinated to two copper atoms has been observed[45] in the copper complex of 8-hydroxyquinoline. Subsequently 2:1 chromium and cobalt complexes of o-amino-o'-hydroxyazo dyes were prepared and formulated as (XLII; X = O, Y = NH).

The loss of a proton from the amino group in the azo compound on metal complex formation is at first sight rather surprising since aromatic amines, such as aniline, form metal complexes with no loss of proton. However, it has been demonstrated[34] that this occurs via the hydrazone form of the azo compound (XLIV).

The acidity of the hydrazone form of the azo compound is considerably enhanced on metal complex formation and this may be compared with the similar effect in other compounds capable of forming complexes with transition metals and having, attached to a nondonor atom, a hydrogen atom whose acidic character is increased by coordination. These include 2,2'-dipyridylamine,[46] 1,3-bis(2'-pyridyl)-2,3-diazaprop-1-ene and related compounds,[47] chelidamic acid,[48] and 4-(2'-pyridylazo)resorcinol.[49]

[42] W. F. Beech and H. D. K. Drew, J. Chem. Soc. pp. 603 and 608 (1940).
[43] R. Grieb and A. Niggli, Helv. Chim. Acta 48, 317 (1965).
[44] H. Jaggi, Helv. Chim. Acta 51, 580 (1968).
[45] J. A. Beran, D. P. Graddon, and J. F. McConnell, Nature 199, 373 (1963).
[46] J. F. Geldard and F. Lions, J. Am. Chem. Soc. 84, 2262 (1962).
[47] F. Lions and K. V. Martin, J. Am. Chem. Soc. 80, 3858 (1958); B. Chiswell, J. F. Geldard, A. T. Phillips, and F. Lions, Inorg. Chem. 3, 1272 (1964); J. F. Geldard and F. Lions, ibid. 2, 270 (1963); R. W. Green, P. S. Hallman, and F. Lions, ibid. 3, 376 (1964).

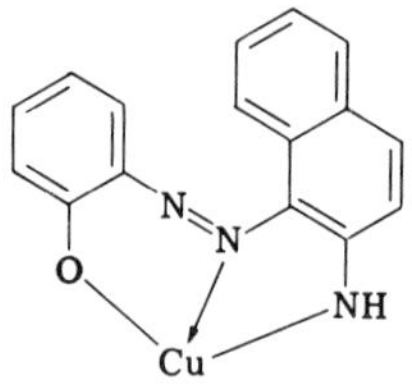

(XLIII)

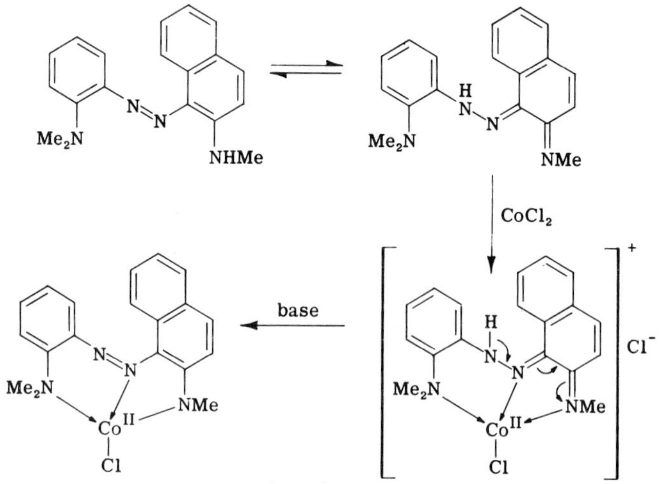

(XLIV)

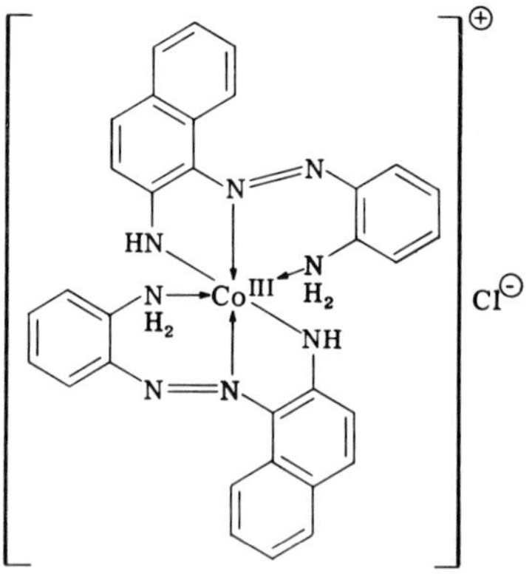

(XLV)

[48] S. P. Bag, Q. Fernando, and H. Freiser, *Inorg. Chem.* **1**, 887 (1962).
[49] A. Corsini, Q. Fernando, and M. Freiser, *Inorg. Chem.* **2**, 224 (1963).

The demonstration that proton loss from an *o*-aminoazo dyestuff on metal complex formation occurs through the hydrazone form of the ligand leads to the conclusion that only one proton should be lost from an *o,o'*-diaminoazo dyestuff on metal complex formation. This has been confirmed[34] in the case of the 2:1 cobalt complex of 1-(2'-aminophenyl-azo)-2-naphthylamine (XLV).

2. Cobalt Complexes

Cobalt complexes of tridentate metallizable azo dyestuffs do not occupy such an important position in the dyestuffs field as chromium complexes. The principal reason for this is, without doubt, the difficulty that has been experienced in the preparation of 1:1 cobalt complexes and, from them, unsymmetrical 2:1 cobalt complexes. So-called unsymmetrical 2:1 cobalt complexes have been prepared[4] by the interaction of cobalt salts and equimolecular mixtures of two different metallizable azo dyestuffs. These are, however, statistical mixtures of the three possible 2:1 complexes.

The preparation of 1:1 chromium complexes of tridentate metallizable azo dyestuffs, in which the coordination sphere of the metal is completed by three molecules of water, depends upon the fact that such complexes are stable in aqueous medium at low pH values (Section II,C,4,*a,i*). Under comparable conditions cobalt complex dyestuffs are unstable and demetallization occurs.[50] It has, therefore, proved impossible to prepare 1:1 cobalt complex dyestuffs in good yield by methods analogous to those used in the preparation of 1:1 chromium complexes.

Recently, however, by taking advantage of the affinity of the cobaltic ion for nitrogen-donor ligands, 1:1 cobalt complexes of tridentate metallizable azo dyestuffs have been prepared[51] in which the coordination sphere of the metal is completed by three molecules of ammonia (XLVI) or various other monodentate nitrogen-donor ligands. Complexes of this type are prepared by the interaction of a tridentate metallizable azo compound and a solution of a cobalt(II) salt in the presence of a large excess of ammonia. The scope of the reaction is wide and 1:1 cobalt complexes have been prepared from a variety of tridentate azo dyestuffs. In every case the product was the diamagnetic cobalt(III) complex and the change in oxidation state of the cobalt was shown[52] to have occurred at the expense of the azo dyestuff, some of which was reduced.

The stability of 1:1 cobalt complexes of this type varies considerably[52]

[50] G. Schetty and H. Ackermann, *Angew. Chem.* **70**, 222 (1958).
[51] A. Johnson, P. A. Mack, R. Price, A. Warwick, and ICI, *BP* 1,094,746.
[52] P. A. Mack and R. Price, *Ind. Chim. Belge* Suppl. (III), p. 31 (1967).

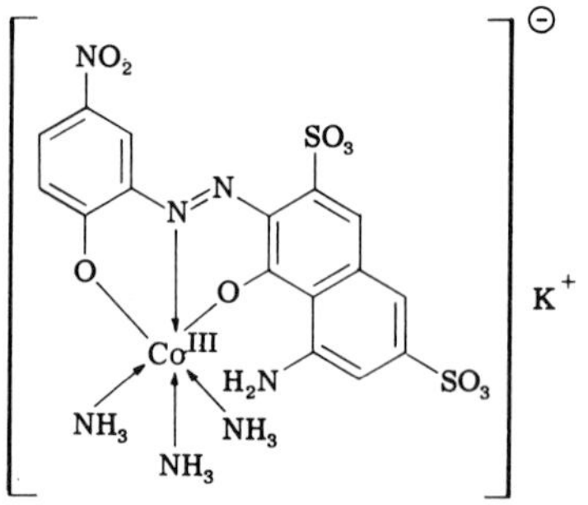

(XLVI)

and is governed by the nature of the metallizable system in the azo compound. Thus, while 1:1 cobalt complexes derived from o-hydroxy-arylazopyrazolones are stable in aqueous solution at 60°, those derived from o,o'-dihydroxyazo dyestuffs slowly disproportionate under comparable conditions, with loss of ammonia and formation of the 2:1 cobalt complex dyestuff. 1:1 Cobalt complexes of o-carboxy-o'-hydroxyazo dyestuffs disproportionate rapidly in aqueous solution at 60°, and those of o-carboxyarylazopyrazolones are unstable in aqueous solution at 20° in the absence of excess ammonia. Unlike 1:1 chromium complex dyestuffs, complexes of this type are insufficiently stable to be of value as dyestuffs in their own right. Such complexes, however, react readily with an equimolecular quantity of the same metallizable azo dyestuff to give a symmetrical 2:1 cobalt complex, or with an equimolecular quantity of a different metallizable azo compound to give an unsymmetrical 2:1 cobalt complex[53] (Chart 3). This provides an excellent method for the preparation of unsymmetrical 2:1 cobalt(III) complexes in a pure state and in good yield.

1:1 Cobalt complex dyestuffs have also been prepared[54] in which the coordination sphere of the metal is partially completed by bidentate nitrogen-donor compounds such as ethylenediamine, 1,3-diaminopropane, biguanide, dipyridyl, and 9,10-phenanthroline (XLVII). Complexes of this type are considerably more stable than those containing only monodentate nitrogen-donor ligands and cannot be used in the preparation of unsymmetrical 2:1 cobalt complex dyestuffs. Even more stable are 1:1 cobalt complex dyestuffs in which the coordination sphere of the cobalt is completed by a tridentate nitrogen-donor ligand[54-56] such as terpyridyl,

[53] A. Johnson, P. A. Mack, R. Price, and ICI, *BP* 1,089,826.
[54] P. A. Mack, R. Price, and ICI, *FP* 1,466,877.
[55] Gy, *BeP* 671,099.
[56] CIBA *FP* 1,486,661.

CHART 3
2:1 Cobalt Complexes

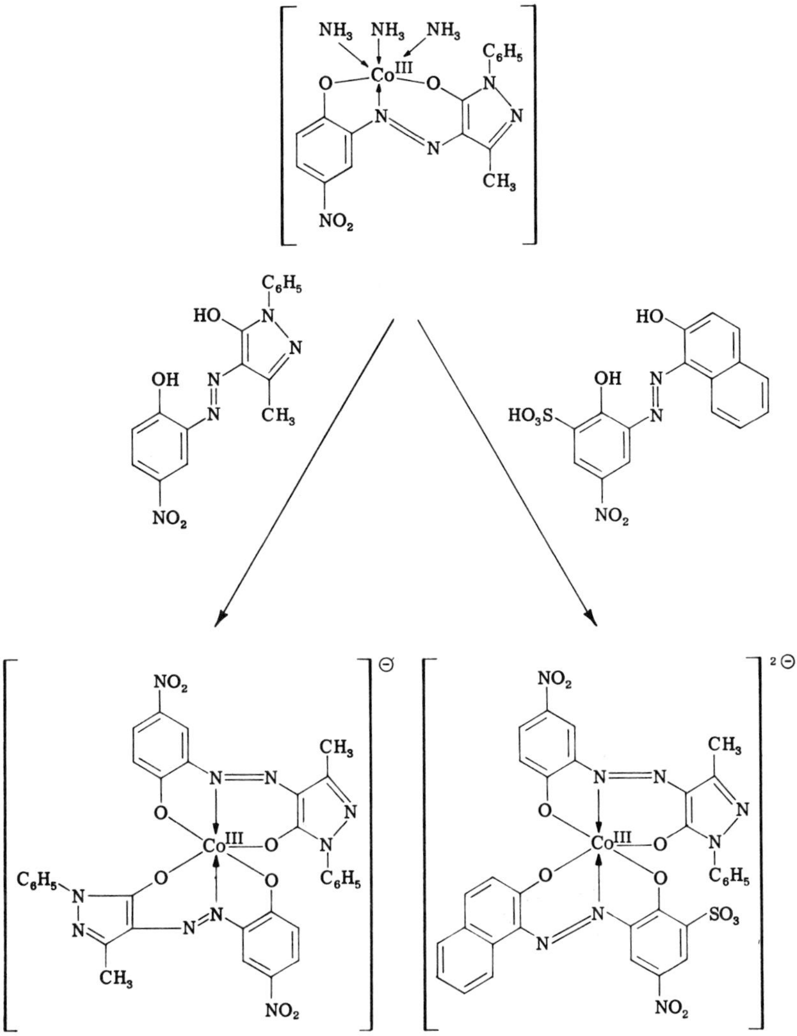

and diethylenetriamine (XLVIII). Complexes of this type are stable compounds and show no sign of degradation in boiling aqueous solution. By varying the degree of sulfonation of the azo compound the net charge on the 1:1 cobalt complex dyestuff can range from +1 (azo compounds devoid of sulfonic acid groups), giving dyes suitable for acrylic fibers; through 0 (monosulfonated azo compounds), giving pigments suitable for lacquers, etc.; —1, —2 (di- and trisulfonated azo compounds), giving dyes suitable for polyamide fibers and wool; to a multiplicity of negative charges, giving dyes which, in the form of their fiber-reactive derivatives, are suitable for cellulosic fibers.[57]

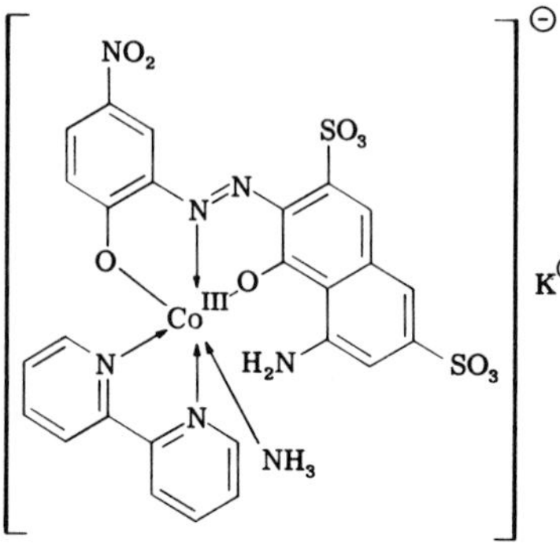

(XLVII) 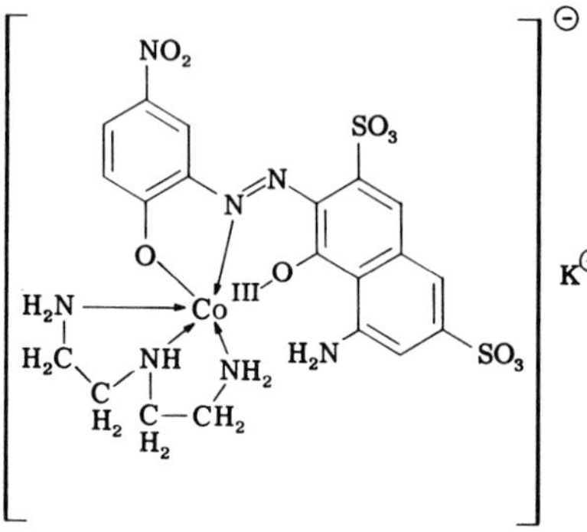 (XLVIII)

3. Stereochemistry of 2:1 Metal Complex Dyestuffs

In 1939 Drew[3] proposed structures for 2:1 chromium complexes of o,o'-dihydroxyazo and o-carboxy-o'-hydroxyazo dyestuffs in which the two dyestuff molecules were mutually perpendicular and octahedrally coordinated to the central metal ion (XLIX). Pfitzner[9a] independently arrived at the same conclusion and 2:1 chromium complexes having this meridial (mer) configuration have been described[58] as Drew-Pfitzner types. However in 1941 Pfeiffer[59] succeeded in resolving the 2:1 chromium complex of the o-carboxy-o'-hydroxyazo dyestuff, 1-phenyl-3-methyl-4-(2'-carboxyphenylazo)-5-pyrazolone, into two isomers which he formulated as octahedrally coordinated complexes in which the donor atoms of each azo compound were situated at the apices of an equilateral triangle forming a face of the valency octahedron of the chromium ion, e.g., (L). 2:1 Chromium complexes having this facial (fac) configuration have been described[60] as Pfeiffer-Schetty types.

o-Carboxy-o'-hydroxyazo dyestuffs form metal complexes in which the metal atom is a member of two annelated six-membered rings (LI) (Section II,I,1). Thus the apparent possibility, which exists in the o,o'-

[57] P. A. Mack, R. Price, and ICI, U.K. Appl. 4530/65.
[58] G. Schetty, Am. Dyestuff Reptr. 54, 589 (1965).
[59] P. Pfeiffer and S. Saure, Ber. 74, 935 (1941).
[60] H. Baumann and H. R. Hensel, Fortschr. Chem. Forsch. 7, 4 (1967).

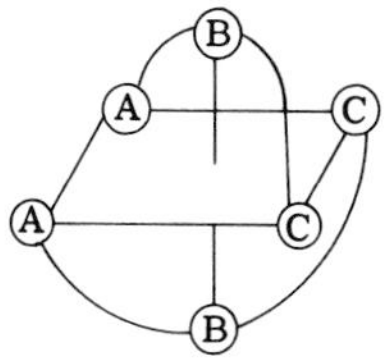

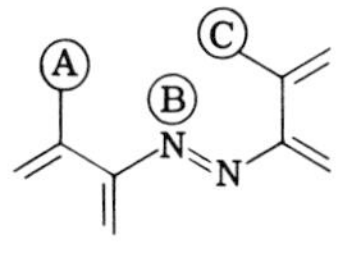

(A) $= -O-,$ $-COO-$
(C) $= -O-$

(XLIX)

(A) $= -COO-$
(C) $= -O-$

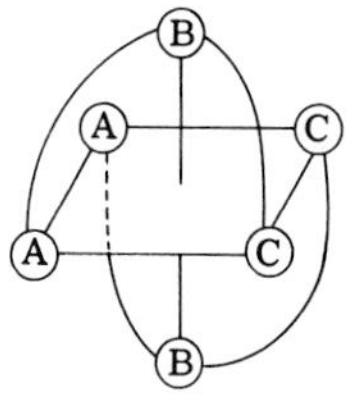

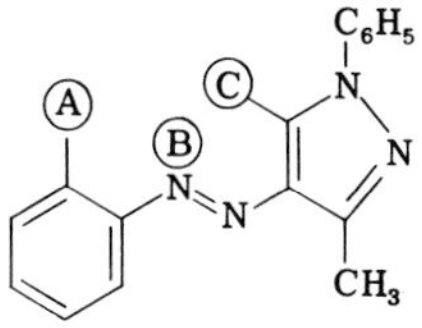

C_6H_5

CH_3

(L)

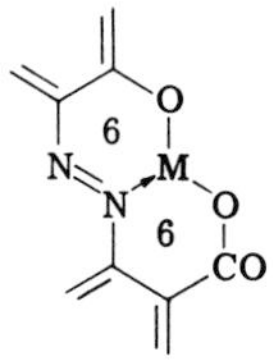

(LI)

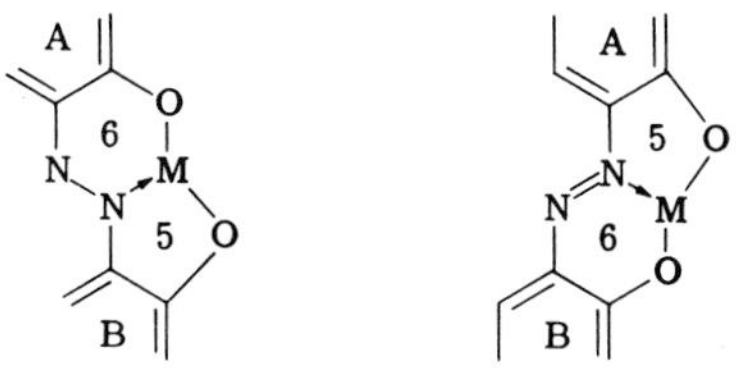

(LII)

dihydroxyazo series (LII), of isomers in which different nitrogen atoms of the azo group are involved in coordination is excluded in the o-carboxy-o'-hydroxyazo series. From this it follows that the two complexes isolated by Pfeiffer must be geometrical isomers.

It can be seen from Chart 4 that the mer configuration permits only an enantiomorphic pair of isomers, while in the case of the fac configuration four enantiomorphic pairs and one centrosymmetric isomer are possible. Thus, the facial configuration proposed by Pfeiffer appeared to be correct. However, it was not until 1961, when the first of a series of papers by Schetty appeared, that any further information on stereochemistry in 2:1 chromium and cobalt complexes of tridentate metallizable azo dyestuffs was published.

In 1961 Schetty[61] succeeded in separating the 2:1 chromium complex of 1-(2'-carboxyphenylazo)-2-naphthol (LIII) into four components by

[61] G. Schetty and W. Kuster, *Helv. Chim. Acta* **44**, 2193 (1961).

R. PRICE

CHART 4
Stereochemistry of 2:1 Chromium and Cobalt Complexes

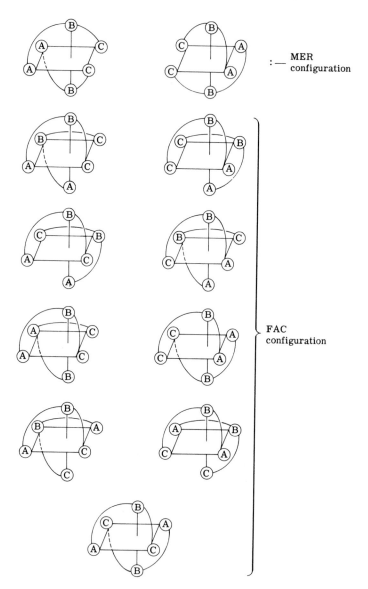

a chromatographic method. The four components each had the same empirical formula but different electronic spectra and solubility properties. Each isomerized readily in solution to an equilibrium mixture of the four components which were considered to be geometrical isomers and,

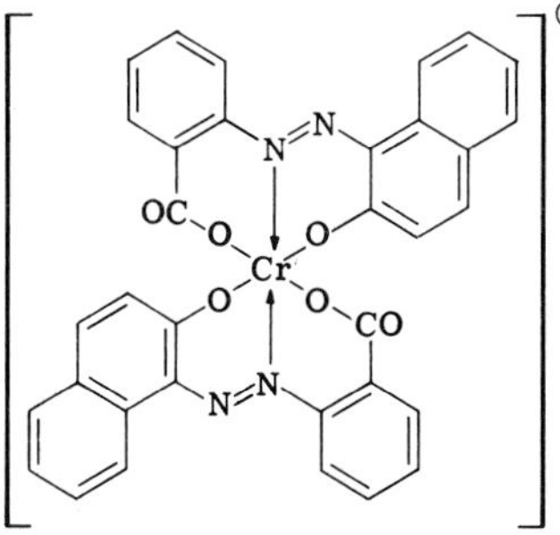

(LIII) 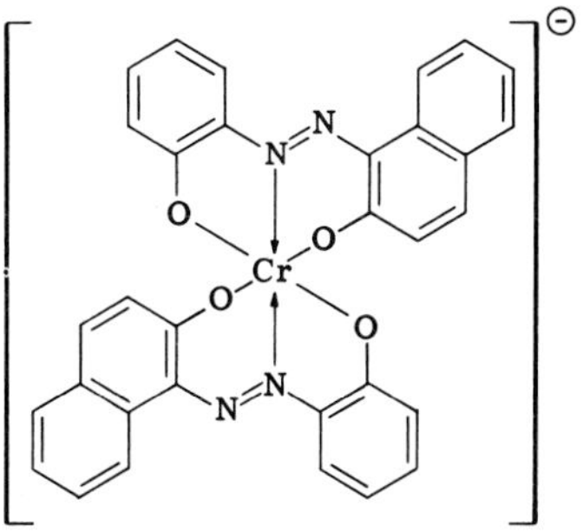   (LIV)

Meridial complexes

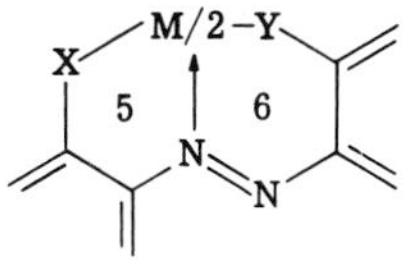

—X— = —O—, —NH—, —N(C_6H_5)—, —N(SO_2R)—
—Y— = —O—

Facial complexes

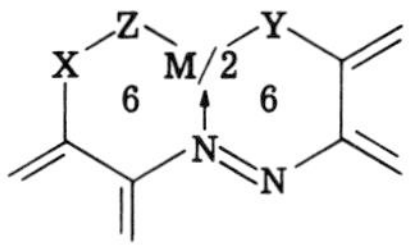

—X—Z— = —C(O)O—, —SO_2N(COC_6H_5)—, —CON($SO_2C_6H_5$)—
—Y— = —O—, —NH—

(LV)

therefore, to have fac configurations. In contrast, the 2:1 chromium complex of 1-(2′-hydroxyphenylazo)-2-naphthol (LIV) consisted of a single component, and no isomers were detected in a chromatographic examination[62] of a series of 2:1 chromium complexes of o,o'-dihydroxyazo dyestuffs. Complexes of this type were, therefore, considered to have a mer configuration.

Following an examination[62,63] of the 2:1 chromium and cobalt complexes of further tridentate azo dyestuffs (LV) Schetty[64] came to the conclusion that (1) all diarylazo dyestuffs which form annelated 5- and 6-membered chelate rings with the metal ion give complexes having a

[62] G. Schetty, *Helv. Chim. Acta* **45**, 1095 (1962).
[63] G. Schetty, *Helv. Chim. Acta* **45**, 1473 (1962).
[64] G. Schetty, *Chimia (Aarau)* **18**, 244 (1964).

mer configuration, and (2) those dyes that form two annelated six-membered chelate rings usually give complexes having a fac configuration. In certain circumstances, however, dyestuffs of this type can adopt a mer configuration. Thus the mer configuration is enforced upon o-carboxy-o'-hydroxyazo dyestuffs in mixed 2:1 chromium complexes with o,o'-dihydroxyazo dyes,[65] e.g., (LVI). o-Carboxyarylazopyrazolones represent a special case[65] of dyestuffs that form 2 annelated six-membered chelate rings with the metal ion and the configuration of 2:1 complexes of dyestuffs of this type is governed by substituents in the azo compound[66] (LVII).

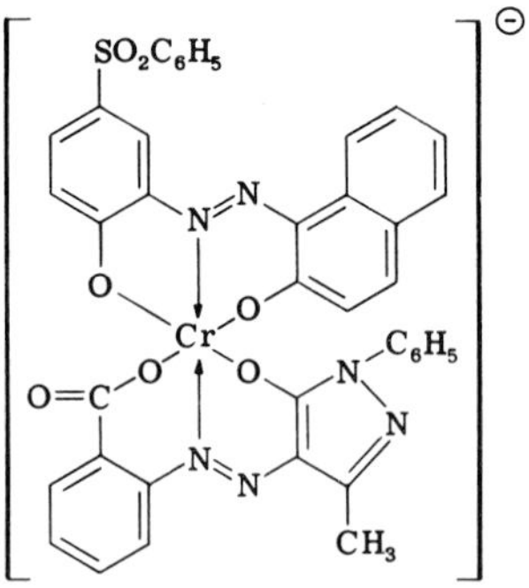

(LVI)

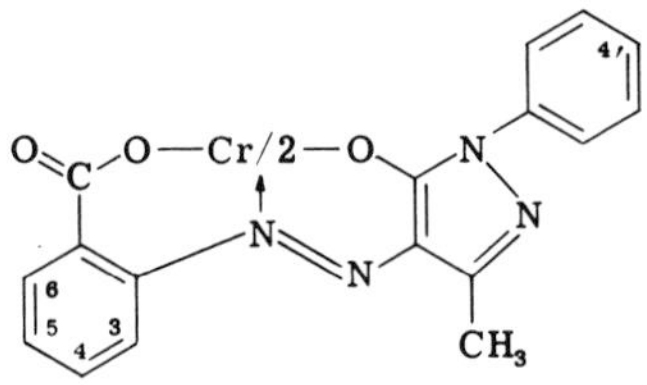

Facial complexes: - 3-Methyl, 6-methyl
Meridial complexes: - 4-Methyl, 5-methyl, 4'-methyl

(LVII)

Very powerful evidence supporting Schetty's postulates has been provided by X-ray crystal structure determinations. Thus, the 2:1 chromium complexes of the two o,o'-dihydroxyazo dyestuffs, 2, 2'-dihydroxy-azobenzene and 1-(2'-hydroxy-4'-nitrophenylazo)-2-naphthol, have been proved[43] to have mer configurations, while the 2:1 chromium complex of

[65] G. Schetty, *Helv. Chim. Acta* **46**, 1132 (1963).
[66] G. Schetty, *Helv. Chim. Acta* **47**, 921 (1964).

the o-carboxyarylazopyrazolone dyestuff, 1-(4'-bromophenyl)-3-methyl-4-(2'-methyl-6'-carboxyphenylazo)-5-pyrazolone has been proved[44] to have a fac configuration. However, the existence of a chromium complex of an o,o'-dihydroxyazo dyestuff having a fac configuration has recently been convincingly demonstrated by Idelson and Karady.[67] These authors converted the 1:1 chromium complex dyestuff Ionochrome Pink N (Francolor) (LVIII) to the sulfonpiperazide and treated the latter with pentane-2,4-dione. Chromatography of the product gave three fractions having identical UV, visible, and IR spectra but significantly different X-ray powder diagrams. Analytical results were in good agreement with the constitution (LIX). If the azo dyestuff was coordinated to the chro-

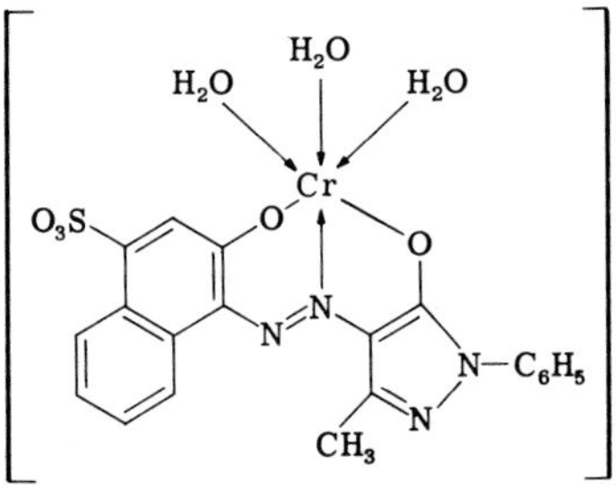

(LVIII)

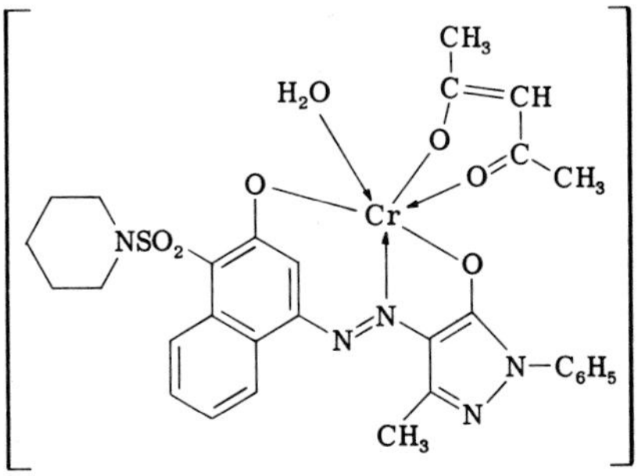

(LIX)

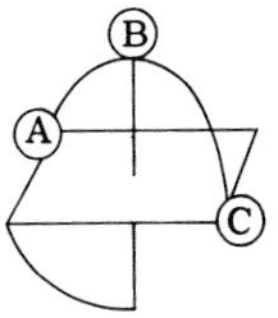

(LX)

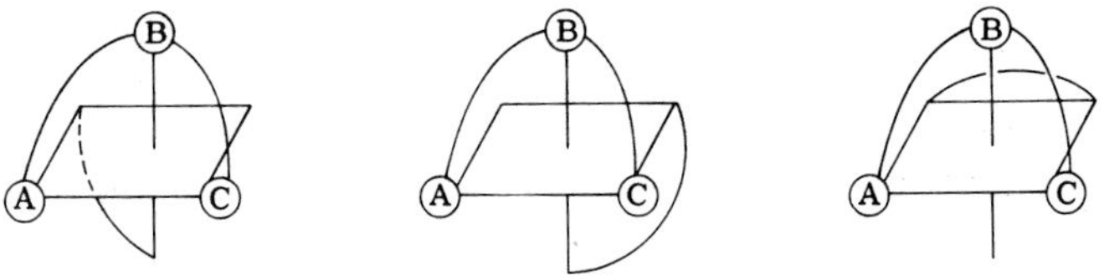

(LXI)

[67] M. Idelson and I. R. Karady, *J. Am. Chem. Soc.* **88**, 186 (1966).

mium atom in the mer configuration in this complex only dl isomerism would be possible (LX). On the other hand three enantiomorphic pairs (LXI) would be possible if the azo compound occupied fac positions. Since three isomeric complexes were isolated it was concluded that the chromium complex (LIX) must have a fac configuration. The similarity of the electronic spectra of the latter and the parent Ionochrome Pink N (LVIII) suggested that this complex also has a fac configuration.

A further example of facial configuration in the 1:1 chromium complex of an o,o'-dihydroxyazo dyestuff was provided by the complex (LXII) which was prepared[68] by two methods. The first involved reaction of the 1:1 chromium complex of the azo dyestuff with diethylenetriamine, and the second reaction of the azo dyestuff with [Cr(CO)$_3$dien]. The diethylenetriamine occupies fac positions in [Cr(CO)$_3$dien][69] and, since the latter reaction took place under very mild conditions, it was assumed that no rearrangement occurred and that the azo compound must occupy fac positions in the product. The existence of these 1:1 chromium complexes of o,o'-dihydroxyazo dyestuffs in a fac configuration is in conflict with the mer structures assigned by Schetty to 2:1 complexes of o,o'-dihydroxyazo dyestuffs, and Idelson et al. suggest that structural changes may occur on formation of 2:1 complexes.

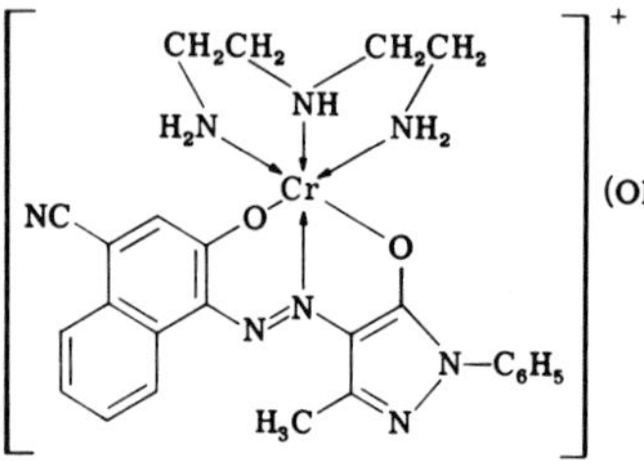

(LXII) 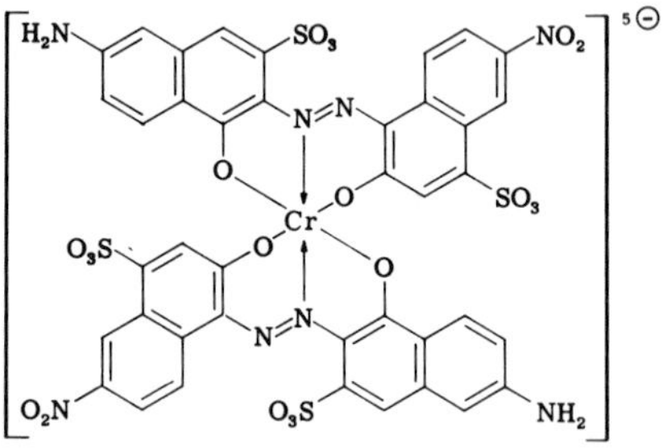   (LXIII)

However, the 2:1 chromium complex of the o,o'-dihydroxyazo dyestuff, 2-amino-6-(2'-hydroxy-6'-nitro-4'-sulfonaphth-1'-ylazo)-5-naphthol-7-sulfonic acid (LXIII), has been separated[70] chromatographically into two isomers. The two isomers had markedly different cellulose substantivity and rapidly reverted to an equilibrium mixture in hot aqueous solution, especially in the presence of small amounts of alkali. The iso-

[68] M. Idelson, I. R. Karady, B. H. Mark, D. O. Rickter, and V. H. Hooper, Inorg. Chem. 6, 450, (1967).

[69] E. W. Abel, M. A. Bennett, and G. Wilkinson, J. Chem. Soc. p. 2323 (1959).

[70] C. Morris, ICI, private communication (1961).

lation of two isomers proves that the o,o'-dihydroxyazo compounds must occupy fac positions in this complex.

From these results it must be concluded that while tridentate azo dyestuffs which form annelated five- and six-membered chelate rings with the metal ion usually form mer complexes, and those which form two annelated six-membered chelate rings with the metal ion usually form fac complexes, both types can adopt either configuration. The method of preparation of the complex and the structure of the parent azo compound govern the configuration assumed. In this connection it is noteworthy that in every case where a fac configuration in a chromium complex of an o,o'-dihydroxyazo compound has been demonstrated the parent azo compound was derived from a 1-amino-2-naphthol diazo component.

The Influence of Stereochemistry on the Properties of 2:1 Metal Complex Dyestuffs. In order to determine the effect of steric configuration on the dyeing properties of 2:1 metal complex dyestuffs it is essential that dyes must be compared in which the structures of the parent azo compounds are very closely related.[71] If this is not done the influence of constitutional differences in the azo compounds cannot be excluded in the interpretation of results, and this places a very serious restriction on any investigation of this type. This problem was overcome by Schetty,[58] who examined the dyeing properties of a series of 2:1 chromium complexes of o-carboxyarylazopyrazolone dyestuffs in which the only structural variation in the parent azo compound was the position of a methyl group. While no definite relationship could be established between stereochemistry and dyeing kinetics on wool, a number of other differences between complexes having fac and mer configurations became apparent. Thus, complexes having a fac configuration had significantly poorer wetfastness properties when dyed on wool but showed less tendency to stain cotton than those having a mer configuration. The former appeared to have marginally superior lightfastness. The physical properties of the two types also differed from each other; complexes having a mer configuration are deeper in shade than those having a fac configuration, show less tendency to aggregate and have greater water solubility.

This work effectively demonstrated the differences shown by 2:1 chromium complexes having fac and mer configurations but provided no information on the behavior of different isomers of the former type, of which five are possible. Recently, however, Morris[70] succeeded in separating two isomers of the 2:1 chromium complex of 2-amino-6-(2'-hydroxy-6'-nitro-4'-sulfonaphth-1'-ylazo)-5-naphthol-7-sulfonic acid

[71] G. Schetty, *SVP Fachorgan Textilveredlung* **1**, 3 (1968).

(LXIII). Each was converted into a fiber-reactive derivative and dyed on cotton under very mild conditions to avoid equilibration to a mixture of isomers. The two isomers showed markedly different cellulose substantivity and this was reflected in the degree of fixation on cotton. While one isomer fixed to the extent of 67%, the other gave only 40% fixation. No information is available on the absolute configuration of the two isomers but each rapidly gave an equilibrium mixture of the two on heating in aqueous solution. For this reason little technical application can be foreseen for this very interesting observation. The very facile equilibration in aqueous solution of single isomers of 2:1 chromium complex dyestuffs to give mixtures of isomers would restrict their use to cold dyeing methods. This could find uses in the field of reactive dyestuffs but, unless simple stereospecific synthetic methods could be devised for the preparation of particular isomers of 2:1 chromium complex dyestuffs, the tedious and commercially unattractive methods employed in their isolation make them of academic interest only.

4. Methods of Preparation

a. *Chromium Complexes.* Chromium complexes of tridentate metallizable azo compounds occupy their position as the most important single class of metal complex azo dyestuffs because of their high stability. This is due to the fact that chromium(III) complexes are kinetically inert.[72] It is partly because of the inertness of chromium(III) complexes and their reluctance to undergo ligand exchange reactions that difficulties are sometimes experienced in the preparation of chromium complex dyestuffs from aquated chromium(III) salts.

In the hexaaquo chromium(III) ion each of the low-energy d orbitals is occupied by a single electron. Since there is only one way to arrange these electrons in the three available orbitals the Jahn-Teller effect does not operate to distort the regular octahedral structure and the ligand field stabilization energy is considerable.[10b] Computation of ligand field stabilization energies[73] indicates that d^3 ions, along with d^6 ions, are more resistant to distortions leading to either five- or seven-coordinate intermediates and thus rates of substitution of chromium(III) complexes are slow[74,74a] whether proceeding by a dissociative or an associative mecha-

[72] H. Taube, *Chem. Rev.* **50**, 69, (1952).

[73] F. Basolo and R. Pearson, "Mechanisms of Inorganic Reactions," p. 109. Wiley, New York, 1958.

[74] F. Basolo and R. Pearson, *Advan. Inorg. Chem. Radiochem.* **3**, 1 (1961); R. Wilkins, *Quart. Rev. (London)* **16**, 316 (1962).

[74a] J. E. Earley and R. D. Cannon *in* "Transition Metal Chemistry" (R. L. Carlin, ed.) p. 34. Arnold, London, 1965.

nism. The inertness of the hexaaquo chromium(III) ion, and its consequences in the synthesis of chromium complexes in general, has been demonstrated by several authors.[75,75a]

A further complicating feature in substitution reactions of the hexaaquo chromium(III) ion in basic or neutral solutions is the formation of hydroxo- and oxo-bridged polynuclear complexes. This was first demontrated by Bjerrum[76] as long ago as 1910 and since that time has been studied by a number of workers.[77] The subject is discussed by Earley and Cannon[74a] in a review on the aqueous chemistry of chromium(III).

Early methods employed in the preparation of chromium complexes of tridentate metallizable azo dyestuffs almost invariably involved the use of an aquated chromium(III) salt in aqueous medium. The reaction was often slow for the reasons outlined above, and in certain cases failed to go to completion unless large excesses of chromium were used. Since that time many methods have been examined in an effort to overcome these difficulties and this is reflected in the very wide patent literature on this subject. Most methods appear to have been designed to overcome the problem of slow displacement of coordinated water from the aquated chromium(III) ion.

i. The use of chromium salts. In this method, which is commonly employed, the metal-free azo dyestuff is treated with an excess of a chromium(III) salt, such as the acetate, chloride, or sulfate, in aqueous medium at the boil, or at higher temperatures under pressure. In the case of azo compounds devoid of sulfonic acid groups it is usual to add organic solvents such as alcohol, ethylene glycol, or formamide. Increasing acidity of the reaction medium favors the formation of 1:1 chromium complexes, and at a pH of 1.9 or below the 1:1 complex is usually the sole product. At higher pH values (approx. 9) the 2:1 complex is usually obtained. The use of a particular chromium salt as a source of chromium is, therefore, determined by the product required. Thus chromium(III) salts of strong acids, such as the sulfate or chloride, which allow the pH of the reaction mixture to fall to low values, are best employed for the

[75] J. P. Hunt and H. Taube, *J. Chem. Phys.* **18**, 757 (1950); **19**, 602 (1951); N. Bjerrum, *Z. Physik. Chem.* **59**, 336 and 581 (1907); C. L. Rollinson and J. C. Bailar, *J. Am. Chem. Soc.* **65**, 250 (1943); F. P. Dwyer and A. M. Sargeson, *J. Am. Chem. Soc.* **81**, 2335 (1959).

[75a] F. P. Dwyer, "Advances in the Chemistry of the Coordination Compounds" (S. Kirschner, ed.), p. 21. Macmillan, New York, 1961.

[76] N. Bjerrum, *Z. Physik. Chem.* **73**, 724 (1910).

[77] E. Stiasny, "Gerbereichemie." Steinkopff, Darmstadt, 1931; H. T. Hall and H. Eyring, *J. Am. Chem. Soc.* **72**, 782 (1950); M. Ardon and G. Stein, *J. Chem. Soc.* p. 2095 (1956); J. A. Laswick and R. A. Plane, *J. Am. Chem. Soc.* **81**, 3564 (1959).

preparation of 1:1 complexes. Chromium salts of weak acids, such as the acetate, exert a marked buffering effect and favor the formation of 2:1 complexes.

The reactions involved in the formation of chromium complex dyestuffs from aquated chromium(III) salts are summarized in (LXIV). Various workers[78] have studied the kinetics of the reaction but have ob-

$$DH_2(\text{or Ion}) + [Cr(H_2O)_6]^{3+} \rightleftharpoons [DCr(H_2O)_3]^+ \xrightarrow[\text{HCl}]{DH_2(\text{or ion})} [D_2Cr]^-$$

(DH$_2$ represents a tridentate medially metallizable azo dyestuff devoid of sulfonic acid groups)

(LXIV)

tained no conclusive results since the system is not suitable for study by the usual titration methods due to the very slow rate of reaction between o,o'-dihydroxyazo dyestuffs and the hexaaquo chromium(III) ion.[79] However, when the reaction between an o,o'-dihydroxyazo dyestuff and an aquated chromium salt is carried out under conditions which favor the formation of 2:1 chromium complex, no 1:1 complex is detected in the reaction mixture, demonstrating that the second stage in the reaction sequence is more rapid than the first. In fact the overall reaction is very much more rapid at high than at low pH values and this is often utilized in practice in the preparation of 1:1 chromium complexes. The metallizable azo compound is first converted to the 2:1 complex at relatively high pH and the latter is treated with mineral acid to obtain the 1:1 complex.

The fact that o,o'-dihydroxyazo dyestuffs react with the aquated chromium(III) ion more rapidly at high than at low pH suggests that reaction occurs more rapidly between the dyestuff ion and the chromium ion than between the un-ionized dyestuff and the chromium ion (see Section II,B,1). This is in agreement with the early observations of Krzikalla[80] that, in general, the more electronegatively substituted the azo compound the more rapidly does chromium complex formation occur. For example, o,o'-dihydroxyazo dyestuffs derived from picramic acid (LXV) usually form chromium complexes relatively rapidly. The presence of suitably situated electronegative groups in o,o'-dihydroxyazo dyestuffs results in enhancement of the acidity of one or both hydroxyl

---

[78] F. A. Snavely, W. C. Fernelius, and B. E. Douglas, *J. Soc. Dyers Colourists* **73**, 491 (1967); R. B. Bentley and J. P. Elder, *ibid.* **72**, 332 (1956); E. Coats and B. Rigg, *Trans. Faraday Soc.* **58**, 88 (1962).

[79] N. Bjerrum, "Metal Ammine Formation in Aqueous Solution." Haase & Sons, Copenhagen, 1941.

[80] H. Krzikalla, BIOS/DOCS/2351/2247/1/11.

groups. Coats[81] has determined the dissociation constants of Solochrome Violet R (LXVI) and has shown that the value of the second dissociation constant is lower than the pH at which chroming reactions designed to give 2:1 complexes are carried out.

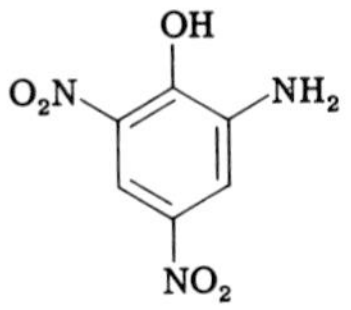

(LXV) 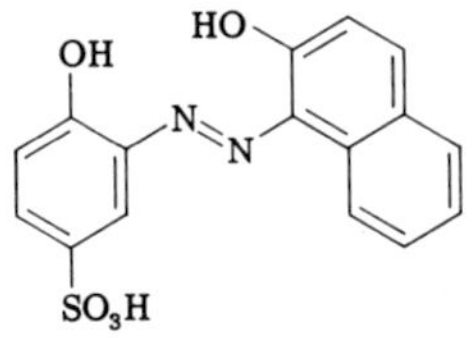 (LXVI)

ii. Chroming in organic solvents. This method is especially suitable for the preparation of chromium complexes of azo dyestuffs devoid of water-solubilizing groups. It also makes possible the use of higher reaction temperatures, and hence more rapid reaction, without the need to use pressure equipment. A variety of solvents has been recommended and the type of complex which is obtained is influenced by the solvent used. For example, chromium chloride in ethylene glycol is reported[82] to give 1:1 complexes rapidly and in good yield. Formamide has been recommended[83] as a solvent and is particularly useful for the preparation of 2:1 complexes since it exerts a buffering action.

It is significant that the solvents used have coordinating properties and it is probable that one of their actions is to displace coordinated water from the aquated chromium(III) salts which are used as the source of chromium in these reactions. In this context the use of chromium salts in urea melts has been recommended[84] as a method for the preparation of chromium complex dyestuffs. Under such conditions chromium chloride hexahydrate reacts with urea to give hexa(urea) chromic chloride, $[Cr(urea)_6]Cl_3$.[85] The latter compound has been shown[29] to be an excellent chroming agent and reacts rapidly and quantitatively with *o,o'*-dihydroxyazo dyestuffs in aqueous medium to give the 2:1 chromium complex of the latter.

iii. The use of complex chromium salts. In this method the metallizable azo compound is treated in neutral or alkaline solution in water and/or organic solvent with a chromium complex of a chelating organic

[81] E. Coats and B. Rigg, *Trans. Faraday Soc.* **57**, 1088 (1961).

[82] Gy, *BP* 790,904; BASF, *BP* 745,474.

[83] E. J. Bourne, M. Stacey, J. C. Tatlow, and ICI, *BP* 748,421; S, *BP* 754,270; 755,576; 787,843.

[84] Gy, *BP* 741,638; 775,005.

[85] E. Wilke-Dörfurt, and K. Niederer, *Z. Anorg. Allgem. Chem.* **184**, 145 (1929).

acid such as oxalic acid,[86] tartaric acid,[87] or salicylic acid,[88] or with a mixture of a chromium salt and a chelating acid.[89] The use of such complexes has a twofold advantage; first the difficulty of displacing strongly coordinated water from the aquated chromium(III) ion is removed, and second, the reaction can be carried out at high pH values without precipitation of chromium hydroxide. The usual product in these cases is the 2:1 chromium complex, although in certain cases 1:1 complexes are obtained in which the coordination sphere of the metal is at least partially completed by the organic ligand, e.g., salicylic acid[90] (Section II,G,1).

In a modification[86,91] of this method an alkaline solution of the metallizable azo dyestuff is treated with the complex chromium compounds formed by the action of alkaline suspensions of chromium hydroxide on organic polyhydroxy compounds such as glycerol. The structures of the chroming agents have not been determined, but the use of the glycerol complex is claimed to eliminate the need for excess chromium since the reaction proceeds quantitatively to give the 2:1 chromium complex of the azo compound.

iv. The use of compounds of Cr(VI). The use of dichromate salts in certain syntheses to overcome the problem of slow displacement of coordinated water from the aquated chromium(III) ion has been known for some time. A typical application[92] is the preparation of potassium bis(oxalato)bis(aquo)chromium(III) from potassium dichromate and oxalic acid. In this case reduction of the chromium(VI) to the trivalent oxidation state is effected by excess oxalic acid. This has been extended to the preparation of chromium complexes of metallizable azo dyestuffs and the reaction is usually carried out in the presence of a reducing agent to avoid oxidation of the azo dyestuff. The reducing agents which have been recommended include furfural,[93] reducing sugars such as glucose,[94] addition compounds of carbonyl compounds and alkali metal bisulfites,[93] and inorganic compounds such as the alkali metal salts of sulfurous acid.[95] It has been claimed that chroming by this method is faster than

[86] A. H. Knight, C. H. Reece, and ICI, *BP* 740,272.

[87] S, *BP* 753,550; R. F. M. Sureau, G. R. H. Mingasson, and Francolor, *BP* 810,207.

[88] Gy, *BP* 756,874; CIBA, *BP* 637,404.

[89] FBy, *BP* 789,126.

[90] G. Schetty, *Helv. Chim. Acta* **35**, 716 (1952).

[91] Gy, *BP* 667,168.

[92] W. G. Palmer, "Experimental Inorganic Chemistry," p. 387. Cambridge Univ. Press, London and New York, 1954.

[93] S, *SP* 370,506; 370,507.

[94] S, *BP* 753,987; FBy, *BP* 796,747; BASF *BP* 793,136; FBy *BP* 813,186.

[95] S, *BP* 807,695.

by any other known process, and that 1:1 complex formation is suppressed.

v. Hydrolytic chroming. In certain cases the preparation of *o,o'*-dihydroxyazo dyestuffs is complicated by the fact that some diazo oxides obtained from *o*-aminophenols react only slowly with coupling components. This results in low yields of impure products. One method of overcoming this problem (see also Section II,C,4,*c,ii*) is to use diazotized *o*-aminophenol sulfuric esters which react readily with coupling components to give the monosulfate ester of the derived *o,o'*-dihydroxyazo dyestuff in high yield.[96] These compounds hydrolyze rapidly in the presence of metal ions to give metal complexes of *o,o'*-dihydroxyazo dyestuffs and chromium complexes can be prepared in this way. The facile hydrolysis of the sulfate ester group in dyestuffs of this type may be compared with the similar reaction undergone by sulfuric and phosphonic esters of 8-hydroxyquinolines in the presence of cupric ions (Section II,B,2).

Another method of overcoming the slow coupling of certain diazo oxides is to use a diazotized *o*-alkoxyaniline in place of the diazotized *o*-aminophenol. *o*-Alkoxy-*o'*-hydroxyazo dyestuffs obtained in this way undergo simultaneous dealkylation and chroming on treatment with chromium salts to give the chromium complexes of the corresponding *o,o'*-dihydroxyazo dyestuffs.[97] Water-soluble *o*-methoxy-*o'*-hydroxyazo dyestuffs can be demethylatively chromed in aqueous acid at 100° but this is a relatively slow process and higher temperatures are preferred.[98] In the case of *o*-alkoxy-*o'*-hydroxyazo dyestuffs devoid of solubilizing groups chromings of this type can be performed in aqueous medium in an autoclave or in a suitable high-boiling solvent such as ethylene glycol.[99]

A further development has been claimed[100] in which 1:1 chromium complexes of *o*-alkoxy-*o'*-hydroxyazo dyestuffs are prepared in ethylene glycol at 120–150° and pH 4.5–5.0 without loss of the alkyl group. Complexes of this type are said to react with an equimolecular quantity of the same or different metallizable azo compound in ethylene glycol at 135–145° and a pH of 7.5–8.0 to give a symmetrical or an unsymmetrical 2:1 chromium complex, respectively. Under these conditions dealkylation occurs and the products are 2:1 chromium complexes of *o,o'*-dihydroxyazo dyestuffs.

[96] R. R. Davies and ICI, *BP* 747,872.
[97] IG, *DRP* 474,997.
[98] CIBA, *BP* 648,364.
[99] Gy, *BP* 740,589.
[100] E. Csendes and DuP, *USP* 2,871,232.

vi. The interaction of 1:1 chromium complexes and metal-free metal-lizable azo dyestuffs. As long ago as 1939 Drew and Fairbairn[3] observed that the 1:1 chromium complex of 1-(2'-hydroxyphenylazo)-2-naphthol would react with a further molecule of the parent azo compound to give the 2:1 chromium complex (LXVII). More recently this has been extended[4] to the preparation of the commercially very important unsymmetrical 2:1 chromium complexes containing a single sulfonic acid group (Section I), e.g., (LXVIII). Thus unsymmetrical 2:1 chromium complexes can be prepared by the interaction of metal-free *o,o'*-dihydroxyazo, *o*-carboxy-*o'*-hydroxyazo, or *o*-amino-*o'*-hydroxyazo compounds with equimolecular quantities of the 1:1 chromium complexes of differ-

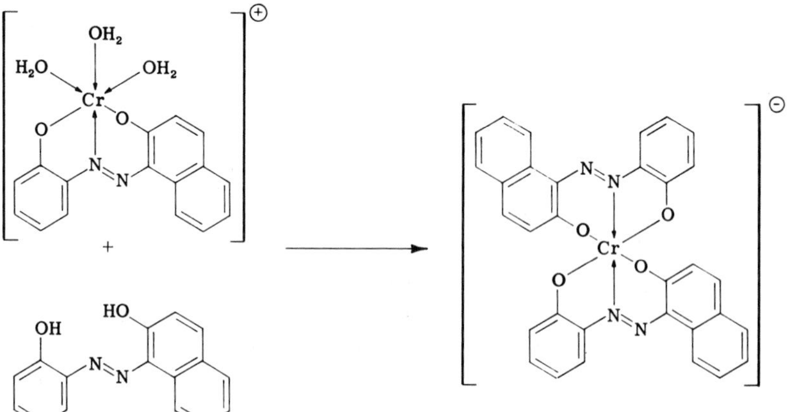

(LXVII)

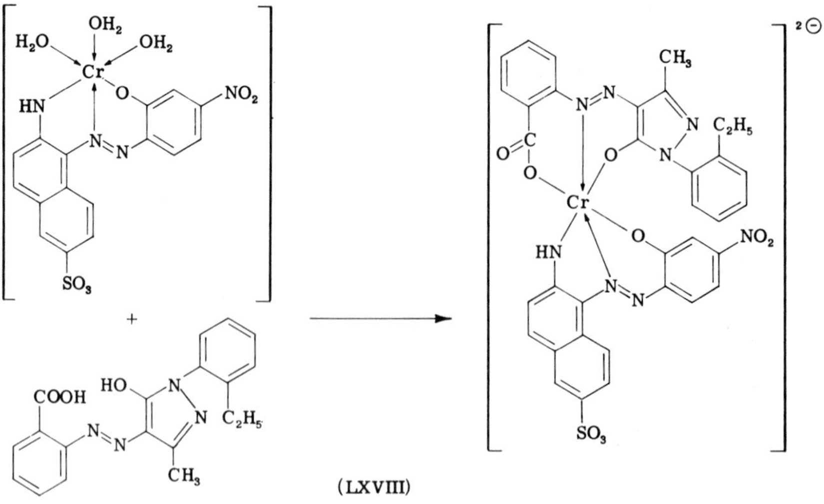

(LXVIII)

ent tridentate metallizable azo dyestuffs. The reaction proceeds under mild conditions and is usually carried out in neutral or weakly alkaline medium at 50–100°.

b. Cobalt Complexes. Like chromium(III) complexes cobalt(III) complexes are kinetically inert (Section II,C,4,*a*). However, although corresponding chromium(III) and cobalt(III) complexes are very similar in behavior the standard methods employed in their preparation are often quite different. In general cobalt(III) complexes are the easier to prepare, the usual method being to oxidize the appropriate cobalt(II) complex. Direct substitution of aqueous cobalt(III) is inconvenient because of its strongly oxidizing character and the slowness of substitution reactions.[75a] Thus, although 2:1 cobalt complexes of tridentate metallizable azo dyestuffs have been prepared by a variety of methods, most involve the interaction of the azo compound and a cobalt(II) salt or complex at relatively high pH. The product is invariably the diamagnetic cobalt(III) complex, the oxidation potential being such that spontaneous oxidation to the cobalt(III) state occurs. If the reaction is carried out under anaerobic conditions partial reduction of the azo compound results[29] and the use of various oxidizing agents has been recommended to avoid this.

A problem which is sometimes encountered in the preparation of 2:1 cobalt complex dyestuffs at relatively high pH values is precipitation of cobalt hydroxide, which can be difficult to remove from the product. This is avoided if the reaction is carried out in the presence of di- or triethanolamine.[101]

The preparation of 1:1 cobalt(III) complex dyestuffs in which the coordination sphere of the metal is completed by mono-, bi-, and tridentate nitrogen-donor ligands, and of unsymmetrical 2:1 cobalt complex dyestuffs has been described in some detail in Section II,C,2.

c. Copper Complexes. The preparation of copper complexes of tridentate metallizable azo dyestuffs presents few difficulties and is usually carried out by the interaction of the azo compound and a copper salt in aqueous medium at 60°. However, certain other methods of preparation are of considerable theoretical as well as technological interest.

i. Simultaneous dealkylation and coppering of o-alkoxy-o'-hydroxyazo dyestuffs. This method[9b] is directly analogous to the demethylative chroming method (Section II,C,4,*a*,*v*) and is particularly valuable for the preparation of copper complexes of *o,o'*-dihydroxazo dyestuffs which are difficult to obtain by coupling a diazotized *o*-aminophenol with a naphthol coupling component. It is usually carried out[102] by heating an

[101] H. Ruckstuhl and S, *FP* 1,469,439.
[102] CIBA, *BP* 644,883.

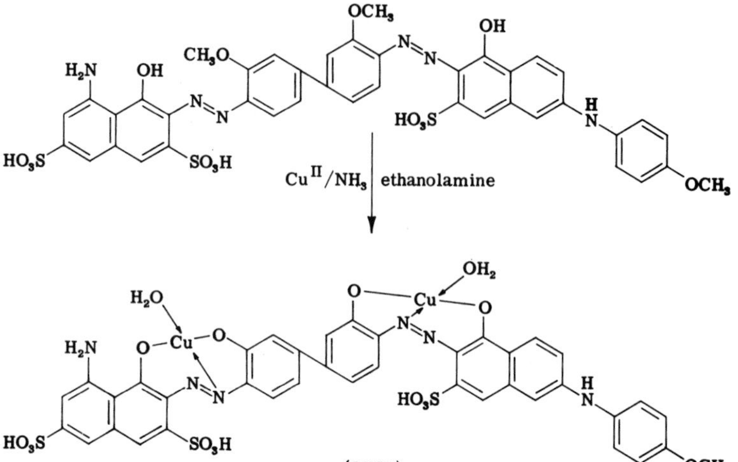

(LXIX)

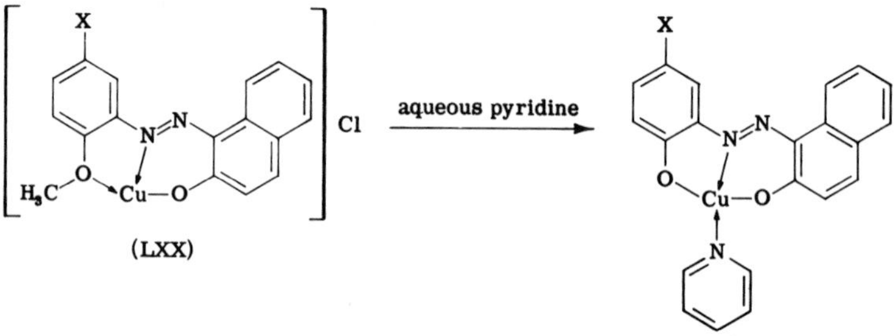

(LXX)   aqueous pyridine

(LXXI)

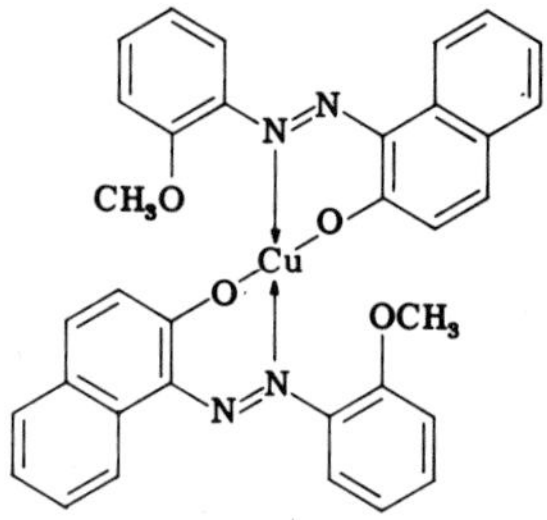

(LXXII)

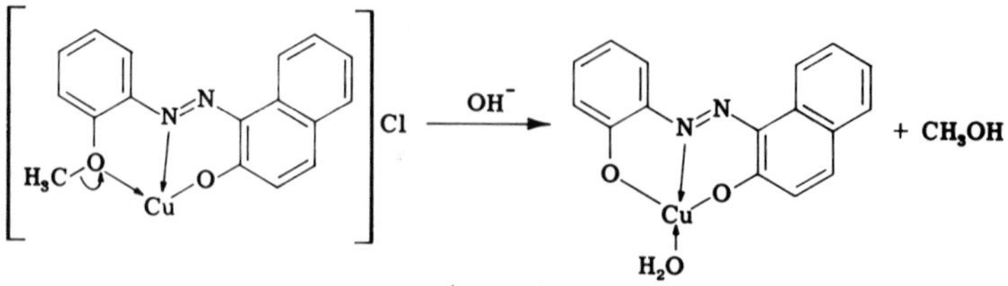

(LXXIII)

aqueous solution of an o-methoxy-o'-hydroxyazo dyestuff with cupra-ammonium sulfate in the presence of an alkanolamine such as diethanol-amine (LXIX).

1-(2'-Methoxyphenylazo)-2-naphthol reacts with cupric chloride in ethanol to give a complex having 1:1 stoichiometry which has been formulated by Mur[103] as (LXX; X = H). This complex readily under-goes demethylation in aqueous pyridine to give the copper complex of 1-(2'-hydroxyphenylazo)-2-naphthol[104] (LXXI). In contrast the 2:1 copper complex of 1-(2'-methoxyphenylazo)-2-naphthol[24b,103] (LXXII) undergoes the corresponding reaction only very slowly,[104] which leads to the conclusion that coordination of the methoxy group is necessary for demethylation to occur.

Mur[104] has also shown that the rate of dealkylation of copper com-plexes such as (LXX) is influenced by substituents para to the methoxy group, the descending order of effect on rate being $X = NO_2 > H > MeO > Me > Cl$. These results could be taken to infer nucleophilic at-tack by hydroxyl ion at the carbon atom attached to the methoxy group, promoted by electron withdrawal due to coordination of the methoxy group and assisted by electron-withdrawing groups in the para position. However, unlike coppering reactions involving replacement of an ortho chloro group (Section iii, below), the methoxy group cannot be replaced by nucleophilic reagents such as ammonia or amines. Therefore it is reasonable to suppose that the methyl group is removed as a carbonium ion (LXXIII), this process being assisted by coordination of the methoxy group and also by electronegative substituents in the para position.

ii. *Oxidative coppering of o-hydroxyazo dyestuffs.* In this method, which has been reviewed by Pfitzner and Baumann,[105] an o-hydroxyazo dyestuff is treated with an oxidizing agent in the presence of cupric ions[106] to obtain the copper complex of an o,o'-dihydroxyazo dyestuff (LXXIV). The oxidizing agent most commonly used is hydrogen peroxide, but salts of peroxy acids, $Na_2S_2O_8$, $NaBO_3$, and Na_2O_2 have also been employed. The reaction is usually carried out in aqueous me-dium at 40–70° and at pH 4.5–7.0.

Recently Idelson et al.[68] have shown that copper complexes of naph-tholazopyrazolones (LXXVI) can be prepared from naphthaleneazopyra-zolones (LXXV) in nearly quantitative yield under very mild conditions by a modification of this procedure. The success of this modi-fication, in which hydrogen peroxide is added to a solution of the copper complex of the naphthalene-azopyrazolone in dimethylformamide at

[103] V. I. Mur, *Zh. Obschch. Khim.* **24,** 572 (1954); *Chem. Abstr.* **49,** 6198 (1955).
[104] V. I. Mur, *Zh. Obschch. Khim.* **28,** 998 (1958); *Chem. Abstr.* **52,** 17197 (1958).
[105] H. Pfitzner and H. Baumann, *Angew. Chem.* **70,** 232 (1958).
[106] BASF, *USP* 2,674,595.

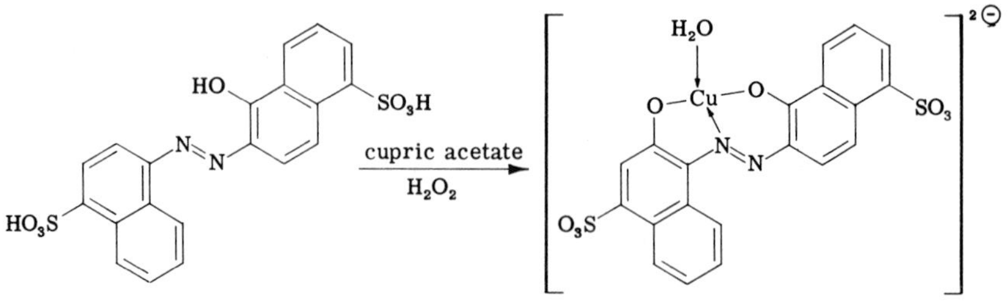

(LXXIV)

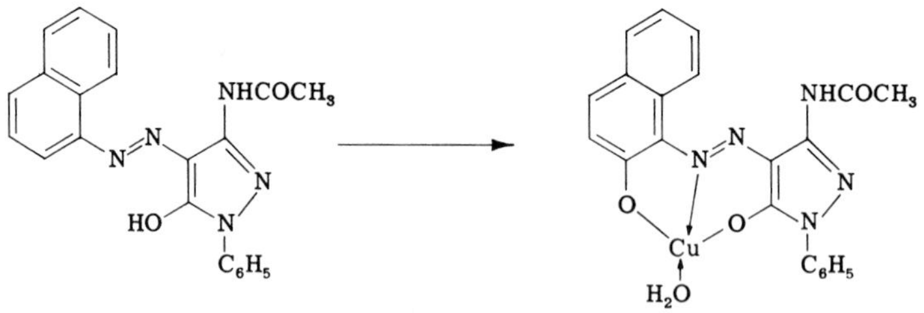

(LXXV)   (LXXVI)

—10° to 0°, is said to depend upon complete conversion of the azo compound to a 1:1 complex. The oxidation of 1:1 copper complexes of
o-hydroxyazo dyestuffs to copper complexes of the corresponding o,o'-
dihydroxyazo dyestuffs has also been reported by Yoshida et al.[107]

Neither Idelson et al. nor Yoshida et al. isolated the 1:1 copper complexes of the o-hydroxyazo compounds before oxidation, but simply
treated solutions containing the azo compound and excess cupric acetate
with hydrogen peroxide. The former authors used dimethylformamide as
solvent, and the latter aqueous acetic acid. The formation of 1:1 copper
complexes of o-hydroxyazo compounds under these conditions appears to
be unlikely since it is known[26] that 1-phenylazo-2-naphthol reacts with
cupric acetate to form a 2:1 complex (XXVI) even in the presence of a
large excess of the latter reagent. However, the use of an equimolecular
quantity of a cupric salt is necessary for the formation of the 1:1 copper
complex of the o,o'-dihydroxyazo compound which is the product of the
reaction.

[107] Z. Yoshida, S. Sagawa, and R. Oda, Kogyo Kagaku Zasshi 62, 1402 (1959);
Chem. Abstr. 57, 13922 (1962); Kogyo Kagaku Zasshi 62, 1399 (1959); Chem. Abstr.
57, 13922 (1962).

Brackman *et al.*[108] have studied the *o*-hydroxylation of monohydric phenols by hydrogen peroxide in the presence of a copper catalyst and have proposed a mechanism for the reaction (Chart 5) in which the position of substitution is controlled by localization of the reagent by copper complex formation. The intervention of a complex having a hydroperoxy radical attached to the cupric ion is in keeping with Glasner's[109] conclu-

CHART 5

Copper Complex Formation in *o*-Hydroxylation

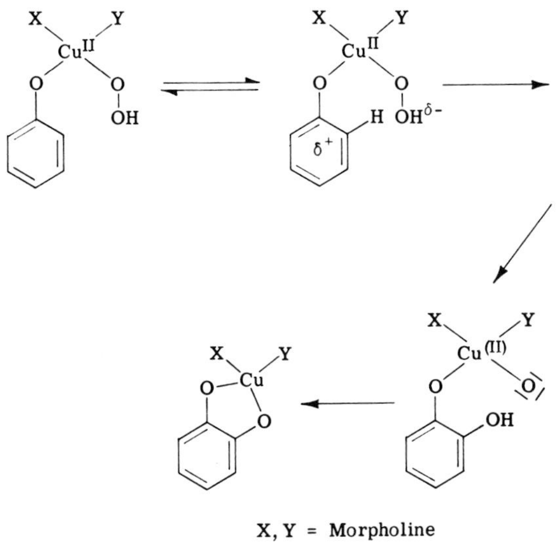

X, Y = Morpholine

sion that copper peroxide is formed by simple addition of –OOH to CuO. It is probable[108] that a similar mechanism is involved in the oxidation of copper complexes of *o*-hydroxyazo dyestuffs to the copper complexes of *o,o'*-dihydroxyazo compounds and that localization of attack by the oxidizing agent is due to its involvement in complex formation.

iii. Preparation from o-chloro-o'-hydroxyazo compounds. The principal application of this method[110] is in the preparation of copper complexes of *o,o'*-dihydroxyazo dyestuffs which are difficult to prepare by coupling a diazotized *o*-aminophenol with a naphthol or pyrazolone coupling component (Section II,C,4,*a,iv*). In practice an *o*-halo, usually *o*-chloro-*o'*-hydroxyazo dyestuff is treated with a copper salt in the presence of an acid-binding agent to obtain the copper complex of the cor-

[108] W. Brackman and E. Havinga, *Rec. Trav. Chim.* **74**, 1107 (1955).

[109] A. Glasner, *J. Chem. Soc.* p. 904 (1951).

[110] IG, *DRP* 571,859; 738,900.

responding *o,o'*-dihydroxyazo dyestuff (LXXVII). The most interesting feature of this method, which has recently been reviewed by Stepanov,[111] is the ease with which the chlorine atom is replaced by a hydroxyl group during the metallization process. The nucleophilic replacement of halogen atoms in aromatic compounds proceeds under mild conditions only if the halogen atom is strongly activated by electronegative substituents in ortho or para positions. However, in the presence of copper salts the chlorine atom in *o*-chloro-*o'*-hydroxyazo dyestuffs can also be replaced by other nucleophiles such as alkoxy, alkylamino, arylamino, and sulfinic acid groups[112] in alkaline medium at 50°. The high mobility of the halogen atoms in *o*-halo-*o'*-hydroxyazo dyestuffs under the conditions described cannot be attributed to the activating effect of the *o*-azo group since available evidence shows this to be low.[113] It is significant that catalytic amounts of copper are ineffective and near-stoichiometric quantities are necessary for reactions of this type to proceed. In this connection Stepanov[114] has demonstrated that the copper complex of the azo compound 1-(2'-chlorophenylazo)-2-naphthol reacts readily with nucleophilic reagents with replacement of the chlorine atom. Stepanov[115] has proposed that the high mobility of the chlorine atom is due to interaction between the chlorine and the metal atom in a complex in which the metal forms a part of a 5-membered chelate ring involving the oxygen atom (LXXVIII). In support of this Stepanov[116] has shown that whereas the Schiff's base (LXXIX) reacts with alcoholates in the presence of cupric ions with replacement of the chlorine atom by an alkoxy group, the isomeric (LXXX) fails to undergo a similar reaction.

However, it has been proved[26,26a] that *o*-hydroxyazo compounds form copper complexes in which the copper atom forms a part of a six-membered chelate ring involving the oxygen atom. The behavior of the two Schiff's bases (LXXIX) and (LXXX) is also rather surprising since it is known that although copper complexes of azomethines of the type

[111] B. I. Stepanov, *in* "Recent Progress in the Chemistry of Natural and Synthetic Colouring Matters and Related Fields" (T. S. Gore *et al.*, eds.) p. 451. Academic Press, New York, 1962.

[112] D. Delfs and IG, *DRP* 658,841.

[113] W. Borsche and I. Exss, *Ber.* **56**, 2353 (1923); G. M. Badger, J. W. Cook, and W. P. Vidal, *J. Chem. Soc.* p. 1109 (1947).

[114] B. I. Stepanov and L. B. Aingorn, *Zh. Obshch. Khim.* **29**, 3436 (1959); *Chem. Abstr.* **54**, 15322a (1960); M. A. Andreevna and B. I. Stepanov, *Zh. Obshch. Khim.* **28**, 2966 (1958); *Chem. Abstr.* **53**, 9162 (1961).

[115] M. A. Andreevna and B. I. Stepanov, *Zh. Obshch. Khim.* **30**, 2748 (1960); *Chem. Abstr.* **55**, 14395d (1959).

[116] B. I. Stepanov, *VIII Mendeleevski Sjezd. Refer. Dokl., Sekcija Org. Khim. i. Technol. Izd. Akad. Nauk SSSR* p. 257 (1959).

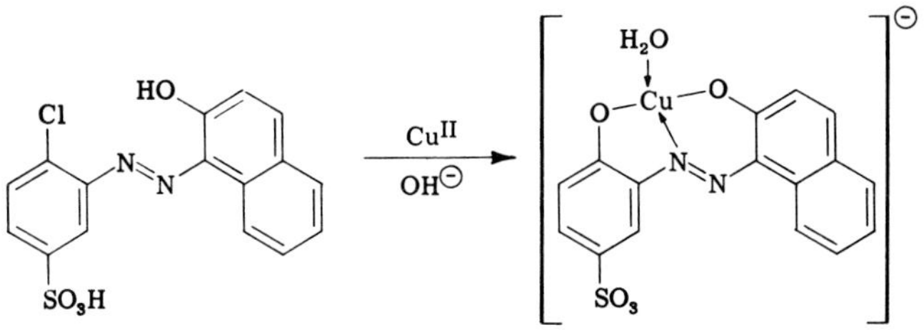

(LXXVII)

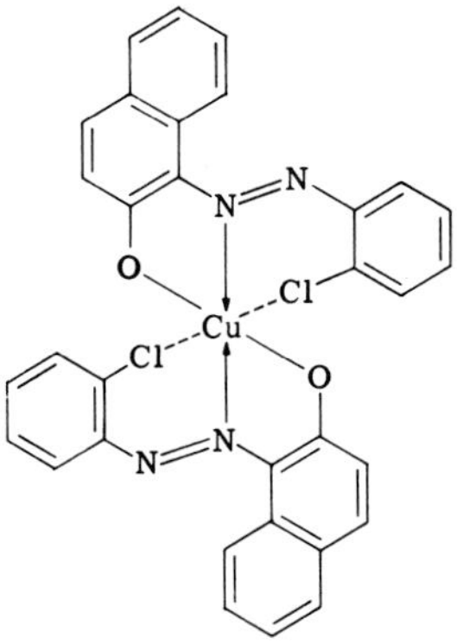

(LXXVIII)

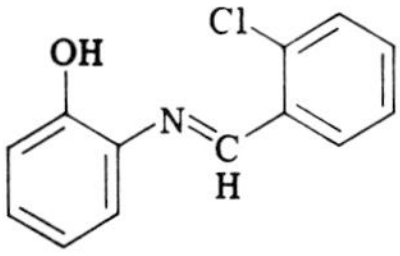

(LXXIX)

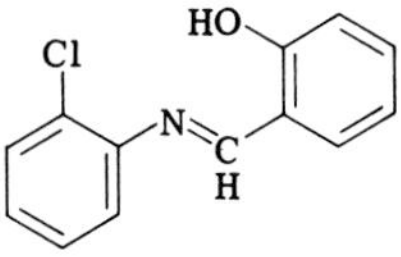

(LXXX)

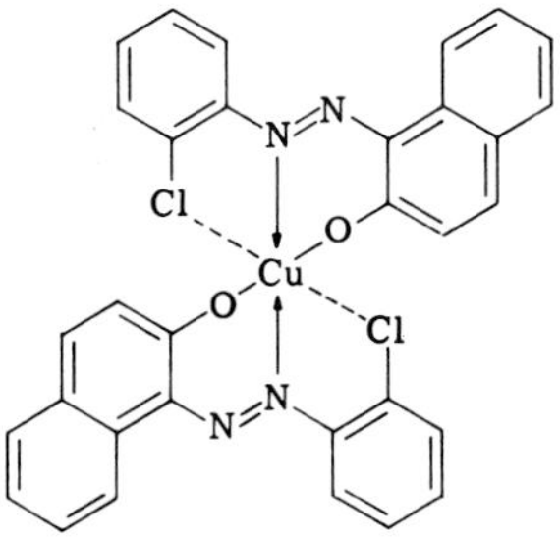

(LXXXI)

(LXXX) are moderately stable, those derived from the isomeric (LXXIX) are not.[117] This is due to activation of the latter towards hydrolysis by the formal positive change on the nitrogen atom associated with coordination.[118]

All available evidence points to activation of the *o*-halogen atoms in copper complexes of *o*-halo-*o'*-hydroxyazo dyestuffs by coordination of the halogen atom to the metal, since the halogen atoms in copper complexes of *m*-, or *p*-chloro-*o'*-hydroxyazo dyestuffs do not exhibit abnormal mobility. However, a structure in which the copper atom forms a part of a 6-membered chelate ring involving the oxygen atom (LXXXI) would be preferred to that proposed by Stepanov. The formation of complex intermediates of this type would result in activation toward nucleophilic attack of the carbon atom attached to the chlorine atom.

5. Less-Common Tridentate Azo Dyestuffs

a. Heterocyclic Types. In recent years a large number of patents has appeared disclosing metal complexes of *o*-hydroxyazo dyestuffs containing a heterocyclic donor atom, usually nitrogen, so situated that the dyestuff functions as a tridentate ligand. One particular application of dyestuffs of this type is in the dyeing of metal-containing poly-*α*-olefins (Section I). The field is too wide to survey in detail here, but in order to illustrate the types of dyestuff which are employed, a few representative patents are listed in Table I.

Certain azo dyestuffs of this type, in particular pyridineazo-*β*-naphthol (PAN) (LXXXII) and pyridineazoresorcinol (PAR) (LXXXIII), have been used in spectrophotometric and titrimetric determination of metal ions, as well as in their separation by solvent extraction techniques. Consequently their metal complexes have been studied in some detail by various workers.[119] The anomalous nature of some of the published results, however, prompted Fernando *et al.*[120] to carry out the X-ray crystal structure determination of the copper complex of pyridylazo-2-naphthol, [Cu(PAN)H$_2$O]ClO$_4$ (LXXXIV). The molecule is very nearly planar and has normal Cu–N and Cu–O interatomic dis-

[117] K. K. Chatterjee, N. Farrier, and B. E. Douglas, *J. Am. Chem. Soc.* **85**, 2919 (1963).

[118] G. L. Eichhorn and J. C. Bailar, *J. Am. Chem. Soc.* **75**, 2905 (1953); G. L. Eichhorn and I. M. Trachtenberg, *ibid.* **76**, 5183 (1954); G. L. Eichhorn, and N. D. Marchand, *ibid.* **78**, 2688 (1956).

[119] S. Shibata, *Anal. Chim. Acta* **25**, 348 (1961); *Nogoya Kogyo Gijutsu Shikensho Hokoku* **12**, 337 (1963); W. J. Geary, G. Nickless, and F. H. Pollard, *Anal. Chim. Acta* **27**, 71 (1962); A. Corsini, I. Mai-Ling Yih, Q. Fernando, and H. Freiser, *Anal. Chem.* **34**, 1090 (1962); H. Wada and G. Nakamura, *J. Chem. Soc. Japan, Pure Chem. Sect.* **85**, 549 (1964).

[120] Shun 'ichiro Ooi, D. Carter, and Q. Fernando, *Chem. Commun.* p. 1301 (1967).

TABLE I

Tridentate Metallizable Azo Dyestuffs Derived
from Heterocyclic Diazo Components

Patent	Firm	Typical azo compound
FP 1,396,150	ClBA	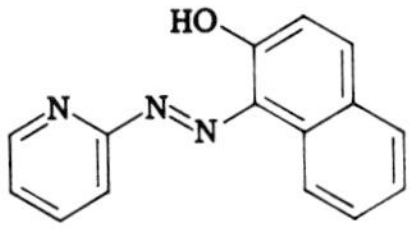
BeP 659,748	FH	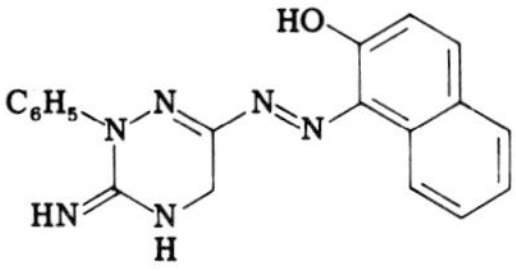
BeP 644,279	Allied Chem. Corp.	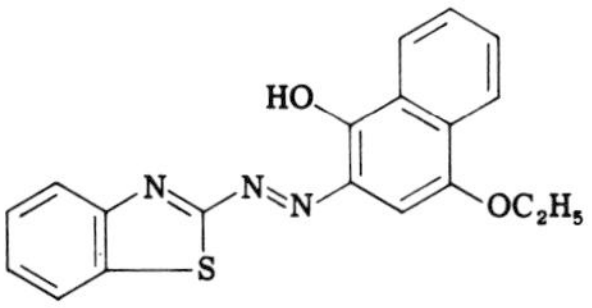
BeP 643,554	Allied Chem. Corp.	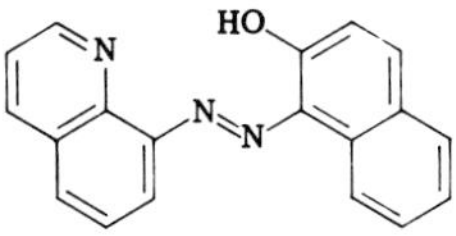
BP 1,038,915	Toyo Rayon	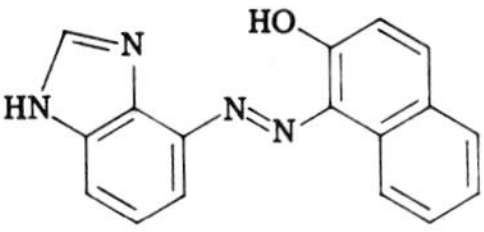
BP 1,016,248	FBy	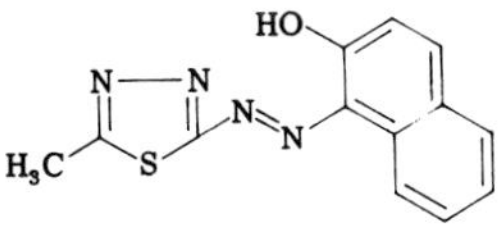
BP 1,016,248	FBy	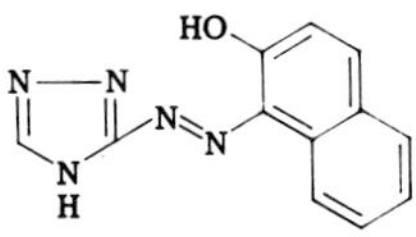

tances. The double-bond character of the azo group is preserved, showing that there is essentially no delocalization of electrons in the chelate ring containing the azo group, and the molecule contains two annelated 5-membered chelate rings.

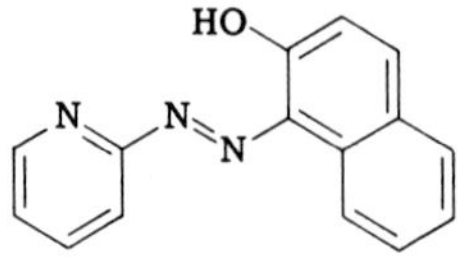

(LXXXII)

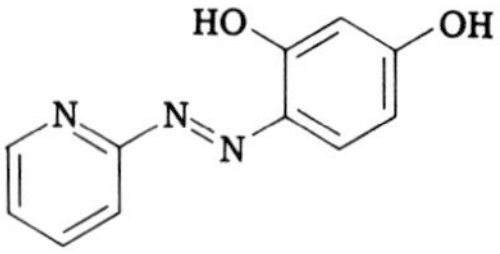

(LXXXIII)

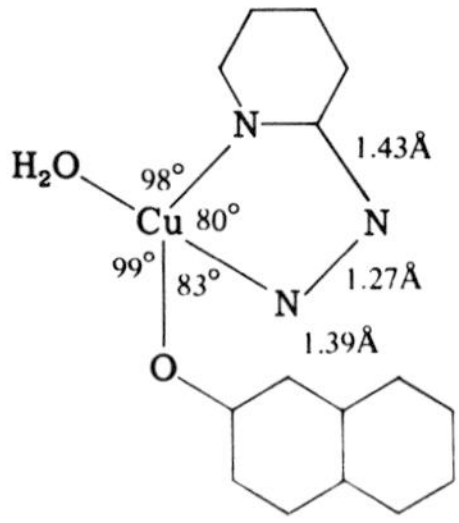

(LXXXIV)

b. o-Alkoxy-o'-hydroxyazo dyestuffs. In 1927 Crippa[24b] prepared a copper complex of 1-(2'-methoxyphenylazo)-2-naphthol with 2:1 stoichiometry in which the methoxy groups were not involved in coordination (LXXXV). More recently Mur[103] has isolated a complex having 1:1 stoichiometry by the interaction of the same azo compound and cupric chloride in ethanol. Mur considered that the methoxy group was coordinated to the copper in this complex which he formulated as (LXXXVI). The complex was rather unstable and was readily converted to a product identical with that obtained by Crippa on shaking with cold ethanolic ammonia, suggesting a very weak bond between the methoxy group and the copper. Confirmation that o-methoxy-o'-hydroxyazo dyestuffs can function as tridentate ligands has been provided by stability measurements.[121]

While metal complexes of o-alkoxy-o'-hydroxyazo dyestuffs are insufficiently stable to be of value as dyestuffs this observation is of importance in connection with the formation of copper and chromium complexes of o,o'-dihydroxyazo dyestuffs by the demethylative metalliza-

[121] F. A. Snavely, B. D. Krecker, and C. G. Clark, *J. Am. Chem. Soc.* **81**, 2337 (1959).

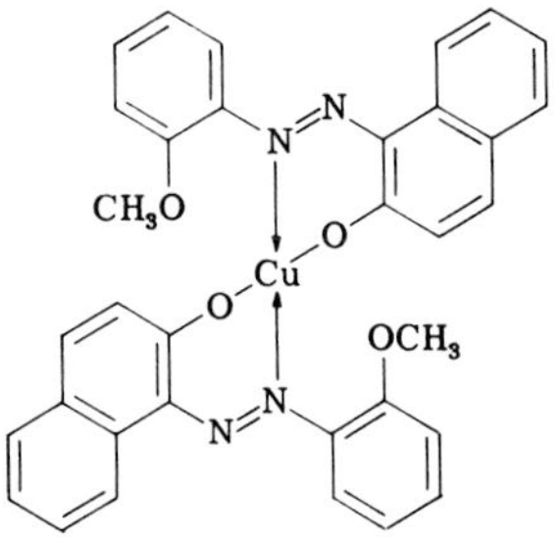

(LXXXV)

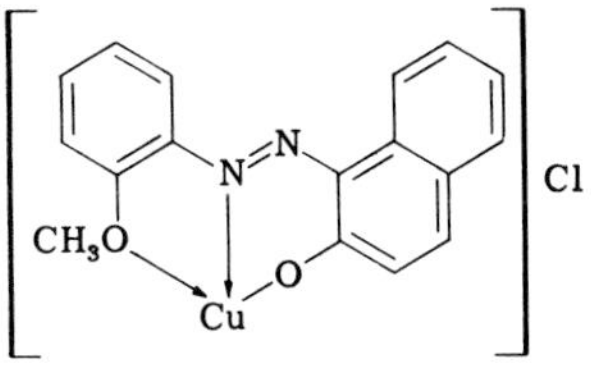

(LXXXVI)

tion of o-alkoxy-o'-hydroxyazo compounds (Sections II,C,5,a,v and c,i).

c. o-Thioalkoxy-o'-hydroxyazo dyestuffs. As in the previous series, evidence for the participation of the o-thioalkoxy group in metal complex formation has been obtained[121] by stability constant determination. Although metal complexes of o-thiomethoxy-o'-hydroxyazo compounds are more stable than those of the corresponding o-methoxy-o'-hydroxyazo compounds, their stability is again too low for them to be of value as dyestuffs. In contrast to o-methoxy-o'-hydroxyazo dyestuffs, o-thiomethoxy-o'-hydroxyazo dyestuffs do not undergo demethylative metallization reactions.[122]

d. o-Hydroxyarylazoaryl arsonic and phosphonic acids. o-Hydroxyazo dyestuffs containing an arsonic acid group in the ortho' position have been recommended as analytical reagents for certain metals. For example, the use of 2-(2'-hydroxy-3',6'-disulfonaphth-1'-ylazo)benzenearsonic acid [LXXXVII; X = AsO(OH)$_2$] in the determination of thorium has been described.[123] However, no metal complexes of compounds of this type, or of the analogous azo compounds containing phosphonic acid groups [LXXXVII; X = PO(OH)$_2$] have been reported as having dyestuff applications. The stabilities of the copper complexes of (LXXXVII) with X = PO(OH)$_2$ and AsO(OH)$_2$ are somewhat lower than those of the copper complex of (LXXXVII) where X = COOH, as a result of the more acidic character of the phosphonic[124] and arsonic acid groups than carboxylic acid groups (Section II,I,1). It is of interest to note, however, that the acidity of the arsonic acid group in the copper complex (LXXXVIII) is enhanced by coordination. As a result of this, complexes of this type have superior solubility compared with their

[122] R. Specklin and J. Meybeck, Bull. Soc. Chim. France 18, 621 (1951).

[123] C. V. Banks and C. H. Byrd, Anal. Chem. 25, 416 (1953); D. W. Margerum, C. H. Byrd, S. A. Reed, and C. V. Banks, ibid. 25, 1219 (1953).

[124] H. H. Jaffé, L. D. Freedman, and G. O. Doak, J. Am. Chem. Soc. 75, 2209 (1953).

carboxylic acid analogs. However, in the 2:1 chromium complex field the increased acidity results in inferior neutral-dyeing properties on wool, and the resulting dyeings have lower fastness to wet treatments than do those of their carboxylic acid analogs.[125]

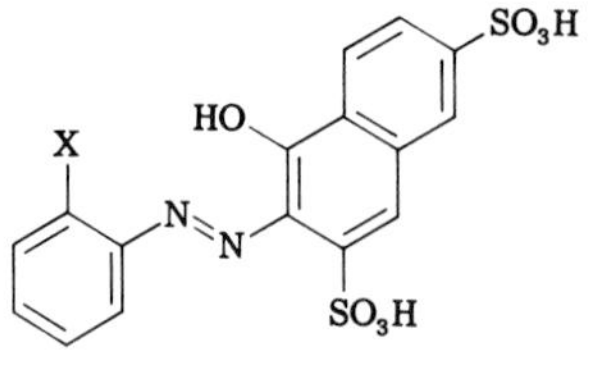

(LXXXVII) 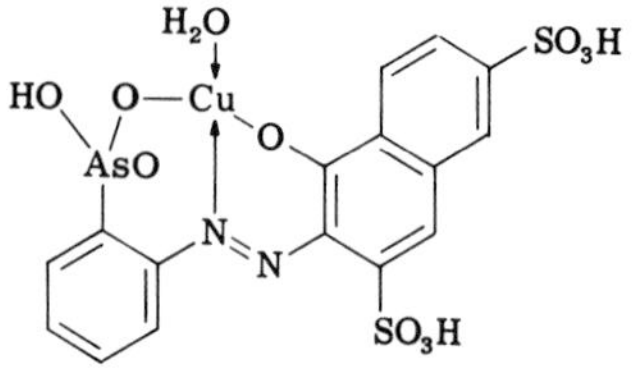   (LXXXVIII)

e. Hydroxyarylazo aryl sulfonic acids and sulfonamides. 2:1-Chromium complexes have been prepared[126] from *o*-hydroxyazo dyestuffs having a sulfonic acid group in the *o'*-position. Despite the strongly acidic character of the sulfonic acid group dyestuffs of this type function as tridentate ligands and give complexes having a fac configuration (Section II,C,3). Not surprisingly complexes of this type are very unstable and readily demetallize. Schetty[71] points out that in these dyestuffs the distance between the donor atoms occupying the positions ortho to the azo group is 0.65 Å shorter than the theoretical distance for the formation of a fac complex, and attributes the lack of stability to strain in the molecule. No doubt this factor does contribute to the lack of stability, but this must be due largely to the very low basicity, and hence donor properties of the sulfonic acid anion (Section II,I,1). Complexes of this type are of no value as dyestuffs[71] and give orange-brown shades on wool having poor wash, perspiration, and lightfastness.

2:1 Chromium complexes with fac configurations have also been obtained[126] from *o*-hydroxyazo compounds having sulfonamide groups in the *o'*-position. These too are very unstable and are of no value as dyestuffs.

f. o-Hydroxy-o'-(alkyl or aryl)sulfonylamino azo dyestuffs. *o*-Hydroxyazo dyestuffs having an alkyl- or an arylsulfonylamino group in the *o'*-position react with chromium and cobalt salts to give 2:1 complexes in which two protons are lost from each molecule of the azo compound[126] (LXXXIX). In both cases only a single isomer has been detected, and from a comparison of their spectra with those of the

---

[125] J. S. Hunter, R. Price, and ICI, unpublished results (1966).
[126] G. Schetty, *Helv. Chim. Acta* **49**, 461 (1966).

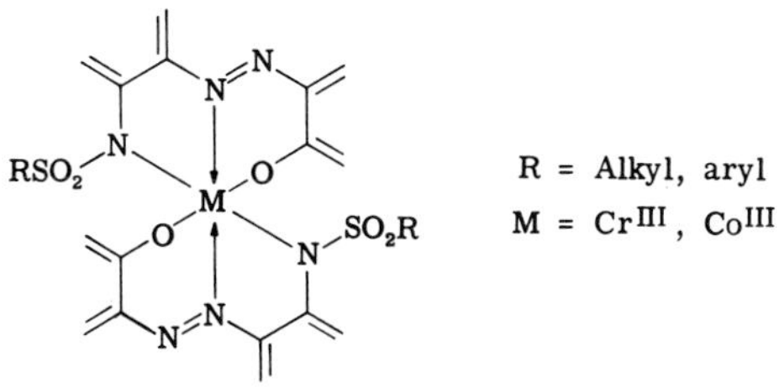

(LXXXIX)

R = Alkyl, aryl

M = Cr[III], Co[III]

corresponding complexes of analogous o,o'-dihydroxyazo dyes, Schetty concludes that they have a mer configuration. In contrast to complexes derived from dyes containing o-hydroxy-o'-sulfonic acid or sulfonamido groups, complexes of this type are sufficiently stable to be of use as dyestuffs.[127]

D. TETRADENTATE AZO DYESTUFFS

o-Hydroxyazo dyestuffs having a glycolic acid group in the o'-position form metal complexes in which the metal is a member of three annelated chelate rings[9a] (XC). The involvement of the carboxyl group in complex formation was originally inferred by Mur[128] and later confirmed[129] by stability constant determinations. Copper complexes of dyes of this type have been employed as direct dyes for cotton (see Chapter VI, by C. V. Stead). Recently, however, Baer[130] has shown that although 2-hydroxy-5-methyl-2'-carboxymethoxyazobenzene (XCI) reacts with copper salts under mild conditions to give the complex (XCII); the complex (XCIII) is obtained under more severe conditions. Loss of the carboxymethyl group from dyes of the type (XCII) under dyebath conditions has also been demonstrated.[130] This may be compared with the demethylative coppering of o-alkoxy-o'-hydroxyazo dyestuffs (Section II,C,4,c,i). In this connection it is of interest to note that the first stage in the light-fading of metal complexes of such dyestuffs appears to involve a breakdown of this type.[26]

Copper complexes of o-hydroxy-o'-(β-aminoethylamino)azo dyestuffs (XCIV) have been prepared[130] by the reaction of o-chloro-o'-hydroxyazo

[127] Gy, FP 1,270,269.
[128] V. I. Mur, J. Gen. Chem. USSR (English Transl.) 24, 585 (1954).
[129] F. A. Snavely and G. C. Craver, Inorg. Chem. 1, 890 (1962).
[130] D. R. Baer, Chimia (Aarau) Suppl. p. 159 (1968).

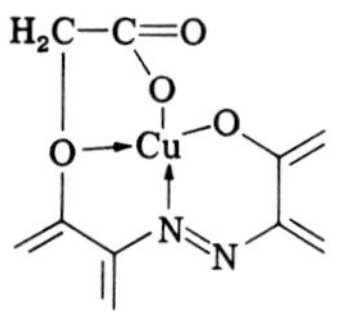

(XC) 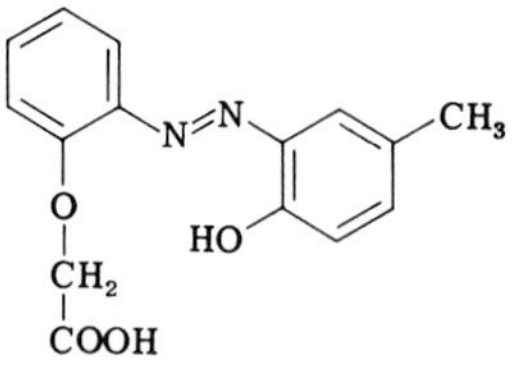　　　　　　　(XCI) 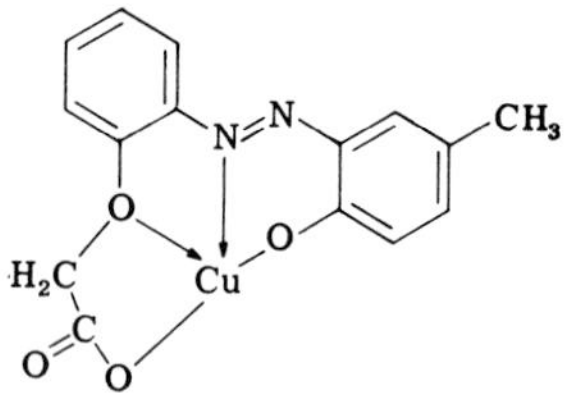　　　　　　　(XCII)

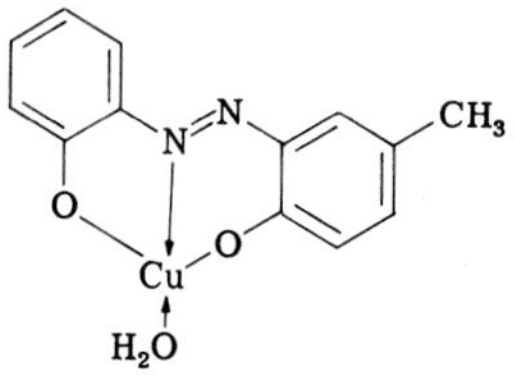

(XCIII) 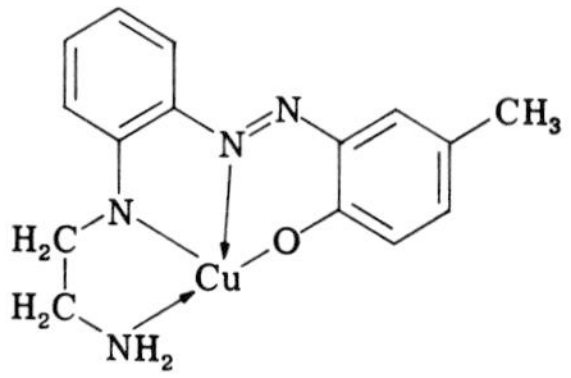　　　　　　　(XCIV)

dyestuffs with ethylenediamine in the presence of cupric ions. Dyestuffs of this type have been evaluated on nylon but are reported[130] to possess very poor fastness properties.

o-Hydroxy-o'-sulfonamidoazo dyestuffs have been shown to function as tridentate ligands but give complexes with inadequate stability to be of value as dyestuffs (Section II,C,5,e). It is known[10a] that of two similar chelating agents, the one forming the greater number of annelated chelate rings with a given metal yields the more stable complex. Therefore in an endeavor to increase the stability of metal complexes of dyestuffs containing this metallizable system Schetty and Ackermann[50] have examined the effect of introducing N-substituents which would permit the formation of a further annelated chelate ring (XCV). Dyestuffs of the type (XCVI) failed to form stable chromium complexes when X = H, but yielded stable complexes (XCVII) when X = OH or COOH. Replacement of the o-carboxy or o-hydroxyphenyl group in (XCVI) by –CH₂COOH gave dyestuffs capable of forming stable metal complexes, but replacement by –CH₂CH₂OH resulted in dyestuffs which did not form stable metal complexes. This is attributable to the feeble coordinating properties of the alcoholic hydroxyl group in comparison to carboxyl or phenolic hydroxyl groups.

Several other variants on this theme have been described and a few typical examples are listed in Table II. In certain cases the coordination sphere of the metal is completed by colorless bidentate ligands (Section II,G,2).

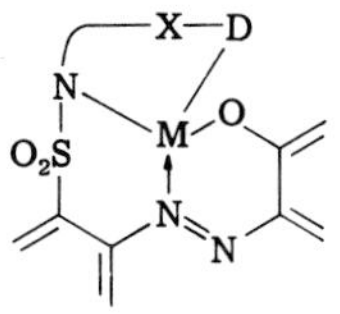

D = Donor group

X = Bridging group such
that the M-N-X-D
chelate ring has 5
or 6 members

(XCV)

X = - O -, - COO -

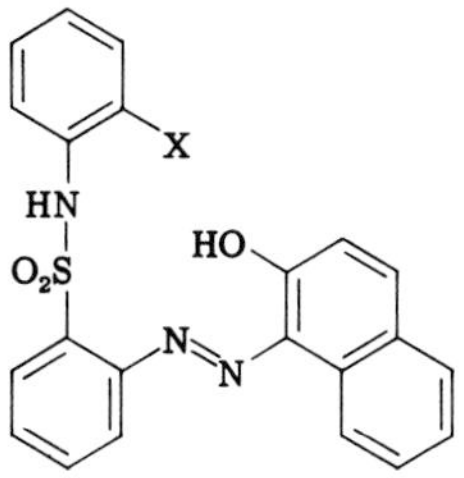

(XCVI)

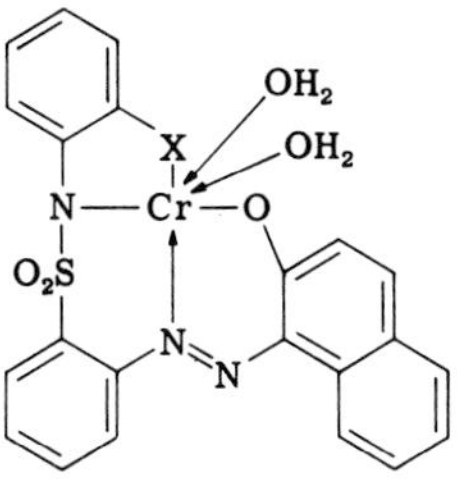

(XCVII)

E. PENTADENTATE AZO DYESTUFFS

Few examples of pentadentate azo dyestuffs capable of forming metal complexes containing four annelated chelate rings are recorded. Dyestuffs of the type (XCVIII), however, are claimed[131] to dye wool in green shades from neutral dyebaths.

F. HEXADENTATE AZO DYESTUFFS

In an extension of their work on metal complexes of o-hydroxy-o'-sulfonamidoazo dyestuffs Schetty and Ackermann[50] succeeded in preparing chromium and cobalt complexes of hexadentate azo dyestuffs of the type (XCIX). In contrast to 2:1 chromium and cobalt complexes of o-hydroxy-o'-sulfonamidoazo dyestuffs (Section II,C,5,e) dyes of this type are stable and are reported[132] to dye wool in brown shades having good wet-fastness properties and very good lightfastness. Schetty[133] concluded that complexes of this type had a fac configuration because of the great similarity of their spectra to that of the 2:1 chromium complex of 1-(2'-carboxyphenylazo)-2-naphthol (Section II,C,3).

Schetty[134] has demonstrated the influence of chelate ring size on sta-

[131] FBy, BeP 581,379.
[132] Gy, BP 766,018.
[133] G. Schetty, Helv. Chim. Acta 48, 1042 (1965).
[134] G. Schetty, Helv. Chim. Acta 50, 2212 (1967).

TABLE II

Metal Complexes of Tetradentate Azo Dyestuffs

Patent No.	Firm	Typical structure	Properties
USP 3,125,561	Gy	(chemical structure: Cr complex with quinoline, O, OOC, CH₃SO₂N, N=N, naphthalene)	Reported to dye wool from a neutral dyebath in pure bluish green shades having very good fastness to light and to wet treatments
BP 812,151	Gy	(chemical structure: Cr complex with quinoline, O, OOC, O₂N, CH₃O₂S, N=N, naphthalene)	Reported to dye wool from acetic acid dyebaths in pure yellowish green shades having good fastness properties
BeP 581,378	FBy	(chemical structure: Cr complex with H₂O, SO₂NH₂, O₂N, CH₃O, N=N, naphthalene)	Reported to dye wool in green shades of good fastness properties. Dyes in which the hydroxyl group in the diazo component is replaced by carboxyl are also claimed
BP 778,262	Gy	(chemical structure: Cu complex with COO, OH₂, O₂S, SO₃, N=N, naphthalene)	Reported to dye wool in bluish red shades having good fastness properties

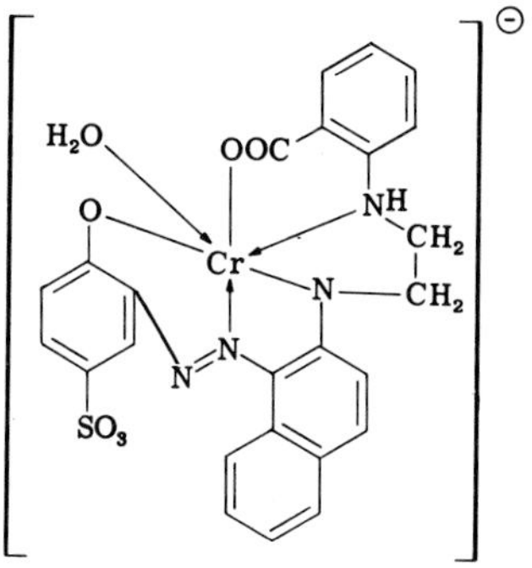

(XCVIII)

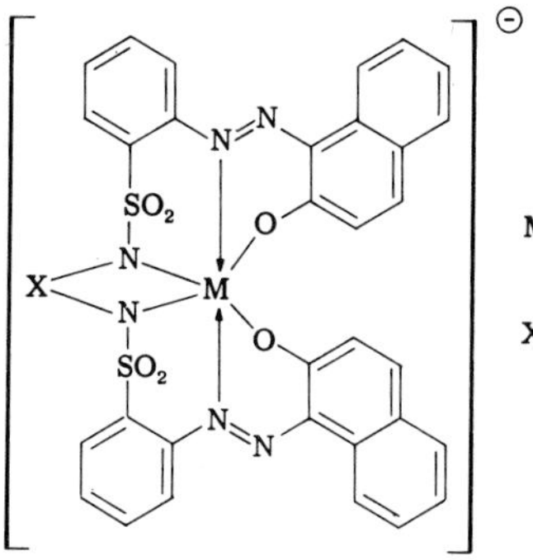

$M = Cr^{III}, Co^{III}$

$X = -(CH_2)_2, (CH_2)_3,$

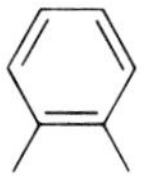

(XCIX)

bility (Section II,I,1) in these complexes by comparing the complexes (XCIX) in which $X = (-CH_2-)_2$, $(-CH_2-)_3$, and $(-CH_2-)_6$ which contain, respectively, five-, six-, and nine-membered "bridging" chelate rings. Whereas those complexes containing five- and six-membered "bridging" rings were stable, and had similar electronic spectra, that containing a nine-membered chelate ring was very much less stable and had a markedly different electronic spectra. Schetty attributes the low stability of the latter to strain in the nine-membered chelate ring.

Pentacyclic 2:1 chromium and cobalt complexes having mer (C) configurations have been prepared[135] from dyestuffs of the type (CI). The electronic spectra of the chromium complexes of (CI; $n = 2$) and (CI; $n = 3$) differed markedly from those of the 2:1 chromium complexes of

[135] G. Schetty, *Helv. Chim. Acta* **50**, 1039 (1967).

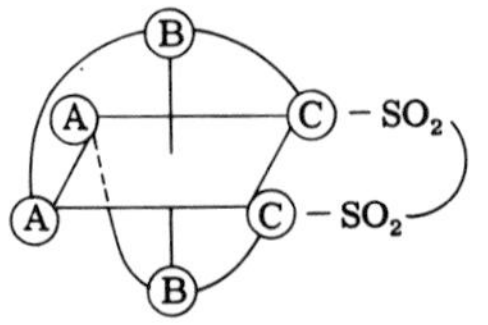

(C)

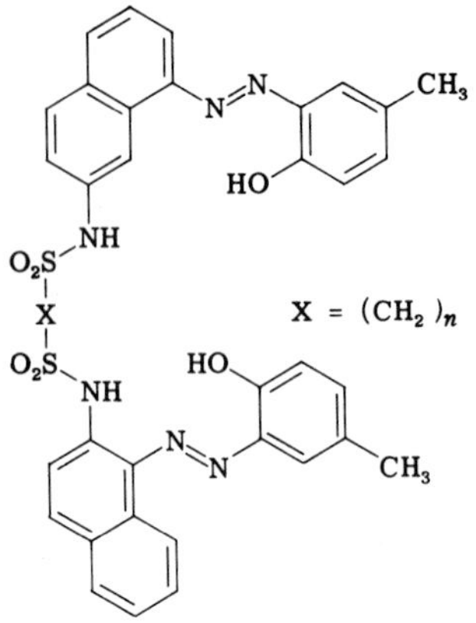

(CI)

the corresponding tridentate *o*-hydroxy-*o'*-alkylsulfonylaminoazo dye-stuffs (Section II,C,5,*f*), and this has been attributed to strain in the seven- and eight-membered "bridging" chelate rings. However, the electronic spectra of the chromium complex of (CI; $n = 10$), which contains a strainless 15-membered chelate ring, was identical with that of the corresponding open-form complex. Schetty[136] has demonstrated the relationship between strain and lightfastness in complexes of this type, the least strained complexes having the higher lightfastness.

G. 1:1 METAL COMPLEX AZO DYESTUFFS WITH METAL COORDINATION SPHERE COMPLETED BY COLORLESS LIGANDS OTHER THAN WATER

1. *Tridentate Azo Dyestuffs*

According to Ender and Müller[137] 1:1 chromium complex azo dyestuffs become attached to wool by the formation of coordinate bonds between the substrate and the chromium ion, a view which is supported by the work of Valko,[138,139] and Rattee.[140] As a result of this, migration of the dyestuff cannot occur once it has become bonded to the wool. Since wool is not a homogeneous fiber certain sites are more readily accessible to the dyestuff than others and there is a tendency for 1:1 chromium complex dyestuffs to become attached to such sites. Thus it is difficult to achieve

[136] G. Schetty, *Helv. Chim. Acta* **50**, 1836 (1967).

[137] W. Ender and A. Müller, *Melliand Textilber.* **19**, 181 (1938).

[138] E. Valko, I. G. Technical Report (Unclassified) Captured German Microfilm FD. 281/51, Frames 1149–1162, Date 21/1/37.

[139] E. Valko, *J. Soc. Dyers Colourists* **55**, 173 (1939).

[140] I. D. Rattee, *J. Soc. Dyers Colourists* **69**, 288 (1953).

level dyeings with dyestuffs of this type. In an attempt to reduce the rate of fixation of 1:1 chromium complex dyestuffs, complexes have been prepared in which the coordination sphere of the metal is at least partially completed by colorless polydentate ligands. Thus the preparation of 1:1 chromium complexes of unsulfonated *o,o'*-dihydroxyazo dyestuffs containing one molecule of an aromatic *o*-hydroxycarboxylic acid, such as salicylic acid or a sulfosalicylic acid, has been described.[141] This entailed the reaction of an *o,o'*-dihydroxyazo dyestuff with a chromium salicylate of the type described by Barbieri.[142] Schetty[143] has investigated this reaction and has shown the products to be complexes of the type (CII).

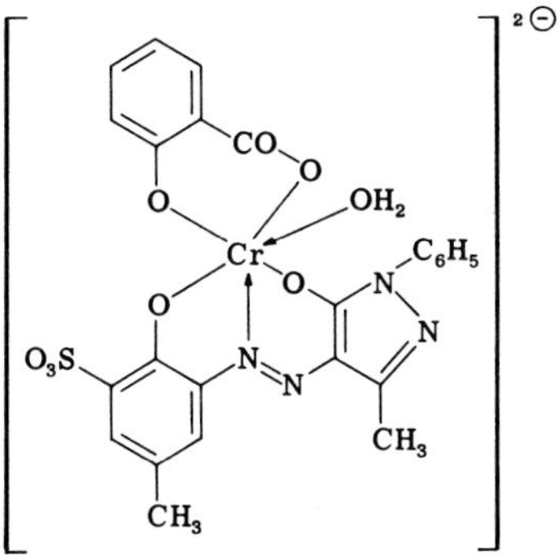

(CII)

However, complexes of this type readily react with a further molecule of the metal-free azo compound to give 2:1 chromium complexes and this makes them difficult to obtain in a pure state. Further disadvantages of such complexes are that they readily undergo disproportionation reactions (CIII) merely on heating in solution, and decompose under acidic conditions to give 1:1 chromium complexes containing coordinated water (CIV).

$$2D\text{—}Cr\text{—}S \rightleftharpoons D_2Cr + S_2Cr \qquad (S \equiv \text{salicylic acid})$$
$$(CIII)$$

$$D\text{—}Cr\text{—}S \rightarrow DCr(H_2O)_3 + S \qquad (S \equiv \text{salicylic acid})$$
$$(CIV):$$

In contrast, 1:1 chromium complexes derived from sulfonated *o,o'*-dihydroxyazo, or *o*-amino-*o'*-hydroxyazo dyestuffs, and containing a molecule of coordinated 8-hydroxyquinoline are reported[144] to be stable, and

[141] A. Conzetti, O. Schmid, and Gy, *DRP* 741,462.
[142] G. A. Barbieri, *Atti Accad. Nazl Lincei* **24**, 605 (1915).
[143] G. Schetty, *Helv. Chim. Acta* **35**, 716 (1952).
[144] CIBA, *BP* 964,800.

suitable for dyeing a wide variety of materials, in particular wool. Thus the chromium complex (CV) is claimed to give level bluish green dyeings on wool having good fastness properties. The greater stability of complexes of this type compared with those containing coordinated salicylic acid is shown by the fact that they can be prepared by reaction of the latter with 8-hydroxyquinoline.

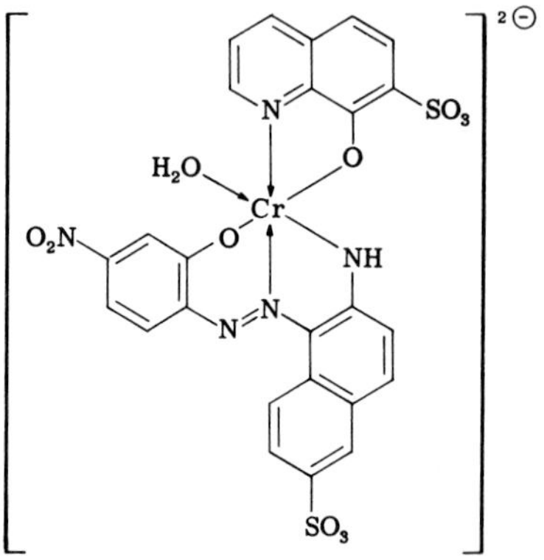

(CV)

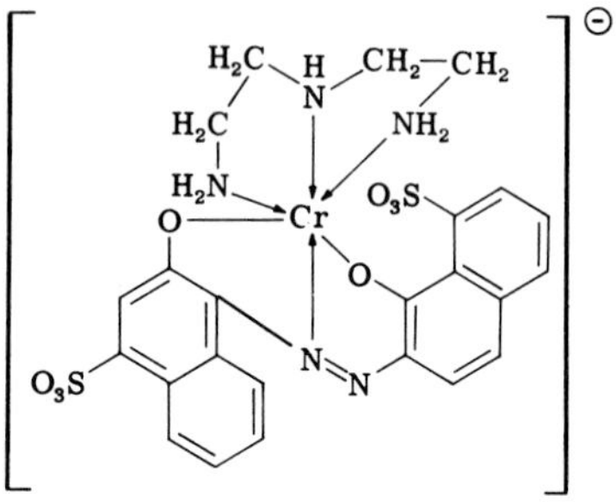

(CVI)

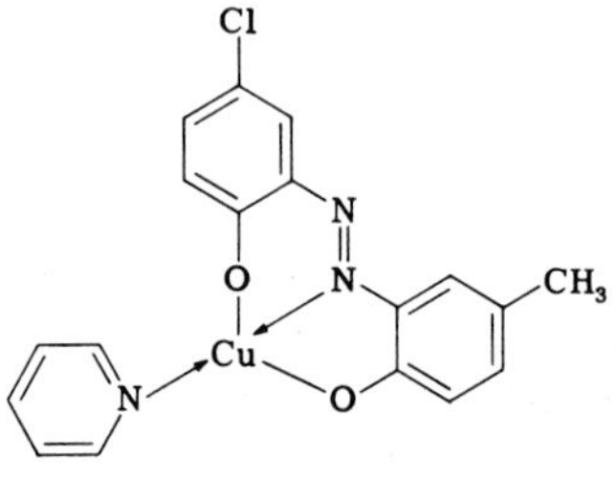

(CVII)

The use of colorless ligands containing water-solubilizing groups has been employed as a means of conferring water solubility on 1:1 chromium complexes of metallizable azo compounds devoid of solubilizing groups. 1:1 Chromium complex dyestuffs have been prepared[145] containing coordinated 1-nitroso-2-hydroxynaphthalene-6-sulfonic acid, salicylic acid 5-sulfonamide, 1,2-dihydroxybenzene-3,5-disulfonamide, and 1,8-dihydroxynaphthalene-3,6-disulfonic acid.

Other compounds that have been reported to occupy two coordination positions in 1:1 chromium complex dyestuffs include oxalic acid, ethanolamine, amino acids such as glycine and alanine, and acetyl acetone.[67,68]

1:1 Chromium complexes of tridentate metallizable azo dyestuffs have

[145] BASF, *BP* 692,073.

been prepared in which the coordination sphere of the chromium ion is completed by colorless tridentate ligands. For example, the dyestuff (CVI) is reported[56] to dye wool from weakly acid dyebaths in level greenish blue shades.

The preparation and properties of 1:1 cobalt complexes of tridentate metallizable azo dyestuffs containing coordinated bi- and tridentate nitrogen-donor ligands are described in Section II,C,2.

Copper complexes of tridentate azo dyestuffs containing coordinated aniline and pyridine have been isolated,[25] and the coordination of other ligands, e.g., propylene glycol,[146] quinoline and 8-hydroxyquinoline,[147] ethanolamine and ethylenediamine[148] to copper complexes of o,o'-dihydroxyazo dyestuffs has been demonstrated in solution. Complexes of this type have relatively low stability, the fourth ligand being relatively easily displaced by other ligands. However, complexes such as (CVII) containing coordinated pyridine or other basic nitrogen-containing heterocyclic compounds are reported[149] to give level dyeings on nylon having excellent fastness properties. In contrast the corresponding copper complexes not containing coordinated pyridine give very uneven dyeings on nylon under comparable conditions.

2. Tetradentate Azo Dyestuffs

1:1 Chromium complexes of tetradentate azo dyestuffs in which the coordination sphere of the metal is completed by a variety of colorless bidentate ligands, such as 8-hydroxyquinoline, salicylaldehyde, o-hydroxyacetophenone, salicylic acid, picolinic acid, and quinaldic acid are

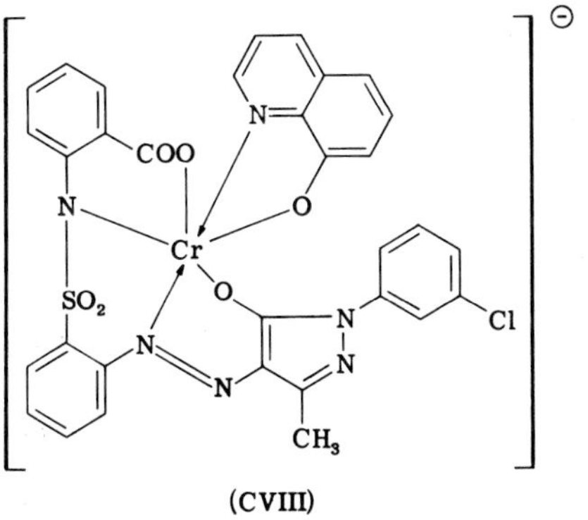

(CVIII)

[146] E. J. Gonzales and H. B. Jonassen, J. Am. Chem. Soc. 79, 4282 (1957).

[147] H. B. Jonassen and J. R. Oliver, J. Am. Chem. Soc. 80, 2347 (1958).

[148] E. J. Gonzales and H. B. Jonassen, J. Inorg. & Nucl. Chem. 24, 1595 (1962).

[149] DuP, FP 1,476,150.

claimed[150] to have a number of advantages over similar 1:1 chromium complexes derived from tridentate azo compounds. Thus they are easier to prepare because of a reduction in the possibilities of side reactions (Section II,G,1) and have considerably enhanced stability. A typical dyestuff of this type (CVIII) is reported to dye wool from a weakly acid dyebath in level greenish yellow shades with good fastness properties.

H. COMPLEXES OF METALS OTHER THAN CHROMIUM, COBALT, AND COPPER

The dullness of chromium and cobalt complexes of medially metallizable azo dyestuffs has been attributed[71] to a broadening of the spectral absorption bands of the deprotonated azo dyestuff by absorptions due to $d \rightarrow d$ transitions in the metal ion. Transitions of this type are excluded in complexes of metals such as titanium(IV) having empty d orbitals and this provides a means of evaluating the hypothesis.[151]

2:1 Titanium(IV) complexes of a variety of tridentate metallizable azo dyestuffs, e.g., (CIX), have been compared[151] with the corresponding

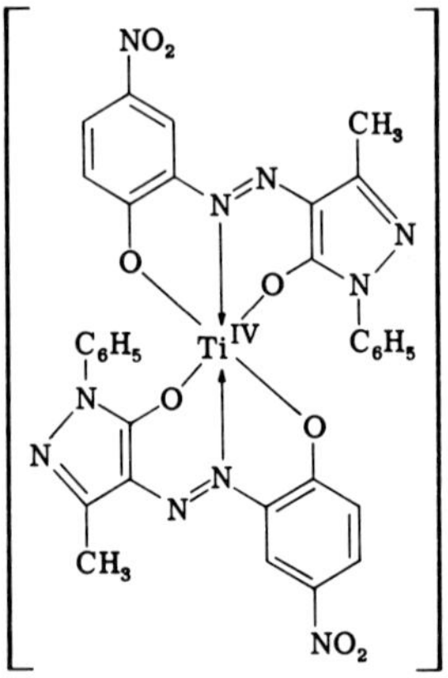

(CIX) 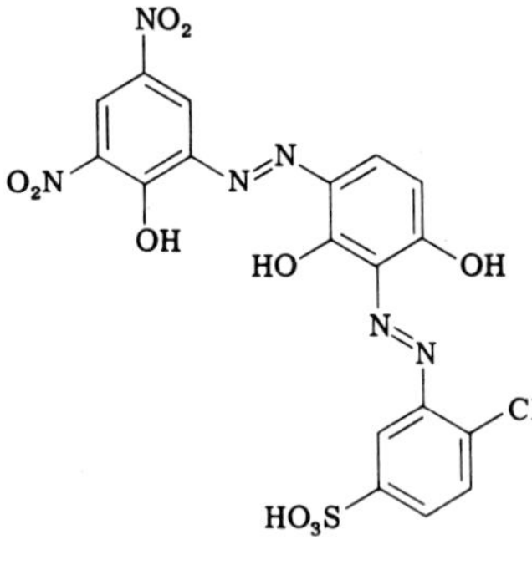   (CX)

chromium complexes on nylon 6, and found to give brighter shades in every case. The fastness properties of the derived dyeings were, however, considerably lower in the case of the titanium complexes and dyestuffs of this type have little commercial interest.

Tin, aluminum, and boron[152] complexes of metallizable azo dyestuffs

[150] Gy, *BP* 812,151.
[151] M. Yamamoto and F. Mashio, *J. Chem. Soc. Japan, Ind. Chem. Sect.* **68**, 688 (A38) (1965).
[152] G. A. Gamlen, ICI, private communication.

are also considerably brighter in hue than the corresponding chromium and cobalt complexes but their stability is inadequate for them to be of much value as dyestuffs. The only application reported is in the dyeing of aluminum-containing polypropylene with metal-free metallizable azo dyestuffs.[153] In this case the aluminum complex of the azo compound is formed within the fiber and is protected from decomposition by common reagents by the hydrophobic nature of the fiber.

Iron complexes of azo dyestuffs have been claimed in the patent literature but do not appear to have many commercial applications in the textile field. However, iron complexes obtained by treating disazo dyestuffs such as (CX) with ferrous sulfate are reported[154] to dye leather in brown shades having good fastness properties.

I. STABILITY

1. *General Considerations*

The factors which influence the stabilities of metal complexes are size of chelate ring, number of chelate rings per ligand molecule, basicity of the ligand, and the nature of the metal.

It has long[155] been a matter of practical experience that a decisive factor in the formation of a chelate ring is the number of atoms involved in ring formation, and that chelates with five- or six-membered rings are the most stable. This has been demonstrated in many fields including that of metal complex azo dyestuffs. For example, terminally metallizable azo dyes derived from salicylic acid (CXI) and 8-hydroxyquinoline (CXII), which form, respectively, six- and five-membered chelate rings with metal ions, form stable metal complexes, whereas those derived from phthalic acid (CXIII), which would form seven-membered chelate rings, do not.[156] Similarly, tridentate azo compounds which form annelated 5:6 (CXIV) or 6:6 (CXV) rings with metal ions give stable complexes, whereas those which would form annelated 6:7 chelate rings [(CXVI) and (CXVII)] with the metal ion give complexes having stabilities comparable to those derived from the corresponding bidentate ligands.[156]

It is an accepted principle[10a,157] that of two similar chelating agents,

[153] ICI, *BeP* 597,032.

[154] G. E. H. Modrow, E. Schick, H. Baumann, and FW, *BP* 1,051,219.

[155] H. Ley, *Z. Elektrochem.*, **10**, 954 (1904).

[156] H. Krzikalla and H. Pfitzner, BIOS/DOCS/2351/2247/1/10.

[157] R. N. Hurd, G. DeLamater, G. C. McElkeny, and J. P. McDermott, *in* "Advances in the Chemistry of the Coordination Compounds" (S. Kirschner, ed.) p. 355. Macmillan, New York, 1961.

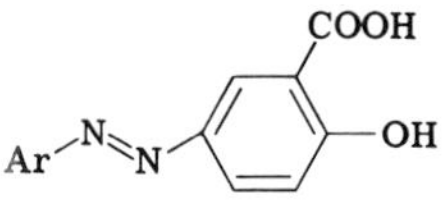

(CXI) 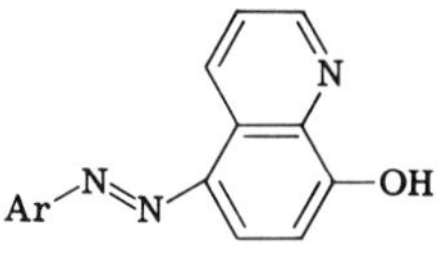   (CXII) 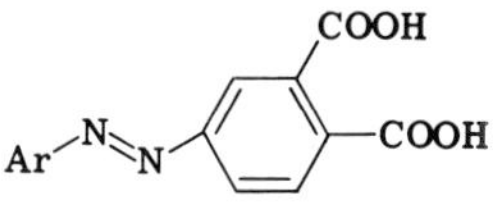   (CXIII)

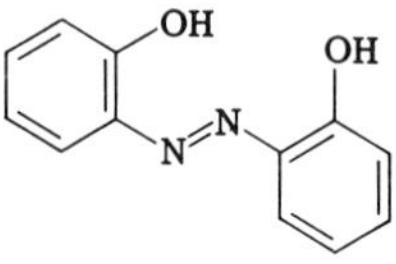

(CXIV) 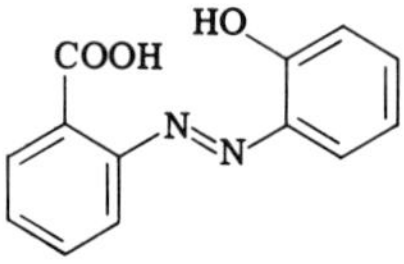   (CXV) 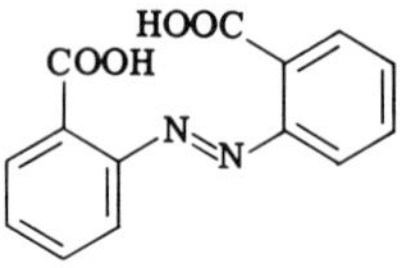   (CXVI)

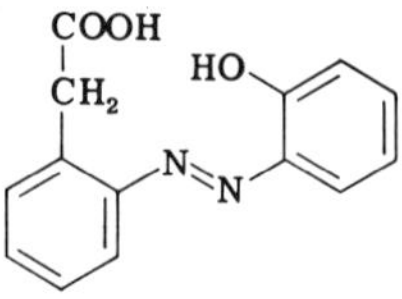

(CXVII)

the one forming the greater number of annelated chelate rings with a given metal ion yields the more stable complex. Thus, although metal complexes of bidentate azo compounds in which the azo group forms a part of the metallizable system have inadequate stability to be of value as dyestuffs, metal complexes of tridentate azo compounds, in which the metal ion is a member of two annelated chelate rings, are stable compounds widely used as dyestuffs.

Chelate stability is also related to the basic strength of the chelating agent, where the term chelating agent is taken to mean the anion with which the metal actually combines, rather than the un-ionized ligand molecule. Thus in a series of related ligands chelated to the same metal, the most strongly ionized will usually form the least stable complex.[33] This generalization is supported by the results of Calvin and Wilson[158] on complexes of substituted salicylaldehydes, and of Calvin and Bailes[159] on complexes of substituted salicylaldimines. This effect has also been

[158] M. Calvin and K. W. Wilson, *J. Am. Chem. Soc.* **67**, 2003 (1945).
[159] M. Calvin and R. H. Bailes, *J. Am. Chem. Soc.* **68**, 949 (1946).

demonstrated with metal complexes of o-hydroxyazo compounds (see next section).

The influences of the metal on complex stability may be classified as donor-atom preference and complex forming ability. Sidgwick[160] has classified metals according to their tendency to form complexes with ligands containing particular donor atoms. Thus Fe^{III} shows a greater tendency to form complexes with oxygen-donor ligands than with nitrogen-donor ligands. The reverse is true of Co^{III} while Cr^{III} has an equal tendency to form complexes with both oxygen-donor and nitrogen-donor ligands. The importance of this is illustrated by the formation of 1:1 Co^{III} complex dyestuffs in which the coordination sphere of the metal is completed by nitrogen-donor ligands (Section II,C,2). Irving and Williams[161] have established the sequence Mn < Fe < Co < Ni < Cu > Zn for the stability of complexes of divalent metals. In this connection it is significant that the only divalent metal finding wide application in the field of metal complex dyestuffs is copper.

The validity of these generalizations has been proved in the case of metal complex dyestuffs by the results of stability studies carried out by a number of workers, in particular, Snavely and his collaborators.

Many methods are available[79,162] for the determination of stability constants, but that most frequently used for metal complexes of azo dyestuffs is the Calvin[158] modification of the Bjerrum potentiometric titration method.

2. Bidentate Azo Compounds

The relationship between acid dissociation constant and chelate stability in a series of 1-(2'-hydroxy-4'-substituted phenylazo)naphthalene-4-sulfonic acids (CXVIII) has been demonstrated by Peters et al.[33] The results obtained by these workers, which are summarized in Table

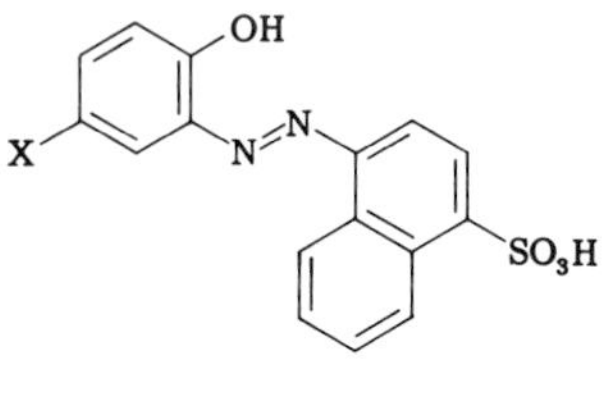

(CXVIII) 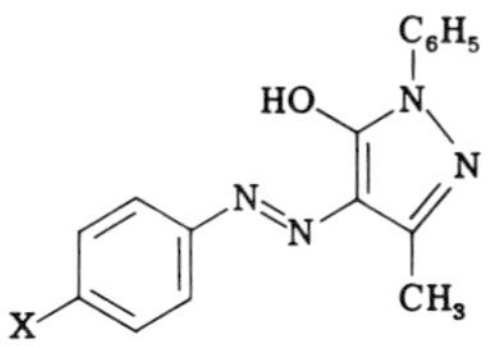   (CXIX)

[160] N. V. Sidgwick, J. Chem. Soc. p. 433 (1941).

[161] H. Irving and R. J. P. Williams, J. Chem. Soc. p. 3192 (1953).

[162] A. E. Martell and M. Calvin, "Chemistry of the Metal Chelate Compounds." Prentice-Hall Englewood Cliffs, New Jersey, 1952.

III, clearly illustrate that the most acidic dyestuff forms the least stable complex.

Comparable results have been obtained by Snavely and his co-workers[121,163,164] in a study of metal complexes of 1-phenyl-3-methyl-4-(4'-substituted phenylazo)-5-pyrazolones (CXIX). In this series the acid

TABLE III

ACID DISSOCIATION (pK) AND COPPER CHELATE STABILITY (log K) FOR
1-(2'-HYDROXY-4'-SUBSTITUTED PHENYLAZO)-NAPHTHALENE-4-SULFONIC
ACIDS (CXVI) IN 40% ETHANOL AT 25°

Substituent X	pK	log K
—NO$_2$	8.1	17.2
—Cl	8.15	17.6
—COCH$_3$	8.2	17.8
—CH$_3$	8.35	18.2
—NH$_2$	8.45	18.9
—OCH$_3$	8.5	19.2

dissociation constants and complex stabilities increase in the order X = NO$_2$ < Cl, Br < I < OCH$_3$ < CH$_3$ < H. These authors also extended their studies to other metals and established the stability sequence for divalent metals to be Cu > Ni > Co > Zn > Pb > Cd > Mn > Mg > Ca > Sr > Ba, which is directly comparable with results obtained with other bidentate ligands.[165]

The relationship between chelate stability and acid dissociation constant is valid only within a strictly comparable series of ligands and cannot be extended to other systems. This is demonstrated by the results of Snavely[166] in the case of the related arylazo-3-pyrazolones (CXX). Although these compounds are stronger acids than the arylazo-5-pyrazolones (CXIX) they form more stable metal complexes than do the latter.

The influence of the nature of the donor atoms in bidentate azo dyestuffs on complex stability has been demonstrated[167] by comparing the

[163] F. A. Snavely, W. C. Fernelius, and B. P. Block, *J. Am. Chem. Soc.* **79**, 1028 (1957).

[164] F. A. Snavely and B. D. Krecker, *J. Am. Chem. Soc.* **81**, 4199 (1959).

[165] M. Calvin and N. C. Melchior, *J. Am. Chem. Soc.* **70**, 3270 (1948); K. Yamasaki and K. Sone, *Nature* **166**, 998 (1950); B. E. Bryant, W. C. Fernelius, and B. E. Douglas, *ibid.* **170**, 247 (1952).

[166] F. A. Snavely, D. A. Sweigant, C. H. Yoder, and A. Terzis, *Inorg. Chem.* **6**, 1831 (1967).

[167] F. A. Snavely, W. S. Trahanovsky, and F. H. Suydam, *Inorg. Chem.* **3**, 123 (1964).

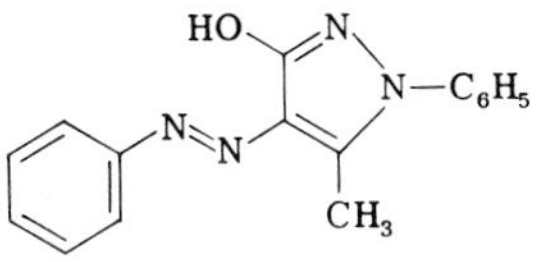

(CXX) 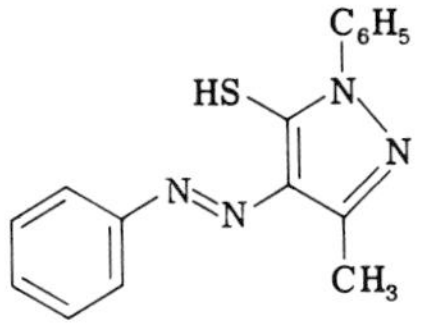   (CXXI)

stability constants of metal complexes of 1-phenyl-3-methyl-4-phenyl-
azo-5-pyrazolones (CXIX) with those of the corresponding complexes
derived from 1-phenyl-3-methyl-4-phenylazo-5-thiopyrazolones (CXXI).
In each case the latter dyestuffs formed the more stable complexes and
since the ligand anions of the oxygen and sulfur analogs have essentially
equal basicity, the tendency of sulfur to bond to the metal ion more
strongly than oxygen is clearly shown.

3. *Tridentate Azo Compounds*

The relationship between ligand basicity and metal complex stability
in a series of *o,o'*-dihydroxyazo dyestuffs has been investigated by
Snavely *et al.*,[78] who established that the first acid dissociation constants
and the stabilities of the copper complexes of a series of 1-(2'-hydroxy-
5'-substituted phenylazo)-2-naphthols (CXXII) followed the sequence
X = NO_2 < Cl < H.
The influence of the nature of the donor atoms in tridentate metalliz-

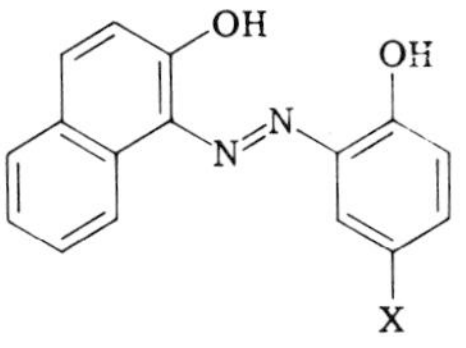

(CXXII) 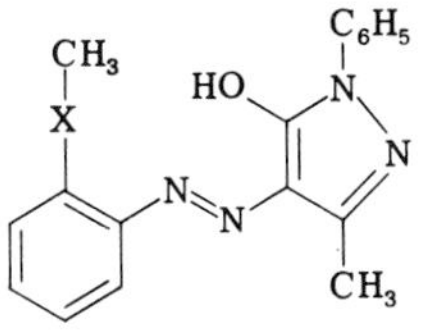   (CXXIII) 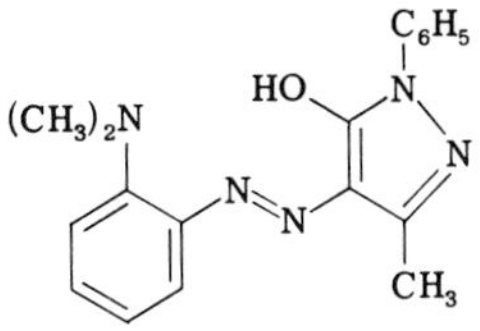   (CXXIV)

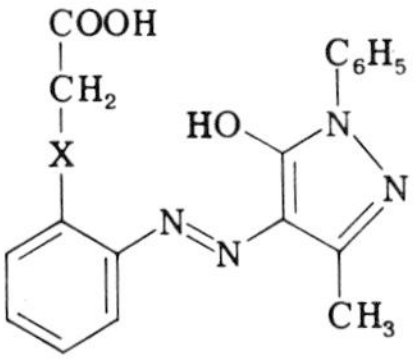

(CXXV) 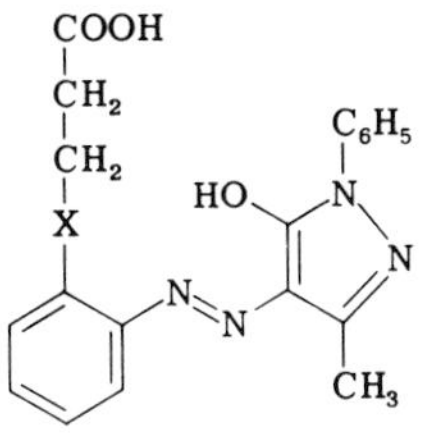   (CXXVI)

able azo dyestuffs on metal complex stability has been demonstrated[121,168] by a comparison of the three azo compounds (CXXIII; X = O), (CXXIII, X = S), and (CXXIV). Although the acid dissociation constants of the dyestuffs (CXXIII; X = S) and (CXXIII; X = O) are practically identical the stability constants of metal complexes of the former are greater than those of the corresponding complexes derived from the latter. This may be compared with the similar result in the bidentate series, and has been attributed[121] to π-bonding[169] in the sulfur analogs. The relative stabilities of divalent metal complexes of the three types of dyestuff follow precisely the same sequence, Cu > Ni > Co > Zn > Cd, but differences are apparent in the case of individual metals. Thus in the case of Ni, Co, and Cd the relative stabilities of complexes of the three dyestuffs are in the order N > S > O. In the case of Zn the order is N > O > S, and Cu, N = S > O.

The relative stabilities of metal complexes of bi- and tridentate azo dyestuffs have been shown[170] to follow the sequence in Chart 6 with regard to the ligand. The sequence for divalent metals is Cu > Ni > Co > Zn > Pb > Cd > Mn > Mg > Ca > Sr > Ba, and for trivalent metals Fe > Cr > Al. However, the position of Cr^{III} in this series must be re-

CHART 6
Stability of Azo Dyestuff Metal Complexes

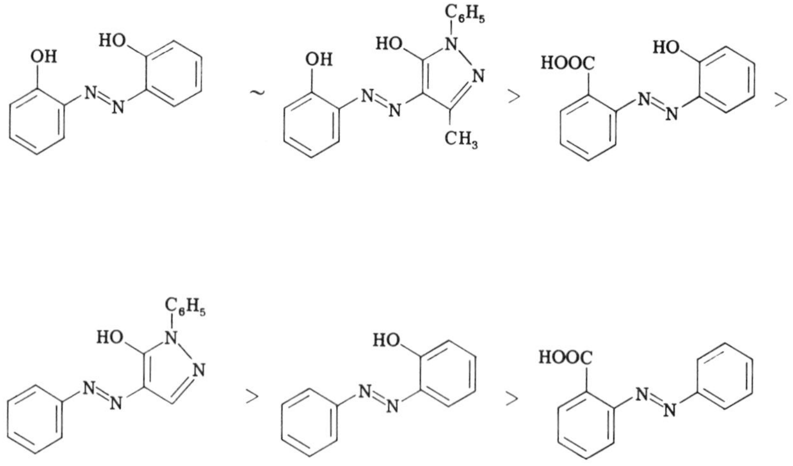

[168] F. A. Snavely, C. H. Yoder, and F. H. Suydam, *Inorg. Chem.* 2, 708 (1963).
[169] S. Ahrland, J. Chatt, N. R. Davies, and A. A. Williams, *J. Chem. Soc.* pp. 264, 276, and 1403 (1958).
[170] F. A. Snavely and W. C. Fernelius, *Science* 117, 15 (1952).

garded as very doubtful since the reaction between *o,o'*-dihydroxyazo dyestuffs and the hydrated chromium(III) ion in aqueous solution is slow, even at 100°, and the system is not suitable for study by the potentiometric method employed.[79]

4. *Tetradentate Azo Compounds*

Determination of the stability constants of metal complexes of tetradentate azo dyestuffs appears to have been restricted to the two series of dyestuffs (CXXV; X = O and S)[129] and (CXXVI; X = O and S).[171] In both cases the sulfur-containing dyestuffs form more stable complexes than their oxygen-containing analogs with divalent Cu, Ni, Co, and Cd, while the reverse is true of Zn, Mg, Mn, Ca, Sr, and Ba.

III. Metal Complexes of Other Dyestuffs

A. *o*-Nitrosonaphthols and Hydroxyindazoles

The first fully synthetic metal complex dyestuff, Pigment Green 12 (CI 10020), which was discovered as long ago as 1885, is the iron complex of 1-nitroso-2-naphthol-6-sulfonic acid (CXXVII). This water-soluble complex dyes wool in fast green shades from strongly acid dyebaths and was the forerunner of premetallized dyes of the Neolan and

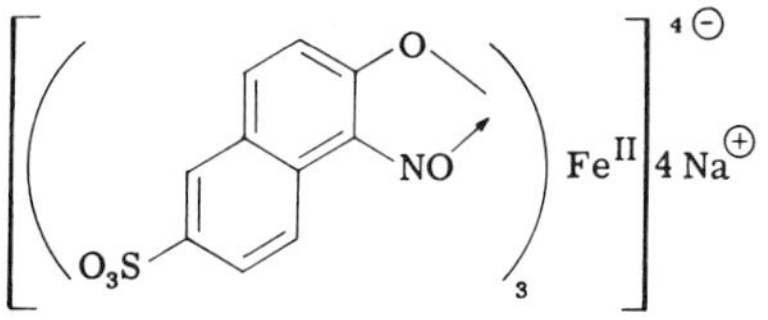

(CXXVII) 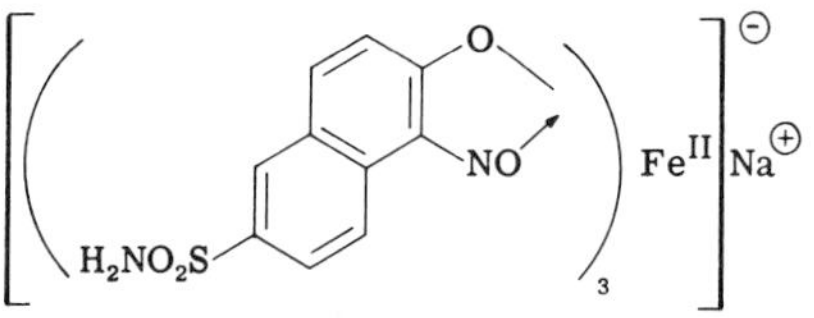   (CXXVIII)

Palatine types (Section I). In line with progress in the field of neutral-dyeing premetallized azo dyes (Section I) iron complexes of nitrosonaphthols containing sulfonamide groups (CXXVIII) have been prepared and reported[172] to be suitable for dyeing wool from neutral or weakly acid dyebaths.

More recently the ferrous complexes of 5-nitroso-6-hydroxy- and 4-nitroso-5-hydroxyindazoles[173] have been found to be sufficiently soluble

[171] F. A. Snavely, W. Magen, and D. Kozart, *J. Inorg. & Nucl. Chem.* **27,** 679 (1965).

[172] *DRP* 869,103.

[173] R. F. M. Sureau, G. R. H. Mingasson, and Fran, *USP* 2,787,515.

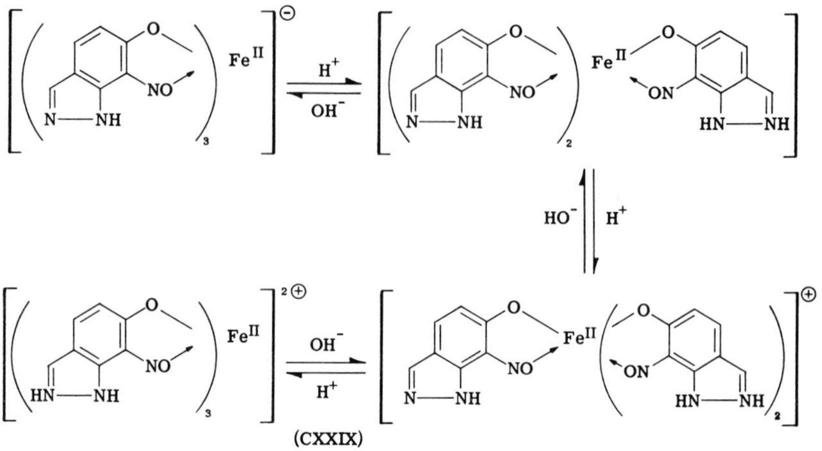

(CXXIX)

in water to permit the dyeing of wool and superpolyamide fibers from weakly acid dyebaths in green to olive shades of very good fastness properties. Sureau[174] has studied these complexes using electrophoretic techniques and has shown that they can be variously charged (CXXIX), depending upon the pH of the medium, because of the amphoteric nature of the heterocyclic nucleus, thus accounting for their water solubility.

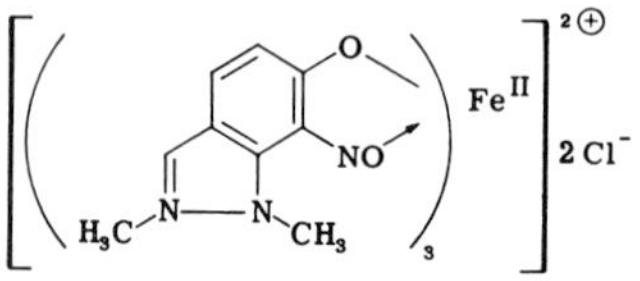

(CXXX) 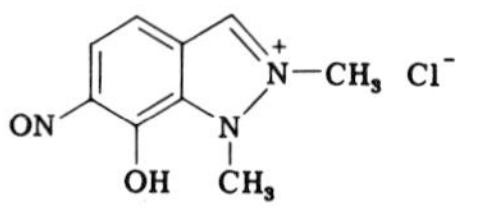   (CXXXI)

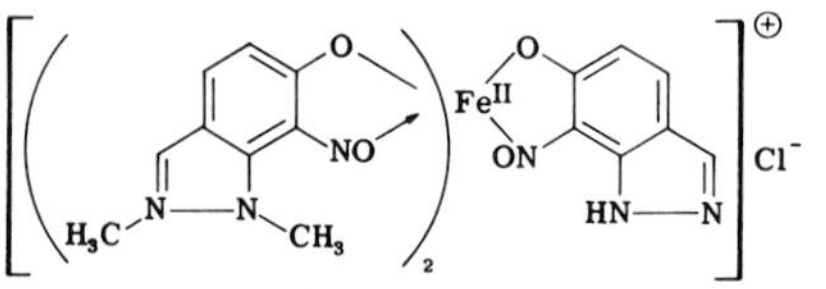

(CXXXII) 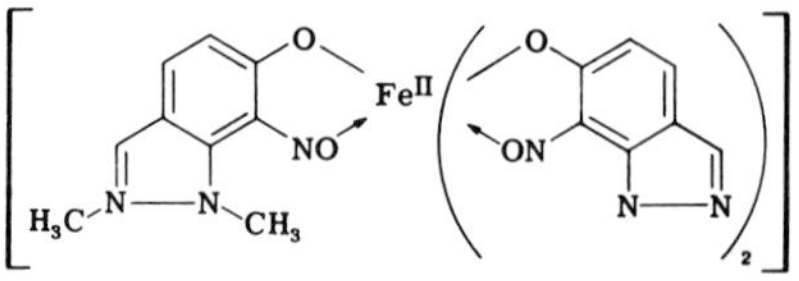   (CXXXIII)

Following this observation Sureau[174] succeeded in preparing cationic ferrous complexes (CXXX) from the quaternary compound (CXXXI), and mixed complexes such as (CXXXII) and (CXXXIII) from the quaternary compound (CXXXI) and the nitroso hydroxyindazole.

It has been reported[175] that ferric complexes of 1-nitroso-2-naphthol-

[174] R. F. M. Sureau, *Chimia (Aarau)* **19,** 254 (1965).
[175] G, *DAS* 1,150,166.

6-alkylsulfones and dialkyl sulfonamides having 3:1 stoichiometry can be prepared by the interaction of the appropriate nitrosonaphthol and a ferric salt in alcohol. Sureau,[174] however, has shown that the products are, in fact, ferrous complexes having 3:1 stoichiometry, e.g., (CXXXIV). The first stage in the reaction between the ferric salt and the nitrosonaphthol is oxidation of the latter, and the resulting ferrous salt then forms a complex with the remaining nitrosonaphthol.

In an interesting development on complexes derived from *o*-nitroso-naphthols and phenols it is claimed[176] that iron, copper, and nickel complexes of the products obtained by the nitrosation of arylazoresorcinol dyestuffs dye leather in brown shades having excellent fastness to light. Certain of the complexes which are disclosed are derived from nitrosated *o*-hydroxyarylazoresorcinol dyestuffs and contain two chelating centers. Examples of dyestuffs of this type include the copper complex of the product obtained by the nitrosation of (CXXXV), and the nickel complex of the product obtained by the nitrosation of (CXXXVI), which are reported to dye leather in light tan, and tan shades, respectively.

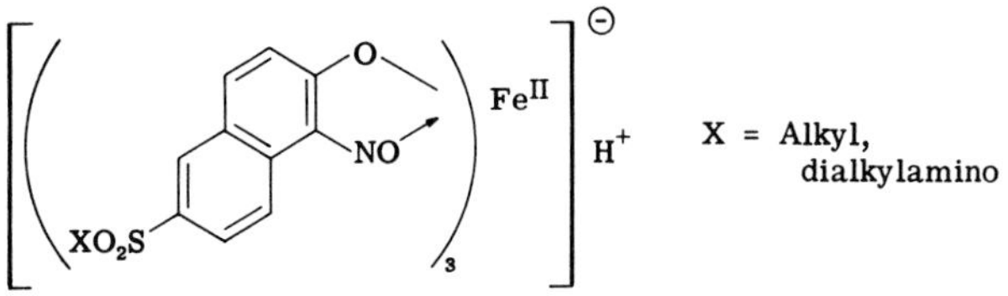

(CXXXIV)

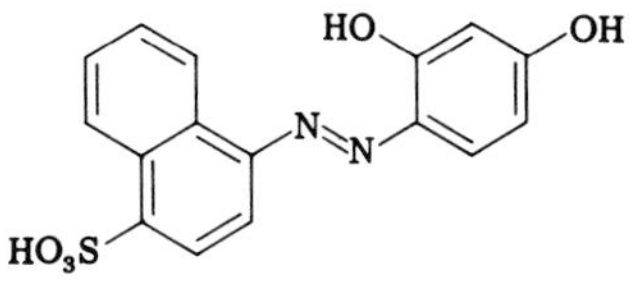

X = Alkyl, dialkylamino

(CXXXV)

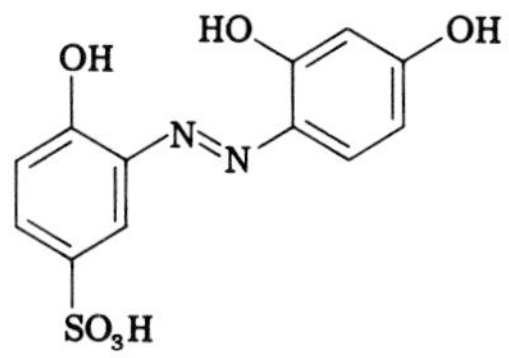

(CXXXVI)

The importance of physical form in the pigment field is effectively illustrated by some recent work on the nickel complex of 1-nitroso-2-naphthol. Nickel chelates of 1-nitroso-2-naphthol are highly colored compounds but are reported[177] to have very poor light stability and,

[176] J. R. Atkinson, D. A. Plant, and ICI, *BP* 668,474.
[177] Hercules, *BP* 3,338,937.

therefore, no value as pigments. However, processes have been claimed[177,178] for the production of a crystalline, light-stable form of the nickel complex of 1-nitroso-2-naphthol, which is reported to be a highly effective pigment.

B. Azomethine Dyestuffs

Azomethines bear a formal resemblance to azo compounds and many parallels exist in the coordination chemistry of the two series of compounds. It is not surprising, therefore, that the possibility of employing metallizable azomethines in the dyestuffs field has been widely investigated, and tridentate diarylazomethines (CXXXVII) having a variety of metallizable substituents (X,Y), such as OH, O-alkyl, SH, S-alkyl, NH_2, COOH, and OCH_2COOH, in ortho positions have been examined.[179]

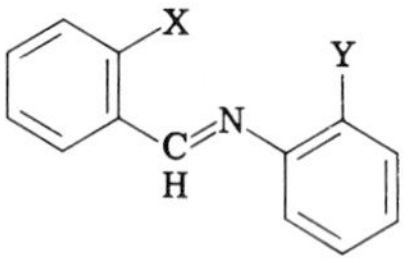

(CXXXVII)

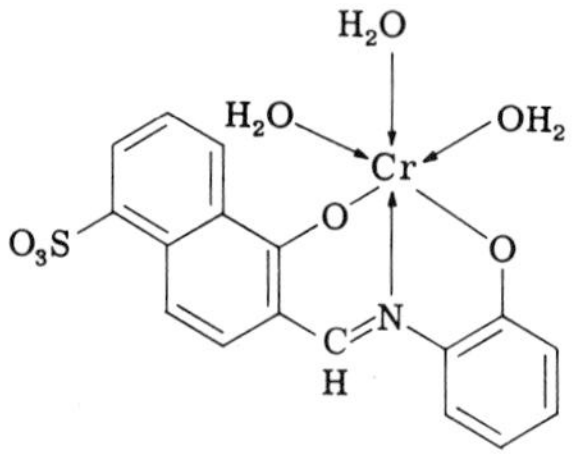

(CXXXVIII) 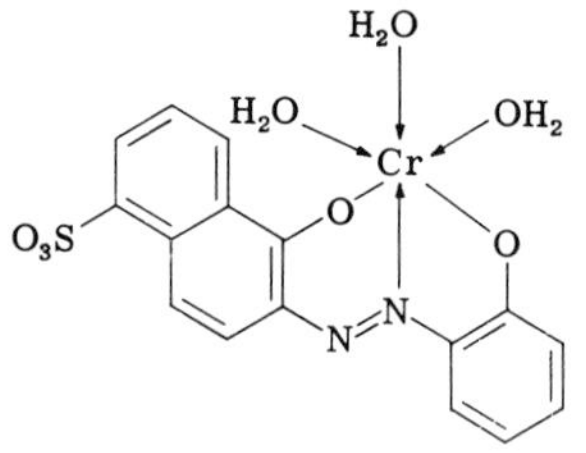   (CXXXIX)

The iron, cobalt, manganese, copper, nickel, and aluminum complexes of azomethines of these types all decompose in mineral acid dyebaths but, despite the facile hydrolysis by acids of the parent azomethines, chromium complexes of o,o'-dihydroxydiarylazomethines are reported to be stable under these conditions. In fact the properties of the chromium complex (CXXXVIII) are stated[179] to be comparable with those of the chromium complex (CXXXIX) of the corresponding o,o'-dihydroxyazo

[178] Hercules, *USP* 3,338,938.
[179] H. Krzikalla and H. Pfitzner, BIOS/DOCS/2351/2247/1/12.

dye. The tinctorial strength of chromium complexes of o,o'-dihydroxy-diarylazomethines is very much lower than that of the corresponding chromium complexes of o,o'-dihydroxyazo dyestuffs, however, and these compounds do not appear to have found much technological application.

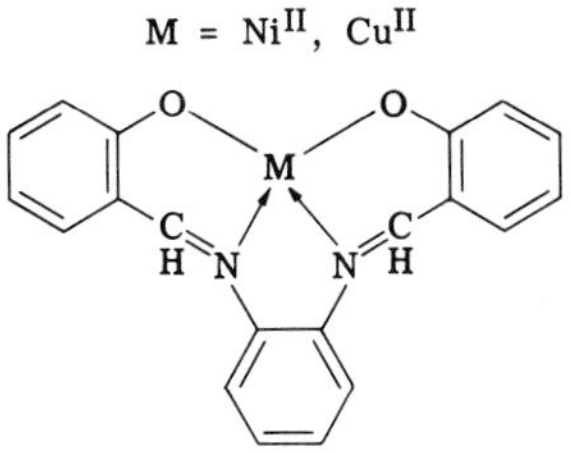

(CXL) 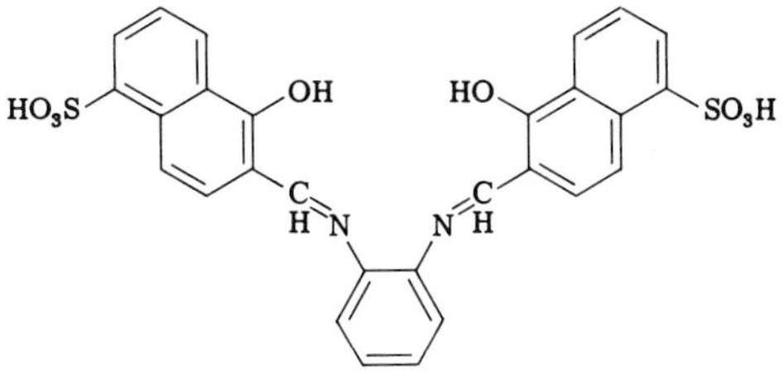   (CXLI)

Metal complexes of tetradentate azomethines are reported[179] to suffer from a similar deficiency. Thus, although the copper and nickel complexes (CXL) have high lightfastness, their tinctorial strength and brightness are inadequate for them to be of value as pigments. Similarly the chromium complexes of sulfonated tetradentate azomethines, such as (CXLI), give dull, tinctorially weak dyeings on wool, possessing poor wet-fastness properties.

C. FORMAZAN DYESTUFFS

The formazans, which were first discovered[180] in 1892, are derivatives of the hypothetical parent compound

$$\overset{1}{N}H=\overset{2}{N}-\overset{3}{C}H=\overset{4}{N}-\overset{5}{N}H_2$$

and bear a formal resemblance to azo compounds. Various methods are available for their preparation,[181] for example, coupling diazonium salts with compounds containing a reactive methylene group, e.g., nitromethane (CXLII), acetoacetic ester, cyanoacetic acid, and malonic acid, but the most convenient involves the reaction of a diazonium salt with a hydrazone in alkaline medium[182] (CXLIII). Unsymmetrical formazans can be synthesized by this method.[183]

[180] H. von Pechmann, *Ber.* **25**, 3175, (1892); E. Bamberger and E. Wheelwright, *ibid.* **25**, 3201 (1892).

[181] A. W. Nineham, *Chem. Rev.* **55**, 355 (1955); H. Wahl and M. T. Le Bris, *in* "Recent Progress in the Chemistry of Natural and Synthetic Colouring Matters and Related Fields" (T. S. Gore *et al.*, eds.), p. 507. Academic Press, New York, 1962; R. Pütter, *Houben-Weyl* **10**, No. 3, 631 (1965).

[182] W. Ried, *Angew. Chem.* **64**, 391 (1952).

[183] R. Wizinger and V. Biro, *Helv. Chim. Acta* **32**, 901 (1949).

In 1941 Hunter and Roberts[184] established that 1,3,5-triphenylfor-mazan functions as a bidentate ligand and forms complexes having 2:1 stoichiometry with divalent copper, nickel, and cobalt (CXLIV). Complexes of this type have low stability towards acids and, following the comparable work on metal complexes of azo compounds,[185] Wizinger[186,186a,b] was prompted to investigate tri- and tetradentate formazans in an endeavor to obtain metal complexes of enhanced stability.

1. Tridentate Formazans

1-(2'-Hydroxyphenyl)- (CXLV), and 1-(2'-carboxyphenyl)-3,5-di-phenylformazans[186,186a,b] (CXLVI) form intensely colored bicyclic complexes having 1:1 stoichiometry with divalent copper and nickel. In both cases a considerable shade change occurs on metal complex formation, and the products have enhanced stability towards acids in comparison

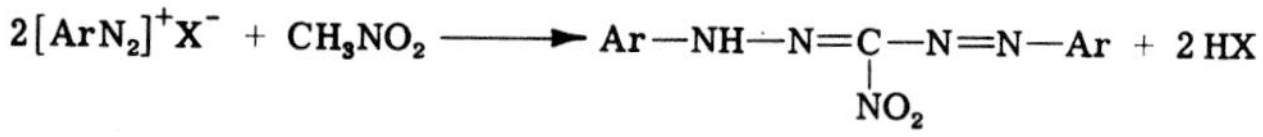

$$2[ArN_2]^+X^- + CH_3NO_2 \longrightarrow Ar-NH-N=\underset{\underset{NO_2}{|}}{C}-N=N-Ar + 2HX$$

(CXLII)

$$[ArN_2]^+X^- + \underset{\underset{R}{|}}{CH}=N-NH-Ar' \longrightarrow Ar-N=N-\underset{\underset{R}{|}}{C}=N-NH-Ar' + HX$$

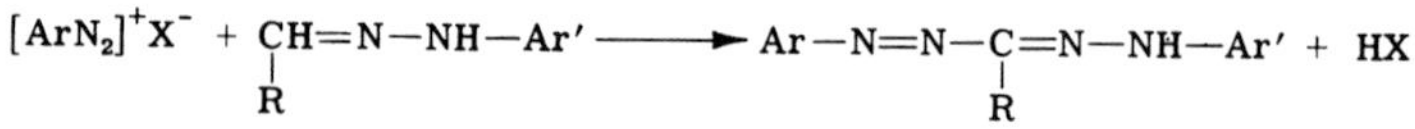

(CXLIII)

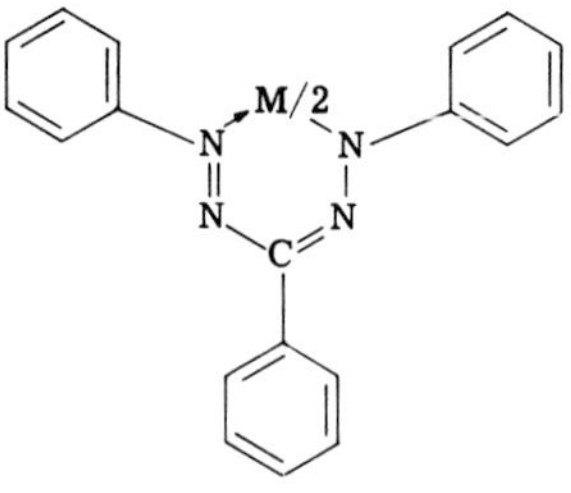

(CXLIV)

[184] L. Hunter and L. B. Roberts, J. Chem. Soc. pp. 820 and 823 (1941).

[185] P. Pfeiffer, T. Hesse, H. Pfitzner, W. Scholl, and H. Thielert, J. Prakt. Chem. [2] 149, 217 (1937).

[186] R. Wizinger, Z. Naturforsch. 9b, 729 (1954).

[186a] R. Wizinger, Chimia (Aarau) Supple. p. 82 (1968).

[186b] H. R. von Tobel and R. Wizinger, in "Recent Progress in the Chemistry of Natural and Synthetic Colouring Matters and Related Fields" (T. S. Gore et al., eds.), p. 495. Academic Press, New York, 1962.

with metal complexes of bidentate formazans. Treatment of the brownish green nickel complex (CXLVII; M = Ni) with pyridine gives the crystalline product (CXLIX) which is violet in color.

Wizinger was unable to isolate products similar to (CXLIX) from 1-(2'-carboxyphenyl)-3,5-diphenylformazan (CXLVI), but replacement of the meso (3) phenyl group by a cyano group gave copper and nickel complexes which reacted with pyridine to give the complexes (CL), and (CLI). In both cases a considerable shade change occurred on treatment with pyridine, the nickel complex changing from green to carmine red.

Analytical evidence on the complexes (CXLVII) and (CXLVIII)

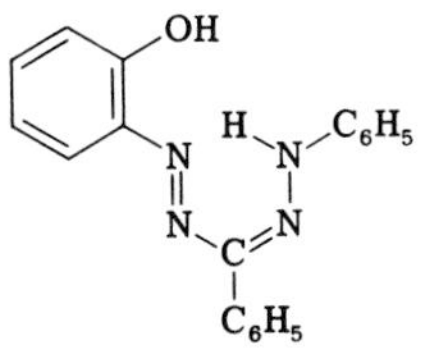

Red
(CXLV)

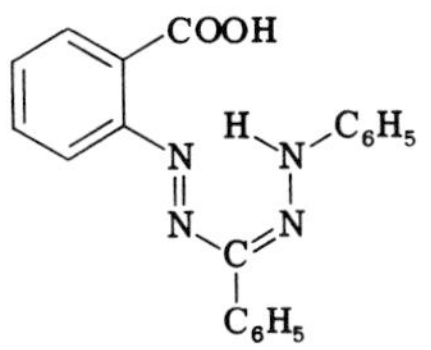

Orange red
(CXLVI)

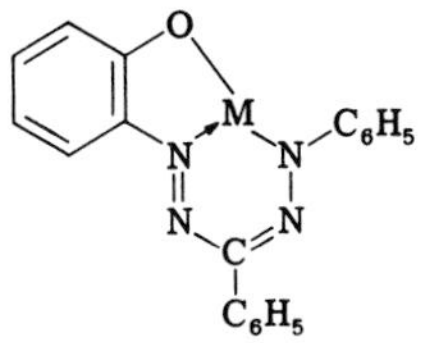

M = Cu, Violet
M = Ni, Brownish green
(CXLVII)

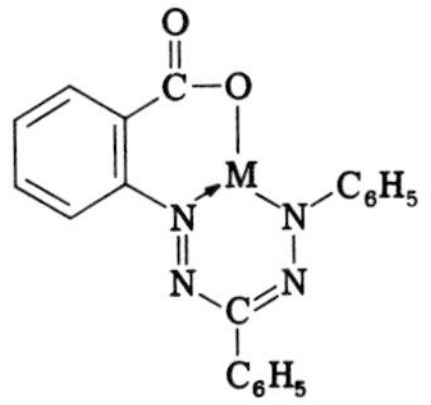

M = Cu, Violet
M = Ni, Leaf green
(CXLVIII)

was in good agreement with these formulations, suggesting that the coordination sphere of the metal is completed by bridging through the oxygen atoms (see Section II,C,1), a view which is supported by the solubilities of the various complexes. Whereas the complexes containing coordinated pyridine are quite soluble, the parent complexes have low solubility. However, molecular weight determinations[187] in benzene showed the latter to be monomolecular.

These observations, together with the very considerable shade changes which occur on addition of pyridine are of considerable theoretical interest and examination of the various products by modern techniques, e.g., reflectance spectra and magnetic measurements, in order to clear up the

[187] A. Grün and W. Freiesleben, Helv. Chim. Acta 41, 574 (1958).

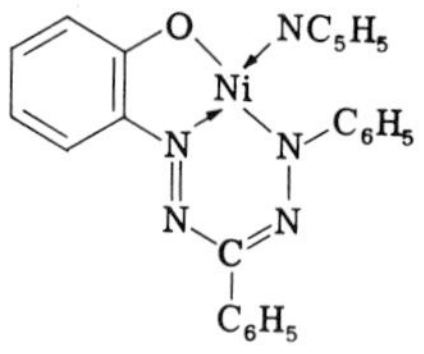

(CXLIX)

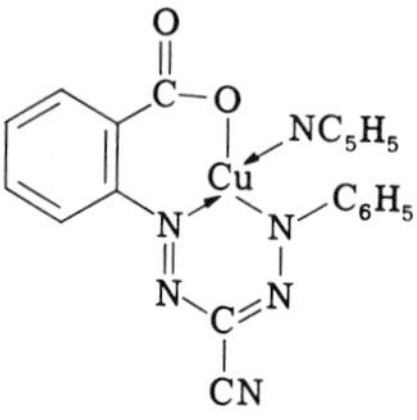

(CL)

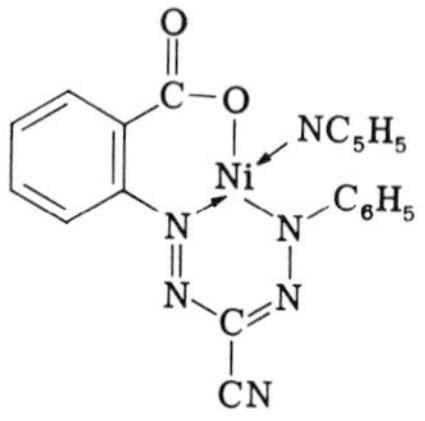

(CLI)

uncertainty regarding coordination number of the metals, and the stereo-chemistry of the complexes, would repay study.

In contrast to copper and nickel, divalent cobalt does not form complexes analogous to (CXLVII) and (CXLVIII), but only complexes of the type (CLII), which are stated[186a,b] to be more stable towards acid than the corresponding copper and nickel complexes.

Various dyestuffs applications have been claimed for 1:1 metal com-

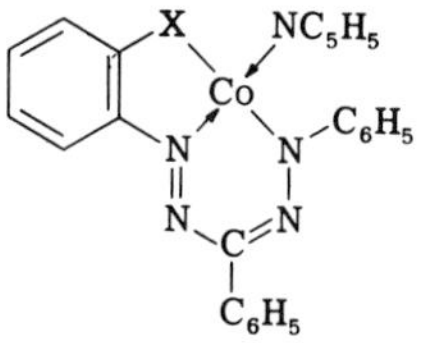

X = − COO −, Bordeaux
X = − O −, Blue

(CLII)

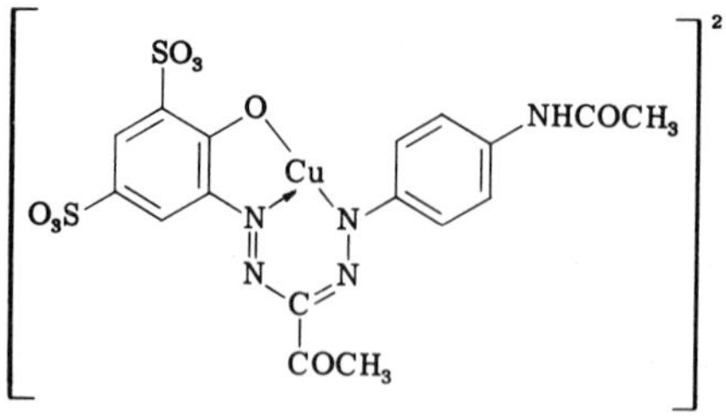

(CLIII)

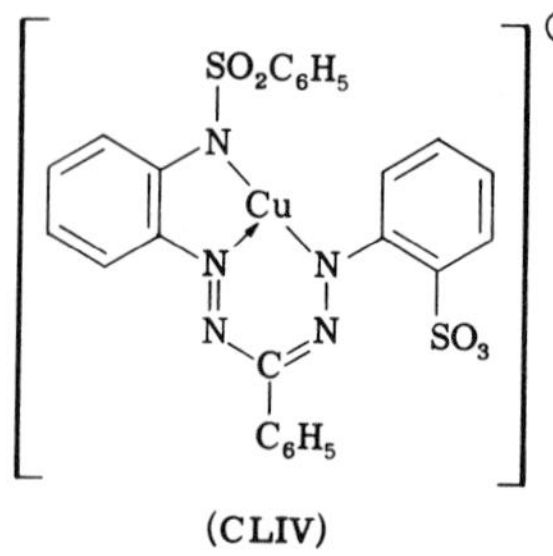

(CLIV)

plexes of tridentate formazans. For example, the copper complex (CLIII) is reported[188] to dye wool from an acid dyebath in blue shades of good fastness properties. Tridentate formazans have also been prepared in which one donor function is an alkyl- or an arylsulfonylamino group (see Section II,C,5,*f*). A typical copper complex (CLIV) derived from a formazan of this type is claimed[189] to dye wool in violet shades from a weakly acid dyebath.

Tridentate formazans behave in a similar manner to tridentate azo compounds and give cobalt(III) and chromium(III) complexes having 2:1 stoichiometry.[190] Some difficulty has been experienced in the preparation of chromium complexes from simple chromium salts but certain methods, e.g., reaction of the formazan with chromium fluoride in formamide, with trichlorotripyridinechromium(III) in boiling pyridine, or with sodium chrome salicylate in alkaline solution are reported[186] to be effective. The colors of the chromium complexes obtained from a particular

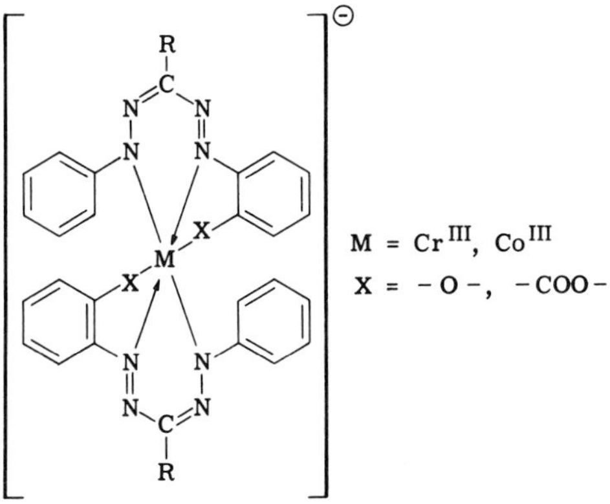

$M = Cr^{III}, Co^{III}$

$X = -O-, -COO-$

(CLV)

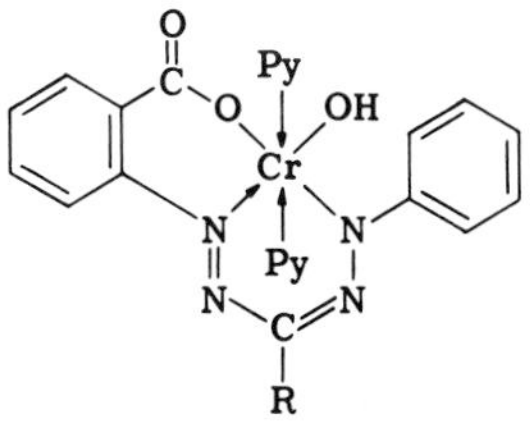

(CLVI)

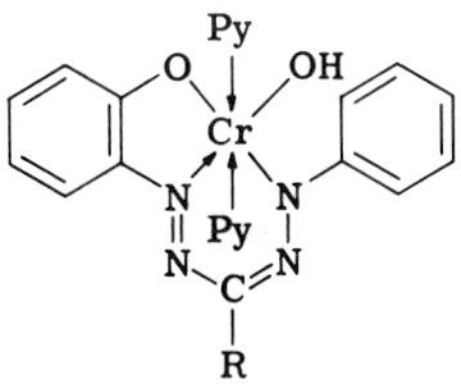

(CLVII)

[188] S, *BP* 984,451.
[189] Gy, *BP* 961,843.
[190] S, *BeP* 603,940.

formazan vary considerably depending upon the method of preparation, and their constitutions have not been fully elucidated. Those obtained by the interaction of tridentate formazans and trichlorotripyridinechromium(III) have been assigned[186,186a] the formulations (CLVI) and (CLVII). In the case of the 2:1 cobalt complexes Schetty et al.[191] have shown that complexes having a fac configuration (Section II,C,3) are formed when the metal ion is a member of two annelated six-membered chelate rings (CLV; X = –COO–), and mer complexes are formed when the cobalt ion is a member of five- and six-membered annelated rings (CLV; X = –O–).

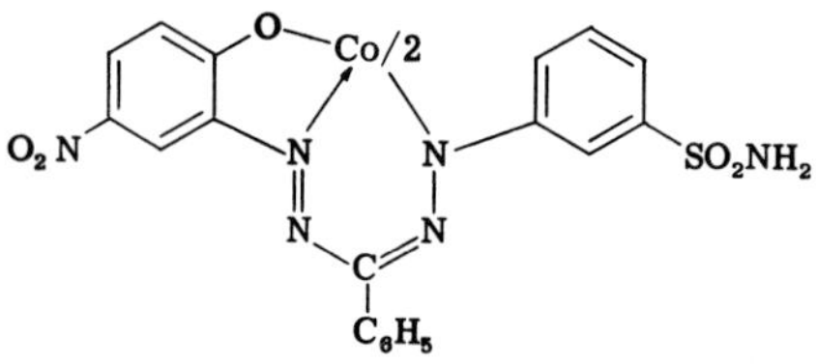

(CLVIII) 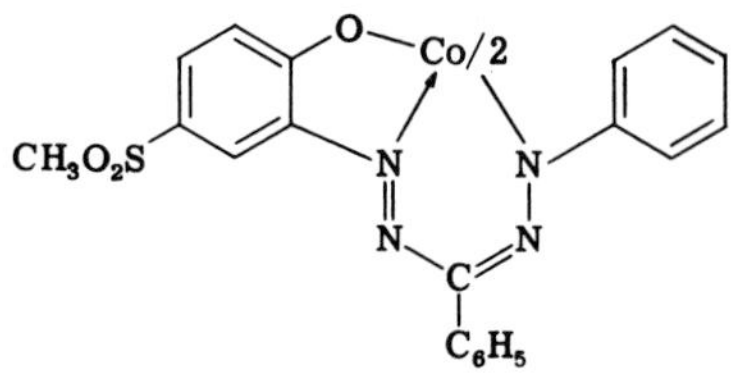   (CLIX)

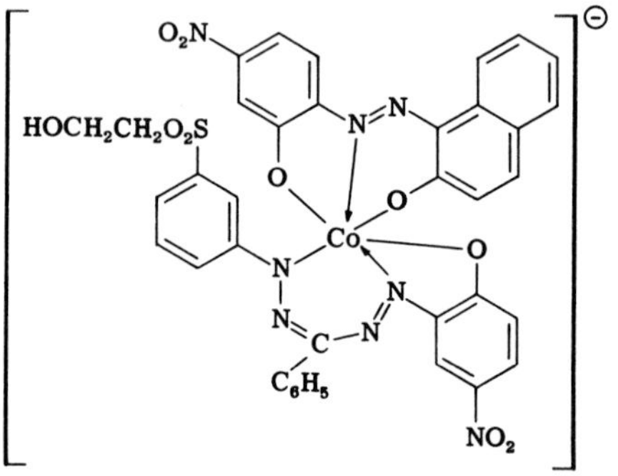

(CLX)

2:1 Cobalt complexes of tridentate formazans which derive their solubility from sulfonamide[192] (CLVIII) or alkylsulfonyl[193] (CLIX) groups may be compared with the analogous 2:1 metal complexes of tridentate azo compounds (Section I), and behave in a similar manner to the latter, giving level dyeings on wool from neutral to weakly acid dyebaths. It

[191] F. Beffa, P. Lienhard, E. Steiner, and G. Schetty, Helv. Chim. Acta 46, 1369 (1963).
[192] Gy, BP 1,019,464.
[193] Gy, BP 1,028,918.

has recently been claimed[194] that metal complex dyestuffs having good dyeing properties, especially on polyamide fibers, are obtained by the interaction of equimolecular quantities of a tridentate azo or azomethine compound, a tridentate formazan compound, and an agent yielding cobalt or chromium. The products obtained in this way are reported to consist essentially of unsymmetrical 2:1 metal complexes, rather than statistical mixtures of the three possible 2:1 metal complexes, and a typical dyestuff of this type (CLX) is claimed to dye wool from a neutral bath in navy blue shades of good fastness properties.

2. Tetradentate Formazans

Metal complex formation by tetradentate formazans has been investigated by Wizinger[186,186a,b] and his co-workers, who studied the reactions of the compounds (CLXI; $R = CN$, C_6H_5), (CLXII; $R = CN$, C_6H_5),

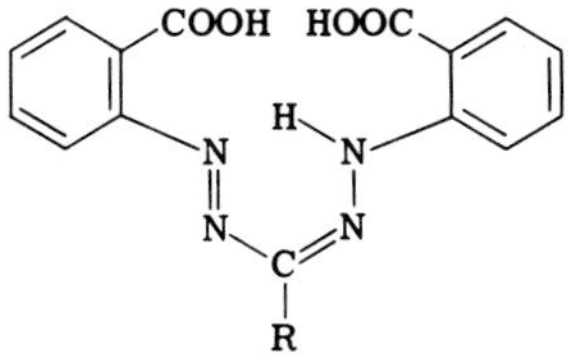

(CLXI)

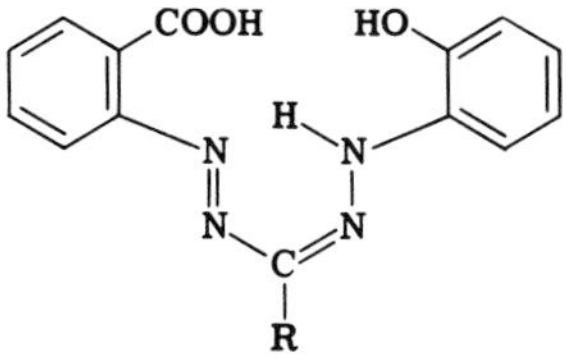

(CLXII)

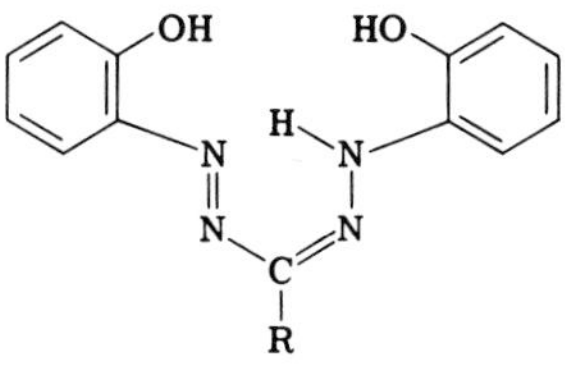

(CLXIII)

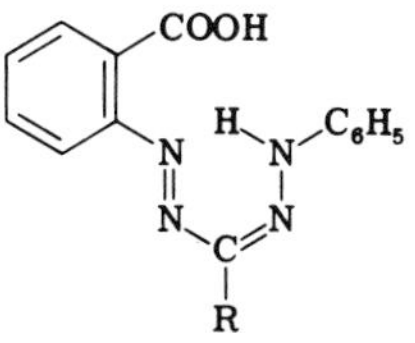

(CLXIV)

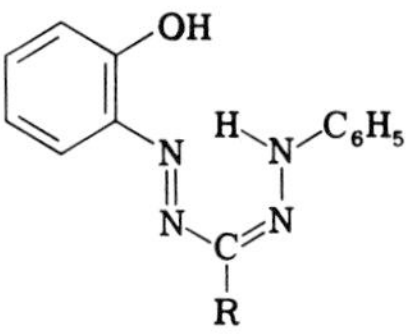

(CLXV)

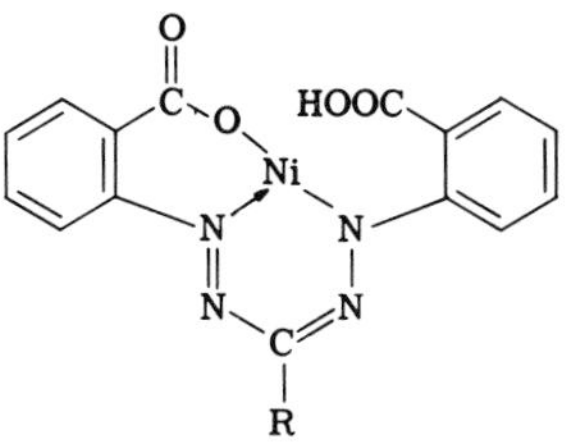

(CLXVI)

[194] F. Beffa, P. Lienhard, E. Steiner, and Gy, *BP* 1,046,649.

and (CLXIII; R = CN, C_6H_5) with salts of nickel, copper, and cobalt. These compounds readily form nickel and copper complexes having 1:1 stoichiometry which are reported to be considerably more stable towards acids than the corresponding complexes derived from the tridentate formazans (CLXIV) and (CLXV). Surprisingly, however, there is little difference in color between the complexes derived from (CLXI) and (CLXIV). For example, (CLXIV; R = CN) forms a green nickel complex which changes to red on reaction with pyridine (Section III,C,*1*), and (CLXI; R = CN) behaves in a similar manner. From these results Wizinger[186,186a,b] concluded that (CLXI; R = CN, C_6H_5) probably functions as a tridentate ligand in these complexes (CLXVI), and attributes their enhanced stability towards acids to the presence of the free carboxyl groups. The situation regarding the nickel and copper complexes of (CLXII) and (CLXIII) also is not fully resolved, although on the

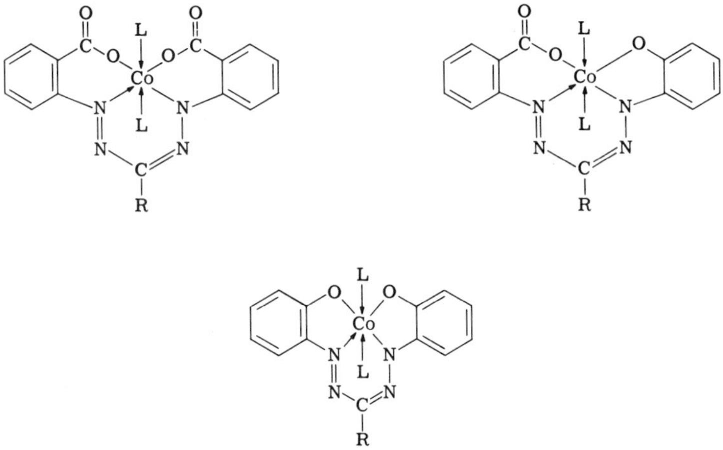

L = Pyridine, ammonia, water

(CLXVII)

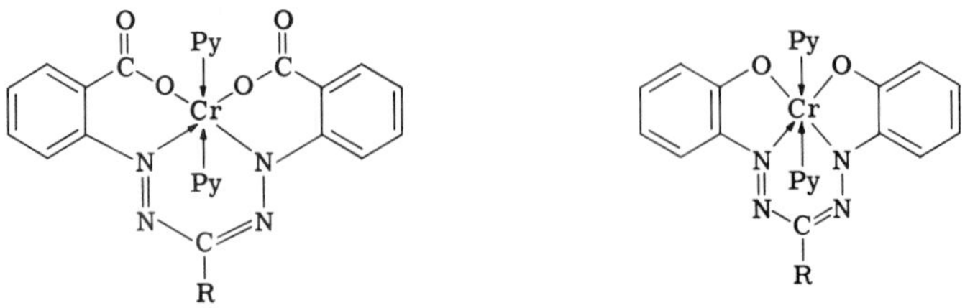

(CLXVIII)

basis of their colors Wizinger suggests that while the nickel complexes may be tricyclic types, the copper complexes almost certainly are bicyclic types. From this it is apparent that these complexes, also, would repay study by currently available techniques in order to elucidate the relationships between structure, color, and stability.

Trivalent cobalt forms tricyclic complexes with tetradentate formazans, the coordination sphere of the metal being completed by a variety of monodentate ligands including pyridine, ammonia, and water (CLXVII). These complexes have greatly increased stability towards acids, and it is reported[186,186a,b] that the complexes derived from formazans containing a meso cyano group are stable in concentrated sulfuric acid at 100° for short periods. Comparable chromium complexes have also been prepared in which the coordination sphere of the metal is completed by pyridine molecules (CLXVIII). Tetradentate formazans containing donor groups other than hydroxyl or carboxyl groups have been synthesized. These include formazans containing alkylsulfonamido groups[195,196] (CLXIX), and formazans containing various heterocyclic nitrogen donor functions, e.g., (CLXX),[186a] and (CLXXI).[186a]

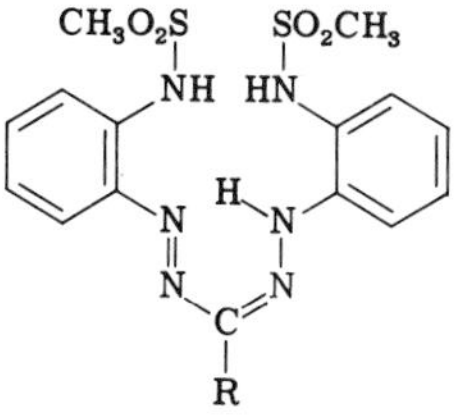

(CLXIX) 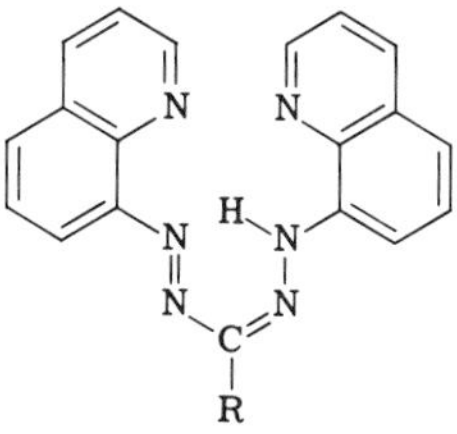   (CLXX) 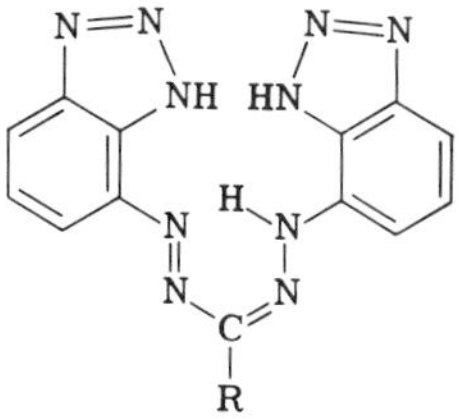   (CLXXI)

Various dyestuffs and pigment applications have been claimed for metal complexes of tetradentate formazans, for example, the copper complex of (CLXXII) is reported[197] to dye nylon from a neutral dyebath in blue shades of good lightfastness. The use of metal complexes of tetradentate formazans in the field of fiber-reactive dyestuffs has also been claimed, and covers a wide variety of fiber-reactive substituents including dichlorotriazinyl, monochloromonometanilinotriazinyl, trichloropyrimidyl, β-chloropropionyl, and β-chloroacryloylamino groups which may be attached to aryl groups in the 1,5- or meso positions of the formazans. A few typical examples include the copper complexes of

[195] Gy, *BeP* 638,128; 638,129.
[196] Gy, *FP* 1,276,586.
[197] R. A. Brooks and DuP, *USP* 2,662,075.

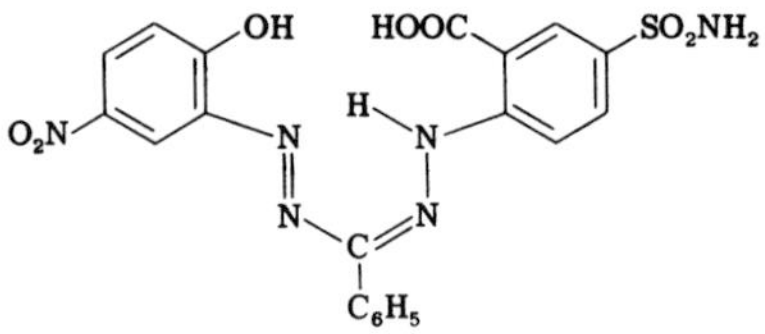

(CLXXII)

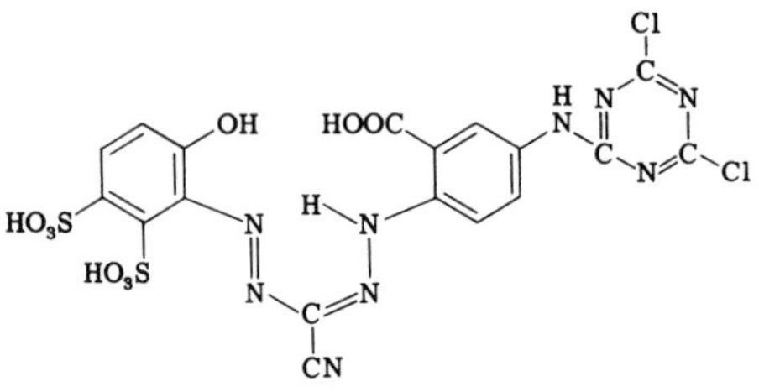

(CLXXIII)

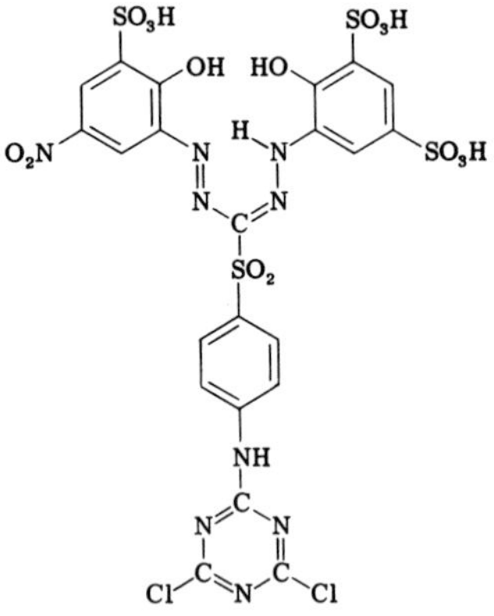

(CLXXIV)

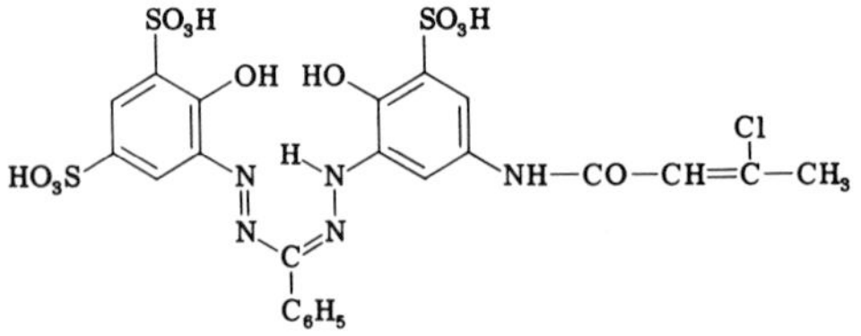

(CLXXV)

(CLXXIII),[198] and (CLXXIV),[199] and the nickel complex of (CLXXV),[200] which are all reported to give fast dyeings on cellulosic fibers.

The intensity of the colors of metal complexes of formazans has found application in the analytical field[201] and 1-(2'-hydroxyphenyl-5'-sulfophenyl)-3-phenyl-5-(2'-carboxyphenyl)-formazan (CLXXVI) can be used in the detection of zinc at a concentration of 1:50,000,000.[202] The formazan (CLXXVII) is reported[203] to be an excellent reagent for the colorimetric determination of copper and nickel, and (CLXXVIII) gives a variety of colors with different metal ions, e.g., Zn, blue; Cu, greenish blue; Co, green; Ag, rubine; Pd green, at very low concentrations.

[198] W. Steinemann and S, *BP* 1,022,043.

[199] W. Steinemann and S, *BP* 984,452.

[200] Gy, *BP* 950,861.

[201] R. Wizinger, *Angew. Chem.* **61**, 33 (1949).

[202] J. H. Yoe, and R. M. Rush, *Anal. Chim. Acta* **6**, 526 (1952).

[203] H. B. Jonassen, V. C. Chamblin, and V. L. Wagner, *Anal. Chem.* **30**, 1660 (1958).

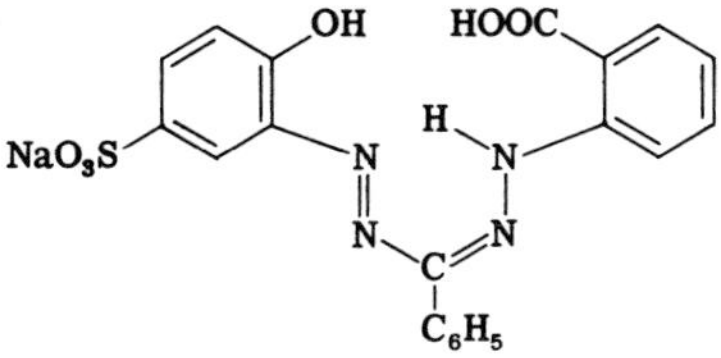

(CLXXVI)

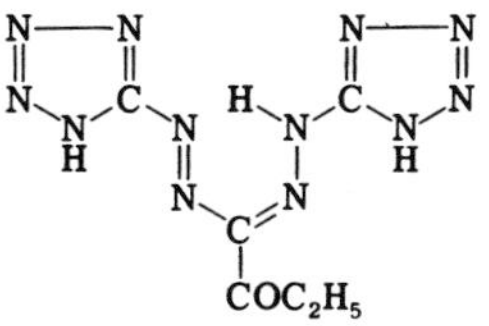

(CLXXVII)

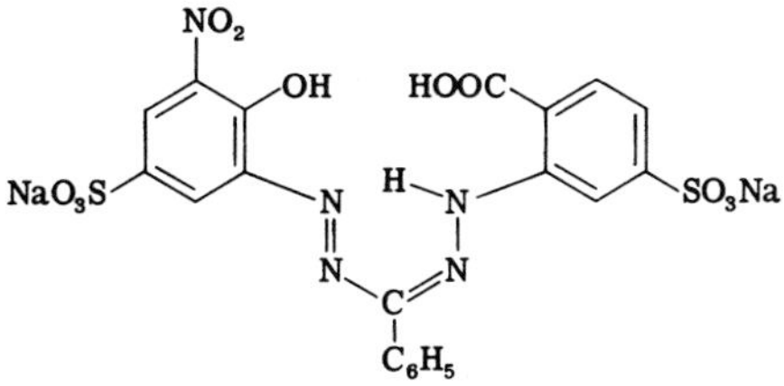

(CLXXVIII)

A series of compounds (CLXXIX) which may be regarded as azomethine analogs of formazans has been synthesized and shown[204,205] to form metal complexes analogous to those formed by the formazans. An interesting example of compounds of this type which form the subject of a recent review[206] is (CLXXX), in which the meso substituent is an arylazo group.[207]

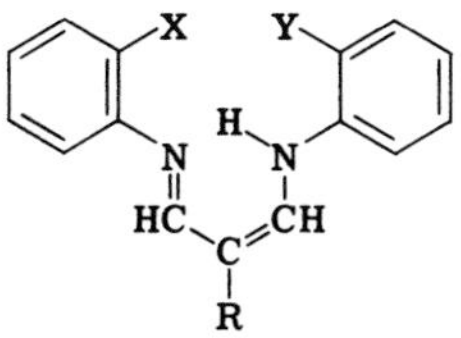

X, Y = Metallizable substituents

(CLXXIX)

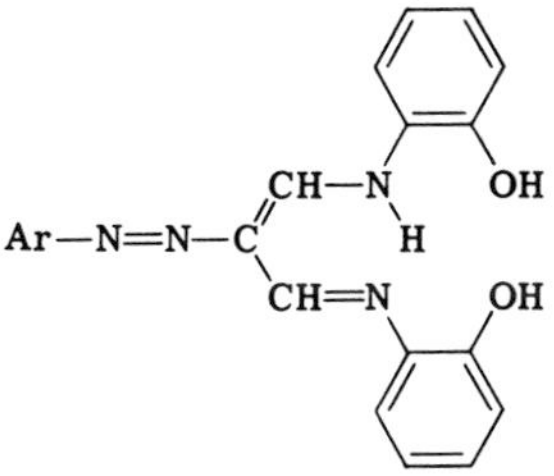

(CLXXX)

[204] B. Hirsch, *Angew. Chem.* **67**, 527 (1955).

[205] H. Baumann, H. R. Hensel, and BASF, *DBP* 1,110,348.

[206] H. Baumann, and H. R. Hensel, *Fortschr. Chem. Forsch.* **7**, No. 4, 1967.

[207] H. R. Hensel, B. Eistert, H. Baumann, J. Dehnert, and BASF, *DBP* 1,047,964; H. R. Hensel, *Ber.* **97**, 96 (1964).

CHAPTER VIII

DISPERSE DYES

J. M. Straley

RESEARCH LABORATORIES, TENNESSEE EASTMAN COMPANY,
DIVISION OF EASTMAN KODAK COMPANY, KINGSPORT, TENNESSEE

I. Introduction

In 1950, disperse, or "acetate," dyes, as they were more commonly called, were used almost entirely on secondary cellulose acetate. There was a small usage on polyamides. Since then their application to fibers other than cellulose acetate has grown steadily. The realization that some disperse dyes cover barré (nonuniformities introduced into the fiber during processing) on nylon has increased their use on that fiber, particularly on the newly popular tufted carpets. Almost all polyester fabrics are dyed with them. They are useful in light to medium shades on acrylic and modacrylic fibers. Acetate dyes are used on certain modified polypropylenes, although not yet in any significant amount. The recently introduced elastomeric fibers can be colored with disperse dyes. There apparently is no reliable way of determining the relative percentages used on these

TABLE I

U. S. FIBER PRODUCTION (IN MILLIONS OF POUNDS)[a]

	1950	1966
Cellulose esters (including triacetate)	440	454
Polyesters	0	485
Polyamides	90	1,066
Polypropylene	0	133
Acrylics and modacrylics	9	353

[a] Does not include industrial fibers, tire cord, or cigarette filter tow.

various fiber classes. Table I shows the growth in the United States of the principal fibers on which disperse dyes are used.[1]

It is apparent that the increase in cellulose esters was of little consequence, so that the dye growth was entirely dependent on the growth of the other fibers.

In 1950 the U. S. disperse dye sales amounted to 8.5 million pounds (12.3 million dollars worth), and in 1966, 14.8 million pounds were sold for 38.1 million dollars. As a result of this growth, competition in this field has heightened sharply. Importation of disperse dyes into the United States in 1950 was negligible, while in 1966 it amounted to 2.5 million pounds. Although no figures are available, an inspection of the literature reveals that both the number of patents and number of their assignees have increased enormously since 1950.

Quite naturally, the increased number of end uses, processing conditions, finishes, etc., introduced by the new fibers have imposed new requirements on their coloring agents with respect to properties. Automotive fabrics need high resistance to light at relatively high temperatures. Polyester/wool blends require use of disperse dyes that stain wool only minimally or that can be removed easily. Otherwise, the disperse-dyed wool, usually poor to light, causes the fabric not to meet specifications. "Gulf Coast" fading of certain colors on nylon carpeting results from exposure to contaminants in areas of high humidity and temperature. Fastness properties must not be adversely affected by the "carriers" used in exhaust dyeing of polyesters and cellulose triacetate. In pleating, heatsetting, and thermal fixation methods of dyeing polyesters and in the curing of latex backings on carpets, the dyes must be able to withstand temperatures often as high as 450°F. In carpet dyeing they must resist the conditions at pH values of 8 to 9, which are necessary to prevent the oils in the jute backing from staining the nylon. Extremely small particle size and uniformity of dispersion are required to prevent specking and

[1] Private survey for Eastman Chemical Products, Inc.

streaking in printing and thermal fixation and filtration in package and beam dyeing. One of the most recent finishing developments is the increasingly popular durable-press treatment of synthetic/cellulosic fabrics. The resin-catalyst system used in that treatment has seriously affected the lightfastness or altered the shade of some of the hitherto most useful disperse dyes. The difficulty of removing greasy soils from these treated garments has caused the detergent manufacturers to add harsh alkalis to their products. Consequently the dyes, particularly on work clothing, must be able to survive severe laundering. No doubt, when the inevitable soil-release, antistatic, and flameproofing finishes arrive, the useful fast dyes will again require alteration.

Visualize, if you can, the poor acetate dye chemist, accustomed to dyeing at a maximum temperature of 180°F and only modest demands regarding fastness to light, washing, sublimation, and gas, suddenly confronted with the above requirements.

II. General Discussion

Although the advent of the truly hydrophobic fibers, the polyesters, imposed new problems for the dyer and dye chemist, it also opened the door to the use of colored chemicals which hitherto were employed only as intermediates, pigments, or dyes of widely differing applications. This was brought about by the use of high temperatures and pressures—wet as in the Burlington beam process, dry as in the Thermosol process—or the use of "carriers" at ambient pressures to augment the kinetic energy of the dye molecule and to increase permeability of the fibers' molecular arrangement. At the same time, many of the acetate dyes were found unsuitable for the newer fibers.

Old intermediates newly described[2,3] for use on polyesters include (I) and (II). An old dye, formerly of only academic interest, introduced as a polyester dye[4] is (III).

Azoic dyes, formerly used only as pigments or developed *in situ*, can be used to provide bright shades, although often of inferior lightfastness, on polyesters. Some of the most popular of these are prepared by coupling variously substituted anilines to 3-hydroxy-2-naphthanilides.[5] Selected vat dyes, generally of low molecular weight, such as the indigoids or anthraquinoid amides or acridones, dye polyesters as dispersions, usually

[2] EKCo., *USP* 3,087,773.
[3] DuP, *USP* 2,757,064.
[4] G, *USP* 2,840,443.
[5] Fran, *FP* 1,164,365; *USP* 3,043,647.

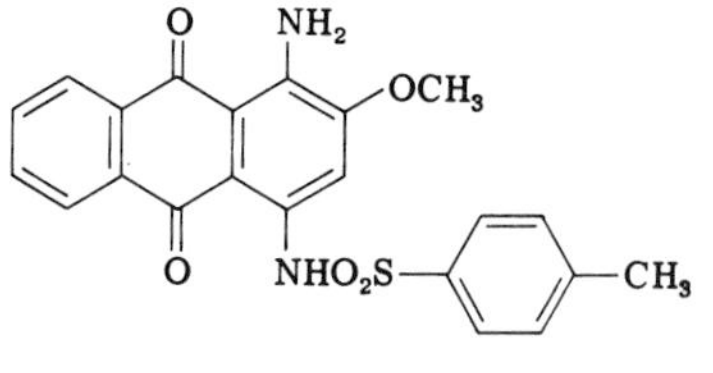

Pink
(I)

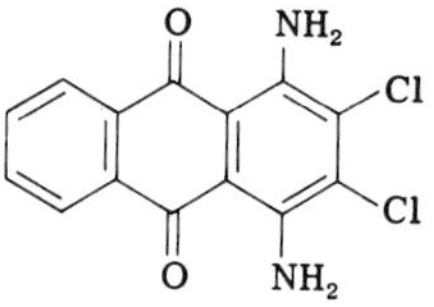

Violet
(II)

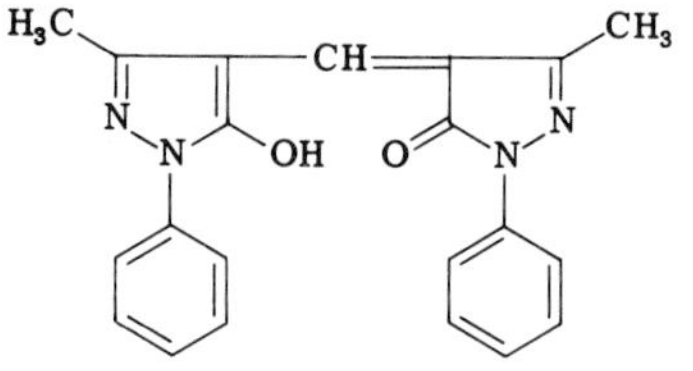

Yellow
(III)

to only medium strengths at best.[6] Their fastness properties are often good to excellent. Application to the fiber is best accomplished by means of thermal fixation techniques at 210–220° or by printing methods. Deep shades, such as navies, browns, and blacks cannot ordinarily be attained.

On the other hand, quite a few of the older acetate colors have retained their popularity on polyamides or polyesters. Some of these are (IV–XI).

The present state of imprecise knowledge does not permit generalities as to fastness properties of the various dye classes. One cannot simply refer to "dye fastness" but must consider these properties as a function of the dye–fiber entity. It is not really surprising, for example, to find that the lightfastness of an individual dye on cellulose esters differs widely from its fastness on polyamides, but it is a bit of a shock to find that some dyes differ dramatically in this property from poly(ethylene terephthalate) to poly(1,4-cyclohexylenedimethylene terephthalate), not always in favor of the same fiber. Several early attempts have been made to establish generalities, such as the influence of hydroxyalkyl groups on lightfastness of polyesters and the correlation of the gas-fastness of anthraquinone dyes on cellulose acetate with their lightfastness on polyesters. These and other generalities do not stand up when a sufficient

[6] H. Musshoff, *J. Soc. Dyers Colourists* **77**, 89 (1961); R. Klein, *Chemiefasern* **13**, 342 (1963); K. Speier, *ibid.* **11**, 668 (1961).

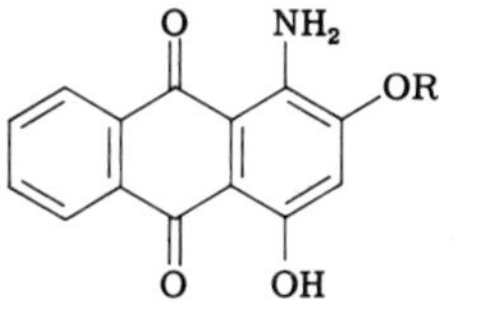

$R = -CH_3, -CH_2CH_2OH, -CH_2CH_2OCH_3$
Pink
(IV)

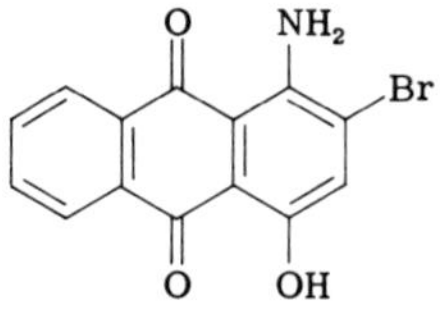

Red-violet
(V)

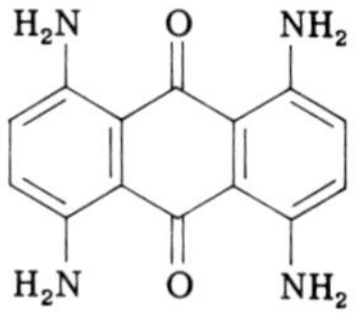

Blue
(VI)

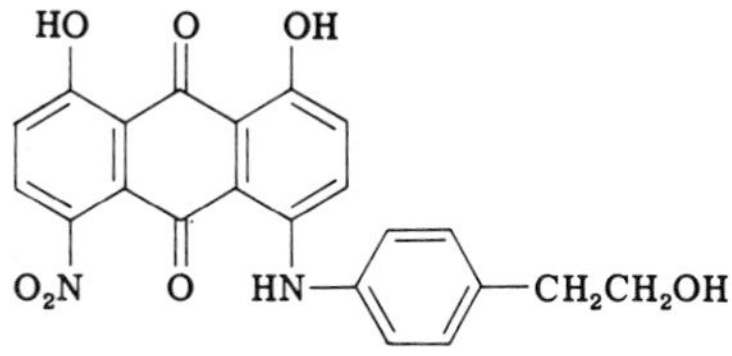

Blue
(VII)

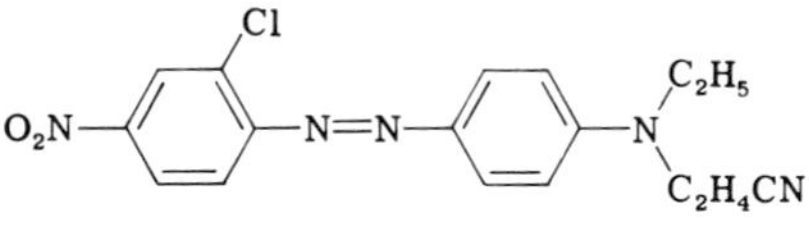

Red
(VIII)

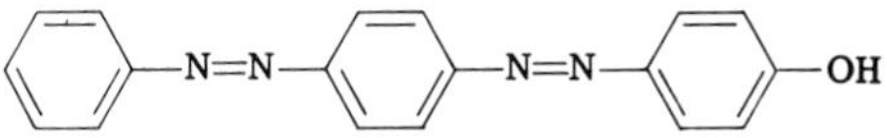

Yellow
(IX)

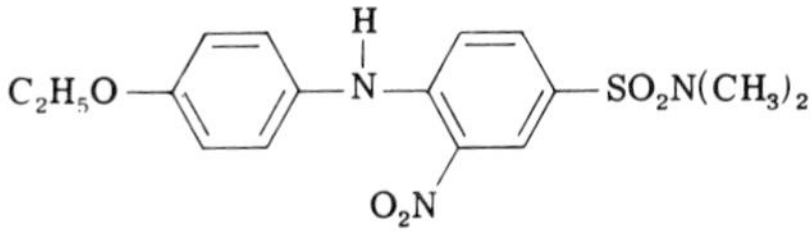

Yellow
(X)

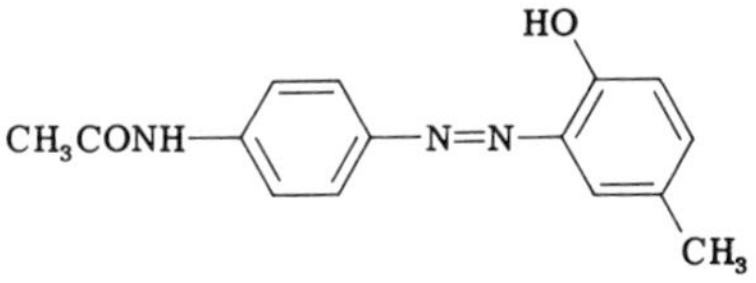

Yellow
(XI)

number of dyes are examined. More recent work[7] indicates that the presence of certain groups, such as –OH, –CONH–, –SO$_2$N–, or –OAlkyl, in the dye nucleus confer affinity and fastness properties on diverse dye–fiber combinations. The properties of a cross section of disperse dyes on cellulose esters, polyamides, and polyesters have been reviewed.[8]

[7] D. Marian, *Am. Dyestuff Reptr.* **49,** No. 11, **37,** (1960); Fran. *FP* 1,166,701; 1,176,871; 1,187,252-3.

[8] J. M. Straley and D. G. Carmichael, *Can. Textile J.* **9,** 3 (1959).

It is not the purpose of this chapter to correlate chemical structure with fastness properties nor to discuss methods of application, but there are some published guides which may be helpful. The subjects include the influence of light on disperse dyes,[9] gas-fastness,[10] sublimation fastness, the effects of thermal fixation and durable-press finishes,[11] and a general treatment of fastness properties.[12]

Papers giving an excellent resumé of color reactions and identification of over 100 disperse dyes,[13] correlations of various properties of anthraquinone dyes,[14] and a discussion of the effects of substitution and cyclization of azo components[15] have been published.

In the future, the necessity of conserving our water resources and avoiding contamination of our environment may lead to dyeing systems employing little or no water. At the same time, considerable savings may be realized by shorter dyeing cycles and recoverable dyeing media. Toward these ends, dyeing from solvents such as alkylene glycols,[16] dimethylformamide,[17] dioxane,[18] and dimethyl sulfoxide[19] have been proposed. The dyes have been padded onto the fabric and then fixed by exposure to the hot vapors of trichloroethylene.[20] An intriguing concept is the utilization of the vapor pressure of the compounds to dye in the gaseous phase without the use of auxiliary chemicals. Level dyeing of polyester packages has already been achieved with this system.[21]

Dye pastes have been printed onto paper which, after drying, can be heated in close contact with synthetic fabrics, again relying on sublimation for the color transfer.[22]

[9] C. H. Giles, J. Soc. Dyers Colourists **73**, 127 (1957); E. Merian, Textile Res. J. **36**, 612 (1966); C. H. Giles and S. M. K. Rahman, ibid. **31**, 1012 (1961).

[10] V. S. Salvin, W. D. Paist, and W. J. Myles, Am. Dyestuff Reptr. **41**, 297 (1952); S. M. Edelstein, ibid. **48**, 35 (1959); Textile Res. J. **28**, 1009 (1958).

[11] V. S. Salvin, Am. Dyestuff Reptr. **56**, 421 (1967); **55**, 490 (1966); J. J. Ionnarone and W. J. Wygand, ibid. **49**, No. 3, 81 (1960); J. Keaton and D. T. Preston, J. Soc. Dyers Colourists **80**, 312 (1964); R. Kern, Melliand Textilber. **48**, 307 (1967); H. B. Goldstein, Textilveredlung **2**, 384 (1967).

[12] H. E. Schroeder and S. N. Boyd, Textile Res. J. **27**, 275 (1957).

[13] D. Haigh, J. Soc. Dyers Colourists **79**, 242 (1963).

[14] Ko Naiki, Seni-i Gakkaishi **15**, 203 (1959); Chem. Abstr. **53**, 9675 (1959).

[15] J. B. Dickey et al., Am. Dyestuff Reptr. **54**, 596 (1965).

[16] G, USP 2,876,061; Fontaine, BP 760,041; DuP, USP 2,882,119.

[17] Ethicon, USP 2,909,177.

[18] DuP, USP 3,098,691.

[19] Crown-Zellerbach, USP 3,120,423.

[20] D. A. Garrett, J. Soc. Dyers Colourists **83**, 365 (1967).

[21] F. Jones and J. Kraska, J. Soc. Dyers Colourists **82**, 333 (1966).

[22] Filatures Prouvost, FP 1,223,330.

III. Anthraquinone Dyes

A. HOMOCYCLIC DYES

The series of 1-hydroxy-4-amino (may be alkylated or arylated) dyes has enjoyed commercial use on several fiber classes by a number of its members. Some of these are structures (XII–XVIII).

These vary from pink to blue-violet in shade, the aryl derivatives usually absorbing at the longer wavelengths. They are usually prepared by the familiar process of condensing equimolar quantities of the amine with quinizarin–leucoquinizarin mixture under mild conditions. Excess

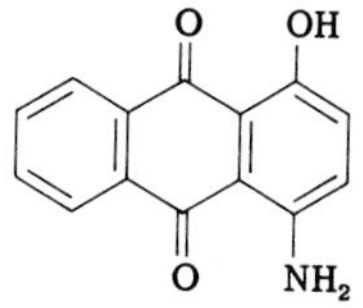

Pink

(XII)

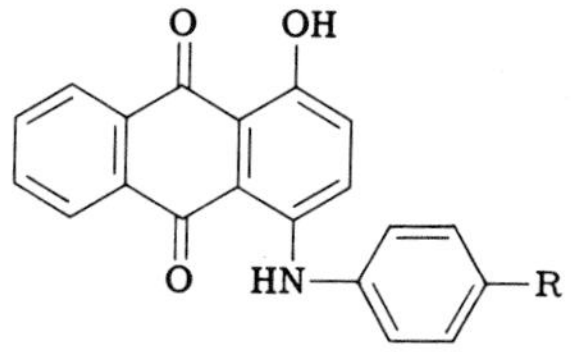

Violet

(XIII) R = H
(XIV) R = (OCH₃)

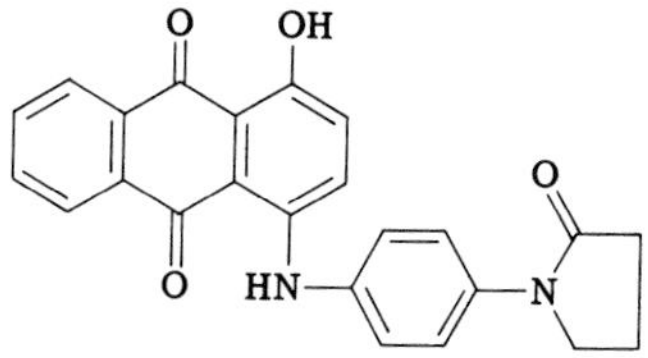

Reddish blue[23]

(XV)

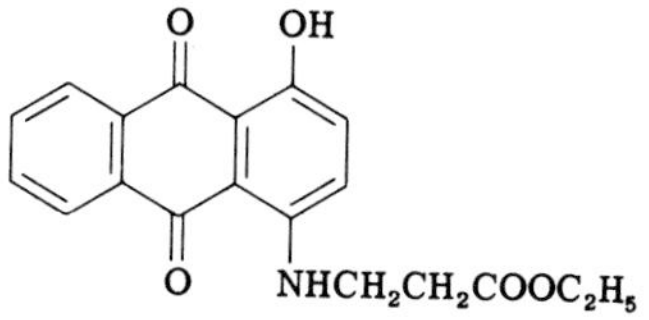

Violet[24]

(XVI)

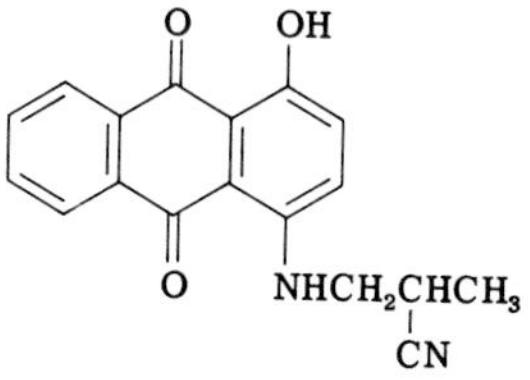

Violet[25]

(XVII)

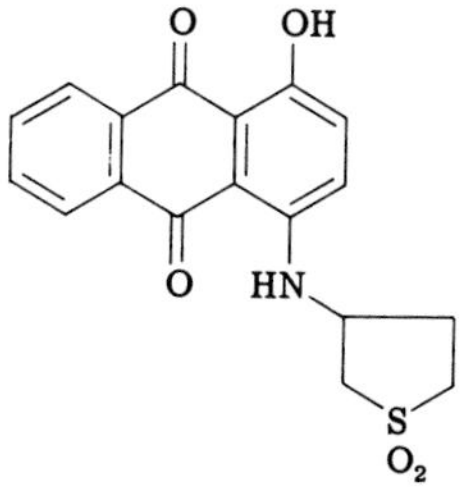

Violet[26]

(XVIII)

[23] EKCo., USP 3,201,415; 3,279,880.
[24] S, BP 841,927; 1,061,424.

amine or too rigorous conditions may result in replacement of the second anthraquinone hydroxyl. This usually produces bluer, duller shades, and in those dyes designed for cellulose acetate, a decrease in gas-fastness. Some can be prepared by the reaction of an unsaturated acid (followed by esterification) with 1-hydroxy-4-aminoanthraquinone.[24] The amides of these acids have also been reported. The β-cyanoethyl group, however, was introduced by condensation in the usual manner with β-cyanoethylamine.[27] 1-Hydroxy-4-(β-alkylsulfonylethylamino)anthraquinones appear in the literature.[28] The reaction of amines with quinizarin in a phenolic solvent eliminates the need for leucoquinizarin and reoxidation.[29]

Much of the effort in this series has been directed to arylamino derivatives. Aryloxy (or thio) phenylamines,[30] N-alkyl-N-acylphenylenediamines,[31] and p-alkyl-m-[(β-hydroxethoxy)methyl]anilines[32] have been used. Dyes derived from aminobenzo-1,3-dioxanes[33] and the cyclic ethylene acetals of aminobenzaldehydes have been disclosed.[34]

The hydroxyalkyl[35] or benzyl[36] esters and various amides[37] of aminobenzoic acids have been used in this condensation. Dyes from the esters of 3-(4-aminobenzoyl) propionic acid[38] and the amides of nuclearly alkylated aminobenzenesulfonic acids[39] have been prepared. The reaction products from quinizarin and aminophenols have been treated with carboxylic acid halides[40] and alkyl- or arylsulfonyl halides.[41]

1-Hydroxy-4-alkylamino-[42] or arylaminoanthraquinones[43] have been halogenated.

The use of compounds prepared by heating boric acid with 2-methyl-2,4-pentanediol, for example, has been said to facilitate the condensation

[25] EKCo., *USP* 2,659,739.
[26] FBy, *USP* 3,249,626.
[27] S, *BP* 765,725.
[28] G, *BP* 968,709.
[29] CCC, *USP* 2,727,045.
[30] Gy, *BeP* 612,278.
[31] S, *USP* 2,894,800.
[32] G, *USP* 2,585,681.
[33] G, *USP* 2,546,121.
[34] G, *USP* 2,612,507.
[35] FBy, *BP* 891,774.
[36] CIBA, *USP* 3,097,909.
[37] Gy, *BP* 1,053,110; *SP* 430,008.
[38] BASF, *BP* 1,061,948.
[39] Gy, *BeP* 612,277.
[40] NSK, *FP* 1,573,869.
[41] Gy, *BP* 1,067,645.
[42] S, *USP* 3,164,615.
[43] EKCo., *USP* 3,106,438.

of quinizarin (and its derivatives) with hindered anilines, such as 2,6-dialkyl derivatives.[44]

The alkylamino dyes are chiefly useful on cellulose acetate, their lightfastness usually not being sufficient on polyesters, with the exception of the sulfolanyl derivative (XVIII). The arylamino derivatives usually have poor affinity for cellulose esters and are used on polyesters, even though their lightfastness sometimes is inferior to that of other (but more expensive) anthraquinones.

The old compound (XIX) was used briefly on polyesters. Dyes of the type (XX) have been proposed,[45] as have those represented by (XXI).[46]

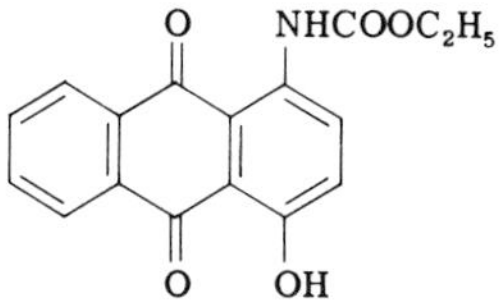

Orange
(XIX)

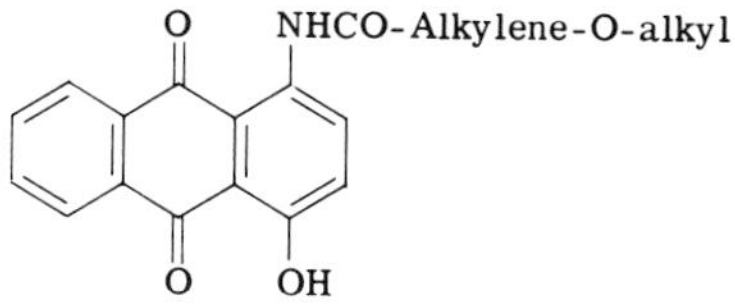

Orange
(XX)

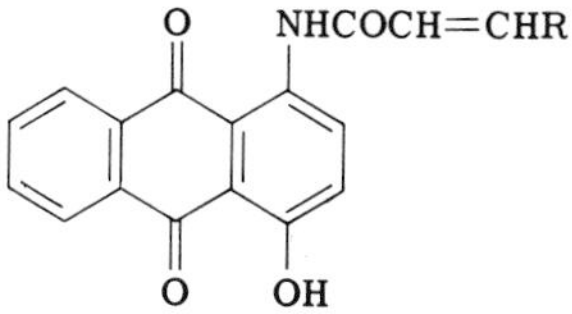

Orange
(XXI)

A family of compounds which provides bright red and pink shades on cellulose esters, polyamides, and polyesters is represented by 1-amino-2-X-4-hydroxyanthraquinone, where X is usually an alkyl or aryloxy or thio substituent. These are readily prepared by the related routes shown in Chart 1.

Route a to the alkyl derivatives, although a step longer, is often more advantageous than the direct route b. Some of the dyes which appeared in the literature long before the marketing of polyesters are in use now on this fiber as well as others. These are structures (IV) and (V), and (IV) where R = phenyl. The prominent deficiency of these dyes is their inadequate sublimation fastness for many applications. Attempts to correct

[44] Gy, *USP* 3,215,710.
[45] S, *USP* 2,794,031.
[46] S, *USP* 2,794,032.

CHART 1

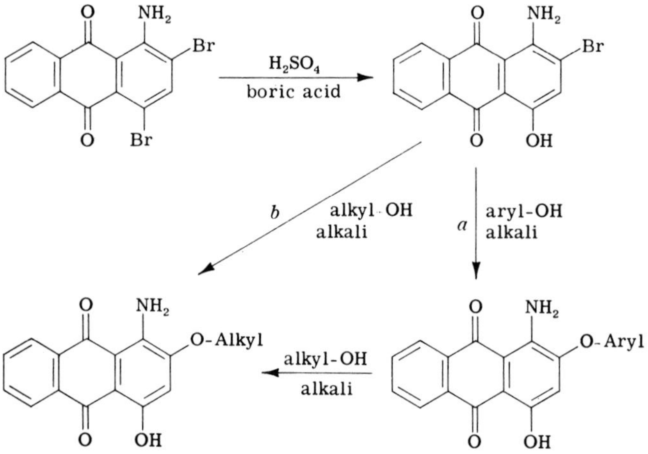

this situation have resulted in the compounds (XXII),[47] (XXIII),[48] (XXIV),[49] and (XXV).

Dye (XXV) is prepared by chlorosulfonating 1-amino-2-phenoxy-4-hydroxyanthraquinone and condensing the product with 3-methoxypropylamine.[50] This reference includes a large number of similar compounds; e.g., where –H, –NH$_2$, etc., replaces the 4-OH group.

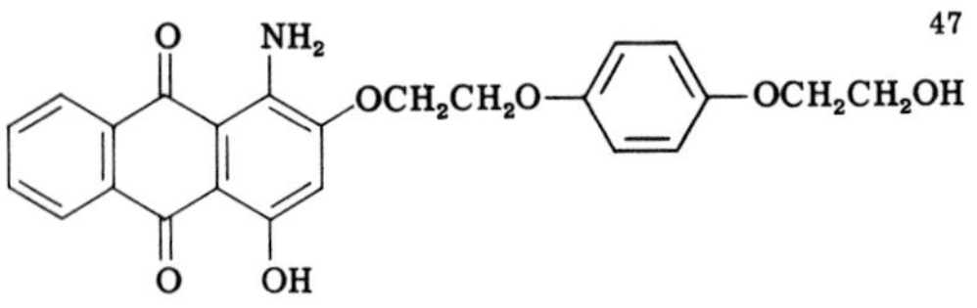

(XXII)

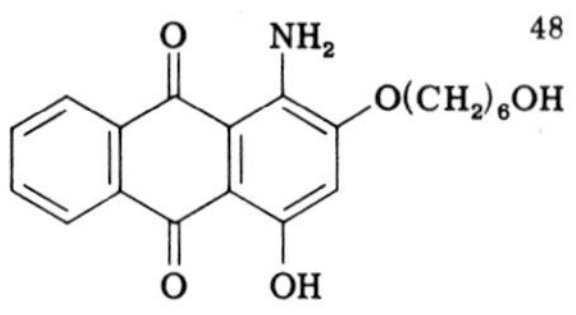

(XXIII)

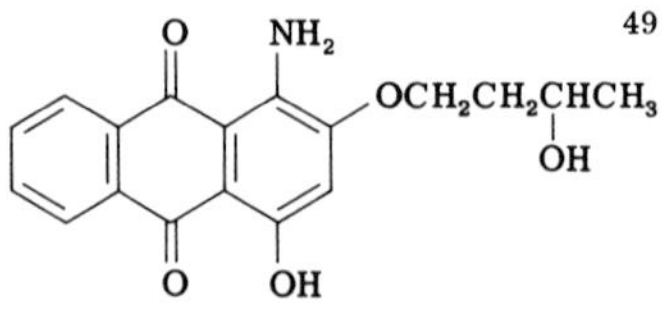

(XXIV)

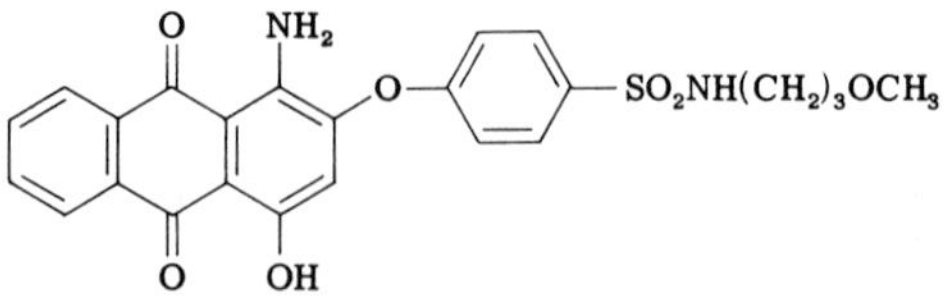

(XXV)

[47] FBy, *BP* 1,093,863.
[48] BASF, *BP* 982,267.
[49] DuP, *FP* 1,356,563.
[50] BASF, *USP* 3,299,103; *BP* 913,902.

Members of the family in which the group in the 2-position is $-OCH_2CH_2X$, $-SCH_2CH_2X$, $-OCH_2CH_2O$ Alkyl, $-O(CH_2CH_2O)_n$ Alkyl, and $-S$ Alkylene X, where X represents a wide variety of substituents, have been proposed.[51]

Use of 1-amino-2-chloro-4-hydroxyanthraquinone instead of the 2-bromo compound is said to give a smoother reaction with fewer impurities in the direct route to the 2-alkoxy derivatives.[52] 1-Aminoanthraquinone is chlorinated in dimethylformamide to produce the 1-amino-2, 4-dichloro compound necessary for the 4-hydroxy intermediate.[53]

Introduction of a 4-(hydroxymethyl)cyclohexylmethoxy group into the 2-position is said to improve sublimation fastness.[54] Aralkoxy or thio residues in the 2-position in which the aryl group bears various substituents including sulfamoyl (may be substituted) groups have been reported.[55] In such compounds, the 4-hydroxy group may be replaced by $-NH_2$ or $-NHR$ groups and the 1-amino group may also be substituted. The 2-aryloxy group may bear $-CN$ or $-$alkyl CN substituents.[56] Tetrahydrofurfuryloxy groups have also occupied the 2-position.[57]

1-Amino (or substituted amino) -2,4-dihydroxyanthraquinones, when treated with organic sulfonyl chlorides, are esterified only on the 2-hydroxyl group.[58]

1-Amino-2-aryloxy-4-hydroxy compounds in which the aryl group bears alkyl (or substituted alkyl) groups,[59] halogen atoms,[60] and alkylthio or arylthio residues[61] have been reported. It may also be substituted by other aryl,[62] β-carbamoylethyl,[63] alkylsulfonyl,[64] or β-chloroethylsulfamoyl[65] moieties. 1-Amino-4-hydroxy dyes with $-OC_6H_4ZC_6H_5$, where Z is $=NH$, $-O-$, $-S-$, $-SO_2-$ have been described. The reference also discloses dyes where the 4-position may contain various amino groups and

[51] CL, *USP* 2,640,062; DuP, *USP* 2,768,052; S, *USP* 2,844,598; ICI, *USP* 2,992,240; CIBA, *BP* 834,949.

[52] CIBA, *BP* 1,085,685.

[53] CIBA, *BP* 1,054,503.

[54] AAP, *BP* 974,404; EKCo., *FP* 1,446,845.

[55] CIBA, *USP* 2,972,622; YDC, *BP* 1,094,791.

[56] CIBA, *USP* 3,329,692.

[57] AAP, *USP* 3,124,601.

[58] NSK, *FP* 1,489,956.

[59] CIBA, *USP* 3,174,983; IC, *USP* 3,189,398; MDW, *BP* 973,262.

[60] BASF, *BP* 900,127.

[61] FBy, *USP* 3,293,270.

[62] CIBA, *USP* 3,178,455.

[63] MCI, *FP* 1,478,865.

[64] FBy, *BP* 1,076,988.

[65] ICI, *USP* 3,147,287.

the 3-position may bear halogen.[66] Hydroxyaryloxy groups *per se*[67] or esterified with a carboxylic or sulfonic acid[68] have occupied the 2-position. The reaction of the 2-aryloxy (or thio) group with N-methylolamides or imides (e.g., N-hydroxymethylphthalimide) is said to improve sublimation fastness.[69] 1-Amino-4-hydroxy(amino, substituted amino) compounds with $-O(CH_2CH_2O)_nCOCH_2CH_2COOH$ in the 2-position have been prepared.[70] 1-Amino-2-carbalkoxy[71] and aroyl[72] 4-hydroxyanthraquinones, the aroyl compound being blue, have been reported, as have 1-fluoroalkylamino-2-bromo-4-hydroxyanthraquinones.[73] 1-Arylamino-3-alkylsulfonyl-4-hydroxyanthraquinones have been prepared,[74] and treatment of 1-arylamino-3-bromo(or alkoxy or sulfo)-4-aminoanthraquinone in a caustic fusion produces 4-arylaminoalizarin.[75]

A few new 1,4-dihydroxy-2-X-anthraquinones and new processes have been reported. The Marschalk[76] procedure for introducing alkyl or substituted alkyl groups into the molecule by condensation of leucoquinizarin with aldehydes in aqueous solution has been adapted to organic solvents,[77] as in Chart 2.

CHART 2

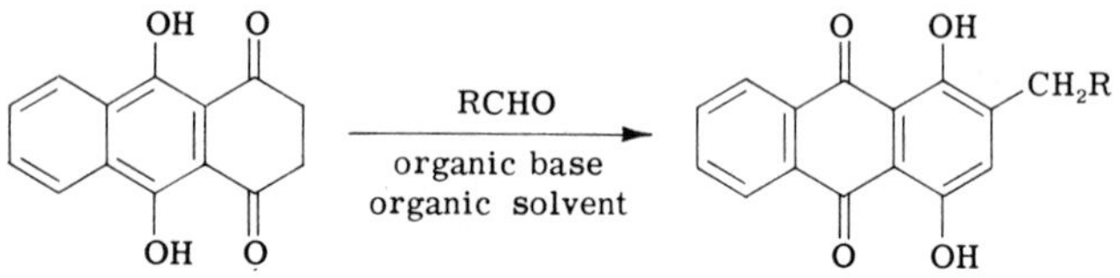

This process does not require an oxidation step. When R = aryl, chlorosulfonation followed by condensation with ammonia or amines results in orange dyes for polyesters.[78]

Replacement of the bromine in 2-bromoquinizarin by Alkyl SO_2(or O)-

[66] FH, *BP* 1,090,259.
[67] ICI, *USP* 2,773,071.
[68] NSK, *FP* 1,497,689.
[69] FBy, *FP* 1,503,493.
[70] CIBA, *BP* 652,453.
[71] BASF, *USP* 2,823,212.
[72] Toms River, *USP* 3,211,755.
[73] EKCo., *USP* 2,624,746.
[74] ICI, *BP* 797,383.
[75] FBy, *BP* 1,090,510.
[76] C. Marschalk, F. Koenig, and N. Ouroussoff, *Bull. soc. chim. France* [5]3, 1545 (1936).
[77] BASF, *FP* 1,503,485.
[78] BASF, *BeP* 674,112; *FP* 1,461,959.

Alkylene-O groups has been accomplished.[79] If the bromine is replaced by aralkylamino, arylamino, aralkylthio, or aralkyloxy groups, the products may be chlorosulfonated and transformed into the corresponding sulfonamides.[80]

The methods of preparing 1,4-diaminoanthraquinones are well known and they will not be discussed in detail here. The most common are

(1) Reaction of amines and ammonia with quinizarin.

(2) Replacement of labile groups (halo, nitro, etc.) with an amine. A modification is the use of a sulfonamide followed by hydrolysis.

(3) Reduction of nitro groups.

(4) Reaction of 1-amino-2-sulfo(or halo)-4-haloanthraquinone with an amine followed by replacement or elimination of the group in the 2-position.

A group of 1,4-bis(alkylamino)anthraquinones, collectively known as Disperse Blue 3, has for years been the work-horse blue for cellulose acetate. In more recent years it has been popular on nylon carpeting because of good barré coverage, although its lightfastness and resistance to atmospheric fading are not good. Its lightfastness on polyesters is poor also.

More recently, quinizarin (plus its leuco) has been condensed with mixtures of ammonia with various amines.[81] 1-Methylamino-4-(β-acetoxyethylamino)anthraquinone has been proposed for dyeing poly(vinyl chloride) fibers.[82] Dyes with bromoalkyl groups on both nitrogens have been disclosed.[83]

The addition reactions shown in Chart 3 have been reported.[84,85]

Workers studying spectral shifts in various 1,4- and 1,5-bis(alkylamino) anthraquinones pointed out an anomalous shift for the dye obtained from quinizarin and 2 moles of ethylenediamine.[86] It was later found that, instead of the expected bis(β-aminoethylamino) compound, structure (XXVI) had been formed.[87]

Fluorinated alkylamino groups in the 1-position of dyes bearing $-HNC_6H_4O(C_2H_4O)_n$Alkyl groups in the 4-position have been prepared.[88]

[79] OBM, *USP* 3,361,772.
[80] BASF, *BP* 1,065,477; *FP* 1,473,794; *DBP* 1,241,016.
[81] CIBA, *USP* 2,731,477.
[82] Fran, *USP* 2,795,477.
[83] ICI, *BP* 836,671.
[84] S, *FP* 1,470,597.
[85] G, *USP* 2,727,903.
[86] M. Simon, *J. Am. Chem. Soc.* **85**, 1974 (1963).
[87] M. S. Simon and D. P. Waller, *Tetrahedron Letters* p. 1527 (1967).
[88] EKCo., *USP* 2,537,975.

CHART 3

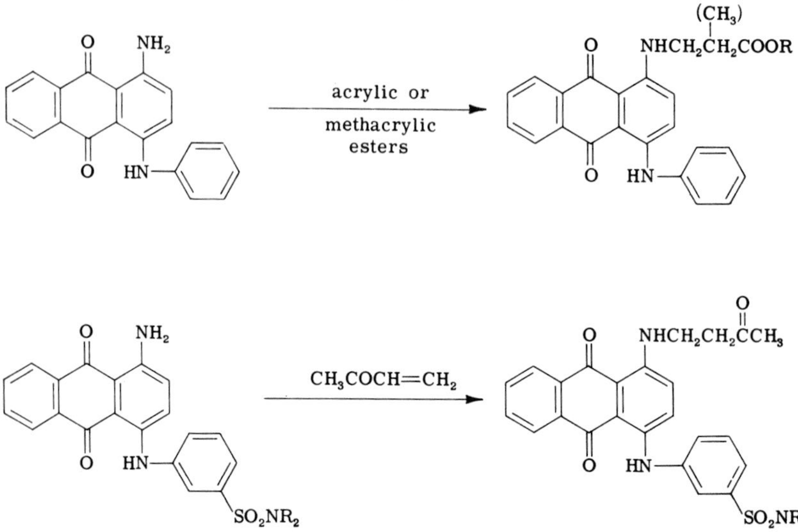

Dyes of structures (XXVIIa,b,c) have been reported. The (XXVIIc) configurations are said to be of special interest on nylon.

1-Amino-4-NHC$_6$H$_4$CH$_2$OCH$_2$CH$_2$OH-anthraquinone has been de-

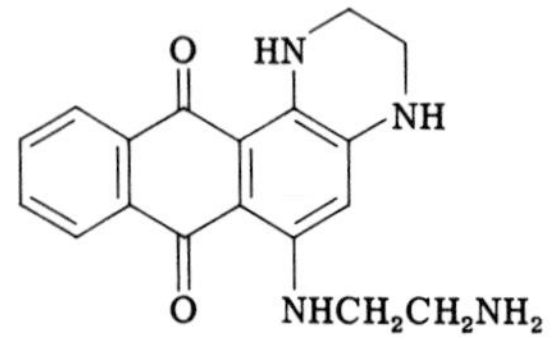

(XXVI)

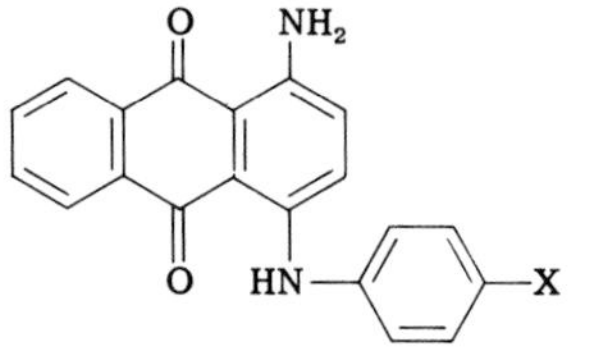

(a) X = — SO$_2$N(C$_2$H$_4$OH)$_2$, etc.[89]
(b) X = — N(Alkyl) SO$_2$C$_2$H$_4$N(Alkyl)$_2$[90]
(c) X = — SO$_2$NHCH$_2$CH$_2$Cl or
       — SO$_2$NHCH$_2$CHOHCH$_2$Cl[91]

(XXVII)

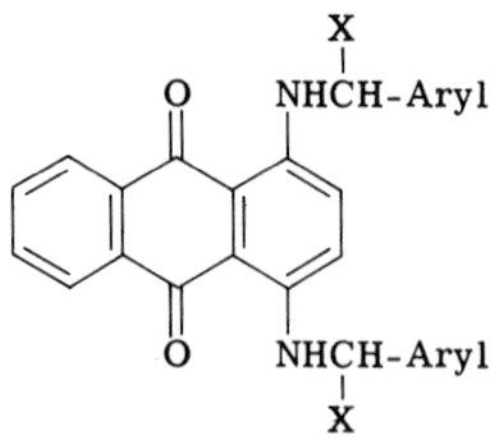

X = Alkyl or —CH$_2$OH

(XXVIII)

[89] G, USP 2,730,534.
[90] FH, USP 3,354,182.
[91] ICI, USP 3,147,287.

scribed.[92] Condensation of 1-amino-4-arylamino dyes with N-(hydroxy-methyl)phthalimide results in attachment of a phthalimidomethyl group to the aryl nucleus.[93] 1-Aroylamido[94] or 1-alkylsulfonamido-4-aryl-amino[95] molecules are violet polyester dyes.

1,4-Bis(arylamino)anthraquinones in which both aryl groups bear $-SO_2NH_2$, $-SO_2NHAlkyl$, etc.,[96] or $-CH_2OCH_2CH_2OH$ groups[97] are known. 1,4-Bis(2,4,6-triethylanilino)anthraquinones are proposed for dyeing polypropylene.[98] Dyes of structure (XXVIII) are said to yield bright blues on polyesters.[99]

Dyes can be prepared by addition of 1,4-diaminoanthraquinones to styrene oxides, the products being phenylhydroxyalkyl derivatives.[100] 1,4-Diaminoanthraquinone can be condensed with acrylic esters or the nitrile to give, for example, the 1,4-bis(β-cyanoethylamino) compound.[101] 1-Cyclohexyl (which may bear $-OH$, $-OAlkyl$, $-NHR$ groups)-4-amino (or substituted amino) compounds are bright blue dyes.[102]

The dyeing properties on nylon and cellulose acetate of 1,4-diamino-anthraquinones which bear butyl groups in the 2- or 6-positions have been studied.[103] Bathochromic shifts compared to the unbutylated nuclei are observed.

Heating 4-amino or substituted aminoalizarins with ammonia under pressure replaces the 1-OH group with an $-NH_2$ group.[104]

Many groups are introduced into the 2-position by replacing groups such as halogen or $-SO_3H$ with $-OR$, $-SR$, $-O_2SR$, or $-CN$. 2-Aryl ethers (or thio ethers) bearing $-SO_2NH_2$ groups, also having other groups such as halogen in the 3-position,[105] are known.

The process of Chart 4 has been described.[106]

Dyes of structure (XXIX) have been reported.[107,108]

[92] G, *USP* 2,560,887.
[93] G, *DBP* 817,625.
[94] FM, *BP* 1,000,887.
[95] AAP, *USP* 3,350,425.
[96] S, *USP* 2,852,535; *DBP* 1,052,604.
[97] G, *USP* 2,585,681.
[98] ICI, *USP* 3,188,163.
[99] ICI, *BP* 1,094,925.
[100] DGS, *DBP* 1,010,215.
[101] A. Vaidyanathan and S. V. Sunthankar, *Indian J. Technol.* **2**, 338 (1964); *Chem. Abstr.* **62**, 5361 (1965).
[102] FBy, *DBP* 1,018,570.
[103] A. T. Peters, Jr. and A. T. Peters, *J. Chem. Soc.* p. 1125 (1960); B. W. Larner and A. T. Peters, *ibid.* p. 1368 (1952).
[104] FBy, *DBP* 1,245,387.
[105] BASF, *BeP* 672,088; *BP* 1,070,117-8.
[106] CL, *USP* 2,640,059.
[107] CCC, *BP* 1,067,538.

CHART 4

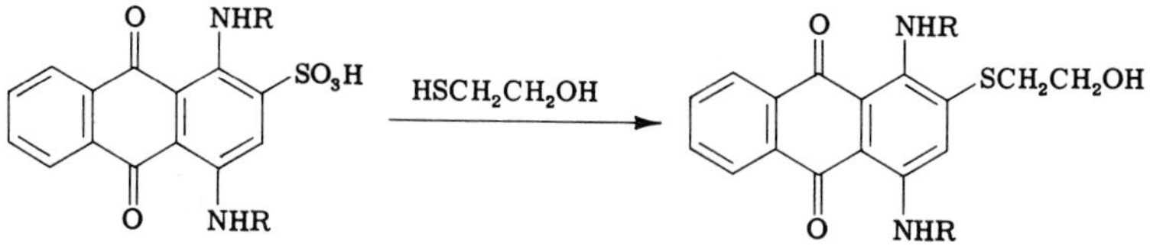

1-Amino-2-alkyl(or aryl)sulfonyl-4-arylaminoanthraquinones,[109] or derivatives in which the 4-position may bear $-NH_2$, $-OH$, $-NHSO_2Aryl$ and the group in the 3-position may be H, halogen, $-CN$, $-SR$, or

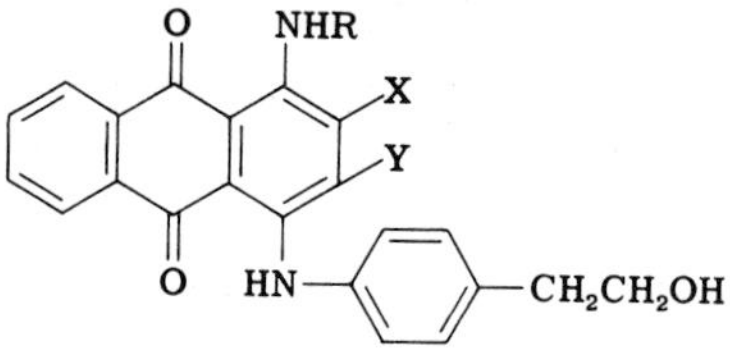

(a) R = $-H$ or $-CH_3$; X = $-Br$
(b) R = $-H$, X = $-OC_6H_4OH$,
    Y = $-H$ or $-Cl$

(XXIX)

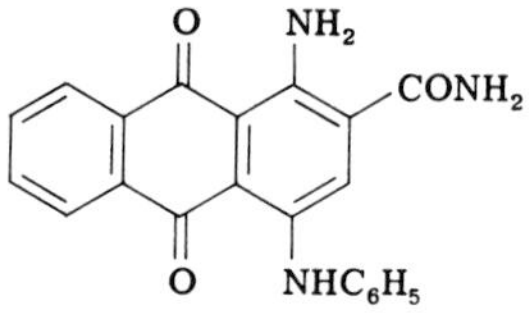

(XXX)

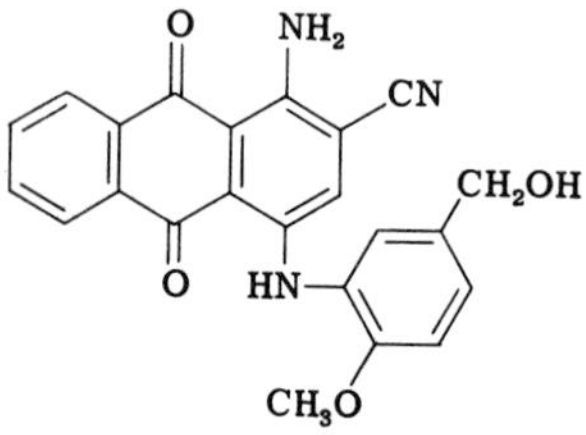

(XXXI)

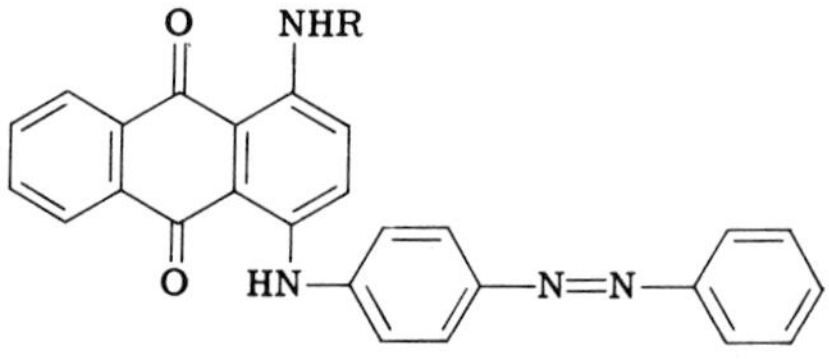

(XXXII)

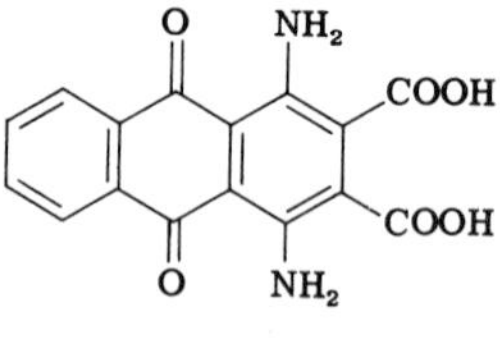

(XXXIII)

[108] IC, *USP* 3,210,383.
[109] FH, *BP* 1,005,730.

–SO$_2$R[110] have recently been described. The –SO$_3$ aryl residue has been introduced into the 2-position in the 1,4-diamino compounds.[111]

Bright blue dyeings on polyesters result from the use of 1,4-diamino-2-nitroanthraquinone.[112] 2 (or 3)-Bromo-1,4-diamino-5-nitroanthraquinone has been prepared by bromination of the 1,4-diamino-5-nitro compound.[113] Nitro derivatives of 1-amino(or alkylamino)-4-alkylamino-anthraquinone have been made.[114]

Several patents are concerned with the preparation of 1,4-diamino-(alkyl or arylamino, etc.)-2-cyano or 2,3-dicyano derivatives,[115] although it is difficult to obtain pure products from any of these processes. Replacement of halogen with cuprous cyanide is more reliable, and some mono-cyano compounds of this type have been proposed for polyester dyeing.[116] Dyes containing –CN, –COOAlkyl, –CO(OCH$_2$CH$_2$)$_n$OH, –CONHAlkyl-eneOH, or –CONH Alkyl (or aryl) in a wide variety of 1,4-diamino derivatives have been proposed.[117]

The following counterbalancing system for cellulose acetate in which (XXX) turns red and (XXXI) turns green with gas fumes has been described.[118]

The treatment of 1,4-diamino-2,3-dicyanoanthraquinone with hydrosulfite is said to improve gas-fastness.[119]

1-Amino-4-amino(or substituted amino or hydroxy)anthraquinones bearing –COOR groups in the 2- or 3-position or in the other ring have been reported as polyester dyes.[120] The use of –COAryl in the 2-position has been claimed,[121] and green dyes are provided by (XXXII).[122] (XXXIII), when treated with methyl esters of arylsulfonic acids, is said to provide disperse dyes of good properties.[123]

The synthesis and spectral properties of a large number of 1,4-di-aminoanthraquinones, N-substituted derivatives, and related compounds have been described.[124]

[110] FBy, *BP* 1,076,988.
[111] FBy, *FP* 1,480,697.
[112] FBy, *USP* 3,099,513.
[113] Vond, *BP* 957,097.
[114] S, *FP* 1,421,095.
[115] CL, *USP* 2,573,732-3; 2,573,811; 2,587,002.
[116] CIBA, *USP* 3,084,015.
[117] ICI, *BP* 721,283; G, *USP* 2,768,183; BASF, *DBP* 1,025,079; Toms River, *USP* 3,203,751.
[118] G, *USP* 2,953,421.
[119] CL, *USP* 2,602,721.
[120] BASF, *BP* 790,728.
[121] CIBA, *BP* 661,045.
[122] Gy, *NeP* 67,102,950.
[123] S, *USP* 2,921,944.

A large series of anthraquinones containing hydroxyalkylamino groups have been esterified with alkyl or arylsulfonyl chlorides. For example, this reaction has been run with 1-isopropylamino-4-(γ-hydroxypropyl-amino)anthraquinone.[125]

1,4-Diamino compounds and many derivatives have been treated with epichlorohydrin to prepare the corresponding β-hydroxy-γ-chloropropyl compounds.[126]

1-Amino-2-X-4-aryl(or alkyl)sulfonamidoanthraquinones, or the corresponding carboxamido derivatives have been investigated. These groups in the 4-position produce shades somewhat similar to those obtained if a hydroxyl occupies the site. Usually, however, the amides are not as sensitive to heavy metals, such as copper and iron, as the hydroxy compounds are. Sublimation fastness is improved in many of the dyes, and as the molecular weight and polarity increase, the products appear to become more suited to thermal fixation rather than to exhaust methods of dyeing. In some dyes, by the proper selection of X and of the substituent on the 4-nitrogen, a practical degree of affinity for cellulose acetate may be realized. Surprisingly, in some instances the gas-fastness is also improved over that of the hydroxy compound. These compounds are obtained by orthodox procedures, i.e., by acetylating a free amino group or by replacing a halogen atom with the appropriate sulfonamide.

1-Amino-2-nitro-4-acylamidoanthraquinones are reddish blue dyes[127] whose color is shifted towards the green by the presence of halogen in the other benzo ring.[128] Dyes in which the nitro group is replaced with –COOR (R = wide variety) are also known.[129] A series of 1-amino-2-alkoxy-4-NHCOOR dyes has been prepared.[130]

A great many compounds having –NHSO$_2$ Alkyl (or Aryl) in the 4-position, –NH$_2$, –OH, or –NHSO$_2$R in the 1-position and –H, –CH$_3$, –OAlkyl or –OAryl in the 2-position are available.[131] Structures (I) and (XXXIV)[132] are typical.

Another large class of dyes is derived from anthraquinones in which all α-positions are occupied, chiefly by hydroxy, nitro, or amino groups

[124] Ko Naiki, *J. Soc. Org. Syn. Chem., Japan* **12**, 108 (1954); *Chem. Abstr.* **51**, 721 (1957).

[125] ICI, *BP* 870,948.

[126] B. Tomchin and L. S. Efros, *Zh. Obshch. Khim.* **33**, 2321 (1963); *Chem. Abstr.* **60**, 694 (1964).

[127] CIBA, *USP* 2,918,344.

[128] CIBA, *BP* 866,062.

[129] BASF, *BP* 964,757; *USP* 3,277,119.

[130] EKCo., *USP* 2,937,190; 2,967,871; CIBA, *BP* 1,099,248.

[131] EKCo., *USP* 3,072,683; 3,324,150; Toms River, *USP* 3,240,551.

[132] FBy, *BP* 1,016,664.

and their derivatives. Quite a few retain nitro groups and others are derived from them. Replacement of one or both nitro groups in dinitro-anthrarufin (1,5-dihydroxy-4,8-dinitroanthraquinone, hereafter called DNA) or dinitrochrysazin (1,8-dihydroxy-4,5-dinitroanthraquinone, hereafter called DNC; if the reference is to both DNC and DNA or to a mixture of them, the symbol will be DNA-C) with amines is ancient.[133] However, none of the products had sufficient affinity for the synthetic fibers available before about 1954. In the early 1950s, it was discovered that replacement of one nitro group with an arylamino-bearing hydroxy-alkyl, hydroxyalkoxy, etc., group produced blue acetate dyes of high affinity and outstanding fastness to light and gas.[134] It was found that those from DNC were slightly greener and faster to light than the 1,5-isomers. Some of these were (XXXV) and (XXXVI).

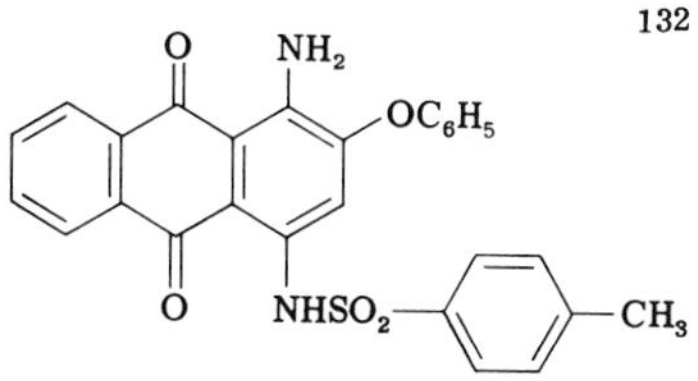

(XXXIV)

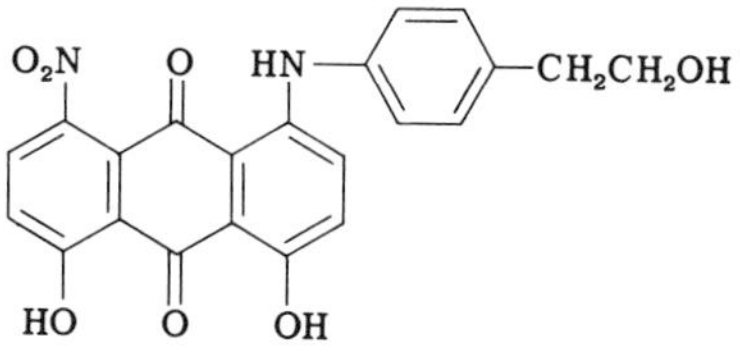

(XXXV)

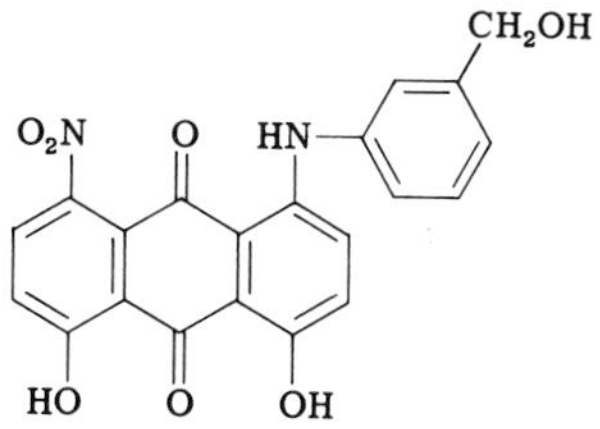

(XXXVI)

These condensations are easily performed in various organic solvents or in excess of amine at temperatures up to about 130°, since the second nitro group is replaced only with considerable difficulty. If the aromatic amine is deactivated by negative groups, replacement of even one nitro is not easy.

During the commercial birth pangs of the polyesters, a blue of satisfactory lightfastness was sorely needed. The above dyes filled this need

[133] FBy, *DRP* 89,090; *DBP* 136,777; BrC, *BP* 420,593.
[134] EKCo., *USP* 2,641,602; 2,651,641; 2,726,251; 2,777,863; CL, *USP* 3,154,568.

admirably. In later years the dyes from DNC and DNA-C condensed with aniline, anisidine, toluidine, etc., have also been widely used. Reduction of the remaining nitro group in these compounds produces brighter dyes with slightly better dyeing properties. On cellulose acetate the dyes have reduced gas-fastness, although the fastness to cold water bleeding is improved.

The intermediates necessary to make these dyes can be prepared by direct nitration of the respective dihydroxy compounds,[135] but better yields of satisfactory quality are realized by use of the sequence[136] shown in Chart 5.

CHART 5

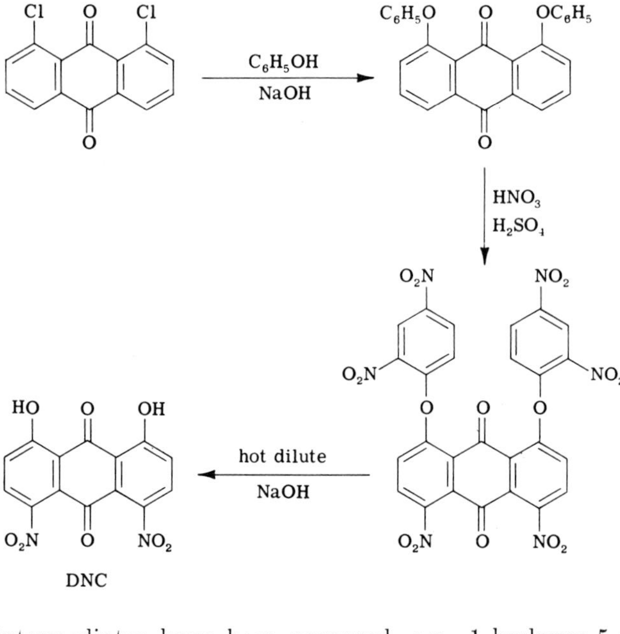

Related intermediates have been prepared, e.g., 1-hydroxy-5-methoxy-anthraquinone, dinitrated and brominated, gives the corresponding 4,8-dinitro-2-bromo compound.[137] Among the amines used to replace one of the nitro groups in DNA-C are anilines bearing $-CH_2(OCH_2CH_2)_n-OH$,[138] aryloxy or arylthio,[139] carbalkoxy, carbalkoxymethylene, car-

[135] C. F. H. Allen, G. F. Frame, and C. V. Wilson, *J. Org. Chem.* **6,** 743 (1941).
[136] *BIOS* **1493,** 8.
[137] FBy, *BP* 980,038.
[138] ICI, *USP* 2,933,508; G, *USP* 2,945,867.
[139] Gy, *USP* 3,214,445; 3,278,563; ACNA, *USP* 3,357,781.

balkoxyalkoxy, etc.,[140] and carbamoyl[141] groups. Aminosalicyclic acids,[142] nitroaniline,[143] and aminobenzenesulfonamides[144] (which may be substituted) have been employed. Aminoazo compounds, dyes in themselves, have been used, producing green shades.[145] p-Phenylenediamines in which one nitrogen bears groups such as alkyl (may be substituted) or acyl groups have been used.[146] If the condensations are run in the presence of tertiary alkylamines, different, and presumably unknown, products are obtained.[147]

Dyes from DNA with halogenated anilines have been reported.[148] DNA condenses with alkylated anilines to produce dyes of better affinity for polypropylene than if DNC is used.[149] Treatment of the dyes from DNC with formaldehyde and sulfuric acid is said to increase the affinity.[150] There is an implication that hydroxymethylation occurs in the anilino ring. Bright, fast dyes are obtained from DNC and β-hydroxyalkyl m-aminobenzoates.[151]

DNA-C has been condensed with 3-aminosulfolane,[152] 2-aminopyrimidines,[153] and anilines bearing triazole, piperidone, pyrrolidone, etc., groups.[154] In the last reference, –OH or –NH$_2$ groups may replace the remaining nitro group.

Both nitro groups in DNA-C have been replaced by hydroxyalkylanilino,[155] –NHC$_6$H$_4$N(Alkyl)SO$_2$Alkyl[156] and –NHC$_6$H$_4$SO$_2$Alkyl.[157] Replacement of one nitro group by an arylamino followed by replacement of the other by an alkylamino has been reported.[158] A violet dye with fascinating possibilities as an intermediate was prepared by reduction of

[140] CIBA, *USP* 3,097,909; ICI, *USP* 2,766,262.
[141] Gy, *BP* 1,015,509.
[142] OBM, *BP* 1,061,025.
[143] ACNA, *BP* 970,356.
[144] G, *USP* 2,722,535.
[145] Crompton & Knowles, *USP* 2,929,810.
[146] G, *USP* 2,722,536; 2,723,279.
[147] CIBA, *USP* 2,819,275.
[148] FBy, *BP* 1,067,768.
[149] IC, *USP* 3,362,966.
[150] ICI, *USP* 2,830,062.
[151] FBy, *USP* 3,098,080.
[152] G, *BP* 968,709.
[153] ACNA, *FP* 1,371,712.
[154] FBy, *USP* 3,184,455.
[155] CIBA, *SP* 325,464.
[156] S, *USP* 2,967,754.
[157] S, *USP* 2,967,753.
[158] G, *USP* 2,850,510.

only one of the nitro groups by means of mild conditions in aqueous ammonia.[159]

A novel reaction[160] involving DNC is shown in Chart 6.

CHART 6

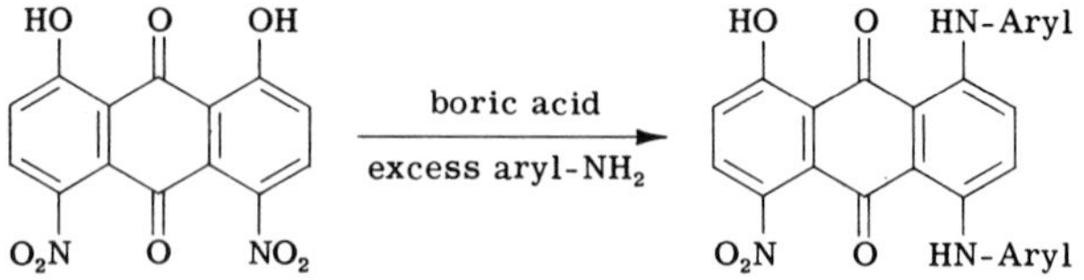

Green

When the mole-per-mole condensation product of DNA-C with an arylamine is treated with sodium sulfide, the remaining nitro group is said to be replaced with an –NHOH group. This group, in turn, is converted to an –N(OH)CH$_2$OH group by treatment with formaldehyde.[161]

Much of the following discussion is concerned with dihydroxydiaminoanthraquinones. If the root is diaminoanthrarufin (1,5-diamino-4,8-dihydroxyanthraquinone), the symbol DAA will be used. If it is diaminochrysazin (1,8-diamino-4,5-dihydroxyanthraquinone), the symbol will be DAC. Where the reference is to either or a mixture, the symbol will be DAA-C.

DAA-C has been monoarylated[162] and treated with formaldehyde to hydroxymethylate one or both of the amino groups.[163] Increased tinctorial power is said to be conferred thereby. Condensation with 2-chlorobenzothiazoles gives violet to blue polyester dyes.[164] The action of formic acid on DAA-C formylates one –NH$_2$ group; the other is formylated later.[165] Arylsulfonamido groups on DAA-C have been reported.[166] An example is (XXXVII).

Nitration of the dibenzoyl derivative of DAA-C, followed by hydrolytic removal of the benzoyl groups, gives a blue mononitro DAA-C.[167] Mixtures of 1-arylamino-4-OH-5(or 8)-OH or –OCOCH$_3$-5(or 8)-NH$_2$ or –NHCORanthraquinones are said to be of value on polyesters.[168]

[159] S, *USP* 3,060,200.
[160] FBy, *BP* 1,026,825.
[161] AAP, *BP* 928,008.
[162] Fran, *BP* 969,721.
[163] FH, *USP* 3,195,973.
[164] Fran, *FP* 1,305,526; 1,311,332.
[165] CIBA, *BP* 880,426.
[166] G, *USP* 2,704,292; Fran, *FP* 1,205,867 and addn. 766,854; *USP* 2,993,917.
[167] S, *SP* 358,178.
[168] ICI, *BP* 1,069,295.

CHART 7

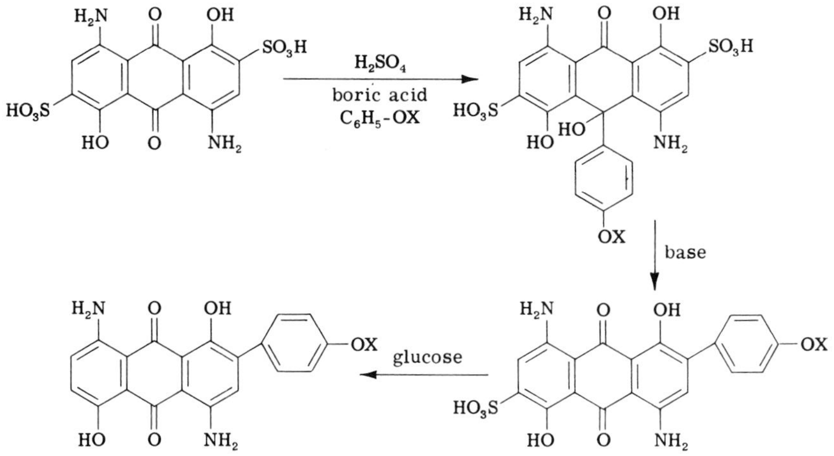

X = —H or lower alkyl

Some old chemistry[169] has been invoked to provide the polyester dyes shown in Chart 7.

Several patents are directed to the use of these compounds.[170] They are characterized by excellent buildup and luster, although their light and sublimation fastness properties are only mediocre. Mixtures of these compounds with various yellows, oranges, and reds to obtain navies, browns, and blacks have been proposed.[171] One or both amino groups have been alkylated and acylated.[172] Treatment of the dye of Chart 7 when X = –H with alkyl sulfates leads to better buildup, particularly on acetate.[173] The –OH groups have also been acylated.[174] Treatment of the dyes with chloroalkyl esters of chloroformic acid, followed by acylation, introduces acyloxyalkyl groups on the nitrogens.[175] Dyes in which the –C_6H_4OX group is replaced by one from an aryl cyclic ether, such as benzo-1,3-dioxane, are known.[176]

When DNA is treated with phenols or their ethers in sulfuric and boric acids, a similar reaction but with different orientation occurs,[177] as in Chart 8.

[169] IG, *FP* 618,309; *USP* 1,652,584.
[170] S, *USP* 3,043,646; CCC, *USP* 3,265,460.
[171] S, *USP* 3,207,568-9.
[172] ICI, *USP* 3,349,104.
[173] YDC, *BP* 1,094,873.
[174] ICI, *FP* 1,373,758.
[175] CIBA, *BeP* 669,879.
[176] ICI, *BeP* 646,061.
[177] FBy, *FP* 1,345,377.

CHART 8

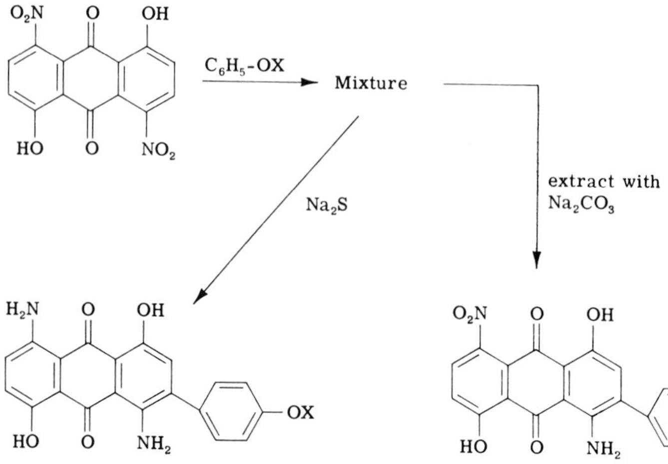

DNA-C and mercaptans may be condensed under various conditions with sodium alkoxides[178] or with organic bases,[179] as shown in Chart 9.

Halogenation of these various compounds has been reported. DAA-C, when halogenated to introduce between 0.4 and 1.5 moles of halogen, particularly bromine, gives a bright, reddish blue polyester dye with good buildup and tinctorial power.[180] Two moles of halogen have also been introduced.[181] DAA in which one amino group bears an alkyl or cycloalkyl has been halogenated in these proportions,[182] as have molecules

CHART 9

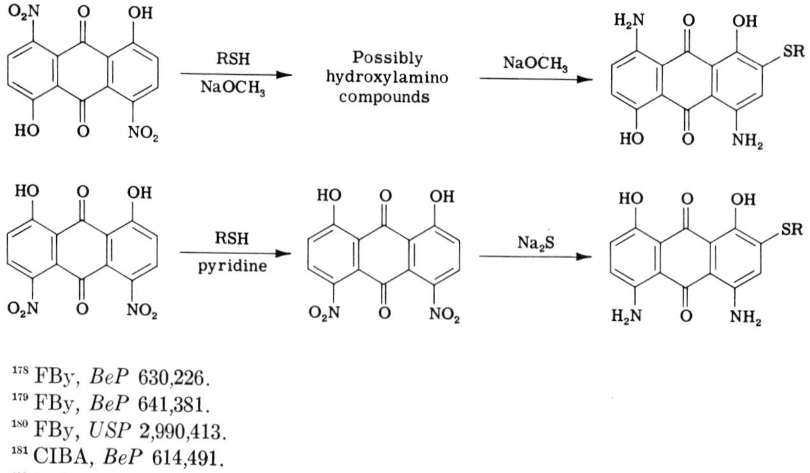

[178] FBy, *BeP* 630,226.
[179] FBy, *BeP* 641,381.
[180] FBy, *USP* 2,990,413.
[181] CIBA, *BeP* 614,491.
[182] S, *BeP* 585,015.

containing two alkylamino groups.[182a,183] These dyes can be prepared by brominating 1,5- or 1,8-diaminoanthraquinone in oleum, and then heating above 120° with boric acid.[184] Alkyl ethers of halogenated DAA-C are known.[185] DAA-C can be treated with aldehydes in the Marschalk[76] reaction to introduce one or two alkyl or substituted alkyl groups[186]; upon halogenation, these intermediates give blue polyester dyes.[187] N-Alkylated derivatives are also available.[188]

In addition to the methods of Chart 9, –SR groups can be introduced into the DAA-C molecules by reaction of their halogen derivatives with RSH(Na),[189] and the products can in turn be halogenated.[190] Carboxy, carbalkoxy,[191] cyano, and carboxamido groups have been introduced into the DAA-C molecules, as in Chart 10.[192]

CHART 10

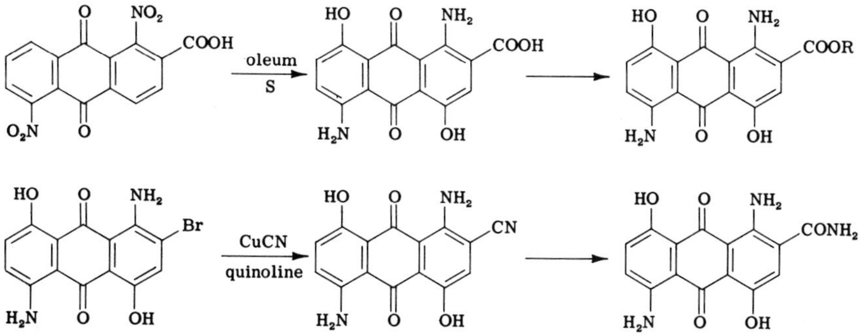

DAA-C, when oxidized to the quinone imine with manganese dioxide adds sulfinic acids to give RSO_2DAA-C.[193] Other aminohydroxy compounds have been treated in this fashion, the RSO_2H addition producing a bathochromic shift.

If the last step in Chart 7 is performed more rigorously, hydrolysis of the amino groups also occurs. This hydrolyzed product can be trans-

[182a] G, BeP 639,591.
[183] Fran, FP 1,320,920.
[184] FH, DBP 1,257,315.
[185] CIBA, BeP 608,772.
[186] CIBA, BP 958,924; BeP 609,899.
[187] CIBA, USP 3,147,284.
[188] CIBA, FP 1,336,997; BP 958,925.
[189] CIBA, BeP 614,120; FP 1,509,490.
[190] CIBA, BeP 621,630.
[191] S, USP 2,967,752.
[192] S, USP 3,033,880.
[193] FBy, BeP 667,985.

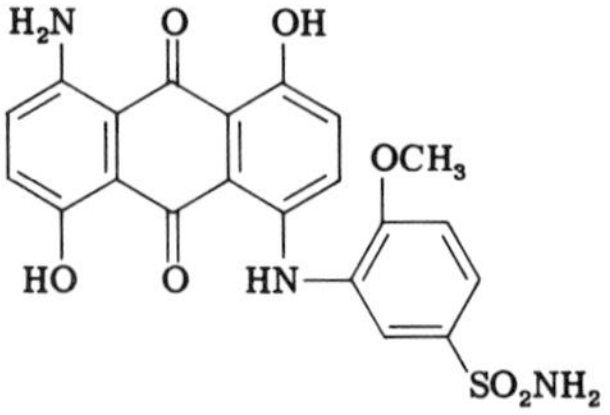

(XXXVII)

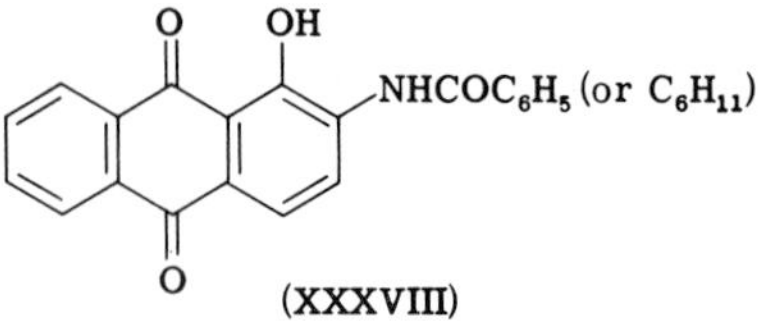

(XXXVIII)

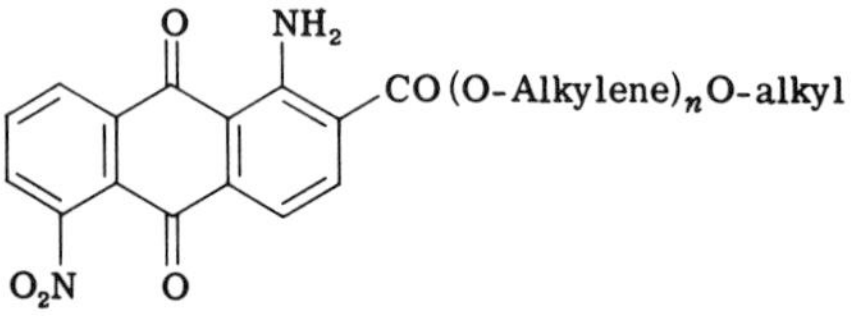

(XXXIX)

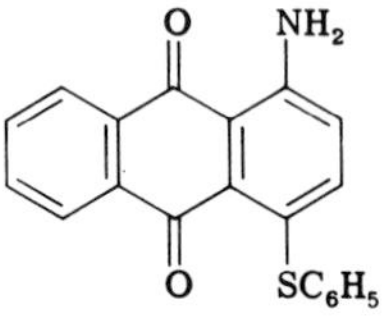

(XL)

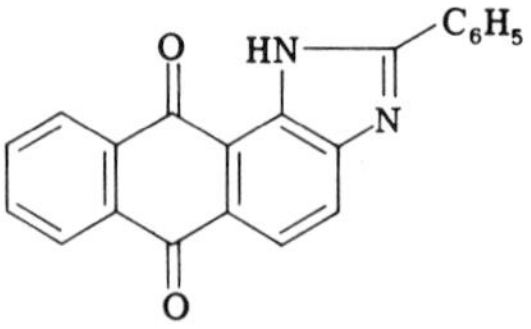

Yellow
(XLI)

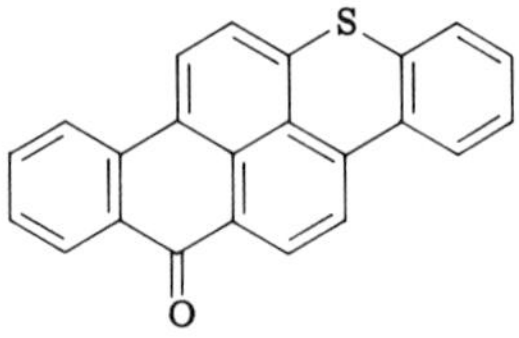

Fluorescent scarlet
(XLII)

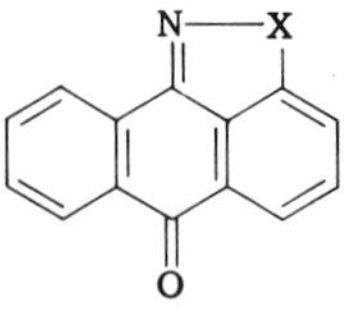

X = —S, —Se,
—NH, —NR, etc.

(XLIII)

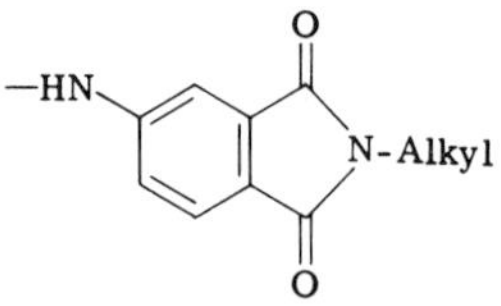

(XLIV)

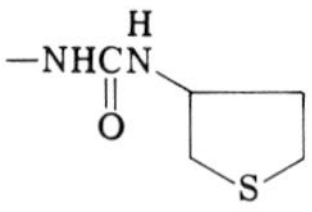

(XLV)

formed into blue dyes, as in Chart 11.[194] Acylation of the final product gives navy blue dyes.[195]

If quinizarin, 1-amino-4-hydroxyanthraquinone, or 1,4-diaminoanthra-

---

[194] CN, *FP* 1,349,890.
[195] CN, *FP* 1,371,886.

CHART 11

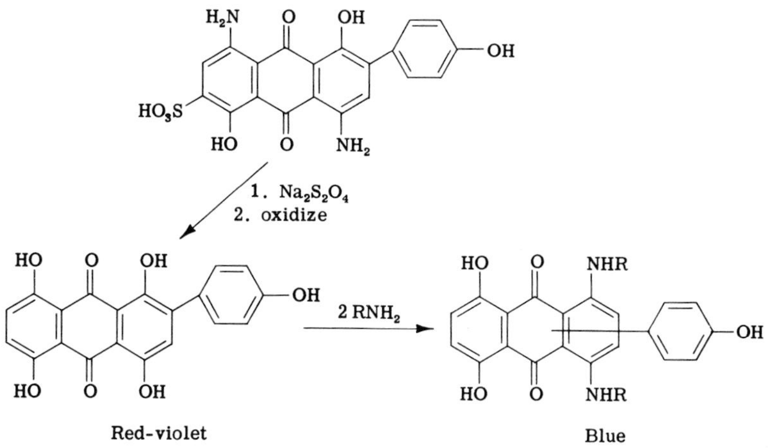

1. $Na_2S_2O_4$
2. oxidize

Red-violet   Blue

quinone is chlorinated in sulfuric–boric acid, chlorine enters the 5,8-positions.[196] The halogens can then be replaced stepwise with amines and mercaptans,[197] as in Chart 12.

CHART 12

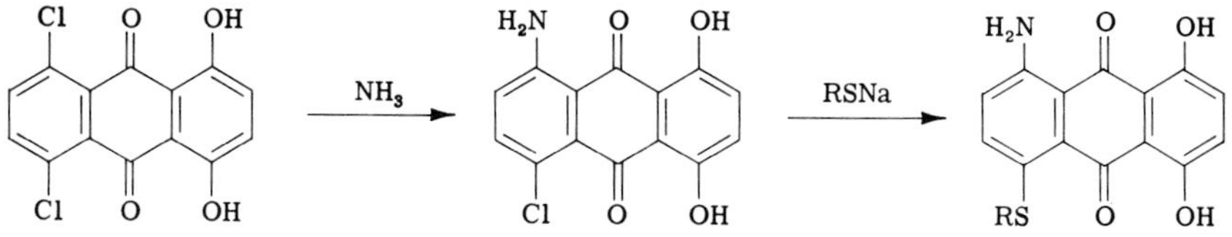

The bromine atom in 1,4-dihydroxy-5-amino(substituted or nonsubstituted)-7-bromo-8-aminoanthraquinone undergoes the usual replacements with RNH_2, ROH, RSH, etc.[198]

1,4,5-Triamino-8-hydroxyanthraquinones and derivatives have been prepared,[199] as in Chart 13.

Dibromo-1,4,5,8-tetraaminoanthraquinone has been diacylated with the same or different acylating agents, which may introduce CO–, ROOC–, RSO_2–, etc.[200] Treatment of 5-nitro-1,4-diaminoanthraquinone with sulfur and oleum gives a mixture of the 1,4,5-triamino-2,8- and 3,8-dihydroxy derivatives, which may be alkylated. Violet to reddish blue dyes

[196] FBY, *BeP* 651,989.
[197] FBy, *BeP* 676,627; 678,128.
[198] FBy, *BP* 1,090,190.
[199] FBy, *FP* 1,488,822; IC, *DBP* 1,258,995.
[200] CIBA, *USP* 3,282,967.

CHART 13

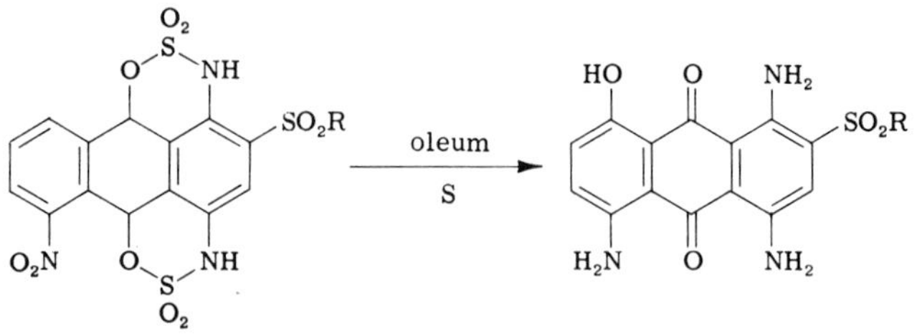

are obtained.[201] A wide variety of anthraquinones containing alkyl or aryl (both may be substituted) sulfonyl groups in the β-position have been enumerated.[202]

Aminoanthraquinones have been condensed with (chloroformyl)phenylphosphoric acid dichloride and hydrolyzed, thus introducing the –NH-$COC_6H_4OP(O)(OH)$ group.[203]

Compound (XXXVIII) gives yellows,[204] while (XXXIX) imparts red shades[205] to polyesters.

1-Amino-2-bromo(or   2,4-dibromo)-5-acetamidoanthraquinone   dyes polyesters orange.[206] 1-Nitroanthraquinone-2-carboxamide gives, when condensed with cyclohexylamine, in addition to the expected 1-cyclohexyl-2-carboxamide, the 1-amino-2-N-cyclohexylcarboxamide, 1-cyclohexylamino- and 1,4-bis(cyclohexylamino)anthraquinones.[207]

1-Hydroxy-4-arylaminoanthraquinones (may be further substituted) are said to acquire increased sublimation fastness when treated with formaldehyde.[208]

1,5-Bis(m-toluamido)-4-hydroxyanthraquinone has been proposed as a disperse dye.[209]

Interest in anthraquinones bearing sulfur derivatives in the α-position has been expressed. In dyes typified by (XL),[210] the arylthio group may occupy the 5- or 8-position; the NH_2 group is replaced by –H, –OH, –OAlkyl, etc.; two –SAryl or –SAlkyl groups may be present; and

[201] IC, BP 979,565.
[202] FBy, BP 1,053,455; 1,076,988.
[203] FH, BP 894,960.
[204] CIBA, USP 2,819,274.
[205] ICI, BP 809,043.
[206] CIBA, BP 1,095,087.
[207] T. Hargreaves and A. T. Peters, Nature 202, 1209 (1964).
[208] CIBA, BP 887,876.
[209] CFM, BP 913,914.
[210] BASF, BP 905,449; 990,290; DBP 1,258,380.

further substituents, such as halogen, –CH₃, and –CN, reside on the nucleus.[210,211]

Reaction of the diazo from 5-nitro-1,4-diaminoanthraquinone with thiocyanic acid replaces one amino group with the –SCN group.[212]

Addition of unsaturated compounds, e.g., styrene, to α-anthraquinonyl-sulfonyl halides yields β-haloalkyl sulfides.[213]

1-Hydroxy-2-alkoxy(or thio)-4-arylthioanthraquinones are red dyes for polyesters.[214]

B. Heterocyclic Dyes

An interesting series of dyes is provided by annellation of heterocyclic rings to the anthraquinone nucleus. Some of the most beautiful blue to turquoise dyes are derived from 1,4-diaminoanthraquinone-2,3-dicarboximides (1,3-dioxo-4,7-diamino-5,6-phthaloylisoindolines). Treatment of the 2,3-dicyano[215] (or dicarbamoyl)[216]-1,4-diamino compound in sulfuric acid, sometimes in the presence of a secondary alcohol, gives the dyes shown in Chart 14.

The intermediate dinitriles and diamides can be obtained by the well-

CHART 14

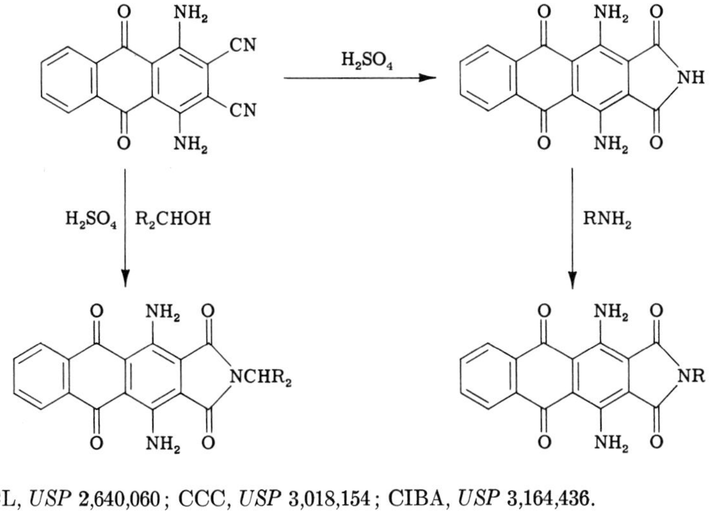

[211] CL, *USP* 2,640,060; CCC, *USP* 3,018,154; CIBA, *USP* 3,164,436.
[212] EKCo., *USP* 3,113,952.
[213] CIBA, *USP* 2,807,630.
[214] BASF, *BP* 1,027,759.
[215] DuP, *USP* 2,628,963.
[216] DuP, *USP* 2,753,356.

known reaction of metallic cyanides on the corresponding sulfonic acids[217] or by reaction of amines with the dicarboxylic acid chlorides.[218] The dinitriles *per se* have been claimed as polyester dyes.[217]

These clean, lightfast colors do not build well, are not completely fast to sublimation, are expensive, and are chiefly used for bright shades and in controlling the tendency for some combinations to flare red in incandescent light. Nevertheless, this is unique dye chemistry and has stimulated keen interest.

Hydroxyalkyl groups may be introduced by treatment of the unsubstituted imide with alkylene carbonates or sulfites.[219] The =NH group can be replaced by =N(CH$_2$)$_n$NR$_2$ by reaction with the proper diamine.[220] The –NR$_2$ group in this side chain may also be cyclic, such as piperidino or piperazino.[221]

CHART 15

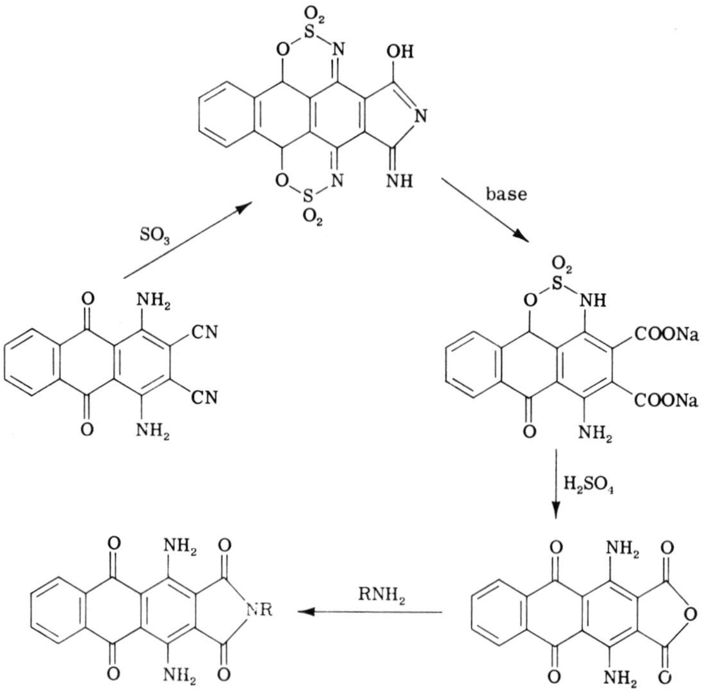

[217] Toms River, *USP* 3,203,751.
[218] DuP, *USP* 2,692,272.
[219] BASF, *USP* 3,086,024.
[220] DuP, *USP* 2,701,802.
[221] BASF, *BP* 899,984.

Another route to these dyes via the cyclic sulfimide intermediate, as in Chart 15, has been reported.[222]

The anhydride has been obtained without going through the sulfimide.[223]

Closely related dyes can be prepared from anthraquinonecarboxamides in the presence of oxidizing agents and inorganic cyanides,[224] as in Chart 16. The process is improved by incorporation of an organic cyanide.[225] 1-Amino-4-nitrocarboxamides can be used in this process.[226]

CHART 16

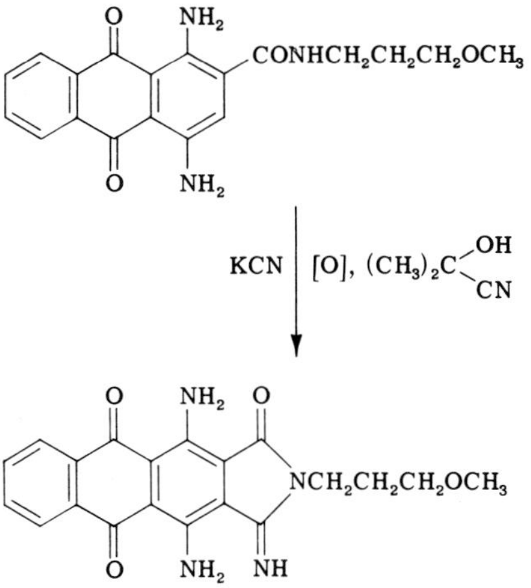

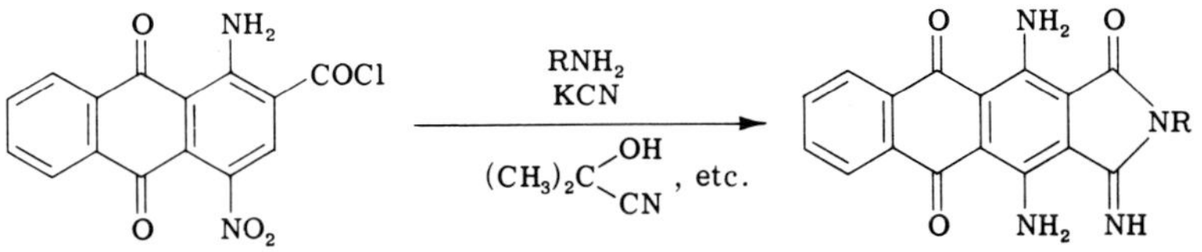

These 3-imino dyes can also be prepared from the intermediates of Chart 14, if milder conditions and sulfuric acid of 100% or higher concentration are employed,[227] as shown in Chart 17. Reaction with an amine replaces the 3-imino group.

[222] NSK, *USP* 3,268,552.
[223] FBy, *USP* 2,770,625.
[224] BASF, *DBP* 1,250,031.
[225] BASF, *USP* 3,294,815.
[226] BASF, *USP* 3,137,699; *BP* 1,063,379.
[227] FBy, *DBP* 1,073,661.

CHART 17

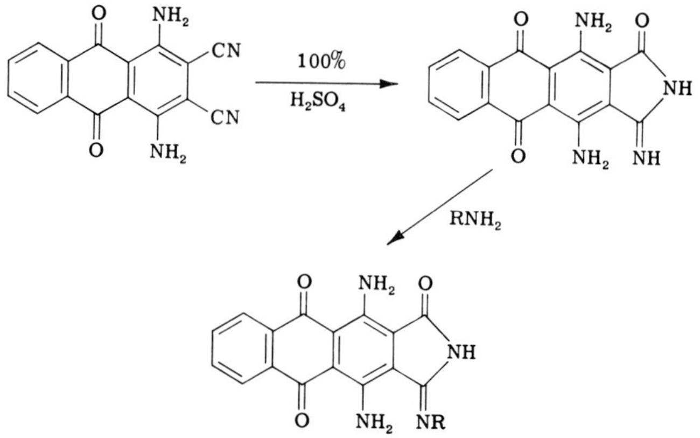

Use of an alkyl halide, a sulfate, etc., replaces the dicarboximide hydrogen[228] in the dyes of Chart 18. Alkylimino groups in both the 1- and 3-positions are possible.[229]

CHART 18

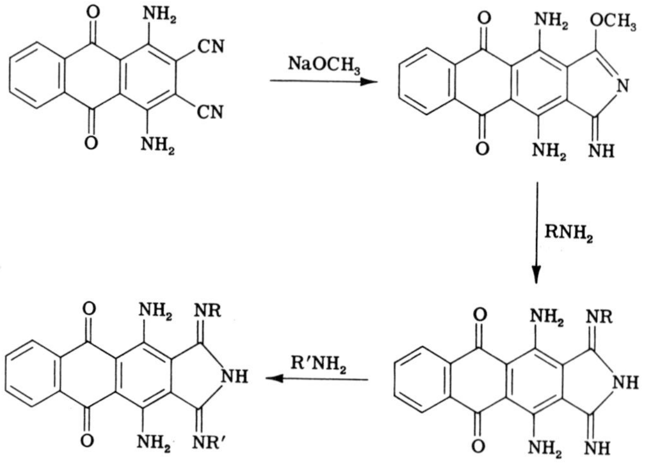

Similar chemistry places other groups, such as –OH and –NHR, in 4- or 7-positions.[225,230]

Another series of heterocycles providing blue to bluish green shades on polyesters are the members of the anthraquinoid 1,2-acridones

[228] NSK, *USP* 3,326,934.
[229] FBy, *BP* 899,709.
[230] DuP, *USP* 2,749,354.

(phthaloylbenzacridones),[231] represented in Chart 19. Compounds where the position ortho to the free –NH$_2$ group is occupied by –CN, –CO-NH$_2$,[232] –OAlkyl, –OCycloalkyl, –OAryl,[231] etc., are known.

CHART 19

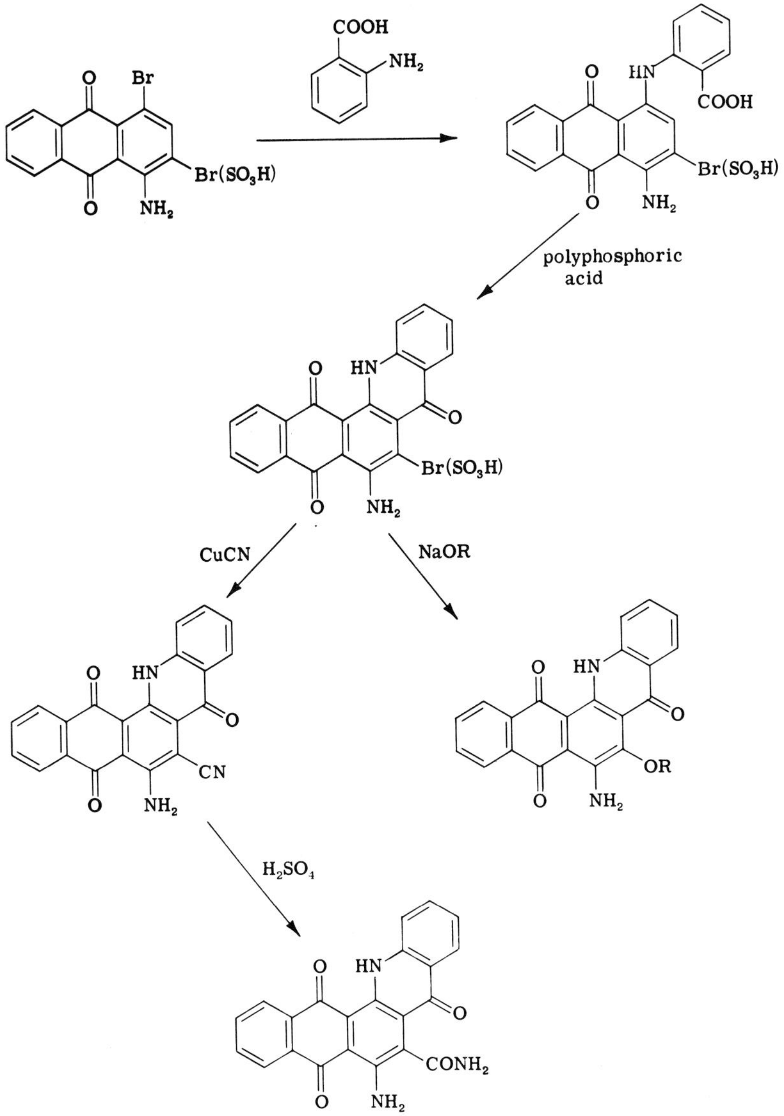

[231] ICI, *BP* 919,270; 944,722.
[232] Toms River, *USP* 3,299,071.

The $-NH_2$ group in the 6-position can be $-NHAlkyl$.[233] Green shades can be obtained by reacting the $6-NH_2$ group with 2,4-dinitrochlorobenzene.[234] Carbalkoxyethylamino groups in the 6-position are obtained by reaction of the $6-NH_2$ with acrylic or methacrylic esters, or the addition can be performed on the starting materials, followed by cyclization.[235] Reddish blue dyes result from the presence of acylamido groups in the 6-position.[236]

Chart 20 shows the preparation of reddish blue dyes.[237]

CHART 20

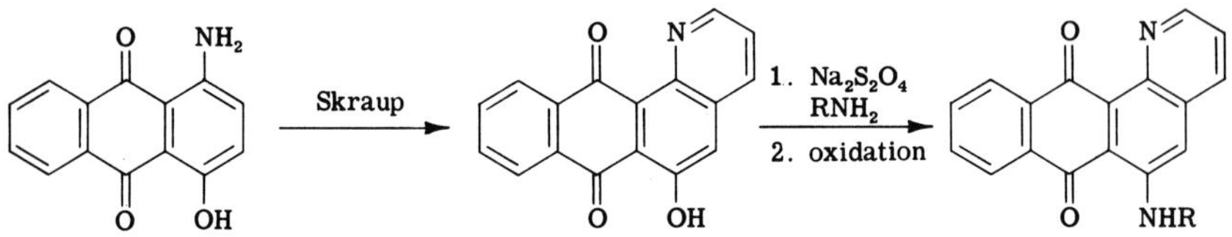

Blue to blue-green polyester dyes are obtained according to the example of Chart 21.[238]

CHART 21

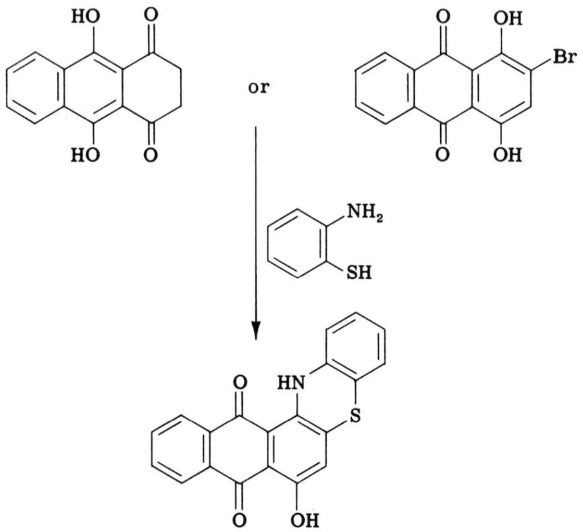

[233] ICI, *BP* 944,513.
[234] CFM, *DBP* 1,187,337.
[235] S, *BeP* 685,699.
[236] CFM, *BP* 930,223; 963,519.
[237] CL, *USP* 2,658,898.
[238] EKCo., *USP* 3,254,078.

Various α-aminoanthraquinones were condensed with alkyl ethoxy-methylenemalonates and cyclized to give fast dyes,[239] as in Chart 22.

CHART 22

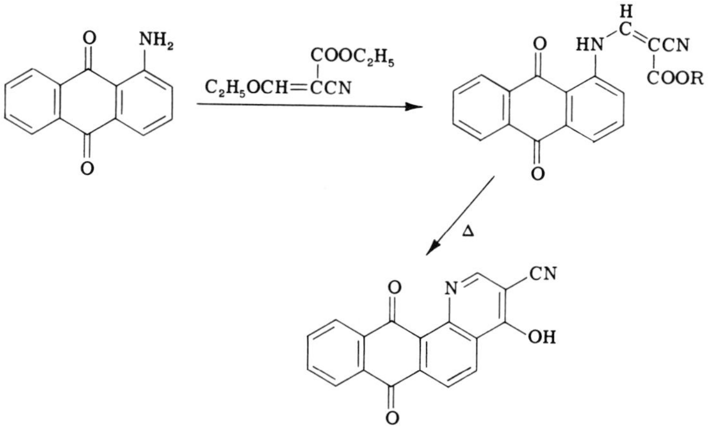

Other angular heterocycles are (XLI)[240] and (XLII).[241]

Ring closures in the 1,2-system from both aliphatic and aromatic amines are reported. For example, 1-(o-nitroanilino)anthraquinone can be cyclized to the corresponding anthraquinonedihydrophenazine.[242]

Compounds in which the heterocyclic atoms link the 1- and 9-positions are well known. Five-membered rings are represented by structure (XLIII).

The isothiazole dyes are prepared by reaction of a 1-halo or 1-sulfo compound with ammonia and a sulfur-yielding material[243] or by treatment of the 1-diazo compound with an ionic thiocyanate and ammonia.[243] 5-Arylisothiazolo derivatives give yellow dyes. In (XLIII), when X is –NH or –NR, the dyes can be obtained by replacement of an α-halogen followed by dehydration, or by reduction of the corresponding diazo compound and dehydration. Introduction of a hydroxyl group into the 5-position produces acetate dyes.[244]

5-Acylamidoisothiazoloanthraquinones yield greenish yellow dyeings.[245] Greenish yellow dyeings are also obtained from 5-(β-chloropropion-

[239] K. Sivasankaran, K. S. Sardesai, and S. V. Sunthankar, *J. Sci. Ind. Res. (India)* **18B**, 164 (1959); K. Sivasankaran and S. V. Sunthankar, *ibid.* **20D**, 336 (1961).

[240] BASF, *DBP* 1,229,034.

[241] FH, *USP* 3,356,687.

[242] H. Koelliker and P. Caveng, *Chimia (Aarau)* **20**, 281 (1966).

[243] CIBA, *DBP* 1,240,202.

[244] CIBA, *USP* 2,805,225.

[245] CIBA, *USP* 2,715,128; 3,100,132.

amido)pyrazoleanthrone.[246] The synthesis in Chart 23 has been reported.[247]

CHART 23

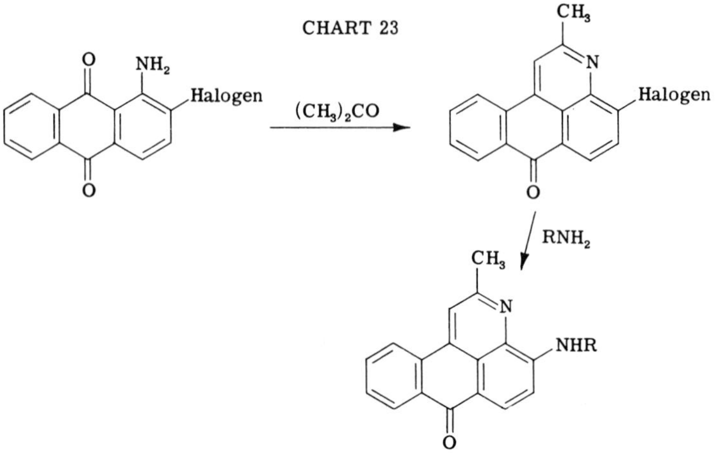

Investigation of an old reaction of sulfur trioxide with 1,4-diaminoanthraquinone, as shown in Chart 24, has led to elucidation of its structure and to new reactions.[248]

CHART 24

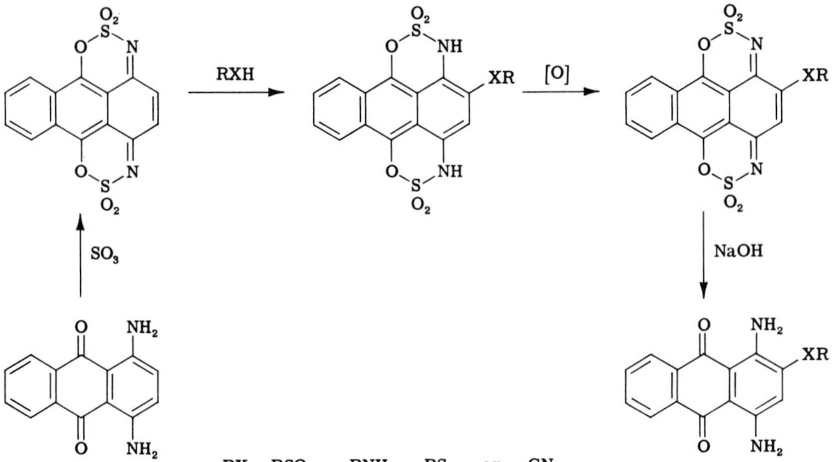

RX = RSO₂—, RNH—, RS—, or —CN

[246] FBy, *USP* 3,324,142.
[247] S. W. Oraluk, *USP* 3,203,956.
[248] H. W. Schwechten, R. Neeff, and O. Bayer, *Ber.* **90**, 1129 (1957); FBy, *BP* 749,677.

1,9-Anthrapyrimidines result from condensation of aryl nitriles with α-aminoanthraquinones.[249]

Some anthraquinone dyes have heterocyclic rings attached laterally in the β-position, as shown in Chart 25.[250-253] Some of these result from ring closures of derivatives of 2-carboxylic acids. The nitro group in the last compound in Chart 25 may be replaced by –NHR, –SR, etc.

CHART 25

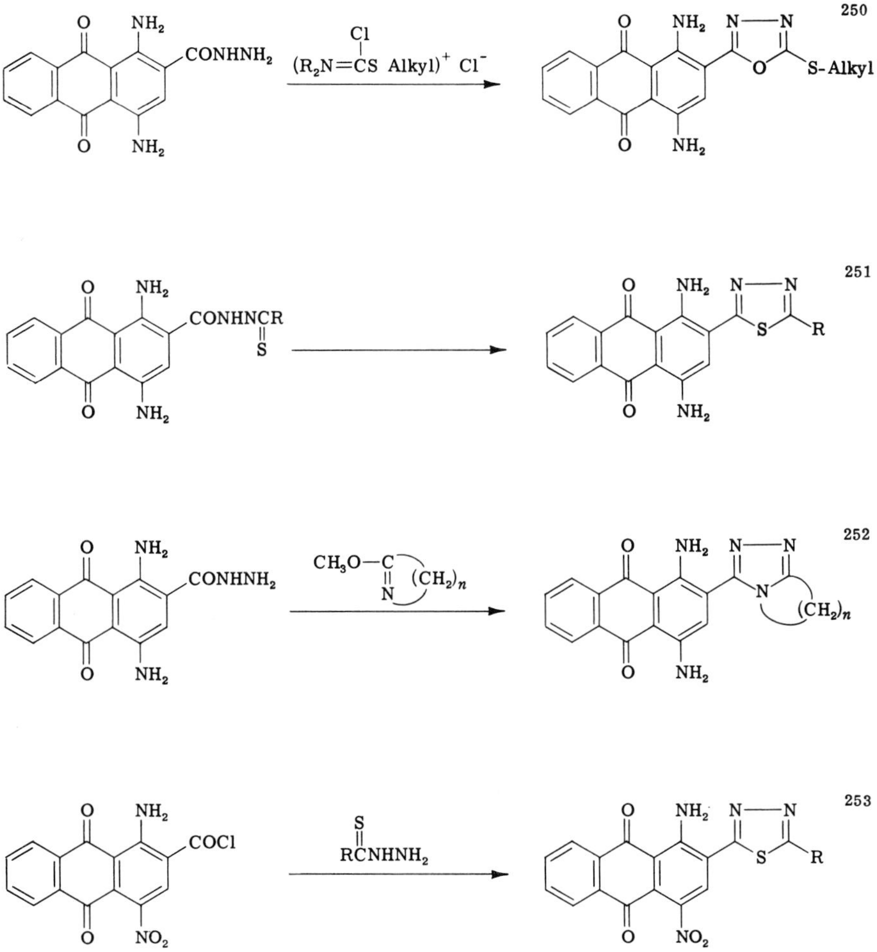

[249] BASF, *DBP* 1,258,000.
[250] BASF, *USP* 3,270,030.
[251] BASF, *BP* 1,001,497.
[252] BASF, *DBP* 1,154,587.
[253] BASF, *DBP* 1,256,188.

Heterocycles without the benzo group, which is present in the example of Chart 26, [254] are also disclosed.

CHART 26

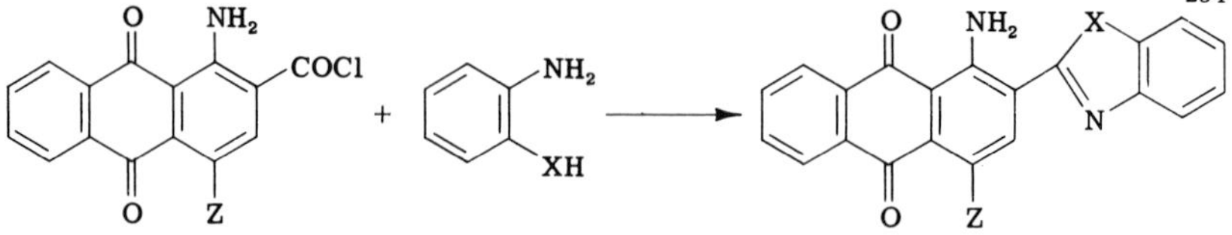

X = —S—, —O—, —NH—
Z = —NH₂, —NHR, —NO₂, —OH, —NCOR, —NCOOR

Chemistry reminiscent of Chart 7 has been used to introduce a thiophene moiety,[255] as in Chart 27.

CHART 27

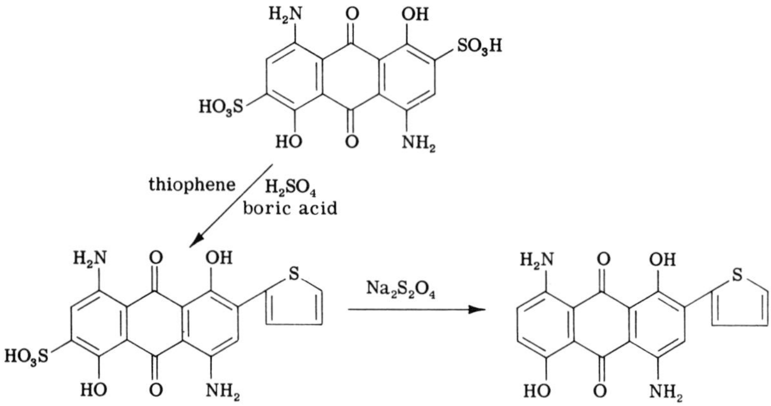

1-Amino-2-oxazolyloxy(thiazolyloxy, etc.)-4-hydroxy(amino, substituted amino)anthraquinones have been disclosed.[256]

There are a number of dyes in which the heterocycle is attached through an α-amino group. For example, treatment of 1-amino-4-hydroxyanthraquinone with 2-chlorobenzothiazole yields the 1-(2-benzothiazolyl)-4-hydroxy derivative.[257] DAA-C reacts similarly.[258] α-Bromo atoms react with these compounds, 2-mercaptobenzothiazole, for example, to intro-

[254] CIBA, *USP* 3,178,252; 3,185,698; *BeP* 628,695.
[255] FBy, *USP* 3,265,709.
[256] CIBA, *BP* 968,259.
[257] CN, *USP* 3,313,823.
[258] Fran, *BeP* 619,722.

duce the benzothiazolylthio residue.[259] In a like manner, α-bromo atoms are replaced with dicarboximido (e.g., succinimido) groups.[260]

Dyes in which amino groups bear 1,3,5-triazine moieties, which in turn bear aryl, $-NR_2$, etc., residues have been reported.[261]

Patents in which the anthraquinone molecule is attached to (XLIV)[262] and (XLV)[263] also disclose attachment to other chromophores.

IV. Azo Dyes

A. MONOAZO DYES

The diazotization and coupling of disperse azo dye components presents nothing new to organic chemists. Those amines basic enough to easily form stable salts with mineral acids are usually diazotized in aqueous solution. With homocyclic amines of low basicity and heterocyclic amines, the use of media low in water content, such as strong sulfuric acid, phosphoric acid, or organic acids, is highly beneficial. The diazotizing agent for these amines is usually nitrosylsulfuric acid. One of the best general procedures is to dissolve the amine in 50–60% sulfuric acid, cool to 0–5°, and add a solution of sodium nitrite in sulfuric acid; this solution is previously heated to 65–70° but cooled before addition. The coupler may be dissolved in 20–30% sulfuric acid, cooled, and the diazo solution stirred in. With these highly negative amines it is often unnecessary to neutralize in order to isolate the dye. If necessary to neutralize, mild alkalies, such as sodium or ammonium acetate, should be used.

Until about 1950, only a few disperse dyes derived from heterocyclic diazos had reached commercial status.[264] These were remarkable chiefly as bright, dischargeable colors, their fastness properties being only mediocre. Since that time, however, the success of a few newcomers on the market has given impetus to extensive study in this area.

One of the earliest innovations was the introduction of dyes from 2-amino-5-nitrothiazole.[265] Examples of these are the dye (XLVI) and dyes from the same diazo and the couplers (XLVII) and (XLVIII). These dyes have very high extinction coefficients. Their lightfastness is rather poor, but their buildup, gas-fastness, and dischargeability are

[259] S, USP 3,318,903.
[260] CIBA, USP 3,234,234.
[261] BASF, USP 3,297,695; CIBA, BP 897,488–9.
[262] BASF, BP 1,092,025; FP 1,495,028.
[263] FBy, BP 1,086,765.
[264] CSD I, p. 641.
[265] EKCo., USP 2,659,719; 2,683,708–9.

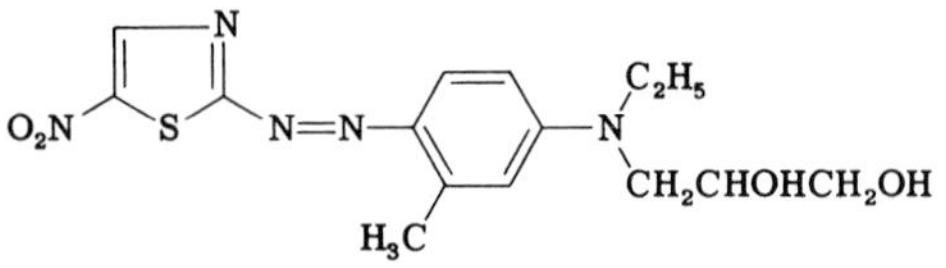

(XLVI)

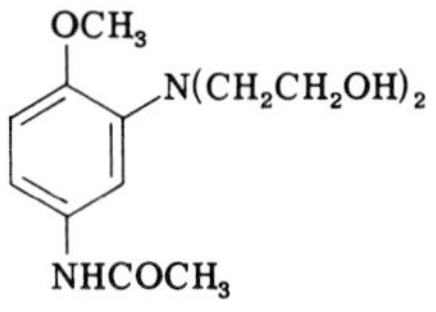

(XLVII)

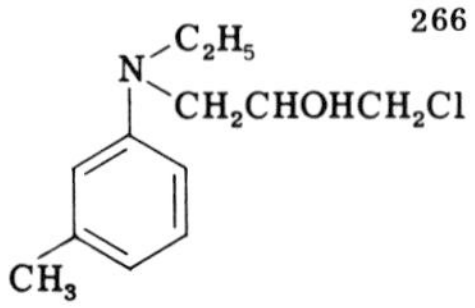

266

(XLVIII)

outstanding. Coupler (XLVIII)[266] gives a blue redder than (XLVI), and (XLVII) gives a greenish blue. Other dyes from this diazo and aniline couplers in which one group attached to the nitrogen is alkyl and the other group is an alkyl bearing a carboxyl or carbamoyl residue,[267] bears one or two acyloxy groups,[268] or is an epoxyalkyl group[269] have been enumerated. Another coupler proposed is *m*-aroylamidoaniline and derivatives.[270]

Dyes from 2-amino-5-alkylsulfonyl-[271] and 4-trifluoromethylthiazoles[272] have been suggested. Other aminothiazoles have been coupled to bis(β-cyanoethyl) anilines,[273] and to anilines on which one N-substituent is alkyl or substituted alkyl and the other is –alkyleneCONH$_2$.[274] The general preparation of 2-aminothiazole and some of its derivatives as well as the properties of the azo dyes from them have been discussed.[275] Preparation of the nitro derivatives is presented in more detail by some of the same authors.[276] Commercially, it has been demonstrated that these reactions can be hazardous.[277] The parent nucleus, 2-aminothiazole, is readily prepared by reaction of 2-chloroacetaldehyde, or its functional

[266] ICI, *BP* 840,903.
[267] CIBA, *USP* 3,335,125; *DBP* 1,245,514; BASF, *USP* 3,287,347.
[268] YDC, *BP* 1,060,240.
[269] ICI, *BP* 856,898.
[270] DuP, *USP* 3,336,286.
[271] S, *USP* 3,007,915.
[272] EKCo., *USP* 2,726,237.
[273] CIBA, *BP* 883,342.
[274] EKCo., *USP* 3,349,075.
[275] J. B. Dickey *et al.*, *J. Org. Chem.* **24**, 187 (1959).
[276] J. B. Dickey, E. B. Towne, and G. F. Wright, *J. Org. Chem.* **20**, 499 (1955).
[277] L. Silver, *Chem. Eng. Progr.* **63**, 44 (1967).

derivatives, with thiourea. The single most interesting observation from the above series is the tremendous color shift from the red of *p*-nitroaniline dyes to the blue of the corresponding 5-nitrothiazole dyes, even though the bathochromism of aminothiazole diazos relative to aniline diazos in azo dyes had already been recognized.[278]

Azo dyes from 2-aminoisothiazoles,[279] 2-amino-3-cyanopyrazoles,[280] and 5-amino-4-nitroimidazoles,[281] amino-1,3,4-thiadiazoles,[282] and 1,2,4-thiadiazoles[283] have been mentioned without achieving any commercial usage. The coupling power of a series of five-membered heterocyclic diazos has been studied.[284] Comparative couplings show that the most powerful, from the 1,3,4- and 1,2,4-thiadiazoles, resemble diazotized 2,4,6-trinitroaniline in this respect.

Some of the most beautiful greenish blue monoazo dyes are derived from 2-amino-3-nitro-5-acyl(or aroyl)thiophenes.[285] Only the lack of economical synthetic procedures has kept them from commercial use.

As previously mentioned,[264] a few azo dyes from 2-aminobenzothiazoles had been marketed before 1950. Apparently because of positive substituents on the benzo ring, these had only modest lightfastness. The use of more negative groups in the 6-position of the benzothiazole nucleus improved this property.[8] Some of the earliest of these were derived from 2-amino-6-alkylsulfonylbenzothiazole.[286] Typical examples are given in Chart 28.[287]

CHART 28

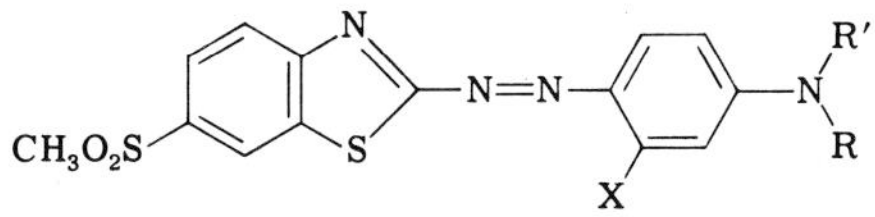

CH_3O_2S ... $N=N$ ... X ... R', N, R

1. X = —H, R = —CH_2CH_2OH, R' = —CH_2CH_2CN
2. X = —H, R = —$CH_2CH_2OCOCH_3$, R' = —CH_2CH_2CN
3. X = —CH_3, R = —CH_2CH_2OH, R' = —CH_2CH_2OH
4. X = —H, R = —CH_2CH_3, R' = —$CH_2CH_2CONH_2$[287]

[278] G. T. Morgan and G. V. Morrow, *J. Chem. Soc.* **107**, 1291 (1915); G, *USP* 2,149,051.

[279] EKCo., *USP* 3,143,540.

[280] EKCo., *USP* 3,336,285.

[281] EKCo., *USP* 3,213,080.

[282] EKCo., *USP* 2,790,791; BASF, *USP* 3,096,320; FBy, *BP* 957,416.

[283] FBy, *USP* 2,791,579; EKCo., *USP* 3,221,006.

[284] J. Goerdeler, H. Hanbrich, and J. Galinke, *Ber.* **93**, 397 (1960).

[285] J. B. Dickey *et al., J. Soc. Dyers Colourists* **74**, 123 (1958); EKCo., *USP* 2,805,218.

[286] EKCo., *USP* 2,785,157.

[287] Kewanee, *USP* 3,342,800.

Several routes to the necessary azo components are available.[286,288] These are outlined in Chart 29.

Route D is obviously quite versatile because of the reactivity of the sodium salt of the mercaptobenzothiazole. In general, 2-aminobenzothiazoles can be prepared by reaction of aromatic amines with "nascent" thiocyanogen. The intermediate thiocyanoanilines are seldom isolated. This chemistry is the topic of a recent interesting review.[289]

CHART 29

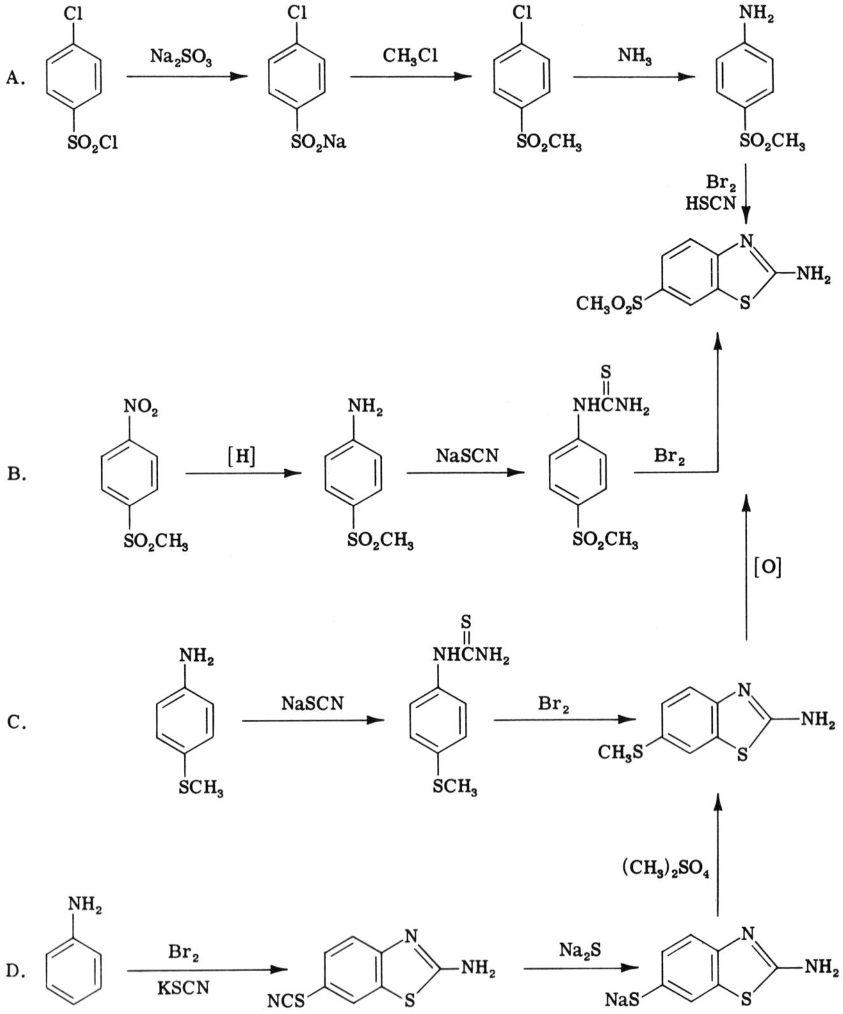

[288] F. E. Johnson and C. S. Hamilton, *J. Am. Chem. Soc.* **71**, 74 (1949).
[289] R. Pohloudek-Fabini and M. Schuessler, *Pharmazie* **22**, 220 and 620 (1967).

These dyes are bright scarlet to red-violets of high tinctorial power and excellent dischargeability. Various individuals of the series have good to excellent fastness to light, gas, and sublimation on acetate, triacetate, and polyesters. Their tendency to stain wool, possibly because of the methylsulfonyl group, is rectified by replacing this group with a cyanoalkylsulfonyl residue.[290]

Similar dyes are obtained from 6-alkylsulfonylbenzothiazoles in which the alkyl group bears several hydroxyls,[291] from 2-amino-5-methyl-6-methylsulfonylbenzothiazole,[292] and from 2-aminobenzothiazolyl-6-sulfonamides.[293] Dyes from 2-amino-6-nitrobenzothiazole[294] have not been neglected (XLIX).

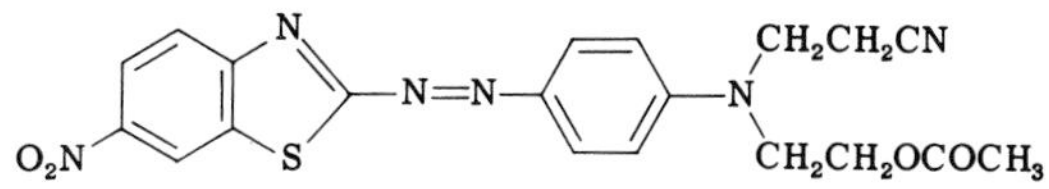

(XLIX)

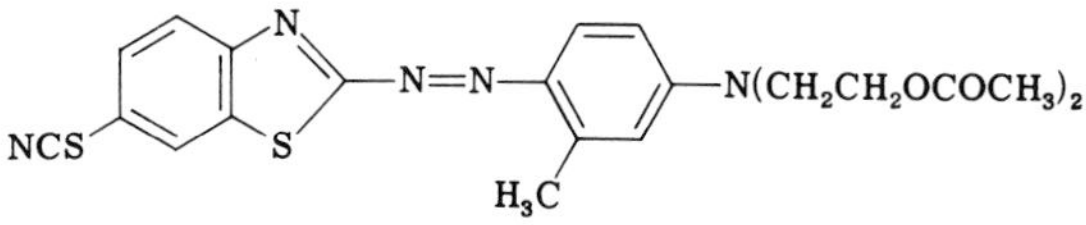

(L)

Dyes from the 6-acyl or aroyl,[295] carbalkoxy,[296] cyano, or thiocyano[297] (L) azo components have been reported. The dyes from the thiocyano compounds are less fast to light than the corresponding dyes from the 6-alkylsulfonyl derivatives. Dyes from 2-amino-4-nitro-6-alkylsulfonyl(or sulfamoyl)benzothiazoles[298] and the 4,6-dinitro derivative[299] have been disclosed. Diazotization of these last two amines is not easy, and the resulting dyes are often contaminated with impurities. Oxotetrahydrobenzothiazoles[300] produce dyes intermediate in absorbency between thiazoles and benzothiazoles. Benzothiazole dyes have been compared

[290] EKCo., *USP* 3,280,101.
[291] ICI, *BP* 953,887.
[292] YDC, *BP* 944,250.
[293] ICI, *BP* 908,656, 919,424; S, *USP* 2,980,666.
[294] H. Dreyfuss, *CP* 479,802; ICI, *BP* 896,232.
[295] DuP, *USP* 3,329,669.
[296] BASF, *BeP* 675,227.
[297] ICI, *USP* 3,084,153.
[298] S, *USP* 3,105,829.
[299] IC, *USP* 3,090,789.
[300] EKCo., *USP* 3,161,632.

with each other and with their aniline counterparts as to absorbency and fastness on polyesters.[301] Generally, in comparison with the aniline dyes, the benzothiazole compounds are bathochromic, have higher tinctorial power, and have better light and sublimation fastness. In the benzothiazole dyes having two substituents in the benzo rings, those having a nitro group appear to have higher sublimation and poorer lightfastness.

A series of metalizable dyes from benzothiazoles coupled ortho to hydroxyl groups in the azo components,[302] while possibly not strictly disperse dyes, were of brief significance for providing fast acetate prints. These should also give fast dyeings on metalized polypropylene if this type of fiber survives the ills besetting it.

Ordinarily, 2-aminopyridines do not undergo the diazotizations and couplings that are considered "normal," but the N-oxides, such as the N-oxide of 2-amino-5-nitropyridine are readily diazotized and coupled to orthodox azo components.[303]

An interesting dye preparation not involving diazotization is the oxidative coupling of a heterocyclic hydrazine,[304] as in Chart 30.

CHART 30

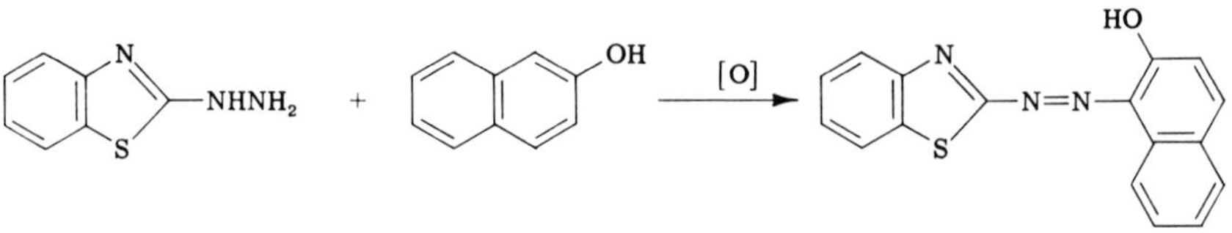

Azo dyes from heterocycles bearing the diazonium in the homocyclic ring are known; for example, from 3-alkyl-6-amino-4-oxo-3,4-dihydrobenzo-1,2,3-triazines,[305] 6-amino-2-hydroxy-4-alkylquinolines,[306] and 2-(6-aminophenyl)benzo-1,2,3-triazine.[307] Benzotriazole 5- or 6-diazos give polyamide dyes when coupled to naphthols and anilines.[308]

With the exception of the metalizable dyes from pyrazolones, 2,4-dihydroxyquinoline, etc., few dyes from heterocyclic diazos coupled directly into the heterocyclic ring have been reported. Those used as dis-

---

[301] M. F. Sartori, J. Soc. Dyers Colourists **83**, 144 (1967).
[302] EKCo., USP 2,832,761; 2,857,371; 2,857,373; 2,865,909; 2,868,775; 3,097,196; 3,099,653.
[303] IC, USP 3,249,597.
[304] BASF, BP 810,736.
[305] FBy, DBP 1,101,658.
[306] ICI, USP 3,137,685.
[307] DuP, USP 3,148,179.
[308] M. Kamel, S. Sharif, and M. M. Kamel, J. Prakt. Chem. [4] **35**, 122 (1967).

perse dyes usually result from coupling into homocyclic rings anellated to heterocycles or into compounds bearing the heterocyclic function attached to an alkylene side chain. Dyes from 2-amino-5-nitrothiazole coupled to 3-alkoxy-N-alkyltetrahydroquinoline,[309] 2-amino-6-alkylsulfonylbenzothiazoles, and 5-amino-1,2,4-thiadiazoles coupled to tetrahydroquinolines and benzomorpholines[310] have been reported. Dyes of general structure (LI) have been described.[311]

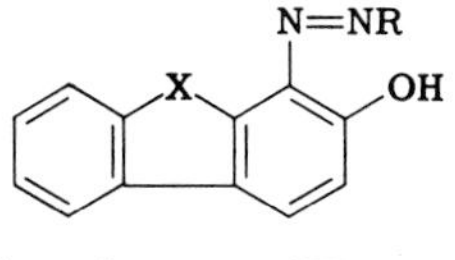

X = —S—, or —NH—

(LI)

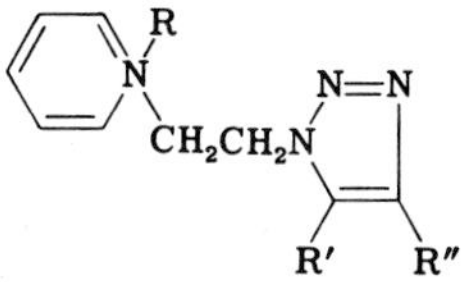

(LIII)

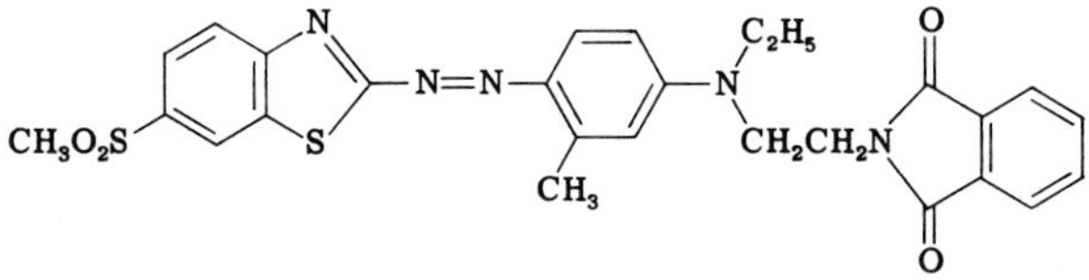

(LII)

Thiazoles and benzothiazoles have been coupled to 2-cyanomethylheterocycles.[312] These diazos have also been coupled to anilines or tetrahydroquinolines having a dicarboximido or pyrrolidinoalkyl group,[313] as in (LII). These dyes have good to excellent fastness properties on polyesters, but their affinity for cellulose acetate is low. The couplers are readily prepared as in Chart 31.

Dyes also result from coupling homo- or heterocyclic diazos to couplers like (LIII).[314] These couplers are prepared by reacting the corresponding alkylene azides with R′C≡CR″. 2-Acylamidothiazoles or thiophenes also couple.[315]

[309] BASF, *DBP* 1,150,465.
[310] EKCo., *USP* 2,773,054; 3,272,791.
[311] Fran, *USP* 3,123,433.
[312] BASF, *DBP* 1,213,549.
[313] EKCo., *USP* 3,148,180; 3,161,631; 3,206,452; 3,213,081; 3,346,552.
[314] FBy, *FP*, 1,501,201.
[315] Chinoin, *USP* 3,102,111.

CHART 31

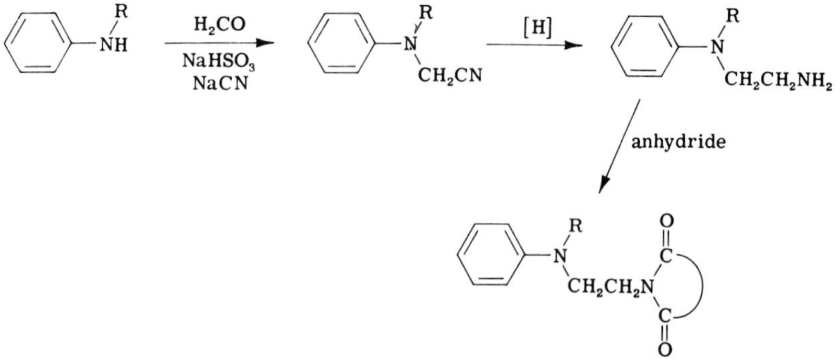

Some unusual syntheses of heterocyclic dyes from homocyclic inter-mediates have been reported.[316,317] Examples are shown in Chart 32.

CHART 32

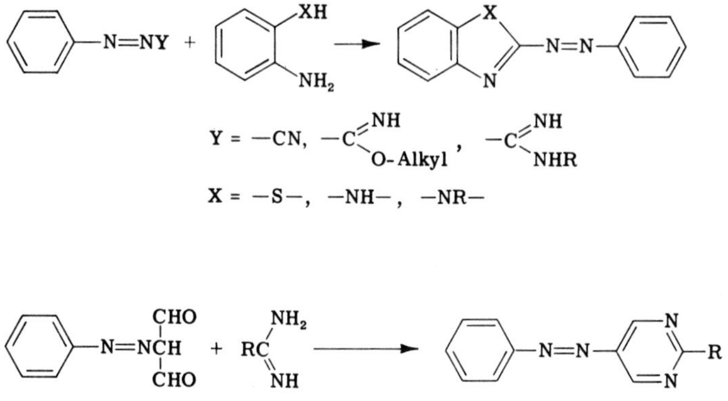

$$Y = -CN, \quad -C\overset{NH}{\underset{O\text{-Alkyl}}{\diagup}}, \quad -C\overset{NH}{\underset{NHR}{\diagup}}$$

$$X = -S-, \quad -NH-, \quad -NR-$$

A large proportion of dyes for the newer synthetic fibers are derived from homocyclic diazo components. Coupled to phenolic compounds they find application on polyolefins. For this purpose, the couplers usually bear *tert*-butyl, hexyl, isooctyl groups, and the like, and the use of poly-phenyl diazos is beneficial.[318,319] Cyanobenzenediazos devoid of nitro groups coupled to 5- or 8-hydroxy-1-naphthylamines have been reported.[320]

[316] BASF, *USP* 3,294,777.
[317] CCC, *USP* 2,675,378.
[318] CIBA, *BeP* 609,898; Ube-Ditto, *DBP* 1,257,735.
[319] Nitto Boseki, *USP* 3,208,813; VGF, *USP* 2,989,358.
[320] FBy, *DBP* 1,126,543.

Yellow dyes of structure (LIV) have been proposed for cellulose acetate.[321]

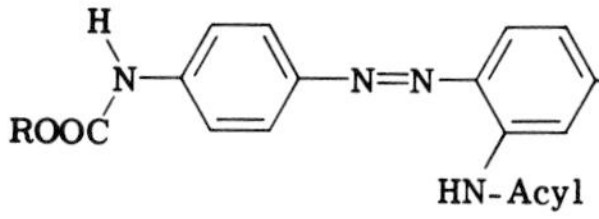

R = Alkyl or alkoxy
R' = Alkyl or acyl

(LIV)   (LV)

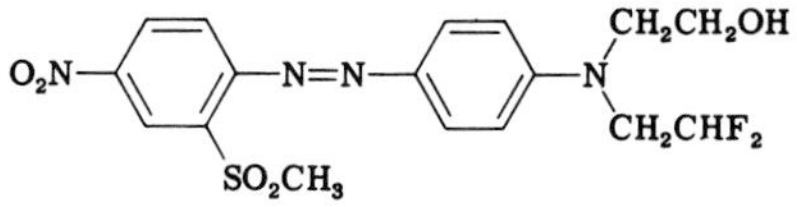

These are prepared by coupling to the free phenol followed by alkylation or acylation.

A variety of dyes derived from phenolic couplers, usually p-alkyl- or p-alkoxyphenols, appear in the literature.[322] The diazos bear substituents such as $ArylCONH-$, $ClCH_2ArylCONH-$, $ClCH_2CH=CHCONH-$, R_2NSO_2NH-, $R_2NSO_2C_6H_4CONH-$, and $RSO_2N(R')C_6H_4CONH-$.

Phenolic dyes have been prepared by ring closure,[323] as in Chart 33.

CHART 33

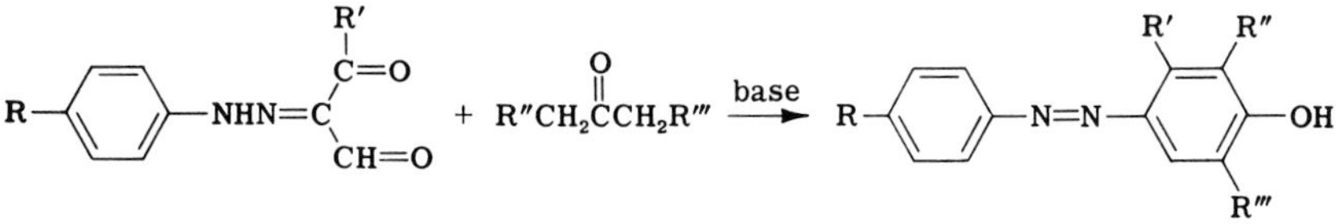

Couplings to arylamides of 3-hydroxy-2-naphthoic acid[324,325] produce bright shades on polyesters in thermal fixation processes, although the lightfastness is usually not of the highest quality. Amides of this same acid in which the nitrogen group is substituted by $-alkyleneOX$, where $X = -H$, $-alkyl$, or $-acyl$, have been reported.[326] Diazotized o-cyano-ethylanilines coupled to various compounds, particularly naphthols, have been reported.[327] The dyes in which $X = alkyl$ are said to have better affinity, but better lightfastness is achieved when $X = acyl$.

The class of monoazo disperse dyes in which substituted anilines are coupled to substituted anilines is, from the aspect of inventorship, the most confusing of all. It may well have been this chemistry which provoked the recent urge for a universal patent system. The practice of the

[321] S, *USP* 2,831,850; 2,870,137.
[322] S, *USP* 2,864,816; 3,112,304; 3,122,533; 3,169,126; Gy, *USP* 3,321,459–60.
[323] BASF, *USP* 3,297,679.
[324] Fran, *USP* 3,043,647.
[325] FH, *FP* 1,292,025; *DBP* 1,238,434; CFM, *BP* 1,063,155.
[326] Gy, *USP* 3,207,747–8; *BeP* 624,898.
[327] CCC, *USP* 3,211,718.

patent offices of some countries to issue whatever they are presented without even a pretense of search has aggravated the confusion, as have inconsistent evaluations of the teachings of the prior art. The result is a snarl which no one who hoped to retain his sanity would attempt to unravel.

About 1950, acetate dye chemists began to realize more fully the bathochromic, and sometimes stabilizing, effect of electron-withdrawing groups when introduced into the diazo component and their hypsochromic influence and often powerful stabilizing effect when residing on the *N*-alkyl groups para to the azo group. Actually, only a few of these groups were new.

One group of chemists quite thoroughly explored the use of fluorine in both components.[328] However, fluorine is expensive, and the methods of introducing it are sometimes complicated and tedious. One red acetate dye (LV), having excellent fastness properties although being somewhat dull and bricky, represented this class in the market for some time.

The unusual stability of the $-SO_2F$ group to the hot aqueous dyebath has been demonstrated.[329]

The simultaneous use of *N*-cyanoalkyl and alkyl (or hydroxyalkyl) groups in the coupler combined with multiple negative groups, such as sulfamoyl, cyano, alkylsulfonyl, nitro, halo, and carbalkoxy, gives dyes said to combine good tinctorial power, affinity, and fastness properties on both acetate and polyesters.[330] Bright dyes of improved lightfastness result from the above diazos coupled to components in which both alkyl groups on the nitrogen bear cyano groups.[331] The preparation of these couplers is often troublesome. The most attractive synthesis would be that shown in Chart 34. When R is hydrogen, alkyl, or a positively sub-

CHART 34

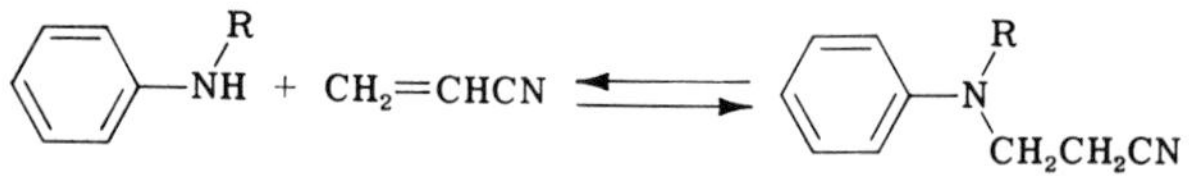

stituted alkyl, such as hydroxyethyl, 2,3-dihydroxypropyl, or alkoxy-alkyl, the reaction proceeds readily. If negative groups, such as halo or cyano, are present, addition is difficult and the equilibrium is shifted to the left.

Although in most diazos the substituents are ortho or para to the diazo

---

[328] EKCo., *USP* 2,491,481; 2,492, 971–2; 2,516,302–3; 2,590,090; 2,590,092; 2,594,297; 2,615,013–4; 2,618,631; 2,757,173.

[329] CCC. 2,576 037; S, *USP* 2,794.833. 2,830.043.

[330] S, *USP* 2,782,186; 2,782,188–9; 2,873,270; 3,042,078; 3,050,576.

[331] DuP, *USP* 2,782,187; CIBA, *USP* 2,941,992.

group, there are a few in which some of the negative substituents are in the meta position.[331,332] From 2-cyano-5-chloroaniline, for example, the dyes produced are said to exhibit equal lightfastness on both acetate and polyamides, whereas from 2,5-dichloro-4-methylsulfonylaniline bright, fast dyes on acetate and polyesters are produced. It has been stated that, to attain light and sublimation fastness simultaneously on polyesters, two cyanoethyl groups on the coupler nitrogen are necessary. The same effect is said to be obtained by the presence of a chlorine atom ortho to the –NHCH$_2$CH$_2$CN group.[333]

The advent of the polyesters increased the use of some of the older, simple dyes, which for one reason or another had found little use on acetate. Some of these are structures (LVI)–(LX).

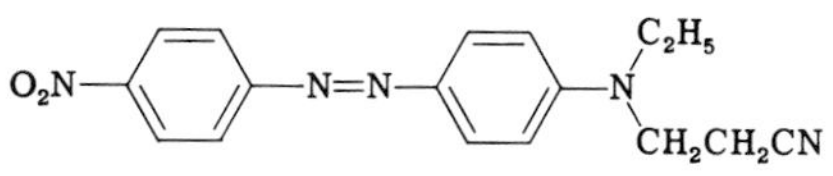

Orange

(LVI)

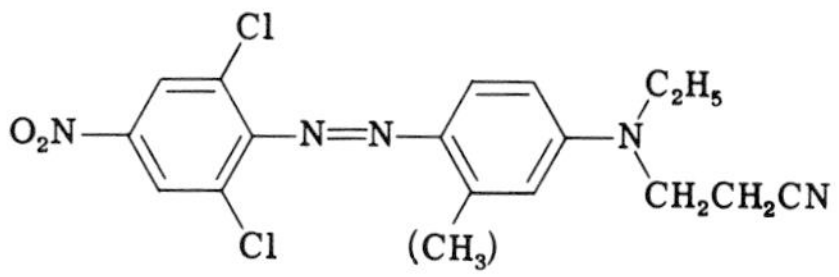

Orange-brown

(LVII, LVIII)

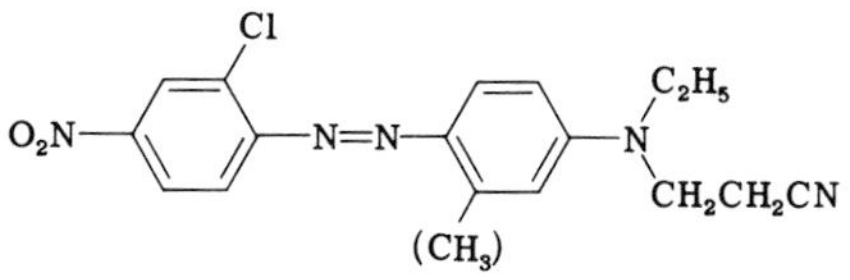

Red to rubine

(LIX, LX)

There are a few recent patents regarding similar types.[334]

In 1935, it was shown[335] that the substitution of an acyloxyalkyl for a hydroxyalkyl or an alkyl group on the 4-nitrogen atom of the coupler results in improved lightfastness. This principle was applied to polyester dyes,[336] resulting in commercial use of dyes such as (LXI) to (LXVIII). An extension of this idea is the reaction of the N-(β-hydroxyethyl) groups with isocyanates to yield urethanes[336] combined with homocyclic and heterocyclic diazos. In most of these alterations of the hydroxyl group, reaction can be with either the precursor coupler or the azo dye.

[332] FBy, *USP* 2,888,450; S, 2,967,858.

[333] DuP, *USP* 3,081,295.

[334] BASF, *DBP* 1,164,971-2; CIBA, *DBP* 957,149.

[335] CIBA, *DRP* 620,648.

[336] FBy, *USP* 3,125,402; *DBP* 953,548; S, *USP* 3,069,408; Gy, *USP* 3,337,522; YDC, *BP* 1,055,399; CFM, *BP* 1,067,040; Carbochemique, *BeP* 685,426; BASF, *USP* 3,117,830; FBy, *DBP* 1,257,314.

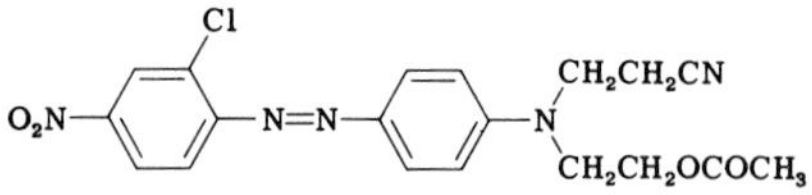

Scarlet
(LXI)

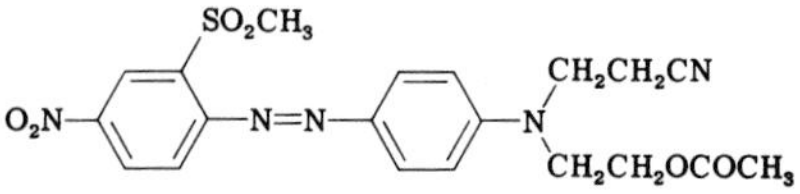

Red
(LXII)

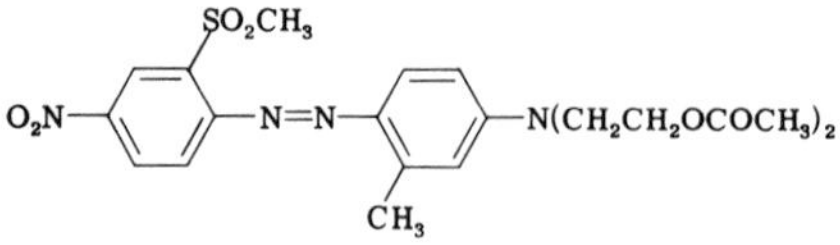

Red
(LXIII)

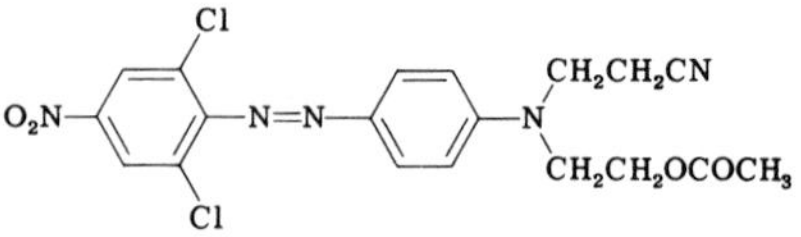

Yellow-brown
(LXIV)

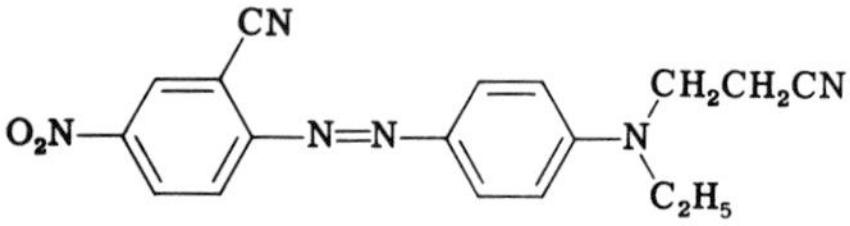

Rubine
(LXV)

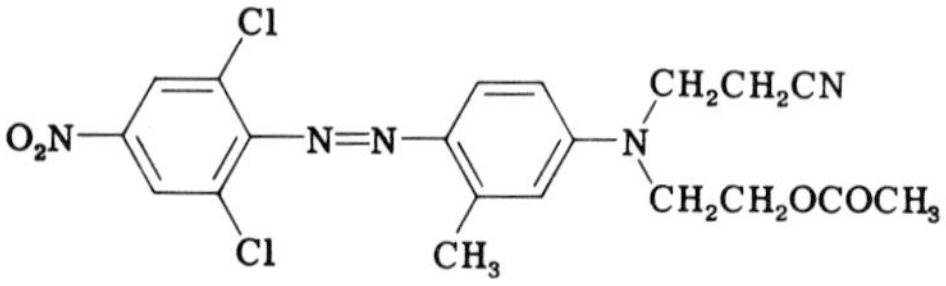

Yellow-brown
(LXVI)

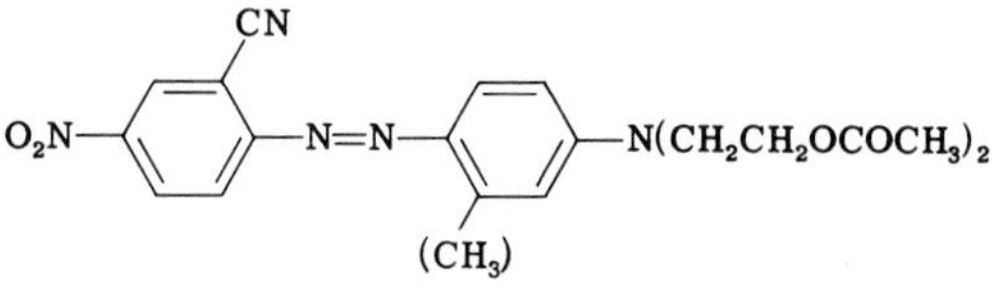

Scarlet-red
(LXVII)

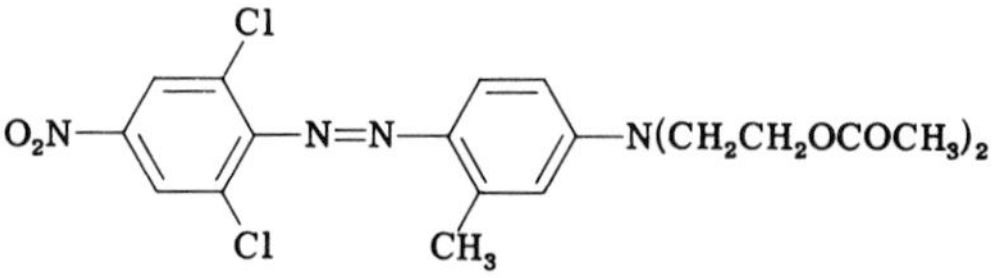

Brown
(LXVIII)

Some of the above find application in the thermofixation and durable-press processes on triacetate.[336] Another class of substituents which had appeared from time to time in the earlier literature is the nuclearly placed acylamido group in the position meta to the coupler –N(R)(R') group. The term "acylamido" embraces –NHCHO, –NHCOAlkyl (or substituted alkyl), –NHCOAryl, –NHCOOAlkyl, –NHCONH₂, –NHSO₂-Alkyl (or aryl). These groups produce bathochromic shifts relative to –H, alkyl, –Cl, –OAlkyl, etc., in the same position. Their use with groups such as –CH₂CH₂CN or –CH₂CH₂OAcyl on the coupler nitrogen is particularly advantageous.[336a,337] Examples are (LXIX) and LXX).

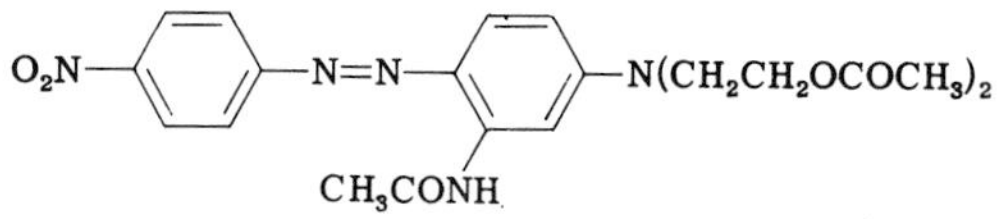

Scarlet

(LXIX)

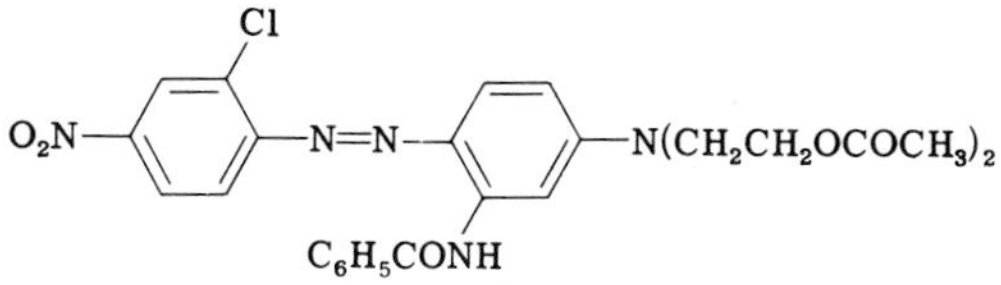

Rubine

(LXX)

These dyes have good to excellent properties on polyesters. The presence of three electron-withdrawing groups in the 2,4,6-positions of the diazo component extends the color range to even greenish blues. Of particular interest are colors prepared by coupling 2,4-dinitro-6-haloanilines to the azo components of Chart 35.[338]

Typical examples are (LXXI), (LXXII), and (LXXIII).

These are fairly dull blues of modest lightfastness, but since they are used only in heavy shades, such as navies or blacks, the inadequacy is hardly noticeable. They are especially suited to thermofixation and durable-press finishes, having excellent buildup and good sublimation

[336a] S, *USP* 2,891,942; *BP* 1,092,057.

[337] CIBA, *USP* 2,971,953; S, *USP* 3,359,256; ICI, *BP* 1,066,085; *USP* 3,139,422; FH, *BeP* 614,027; *DBP* 1,205,213; FBy, *USP* 3,268,507; *BP* 995,306.

[338] S, *USP* 3,122,410; Neth. Appl. 67/10804; E. Merian, *USP* 3,178,405; BASF, *USP* 3,232,693; FH, *USP* 3,250,762-3; 3,284,437; *DBP* 1,213,551; Neth. Appl. 67/10247; CIBA, *USP* 3,325,471; 3,342,803; EKCo., *USP* 2,249,749.

CHART 35

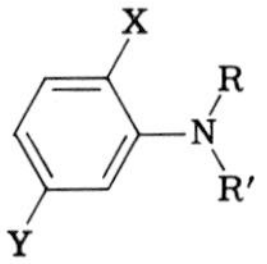

R = —H, —CH₂CH₂O-Acyl, —CH₂CH₂OH,
—CH₂CH₂CO-Alkyl, —CH₂CH₂OCH₂CH₂CN

R' = Alkyl, —CH₂CH₂CN, —CH₂CH₂O-Acyl,
— CH₂CH₂OCH₂CH₂CN, —CH₂CHOHCH₂-Halogen, —CH₂— (phenol ring with OH)

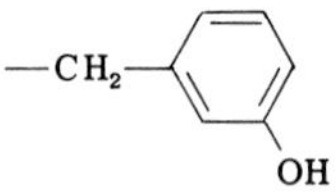

X = —H, Alkyl, lower alkoxy, —CH₂CH₂OH, —OCH₂CH₂O-Acyl

Y = Acylamido as previously defined

fastness. They also resist the shade change often caused by the resin–catalyst systems used.

2,4-Dinitro-6-methoxyaniline has been used with this type of coupler, one of the coupler *N*-alkylene groups bearing a –COOR or –OCOR residue.[339]

Some attention has been paid to the use of 2-cyano-4-nitro-6-halo-

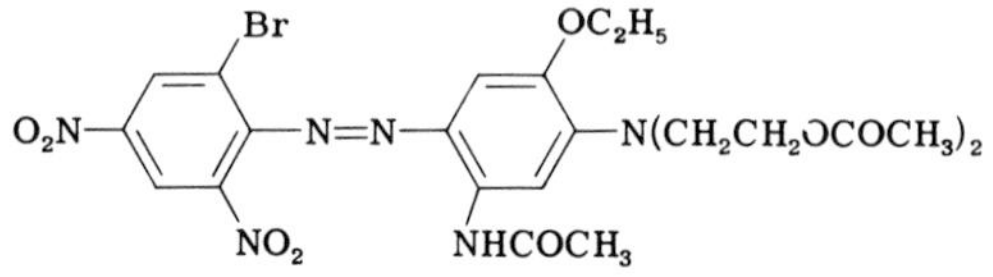

(LXXI)

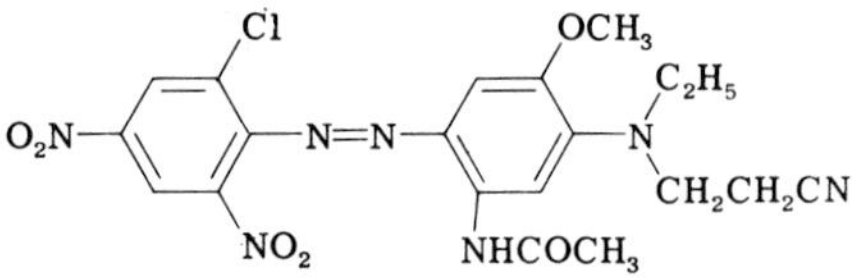

(LXXII)

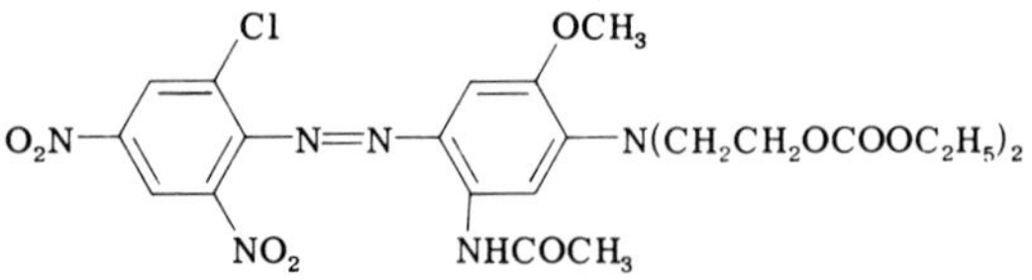

(LXXIII)

[339] S, *FP* 1,513,947.

diazos (among others)[340] coupled to acylamides. These impart violet to blue shades to hydrophobic fibers. Blue to blue-green dyes result from the use of 2,4-dinitro-6-cyanoaniline as the diazo component.[341] Dyes from both heterocyclic and homocyclic diazos in which the hydrogen on the coupler acylamido group is replaced by alkyl have been reported.[342] Dyes in which either the acylamido group is –NHSO$_2$Alkyl or one of the coupler N-alkyls bears this group have been described.[343]

Other dyes which may or may not bear the acylamido, cyanoalkyl, or acetoxyalkyl groups have been investigated. In one type, novelty is provided by diazos from 4-nitro-2-alkylsulfinylanilines.[344] In another, the diazo components are 4-nitro-2-carbalkoxyanilines, and one of the coupler's N-alkyl groups also bears a carbalkoxy group.[345] Dyes from 3-halo-5-nitroanthranilic acid esters[346] are known. In others, the new feature is the stipulation that at least one of the coupler's N-alkyl groups be –CH$_2$CH$_2$COOAlkyl.[347] Homocyclic and heterocyclic diazos have been coupled to C$_6$H$_5$N(CH$_2$CH$_2$CN)(Alkylene-O-Alkyl) and derivatives.[348]

Other negatively substituted diazo components which have been suggested include 2,4-dicyanoanilines (and derivatives),[349] anilines with carbalkoxy groups,[350] or 2-alkylsulfonylanilines with halo or nitro groups in the 4,6-positions.[351]

Many investigators have dealt with dyes in which the azo component is the novel feature. 3-Dialkylaminobenzonitriles or couplers which have an RSO$_2$NH– group in either the dialkylamino group or meta thereto have been proposed.[352] In others the alteration is in the alkyl groups on the coupler nitrogen. In the structure C$_6$H$_5$N(R)R', where the benzene ring may bear other substituents, one R group may be –Alkylene NHCOAlkyl, etc.,[353] –Alkylene COAlkyl,[354] –Alkylene C≡CAlkyl,[355]

[340] S, *USP* 3,342,804; *DBP* 1,248,190; *BP* 971,167; 1,087,664-5; FBy, *DBP* 1,232,292; *FP* 1,490,035.
[341] CN, *BP* 1,080,480.
[342] ICI, *BP* 1,053,830.
[343] FBy, *USP* 2,955,901.
[344] BASF, *BeP* 675,228.
[345] ICI, *USP* 3,335,126.
[346] BASF, *DBP* 1,257,311.
[347] Fby, *DBP* 1,257,313.
[348] CIBA, *FP* 1,498,812.
[349] FBy, *DBP* 942,221; 951,525.
[350] BASF, *DBP* 1,052,081; 1,150,466; 1,241,013.
[351] S, *DBP* 931,428; *FP* 1,463,508.
[352] S, *BP* 1,087,276; *DBP* 1,078,992.
[353] FBy, *DBP* 963,457.
[354] BASF, *BP* 976,239.
[355] BASF, *BP* 928,492.

–CH$_2$CH(COAlkyl or Aryl)CH$_2$CN,[356] –Alkylene NHSO$_2$N(Alkyl)$_2$,[357] –Alkylene SO$_2$ Aryl,[358] –Alkylene SO$_2$CH=CH$_2$,[359] –CH$_2$CH(OH)Aryl,[360] –CH(CH$_2$NO$_2$)Aryl,[361]   –AlkyleneCOOAlkyleneCN,[362]   –Alkylene-OOCRCOOAlkyl where R=nothing or Alkyl,[363] –AlkyleneOOCAlkylene –SO$_2$Alkyl or Aryl,[364] –AlkyleneOOCCH$_2$O (or S)Aryl or Alkyl.[365] Silicon atoms have been introduced into the N-Alkyl residues.[366] R can be –AlkyleneOAlkyl, R' is –AlkyleneCOOAlkyl,[367] or, when R' is this latter moiety, R is –AlkyleneOOCAlkyl or Aryl.[368] Couplers have been prepared by condensing ArylNHAlkyl with from 2 to 10 moles of ethylene oxide.[369] Nonalkylated anilines can be coupled and the –NH$_2$ group then transformed into ureas, etc.[370] Dyes from couplers bearing β-chloroethyl, β,γ-dihalopropyl, γ-chloro-β-hydroxypropyl, epoxyalkyl, etc., groups have been disclosed.[371]

Some novel azo syntheses have been reported. For example, heating nitrobenzene with caustic and methanol yields azobenzene.[372] Treatment of isocyanates with peroxides yields azo dyes,[373] possibly by the route of Chart 36.

CHART 36

$$2\,RNCO\ +\ H_2O_2\ \longrightarrow\ \underset{\underset{O}{\|}\ \underset{O}{\|}}{RNHCOOCNHR}\ \xrightarrow{-2\,CO_2}\ 2\,RN\cdot H\ \xrightarrow{H_2O_2}\ RN{=}NR\ +\ 2\,H_2O$$

Replacement of certain phenolic groups by amino groups has been reported,[374] as illustrated in Chart 37.

[356] ICI, *USP* 3,117,118.
[357] S, *USP* 3,206,454.
[358] FH, *USP* 3,118,873.
[359] EKCo., *BeP* 683,219.
[360] PCC, *USP* 2,882,269.
[361] FB, *DBP* 927,286.
[362] ICI, *USP* 3,097,198.
[363] FBy, *BP* 959,260.
[364] CFM, *BeP* 672,259.
[365] BASF, *BeP* 675,138.
[366] UCC, *USP* 2,925,313; 2,927,839; 2,931,693.
[367] BASF, *BP* 1,090,768.
[368] FBy, *BP* 944,410.
[369] ICI, *BP* 1,061,268.
[370] FBy, *DBP* 953,549.
[371] FW, *BP* 1,097,330; ICI, *USP* 2,944,871; 3,314,935.
[372] BASF, *DBP* 948,978.
[373] PHO, *DBP* 963,154.
[374] CIBA, *USP* 3,352,847.

CHART 37

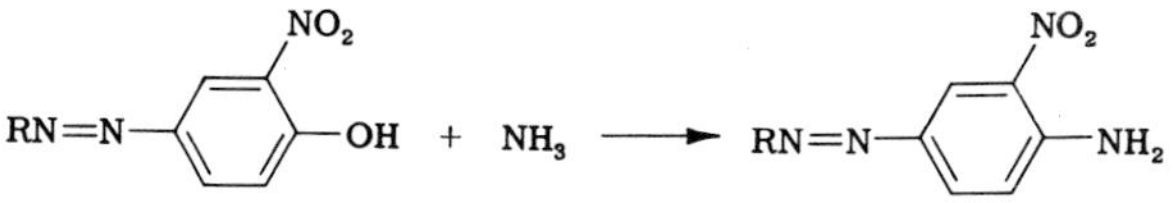

RN=N—〈benzene ring with NO₂ and OH〉 + NH₃ ⟶ RN=N—〈benzene ring with NO₂ and NH₂〉

2-Nitrodiphenylamine, when treated with zinc and caustic, yields **2,2′-dianilinoazobenzene.**[375]

o-Nitrophenyl diazos have been coupled to indanediones.[376] Dyes of the type illustrated by (LXXIV) are bright blue dyes having poor lightfastness on polyesters.[377] In black mixtures on certain fabric constructions they provide cheap coloration. 2-Naphthylamines bearing alkyl(aryl) sulfonyl groups have been employed as the azo components.[378]

Azo dyes in which at least one of the coupler's N-alkyl groups has a heterocyclic ring have been studied. The dyes of structures (LXXV) have been proposed.[379]

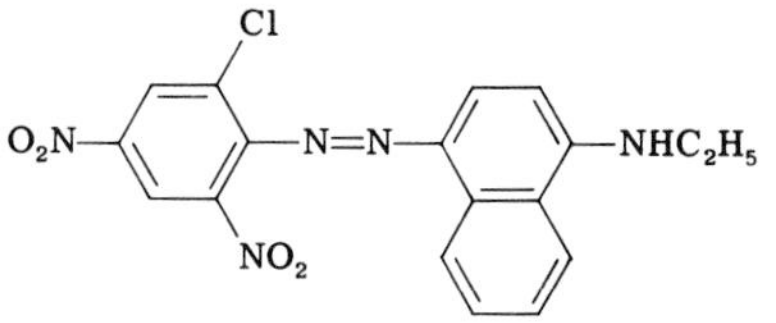

(LXXIV)

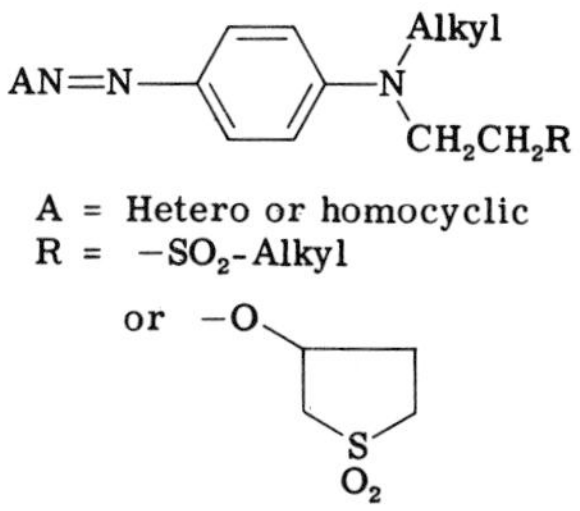

A = Hetero or homocyclic
R = —SO₂-Alkyl

or —O〈sulfolane ring, S, O₂〉

(LXXV)

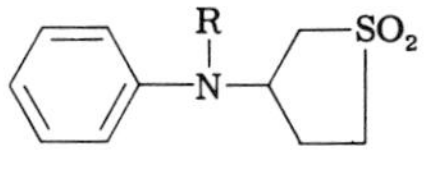

(LXXVI)

The sulfolane group is formed by reaction of butadiene with sulfur dioxide followed by addition of the coupler's alkylhydroxy group to the 3-sulfolene thus prepared.[380] The sulfolane ring can reside on the nitrogen atom (LXXVI),[381] or the nitrogen atom and the sulfur dioxide may be part of the same heterocycle.[382] Structure (LXXVII) has excellent fastness properties. The coupler can be prepared by reaction of 1 mole

[375] C. T. Allen and G. H. Swan, J. Chem. Soc. p. 3892 (1965).
[376] S, BP 952,463; FP 1,222,237; USP 3,093,437; 3,153,643.
[377] YDC, BP 985,254.
[378] Gy, BP 992,981.
[379] FBy, USP 3,177,198.
[380] Shell, USP 2,504,098.
[381] FBy, DBP 1,217,523.
[382] EKCo., BeP 701,155.

of divinyl sulfone with aniline; however, use of this toxic intermediate can be avoided by condensation with the cheaper bis(β-hydroxyethyl) sulfone.

Oxygen-containing rings have been mentioned (LXXVIII).[383]

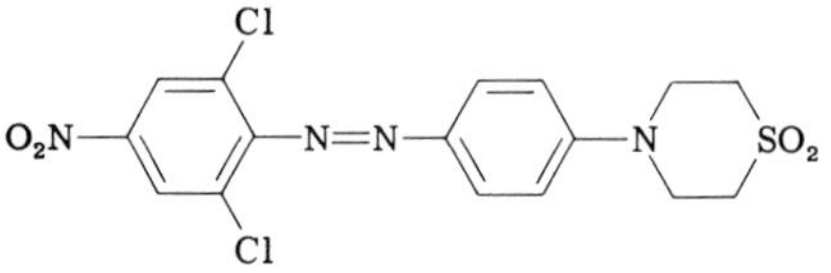

(LXXVII) 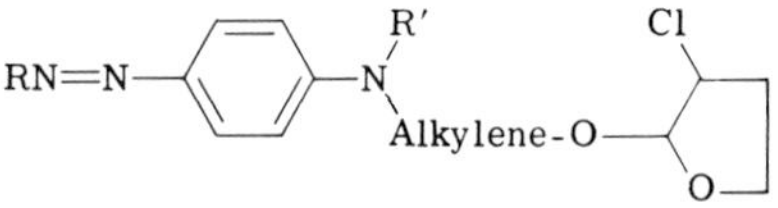   (LXXVIII)

The chlorotetrahydrofuran residue may be introduced by reaction between the hydroxyl group and 2,3-dichlorotetrahydrofuran.

Other dyes in which the heterocycle in (LXXVIII) is replaced by pyrrolidinone or dicarboximido groups, which themselves may contain hetero atoms, are known.[384] The pyrrolidinone group is produced by reaction of a γ-butyrolactone with an ω-aminoalkyl compound, while the dicarboximido group results from reaction of an anhydride with the same function. Typical of these dyes are (LXXIX) and (LXXX).

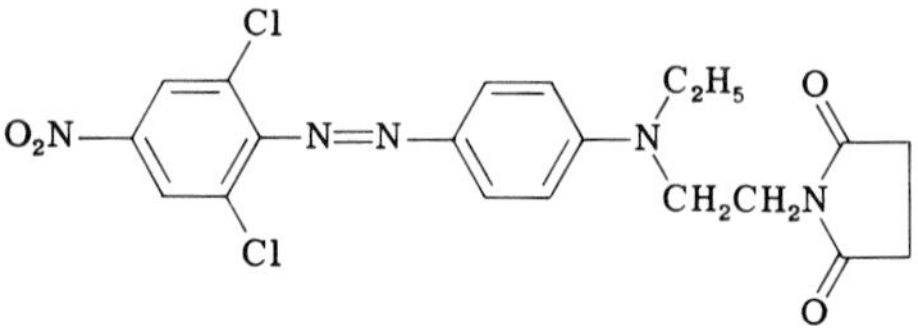

Orange

(LXXIX)

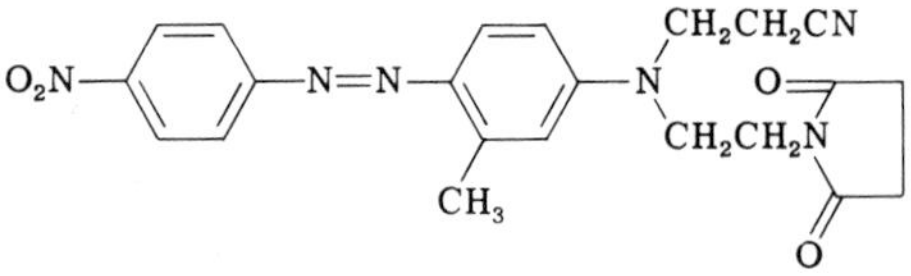

Orange

(LXXX)

The 1,2,3-triazole nucleus has also been appended to the N-alkyl group.[385]

One of the most familiar heterocyclic coupler classes used in azo dye chemistry is the pyrazolone series, and it has not been neglected in the

[383] BASF, USP 3,117,956.
[384] EKCo., USP 3,148,178; 3,342,799; 3,349,076.
[385] FBy, FP 1,501,201.

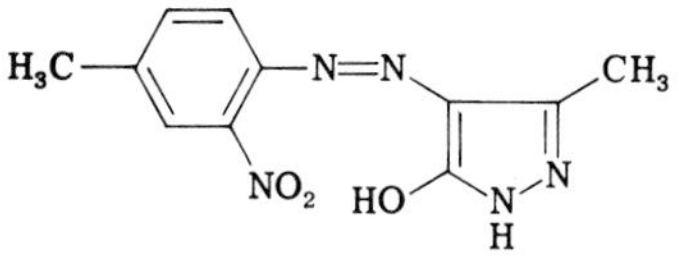

(LXXXI)

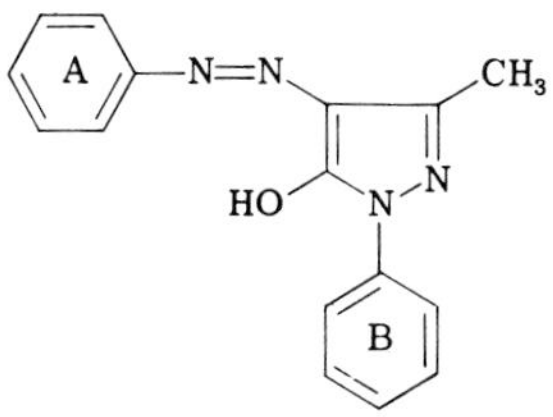

(LXXXII)

disperse dye field. Structure (LXXXI) is a yellow polyester dye.[386] It also provides dischargeable grounds on cellulose acetate. Many other pyrazolone couplers and aryl diazos are mentioned, the prime stipulation being the presence of an ortho nitro group in the diazo. In the structure (LXXXII), either ring A or B can bear an –SCN group,[387] an –SO₂NH₂ or –SO₂NR₂ group,[388] or an –SO₃R group, and A can be replaced by ArylN=NAryl–.[389] Ring B may be substituted by –NHSO₂N(Alkyl)₂,[390] or may have a fluorine atom ortho to the N linkage.[391] The pyrazolone methyl group may sometimes be replaced by aryl, –COOR, –CONH₂, etc. A specific dye, 4-(2,4-dichloro-6-methylphenylazo)-1-(o-chlorophenyl)-3-methyl-5-pyrazolone, has been disclosed.[392] Much attention has been given to dyes of this class in which the typical feature is a –COOR or –CONR(R′) group in the 3-position of the pyrazolone.[393] In some of these, heterocyclic as well as homocyclic diazos are employed. Dyes in which the pyrazolone nitrogen bears a substituted triazine ring,[394] a –CH₂CH(OH)Aryl group,[395] a 3-sulfolane ring,[396] an –SO₂N(Alkyl)₂,[397] –CH₂CHOCOAryl,[398] or an –SO₂Aryl[399] have been reported. A variation is a class in which the diazo component bears a –COOR or –CONR₂ group.[400]

[386] CIBA, *BP* 867,535.

[387] FBy, *BP* 852,400.

[388] Fran, *USP* 3,012,843.

[389] Gy, *BP* 1,009,363; *USP* 3,341,843.

[390] S, *USP* 3,206,453.

[391] Gy, *BeP* 605,507.

[392] FH, *BP* 895,392.

[393] Fran, *BP* 967,545; ICI, *USP* 3,164,437; 3,316,240; 3,325,469; CCC, *USP* 3,019,217; *USP* 3,198,783; S, *USP* 3,130,190.

[394] Gy, *USP* 3,330,232.

[395] Gy, *BP* 955,520.

[396] FBy, *USP* 2,957,863.

[397] S, *BP* 1,067,518.

[398] FBy, *USP* 3,324,105.

[399] Toms River, *USP* 3,342,801.

[400] CFM, *BP* 1,064,596; FBy, *USP* 2,898,178; G, *USP* 3,246,945; CIBA, *USP* 3,305,541.

Azo dyes from aryl diazoniums coupled to 5-amino-3-alkyl(aryl)-1-alkyl(aryl, etc.)pyrazoles give yellow to scarlet shades on polyesters.[401] Similar dyes, except that an alkoxy group occupies the 3-position, are known.[402] These interesting intermediates are prepared by the typical reaction of Chart 38.[403]

CHART 38

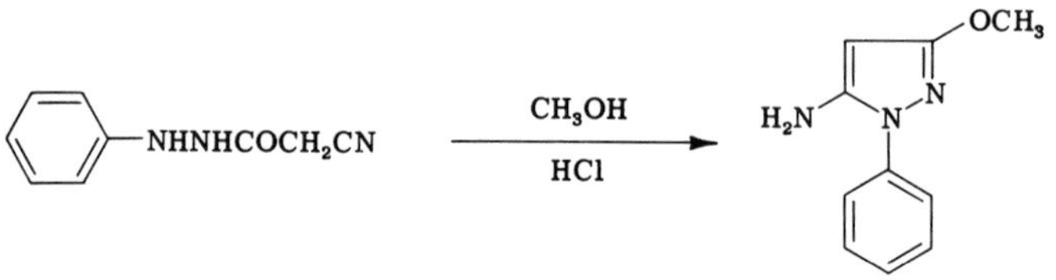

Diazos bearing cyano and hydroxyalkylsulfamoyl groups have been coupled to 1,2-disubstituted indoles.[404] Trichlorophenyldiazos have also been mentioned with these couplers.[405] Fluorinated diazos coupled to 2,6-diaminopyridine[406] and dyes from 2,6-dihydroxy-3-cyano-4-methylpyridine[407] have been proposed. This coupler is prepared by condensation of ethyl cyanoacetate and acetoacetic ester with ammonia.[408]

Treatment of diketene with o-aminobenzenethiol gives 4-methyl-6,7-benzo-1-thia-5-aza-4,6-cycloheptadien-2-one, which yields yellow to orange dyes.[409] Coupling of aryl diazos substituted by nitro, carbamoyl, carbalkoxy, or chloro, to 1,2-diaryl-3,5-dioxopyrazolidines gives yellow dyes which are said to be exceptionally good in combinaton with blue anthraquinone dyes.[410]

Although the dyes from chloro- or alkoxy-5-sulfamoylanilines coupled to hydroxypyrimidines are more suitable for the Basazol process, they can be used as disperse dyes.[411] Acetate dyes from homocyclic diazos coupled to 2,6-dihydroxypyrimidines have been described.[412] Aryl diazos coupled to 4-hydroxycoumarins give yellow shades on polyesters.[413]

[401] Gy, USP 3,344,133.
[402] Gy, USP 3,356,673.
[403] Gy, DBP 1,120,453.
[404] FBy, BP 850,422; 969,445.
[405] FBy, BeP 702,241.
[406] Nepera, USP 3,357,968.
[407] CFM, BP 1,095,829.
[408] I. Guareschi, Ber. 29, 655 (1896).
[409] EKCo., USP 3,125,563.
[410] S, USP 3,124,567.
[411] BASF, USP 3,352,846.
[412] EKCo., USP 2,578,290.
[413] FBy, BP 1,016,525; USP 3,344,132.

Some azo components couple elsewhere than in the hetero ring. Examples of these are (LXXXIII),[414] (LXXXIV),[415] (LXXXV),[416] (LXXXVI),[417] (LXXXVII),[418] (LXXXVIII),[419] and (LXXXIX).[420]

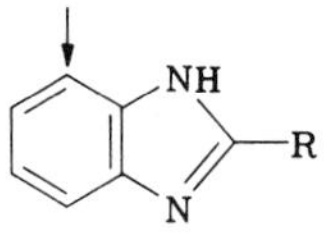

(LXXXIII) 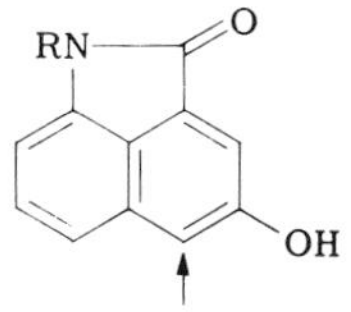　　　　(LXXXIV) 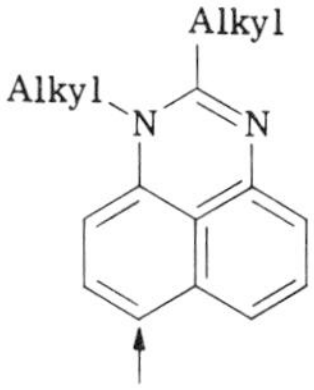　　　　(LXXXV)

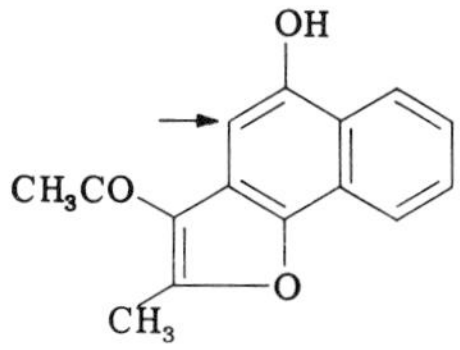

(LXXXVI) 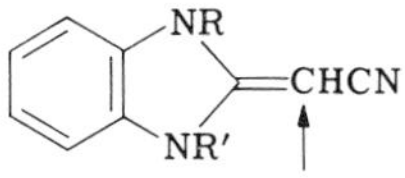　　　　(LXXXVII) 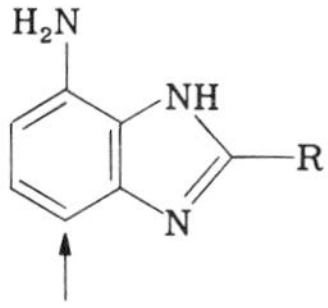　　　　(LXXXVIII)

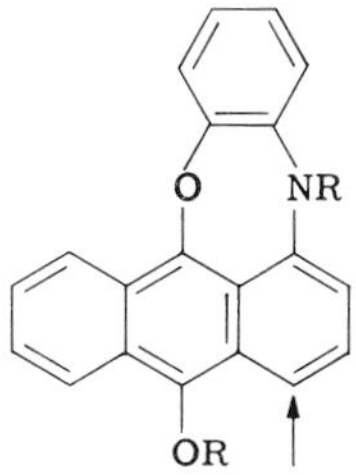

(LXXXIX)

Dyes related to these structures can be prepared as shown in Chart 39.[421] Arylazoanilines have been condensed with ethoxymethylenemalonates

[414] FH, *USP* 3,132,131.
[415] FBy, *USP* 2,961,438.
[416] BASF, *BP* 914,505.
[417] S, *BeP* 697,944.
[418] BASF, *USP* 3,313,998.
[419] FH, *BeP* 611,984.
[420] E. P. Fokin and V. Y. Danisov, *Izv. Akad. Nauk SSSR* p. 2073 (1965); *J. Soc. Dyers Colourists* **82,** 107 (1966).
[421] FBy, *FP* 1,390,113.

CHART 39

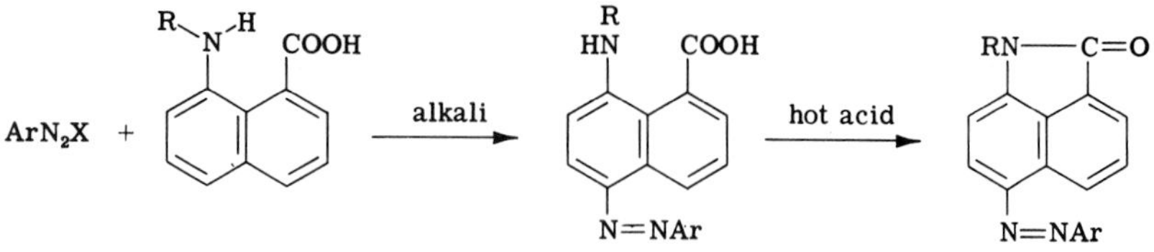

or ethoxymethylenecyanoacetates to yield finally arylazoquinoline dyes,[422] as in Chart 40.

CHART 40

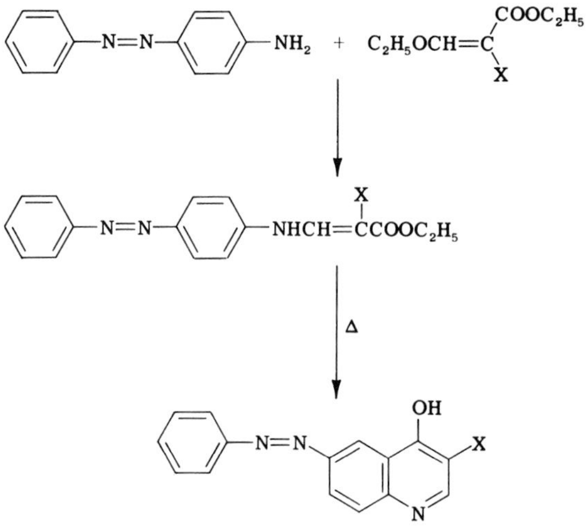

X = —COOC$_2$H$_5$ or —CN

B. Disazo Dyes

A class represented by only a few members in the acetate dye series has benefited by the use of more rigorous dyeing methods. Some of these are (XC), (XCI), (XCII), and (XCIII). These impart yellow to orange coloration to polyester fibers.[423] In addition to these compounds, the aminoazobenzene component may bear acetamido,[424] hydroxy,[425] cyano-alkoxy,[426] alkoxyalkylcarbonyl,[427] or sulfamoylalkyl, or arylsulfonyl, or esterified sulfonic acid groups.[428]

[422] S. N. Nagaraja and S. V. Sunthankar, *J. Sci. Ind. Res. (India)* **20D,** 374 and 407 (1961).

[423] CIBA, *USP* 2,954,371.

[424] CL, *USP* 2,563,091.

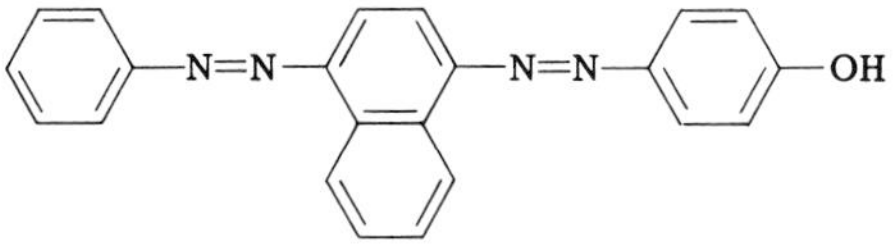

(XC)

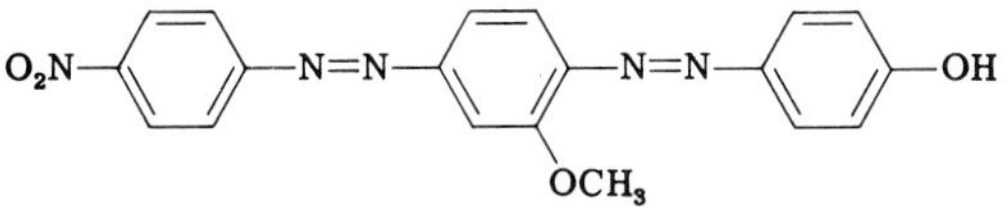

(XCI)

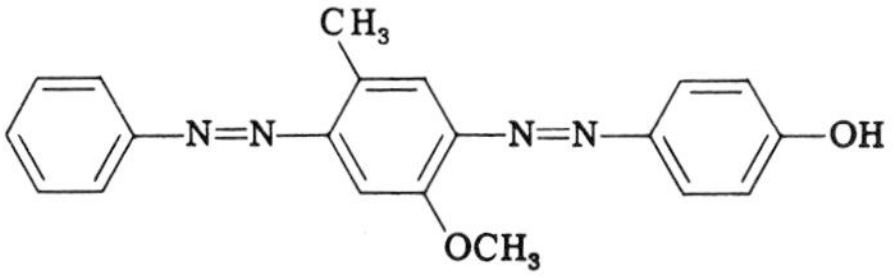

(XCII)

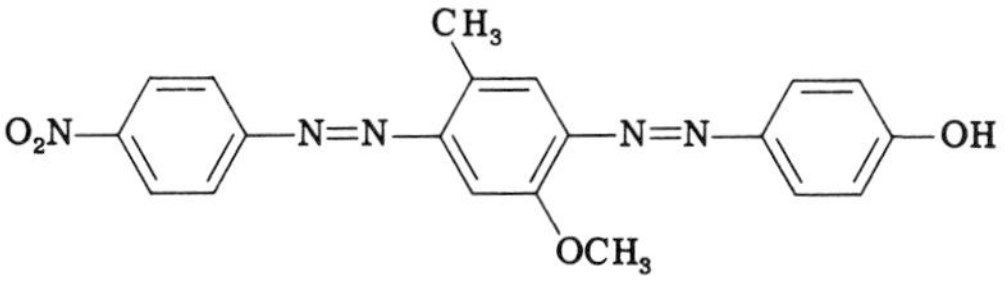

(XCIII)

A wide variety of aminoazobenzenes have been coupled to phenols and naphthols which may bear carboxyl groups.[429] Some of these are said to have affinity for polypropylene.

Mixtures of disazo dyes[430] and those with alkoxy groups ortho to the azo linkage[431] are said to have better affinity than those previously in use.

Other aminoazoaryl compounds are coupled to amides of salicylic

[425] FH, *USP* 3,186,787.

[426] CIBA, *USP* 3,060,168.

[427] CIBA, *USP* 3,037,014.

[428] CIBA, *BP* 966,826; *USP* 3,310,550; S, *USP* 3,134,766.

[429] ACNA, *USP* 3,049,532; 3,089,868; 3,090,780; 3,098,847; 3,125,565; OBM, *USP* 3,236,829; 3,302,992; NSK, *USP* 3,214,424; 3,274,174; 3,282,638.

[430] EKCo., *USP* 3,253,876.

[431] S, *USP* 2,782,185.

acid,[432] α- or β-naphthols bearing sulfamoyl groups, particularly in the 6- or 7-positions.[433] 4-(o-Carboxyphenylazo) aniline coupled to phenols, preferably nuclearly alkylated, has been proposed for polyolefin fibers.[434] Several patents are concerned with aminoazobenzene with a nitro group ortho to the –NH₂ coupled to naphthols, naphtholcarboxamides, active methylene compounds, naphthylamines, etc.[435] 4-(p-Formylphenylazo) anilines have been used as the diazo components.[436] Aminoazobenzenes have been coupled to dialkylanilines in which one of the alkyl groups bears a terminal dicarboximide or pyrrolidinone radical.[437] Other disazo dyes using substituted anilines as azo components have been proposed.[438]

Aminoazobenzenes coupled to heterocyclic compounds are of use chiefly on polyesters. Pyrazolones with 3-carboxamido groups[439] or with sulfamoylaryl groups on the 1-nitrogen[440] have been cited. Barbituric acid derivatives,[441] 4-hydroxyquinolones,[442] and substituted indoles[443] have served as couplers. Dyes in which different types of heterocyclic couplers are used are said to have affinity for polyolefins.[444]

Bispyrazolones, prepared by condensation of 4,4'-hydrazinobenzo-phenones (or sulfones), have been coupled to aminosulfonamides and sulfones.[445] Disazo dyes have been formed by coupling a diazo to 1-(aminophenyl) pyrazolones and, in turn, diazotizing these dyes and coupling them to phenols.[446]

Bis(4-aminophenyl)ureas or thioureas have been coupled to ortho-coupling phenols.[447]

Diazotized anilines bearing arylsulfonyl or arylsulfonic ester groups, when coupled to compounds such as (XCIV), give dyes said to have excellent properties on polyamides.[448]

[432] CN, USP 3,331,829.
[433] Gy, USP 3,338,880.
[434] NSK, USP 3,351,580.
[435] CIBA, BP 987,740; USP 3,234,206; 3,359,255.
[436] FBy, BP 871,633.
[437] EKCo., USP 3,254,073; FP 1,503,466.
[438] ACNA, USP 3,092,616; 3,096,140; 3,222,355; NSK, USP 3,293,240; 3,351,580.
[439] CN, USP 3,254,073.
[440] Fran, USP 3,066,134.
[441] Gy, 3,341,512.
[442] BASF, USP 3,117,959.
[443] BASF, USP 3,070,592.
[444] Montecatini, USP 3,158,435.
[445] Gy, USP 3,197,455.
[446] CIBA, USP 3,137,687.
[447] BASF, BP 973,930.
[448] Whitten, USP 3,325,468.

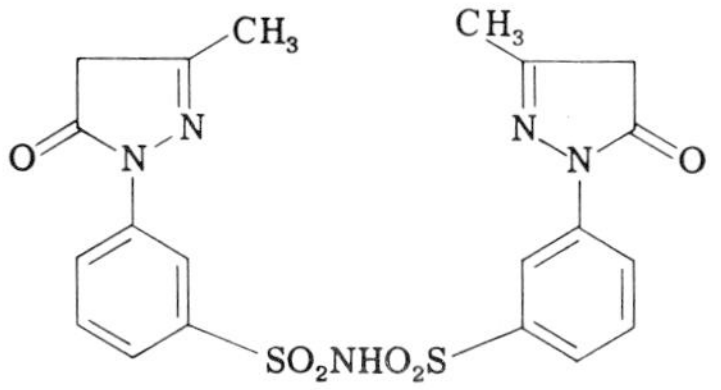

(XCIV) 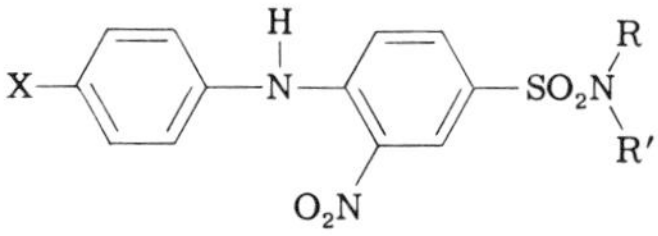   (XCV)

Coupling of 3-aminoazobenzene to 5-pyrazolones is said to provide polyester dyes.[449]

Coupling of erythritol esters of *m*-aminobenzoic acids to active methylene compounds has been suggested.[450] 4-(Aminophenylazo)benzodioxanes have been coupled to phenols.[451]

Clathrate compounds, prepared by adding *p*-[*p*-(phenylazo)phenylazo]phenols to molten thiourea, have been proposed for dyeing polypropylene.[452]

Trisazo dyes in which the 4-position in both terminal aryl rings bear –OH or –NH₂ are suggested for polyolefins.[453]

V. Nitrodiphenylamine Dyes

A class of yellow dyes with rather poor tinctorial power has survived because of generally excellent lightfastness combined with inexpensive methods of manufacture. This class is the *o*-nitrodiphenylamine series. Although in the past, dyes bearing other nitro groups, as well as hydroxyl, alkyl, or other groups found commercial use, the major recent interest involves dyes of structure (XCV).

On polyesters, the representatives are (1) X = –H, R = –H, R′ = –C₆H₅; (2) X = –OC₂H₅, R and R′ = –CH₃. On cellulose esters, the dyes that predominate are[454] (3) X = –OC₂H₅, R and R′ = –H; (4) X, R, and R′ = –H.

The synthesis, lightfastness, spectral characteristics, and their relation to structure have been thoroughly discussed.[455] The superior lightfastness

[449] FH, *BP* 896,605.
[450] G, *USP* 3,211,717.
[451] FBy, *BP* 1,091,464.
[452] MCI, Jap. Appl. 26813/67.
[453] ACNA, *BP* 903,369.
[454] EKCo., *USP* 2,422,029; 2,466,011; P. Fischer, *Ber.* **24**, 3794 (1891).
[455] R. S. Asquith and B. Campbell, *J. Soc. Dyers Colourists* **79**, 678 (1963); R. S. Asquith, I. Bridgeman, and A. T. Peters, Jr., *ibid.* **81**, 439 (1965); **82**, 410 (1966); **83**, 132 (1967); J. F. Corbett, *ibid.* **83**, 273 (1967).

is due to the stabilization of the *ortho*-quinoid charge-transfer form of the *o*-nitroamine system. The skeletal structure may be expressed as in Chart 41.

CHART 41

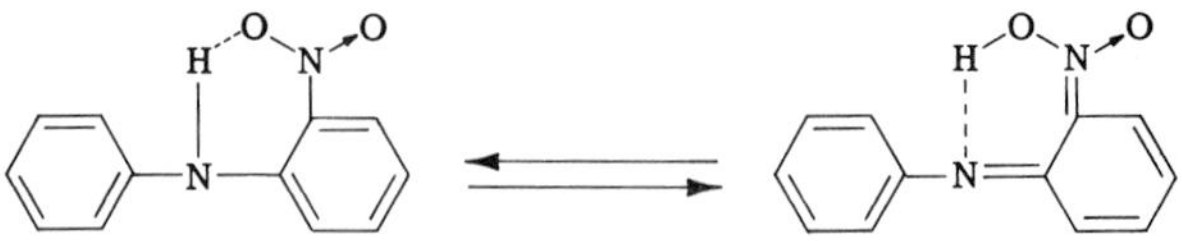

An earlier paper[456] correlating the constitution of a large number of these dyes with the absorption, molar extinction, and other properties on various fibers will be of interest to the industrial chemist. The poor sensitivity of the human eye in this spectral range is cited, and fading by artificial light and by sunshine are compared. Other aspects of the effect of configuration on properties have been presented.[457]

In general, the preparation of these dyes is easily effected by reaction of an aromatic amine with an *o*-halonitrobenzene in an inert solvent, such as chlorobenzene. The use of relatively unreactive amines in solvents such as dimethylformamide is apt to result in replacement of the halogen atom by the dimethylamino group. The use of an emulsifying agent in an aqueous solvent to reduce agglomeration and produce easily filtered crystals has been reported.[458]

The sulfonamido substituent groups have been singled out for attention. Improved wash-fastness has been reported where R and R′ combine to form a morpholine ring,[459] as well as where R = Aryl and R′ = –CH$_2$-CH$_2$OH.[460] A dye in which R = –H, and R′ = C$_6$H$_4$SO$_3$H has been reported to dye cellulose acetate.[461] Other dyes where R = –H or Alkyl and R′ is –AlkyleneCN[462] or a branched butyl group have been suggested.[463]

Interest has been directed to the ring not containing the nitro residue. The addition of an aryl group is said to increase the tinctorial power and provide a bathochromic shift.[464] The fact that the necessary aminobiphenyls are considered to be carcinogenic may have kept such dyes from

[456] E. Merian, *Angew. Chem.* **72,** 766 (1960).

[457] V. S. Salvin and J. Adams, *Am. Dyestuff Reptr.* **48,** No. 7, 43 (1959).

[458] CL, *BP* 659,172.

[459] CL, *USP* 2,569,172.

[460] CL, *USP* 2,922,796.

[461] CL, *USP* 2,595,359.

[462] CCC, *USP* 3,239,543.

[463] CL, *BP* 794,176.

[464] EKCo., *USP* 2,725,390.

the market. Alkylphenoxy groups para to the $=NH$[465] and the use of $-O(CH_2CH_2O)_n$Alkyl groups have been reported.[466] Carboxyl or carboalkoxy groups on this ring[467] or optionally on this ring or on a sulfonamidoaryl ring are disclosed.[468]

Dyes in which the $-SO_2N(R)R'$ group is replaced by $-SO_3$Aryl[469] (said to have good fastness properties) or $-SO_2CH=CH_2$[470] have been reported. The sulfonamido group has also been replaced by $-CF_3$,[471] acyl,[472] or phosphoryl[473] residues. Dyes especially suited for polyamides bear a $-COCHClAlkyl$ group.[474] Dyes containing 2-nitroarylamino residues joined by $-CH_2-$ between the two amino nitrogens are disclosed.[475]

Diphenylamine dyes containing additional chromophoric systems have been prepared. Azonitrodiphenylamines prepared by condensing a 4-chloro-3-nitrobenzenesulfonamide with an aminoazo compound[476] or conversely from arylamines and 4-chloro-3-nitroazobenzenes[477] are reported. Reaction of (4-chloro-3-nitrobenzylidene) cyanoacetic esters (or nitrile) with arylamines gives products of bright shades on acetate and nylon.[478]

The closely related 4-nitroacridones have been claimed for dyeing polypropylene,[479] and members of this family bearing β-chloroethyl groups are suggested for nylon.[480] The addition of an $RS-$ (where $R =$ alkyl, aryl, heterocyclic) para to the 4-nitro group is said to be beneficial for polyester dyeing.[481]

VI. Methine Dyes

The methine, or styryl, class of dyes contains some of the brightest, most lightfast dyes for acetate and polyesters. The spectral range does

[465] S, *USP* 2,879,269.
[466] S, *USP* 2,977,376.
[467] S, *USP* 3,215,485.
[468] CL, *BP* 794,177.
[469] CIBA, *BP* 790,921.
[470] FH, *USP* 2,784,204.
[471] N. Kartinos and A. Stark, *USP* 2,769,816.
[472] G, *USP* 2,708,149.
[473] EKCo., *USP* 2,596,660.
[474] ICI, *BP* 868,471.
[475] BASF, *DBP* 1,088,020.
[476] YDC, *BP* 1,037,163.
[477] BASF, *FP* 1,486,827.
[478] G, *USP* 2,894,447.
[479] IC, *USP* 3,188,164.
[480] ICI, *USP* 2,938,905.
[481] Gy, *USP* 1,509,386.

not extend beyond greenish yellow, and they tend to hydrolyze under alkaline conditions. Those most used commercially are prepared by condensation of an aryl aldehyde, bearing $-NR(R')$ in the para position, with derivatives of cyanoacetic acid. The aldehydes may be prepared by the familiar Vilsmeier method or generated *in situ* from the Schiff's base, as in Chart 42.[482]

CHART 42

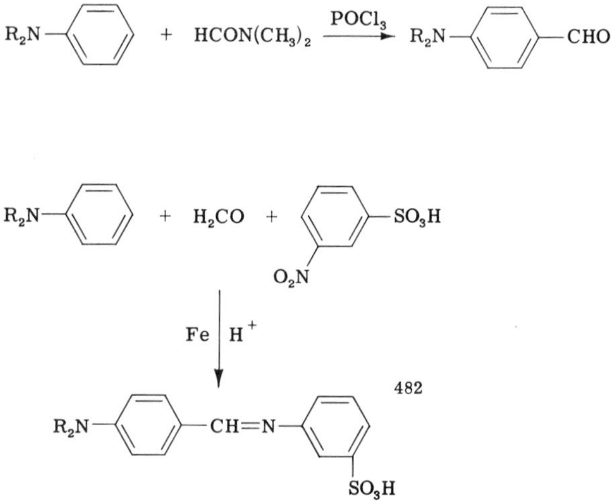

The presence of an alkyl or alkoxy group ortho to the formyl group appears to increase the tinctorial power, as does the use of β-acyloxy groups on the R groups in Chart 42. The dyes from malononitrile also appear stronger than those from cyanoacetic esters. The introduction of ClAlkyleneCOO–[483] or ArylNHCOO–,[484] on the R groups, although not readily understood, appears to stabilize the dye against hydrolysis. Some of the more interesting new dyes are (XCVI),[482] (XCVII),[484] and (XCVIII).[485]

These dyes are used for the preparation of bright Kelly greens, chartreuse, and similar shades. (XCVII) and (XCVIII) find particular use on polyesters because of their resistance to hydrolysis and sublimation.

Many ramifications of these structures are possible. In (XCVII) the *N*-ethyl has been replaced by aryl and the *o*-CH₃ by OAlkyl.[485] The replacement of $C_6H_5NHCOO-$ by dicarboximido (succinimido, phthal-

[482] EKCo., *USP* 2,583,551.
[483] EKCo., *USP* 2,776,310.
[484] S, *USP* 2,850,520; EKCo., *USP* 3,247,211.
[485] EKCo., *USP* 3,326,960.

CN 482

$(CH_3COOCH_2CH_2)_2N$—⟨benzene ring⟩—CH=C—COOCH$_3$

CH$_3$

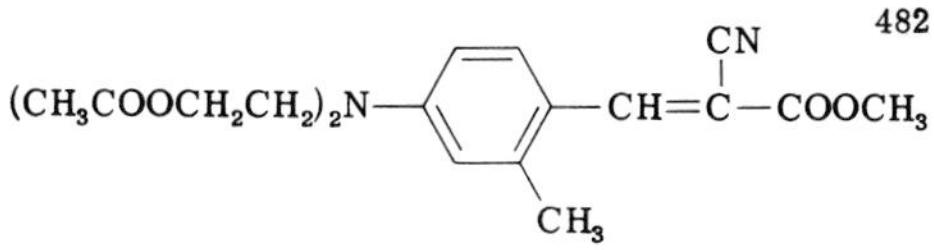

(XCVI)

C$_6$H$_5$NHCOOCH$_2$CH$_2$ 484

N—⟨benzene ring⟩—CH=C⟨CN / CN⟩

C$_2$H$_5$

CH$_3$

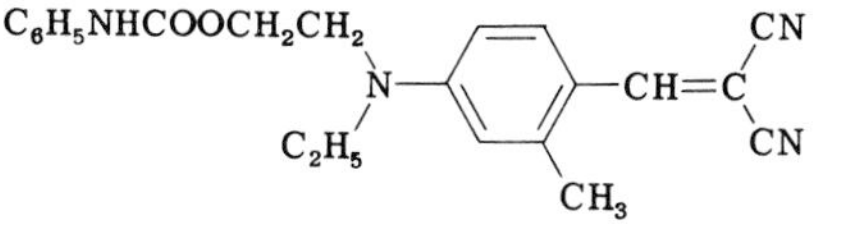

(XCVII)

CH$_3$ 485

CH=C⟨CN / CN⟩

(CH$_3$)$_2$—N—CH$_3$

C$_6$H$_5$NHCOOCH$_2$CH

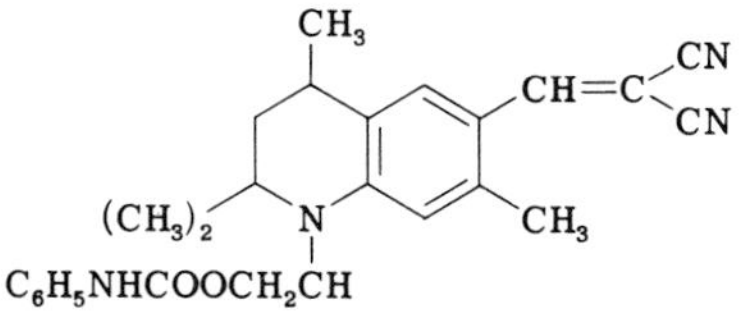

(XCVIII)

imido, etc.) in both (XCVII) and (XCVIII) has been investigated.[486] The use of 4-dialkylamino-1-naphthaldehydes in the synthesis has been suggested.[487] Dyes in which one or both of the N-alkyls contain RCOO– (R = aryl or heterocyclic),[488] or RSO$_2$N(R′)– (where R = alkyl or aryl and R′ = –H or alkyl)[489] have been reported. In the dicarboximido derivatives just mentioned, one of the –CO– linkages has been replaced by –SO$_2$–.[490] Increased tinctorial power and sublimation fastness have been reported for dyes in which the active methylene compound is β-cyanoethyl cyanoacetate.[491] This intermediate is prepared by ester interchange with simple alkyl esters.[492]

Dyes in which the aryl residue and the =C(CN)$_2$ group are separated by a plurality of vinylene groups, some substituted by CN, have been reported.[493] Products from the usual aldehydes condensed with 1,2-di-

[486] EKCo., USP 3,240,783; 3,349,098.
[487] G, USP 2,914,551.
[488] CIBA, BP 1,036,079.
[489] FBy, BeP 657,304; BP 1,025,918.
[490] ICI, BP 1,053,997.
[491] G, USP 2,789,125; 2,811,544.
[492] G, USP 2,806,872.
[493] S, BeP 574,780-1.

phenyl-3,5-dioxopyrazolidine have been suggested.[494] Dyes of structure (XCIX) have been prepared.[495] Dyes which bear two styryl groups (C), (CI) are known.[496,497] Structure (C) is said to dye polyesters, reserving wool, while (CI) has improved lightfastness on polyesters.

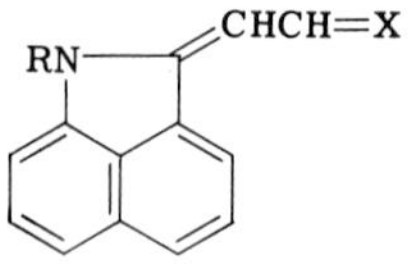

R = Alkyl, substituted alkyl
X = Active methylene

(XCIX)

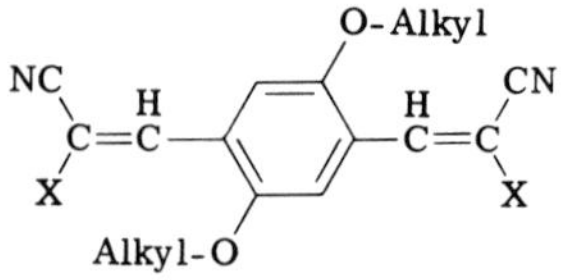

X = —CN, —COO-Alkyl

(C)

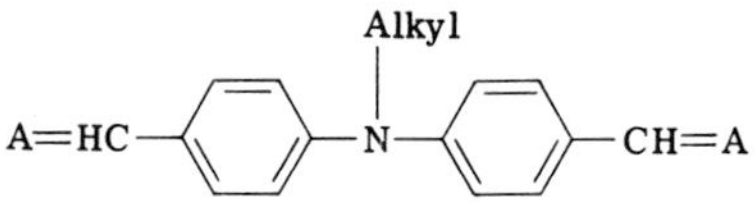

A = Active methylene,
same or different

(CI)

Some interest has been shown in the dyes of structure (CII).[498]

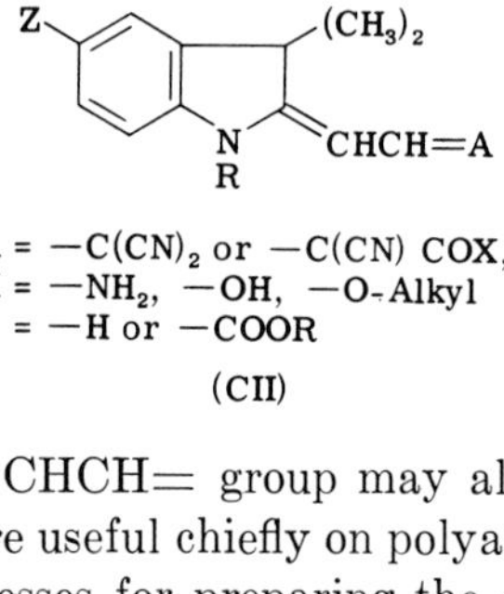

A = —C(CN)$_2$ or —C(CN) COX, where
X = —NH$_2$, —OH, —O-Alkyl
Z = —H or —COOR

(CII)

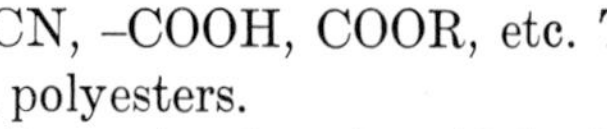

$(CN)_2C=C$-Aryl-N=N-Coupler
             |
            CN

(CIII)

The =CHCH= group may also bear –CN, –COOH, COOR, etc. These dyes are useful chiefly on polyamides and polyesters.

Processes for preparing the dyes by (1) condensing the aldehyde and active methylene without a solvent,[499] and (2) reacting –(Aryl) N(Alkyl)– with a 4-chloro-3-nitrostyryl molecule[500] are available.

[494] S, *BeP* 626,369.
[495] FBy, *BeP* 647,036; 647,743.
[496] S, *USP* 3,027,220.
[497] G, *USP* 2,766,233; FBy, *USP* 3,189,641.
[498] FBy, *USP* 3,184,453; 3,255,204; *BP* 1,063,320; *FP* 1,460,912.
[499] G, *USP* 2,649,471.
[500] G, *USP* 2,894,447.

The use of oxonol dyes of the pyrazolone type first mentioned in 1897[501] on polyesters has met with favor.[502] These are prepared by condensing 2 moles of a pyrazolone with an agent [$HCONH_2$, $HC(OC_2H_5)_3$] yielding $-CH=$ to give, as the simplest structure, (III). The pyrazolone nuclei may differ from each other,[503] and the reaction may be between a pyrazolone, or other active methylene, and a 4-formylpyrazolone prepared prior to the final condensation[504] or *in situ.*[505]

One school of chemists has extensively investigated reactions leading to orange to blue dyes containing tricyanovinyl groups. Many of these dyes are bright, bathochromic to the unsubstituted dye, and of high tinctorial power. Several routes are available, as shown in Chart 43.[506-510]

CHART 43

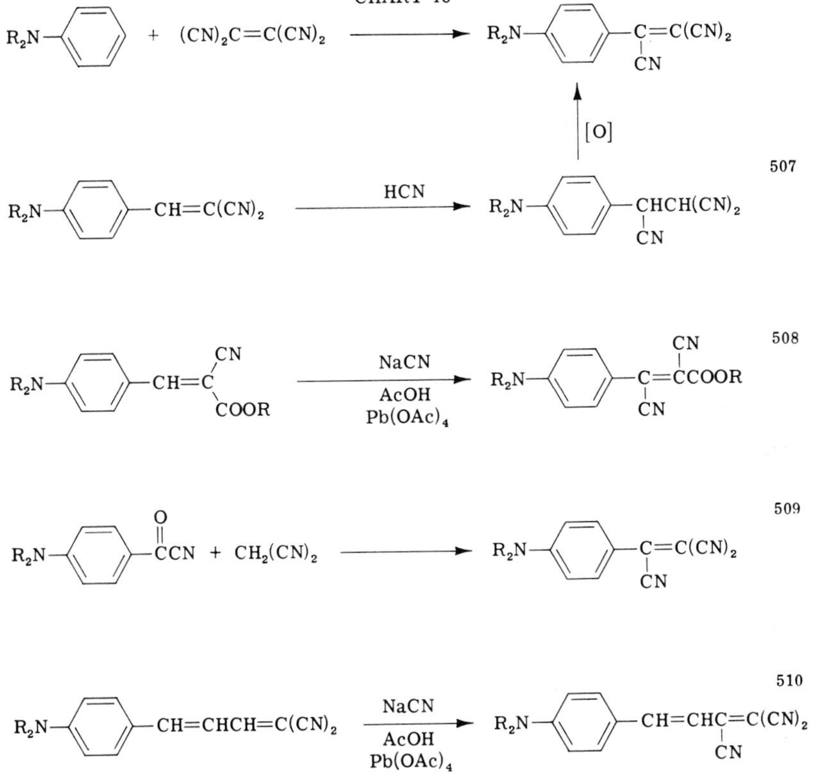

[501] L. Claisen, *Ann.* **297**, 37 (1897).
[502] G, *USP* 2,894,447.
[503] FBy, *DBP* 1,157,582; 1,164,973.
[504] FBy, *FP* 1,240,930.
[505] BASF, *DBP* 1,174,787.
[506] DuP, *USP* 2,762,810.

The last dyes in Chart 43 are blue on acrylic fibers and violet with high hydrolytic stability on polyesters. Further reactions of tetracyanoethylene (TCE) are given in Chart 44.[511-514]

CHART 44

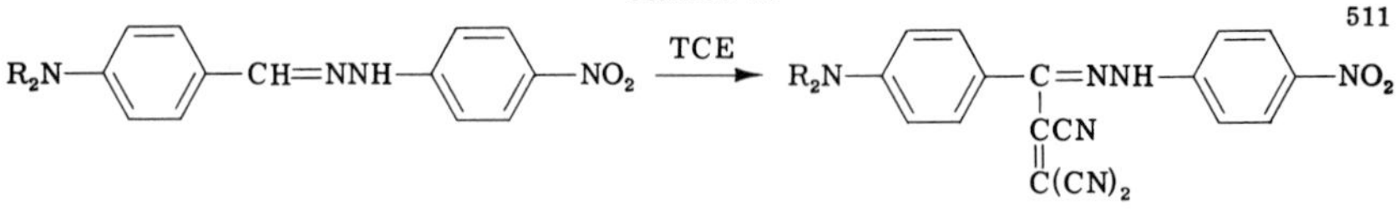

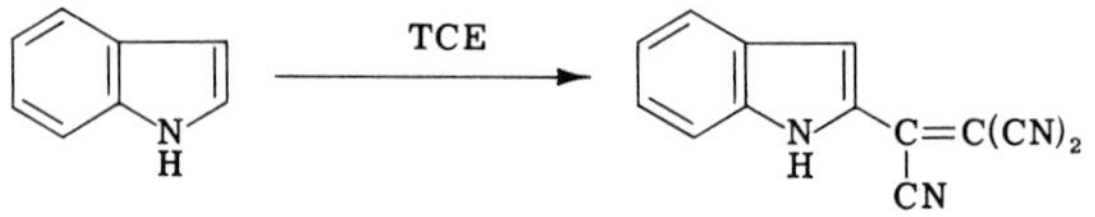

The last dye in Chart 44 is said to be valuable for dyeing polypropylene. Dyes (CIII) containing both methine and azo linkages are known.[515]

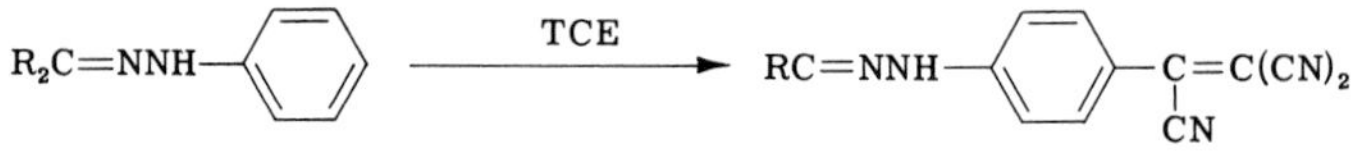

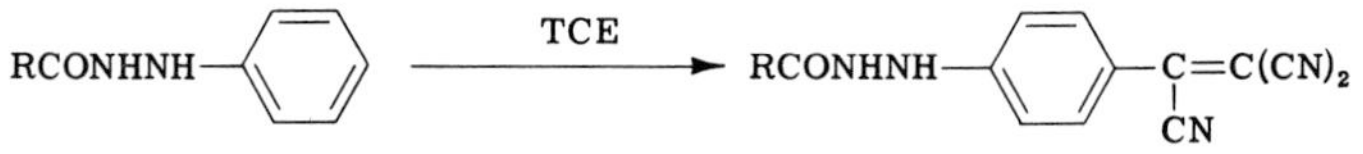

VII. Quinophthalone Dyes

Quinoline yellow is one of the oldest dyes for natural fibers, although its lightfastness is not good. This fault has been corrected by introduction of a hydroxyl group into the 3'-position. Omission of the sulfonic acid

[507] DuP, *USP* 2,889,335.
[508] DuP, *USP* 2,803,640.
[509] DuP, *USP* 2,813,116.
[510] DuP, *USP* 2,798,811.
[511] DuP, *USP* 3,026,326.
[512] DuP, *USP* 3,058,977.
[513] DuP, *USP* 3,168,551.
[514] VGF, *USP* 3,100,133.
[515] DuP, *USP* 2,824,096.

group leads to a polyester yellow of excellent lightfastness and buildup, although resistance to sublimation is only fair. A recent review of this series, termed quinophthalones, gives an analysis of their structure.[516] The deficiencies of the previously proposed structures are discussed, and a simplified polar structure is suggested. The parent quinophthalone and the commercial dye are portrayed as (CIV) and (CV).

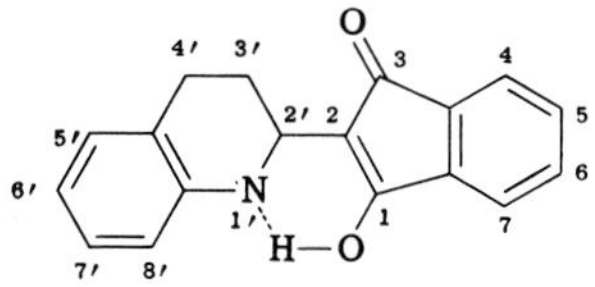

(CIV) 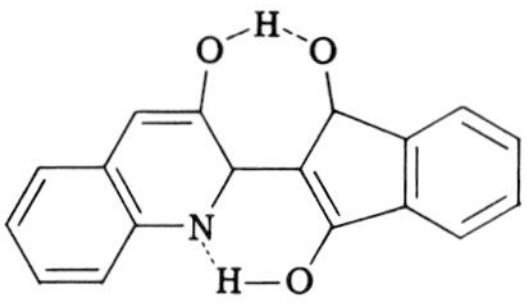   (CV)

The unhydroxylated compound has poor stability to light. The tremendous increase in fastness conferred by the 3'-hydroxyl group in (CV) is perhaps explained by stabilization caused by the hydrogen bonding between the 3- and 3'-oxygen atoms.

Quinophthalones are readily prepared by condensation of quinaldine derivatives with the aromatic *ortho*-dicarboxylic anhydrides. The 3'-hydroxylated dye is prepared as in Chart 45, a decarboxylation occurring in the final step.[517,518]

CHART 45

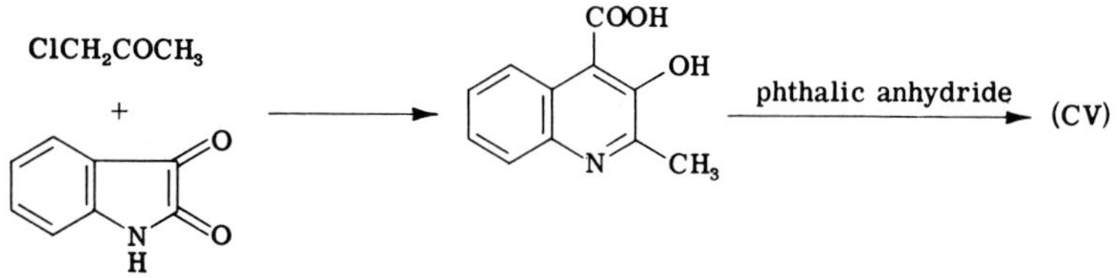

The use of 3 (or 4)-nitrophthalic anhydride results in the 4 (or 5)-nitro derivative, which can be reduced to the corresponding amine.[519] This can be treated with alkylating agents, such as epichlorohydrin, yielding the β-hydroxy-γ-chloropropylamino compound.[520] Reaction of the quinaldines with pyromellitic dianhydride gives the dicarboxy dyes,[521] while trimel-

[516] F. Kehrer, P. Niklaus, and B. K. Manukian, *Helv. Chim. Acta.* **50**, 2200 (1967).
[517] G, *USP* 2,082,358.
[518] PB No. 70,256, Frame 9591.
[519] DuP, *USP* 2,818,410.
[520] DuP, *USP* 2,818,409.
[521] DuP, *USP* 2,592,370.

litic anhydride provides the 5-carboxyquinophthalones.[522] These can be converted into esters, amides, etc., by conventional means.

Several methods of preparing the halogenated quinophthalones have been proposed. Halogenation of the 3'-hydroxy compound in inert solvents is said to improve the fastness properties.[523] Bromination during fusion of the two reactants yields 3'-hydroxy-4'-bromoquinophthalone.[524] Quinaldines, picolines, etc., have been condensed with halogenated phthalic anhydrides.[525]

VIII. Naphthoquinone Dyes

Naphthazarin (5,8-dihydroxy-1,4-naphthoquinone) was discovered in 1861, and the compound and many of its derivatives have been used as coloring agents in a variety of applications. It is interesting to note that, although nylon was introduced in the late 1930's, the use of this old dye (to produce a black) on the oldest of the truly synthetic fibers was reported only recently.[526]

A number of acetate dyes prepared by reaction of naphthazarin with amines or ammonia were proposed,[527] but all had inadequate lightfastness. (This reference is an excellent review of aminonaphthoquinone chemistry.) The amino groups entered the β-positions in the nucleus, as did the groups from thiophenols and sulfinic acids.[528] One or two moles could be added, and although the reaction was said to proceed more easily than with aniline, the yields were not as high.

Another naphthazarin sulfur-containing intermediate (CVI) was synthesized from hydroquinone and thianaphthene-2,3-dicarboxylic anhydride in an aluminum chloride melt.[529] This product behaves like quinizarin in its replacement of the 1- and 4-hydroxy groups by amino groups.

Novel dye syntheses employing Diels-Alder reactions with naphthazarin have been reported,[530] as shown in Chart 46.

The compound usually called simply "naphthazarin intermediate" formed by the reaction between 1,5-dinitronaphthalene and sulfur ses-

[522] DuP, *USP* 3,023,212–4.
[523] BASF, *BP* 865,308; *USP* 3,036,876.
[524] BASF, *DBP* 1,229,663.
[525] FH, *DBP* 1,252,168.
[526] BASF, *USP* 3,311,444.
[527] E. Merian, *Am. Dyestuff Reptr.* **48**, No. 20, 31 (1959).
[528] D. B. Brice and R. H. Thomson, *J. Chem. Soc.* p. 1429 (1956).
[529] A. T. Peters and D. Walker, *J. Chem. Soc.* p. 1429 (1956).
[530] R. E. Winkler, *Chimia (Aarau)* **21**, 575 (1967).

CHART 46

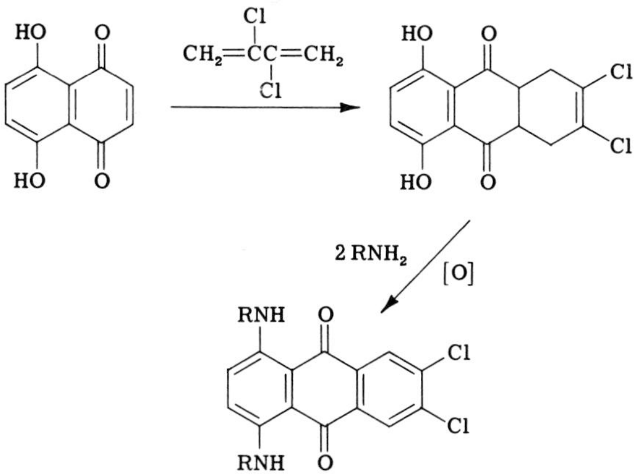

quioxide, is difficult to isolate, because of its solubility properties. It can be isolated as its zinc chloride salt,[531] and other purifications are known.[527] Its structure was formerly portrayed as (CVII), but the fact that its reactions are not consistent with those of quinones, phenols, or amines points to the strongly hydrogen bonded (CVIII).

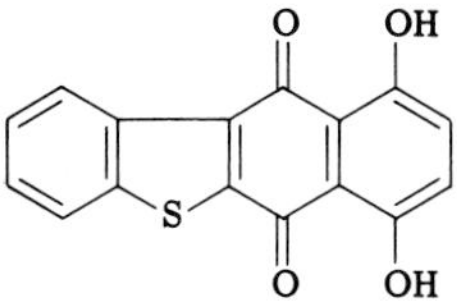

(CVI) 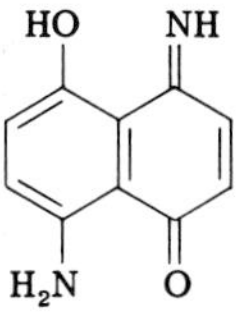　　　　　(CVII) 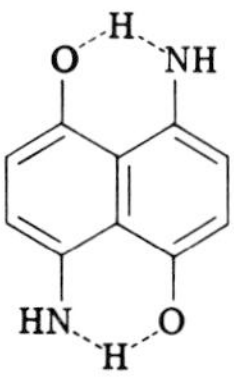　　　　　(CVIII)

By recent terminology the compound is named "naphthoxidine." In contrast to naphthazarin, amines usually replace one of the –NH– groups. Blue to green dyes have been prepared by replacement by one of two arylamines.[532] Replacement of the –NH– group with aminoazobenzenes gives green dyes.[533] Attachment of aryl and azobenzene moieties to β-carbon atoms has been accomplished by the Gomberg reaction.[534]

The first commercial blue disperse dye to possess good fastness to both light and gas resulted from bromination of the unisolated naphthazarin intermediate,[535] although it, of course, can be run in organic solvents.

[531] PB No. 73,377, Frame 2226.
[532] S, USP 2,555,973; 2,982,956.
[533] S, USP 2,553,049.
[534] Gy, USP 3,320,234; 3,338,659.
[535] S, USP 2,553,048.

CHART 47

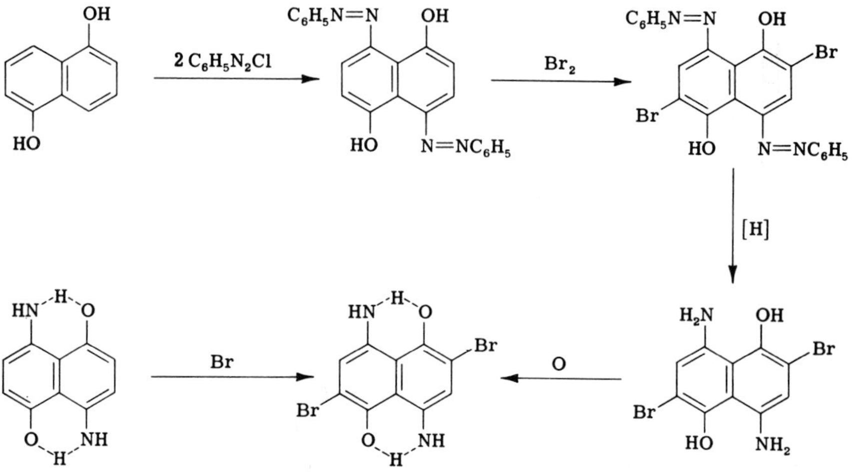

As is often true, the reaction product, which contains other materials, dyes better than the pure main component, 3,7-dibromonaphthoxidine does.[527] The configuration was established as in Chart 47.[536]

The –NH– in the brominated compound can also be replaced with amines, such as aminoazobenzene, in acetic acid.[537] If sodium acetate is added, one of the bromine atoms can be replaced. Arylamino compounds have replaced the bromines.[538] One of the –NH₂ groups can be hydrolyzed to an –OH residue.[539] The 2,3-dihalo isomer of the directly halogenated naphthoxidine is prepared by treatment of 2,3-dichloro-5-nitro-1,4-naph-

CHART 48

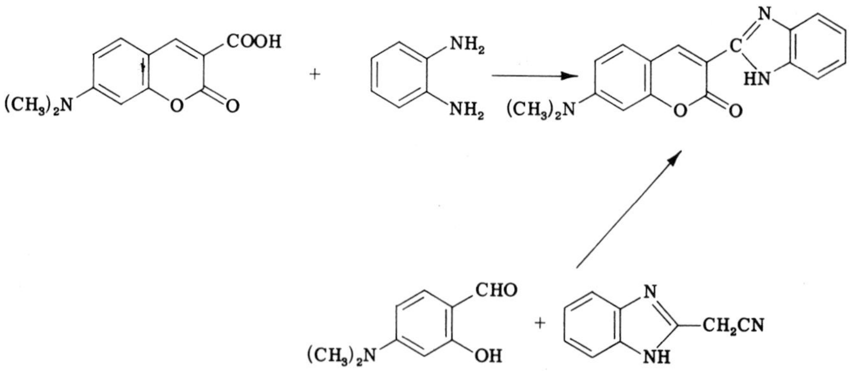

[536] S, *USP* 2,623,872.
[537] S, *USP* 2,553,050.
[538] S, *USP* 2,553,046.
[539] S, *USP* 2,538,005.

CHART 49

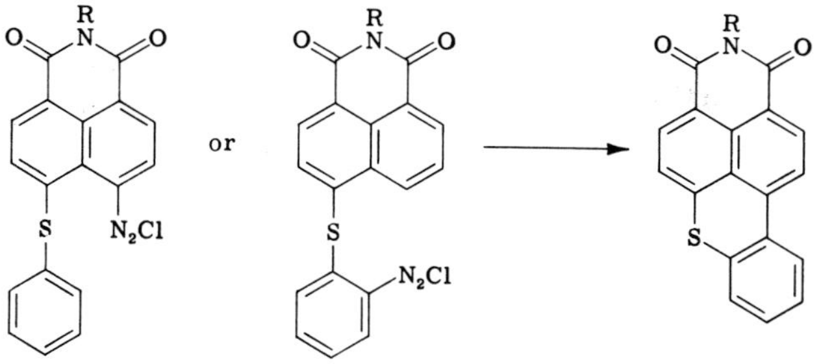

thoquinone with sulfur sesquioxide.[540] The dyes resulting from this fascinating chemistry unfortunately are not completely stable to commercial dyeing conditions, particularly in the presence of heavy metals. This disadvantage is also encountered with some of the supposedly highly stable anthraquinone dyes.

The blue 2,3-dimethyl-6-bromo-5,8-diamino-1,4-naphthoquinone has been prepared by a series of reactions commencing with nitration of 2,3-dimethyl-1,4-naphthoquinone.[541] A bluish red dye, 4-amino-2-chloro-3,6,8-tribromo-1,4-naphthoquinone has also been prepared.[542] A paper discussing this type of chemistry has been published.[543]

The relation of affinity to the degree of planarity of the naphthoquinone dyes has been published.[544]

CHART 50

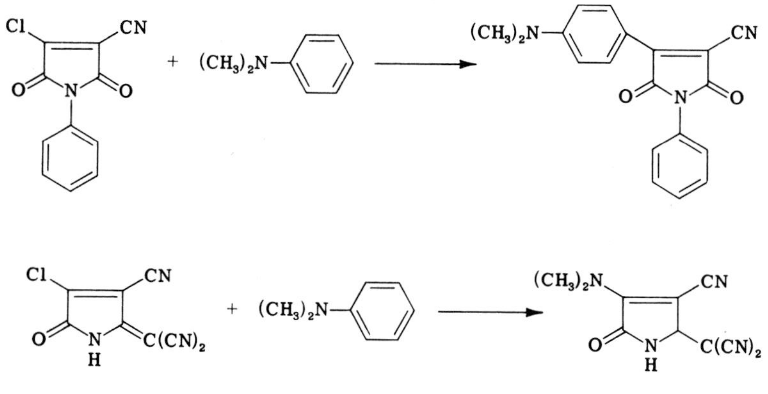

[540] S, *USP* 2,764,600.
[541] DuP, *USP* 2,687,939.
[542] DuP, *USP* 2,687,940.
[543] M. F. Sartori, *Ann. Chim. (Rome)* **49**, 2157 (1959).
[544] E. H. Daruwalla, S. S. Rao, and B. D. Tilak, *J. Soc. Dyers Colourists* **76**, 418 (1960).

IX. Miscellaneous Dyes

There are a number of dyes which do not fit into the classes usually used on cellulose acetate. For example, 2,3',4-trichloro-5,5'-dimethyl-thioindigo has been suggested for this application.[545] Dinitrophenyl-

CHART 51

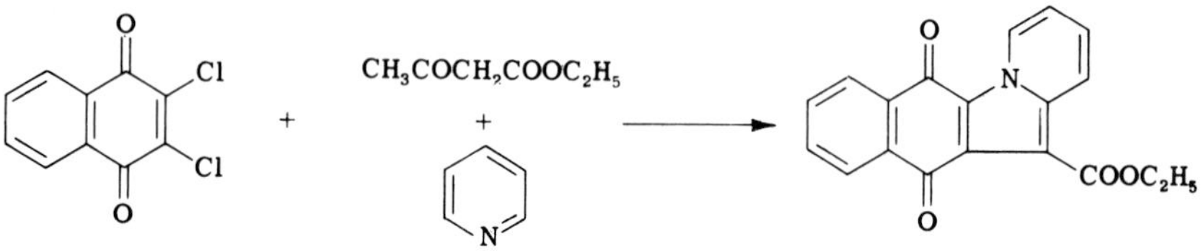

hydrazones of various aldehydes and ketones have been proposed.[546] Several patents are concerned with the presence of groups such as carbamoyl, sulfamoyl, sulfatooxyalkylsulfonyl, and **3-pyridinosulfo** on dye structure in general.[547]

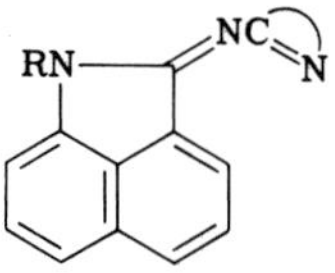

(CIX)

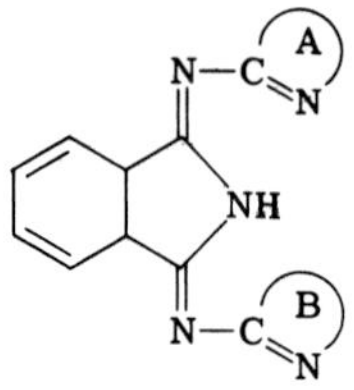

(CX)

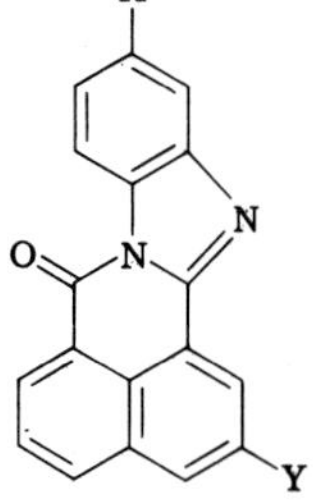

(CXI)

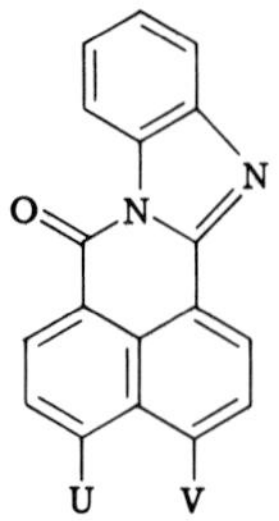

(CXII)

[545] FH, *SP* 430,649.
[546] CFM, *BP* 940,256; 1,056,610.
[547] Gy, *BP* 1,048,908; FH, *DBP* 1,240,809; ICI, *USP* 3,171,710.

Amino heterocycles condensed with naphthostyryls[548] and 1,4-diimino-isoindoline[549] produce (CIX) and (CX).

Rings A and B may be the same or different. The diiminoisoindolines may be prepared by reaction of phthalonitriles with ammonia.[550] Chart 48 illustrates the preparation of some fluorescent dyes of only moderate lightfastness.[551]

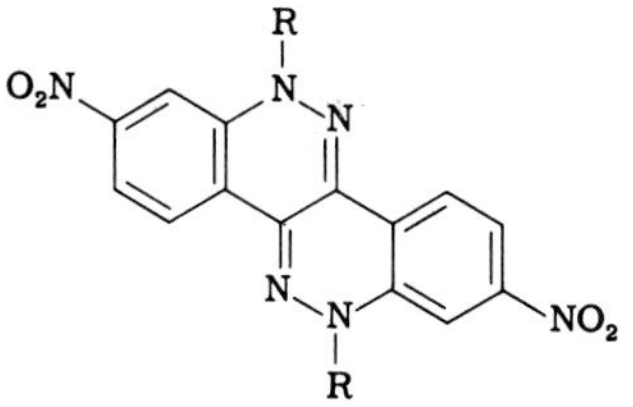

(CXIII)

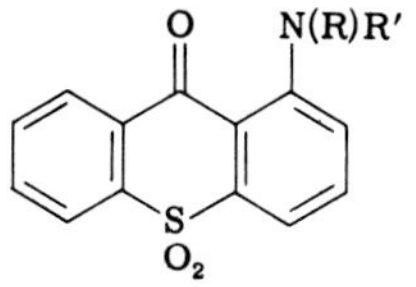

R and R' = —H, Alkyl

(CXIV)

The phthaloperinone series is also represented by (CXI)[552] and (CXII),[553] where X and/or Y = –OH, –OCH$_2$CH$_2$OH, –OAlkyl, halogen, –SR, carbalkoxy, sulfamoyl, etc., and the mixture where U or V = arylthio. Related types are prepared by the ring closures of Chart 49.[554]

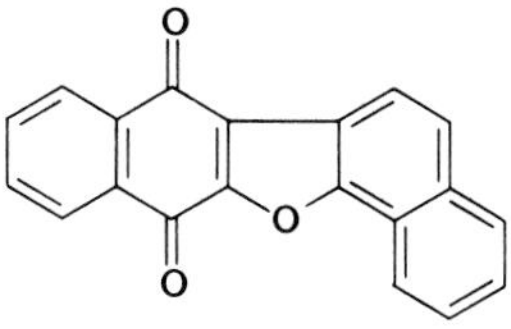

(CXV)

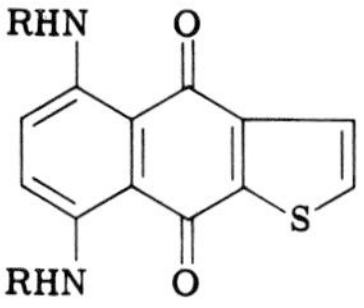

(CXVI)

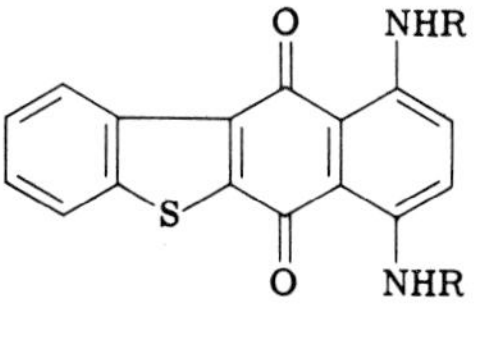

(CXVII)

[548] FBy, *USP* 3,287,465.
[549] FBy, *FP* 1,501,546; BASF, *BP* 1,090,061; *DBP* 950,800.
[550] FBy, *BP* 698,039–49.
[551] Gy, *BP* 1,085,456; *USP* 3,014,041.
[552] BASF, *BP* 1,062,368; 1,095,035; FH, *USP* 2,994,697.
[553] FH, *USP* 3,322,769.
[554] FH, *BP* 1,095,784.

These are said to be bright yellow polyester dyes. Red to green dyes are prepared by the condensation of nitro-*o*-halobenzils with assorted hydrazines (CXIII).[555] Substituted aminothioxanthone dioxides have been disclosed (CXIV).[556]

Dyes may be prepared from certain halogenated maleimides,[557] as in Chart 50.

Yellow to red polyester phthaloylpyrrocoline[558] dyes are prepared as in Chart 51. The ester can be converted to the usual derivatives.

Structures (CXV),[559] (CXVI) and (CXVII)[560] appear in the literature. The thiophene derivatives (CXVI) are bathochromic relative to their anthraquinone counterparts.

Finally, DNHCOC=CXY, where D is a chromophoric system, Z and X = –H or halogen, and Y = halogen or halogenated alkyl,[561] has been mentioned.

[555] CFM, *DBP* 1,121,038; 1,185,322.

[556] BASF, *USP* 2,884,300.

[557] DuP, *USP* 3,013,013; 3,096,339.

[558] M. S. Mathur and B. D. Tilak, *J. Sci. Ind. Res. (India)* **17B**, 33 (1958); CCC, *USP* 2,863,714.

[559] DuP, *USP* 2,940,983.

[560] A. T. Peters and D. Walker, *J. Chem. Soc.* p. 1429 (1956); p. 1525 (1957).

[561] S, *USP* 3,122,533.

AUTHOR INDEX

Numbers in parentheses are reference numbers and indicate that an author's work is referred to although his name is not cited in the text.

SUBJECT INDEX